Dual Nationality in the European Union

Immigration and Asylum Law and Policy in Europe

Edited by

Jan Niessen
Elspeth Guild

VOLUME 26

The titles published in this series are listed at brill.nl/ialp

Dual Nationality in the European Union

A Study on Changing Norms in Public and Private International Law and in the Municipal Laws of Four EU Member States

By

Olivier W. Vonk

MARTINUS NIJHOFF PUBLISHERS

LEIDEN • BOSTON
2012

Library of Congress Cataloging-in-Publication Data

Vonk, Olivier W.
Dual nationality in the European Union : a study on changing norms in public and private international law and in the municipal laws of four EU member states / by Olivier W. Vonk.
p. cm. -- (Immigration and asylum law and policy in Europe ; vol. 26)
Includes bibliographical references and index.
ISBN 978-90-04-22720-0 (hardback : alk. paper) 1. Dual nationality--France. 2. Dual nationality--Netherlands. 3. Dual nationality--Germany. 4. Dual nationality--Spain. I. Title.

KJE5124.V66 2012
342.2408'3--dc23
2012004551

ISSN 1568-2749
ISBN 978-90-04-22720-0 (hardback)
ISBN 978-90-04-22721-7 (e-book)

This book is printed on acid-free paper.

Contents

Acknowledgments

This book is based on a PhD thesis defended at the European University Institute (Florence, Italy) in November 2010. I am particularly grateful to Prof. Marie-Ange Moreau, my supervisor at the EUI, for taking an interest in the subject of dual nationality and for giving me the chance to write a dissertation at one of the best places to conduct interdisciplinary and comparative research. I am also greatly indebted to Prof. Gerard-René de Groot, whose enthusiasm for everything related to nationality law inspired me to write this book. I feel privileged to have studied with him in Maastricht and thank him for his guidance and support from the very start of my PhD project.

I also wish to thank the two other members of the examining board, Prof. Rainer Bauböck and Prof. Bruno Nascimbene, for their detailed comments. This book would certainly have looked very different had I not been able to benefit from Prof. Bauböck's seminars in the Department of Political and Social Sciences at the EUI. My gratitude also goes to the EUI and the Spanish government for funding research missions in France and Spain respectively.

Special thanks are also in order to René Bruin, Karel Hendriks and Dr Maarten Vink. I feel privileged to have been given the chance to further specialize in nationality law this last year by working with them on the subject of statelessness.

On a personal level I especially wish to thank Costanza Margiotta and Luca Paulesu for their friendship, their stories about Italy and their interest in my work. My time at the EUI would not have been the same without you.

It is to my family, and my parents in particular, that I want to dedicate this book. Thank you so much for your unremitting support and encouragement—in good times and bad times.

Olivier Vonk
17 September 2011

Summary

The main objective of this book is to examine the phenomenon of dual nationality in the European Union (EU), particularly against the background of the status of European citizenship—a status that is linked to the nationality of each EU Member State. (Article 20(1) of the Treaty on the Functioning of the European Union provides that 'citizenship of the Union shall be additional to and not replace national citizenship'.)

The study consists of two parts. The first part (Chapters 1 and 2) sets out the approach towards (dual) nationality in Public and Private International Law as well as in EU Law, in particular by analysing the case law of the Court of Justice of the European Union (CJEU). The second part (Chapters 3–6) consists of an overview of the dual nationality regimes in four EU Member States—France, Italy, the Netherlands and Spain—and their possible effects on the EU as a whole.

Chapter 2 of the book is entitled the 'intra-EU context', since it primarily deals with the CJEU's approach towards a dual nationality consisting of two Member State nationalities. The country reports, on the other hand, deal with the 'extra-EU context' because the dual nationality policies of the countries under consideration predominantly affect non-Member State nationals. Thus, France and the Netherlands have for some time already faced the question how to integrate the (Muslim) immigrant population; Italy and Spain have long since adopted a system of preferential treatment for (Latin American) former emigrants and their descendants. The country reports demonstrate how dual nationality is used (or rejected) in these four countries.

Finally, the question whether the EU should in time acquire (limited) competence in the field of European nationality law is one of the major themes of this study. Regardless of one's stance on this question, it must be readily admitted that the subject of Member State autonomy in nationality law is becoming ever more salient with the enlargement of the Union and the growing relevance of European citizenship in the case law of the CJEU. In the opinion of this author, the study shows that the almost absolute autonomy of Member States in the field of nationality law is becoming increasingly problematic for the EU as a whole. Based *inter alia* on the findings from the country reports, the author takes the position that there is arguably a need for the (minimum) harmonization of European nationality laws.

General Introduction

The main objective of this study is to examine the phenomenon of dual nationality[1] in the European Union (EU), particularly against the background of the status of European citizenship—a status that is linked to EU Member State nationality. It is essential to stress at the outset that EU citizenship (also called Union citizenship) is additional to and does not replace Member State nationality.[2] EU citizens have, *inter alia*, the right to move and reside freely within the territory of the Member States.[3] The EU has no mandate to act in the field of nationality law, however, and the Member States have always jealously guarded their exclusive competence. Yet the fact that the EU lacks competence to interfere with the conditions placed by Member States on the acquisition and loss of their nationality does obviously not mean that questions of (dual) nationality have not arisen.

The following analysis of the role of dual nationality in the EU consists of two parts. The first part (Chapters 1 and 2) sets out the approach towards

---

1 A number of points need to be made clear at the outset. First, there is no substantive difference between dual nationality, on the one hand, and multiple and plural nationality, on the other, beyond the obvious fact that the latter can refer to more than two nationalities. For the sake of variety, this study uses all terms interchangeably. Second, the term 'nationality' will be consistently employed to denote the legal relation between an individual and a State. In the writings of many political and social scientists, however, the term 'citizenship' is often used to describe this legal relation. Although we will never use citizenship as a substitute for nationality in this study, the former term may come up in some of the citations.

Finally, the traditional pillar structure in EU law ceased to exist with the entry into force of the Treaty of Lisbon on 1 December 2009. Although one therefore no longer speaks of the 'Community' but of the 'Union', we have kept intact the references to the Community as used in the pre-Lisbon literature and case law, as well as to the European Court of Justice (ECJ), at present called the Court of Justice of the European Union (CJEU). The EU after the entry into force of the Treaty of Lisbon is based on two Treaties of equal value: the Treaty on European Union (TEU) and the Treaty on the Functioning of the European Union (TFEU). The latter is a revised form of the former EC Treaty. For a detailed overview of the Treaty of Lisbon see Michael Dougan, "The Treaty of Lisbon 2007: winning minds, not hearts", *Common Market Law Review* 45 (2008): 617–703.

2 Article 20(1) TFEU/ex Article 17(1) EC reads: 'Citizenship of the Union is hereby established. Every person holding the nationality of a Member State shall be a citizen of the Union. Citizenship of the Union shall be additional to [the EC Treaty read 'shall complement', author's addition] and not replace national citizenship'.

3 Under Article 21(1) TFEU/ex Article 18(1) EC, 'every citizen of the Union shall have the right to move and reside freely within the territory of the Member States, subject to the limitations and conditions laid down in the Treaties and by the measures adopted to give them effect'.

(dual) nationality in EU law, in particular by analysing the case law of the Court of Justice of the European Union (hereafter referred to as the 'CJEU' or 'the Court' and until 1 December 2009 known under the name European Court of Justice (ECJ)). The second part (Chapters 3–6) consists of an overview of the national attitude towards dual nationality in four EU Member States, namely France, Italy, the Netherlands and Spain. Yet we begin Chapter 1, by way of introduction, with a general overview of the role of nationality law in municipal and international law, explain our choice for dual nationality as the subject of this book and, finally, discuss nationality law in a European context. This European context not only refers to the position of Member State nationality in EU law, but also to the part played by the Council of Europe in the area of nationality law: the latter has since long been active in nationality matters. The last section of Chapter 1, dedicated to *nationality* in the European context, provides a stepping stone to the actual subject of this study, to wit the specific role of *dual nationality* in the EU.

In Chapter 2 we therefore analyse the (relatively few) cases of the CJEU that involve questions of dual nationality. As most of them address issues of Private International Law (PIL), Chapter 2 examines in detail the place occupied by dual nationality in this area of law—both on the national and the European level. As for the CJEU case law, it was in particular the dual nationality case *García Avello*[4] and its follow-up case *Grunkin-Paul*,[5] both concerning the law on surnames, which triggered a debate on the need for uniform conflict and recognition rules in respect of personal status.[6] More recently, *Hadadi*[7] raised interesting questions as regards dual nationality in the framework of the Brussels IIbis Regulation.

García Avello and *Hadadi* address a particular case of dual nationality: both judgments involved dual nationals who held two Member State nationalities. We have therefore called this part of the discussion on dual nationality the 'intra-EU context'. The country reports, on the other hand, have been given

[4] Case C-148/02 *García Avello* [2003] ECR I-11613.

[5] Case C-353/06 *Grunkin-Paul* [2008] ECR I-07639. This case will be remembered, according to Meeusen, 'as the first case where the ECJ really interfered with the Member State choice-of-law process in matters of personal status and family relations'. Johan Meeusen, "The Grunkin and Paul Judgment of the ECJ, or How to Strike a Delicate Balance between Conflict of Laws, Union Citizenship and Freedom of Movement in the EC", *Zeitschrift für Europäisches Privatrecht* 18, no. 1 (2010): 200.

[6] The close relationship between nationality and personal status will be explained in Chapter 2. For a study combining the two fields see Michel Verwilghen, ed., *Nationalité et statut personnel. Leur interaction dans les traités internationaux et dans les législations nationales* (Bruxelles: Bruylant, 1984).

[7] Case C-168/08 *Hadadi* [2009] ECR I-06871.

the subtitle 'extra-EU context'. The reason is plain: the dual nationality policies of the countries under consideration predominantly affect non-Member State nationals. France and the Netherlands have already for some time faced the question of how to integrate the (Muslim) immigrant population, and Italy and Spain have long since adopted a system of preferential treatment for (Latin American) former emigrants and their descendants. The four country reports will demonstrate how dual nationality is used (or rejected) as an instrument for meeting these different objectives.

In the country reports we thus assess the place occupied by dual nationality in two traditional immigration countries (France and the Netherlands) and two traditional emigration countries (Italy and Spain). Although the latter two have also become immigration countries in recent decades, this development in not reflected in their nationality laws; rather, Italy are Spain are characterised by a strong focus on former emigrants and their descendants. The goal in these country reports is not just to provide a one-to-one comparison of legal provisions which have a bearing on the issue of dual nationality. Rather, the main aim of the case studies is try to find out what issues have arisen in relation to this phenomenon from the beginning of the previous century up to the present. In so doing, we will test—at least for the countries under discussion—the academic claim that both immigration and emigration countries increasingly tolerate dual nationality. (This claim is subject to the caveat, however, that it certainly does not hold true for all countries.[8]) Our discussion of dual nationality in the comparative chapters will also allow us to illustrate some of the problems related to dual nationality which are identified in the course of Chapter 1.

Perhaps stating the obvious, the comparative case studies show that multiple nationality occupies a different position in each of the States discussed, which can be accounted for by the different challenges to which they are exposed. Although this makes it somewhat difficult to draw comparative conclusions, it is also evidence of the fact that the attitude towards dual nationality is, to a large extent, rooted in the countries' different historical pasts. Nevertheless, it will also become clear that their position regarding dual nationality has not always been fixed, but has been subject to change over time too.

The decision to limit the comparative part to four countries means that this book is not a comprehensive study of the approach to dual nationality in all the Member States of the EU. The nationality laws of other (Member) States

---

[8] Thomas Faist, "Dual citizenship: Change, Prospects, and Limits", in *Dual Citizenship in Europe: From Nationhood to Societal Integration*, ed. Thomas Faist (Aldershot: Ashgate, 2007), 173.

will, however, sometimes be subject of discussion (particularly in Chapter 1) where relevant to the present study, but they are not described in any detail. The four countries were chosen not only because they are of particular interest for the subject under scrutiny—they represent a mix of immigration and emigration countries and therefore faced different challenges throughout the 20th century—but also because of the language barriers and other obstacles inherent in other pertinent cases (for example in Eastern Europe) or because these had already been recently investigated and described in English (Germany).[9] Yet, by confining ourselves to a limited number of countries in the comparative chapters we can, hopefully, provide a more thorough overview of the historical development of dual nationality than would have been feasible had more country studies been included. At the same time, the decision to only look at four countries in a detailed fashion should not affect in any way the overarching background of this study, namely the interaction between the nationality laws of the Member States and the European citizenship attached to Member State nationality.

As nationality law is still firmly within the competence of each individual State, studying the legal regime on nationality in different countries is by definition a comparative undertaking of different domestic rules.[10] Hence, half of this study is made up of the respective country reports. In addition, EU law

---

[9] See for example, on the situation in Eastern Europe and Germany, Simon Green, "Between Ideology and Pragmatism: The Politics of Dual Nationality in Germany", *International Migration Review* 39, no. 4 (2005); Jürgen Gerdes, Thomas Faist, and Beate Rieple, "'We are All "Republican" Now': The Politics of Dual Citizenship in Germany", in *Dual Citizenship in Europe: From Nationhood to Societal Integration*, ed. Thomas Faist (Aldershot: Ashgate, 2007); Enikö Horváth, *Mandating identity: citizenship, kinship laws and plural nationality in the European Union*, Dissertation European University Institute (Alphen aan den Rijn: Kluwer Law International, 2007); Rainer Bauböck, Bernhard Perchinig, and Wiebke Sievers, eds., *Citizenship policies in the New Europe* (Amsterdam: Amsterdam University Press, 2009).

[10] Consequently, there is long tradition of books with comparative analyses of nationality laws, among which Verwilghen, ed., *Nationalité et statut personnel. Leur interaction dans les traités internationaux et dans les législations nationales*; Gerard-René de Groot, *Staatsangehörigkeitsrecht im Wandel* (Köln: Heymanns, 1989); Bruno Nascimbene, ed., *Nationality laws in the European Union - Le droit de la nationalité dans l'Union Européene* (Milano: Giuffrè Editore, 1996); Patrick Weil and Randall Hansen, eds., *Towards a European Nationality. Citizenship, Immigration and Nationality Law in the EU* (Hampshire: Palgrave Publishers, 2001); Rainer Bauböck et al., eds., *Acquisition and Loss of Nationality, Policies and Trends in 15 European Countries* (Amsterdam: Amsterdam University Press, 2006). These studies are complemented by others that explore particularly the relation between municipal nationality law and European citizenship. See for example Maarten Vink, *Limits of European Citizenship. European Integration and Domestic Immigration Policies* (Hampshire: Palgrave Macmillan, 2005).

plays a big part in this book—despite the fact that the Union lacks competence to act in nationality matters—as only possession of the nationality of a Member State of the EU gives access to European citizenship. We shall see, however, that the CJEU has imposed some constraints on the Member States' autonomy in matters of nationality. Thus, in *Micheletti*[11] the Court ruled that State competence in nationality law must be exercised with due regard to Community law. This was recently confirmed again in *Rottmann*,[12] a case in which Advocate General (AG) Maduro also stressed that although the acquisition and loss of nationality are in themselves not governed by Community law, 'the conditions for the acquisition and loss of nationality must be compatible with the Community rules and respect the rights of the European citizen'.[13]

The question whether the EU should in time acquire (limited) competence in the field of European nationality law is one of the major themes of this study. Regardless of one's stance on this question, it must be readily admitted that the subject of Member State autonomy in nationality law is becoming ever more salient with the enlargement of the Union and the growing relevance of European citizenship in the case law of the CJEU. In this writer's opinion, the study shows that the almost absolute autonomy of the Member States is becoming increasingly problematic for the EU at large. Basing ourselves *inter alia* on the findings from the country reports, we take the position that there is arguably a need for the (minimum) harmonization of European nationality laws.[14]

In light of the above, dual nationality is a relevant subject to study in an EU context for at least two reasons. First, Member State policy towards multiple nationality has an effect on access to European citizenship for third country nationals (TCNs). After all, the toleration of dual nationality in combination with a preferential regime for certain groups living outside the EU removes some of the hurdles to becoming a Member State national and thus has a direct effect on access to European citizenship. Such a regime of facilitated access is in place in several Member States. Juxtaposed to this privileged

---

[11] Case C-369/90 *Micheletti* [1992] ECR I-04239.

[12] Case C-135/08 *Rottmann* [2010] ECR I-01449.

[13] Para. 23 of AG Maduro's Opinion.

[14] The harmonization debate is in full swing. See for example Rainer Bauböck et al., "Introduction", in *Acquisition and Loss of Nationality, Policies and Trends in 15 European Countries*, ed. Rainer Bauböck, *et al.* (Amsterdam: Amsterdam University Press, 2006). The interaction between the nationality laws of the Member States and European citizenship is also currently being investigated in the framework of EUDO citizenship (http://eudo-citizenship.eu/), which is part of the European Union Democracy Observatory.

category is the category of non-privileged TCNs, who often have to meet stringent conditions to acquire the nationality of a Member State (and thus EU citizenship). As said, this part of the discussion has been called the extra-EU context.

Second, the case law on European citizenship—in particular the *García Avello* judgment (a case concerning the surname of children who held both Belgian and Spanish nationality)—shows that within a purely intra-EU context the possession of dual Member State nationality can have far-reaching consequences. *García Avello* is one of the cases discussed in Chapter 2 in relation to the role of dual nationality in PIL and EU law. There is a burgeoning literature on dual nationality, including several monographs and edited volumes,[15] but we are not aware of recent studies that have addressed dual nationality in a detailed fashion for these two specific contexts.[16]

Dual nationality is one of the most topical subjects among those who are currently studying nationality law. It is particularly interesting to note that dual nationality takes a middle road between two positions that in our opinion are no longer tenable today. On the one hand we have the ancient conception of nationality as the expression of an undivided allegiance of an individual to one (and only one) State, and on the other the postnational idea that the end of the nation-state—and thus the concept of nationality itself—is near. The first view can no longer hold true in our present age of large-scale migration and European integration, while the second neglects the fact that nationality is often still essential for the exercise of certain rights, and that the

---

[15] Patrick Weil and Randall Hansen, eds., *Dual Nationality, Social Rights and Federal Citizenship in the US and Europe* (New York: Berghahn Books, 2002); David A. Martin and Kay Hailbronner, eds., *Rights and duties of dual nationals: changing concepts and attitudes* (The Hague: Kluwer Law International, 2003); Mohsen Aghahosseini, *Claims of Dual Nationals and the Development of Customary International Law. Issues Before the Iran-United States Claims Tribunal* (Leiden/Boston: Martinus Nijhoff Publishers, 2007); Alfred Michael Boll, *Multiple Nationality and International Law* (Leiden/Boston: Martinus Nijhoff Publishers, 2007); Thomas Faist, ed., *Dual Citizenship in Europe: From Nationhood to Societal Integration* (Aldershot: Ashgate, 2007); Thomas Faist and Peter Kivisto, eds., *Dual Citizenship in Global Perspective, From Unitary to Multiple Citizenship* (New York: Palgrave Macmillan, 2007).

[16] The conspicuous absence in Boll's study of multiple nationality in the context of PIL and EU law has been noted in various book reviews. See Hans Ulrich Jessurun d'Oliveira, "Book review of Alfred Boll's 'Multiple Nationality and International Law'", *The American Journal of International Law* 101 (2007); Ko Swan Sik, "Book review of Alfred Boll's 'Multiple Nationality and International Law'", *Netherlands International Law Review* 55 (2008): 408. See also Olivier Vonk, "De rol van dubbele nationaliteit voor toegang tot het Unieburgerschap en voor rechts- en forumkeuzebevoegdheid in het Europese internationaal privaatrecht", *Nederlands Juristenblad*, no. 27 (2011).

acquisition of the nationality of the host State provides a migrant with a secure residence status.

The phenomenon of dual nationality sits somewhere between these two positions. On the one hand, our age of migration can easily lead to bonds with more than one State; this is becoming increasingly recognized through the growing toleration of dual nationality (other important factors which have influenced this toleration are gender equality in nationality law and human rights considerations). On the other hand, it is a phenomenon that does not underplay the important role that nationality still fulfils today, notwithstanding the fact that a substantial number of rights have become dependent on residence rather than nationality over the years. In discussing this theme in Chapter 1, we have tried to give due regard to the abundant literature on dual nationality from disciplines other than law.[17] Consequently, although the chief focus of the study lies in examining the legal implications of dual nationality in EU law (and therefore PIL), other perspectives will occasionally be adopted as well. We feel it is essential to take a multi-disciplinary approach to dual nationality by not only studying it from a legal perspective but also by paying attention to the political, sociological or even psychological dimension; from a legal perspective, the phenomenon can again be approached from at least two different viewpoints: the individual and the State. In the course of this study we shall see how dual nationality impacts on both the individual and the State, at the municipal, international and European levels.

The opening sections of Chapter 1 concern general remarks on issues and principles of nationality; these preliminary observations are essential for a good understanding of the ensuing chapters. They address the legal notion of nationality, its historical background, the difference between nationality and citizenship, and the function of nationality in municipal and international law. Section 6 then moves on to explain the choice for multiple nationality as the subject of this book. It will be demonstrated that the number of persons holding multiple nationalities has tremendously increased over the last couple of decades, that dual nationality has become more accepted, but also that strongly divergent views on dual nationality still exist. The phenomenon is not only opposed for emotional reasons, but also for the legal difficulties it allegedly creates. The areas where possible problems may arise shall therefore be identified in Section 9. The inconveniences traditionally associated with dual

---

[17] Although we feel that the growing interaction between the legal and other disciplines in the field of nationality/citizenship is very valuable, the present study is nonetheless meant as a legal analysis of dual nationality. The input from other disciplines primarily serves to provide a broader perspective on the subject and is thus, by necessity, not a comprehensive discussion of the vast literature on dual nationality in non-legal disciplines.

nationality concern loyalty, voting rights, diplomatic protection, military service, and personal status; these issues are subsequently further illustrated in the country reports. Suffice it to say for now that we will argue that the supposed problems are less significant than might be believed and that they do no longer hold the same force as they used to. In addition, the changing role of the nation-state (and the part played by multiple nationality in this development) is thoroughly examined. Many commentators have rightly pointed out that it is remarkable how dual nationality, until only a few decades ago strongly out of favour, has been the object of growing toleration in recent years. In connection with the changing role of the nation-state we also explore concepts such as transnationalism, postnationalism and—most importantly—European citizenship (Sections 7 and 8). The final section focuses on the activities of the Council of Europe in the field of nationality law and on the role of nationality in the European Union, thereby creating a link with Chapter 2 which deals explicitly with multiple nationality in EU law. As said, investigating dual nationality in EU law also entails looking at it from a PIL perspective. Consequently, we will devote much attention to examining the solutions in this area of law to so-called 'conflicts of nationalities'.

Part I

The Legal Concept of (Dual) Nationality

Chapter 1

General Observations on (Dual) Nationality and its Role in Municipal and International Law

1. *Nationality and Citizenship: Their Historical Roots*

As States need a population, there has always been the need to define who belongs to a given State. For this purpose the concept of nationality is used and this section will give a description of the historical roots of two related concepts: nationality and citizenship. The origin of citizenship is generally traced back to ancient Greece and Rome. Yet neither the Greek City State nor the Roman Empire was a State, that is, a society whose political organization corresponded to the concept of a nation. What was essential to the Greek and Roman status of citizenship were the 'rights of participation in the political activities of what were then small communal communities'.[1] Citizenship primarily expressed a (personal) status rather than a belonging to a territorially defined nation.[2] According to Boll, the Greek and Roman ideas on citizenship—although directly relevant to current definitions of citizenship[3]—are therefore not the direct predecessors of nationality as it is now used under international law.[4] He argues that 'the modern concept of nationality is of recent origin … and essentially related to power over territory as well as natural persons'.[5]

Making a big leap to the time of the French Revolution, we see that the concept of nationality arose as a result of the nation-state becoming the principal political construct. When speaking about nationality as a post-revolutionary concept, Wihtol de Wenden refers to the close link that was established between nationality and the exaltation of the nation—a nation whose need for

---

[1] Síofra O'Leary, *The evolving concept of Community citizenship: from the free movement of persons to Union citizenship* (The Hague: Kluwer Law International, 1996), 5.

[2] 'À Athènes comme à Rome, la qualité de citoyen est liée, moins à la territorialité qu'à la liberté'. See Catherine Wihtol de Wenden, *Citoyenneté, nationalité et immigration* (Paris: Arcantère Éditions, 1989), 43.

[3] See for an historical overview of the concept of citizenship Paul Magnette, *Citizenship: the history of an idea* (Colchester: ECPR Press, 2005).

[4] Boll, *Multiple Nationality and International Law*, 61.

[5] Ibid. See also David Miller, *On Nationality* (Oxford: Clarendon Press, 1995), 29–31.

sacralisation[6] became increasingly dependent on the sentimental dimension of nationality.[7] Transcendence and differentiation thus became the basic characteristics of the nation.

Although the fundamental importance of national allegiance, which implied a general distrust of multiple attachments, would seem incompatible with the existence of dual nationality,[8] the hostility towards different allegiances was never excessive. Thus, the 1803 Civil Code did not link automatic loss of French nationality to simply possessing another passport. Only an explicit voluntary act in favour of a foreign nationality would end one's attachment with France. In the absence of such an act, possession of another nationality was without consequence. Moreover, the acquisition of French nationality was not conditional upon loss of the nationality of origin.[9] This attitude can be seen as an early manifestation of the French indifference towards dual nationality.[10]

The concept of nationality was developed in France at the end of the 18th and beginning of the 19th centuries and only then did it become the object of detailed legislation as is the case today.[11] At that specific time in history a rapid growth in international relations occurred, but it was also the time

---

6 Closa describes the process that the nation went through over time. Originally, nations were defined as 'communities of people of the same descent, who are integrated geographically in the form of settlements or neighbourhoods and culturally by their common language, customs and traditions, but who are not yet politically integrated in the form of state organization … Progressively, however, the concept of nation evolved to embody a transcendent meaning which referred to something other than the sum of many concrete and precise individuals'. Carlos Closa, "Citizenship of the Union and nationality of Member States", *Common Market Law Review* 32 (1995): 488.

7 Wihtol de Wenden, *Citoyenneté, nationalité et immigration*, 44–45. Terré articulates the idea as follows: '[After the French Revolution] le citoyen nouveau—on dira le national—c'est celui qu'unit un lien d'appartenance à une nation souveraine. A une nation, plûtot qu'à un État'. François Terré, "Réflexions sur la notion de nationalité", *Revue critique de droit international privé* 64 (1975): 205.

8 Terré, "Réflexions sur la notion de nationalité": 211.

9 Géraud de Geouffre de La Pradelle, "Dual Nationality and the French Citizenship Tradition", in *Dual Nationality, Social Rights and Federal Citizenship in the US and Europe*, ed. Randall Hansen and Patrick Weil (New York: Berghahn Books, 2002), 198.

10 Ibid.

11 Gerard-René de Groot and Matjaz Tratnik, *Nederlands nationaliteitsrecht* 4th ed., Studiepockets privaatrecht (Deventer: Kluwer, 2010), 38. De Groot and Tratnik remark that even during the negotiations at the Congress of Vienna (1814–1815) the idea prevailed that subjecthood was simply determined by residence. An independent concept of nationality which was independent from residence had still not taken root because there was as yet no

when strong national identities came into being.[12] The debate on the definition of the nation was also aroused by the transfer of sovereignty from the king to the nation.[13] Nonetheless, as Brubaker writes, 'the subjective "identity" of the vast majority of the population throughout Europe was no doubt largely local on the one hand[14] and religious on the other until at least the end of the eighteenth century. For most inhabitants local and regional identities continued to be more salient than national identity until late in the nineteenth century'.[15]

In late 18th century France, the legal structures dividing the population into different groups—guilds, for example—were abolished. The disappearance of these structures rendered the legal bond of State membership more important.[16] At the same time, the regulation of nationality became essential because important rights and duties ensued from it. The political rights that were gained after the French Revolution were reserved for French nationals, but the status of French national also entailed duties like compulsory military service, which was introduced in a great many countries around that time.[17] Nationality played a role in both public and private law. Whilst the French Constitution contained provisions on nationality as a condition for the exercise of political rights, the Civil Code laid down rules in respect of nationality as a condition for the exercise of civil rights. Only decades later would

---

general awareness that persons living in State X should under certain circumstances be regarded as belonging to State Y. See in this context also Zamoyski, who notes that the fact that a State had come to be seen as a moral entity with a right to a life of its own in the two or three decades preceding the Vienna Congress had no bearing on the negotiations. Consequently, the feudal concept of treating people as appurtenances to land still prevailed; in dividing territories the Great Powers treated the inhabitants as mere cattle: 'The political value of land was calculated not in acres or hectares, but in numbers of inhabitants, commonly referred to as "souls"'. Adam Zamoyski, *Rites of Peace. The Fall of Napoleon & the Congress of Vienna* (London: Harper Perennial, 2007), 386, 562.

12 Haro F. van Panhuys, *The Rôle of Nationality in International Law* (Leiden: A.W. Sühoff, 1959), 33.

13 Roger Price, *A concise history of France* 2nd ed. (Cambridge: Cambridge University Press, 2005), 98.

14 People belonged to a local commune. Peasants were bound to the land of their lords and lived in a state of hereditary subjection. It was thus the lords (the landowners) who decided where their subjects would live.

15 Rogers Brubaker, *Citizenship and Nationhood in France and Germany* (Cambridge, Massachusetts: Harvard University Press, 1992), 4–5.

16 Alexander Makarov, "Règles générales du droit de la nationalité", in *Recueil des cours de l'Académie de droit international de la Haye* (Leiden: Sijthoff, 1949), 277.

17 Ibid., 277–278.

nationality be regulated in special nationality laws.[18] In the mid-19th century French nationality law would be exported throughout Europe.[19]

A legal concept of membership already existed under the *Ancien Régime*. For this purpose the word *citoyenneté* was used, which was primarily perceived in terms of allegiance and attachment to the Kingdom of France.[20] In the words of Peter Sahlins, under the *Ancien Régime* 'individuals shared no common status except as subjects of the king'.[21] The distinction between citizens and foreigners was mainly relevant as a question of private law: the *aubain*, someone foreign to the kingdom, had neither the capacity to inherit nor to bequeath.[22] Problems over inheritance and succession made people contest their alien status before the courts (*parlements*); the ensuing judgments were the beginning of the evolution of the definition of the French person.[23] The above shows that French citizens were basically defined in the

---

[18] Ibid., 278–279. The Netherlands, heavily influenced by France, used a similar construction. The nationality provisions in the 1838 Dutch Civil Code were used in matters concerning civil law; the special nationality law of 1850 (*Wet op het Nederlanderschap*) defined Dutch nationality for the exercise of civic rights (active and passive suffrage and the appointment to government functions). This division was abolished on 1 July 1893, when the *Wet op het Nederlanderschap en het ingezetenschap 1892* came into force. See Gerard-René de Groot, *Handboek Nieuw Nationaliteitsrecht* (Deventer: Kluwer, 2003), 32–36; Gerard-René de Groot, "Geschiedenis van het Nederlandse nationaliteitsrecht in de negentiende eeuw", in *Wordt voor Recht gehalden, Opstellen ter gelegenheid van vijfentwintig jaar Werkgroep Limburgse Rechtsgeschiedenis*, ed. A.M.J.A. Berkvens and Th.J. van Rensch (Maastricht: Werkgroep Limburgse Rechtsgeschiedenis, 2005), 409. See also Chapter 4, Section 2.

[19] The French innovations in the field of nationality law—in particular the *ius sanguinis* principle—would be adopted by various countries in continental Europe in the mid-19th century. Britain maintained its 'feudal' tradition of *ius soli*, however; this tradition would later be transplanted to the British colonies. Patrick Weil, *How to Be French: Nationality in the Making since 1789*, trans. Catherine Porter (Durham: Duke University Press, 2008), 182. See also Hellmuth Hecker, *Staatsangehörigkeit im Code Napoléon als europäisches Recht: die Rezeption des Französischen Code Civil von 1804 in Deutschland und Italien in Beziehung zum Staatsangehörigkeitsrecht* (Hamburg und Frankfurt am Main: A. Metzner, 1980).

[20] The terms *citoyen, naturel, régnicole* and *sujet* were often used interchangeably at the time. See Benoît Guiguet, *Citoyenneté et nationalité: limites de la rupture d'un lien*, Thèse pour le doctorat en droit (Florence: European University Institute, 1997), 22–23.

[21] Peter Sahlins, *Unnaturally French. Foreign Citizens in the Old Regime and After* (Ithaca: Cornell University Press, 2004), 1.

[22] Christian Bruschi, "Droit de la nationalité et égalité des droits de 1789 à la fin du XIXe siècle", in *Questions de nationalité. Histoire et enjeux d'un code*, ed. Smaïn Laacher (Paris: Éditions l'Harmattan, 1987), 23; Brubaker, *Citizenship and Nationhood in France and Germany*, 36.

[23] Weil, *How to Be French: Nationality in the Making since 1789*, 11. Brubaker points out that over time the *parlements* under the *Ancien Régime* came to adopt a much more inclusive definition of the 'qualité de français'. Hence, by the 18th century 'many persons who formerly would have been considered aubains were now considered français'. As the 1791 Constitution

negative: 'Citizens of the kingdom were all those *not* subjected to the disabilities, incapacities, and liabilities of being an alien resident in France. Their identity was determined tacitly ....'[24]

The determination of *citoyenneté* under the *Ancien Régime* was based on the criterion of *ius soli*, which was never seriously challenged by the competing principle of *ius sanguinis*.[25] The French Revolution broke the feudal and monarchic tradition by creating 'a class of persons enjoying common rights, bound by common obligations, formally equal before the law',[26] and by introducing individual participation in the elaboration of national sovereignty.[27] Therefore, what mattered after the Revolution was not to define the French—which was just a question of fact—but the citizen, a status which now also came to be used to denote those who had political rights.[28] As a result, the meaning of the term citizen became confused: in customary usage it described a member of the people (which included women, children and the poor), while it was used in a legal sense to identify those who possessed political rights, namely men who had reached the age of majority and who possessed

---

codified the courts' case law, Brubaker argues that the French Revolution did not really change much with regard to the rules of attribution of French nationality. Brubaker, *Citizenship and Nationhood in France and Germany*, 37–38, 87.

24 Sahlins, *Unnaturally French. Foreign Citizens in the Old Regime and After*, 5.

25 Jean-Michel Belorgey, "Le droit de la nationalité: évolution historique et enjeux", in *Questions de nationalité. Histoire et enjeux d'un code*, ed. Smaïn Laacher (Paris: Éditions l'Harmattan, 1987), 62; Benoît Guiguet, "Citizenship and nationality: tracing the French roots of the distinction", in *European Citizenship: A European Challenge*, ed. Massimo La Torre (The Hague: Kluwer Law International, 1998), 96–97. Weil also shows that the *ius sanguinis* principle was not unfamiliar in 16th century France. In the Mabile decision (1576), a French court recognized as French a woman born in England to French parents, thereby allowing her to inherit her parents' property in France. Weil summarizes the situation under the *Ancien Régime* as follows: 'Anyone who resided in France was French, provided that he or she had been born in France, or had been born to French parents, or else had been naturalized. Birth on French soil, jus soli, remained the dominant criterion, however'. Weil, *How to Be French: Nationality in the Making since 1789*, 11–12.

26 Brubaker, *Citizenship and Nationhood in France and Germany*, 39.

27 The idea of popular sovereignty is laid down in Article 4 of the 'Déclaration des droits de l'homme et du citoyen' and provides that 'le principe de toute souveraineté réside essentiellement dans la nation; nul corps, nul individu ne peut exercer d'autorité qui n'en émane expressément'.

28 Weil notes that 'under the Revolution the definition of a French national was made explicit for the first time, but it was embedded in the definition of a citizen'. A turning point was reached with the 1803 Civil Code when 'nationality took on autonomy: it was defined independently of citizenship and became a personal right'; nationality would be transmitted through parentage and was no longer lost by establishing residence outside France. Weil, *How to Be French: Nationality in the Making since 1789*, 168.

sufficient resources. In other words, the term citizenship introduced semantic confusion as it referred to both passive and active citizens.[29]

The French Revolution, by shifting emphasis from membership to participation, established the participatory element of citizenship as being paramount.[30] Consequently, the post-revolutionary Constitutions placed great emphasis on the right to vote, which had an impact on the concept of citizenship. The status of citizen now came to be understood as the status of those who formed the nation, the latter being defined as a political construct.[31] Citizenship only partly denoted membership of a given community of origin, language and culture, which may explain why nationality had always remained a secondary question in the years immediately after the Revolution.[32]

Nevertheless, a solution had to be found to prevent one from being a citizen without having the civil rights and duties attached to the quality of being French. After all, only Frenchmen enjoyed equal civil rights; foreigners only enjoyed civil rights on the basis of reciprocal agreements with other States.[33] The question of how to regulate the quality of being French—or *nationality*, as State membership was then being increasingly called[34]—in the Civil Code (also known as Code Napoléon[35]) was heavily debated from 1801 onwards. Tronchet, head of the commission preparing the Civil Code, together with a majority of jurists and members of the Parliament opposed *ius soli* and pleaded for *ius sanguinis*. Napoleon Bonaparte, on the other hand, favoured *ius soli*

---

29 Guiguet, "Citizenship and nationality: tracing the French roots of the distinction", 98–101. The Constitution of 1791 makes a distinction between passive and active citizens, but this method was abandoned in subsequent Constitutions. The 1793 Constitution no longer defined the native French but only the French citizen who enjoyed political rights. It was only when the 1803 Civil Code introduced the conditions of French nationality that it became possible to identify that part of the population who did not have political rights. See also Brubaker, *Citizenship and Nationhood in France and Germany*, 87.

30 Edwige Liliane Lefebvre, "Republicanism and Universalism: Factors of Inclusion or Exclusion in the French Concept of Citizenship", *Citizenship Studies* 7, no. 1 (2003): 16–17.

31 Claire Marzo, *La dimension sociale de la citoyenneté européenne*, Thèse pour le doctorat en droit (Florence: European University Institute, 2009), 49.

32 Guiguet, "Citizenship and nationality: tracing the French roots of the distinction", 104–105.

33 Brubaker, *Citizenship and Nationhood in France and Germany*, 87.

34 Weil, *How to Be French: Nationality in the Making since 1789*, 30. Brubaker, however, traces the use of the term nationality back to the mid-19th century, when 'members of the French state were first routinely called nationaux, and state-membership first called nationalité'. In his view, the term nationality became used in the 'nationalist' 19th century because it designated an ethnocultural community. The late-19th century idea was that the ethno-cultural and political community should coincide, although this idea was never as strong in France as it was in Germany. Brubaker, *Citizenship and Nationhood in France and Germany*, 98–99.

35 Bruschi, "Droit de la nationalité et égalité des droits de 1789 à la fin du XIXe siècle", 33.

because a larger population meant a larger reservoir of people to conscript.[36] It was finally decided, however, to make the *ius sanguinis* principle *the exclusive criterion* in the Civil Code for the attribution of French nationality at birth.[37]

Yet in the course of the 19th century it became evident that the exclusive use of *ius sanguinis* also had its downsides: children born in France to non-French parents were no longer becoming French. After reaching the age of majority they could apply for naturalization, but this was a long and costly procedure. Moreover, for young foreign men the French conscription was a strong disincentive for naturalization.[38] Large numbers of foreign men who lived on French territory and who had neither been attributed French nationality at birth nor been naturalized into French nationality were, accordingly, exempt from military service. From 1818 this exemption was increasingly viewed as an unacceptable privilege.[39] The resentment about the exemption of long-settled foreigners from military service intensified in the 1870s and 80s, and in 1889 *ius soli* was again introduced in the Civil Code.[40] In the 1889 law

---

[36] Weil, *How to Be French: Nationality in the Making since 1789*, 24–27. Jurists primarily pleaded for *ius sanguinis* because they had the practical experience of representing clients who had been born abroad to French parents and whose French status had been called into question. The parliament's opposition to *ius soli* was primarily based 'on the determination to break with the feudal approach in order to make the nation the sole source of the quality of being French. The nation is like a family, and nationality must be transmitted the way the family name is transmitted: by parentage'.

[37] Ibid., 29. Some have pointed at the invention of *ius sanguinis* as the cause of the problem of dual nationality. Baty for example expressed a clear preference for *ius soli*, not because he longed to go back to feudal times but because 'la verité est que les êtres humains sont soumis à une souveraineté qui est limitée par rapport au territoire, et moins l'intrusion d'autres souverainetés viendra ajouter de confusion dans le problème, mieux cela vaudra pour tous les intéressés'. Thus, he lamented the introduction in France of *ius sanguinis* because it also created the problem of dual nationality: children born abroad to French parents were now French while they also belonged to another State by reason of their birth on its territory. See Th. Baty, "La double nationalité est-elle possible?", *Revue de droit international et de législation comparée* 7 (1926): 624–625.

[38] Weil, *How to Be French: Nationality in the Making since 1789*, 30–38.

[39] Ibid., 41.

[40] Brubaker, *Citizenship and Nationhood in France and Germany*, 85; Weil, *How to Be French: Nationality in the Making since 1789*, 41–52. Weil points to several factors which explain the rather late reintroduction of *ius soli* in the French Civil Code. *First*, the Civil Code was considered the foundation of modern law. With the reintroduction of *ius soli*—and thus the jettison of *ius sanguinis* as the exclusive principle for the attribution of French nationality—one of the core features of the Civil Code would be prejudiced. *Second*, under the international law principle of reciprocity the effect of imposing French nationality on foreign children could be that other countries would impose their nationality on French children born

ius soli was re-established at the heart of the nationality legislation and French nationality was attributed to foreigners born on French territory based on their degree of socialization: foreigners born in France to a parent who was also born in France were automatically French (double *ius soli*); the first generation foreigners born in France became French upon reaching the age of majority, yet French nationality could still be repudiated during the year that the foreigner reached the age of majority.[41]

It should be kept in mind that French nationality was only defined in the Civil Code with the objective of establishing who enjoyed the private law rights laid down therein;[42] only French nationals could exercise these civil rights.[43] Nationality thus took legal shape, but existed independently from citizenship.[44] These two concepts were thus clearly distinguishable, citizenship being part of the domain of constitutional and public law.[45]

Ultimately, however, the enjoyment of both civil and political rights ended up being dependent on nationality. Guiguet presumes this was done in an effort to eliminate the incoherence surrounding the whole topic and 'in aid of the "normalization", and the organization, of society'. He remarks, however, that using the criterion of nationality to also determine one's political rights

---

abroad. *Third and finally*, in the course of the 19th century France became increasingly preoccupied with its demographic shortage as well as with the growing concentration of foreigners living in its border regions. These trends called for a stronger role of *ius soli* in the nationality legislation.

41 Weil, *How to Be French: Nationality in the Making since 1789*, 49–51. It should be noted that a law of 1851 had already introduced double *ius soli* in French nationality law. However, this law had little success for it still allowed the option of repudiating French nationality at the age of majority. This 'conditional' attribution can be explained, according Brubaker, by France's fear that 'foreign governments would respond by attributing their citizenship to, and imposing military service on, the French residing abroad'. See Brubaker, *Citizenship and Nationhood in France and Germany*, 93; Patrick Weil and Alexis Spire, "France", in *Acquisition and Loss of Nationality, Policies and Trends in 15 European Countries*, ed. Rainer Bauböck, *et al.* (Amsterdam: Amsterdam University Press, 2006), 189.

42 In the words of Bruschi, the Civil Code 'répondait seulement à une question: Qui jouira des droits civils? L'égalité des droits n'était reconnue qu'aux Français'. Bruschi, "Droit de la nationalité et égalité des droits de 1789 à la fin du XIXe siècle", 33.

43 Thus, in the past the *citizen* had to be distinguished from the foreigner with regard to the enjoyment of civil rights; the introduction of *nationality* now served to distinguish the national from the foreigner for the same purpose.

44 Bruschi, "Droit de la nationalité et égalité des droits de 1789 à la fin du XIXe siècle", 33.

45 Guiguet, "Citizenship and nationality: tracing the French roots of the distinction", 107. The fact that private law and constitutional law were distinct realms is clearly evidenced in Article 7 of the Civil Code, which read that 'the exercise of civil rights is independent of the quality of citizen, which is acquired and retained only in conformity with constitutional law'. Quoted in Weil, *How to Be French: Nationality in the Making since 1789*, 196.

was not the only option. In fact, the Constitutions that were enacted in the aftermath of the French Revolution provided no justification for the requirement of nationality as a necessary condition for citizenship.[46]

2. *Terminological Observations in Respect of Nationality and Citizenship*

Great confusion exists as to the exact meaning of the terms 'nationality' and 'citizenship'. Not only does this follow from the fact that the legal and political science literature attach different meanings to them, but also because the terms do not have the same meaning in the different legal traditions. One must thus be mindful of the sense in which the terms are used. A similar problem frequently arises in respect of the terms 'Nation' and 'State'. These terms are sometimes used as synonyms, but we agree with Miller that a clear distinction should be made: '"Nation" must refer to a community of people with an *aspiration* to be politically self-determining, and "State" must refer to the set of political institutions that they may aspire to possess for themselves' (emphasis in original).[47]

It is first and foremost in the English language that confusion with respect to nationality and citizenship arises.[48] Though nationality is used in English to describe the legal link between an individual and a State, it is the status of British *citizen* that is the most privileged status that one can acquire in that it entails the right to enter the UK.[49] This status would correspond to being, for example, a French *national*. Confusingly, the English language also uses the term citizen to denote political membership.

In the continental tradition the distinction between the two notions is fairly straightforward. Nationality (*nationalité*, *nacionalidad*) is normally used to indicate a formal, legal bond between an individual and a State; the term citizenship (*citoyenneté*, *ciudadanía*) is used to denote political membership of a State. Or as Closa has put it: 'Nationality means the affiliation of an individual from the point of view of international law, whilst citizenship implies the host of domestic rights attached to that affiliation'.[50] There are, however, exceptions

---

46 Guiguet, "Citizenship and nationality: tracing the French roots of the distinction", 110–111.

47 Miller, *On Nationality*, 19.

48 See generally on these terminological issues Gerard-René de Groot, "Towards a European Nationality Law", in *Migration, Integration and Citizenship, A Challenge for Europe's Future*, ed. Hildegard Schneider (Maastricht: Forum, 2005), 14 ff.

49 Caroline Sawyer, "Report on the United Kingdom", EUDO Citizenship Observatory Country Reports (2009), 1.

50 Closa, "Citizenship of the Union and nationality of Member States": 492.

to this basic distinction. In Germany and Italy the terms *Staatsangehörigkeit* and *cittadinanza* are employed to describe a legal link; Italy also uses this term to denote 'political' citizenship. The words *Nationalität* and *nazionalità* are not used by reason of their ethnic connotation.[51] The double meaning of the term nationality makes some authors regret the prevalence of this word to describe the legal bond between an individual and a State; they expresses envy at the German term *Staatsangehörigkeit* which, while perfectly describing this bond, at the same time avoids the confusion that is associated with the terms nationality and citizenship.[52]

The difference between nationality in a legal and an ethnic sense is also reflected in the distinction made by Verwilghen between a '*nationalité de fait*' and a '*nationalité de droit*'.[53] The first refers to the sociological and ethnic meaning of the term in the sense of belonging to a *Volkstum* (nationality as a historic-biological term). Under this definition of nationality, a State can thus be comprised of more nationalities. A '*nationalité de droit*' has a different meaning and refers to the politico-legal bond between individual and State. At many points in the past there was a strong wish to merge the two notions, the idea being that in an ideal world each State would be composed of one ethnic 'nationality'.[54] Today this idea has lost much of its popularity and is identified with virulent nationalism. The collapse of Yugoslavia has been conceived by some, however, as proof that the idea that 'State' and 'Nation' should overlap is still alive.[55]

France has historically been identified as the model of the civic-republican nation, adhering to a conception of nationality which is open towards

---

[51] Ulrich K. Preuss, "Citizenship and the German Nation", *Citizenship Studies* 7, no. 1 (2003): 37–38. In the Italian literature on nationality law one will thus rarely find cases in which the term *nazionalità* is consistently used to denote the legal relationship between an individual and a State. See for such a rare case Anna Maria Del Vecchio, "Alcuni rilievi in tema di nazionalità e di cittadinanza nel contesto internazionale", *Rivista internazionale dei diritti dell'uomo* 10, no. 1 (1997): 9.

See in this context also Miller who notes that nationality (in his own non-legal definition which links this concept more to national identity) and ethnicity are phenomena that are of the same general type. Although he admits that a nation typically emerges from a (dominant) ethnic community, he thinks it is perfectly possible for ethnicity and nationality to co-exist because a nation is not an ethnically-homogeneous community. A succesful co-existence will depend on whether each ethnic group feels secure and comfortable with the State's common national identity and its political institutions. Miller, *On Nationality*, 19–21.

[52] Michel Verwilghen, "Conflits de nationalités, plurinationalité et apatridie", in *Recueil des cours de l'Académie de droit international de la Haye* (Leiden: Sijthoff, 1999), 75.

[53] Ibid., 67–74.

[54] Ibid., 96.

[55] Boll, *Multiple Nationality and International Law*, 67.

immigrants. France is then contrasted with Germany, a country which is said to be closed to immigrants because it primarily perceives its national identity in a romantic, ethno-cultural sense.[56] This makes it difficult for foreigners to become part of the German nation.[57] Under this view, France adheres to the concept of nationality as a '*nationalité de droit*' and Germany to that of a '*nationalité de fait*'. In other words, 'the French understand their nation as the creation of their state, the Germans their nation as the basis of their state'.[58]

These different understandings of nationhood led, in Brubaker's view, to radically different nationality laws in France and Germany. 'The expansive, assimilationist citizenship law of France, which automatically transforms second-generation immigrants into citizens, reflects the state-centered, assimilationist self-understanding of the French. And the German definition of the citizenry as a community of descent, restrictive toward non-German immigrants yet remarkably expansive toward ethnic Germans from Eastern Europe and the Soviet Union, reflects the pronounced ethnocultural inflection in German self-understanding'.[59] Thus, according to Brubaker—who wrote his book before the significant reforms of German nationality law in 2000—the key difference between France and Germany lay in the differing significance attached respectively to birth and to prolonged residence in the territory. Brubaker ascribed the fact that France accorded its nationality to children

---

56 Both models define membership differently. Under the civic-republican concept, membership is dependent on subjective will; under the ethno-cultural view it is dependent on criteria such as descent and language.

57 While around 1800 the idea prevailed in France that citizenship dominated over nationality and that a political conception of nationhood dominated over an ethno-cultural one, the German understanding of nationhood was fundamentally ethno-cultural. In other words, in France 'political unity has been understood as constitutive, cultural unity as expressive of nationhood' whilst in Germany 'the Volksgeist is constitutive, the state merely expressive, of nationhood'. See Brubaker, *Citizenship and Nationhood in France and Germany*, 7–10.

58 Ibid., 184. For a discussion on the use of the civic-republican/ethno-cultural distinction in our present time see Faist, "The Fixed and Porous Boundaries of Dual Citizenship", 2.

59 Brubaker, *Citizenship and Nationhood in France and Germany*, 14,78–79. Brubaker argued that French law was not only more inclusive towards immigrants because it contained *ius soli* elements (whereas Germany did not when he wrote his book), but also because the naturalization rates were much higher in France than in Germany. Brubaker thinks this can be explained by the fact that dual nationality was accepted in France and not in Germany, but certainly also by the different understanding of naturalization by immigrants in France in Germany. While immigrants in France had adopted an instrumental, 'desacralized' understanding of nationality, in Germany naturalization was perceived as involving 'not only a change in legal status, but a change in nature, a change in political and cultural identity'. Hence in Brubaker's view, the barriers to naturalization in Germany lay 'not only in the restrictiveness of legal provisions but equally in the political culture of naturalization'.

born in France to foreign parents to its assimilationist understanding of nationality while Germany, due to its ethnic conception of nationality, exclusively accorded German nationality on the basis of descent from German parents.[60]

Brubaker's principal claim was that the 'affinity between definitions of citizenship and conceptions of nationhood makes it difficult to change the former in fundamental ways', and that elite understandings of nationhood 'limit the universe of debate and make a fundamental restructuring of citizenship improbable.'[61] He argued that nationality in a nation-state is 'inevitably bound up with nationhood and national identity, membership of the state with membership of the nation' and concluded that the discussion on nationality in both France and Germany was primarily one of national identity and self-understanding, and not of State interests.[62] As a result, their nationality laws must to a large extent be inherently stable: just as an exclusive use of *ius sanguinis* in France is incompatible with the prevalent assimilationist view of the French nation, so Germany will always reject *ius soli* as foreign to the ethnic perception of the German State.[63]

Brubaker's view—in particular his prediction that *ius soli* would be unthinkable in Germany—could not stand the test of time, since already in 2000 *ius soli* was introduced into German law.[64] Brubaker certainly has a point when he refers to the importance of legal tradition for the continuity in French and German nationality law (nationality laws generally became 'legal traditions or objects of belief within legal traditions'[65]), but his explanation for the exclusive use of *ius sanguinis* in Germany seems to be flawed, for it does not acknowledge the close similarity between French and Prussian nationality law in the

---

60 Ibid., 81. Weil agrees and points out that the late-19th century idea of socialization as the basis for acquisition of French nationality was not a passing trend. On the contrary, it 'structured French nationality and gave it its permanence'. See Weil, *How to Be French: Nationality in the Making since 1789*, 53.

61 Brubaker, *Citizenship and Nationhood in France and Germany*, 184–185.

62 Ibid., 181. In Brubaker's view, long-term resident foreigners have such a strong position in terms of access to the labour market and social benefits that acquisition of either French or German nationality is only of modest import and does not really affect their life chances. He therefore holds the opinion that a country's nationality law is not primarily a reflection of State interests—after all, long-term residents have almost equal rights with nationals—but a reflection of its idea of national identity.

63 Ibid., 183.

64 Kay Hailbronner, "Germany", in *Acquisition and Loss of Nationality, Policies and Trends in 15 European Countries*, ed. Rainer Bauböck, *et al.* (Amsterdam: Amsterdam University Press, 2006).

65 Weil, *How to Be French: Nationality in the Making since 1789*, 178, 191.

mid-19th century. The common distinction between France and Germany has therefore also been called a 'false opposition'.[66] In fact, Weil has shown that in the mid-19th century Prussia (the most influential German state of a Germanic Confederation which consisted of another thirty-eight German States and whose nationality law would be extended to the entire German territory in 1871) came very close to attributing nationality on the basis of residency, which was the system adopted by Austria at the time. Instead of copying the Austrians, Prussia decided to adopt the French model of naturalization in 1842. As has been shown above, however, France did not have *ius soli* at that time.[67] The fact that the German elite nearly implemented a rule which made residence the decisive factor for acquisition of nationality seems incompatible with Brubaker's analysis that the exclusive use of *ius sanguinis* is an inherent feature of Germany's own ethnic self-understanding. Germany in fact came very close to adopting the principle of *ius soli* at a time when this was still very much opposed by France.

Also the political science and sociological literature uses the terms nationality and citizenship, the latter much more frequently than the former as these disciplines are not predominantly interested in membership as a legal status. When reading about 'dual citizenship' in this literature, it may therefore not refer to multiple nationality in the sense used in this study. More likely, it tries to describe phenomena like transnationalism or varying forms of citizenship in a federal State, and thus denotes multiple (political) memberships rather than multiple legal links with different States. In this connection, it is worth pointing out that the sociologist Faist emphatically positions 'dual citizenship' among recent academic conceptualizations like transnationalism,

---

66 Ibid., 173, 191.

67 Ibid., 173–178. Weil points out that the question of Prussian nationality became much more important when serfdom was abolished in 1807. This meant that Prussian peasants were no longer bound to the land of their lords but could settle anywhere in Prussia. This, in turn, led to massive immigration within Prussia, but it also triggered migration into Prussia from other German States. Finally, the Prussian Nationality Code as promulgated on 31 December 1842 attributed Prussian nationality to children born to a Prussian father; foreigners could acquire Prussian nationality through naturalization.

Significantly, however, Weil also mentions that in the mid-1830s a nine-member commission, charged with studying the question of access to Prussian nationality by foreigners, only decided by a five-to-four vote not to automatically grant access to Prussian nationality after ten years' residence (the 'Austrian model'). Instead, the 'French model' was opted for, which meant that an explicit decision by the public authorities (naturalization) was required to acquire Prussian nationality. Consequently, it was only by a single voice that the 'French model'—which was emphatically not based on *ius soli* at the time!—was chosen over the 'Austrian model' of automatic acquisition of nationality by virtue of residence.

postnationalism, nested citizenship,[68] cosmopolitan citizenship, extra-territorial citizenship etc.[69]

Finally, a more philosophical definition of nationality can be given. According to Miller, who has extensively written in defence of the concept of nationality,[70] nationality comprises three interconnected propositions. These concern *personal identity* ('if a person is invited to specify those elements that are essential to his identity … it is in order to refer to nationality'), an *ethical* dimension to nationality[71] ('the duties we owe to our fellow-nationals are different from, and more extensive than, the duties we owe to human beings as such'), and finally a *political* dimension ('people who form a national community in a particular territory have a good claim to political self-determination; there ought to be put in place an institutional structure that enables them to decide collectively matters that concern primarily their own community').[72]

---

68 See on this concept (and its relation with the nationality laws of the EU Member States) Thomas Faist, "Social Citizenship in the European Union: Nested Membership", *Journal of Common Market Studies* 39, no. 1 (2001): 48, 55.

69 Faist, "Dual citizenship: Change, Prospects, and Limits", 172.

70 In Miller's view, 'nationality answers one of the most pressing needs of the modern world, namely how to maintain solidarity among the populations of states that are large and anonymous, such that their citizens cannot possibly enjoy the kind of community that relies on kinship or face-to-face interaction'. In spite of the mythical and imaginary elements in the idea of nationality, people from different political backgrounds can define themselves against the common background as provided by nationality. Thus, rather than being a conservative and perhaps even a dangerous idea, nationality can be reshaped *par excellence* to meet new challenges and new needs. Miller also stresses the importance of a nation's mythical self-conception as expressed in the perception of its own nationality, even if this conception is proved to be founded on false myths. First, such myths 'provide reassurance that the national community of which one now forms part is solidly based in history, that it embodies a real continuity between generations'; second, these myths 'perform a moralizing role, by holding up before us the virtues of our ancestors and encouraging us to live up to them'. Miller, *On Nationality*, 35–36; David Miller, "In Defence of Nationality", in *Citizenship and National Identity* (Cambridge: Polity Press, 2000), 31–32. See also Brian Barry, *Culture and Equality. An Egalitarian Critique of Multiculturalism* (Cambridge: Polity Press, 2001), 80. Barry describes this understanding of nationality as 'civic' nationality.

71 David Miller, "The Ethical Significance of Nationality", *Ethics* 98, no. 4 (1988); Miller, *On Nationality*, 68 ff.

72 Miller, "In Defence of Nationality", 27. Miller here employs and develops the term 'nationality' as used by J.S. Mill who, though acknowledging that a feeling of nationality could be generated by race, descent, language, geographical limits and a common religion, pointed to common political and historical antecedents (a community of recollections) as the strongest factor to foster such a feeling. John Stuart Mill, "Nationality", in *Utilitarianism, Liberty, Representative Government*, ed. H.B. Acton (London: Dent, 1972), 360.

If these propositions alone do not serve to define the concept of nationality, Miller also identifies five elements which distinguish nationality from other collective sources of personal identity. Nationality refers to 'a community constituted by mutual belief, extended in history, active in character, connected to a particular territory, and thought to be marked off from other communities by its members' distinct traits'.[73]

3. *The Role of Nationality in Different Fields of Law*

Nationality plays distinct roles in different fields of the law. It is a traditional subject of discussion whether nationality law is in the first place part of public or private law.[74] In any case, nationality plays (or has played) a role in public and private law, but is also of great relevance to both public and private international law.[75] We shall briefly look at the meaning of nationality in these respective areas. The specific role of *multiple* nationality in each of these fields is further examined in the course of this book.

Until far into the 19th century, nationality played a significant role in private law. In the Netherlands, for example, it is only since 1869 that the rules of Dutch private law have applied equally to Dutch nationals and foreigners.[76] In his work on the origin of the notions nationality and citizenship, Guiguet shows that matters of private law called for a distinction between citizens and foreigners in 16th century France. This followed from the fact that the latter could neither inherit nor bequeath.[77] The determination of one's status as a citizen or foreigner was therefore important from the perspective of private law, and not from that of public law. After all, at that point in time the individual was still seen as a subject and not yet as a member of a sovereign people enjoying political rights.[78] It was for the purposes of succession law that the need arose to distinguish the citizen from the foreigner.[79] In today's world,

---

[73] Miller, *On Nationality*, 22–25; Miller, "In Defence of Nationality", 28–31.

[74] Terré, "Réflexions sur la notion de nationalité": 197–203; Paul Lagarde, *La nationalité française* 3rd ed. (Paris: Dalloz, 1997), 7. Although Lagarde acknowledges that nationality belongs to both public and private law, he stresses its private law dimension because 'la nationalité, comme la majorité, fait accéder l'individu à un certain statut et constitue donc un élément de son statut personnel'.

[75] Verwilghen, "Conflits de nationalités, plurinationalité et apatridie", 88–121.

[76] de Groot and Tratnik, *Nederlands nationaliteitsrecht*, 29.

[77] See also *supra* Section 1.

[78] Guiguet, "Citizenship and nationality: tracing the French roots of the distinction", 98.

[79] Guiguet, *Citoyenneté et nationalité: limites de la rupture d'un lien*, 23.

nationality is no longer determinative for the application of rules of private law. Yet it should not be forgotten that many subjects belonging to the realm of private law—such as the rules on descent and adoption—are important for nationality law.

Nationality is used in public law to distinguish nationals from aliens. This is done for the purpose of restricting certain rights—such as the right of sojourn or voting rights—to nationals. However, a development can be discerned, in the Netherlands at least, to grant rights to aliens that were traditionally reserved for nationals.[80] The distinction between national and alien has also become less salient for those possessing the status of European citizen: European citizens have the right to vote and be elected on a local level in other EU Member States.

Several writers—especially those writing in French—distinguish between a vertical and a horizontal aspect to nationality when describing the public law dimension of nationality.[81] The vertical aspect recalls the notion of allegiance, which forms the basis for the notion of a people as the body of subjects of a State;[82] the purpose of defining the own population reflects the (vertical) public law and international law dimension of nationality. The domestic (horizontal) dimension comes to the fore when nationality is used to identify a national in the sociological sense as a member of the population.[83] Pérez Vera also

[80] de Groot and Tratnik, *Nederlands nationaliteitsrecht*, 29. It is worthy of note that in 1988 the Netherlands abolished the nationality requirement for a lot of public functions. Certain State facilities, such as a number of subsidies, allocations and licenses as well as medical care and education are also dependent on legal residence and not on nationality. See C.A.J.M. Kortmann, "La nationalité et les fonctions politiques et publiques aux Pays-Bas", in *La condition juridique de l'étranger, hier et aujourd'hui. Actes du Colloque organisé à Nimègue les 9–11 mai 1988 par les Facultés de Droit de Poitiers et de Nimègue* (Nijmegen: Faculteit der Rechtsgeleerdheid, 1988), 64; G.G. Lodder, *Vreemdelingenrecht in vogelvlucht* 3rd ed. (Den Haag: Sdu uitgevers, 2008), 15–16.

In other countries, however, nationality seems to matter more because foreigners have fewer rights. In discussing the effects of not possessing French nationality, Lagarde mentions that non-nationals do not have political rights, have more limited freedom of press and cannot exercise public functions. Lagarde, *La nationalité française*, 4.

[81] Terré, "Réflexions sur la notion de nationalité": 203, 208; Elisa Pérez Vera, "Citoyenneté de l'Union européene, nationalité et conditions des étrangers", in *Recueil des cours de l'Académie de droit international de la Haye* (Leiden: Sijthoff, 1996), 278–283; Lagarde, *La nationalité française*, 3.

[82] Allegiance is not used here in its outdated historical meaning, but rather indicates the collectivity of persons who have a stable and permanent link with a State and can therefore be considered to constitute its population.

[83] Lagarde, *La nationalité française*, 3. Whereas the vertical dimension reflects 'une situation de subordination du national envers son État', the horizontal dimension 'fait du national le

notes that the *Nottebohm* judgment makes mention of this aspect of nationality.[84]

Nationality is used in private international law (PIL) as a connecting factor, especially in the field of personal status and family law.[85] (The observations made here introduce a theme that will be explored in greater detail in Chapter 2.) It designates the legal system that should deal with a case which is linked to several jurisdictions.[86] As a connecting factor, however, it has lost ground over time to habitual residence.[87] An obvious problem arises when nationality is the connecting factor in cases which concern a dual or multiple national.[88] Some have therefore stated that the equality of the sexes in nationality law, as a result of which different persons within a family can possess different nationalities, has caused great difficulties in the field of PIL.[89] The problem of dual nationality in this field has also been raised in the context of a more inclusive nationality policy towards immigrants who are, for example, allowed to retain their nationality of origin upon naturalization or are attributed the host country's nationality at birth.[90]

---

membre d'une communauté, la population constitutive de l'État, dont sont exclus les étrangers, et le fait bénéficier du status réservé à cette communauté'.

84 Pérez Vera, "Citoyenneté de l'Union européene, nationalité et conditions des étrangers", 280–281. The ICJ ruled in *Nottebohm* (see also *infra* Section 5.1) that 'nationality is a legal bond having as its basis a social fact of attachment, a genuine connection of existence, interests and sentiments, together with the existence of reciprocal rights and duties. It may be said to constitute the juridical expression of the fact that the individual upon whom it is conferred, either directly by the law or as the result of an act of the authorities, is in fact more closely connected with the population of the State conferring nationality than with that of any other State'.

85 Saarloos argues, however, that 'nationality as a connecting factor for personal status … does not seem to be in line with the European idea of an area of freedom, security and justice'. He submits that habitual residence is a more suitable criterion. Kees Jan Saarloos, *European private international law on legal parentage? Thoughts on a European instrument implementing the principle of mutual recognition in legal parentage*, Dissertatie Universiteit Maastricht (Maastricht: Océ Business Services, 2010), 315.

86 Jean-Yves Carlier, *Autonomie de la Volonté et Statut Personnel* (Bruxelles: Bruylant, 1992), 196.

87 Luc Strikwerda, *Inleiding tot het Nederlandse internationaal privaatrecht*, 78–79.

88 In a French textbook the example is given of a 19-year-old dual national who possesses both French and Algerien nationality. As both countries refer to their national law concerning questions of personal status, this person's legal capacity is uncertain: under French law one reaches the age of majority at eighteen and in Algeria at the age of twenty-one. See Marie-Laure Niboyet and Géraud De Geouffre de La Pradelle, *Droit international privé* 2nd ed. (Paris: LGDJ, 2009), 528–530.

89 Isabella Castangia, *Il criterio della cittadinanza nel diritto internazionale privato* (Napoli: Casa Editrice Dott. Eugenio Jovane, 1983), 61.

90 See on this issue in the context of plans (which materialized by the law reform of 2000) for a more inclusive German nationality policy towards long-term immigrants: Dieter Martiny,

It has been suggested that in practice it is the judge, much more than the legislator, who must confront the difficulties that result from dual nationality by deciding on the applicable law concerning dual nationals.[91] Common practice in such a situation, and allowed under Article 3 of the 1930 Hague Convention, is that a national court disregards the foreign nationalities that their own national may possess.[92] The foreign nationality will, accordingly, have no bearing on the case. The other nationality is merely the result of the wide State discretion in nationality law, which allows States to decide autonomously who to grant their nationality to; the national court seized is under no obligation to pay any attention to this foreign nationality.[93] Yet by defining a person as the national of a single State, courts in a way refuse to accept dual nationality as a fact, which *in practice* has the effect of 'stripping' someone

---

"Probleme der Doppelstaatsangehörigkeit im deutschen Internationalen Privatrecht", *Juristenzeitung*, no. 23 (1993): 1149; Nina Dethloff, "Doppelstaatsangehörigkeit und Internationales Privatrecht", ibid., no. 2 (1995): 64.

Martiny concludes that cases of dual Turkish-German nationality already exist and that an increase of the number of Turkish-German nationals would not cause problems in the field of PIL. After all, the systematic preference for the German nationality would, quite simply, lead to the application of German instead of Turkish law. He points out however (as does Dethloff) that the reform plans paid no attention to the subject of dual nationality in private international law; dual nationality was merely discussed in the context of public law rights. See also Helmut Rittstieg, "Dual Citizenship: Legal and Political Aspects in the German Context", in *From Aliens to Citizens. Redefining the Status of Immigrants in Europe*, ed. Rainer Bauböck (Aldershot: Avebury, 1994), 116–117.

91 de Geouffre de La Pradelle, "Dual Nationality and the French Citizenship Tradition", 202.

92 Verwilghen, "Conflits de nationalités, plurinationalité et apatridie", 429; Anna Maria Del Vecchio, "La considerazione del principio di effettività nel vincolo di nazionalità e di cittadinanza doppia o plurima (e problematiche relative)", *Rivista internazionale dei diritti dell'uomo* 13, no. 1 (2000): 13–14; Stefan Oeter, "Effect of nationality and dual nationality on judicial cooperation, including treaty regimes such as extradition", in *Rights and Duties of Dual Nationals*, ed. David A. Martin and Kay Hailbronner (The Hague: Kluwer Law International, 2003), 66.

In Oeter's view, what lies behind this doctrine, which essentially comes down to a claim of exclusive jurisdiction, is the traditional concept of nationality as an exclusive bond of allegiance. Although the German Supreme Court, by opting for the principle of the effective nationality in a decision of 1979, reversed the doctrine that the foreign nationality of a German dual national may be disregarded, it was subsequently overruled by the legislator, who again declared German nationality to be the only and decisive factor for deciding on the applicable law.

93 In the words of de La Pradelle, 'la préférence donnée presque systématiquement à [la nationalité française] signifie qu'en principe, un Français ne peut faire reconnaître en France qu'il possède une autre nationalité'. Géraud de Geouffre de La Pradelle, "Nationalité française, extranéité, nationalités étrangères", in *Mélanges dédiés à Dominique Holleaux* (Paris: Librairie de la Cour de Cassation, 1990), 146.

of his or her other nationality.[94] This attitude contrasts with the growing tolerance of dual nationality on the legislative level. De la Pradelle has expressed this as follows: 'It is hardly logical to adopt, through the legislature, rules of attribution that increasingly expand multiple belonging, while simultaneously refusing, through the courts, to sanction the majority of concrete manifestations of these belongings'.[95] In the next chapter we will address in more detail the question whether a national court should always automatically apply the law of the forum to a dual national, and whether there should be room for the recognition of foreign judgments which have an impact on the personal status of a dual national.

Finally, if all nationalities are foreign, the solution commonly adopted is to determine a person's dominant or effective nationality.[96] In so doing, the judge will take into consideration various factors such as residence, spoken languages, identity documents and the fulfilment of military obligations.[97] In Section 9 we will see that the principle of the effective nationality, as used in private international law, was transplanted to the realm of public international law by Article 5 of the 1930 Hague Convention.[98]

Lastly, nationality is used to define the personal substratum of the State and is therefore of preeminent importance in public international law. The position of nationality seems to be strongest in this field of the law as it is *the* factor which decides who belongs to a given State.[99] The next sections will explore the role of nationality under international law in greater depth.

From this short overview on the role of nationality in different fields of the law, it may be concluded that nationality is of great importance but that some of its functions are waning. Certain classic public law rights are now also given to aliens or European citizens. As a connecting factor in private international law, nationality is faced with competition from habitual residence—even in the field of personal status and family law.

---

94 de Geouffre de La Pradelle, "Dual Nationality and the French Citizenship Tradition", 205.

95 Ibid., 196. See also Verwilghen, who refers to this practice as 'jouer sur deux tableaux à la fois', in other words, 'accepter l'accroissement des pluripatrides possédant la nationalité du for, mais décider de ne jamais tenir compte des nationalités étrangères de ceux-ci'. Verwilghen, "Conflits de nationalités, plurinationalité et apatridie", 446.

96 Paul Lagarde, "Le principe de proximité dans le droit international privé contemporain. Cours général de droit international privé", ibid. (1986), 78.

97 Patrick Courbe, *Le nouveau droit de la nationalité* 2nd ed. (Paris: Dalloz, 1998), 30.

98 Katharina Boele-Woelki, *Die Effektivitätsprüfung der Staatsangehörigkeit im niederländischen internationalen Familienrecht*, Dissertation Freie Universität Berlin (Deventer: Kluwer, 1981), 39–40.

99 de Groot and Tratnik, *Nederlands nationaliteitsrecht*, 32.

4. *The Function of Nationality under Municipal and International Law*

This section is concerned with the function of nationality at the national and international levels and should show us whether its function is the same in both cases. Another question is whether certain rights and duties are inherent in the concept of nationality or not. The legal doctrine is divided on this question. We subscribe to the view of those who argue that both at the municipal and at the international level nationality must be regarded as an 'empty' notion, entailing no inherent rights or duties.

It was suggested above that the position of nationality is strongest in public international law; the primary function of nationality is to define who is a national of a given State. Whilst on the *international* plane nationality serves to discern the personal substrata of States, on the *municipal* level it distinguishes the national from the alien.[100] The personal substratum (*le patrimoine humain de l'État*) is one of three classic elements of a State, the other two being a territory and authority over people and territory.[101] These remarks immediately show that multiple nationality is incompatible with the primary function of nationality under international law: a multiple national by definition belongs to the personal substratum of more than one State.[102] On the other hand, a prohibition on multiple nationality would contradict another principle of international law, namely the principle that every State is free—within the limits set by international law—to determine rules with regard to its own nationality. One can therefore argue that the exclusive competence in the area of nationality law provides a justification for the existence of dual nationality. In other words, dual nationality, as the inevitable consequence of States exercising their legitimate autonomy, cannot be condemned under international law.[103]

Nationality plays a role on both the municipal and the international planes. According to Weis, 'nationality, in the sense of membership of a State, the "belonging" of an individual to a State, presupposes the co-existence of States. Nationality is, therefore, a concept not only of municipal law but also of international law'.[104] As the content of nationality is defined by municipal law,

---

[100] Ko Swan Sik, *De meervoudige nationaliteit* (Leiden: Sijthoff, 1957), 7.

[101] Ibid.

[102] Ko Swan Sik, "Nationaliteit en het volkenrecht", in *Nationaliteit in Volkenrecht en Internationaal Privaatrecht, Preadvies voor de Nederlandse Vereniging voor Internationaal Recht* (Deventer: Kluwer, 1981), 34.

[103] de Geouffre de La Pradelle, "Dual Nationality and the French Citizenship Tradition", 193.

[104] Paul Weis, *Nationality and statelessness in international law* 2nd revised ed. (Alphen aan den Rijn: Sijthoff & Noordhoff, 1979), 29.

however, no generally accepted definition of nationality exists. Weis does attempt to give one and refers to nationality as 'a specific relationship between individual and State conferring mutual rights and duties as distinct from the relationship of the alien to the State of sojourn'.[105] Another oft-cited definition of nationality for municipal purposes can be found in the 1955 *Nottebohm* judgment of the International Court of Justice (ICJ), which expresses the idea that nationality should be a manifestation of a clear relation between a person and a State. This position is now commonly accepted and it is agreed that a State should not accord its nationality in the absence of such a relation. The ICJ writes in *Nottebohm*:

> Nationality is a legal bond having as its basis a social fact of attachment, a genuine connection of existence, interests and sentiments, together with the existence of reciprocal rights and duties. It may be said to constitute the juridical expression of the fact that the individual upon whom it is conferred, either directly by the law or as the result of an act of the authorities, is in fact more closely connected with the population of the State conferring nationality than with that of any other State.[106]

Coming back to the question whether nationality in itself has a specific content, we disagree with Weis's abovementioned remark that certain rights and duties form an intrinsic part of the notion of nationality. It is tempting to consider certain rights or obligations—such as voting rights or military service—to be dependent on or inherent to nationality, yet this has been shown not to always be the case.[107] There are examples of States that also force resident non-nationals to fulfil military obligations, and some States grant voting rights to non-nationals on a local level. Another example concerns access to public functions. There is often a nationality requirement for the exercise of certain functions, but this is not necessarily the case. Lastly, we may point to the situation in the United Kingdom. Although the right to live in the country of which you are a national is by many regarded as inherent to nationality, the example of the UK demonstrates that this is not necessarily true.

---

[105] Ibid. Boll also comes to the conclusion that certain rights and duties are inherent to nationality because they directly ensue from it. See Boll, *Multiple Nationality and International Law*, 95.

[106] Nottebohm case (second phase), 6 April 1955, ICJ Reports 4, page 23. D'Argent makes the following interesting comment: 'Remarquons la double insistance sur le "fait" qu'est le rattachement [he refers to the term "fact" in the second sentence], non pas à l'État conférant la nationalité, mais à la *population* de cet État, ce qui ne manque pas d'être quelque peu circulaire puisque cette population n'est celle de cet État que parce que les individus qui la composent en ont la nationalité' (emphasis in original). Pierre d'Argent, "Nationalité et droit international public", *Annales de Droit de Louvain* 63, no. 3 (2003): 225.

[107] Ko Swan Sik, "Nationaliteit en het volkenrecht", 13.

The UK knows several categories of citizens not having the right of abode in the UK.[108]

These examples show us that nationality in itself does not entail specific rights and/or duties for individuals or States. We therefore agree with writers such as Makarov[109] and De Groot who see nationality as an 'empty notion' (this view is wholly compatible, however, with the fact that international law requires a 'genuine link' between an individual and a State for a nationality to have effect on the international plane). In De Groot's definition, 'the concept of nationality only acquires substantial meaning as a result of the legal consequences which national … legal systems connect with it.'[110] We also find this idea of nationality as an empty notion confirmed in the statement by the ICJ in *Nottebohm* that 'nationality serves above all to determine that the person upon whom it is conferred enjoys the rights and is bound by the obligations which the law of the State in question grants to or imposes on its nationals.'[111]

Our support, in what may perhaps be a mere academic debate, for the *theoretical* idea that nationality itself should be regarded as 'empty', does not prevent us from acknowledging that *in practice* nationality may not be so empty at all. Though one can say that nationality does not entail duties and rights per se, certain rights and obligations must be commonly understood as being attached to nationality, despite the exceptions mentioned above. Why would statelessness and (in the past) multiple nationality otherwise meet with such great opposition?[112] Is the opposition to multiple nationality not based on the multiplication of rights and duties that are understood to be intrinsically linked to nationality? This line of reasoning is used by d'Oliveira who criticizes De Groot by submitting that just because nationality may not contain a

---

108 See in this connection Case C-192/99 *Kaur* [2001] ECR I-01237. We will come back to this case in Section 11 *infra* when discussing the role of nationality in the European Union.

109 Alexander Makarov, *Allgemeine Lehren des Staatsangehörigkeitsrechts* 2nd ed. (Stuttgart: Kohlhammer, 1962), 31–33. Makarov writes that 'jedes neue Gesetz, das in einem Staate erscheint, kann eine Änderung des Inhalts der an die Staatsangehörigkeit angeknüpften Rechte und Pflichten mit sich bringen'. Makarov also mentions that especially the older literature supported the view that some rights and duties were inherent in the concept of nationality. The abstract character of nationality is an idea of later date.

110 See the English summary in de Groot, *Staatsangehörigkeitsrecht im Wandel*, 342. See also Rolando Quadri, "Cittadinanza", in *Novissimo Digesto Italiano*, ed. Antonio Azara and Ernesto Eula (Torino: Unione Tipografico, 1957), 310; Ko Swan Sik, "Nationaliteit en het volkenrecht", 13.

111 Nottebohm case (second phase), 6 april 1955, ICJ Reports 4, page 20.

112 This also seems to be Makarov's opinion, who defines nationality itself as empty but at the same time observes that the regulation of nationality gained importance after certain rights and duties were attached to it, such as political rights and military obligations. Makarov, "Règles générales du droit de la nationalité", 278.

definite set of rights and obligations does not make it an empty notion; in metaphorical terms, a bottle which contains different liquids is not empty.[113] To his mind, nationality does imply rights and obligations, such as diplomatic protection, although admittedly *à contenu variable*. The exact set of rights and obligations of which nationality is comprised will thus always be a surprise to some extent. Makarov and De Groot will probably agree with this analysis, but rebut that these rights and obligations are still deliberately made *dependent* on nationality. They could have been made dependent on another criterion than nationality—for example residence—and thus do not form an intrinsic part of the concept of nationality. On the other hand, d'Oliveira rightly points to some important consequences of defining nationality as an empty notion; not only does it make the concept of nationality unusable for normative evaluations, it also renders nationality unsuitable as a criterion to, for example, measure (or punish) (un)patriotic behaviour.[114]

This discussion on the interpretation of nationality on the municipal plane can be applied equally to the international plane. For the international level as well, the question arises whether nationality is merely a formal, empty status, or whether it directly entails rights and duties.

Weis defines nationality on the international plane as a term 'denoting the allocation of individuals, termed nationals, to a specific State—the State of nationality—as members of that State, a relation which confers upon the State of nationality ... rights and duties in relation to other States'.[115] This idea—rights and duties exist, but only between States and not between an individual

---

[113] Hans Ulrich Jessurun d'Oliveira, "Europees burgerschap: dubbele nationaliteit?", in *Asser Colloquium Europees Recht, 33e zitting, 2003* (The Hague: T.M.C. Asser Press, 2004), 114–115. Van Panhuys makes a distinction between nationality in a formal sense (membership of a State as a formal status) and nationality in the material sense (the substance of nationality). Not willing to take sides in the debate on whether nationality is a purely formal category or whether it should be characterized according to its substance, Van Panhuys nevertheless seems to have a slight preference for the latter opinion by submitting that 'both aspects should be taken into account, although, of course, the formal aspects are but the shadows of the substance'. See van Panhuys, *The Rôle of Nationality in International Law*, 20–21.

[114] Hans Ulrich Jessurun d'Oliveira, "Tendenzen in Europees nationaliteitsrecht", *Nederlands Juristenblad*, no. 11–12 (1989): 360. He argues as follows: 'Van tweeën één: òf men ontwikkelt de theorie waarin de nationaliteit optreedt als een begrip dat beschikbaar is, zich leent voor onvoorspelbare attributies van rechten en plichten aan een persoon, en dan is dit begrip ook niet te gebruiken als beoordelingsmaatstaf van bestaande regelingen zoals over onvaderlandslievend gedrag ...; òf men ontwikkelt een normatief nationaliteitsbegrip, waarbij de statelijke willekeur in attributie wordt ingedamd, en het begrip beschikbaar raakt voor normatieve evaluaties van bestaande regelingen'.

[115] Weis, *Nationality and statelessness in international law*, 59.

and a State—is also emphasized by Boll.[116] The rights and duties are generally understood to entail the following: the duty for the State is the obligation to allow its nationals entry and residence on its territory; the right that is conferred upon the State of nationality refers to the right to exercise diplomatic protection for the benefit of its nationals.[117] Both authors seem to agree on the inherent nature of these rights and duties to nationality. This is also reflected in Weis's contestation of Koessler's statement that '"nationality", as a conception of international law, does not mean any specific rights/and or duties, nor an aggregate of either or both, but is a purely formal proposition.'[118] In Weis's view, nationality does confer certain rights and duties under international law and is not just a purely formal concept.[119]

However, we take the position that also under international law nationality should be seen as an empty concept which merely connects to certain legal consequences. These consequences do not ensue from the nature of nationality, but follow from the decision to attach these consequences to nationality and not, for example, to place of residence.[120] It may be properly assumed that nationality is still perceived as the most suitable criterion on which to ground certain rights and duties.[121] It has nonetheless been shown that other criteria than nationality can be decisive in granting, for example, diplomatic protection—a right often regarded as being dependent on nationality.[122]

---

116 Boll, *Multiple Nationality and International Law*, 95, 151. He also points out that the rights and duties incumbent on the State seem to provide a benefit for the individual. However, he stresses that few States actually provide in their municipal law for the possibility to claim these rights.

117 Weis, *Nationality and statelessness in international law*, 59; Boll, *Multiple Nationality and International Law*, 95. Boll discusses at length (pages 113–148 of his monograph) a number of other consequences of nationality under international law. He mentions the following categories where nationality is of international importance: State responsibility for nationals; allegiance; right to refuse extradition; determination of enemy status in war time; and exercise of jurisdiction.

118 Weis, *Nationality and statelessness in international law*, 60. See in a similar vein as Weis the following quote by Randelzhofer: 'As far as nationality as a concept of international law is concerned, rights and duties of the State (not of the individual) are immediately derived from nationality: the right of diplomatic protection and the duty of admission'. See Albrecht Randelzhofer, "Nationality", in *Encyclopedia of Public International Law*, ed. R. Bernhardt (Amsterdam: Elsevier, 1997), 502.

119 Weis, *Nationality and statelessness in international law*, 239.

120 de Groot and Tratnik, *Nederlands nationaliteitsrecht*, 3.

121 Ko Swan Sik, "Nationaliteit en het volkenrecht", 15.

122 Clive Parry, "Some considerations upon the protection of individuals in international law", in *Recueil des cours de l'Académie de droit international de la Haye* (Leiden: Sijthoff, 1956), 699 ff. Parry points to the Anglo-Saxon practice to refuse diplomatic protection when a

5. *Nationality Under International Law*

In this section we shall further determine the place of nationality under international law. For this purpose two distinct issues will be discussed. First, we shall examine the important principle of State autonomy in nationality law as well as the recognition of nationality for the purposes of international law (Section 5.1). Subsequently, we shall address the question whether (and in what way) international law may nonetheless circumscribe national autonomy in nationality matters, whether through conventions, rules of customary international law or general principles of law (Section 5.2).

5.1. *State Autonomy and Nationality as a Human Right*

The starting point is the general rule under international law that each State is autonomous in deciding who its nationals are.[123] Although it has been noted by some commentators that 'the "legal bond" of nationality has become less a "tie of allegiance" and more a matter of reciprocal rights and duties between individuals and States', it is at the same time acknowledged that an enforceable right to a nationality does not exist.[124] In other words, an individual cannot rely on a principle of international law which would allow an effective claim to the nationality of a given State.[125] This state of affairs is particularly troubling because nationality is of primordial importance for membership and participation in a national community. The right to a nationality has therefore been described as 'a civil and political meta-right of the most far reaching importance ... It is a right to have rights'.[126]

The rule of State autonomy in nationality law is not altered by Article 15(1) of the Universal Declaration of Human Rights which states that everyone is entitled to a nationality. This provision has no binding force under

national was domiciled abroad. He also mentions that the reverse sometimes occurred: it used to be frequent practice in the US to give protection to aliens who had applied for naturalization but were not yet granted nationality.

123 Michel Verwilghen, "Conflits de nationalités, plurinationalité et apatridie", ibid. (1999), 122.

124 Z.W. Galicki, "Does the right to a nationality belong to the catalogue of human rights?", in *Feestbundel Zilverentant*, ed. F.J.A. van der Velden (Den Haag: Ministerie van Justitie-Directie Wetgeving, 1998), 70.

125 Paul Lagarde, "Le droit à une nationalité", in *Droit et libertés fondamentaux*, ed. Rémy Cabrillac, Marie-Anne Frison-Roche, and Thierry Revet (Paris: Dalloz, 1996), 145.

126 Stephen Hall, "The European Convention on Nationality and the right to have rights", *European Law Review* 24 (1999): 587–588. The aphorism 'a right to have rights' was coined by Arendt. See Hannah Arendt, *The Origins of Totalitarianism* (New York: Schocken Books, 2004), 376.

international law, nor does it say to what nationality someone is entitled.[127] Chan is therefore correct in writing that 'as long as no State [can] be compelled to grant its nationality to the individual, the right to nationality is largely meaningless.'[128] At present, the right to a nationality is no more than an ideal that States should aspire to.[129]

Some conventions have provisions on nationality that focus specifically on the child. Thus, both the 1966 International Covenant on Civil and Political Rights and the 1989 Convention on the Rights of the Child provide that every child has the right to acquire a nationality (Articles 24(3) and 7(1) respectively). Although this means that the Contracting Parties have explicitly committed themselves to transposing this rule in their internal legislation,[130] 'it does not necessarily make it an obligation for States to give their nationality to every child born in their territory. States are required to adopt every appropriate measure, both internally and in co-operation with other States, to ensure that every child has a nationality when he is born.'[131]

A general right to nationality is not part of the human rights catalogue of the 1950 European Convention for the Protection of Human Rights and Fundamental Freedoms (ECHR). Although Article 4 of the European Convention on Nationality (ECN) provides that everyone has the right to a nationality, this right is not protected under the ECHR.[132] An attempt to draft a Protocol to the ECHR on the right to nationality failed in 1988, mainly because the Protocol provided for supervision by the European Court of

---

[127] Randelzhofer, "Nationality", 508; Kay Hailbronner, "Nationality in public international law and European law", in *Acquisition and Loss of Nationality, Policies and Trends in 15 European Countries*, ed. Rainer Bauböck, *et al.* (Amsterdam: Amsterdam University Press, 2006), 37.

[128] Johannes M.M. Chan, "The right to a nationality as a human right. The current trend towards recognition", *Human Rights Law Journal* 12, no. 1–2 (1991): 3.

[129] Lagarde, *La nationalité française*, 13. The non-enforceability of the right to nationality does not mean, though, that the individual's right to nationality against the claims of States to exclusively define their rules on nationality has not been strengthened in several respects over the years. This concerns in the first place the issues of statelessness and gender equality; however, Faist also interprets the increasing tolerance of dual nationality as the result of an emerging trend of nationality as a human right. See Faist, "Dual citizenship: Change, Prospects, and Limits", 175–176.

[130] Verwilghen, "Conflits de nationalités, plurinationalité et apatridie", 162. Paragraph 29 of the ECN also makes a reference to human rights: 'With the development of human rights law since the second world war, there exists an increasing recognition that State discretion in the field [of nationality law] must furthermore take into account the fundamental rights of individuals.'

[131] Chan, "The right to a nationality as a human right. The current trend towards recognition": 5.

[132] Galicki, "Does the right to a nationality belong to the catalogue of human rights?", 72; Nuala Mole, "Multiple nationality and the European convention on human rights", Report for the 2nd European conference on nationality, Challenges to national and international law on

Human Rights on questions of nationality. It proved politically unfeasible for States to forgo their sovereignty in the realm of nationality law.[133] Although many see this as a missed opportunity, we share their hope that all the efforts to establish a right to nationality contribute to the perception of nationality as a human right so that it will one day be enforceable.[134]

A corollary to State autonomy in the domain of nationality is that States may not intervene in each other's sovereignty to regulate matters of nationality. Another consequence is the absence of hard and fast rules of international law as to the criteria for both acquisition and loss of nationality; it is nonetheless possible to give an enumeration of common modes of acquisition and loss that are recognized by customary international law. International law does not, however, require the application of these principles.[135]

As far as the principles of acquisition and loss under international law are concerned, some short remarks must be devoted to the relation between the

---

nationality at the beginning of the new millenium (2001), 139. Hall argues that in the absence of a dispute settlement mechanism, aggrieved individuals have two options: 'They may try to have their complaints pursued politically through the Council of Europe's Parliamentary Assembly', or, 'inside the EU they may be able to seek vindication of their violated ECN rights, as transposed into general principles of Community law, before the Court of Justice'. See Hall, "The European Convention on Nationality and the right to have rights": 601.

De Groot and Vink, referring to a decision by the Dutch Council of State in 2004, also come to the conclusion that certain provisions of the ECN can have direct effect and can be invoked before a national court. Gerard-René de Groot and Maarten Vink, *Meervoudige nationaliteit in Europees perspectief: een landenvergelijkend overzicht*, Voorstudie voor de Adviescommissie voor Vreemdelingenzaken (Den Haag: ACVZ, 2008), 31.

133 Chan, "The right to a nationality as a human right. The current trend towards recognition": 9,14.

134 Ibid., 10; Lagarde, *La nationalité française*, 14; Yaffa Zilbershats, *The Human Right to Citizenship* (Ardsley, New York: Transnational Publishers, Inc, 2002), 181–182.

135 Randelzhofer, "Nationality", 503–505; Boll, *Multiple Nationality and International Law*, 99. Randelzhofer gives the following enumeration of common modes of conferment recognized by international law: Conferment by *ius sanguinis* and *ius soli*; acquisition of domicile with the intention of establishing permanent residence; entry into State service; changes in civil status such as adoption or marriage; voluntary naturalization.

Modes of acquisition that are *not* recognized by international law are the naturalization by a State of persons unconnected with its territory or the (hypothetical) case of naturalization of all persons in the world based on criteria such as religion or language. Also incompatible with international law is legislation that automatically confers nationality upon acquisition of real estate that was acquired prior to this legislation; conferment of nationality in future cases would be allowed, however. Moreover, it is incompatible with international law to confer nationality on the inhabitants of mandated and trust territories by an administering authority, as well as conferment on inhabitants of an occupied territory. We shall see in the chapter on Italy (Chapter 5, Section 3) that the Brazilian 'Great naturalization' in 1889

general modes of loss of nationality[136] and the issue of statelessness.[137] Statelessness and multiple nationality have in common that the literature often deals with them together under the heading 'conflict of nationality laws'.[138] They are seen as anomalous situations, in comparison to the 'normal' situation of every person having one nationality. Both phenomena are the result of the concurrent competence of States to regulate their nationality. Statelessness is normally described as a negative conflict of nationalities, whereas multiple nationality represents a positive conflict.[139] Yet this 'conflict of nationality laws' should be distinguished from the separate legal discipline of Conflict of Laws or Private International Law.[140] We return to this 'conflict of nationality laws' when discussing the 1930 Hague Convention (*infra* Section 5.2.1).

There is disagreement on the question whether an obligation to avoid statelessness is part of customary international law. According to Weis, 'neither the view that denationalisation [loss of nationality by a unilateral act of the State] is inconsistent with international law because it creates statelessness nor the view that it encroaches upon the rights of the individual finds support in the rules of international law. Statelessness is not inadmissible under international law—although it may be considered undesirable'.[141] This undesirability has led to a number of treaties that endeavour a reduction of instances of statelessness. They are, however, only binding on a restricted number of States and only deal with specific instances of statelessness.[142] Whereas Weis does not conclude from these treaties that a general principle of customary law

was claimed to be a violation of international law according to a number of European States. See also Verwilghen, "Conflits de nationalités, plurinationalité et apatridie", 141.

136 Randelzhofer, "Nationality", 505–506. He points out that renunciation by the individual is only valid if accepted by the State. As general modes of loss by unilateral act of the State he indicates the voluntary acquisition of a foreign nationality; entry into foreign civil or military service; the conviction for certain crimes. As regards the ECN, see Article 7(1) for what is meant to be an exhaustive list of grounds for loss of nationality.

137 See Laura van Waas, *Nationality Matters. Statelessness under international law* (Antwerp: Intersentia, 2008); Caroline Sawyer and Brad K. Blitz, eds., *Statelessness in the European Union* (Cambridge: Cambridge University Press, 2011); Karel Hendriks and Olivier Vonk, "Mapping statelessness in the Netherlands", UNHCR report (2011).

138 Weis, *Nationality and statelessness in international law*, 161.

139 Lagarde, *La nationalité française*, 20–21.

140 Weis, *Nationality and statelessness in international law*, 161.

141 Ibid., 125. See similarly, Verwilghen, "Conflits de nationalités, plurinationalité et apatridie", 165.

142 Hailbronner, "Nationality in public international law and European law", 65. Hailbronner gives the following overview of treaties containing obligations to avoid statelessness: The 1954 Convention on the Status of Stateless Persons; the 1957 UN Convention on the Status of Married Women; the 1961 UN Convention on the Reduction of Statelessness; the 1966

has developed which imposes the duty to avoid statelessness, other authors have recently provided a more nuanced view. Hailbronner, for example, agrees with the explanatory report to the 1997 European Convention on Nationality (ECN) which provides in paragraph 33 that an obligation to avoid statelessness exists under customary international law.[143] Boll, on the other hand, is less sure and comments that 'a claim that there exists an obligation to avoid statelessness may overstep the requirements of international law'.[144] Nevertheless, he notes that the unwelcome effects brought about by statelessness seem to affect a State's discretion to withdraw nationality.[145]

Let us return to the rule of customary international law providing that it is within the discretion of a State to regulate its own nationality law.[146] This rule can be traced back to the case on the *Tunis and Morocco Nationality Decrees*.[147] In that particular case, the Court stated in its Advisory Opinion that 'the question whether a certain matter is or is not solely within the jurisdiction of a State is an essentially relative question; it depends upon the development of international relations. Hence, in the present state of international law, questions of nationality are, in the opinion of the Court, in principle within this reserved domain'.[148]

International Covenant on Civil and Political Rights; the 1966 Convention on the Elimination of all Forms of Racial Discrimination; the 1979 Convention on the Elimination of all Forms of Discrimination against Women; the 1989 Convention on the Rights of the Child; and the 2006 Convention on the Avoidance of Statelessness in Relation to State Succession. See further on these conventions (and others) in the field of nationality law, Gerard-René de Groot and Nicole Doeswijk, "Nationaliteitsrecht en het Internationale Recht", in *De Nationaliteit in Internationaal en Europees Perspectief. Preadviezen van Prof. Mr Frans J.A. van der Velden, Prof. Mr Gerard-René de Groot en Mr Nicole Doeswijk* (Den Haag: T.M.C. Asser Press, 2004).

143 Hailbronner, "Nationality in public international law and European law", 65.

144 Boll, *Multiple Nationality and International Law*, 103.

145 Ibid.

146 Although this is a widely recognized and uncontested rule, Karamanoukian has made a plea for posing limits to State discretion in the interest of the fight against dual nationality. He called on all jurists 'dans leur poste de conseillers des gouvernants ou sur leur banc de parlementaires, dans leur chaire de faculté ou dans leur écrits' to 's'élever énergiquement contre la liberté absolue et abusive avec laquelle les États déterminent discrétionairement l'attribution de leur nationalité'. Aram Karamanoukian, "La double nationalité et le service militaire", *Revue générale de droit international public* 78 (1974): 483–484.

147 Permanent Court of International Justice, *Tunis and Morocco Nationality Decrees Case*, (1923) See on this advisory opinion by the Court Wolfgang Benedek, "Nationality decrees in Tunis and Morocco (Advisory Opinion)", in *Encyclopedia of Public International Law*, ed. R Bernhardt (Amsterdam: Elsevier, 1997), 510–511.

148 Permanent Court of International Justice, *Tunis and Morocco Nationality Decrees Case*, (1923) at 24.

Although this judgment, by emphasizing the relativity of the reserved domain, implies that this jurisdiction may be susceptible to change as a result of developments in international law, the principle as articulated by the Court is still valid and is codified in both the 1930 Hague Convention and the 1997 European Convention on Nationality (ECN). Article 1 of the Hague Convention expresses the principle as follows: 'It is for each State to determine under its own law who are its nationals. This law shall be recognized by other States in so far as it is consistent with international conventions, international custom, and the principles of law generally recognized with regard to nationality'. Article 3 ECN provides: 'Each State shall determine under its own law who are its nationals. This law shall be accepted by other States in so far as it is consistent with applicable international conventions, customary international law and the principles of law generally recognized with regard to nationality'.

This autonomy was confirmed in a case of 1955, *Nottebohm*,[149] in which the Court ruled that it was for the sovereign State of Liechtenstein to 'settle by its own legislation the rules relating to the acquisition of its nationality'. The case is of relevance for the application of the principle of the 'effective (or genuine) nationality' in a case concerning the possession of only one nationality. This principle had until then only been applied in situations involving multiple nationality.[150] It follows from *Nottebohm* that a nationality is only relevant under international law if the person holding a given nationality has a 'genuine link' with the State granting that nationality.[151] The principle of the

---

[149] *Nottebohm* case (second phase), 6 April 1955, ICJ reports 4. In *Nottebohm*, a case concerning a German national who in 1939 had acquired Liechtenstein nationality through naturalization (thereby losing German nationality) while habitually resident in Guatemala, the Court had to decide whether his newly acquired nationality had to be recognized by Guatemala under international law so that Liechtenstein could exercise diplomatic protection on his behalf as against Guatemala. As a national of a belligerent State (Germany), Nottebohm had been expelled by Guatemala and had his property seized. The Court concluded that a 'genuine link' with Liechtenstein was lacking and that Nottebohm's actual connections with that State were extremely tenuous. In the Court's view, Nottebohm had applied for Liechtenstein nationality 'to enable him to substitute for his status as a national of a belligerent State that of a national of a neutral State, with the sole aim of thus coming within the protection of Liechtenstein'.

[150] The Court states that it takes different factors into consideration for the purpose of establishing the effective nationality; their importance depends on the particular context. Factors mentioned by the Court are habitual residence, the centre of one's interests, family life, participation in public life and attachment shown to a particular country (*Nottebohm*, at 22).

[151] Notice, however, that the International Law Commission in its seventh report on diplomatic protection (2006) proposes to do away with the genuine link criterion as an additional factor for the exercise of diplomatic protection (see Article 4 of the report). The Commission took the view that *Nottebohm* should be limited to the particular facts of the case because 'if the

'genuine link' should not be construed however as circumscribing national autonomy for the purpose of municipal law: the Court did not go into the (in) validity of Mr Nottebohm's acquisition of Liechtenstein nationality for domestic purposes. The Court did decide that an effective link with Liechtenstein had to exist for that country to be allowed under international law to grant diplomatic protection.[152]

The scope of *Nottebohm* is disputed. Whereas Randelzhofer strictly limits the case to the problem of diplomatic protection consequent on conferment of nationality by naturalization, Verwilghen's estimation of subsequent doctrinal developments leads him to claim that the principle of the 'genuine link' has been extended under international law beyond the issue of diplomatic protection.[153]

Finally, a word on the issue of the recognition of nationality on the international plane. There are relatively few exceptions to the freedom of a State to accord its nationality according to the varying, internationally accepted, modes of attribution, yet international law must find an answer for situations in which this freedom is abused. In this connection, Boll states that 'rather than obliging states not to legislate in a certain way with respect to attribution of nationality, international law dictates that when the consequences of such attribution are felt on the international level, it is up to international law whether a bestowal or removal of nationality must be recognized by other states'.[154]

5.2. *Limitations Imposed by International Law on State Autonomy in Nationality Law*

International law may circumscribe State autonomy in nationality matters. This is clearest when States agree on such limitations themselves by signing international treaties. We have already referred to provisions in the 1930 Hague Convention and the ECN, but there are numerous other conventions

genuine link requirement proposed by Nottebohm was strictly applied it would exclude millions of persons from the benefit of diplomatic protection'.

152 *Nottebohm*, 20–21.

153 Randelzhofer, "Nationality", 504. In a similar vein Weis, *Nationality and statelessness in international law*, 180. After stating that the importance of the case lies for him in the fact that the effective link criterion was applied in respect of a mono-national, Randelzhofer goes on to submit that the exceptional circumstances of the case do not lend themselves for a generalization of the effective link theory. For a different view see Verwilghen, "Conflits de nationalités, plurinationalité et apatridie", 95.

154 Boll, *Multiple Nationality and International Law*, 107.

which attempt to limit State sovereignty. Examples of conventions concerned with human rights issues in nationality law include those on the position of married women and those which endeavour to reduce statelessness. There are, however, also rules of customary international law and general principles of law that have the effect of limiting State sovereignty.[155] Before examining these rules and principles, we first provide a short description of the Hague Convention.

5.2.1. *The 1930 Hague Convention on Certain Questions Relating to the Conflict of Nationality Laws*

This Convention, concluded in 1930 at the Hague Conference which was held under the auspices of the League of Nations, was the first *multilateral* treaty on nationality.[156] Ancel has expressed the view that the Convention was in a sense the culmination of all the preparatory work done by institutions such as the l'Institut de Droit International (sessions in Venice (1896) and Stockholm (1928)) and the Harvard Law School (1929). The efforts by these institutions to come to a solution to the problem of dual nationality were not successful in themselves, but were significant in laying the foundation for the 1930 Convention.[157] According to Chan the importance of the Convention lay first of all 'in the recognition that nationality was no longer within the sole purview of State sovereignty'.[158] All these efforts had little effect in the fight against dual nationality, however.[159]

Already in the 19th century a number of *bilateral* agreements concerning nationality had been concluded with an eye to resolving the problems that stemmed from the emigration of Europeans to North and South America. The Bancroft Treaties, signed between the US and German States in 1868 (Prussia was the first to sign and other German States followed the same year),

---

155 Verwilghen, "Conflits de nationalités, plurinationalité et apatridie", 136–137.

156 José Francisco Rezek, "Le droit international de la nationalité", ibid. (1986), 370; Chan, "The right to a nationality as a human right. The current trend towards recognition": 2.

157 Marc Ancel, "Les conflits de nationalités. Contribution à la recherche d'une solution rationnelle des cas de multi-nationalité", *Journal de droit international* 64 (1937): 27–28. See for the activities of these institutions also Makarov, *Allgemeine Lehren des Staatsangehörigkeitsrechts*, 69–71.

158 Chan, "The right to a nationality as a human right. The current trend towards recognition": 2.

159 As Hool has stated, 'pour louables qu'ils soient, tous ces projets et recommandations resteront sans doute lettre morte. La double nationalité ne disparaîtra pas, aussi longtemps que les lois nationals sur la nationalité et une notable partie du droit privé … n'auront pas été unifiées'. Frédéric-Henri Hool, *Les effets de la double nationalité en droit suisse* (Neuchâtel: Editions du Griffon, 1949), 4.

provide an example.[160] The principle acknowledged in these treaties is that 'the citizens or subjects of one of the contracting parties who become naturalized within the jurisdiction of the other, and who shall have resided therein uninterruptedly for five years, are to be treated as naturalized citizens or subjects of the latter'.[161] The treaties were called a decisive victory on the part of American diplomacy because, although based on reciprocity, the advantages were all on the side of the United States.[162] Another example of bilateral treaties in the field of nationality law are the treaties that were concluded after the first World War which explicitly dealt with the nationality of the population in successor States.[163]

It has already been mentioned that certain international case law (e.g. the *Tunis and Morocco Nationality Decrees* case) was codified in the Hague Convention and that academic writers commonly agree that the general principles found in chapter 1 of the Convention have become part of customary international law.[164] This is relevant as the convention was only ratified by a very few States. The aim of the Convention in respect of dual nationality is somewhat ambiguous. Though the preamble seems to take a clear position when stating that 'the ideal towards which the efforts of humanity should be directed ... is the abolition of all cases both of statelessness and of double nationality', it in fact makes little effort to prevent cases of multiple nationality from arising.[165] Verwilghen accordingly concludes that the Convention is

---

160 See on these treaties for example Alfred Weil, "La nationalité dans les rapports de l'Allemagne avec les Etats-Unis et les traités Bancroft", *Journal de droit international* 44 (1917); Theo. H. Thiesing, "Dual allegiance in the German law of nationality and American citizenship", *Yale Law Journal* 27, no. 4 (1918): 496–499; Aurelia Alvarez Rodríguez, *Nacionalidad y emigración* (Madrid: La Ley, 1990), 86–91; Rey Koslowski, "Challenges of international cooperation in a world of increasing dual nationality", in *Rights and Duties of Dual nationals - Evolutions and Prospects*, ed. D.A Martin and Kay Hailbronner (The Hague: Kluwer Law International, 2003), 158–159.

161 Thiesing, "Dual allegiance in the German law of nationality and American citizenship": 486.

162 Ibid., 496.

163 Hailbronner, "Nationality in public international law and European law", 49 ff.

164 This seems to be questioned by Lagarde, who writes that the Hague Convention's 'force obligatoire' is limited to only the small group of Contracting Parties. Lagarde, *La nationalité française*, 18.

165 Moreover, the rare provisions that do make a concrete attempt at abolishing multiple nationality have become obsolete by subsequent Conventions. We refer to the provisions in the Hague Convention which state that the wife loses her original nationality upon marriage with a foreigner. These provisions are incompatible with the 1957 Convention on the Nationality of Married Women, which provides in its first article that marriage does not affect a woman's nationality. Many States, among which the United States, refused to ratify

resigned to the unavoidability of multiple nationality. The Hague Convention merely makes an effort, so he argues, to provide a practical solution to problems created by multiple nationality. In Verwilghen's view, the Convention finally decided on a rather modest aim, at least more modest than the wording of the preamble suggests.[166]

Makarov has expressed himself in a somewhat similar vein. When discussing Article 6 of the Convention, which deals with the option right in cases of dual nationality, he calls the final text rather meagre if the drafters were serious about preventing cases of dual nationality from arising.[167] Article 6 grants a dual national the right to renounce a nationality on condition that the person had not become a dual national of his free will ('a person possessing two nationalities acquired without any voluntary act on his part may renounce one of them with the authorisation of the State whose nationality he desires to surrender'). The preparatory commission's proposal, however, was of a much broader scope as it argued for a general renunciation right for all dual nationals.[168]

The foregoing again attests to the difficulties in trying to reach an international agreement in nationality matters. This is also the opinion of Guerrero, who attributes the failure of the Convention to its overambitious objectives. Taking into account the widely divergent opinions of the different States, he argued that an in-depth discussion of a limited number of core principles in the field of nationality would have been more fruitful than the attempt to solve a great number of ticklish issues.[169]

The ambiguous attitude of the Convention reinforces the confusion about multiple nationality under international law. On the one hand, the Hague

---

the Hague Convention on account of the discriminatory provisions on women. See Verwilghen, "Conflits de nationalités, plurinationalité et apatridie", 158.

166 Ibid., 169. It should also not be forgotten that the draft convention as prepared by the Harvard Law School did contain provisions that would have prevented many cases of multiple nationality from arising. These were not incorporated in the Hague Convention itself, however. Articles 13 and 16, for example, provided for the loss of nationality upon naturalization and upon resumption of a former nationality. See on this point Boll, *Multiple Nationality and International Law*, 196.

167 Alexander Makarov, "Le droit d'option en cas de double nationalité dans les conventions internationales", in *Liber amicorum J.P.A. François* (Leiden: Sijthoff, 1959), 196.

168 Ibid., 195. Makarov also quotes the preparatory commission's summary of State opinions submitted to it, which clearly shows the different State interests: 'Si certains croient trouver dans une large faculté de renonciation ouverte à l'intéressé la solution du problème de la double nationalité, d'autres envisagent seulement la faculté de rejeter la nationalité acquise jure soli et d'autres, enfin, relèvent le danger que peut présenter le libre choix de l'intéressé.'

169 José Gustave Guerrero, *La Codification du Droit International. La Première Conférence (La Haye, 13 mars - 12 Avril 1930)* (Paris: A. Pedone, 1930), 34.

Convention's preamble and other Conventions that expressed the aim to abolish all cases of multiple nationality—such as the 1963 Convention on the Reduction of Cases of Multiple Nationality and Military Obligations in Cases of Multiple Nationality (see *infra* Section 11.1)—could be interpreted as expressing international consensus on the undesirability of multiple nationality. On the other hand, the pragmatic approach of the Hague Convention as hinted at by Verwilghen, the relatively low number of signatory States, and Verwilghen's claim that other Conventions which combat multiple nationality cannot be seen as general rules of international law because they are only valid among the signing parties, may just as well lead to the conclusion that international law is in fact neutral on the issue of multiple nationality.[170]

5.2.2. *Customary International Law and General Principles of Law in the Field of Nationality*

It is hard to identify customary rules or general principles that are specific to nationality law.[171] One may think of acquisition *iure sanguinis* or *iure soli*—the two predominant modes conferring nationality—as principles that must be recognized by other States under customary international law.[172] Writers like Ko Swan Sik consider as being incompatible with customary international law the grant of nationality in the absence of a factual bond between State and individual.[173] Others point to general principles of law that are also applicable to nationality law, examples being the prohibition on arbitrariness and the prohibition on interference. Importantly, the equality of the sexes and the equality of children are emphatically not (yet) general principles of nationality law.[174]

States can also not regulate their nationality laws in a way that violates fundamental human rights.[175] Hailbronner remarks in this context that a State's

[170] Boll, *Multiple Nationality and International Law*, 204. Boll seems to agree with Verwilghen on the neutrality of international law with regard to multiple nationality: 'It would appear that the impact of multilateral and regional treaties in relation to nationality and multiple nationality is limited both in terms of the treaties as evidence of state practice, and their effect on state practice. Above all paucity in ratification, but also lack of agreement on scope, limitation to specific regions, cultural or political contexts, and fundamental changes in approach over time, indicate that no clear consensus evidenced by consistent treaty practice can be cited as evidence of either a particularly tolerant or intolerant attitude by even a relatively small number of states vis-à-vis multiple nationality'.

[171] Verwilghen, "Conflits de nationalités, plurinationalité et apatridie", 146.

[172] Ian Brownlie, *Principles of Public International Law* 6th ed. (Oxford: Oxford University Press, 2003), 378.

[173] Ko Swan Sik, "Nationaliteit en het volkenrecht", 20.

[174] Verwilghen, "Conflits de nationalités, plurinationalité et apatridie", 158.

[175] de Groot and Tratnik, *Nederlands nationaliteitsrecht*, 22.

right to regulate its own nationality does not mean that this right 'has remained unaffected by the development of human rights and human dignity, which has shifted the very foundation of public international law from a system of coordination of sovereign states to the well-being of human beings'.[176]

Several human rights considerations can be observed in the ECN, particularly in Article 4.[177] However, Hailbronner argues that also several other articles have a human rights dimension because they give flesh to the rule laid down in Article 4 that everyone has the right to a nationality.[178] Article 6(3) of the Convention, for example, contains a rule providing that lawfully and habitually resident foreigners should be able to be naturalized and that the residence period that States are allowed to impose for naturalization may not exceed ten years. The Convention also lays down a duty to facilitate[179] the acquisition of nationality for stateless persons and for recognized refugees who are lawfully resident on a State's territory (Article 6(4)). The same facilitated access must be provided to several other categories as well. Also relevant is Article 5 which contains the principle of non-discrimination between nationals: a State cannot differentiate between nationals by birth and those who acquired its nationality subsequently.[180] Finally, procedural fairness and review in administrative procedures can be considered human rights; therefore, 'the procedural provisions of art. 10–12 ECN … support the human rights character of nationality law'.[181]

---

176 Hailbronner, "Nationality in public international law and European law", 38.

177 Article 4 of the ECN provides that 'the rules on nationality of each State Party shall be based on the following principles: a) everyone has the right to a nationality; b) statelessness shall be avoided; c) no one shall be arbitrarily deprived of his or her nationality; d) neither marriage nor the dissolution of a marriage between a national of a State Party and an alien, nor the change of nationality by one of the spouses during marriage, shall automatically affect the nationality of the other spouse'. The explanatory report provides further clarification by specifying that the right to a nationality under Article 4(a) 'can be seen as a positive formulation of the duty to avoid statelessness and is thus closely related to paragraph b of the same article. While there is a recognition that a right to a nationality exists, the right to any particular nationality is determined by the rules on nationality of each State Party, consistent with Article 3 of the Convention which provides that States shall determine who are their nationals'.

178 Hailbronner, "Nationality in public international law and European law", 37–38.

179 According to the explanatory report on the ECN, facilitated acquisition for the purpose of Article 6(4) means that 'it is sufficient for a State Party to ensure favorable conditions for the acquisition of nationality for the persons belonging to each of the categories listed in the sub-paragraphs. Examples include a reduction of the length of required residence, less stringent language requirements, an easier procedure and lower procedural fees'.

180 Favourable treatment to nationals of certain States is allowed, however, because this constitutes 'preferential treatment on the basis of nationality and not discrimination on the ground of national origin' (see the explanatory report on Article 5).

181 Hailbronner, "Nationality in public international law and European law", 45.

6. *Why a Study on Dual Nationality?*

Having discussed the general principles of nationality law in the previous sections, it is time to comment on the choice of dual nationality as the subject of this study. We will also try to explain why it such a topical subject and give an overview of the questions raised in respect of multiple nationality in the legal literature, as well as in the political science scholarship.

Jurists often ask the question whether multiple nationality—which was predominantly regarded as a legal anomaly in the past but is today more accepted—occasions legal problems and whether these can be overcome.[182] In other words, the legal discipline inquires into multiple nationality in light of its presumed legal inconveniences.

In the field of political science, multiple nationality is often examined in the context of political communities and is studied alongside theories on political membership such as transnational and postnational citizenship.[183] Political science often raises the question how dual nationality should be interpreted in comparison with these other theories and how it affects the relation between individuals and a State. In this connection, the growing toleration of multiple nationality has been called by a 'truly seminal development' due to the fact that only a few decades ago nationality and *political* loyalty, towards a specific national *political* community, were considered inseparable.[184] Consequently,

> what makes multiple nationality so interesting is that it neither deals with 'exclusive citizenship in tightly bounded political communities nor with denationalised citizenship, but rather with a sort of multinationalised citizenship [because dual nationals combine different legal, political and social memberships]. In short, dual citizenship is an instance of internal globalisation: it is an example of how nation-state regulations implicitly or explicitly respond to ties of citizens across states … Recognition of dual citizenship may contribute to the further blurring of the boundaries between immigrants and citizens across borders'.[185]

The study of dual citizenship is therefore crucial for 'understanding how fixed or permeable the boundaries of membership in democratic policies have

182 David A. Martin, "Introduction: The trend toward dual nationality", in *Rights and Duties of Dual nationals—Evolutions and Prospects*, ed. David A. Martin and Kay Hailbronner (The Hague: Kluwer Law International, 2003), 11–18.

183 See for example Linda Bosniak, "Multiple nationality and the postnational transformation of citizenship", ibid.; Rainer Bauböck, "Stakeholder Citizenship and Transnational Political Participation: a Normative Evaluation of External Voting", *Fordham Law Review* 75, no. 5 (2007): 2395.

184 Thomas Faist, Jürgen Gerdes, and Beate Rieple, "Dual Citizenship as a Path-Dependent Process", *International Migration Review* 38, no. 3 (2004): 913.

185 Faist, "The Fixed and Porous Boundaries of Dual Citizenship", 3.

become over the past few decades'.[186] Or as others have put it: 'The acceptance or promotion of dual citizenship represents a crucial step away from the conceptualization of political communities as exclusive and non-overlapping entities';[187] 'dual citizenship highlights specific problems with the citizenship concept, especially the foreigner-citizen dichotomy and the assumed congruence between the demos, the nation and the state'.[188]

For several reasons, today's society is confronted with more cases of multiple nationality than ever before. First, the coincidence of the two ways of acquiring a country's nationality at birth—by application of the principles of *ius soli* (place of birth) and *ius sanguinis* (descent from a national)—may lead to instances of multiple nationality. This concurrence was the main cause for dual nationality at the turn of the 20th century (the idea of gender equality in nationality law had not yet taken root at the time and therefore did not create dual nationals). It was thus in the context of emigration—receiving States often applied *ius soli* whereas sending States adhered to *ius sanguinis*—that the older literature discussed dual nationality.[189] However, this cause for dual nationality may presently be even more important in our age of increasing migration.

Second, the equality of the sexes in nationality law, which was only secured in Western Europe from the 1970s onwards, entails the logical consequence that both parents can transmit their nationality to their children. This results in multiple nationality for children from mixed marriages.[190]

Third, in a globalizing world with increasing migration, not only sending and receiving States can have good arguments for allowing multiple nationality, but also immigrants may have sound motives for supporting dual nationality, as the requirement of relinquishing the nationality of origin is often an obstacle to requesting naturalization in the host State. What is more, acquisition of the host State's nationality may prove to be financially beneficial and

---

186 Faist, "Dual citizenship: Change, Prospects, and Limits", 196.

187 Joachim K. Blatter, "Dual Citizenship and Democracy", 2009; available from http://www.unilu.ch/files/Dual-Citizenship-and-Democracy-wp01.pdf.

188 Tanja Brøndsted Sejersen, "'I Vow to Thee My Countries'—The Expansion of Dual Citizenship in the 21st Century", *International Migration Review* 42, no. 3 (2008): 543.

189 Ancel, "Les conflits de nationalités. Contribution à la recherche d'une solution rationnelle des cas de multi-nationalité": 22.

190 See further on this issue Chapter 4, Section 4. In 1966 only 3,9 percent of the marriages concluded in the Netherlands were mixed marriages. By 1997 this had increased to 13 percent. See Betty de Hart, *Onbezonnen vrouwen. Gemengde relaties in het nationaliteitsrecht en het vreemdelingenrecht*, Dissertatie Katholieke Universiteit Nijmegen (Amsterdam: Aksant, 2003), 241. A good overview of the development in Europe of the equality of the sexes in nationality can be found in de Groot, *Staatsangehörigkeitsrecht im Wandel.*

gives immigrants full political rights. This short overview of the causes of dual nationality thus makes it clear that the increase of cases of dual nationality is, in one way or the other, linked to migration. Consequently, some further comments on the specific role of migration are in order.

The acceptance of dual nationality by receiving as well as sending States corresponds to what Joppke has called a de- and re-ethnicization of nationality law.[191] The de-ethnicization process in immigrant receiving States is caused by the emergence of universal rights which have made it increasingly difficult for States to adhere to an ethnic conception of the nation. Universal human rights and inclusive, liberal norms have had a self-limiting effect on the leeway that States have in the domain of nationality law, in the sense that the exclusive attitude towards certain groups—which seemed self-evident in the past—now has to be justified. In addition to this process, a 'territorial' view of the State has taken root, meaning that membership ought to be dependent on residence instead of descent. This view, which was inspired by the effects of global migration, was part of the cause in many countries for the introduction of *ius soli* elements, the liberalization of naturalization policies, and the acceptance of dual nationality. In Part II of this study we look at the approach to dual nationality in two traditional immigration countries: France and the Netherlands.

Attempts at de-ethnicizing nationality law are mostly made by parties from the political left, whereas those from the right are usually strong supporters of a re-ethnicization of nationality law. More than left wing parties, the political right perceives the State not only as a territorial unit but also—and perhaps even predominantly—as a membership unit or community of descent.[192] From this point of view, nationality law must be especially inclusive towards emigrants and their descendants. The same global migration which played a role in triggering the de-ethnicization of nationality law in respect of immigrants is thus also the cause for the process of re-ethnicization towards emigrants.

Within the migration literature the role of sending States has only recently become the subject of detailed study.[193] Traditionally, the research in this field focused on receiving countries, due to the fact that they have a decisive say in matters concerning immigration, visa policy and asylum. The interest in sending countries was raised primarily by the burgeoning literature on

191 Christian Joppke, "Citizenship between De- and Re-ethnicization (1)", *European Journal of Sociology* 44, no. 3 (2003): 429–458.

192 Ibid., 443.

193 Eva Østergaard-Nielsen, "International Migration and Sending Countries", in *International Migration and Sending Countries: Perceptions, Policies and Transnational Relations*, ed. Eva Østergaard-Nielsen (New York: Palgrave Macmillan, 2003), 3.

transnational communities and diasporas. Sending States with a large emigrant population are often inclined to maintain bonds with their nationals abroad, especially when this results in remittances by a prosperous émigré community. These remittances can have a significant impact on the home country economy.[194] A development in nationality law is the acceptance and use of dual nationality by sending countries for this purpose.[195]

The endeavours by two sending States (Italy and Spain) to maintain links with their emigrants living abroad—in particular in Latin America—will be the subject of Chapters 5 and 6. We will see that these countries have tried to right historical wrongs by modifying their nationality law in a way which considerably facilitates the acquisition of Spanish and Italian nationality by emigrants and their descendants. However, rather than the recognition of multiple ties among its emigrant population—which would be a transnational view—the acceptance of dual nationality by emigration countries is primarily driven by economic interests or the moral feeling to redress past wrongs to nationals who were forced to emigrate for political or economic reasons.

It can also be claimed that the bilateral treaties that were concluded between Spain and certain Latin American countries (see Chapter 6) had another objective, namely to strengthen the ties within the Hispanic world. The intensification of such bilateral relations between States has even been called the principle advantage of dual nationality.[196] It is also in this light that we should read the joint declaration on 22 January 2003 of the French president and the German Chancellor in which they stated that Germans should be able acquire

[194] Michael Jones-Correa, "Seeking shelter: Immigrants and the Divergence of Social Rights and Citizenship in the United States", in *Dual Nationality, Social Rights and Federal Citizenship in the US and Europe*, ed. Randall Hansen and Patrick Weil (New York: Berghahn books, 2002), 1009–1013. One can take different perspectives on these remittances. The money sent back to the sending country can promote stability there and can thus be seen as a form of foreign aid by the receiving country to the sending country. On the other hand, these remittances may undermine democracy in the sending country because the financially strong entrepreneurs who decided to leave the country can exert a dominant influence over their country of origin.

[195] José Itzigsohn, "Migration and Transnational Citizenship in Latin America: The Cases of Mexico and the Dominican Republic", in *Dual Citizenship in Global Perspective, From Unitary to Multiple Citizenship*, ed. Peter Kivisto and Thomas Faist (New York: Palgrave Macmillan, 2007), 118.

[196] Georges Olekhnovitch, "La double nationalité", *Droit et économie* (1991): 22. Similarly, it has been argued that dual nationals make a valuable contribution to the global economy because their knowledge of different languages and cultures makes them particularly well-equiped to improve economic relations between States. See Ezequiel Cabaleiro, "La doble nacionalidad", *Revista general de legislación y jurisprudencia*, no. 212 (1962): 73.

French nationality without losing their German nationality and vice versa.[197] Similar ideas, but in the France-Great Britain relationship, had already been brought forward during the Second World War. In 1940 Winston Churchill made the French the unique offer of creating a French-British Union. Had the offer been accepted, this Union would have had one common government, the countries' parliaments would have merged, and all French and British subjects would have become dual nationals.[198]

The trend that emigration countries try to maintain ties with nationals abroad who wish so, instead of opposing multiple nationality and providing for loss of the original nationality upon naturalization elsewhere, is confirmed by several authors.[199] A number of Latin American countries, for example, have reconsidered their opposition to dual nationality. Mexico, a country traditionally opposed to multiple nationality, changed its attitude in order to better protect Mexican nationals working in the US at a time when US federal law-makers were introducing anti-immigrant legislation.[200] Brazil has allowed dual nationality since 1993, in order to allow its nationals abroad to gain access to social services.[201] Jones-Correa has shown that the ten Latin American countries which have now adopted dual nationality can be divided

197 Gerard-René de Groot and Hildegard Schneider, "Die zunehmende Akzeptanz von Fällen mehrfacher Staatsangehörigkeit in West-Europa", in *Japanischer Brückenbauer zum deutschen Rechtskreis* (Berlin: Duncker & Humblot, 2006), 74.

198 H.L. Wesseling, *Frankrijk in oorlog, 1870–1962* (Amsterdam: Uitgeverij Bert Bakker, 2007), 227. Churchill writes in his memoirs that something dramatic was necessary in 1940 to keep the French going. A Declaration of Union was therefore drafted by the British and sent to General de Gaulle. It read: 'At this most fateful moment in the history of the modern world the Governments of the United Kingdom and the French Republic make this declaration of indissoluble union and unyielding resolution in their common defence of justice and freedom against subjection to a system which reduces mankind to a life of robots and slaves. The two governments declare that France and Great Britain shall no longer be two nations, but one Franco-British Union. The constitution of the Union will provide for joint organs of defence, foreign, financial, and economic policies. Every citizen of France will enjoy immediately citizenship of Great Britain; every British subject will become a citizen of France …'. Winston S. Churchill, *The Second World War, vol. 2* (London: Cassell & Co., 1949), 183.

199 Verwilghen, "Conflits de nationalités, plurinationalité et apatridie", 189; Boll, *Multiple Nationality and International Law*, 263.

200 Martin, "Introduction: The trend toward dual nationality", 7; Itzigsohn, "Migration and Transnational Citizenship in Latin America: The Cases of Mexico and the Dominican Republic", 121.

201 Peggy Levitt, "Variations in Transnational Belonging: Lessons from Brazil and the Dominican Republic", in *Dual Nationality, Social Rights and Federal Citizenship in the US and Europe*, ed. Randall Hansen and Patrick Weil (New York: Berghahn books, 2002), 264–289.

into two groups: early adopters and late adopters.[202] Whereas the acceptance of dual nationality by the early adopters was primarily the result of a top-down and state-driven policy, the late adopters show a mix of top-down and bottom-up influences—concretely meaning that Colombian, Ecuadorian and Dominican immigrants in the United States lobbied intensively for dual nationality in their home countries. The African countries are also becoming increasingly aware of the economic benefits that follow from allowing dual nationality for their diaspora communities.[203] Asian countries on the other hand are still hesitant to allow dual nationality.[204]

The Turkish acceptance of dual nationality appears to be motivated by the same reasons sketched out in the Latin American cases. The remittances of the large community of Turkish nationals living abroad (predominantly in Europe), and their potential as lobbyists for the Turkish cause, were grounds for beginning to tolerate dual nationality in 1981.[205] In contrast to past decades, Turkey now encourages Turkish emigrants to acquire the host country's nationality.[206]

Immigrants themselves can also lobby in the receiving country for the toleration of dual nationality, as is evidenced by the example of the Netherlands. The Turkish Immigrant Organization (IOT), the official representative of the Turkish community to the Dutch government, successfully lobbied for the abolishment of the renunciation requirement in the 1990s.[207] Turkish immigrants in Germany also pleaded for the acceptance of dual nationality by their

---

202 Michael Jones-Correa, "Under Two Flags: Dual Nationality in Latin American and its Consequences for Naturalization in the United States", *International Migration Review* 35, no. 4 (2001): 1000. Early adopters were Uruguay (1919), Panama (1972), Peru (1980) and El Salvador (1983). Latin American countries which only accepted dual nationality in the 1990s (late adopters) are Colombia (1991), the Dominican Republic (1994), Costa Rica (1995), Ecuador (1995), Brazil (1996) and Mexico (1998).

203 Tanja Brøndsted Sejersen, "'I Vow to Thee My Countries'"—The Expansion of Dual Citizenship in the 21st Century", ibid. 42, no. 3 (2008): 530.

204 Ibid., 542.

205 Zeynep Kadirbeyoglu, "National Transnationalism: Dual Citizenship in Turkey", in *Dual Citizenship in Europe: From Nationhood to Societal Integration*, ed. Thomas Faist (Aldershot: Ashgate, 2007), 128–132; Zeynep Kadirbeyoglu, "Changing conceptions of citizenship in Turkey", in *Citizenship policies in the new Europe* ed. Rainer Bauböck, Bernhard Perchinig, and Wiebke Sievers (Amsterdam: Amsterdam University Press, 2007), 295.

206 Østergaard-Nielsen, "Turkey and the 'Euro-Turks': Overseas Nationals as an Ambiguous Asset", 83.

207 Betty de Hart, "The End of Multiculturalism: The End of Dual Citizenship? Political and Public Debates on Dual Citizenship in the Netherlands (1980–2004)", in *Dual Citizenship in Europe: From Nationhood to Societal Integration*, ed. Thomas Faist (Aldershot: Ashgate, 2007), 96.

host State. However, a general toleration of dual nationality was not part of the German nationality law reform in 2000, although the law did become more flexible by allowing a number of exceptions to the general prohibition of dual nationality. After it had become clear that Turks still had to relinquish their nationality upon naturalization in Germany, they turned their attention to their home State and pleaded for a provision which made it impossible to lose Turkish nationality. A Turkish refusal to accept the renunciation of Turkish nationality would cause Turkish immigrants in Germany to fall within one of the exceptions to the prohibition of dual nationality under German law.[208]

Receiving States, on the other hand, can have an interest in immigrants acquiring their nationality because this is considered by some to stimulate the immigrants' integration. Not including the growing number of permanent resident aliens will also undermine a State's democratic inclusiveness.[209] More generally, the requirement of congruence between the people and the resident population is commonly acknowledged.[210] These considerations have led in some countries to the introduction of *ius soli* elements in the nationality legislation so that children of immigrants at some point automatically acquire the nationality of the country of birth.[211] More and more States have also come to the conclusion that asking immigrants to renounce their previous nationality upon naturalization is unjust. In other words, the wish to retain the nationality of origin should not be an obstacle to access to the nationality of the

---

208 Zeynep Kadirbeyoglu, "National Transnationalism: Dual Citizenship in Turkey", ibid., 133.

209 The same argument applies to newly independent States which deny long-term resident minorities the right to nationality. Orentlicher refers in this connection to reports by the Council of Europe and the United Nations which assessed the nationality laws of the newly independent Baltic States in the early 1990. Both reports (reluctantly) concluded that these laws were compatible with international law but the Council of Europe, for example, observed that 'if substantial parts of the population of a country are denied the right to become citizens, and thereby are also denied for instance the right to vote in parliamentary elections, this could affect the character of the democratic system in that country'. See Diane F. Orentlicher, "Citizenship and National Identity", in *International Law and Ethnic Conflict*, ed. David Wippman (Ithaca: Cornell University Press, 1998), 304–309.

It has more recently been pointed out, however, that at least Estonia and Latvia offered these long-term residents the right to acquire nationality through fairly basic procedures. Nonetheless, the question remains whether the time taken to develop these procedures was legally and politically justified. See Ineta Ziemele, *State Continuity and Nationality: The Baltic States and Russia. Past, Present and Future as Defined by International Law* (Leiden/Boston: Martinus Nijhoff Publishers, 2005), 332.

210 Faist, Gerdes, and Rieple, "Dual Citizenship as a Path-Dependent Process": 914. See also Miller, *On Nationality*, 72–73.

211 Rey Koslowski, *Migrants and Citizens. Demographic Change in the European State System* (Ithaca, NY: Cornell University Press, 2000), 144.

country of residence.[212] Though in many countries the abolishment of the renunciation requirement was introduced to encourage naturalization requests, it also reveals an increasing awareness that the ties with the original country are not cut by naturalization in another country. Thus, the renunciation requirement is becoming increasingly regarded as a denial of a factual reality: an application for naturalization is often based on pragmatic reasons and hardly ever means that the applicant no longer feels attached to the country of origin. This is especially true today, where due to modern technology and affordable transport, emigration is no longer by implication a choice for life. Circular migration and remigration are much more frequent phenomena than in the past.

From the viewpoint of the individual there are several reasons why dual nationality can be very desirable. The reason why immigrants apply for the nationality of the receiving country in the first place, is to be treated on exactly the same footing as the nationals of that country. Moreover, nationality is often a condition for the exercise of certain professions and it provides a secure residence status—in other words, one can no longer be expulsed.[213] In addition, Devoretz has shown that the acquisition of nationality by immigrants (in his study of Canadian nationality) often entails significant economic gains.[214] Loss of the original nationality is a very big obstacle to naturalization, however. The policy of both the receiving and sending State in respect of dual nationality will therefore often be decisive for someone's choice to become naturalized or not.

---

212 One of the most striking examples is the Luxembourg nationality law reform of 2008. Having a foreign population that exceeded 40 percent of the total population, Luxembourg decided to make its nationality law more inclusive *inter alia* by accepting dual nationality. See Le Gouvernement du Grand-Duché de Luxembourg, *The Luxembourg Nationality Law of 23 October 2008* (Luxembourg: Imprimerie Centrale, 2009), 10.

213 Paul Lagarde, "L'accession des immigrés à la nationalité du pays d'accueil de le problème de la double nationalité", in *Immigrés et réfugiés dans les démocraties occidentales, défis et solutions*, ed. D. Turpin (Paris: Economica, 1989), 199.

214 Don J. Devoretz, "The Economics of Citizenship: A Common Intellectual Ground for Social Scientists?", *Journal of Ethnic and Migration Studies* 34, no. 4 (2008): 683. If the immigrant expects to gain financially from naturalization, he will probably invest in acquiring more human capital (e.g. language skills) during the waiting period for naturalization. The knife thus cuts both ways: the benefits that already result from naturalization are reinforced by the effort made by the immigrant in the period prior to naturalization to acquire more human capital. Although it does not become clear from the Devoretz's article why exactly naturalization is economically beneficial for immigrants, one can assume that employers prefer naturalized immigrants for high-skilled, permanent jobs. On the other hand, naturalization does not matter much with regard to jobs of a low-skilled, flexible and temporary nature.

The importance of nationality for migrants can be further illustrated by two examples. It is shown that nationality still matters a great deal in Austria: 'Contrary to the well-known arguments about the "denationalisation" of citizenship rights [the authors refer to Soysal's much-quoted book of 1994 called 'Limits of Citizenship'], acquisition of Austrian nationality still matters a lot with respect to immigrants' security of residence, access to the labour market and social and political rights'.[215] The importance of Austrian nationality for immigrants led to a surge of naturalizations in the early 1990s. Another example is the retreat in the United States in the mid 1990s from a policy which guaranteed full social rights (e.g. social welfare benefits and education) to permanent non-nationals. This shows the migrant's vulnerable position regarding social rights when not possessing the nationality of the host country.[216] Consequently, when Hispanic Americans saw their social rights under attack, naturalization rates among this group rapidly increased—without a parallel increase in political participation, however.[217] This development shows that these migrants primarily perceived US nationality in an instrumental way. It also contradicts the postnationalist idea that nationality is increasingly becoming devoid of importance. The US case demonstrates that mere postnational citizenship (i.e. rights which are grounded on residence instead of nationality) does not give sufficient protection to migrants; nationality still matters a great deal because rights that are not grounded in nationality can be modified or withdrawn at the whim of the State. Despite the postnationalists' claim of rights becoming increasingly dependent on residence rather than nationality, postnationalism provides no mechanism for their enforcement. Jones-Correa is therefore right in saying that 'for the present, there is no substitute for nationality in the nation-State'.[218]

---

[215] Dilek Çinar and Harald Waldrauch, "Austria", in *Acquisition and Loss of Nationality, Policies and Trends in 15 European Countries*, ed. Rainer Bauböck, *et al.* (Amsterdam: Amsterdam University Press, 2006), 51.

[216] Christian Joppke, *Immigration and the Nation-State. The United States, Germany, and Great Britain* (Oxford: Oxford University Press, 1999), 274.

[217] Jones-Correa, "Seeking shelter: Immigrants and the Divergence of Social Rights and Citizenship in the United States", 234. Jones-Correa also mentions other causes for the increase of naturalization rates, such as the fact that large numbers of illegal migrants who had been granted amnesty in the 1980s became eligible for naturalization around the time the naturalization rates rapidly increased.

[218] Ibid., 255. See also Marc Morjé Howard, "Variation in Dual Citizenship Policies in the Countries of the EU", *International Migration Review* 39, no. 3 (2005): 716–717; Marc Morjé Howard, "Comparative Citizenship: An Agenda for Cross-National Research", *Perspectives on Politics* 4, no. 3 (2006): 445.

The previous remarks on sending and receiving States addressed moving persons. However, also moving borders can be the cause of multiple nationality.[219] Expatriate populations may not only be produced by 'people moving across international borders' but also by 'international borders moving across people'.[220] In such a case, States sometimes allow multiple nationality to their national minorities who live across the national border but are culturally attached to their home country. On this subject the situation in Central and Eastern Europe is particularly interesting on account of the strong cultural, ethnic and linguistic diversity in this part of Europe where national borders moved frequently in the course of the 20th century.[221]

In summary, we can indicate three main reasons for the growing incidence of multiple nationality: the combination of the *ius soli* and *ius sanguinis* principles, the equality of the sexes and, finally, the interest that individuals as well as sending and receiving States have in tolerating—or sometimes even pursuing—multiple nationality. Some of these grounds are of fairly recent origin, however. In Western Europe the equality of the sexes in nationality law only became widely accepted from the 1970s onwards—in the Netherlands, for example, only as of 1 January 1985.[222]

The growing instances of multiple nationality does not mean that the phenomenon is not still heavily contested, however. The sometimes controversial and sensitive nature of nationality law also renders the subject susceptible to

---

219 Thomas Faist, "Introduction: The Shifting Boundaries of the Political", in *Dual Citizenship in Global Perspective, From Unitary to Multiple Citizenship*, ed. Thomas Faist and Peter Kivisto (New York: Palgrave Macmillan, 2007), 2.

220 Bauböck, "Stakeholder Citizenship and Transnational Political Participation: a Normative Evaluation of External Voting": 2438.

221 As Kovács points out, nearly a quarter of all Hungarians live outside Hungary's borders in neighbouring States. See generally Horváth, *Mandating identity: citizenship, kinship laws and plural nationality in the European Union*; Mária M. Kovács, "The Politics of Dual Citzenship in Hungary", in *Dual Citizenship in Global Perspective, From Unitary to Multiple Citizenship*, ed. Peter Kivisto and Thomas Faist (New York: Palgrave Macmillan, 2007), 93; André Liebich, "Introduction: the vicissitudes of citizenship in the new EU states", in *Citizenship Policies in the New Europe*, ed. Rainer Bauböck, Bernhard Perchinig, and Wiebke Sievers (Amsterdam: Amsterdam University Press, 2007); André Liebich, "How Different is the "New Europe"? Perspectives on States and Minorities", *CEU Political Science Journal* 3, no. 3 (2008).

222 Gerard-René de Groot, "Vingt et un ans après: De gelijke behandeling van man en vrouw in het nationaliteitsrecht", in *De meerwaarde van de rechtsvergelijking. Opstellen aangeboden aan prof. H.U. Jessurun d'Oliveira bij gelegenheid van zijn afscheid als bestuurslid van de Nederlandse Vereniging voor Rechtsvergelijking*, ed. E.H. Hondius (Deventer: Kluwer, 1999), 71–72. See more recently de Groot and Vink, *Meervoudige nationaliteit in Europees perspectief*, 18.

political exploitation for reasons of electoral gain and, consequently, to rapid and frequent change. Nationality law in general, and multiple nationality in particular, have become very politicized in recent years.[223] On the one hand, left wing liberals are unwilling to compromise on their ideal of democratic inclusiveness; right wing conservatives, on the other hand, fear the threat of dual nationality to their ideal of undivided loyalty to the State.[224] The politicisation of nationality law means that multiple nationality is a recurrent topic characterized by waves of toleration or fierce opposition. Let us therefore stress the unlikelihood that the discussion on multiple nationality will ever end. This is inherent to the fact that the position taken on the subject of multiple nationality is mainly dictated by political and psychological motives; legal considerations often seem to be only of minor importance.[225]

It is also a remarkable and intriguing fact that there is such a divergent attitude towards dual nationality in countries that broadly share the same liberal and democratic values. The fierce debate in some countries on dual nationality—think of Germany—is completely absent in the UK for example.[226] In addition, the attitude towards dual nationality is contradictory in many countries; dual nationality may be accepted when it comes to the State's own nationals who naturalize elsewhere, but prohibited with respect to immigrants who apply for naturalization.[227] What is more, countries that officially

---

The equality of the sexes in nationality law was introduced much earlier in Eastern Europe. Already in 1918 the law in the Soviet Union gave women an independent position in nationality matters by both ensuring that marriage would not affect the nationality of women and by allowing women to transmit their nationality to their children on the same conditions as men. The example of the Soviet Union was followed by many States in Eastern Europe in the 1940s and 50s. See Matjaz Tratnik, *Het Nationaliteitsrecht in de Oosteuropese Landen*, Dissertatie Universiteit Maastricht (Deventer: Kluwer, 1989), 393; Gerard-René de Groot, "The background of the changed attitude of Western European States with respect to multiple nationality", in *New concepts of citizenship: residential/regional citizenship and dual nationality*, ed. Atsushi Kondo and Charles Westin (Stockholm: CEIFO, 2003), 101–102.

223 This was different in the past: 'The domination of legal professionals over politicians, and the resulting perception of nationality as a specialized legislation independent of politics, was fundamental in the 19th century'. See Weil, *How to Be French: Nationality in the Making since 1789*, 180.

224 Koslowski, *Migrants and Citizens. Demographic Change in the European State System*, 144.

225 Ko Swan Sik, "Nationaliteit en het volkenrecht", 37.

226 Randall Hansen and Patrick Weil, "Introduction", in *Dual nationality, Social Rights and Federal Citizenship in the US and Europe*, ed. Randall Hansen and Patrick Weil (New York: Berghahn Books, 2002), 6.

227 Or the other way round. Prior to 4 April 2002, Australian nationals naturalizing abroad automatically lost Australian nationality. Dual nationality was tolerated, however, for naturalizing immigrants in Australia. In short, asymmetric treatment of dual nationality may go

require the renunciation of the previous nationality upon naturalization often do not enforce it. This seems to be the case in Spain and the US for example. In the first country only a formal renunciation requirement exists, the legal practice since 1971 being that one can keep the other passport with the possibility of renewal upon naturalization in Spain. Spain does not inform the country of origin of the naturalization of one of its nationals in Spain. If the country of origin provides for the automatic loss of nationality for nationals who naturalize abroad, the Spanish practice thus has the effect that such a provision is not activated.[228] In the US the Immigration and Naturalization Service (INS) is officially opposed to dual nationality, but the pledge that the INS requires from individuals who naturalize to abandon the original nationality is non-enforceable. The US feel they cannot do anything about dual nationality.[229]

The next sections will look more closely at multiple nationality by addressing two specific issues. The first point concerns the possible positions that can be taken as regards the (un)desirability of multiple nationality. In this connection it is also worth considering dual nationality in the context of transnationalism, postnationalism and EU citizenship (Sections 7 and 8). Section 9 then goes on to investigate whether the legal problems resulting from multiple nationality, if any, are insurmountable.

7. *Attitudes Towards Multiple Nationality: Rejection or Embrace?*

Throughout history, dual nationality has often been the object of demonization and some still approach it with hostility today.[230] The discourse on dual nationality has considerably changed over time, however, and no one any longer takes the view that dual nationality is a legal impossibility.[231] The legal

both ways. See on dual nationality in Australia http://www.citizenship.gov.au/current/dual_citizenship/.

228 Aurelia Alvarez Rodríguez, *Nacionalidad española: normativa vigente e interpretación jurisprudencial* (Cizur Menor, Navarra: Thomson/Aranzadi, 2008), 142.

229 Jones-Correa, "Under Two Flags: Dual Nationality in Latin American and its Consequences for Naturalization in the United States": 1012; Hansen and Weil, "Introduction", 6. See very critically on the growing number of dual nationals with dual loyalties in the US, Samuel P. Huntington, *Who are we? The challenges to America's national identity* (New York: Simon & Schuster, 2004).

230 See for some historical remarks Paul Lagarde, "La pluralité de nationalités comme moyen d'intégration des résidents étrangers: Développements en France", in *Plural Nationality: Changing attitudes* (Conference at the European University Institute, Florence: 1992), 1.

231 Thomas M. Franck, "Multiple citizenship: autres temps, autres moeurs", in *Mélanges en l'honneur de Nicolas Valticos* (Paris: Éditions A. Pedone, 1999), 149.

literature at the end of the 19th and beginning of the 20th century traditionally thought of multiple nationality as a legal anomaly, although primarily for emotional and psychological reasons.[232] Legal arguments for the inconceivability of dual nationality were not really brought to the fore, apart from the claim that dual nationality troubled interstate relations.[233] It is in this hostile context that François Laurent wrote that the dual national was a contradictory element in the divine work that was the nation,[234] and that André Weiss made the oft-quoted statement that 'on ne peut avoir deux patries, comme on ne peut pas avoir deux mères'.[235] These authors did not primarily advance legal arguments for their opposition to multiple nationality, but alleged that the emotional loyalty between individual and State stood in the way of the existence of dual nationality. In other words, they dismissed the possibility that a person may legitimately feel connected to more than one State.

Although these arguments have lost popularity over time, some still hold the view that dual nationality is incompatible with loyalty towards the State and national belonging. In 1986 Darras expressed his hostility towards dual nationality in a PhD thesis on that topic because it would encourage immigrants to maintain ties with their home country at the expense of establishing and deepening ties with the country of residence.[236] This line of reasoning, which still has many supporters, is often characterized by one fundamental

---

232 That the psychological element should nonetheless be regarded as a valid aspect of nationality is recognized by Miller, who from his non-legal perspective writes that 'philosophers may find it restricting that they have to conduct their arguments about justice with reference to national identities at all. My claim is that unless they do they will lose contact with the beliefs of the people they seek to address'. Miller also makes the plausible argument that 'people may vary less in the extent to which nationality is an important part of their identity than in how far they see it as legitimate to acknowledge that fact about themselves. The nationalist celebrates his attachment to an historic community; the progressive liberal concedes it with reluctance and shame'. Miller, *On Nationality*, 15; Miller, "In Defence of Nationality", 39.

233 George Cogordan, *La nationalité au point de vue des rapports internationaux* (Paris: L. Larose et Forcel, 1890), 14.

234 Quoted in Rui Manuel Moura Ramos, "La double nationalité d'après le droit portugais", *Boletim da facultade de direito da Universidade de Coimbra* 59 (1983): 182.

235 Quoted in de Groot and Schneider, "Die zunehmende Akzeptanz von Fällen mehrfacher Staatsangehörigkeit in West-Europa", 65.

236 'L'acceptation de la binationalité a sans doute contribué à la désagréger le sentiment d'appartenance à la communauté nationale en laissant l'intéressé sous la dépendance d'une allégeance concurrente … La France ne peut se contenter d'un attachement minimum mais doit veiller à l'existence d'un engagement réel du nouveau Français, ce qui laisse supposer un dessaisissement progressif du lien de sujétion étranger'. See Loïc Darras, *La double nationalité*, Thèse pour le doctorat en droit (Paris: Université Paris II, 1986), 956.

flaw however: emigrants are always treated differently from immigrants. Whilst Darras thus vehemently opposes dual nationality for immigrants in France—French national identity is at stake!—he does not mind burdening other States with the problem of dual nationality; he argues that French expatriates should be allowed to retain their original nationality upon acquiring another one if this is in the French interest.[237] How one can accuse immigrants of a dual allegiance and at the same time plead for the retention of French nationality for French expatriates is rather puzzling.

Similarly, it has been claimed that dual nationality is a 'sociological incongruity' because individual and State have a mutual responsibility towards each other: the individual should contribute to the welfare of the State, while the State has a duty to care for the individual's welfare.[238] Moreover, the older literature did not only strongly oppose dual nationality for its anomalous character, it also—and this is a big difference compared to today's ideas on dual nationality which stress the benefits of having a dual nationality—thought that dual nationals were hardly in an enviable position.[239]

One expression of the psychological dimension of (dual) nationality is the idea that it is an honour to have the nationality of a given State. An example is the statement by the Dutch Minister of Alien Affairs and Integration in 2003 that acquisition of Dutch nationality should be considered 'the first prize'.[240]

---

[237] Ibid., 957–959. In Darras's view, the French policy should 'consentir aux Français d'origine installés à l'étranger la conservation de la nationalité française et sa juxtaposition à la nationalité du pays d'accueil lorsque notre intérêt national y trouve une utilité … Il convient donc d'accorder une préférence incontestable à la création d'une binationalité à l'avantage des Français de souche expatriés. Prétendre actuellement constituer une plurinationalité élargie reviendrait à compromettre à terme l'identité française. L'avenir de la France dépend de ce choix politique'.

[238] This opinion is expressed by Griffin, who is paraphrased in Ruth Donner, *The Regulation of Nationality in International Law* 2nd ed. (New York: Transnational Publishers Inc., 1994), 201.

[239] According to Thiesing, 'any individual who intentionally or unintentionally possesses such dual nationality, is hardly in an enviable position. Two different states claim his allegiance and demand the duties and obligations owed under it. Awkward as his position is under ordinary circumstances, his status will make him the subject of an irreconcilable conflict of duties in case a serious controversy should engage the two countries'. Thiesing, "Dual allegiance in the German law of nationality and American citizenship": 483. See in the same vein Henri Fromageot, *De la double nationalité des individus & des sociétés* (Paris: A. Rousseau, 1892), 102.

[240] Ricky van Oers, Betty de Hart, and Kees Groenendijk, "Netherlands", in *Acquisition and Loss of Nationality, Policies and Trends in 15 European Countries*, ed. Rainer Bauböck, *et al.* (Amsterdam: Amsterdam University Press, 2006), 403. The Dutch government also saw naturalization as the 'crown on a succesful integration process' (Tweede Kamer 2003–2004, 19 637, nr 837).

This statement corresponds to the view that nationality is an essential element in community identification; or, put negatively, that dual nationality (and consequently dual loyalties) will have a damaging effect on the national public spirit. Yet this position does not permit, in our view, the different degrees of connectedness to which today's migration gives rise. In its attempt to enforce a national identity, this stance neglects the 'scalar' possibilities of identification with both country of residence and country of origin.[241] It also clearly entails the danger of pitting 'us' against 'them', while the acceptance of multiple nationality would help to erode this distinction.[242]

Lagarde also points to this danger and stresses that nationality is first and foremost 'l'expression juridique d'un fait social de rattachement'.[243] Indeed, in cases where the bond between State and individual is still weak, it may be required for the individual to express his will so as to confirm this 'rattachement'. Yet in cases where this bond is an objective fact, asking for an act of will rather than automatically attributing nationality is not only superfluous but indirectly stresses the immigrant's 'foreignness' (*extranéité*). Nor does it contribute to the integration of immigrants since many of them are unaware of the formalities required for acquiring the nationality of the country of residence. Accordingly, large groups of immigrants will continue to occupy a marginal position in society whereas nationality should, in Lagarde's view, be a step towards full integration and equality.[244] The acceptance of dual nationality will 'soften' the integration process because the traumatic experience of completely severing the ties with the country of origin—often felt as a form of treason by the persons concerned—is avoided.[245] This idea that nationality is an instrument in the integration process is vehemently opposed by others,

---

241 Peter J. Spiro, "Dual Citizenship: A Postnational View", in *Dual Citizenship in Global Perspective, From Unitary to Multiple Citizenship*, ed. Thomas Faist and Peter Kivisto (New York: Palgrave Macmillan, 2007), 197.

242 Ibid.

243 See also *supra* Section 4 on the function of nationality under municipal and international law.

244 Lagarde, "L'accession des immigrés à la nationalité du pays d'accueil de le problème de la double nationalité", 199–210. We wholeheartedly agree with Lagarde when he makes the following observation: 'Ce serait faire preuve d'angélisme que de penser que l'immigré qui accède à la nationalité du pays d'accueil, par example à la nationalité française, va se sentir immédiatement en parfaite communion d'esprit avec les nationaux de ce pays et qu'il va se découvrir spontanément des ancêtres gaulois. Du moins, devenu français, se sentira-t-il moins étranger parce que plus égal. La disparition de la situation juridique d'inégalité devrait rendre possible une assimilation véritable'.

245 Lagarde, "La pluralité de nationalités comme moyen d'intégration des résidents étrangers: Développements en France", 2.

who maintain that the acquisition of French nationality by immigrants has not contributed to 'attenuating the socio-cultural divergences'.[246] As we will see in the chapter on France, Darras took this conclusion to the extreme and pleaded for the abolishment of all *ius soli* elements from French law.

At the opposite end of the spectrum are those who take the view that there are no reasons which prevent a person from legitimately possessing more than one nationality. We agree with this view, and so do (apparently) most nationality law specialists.[247] Indeed, if we perceive of nationality as being primarily a legal bond between an individual and a State, it is unclear why one should not be able to maintain legal bonds with more than one State.[248] Multiple nationality would just be a further example of a person having multiple allegiances.[249] In this connection, it should be noted that people possess many non-State loyalties, for example to the family or ethnic and religious communities. These loyalties can even conflict with loyalty to the State, yet no one would argue that these loyalties are incompatible with the status of national/citizen. Is it perhaps not time to accept concurrent attachments and loyalties to different States, just as non-State loyalties to whatever group or organization are accepted?[250] Hailbronner continues along these lines and points to the changing role of the sovereign State, having the effect that States are beginning to recognize the possibility of political membership of more than one State.[251]

---

246 Darras, *La double nationalité*, 953–955; Yves Lequette, "La nationalité française dévaluée", in *L'avenir du droit. Mélanges en hommage à François Terré* (Paris: Dalloz, 1999), 368 ff.

247 See for example Lagarde, "La pluralité de nationalités comme moyen d'intégration des résidents étrangers: Développements en France", 3; Gerard-René de Groot, "Een pleidooi voor meervoudige nationaliteit", *Migrantenrecht* 21, no. 3 (2006): 100–105. In Lagarde's view, 'la double nationalité est aujourd'hui une donnée historique et culturelle qu'on ne peut ignorer et qu'il faut à la fois identifier et gérer au mieux'.

248 Giovanni Kojanec, "Report on Multiple Nationality", (2000), 13. Rigaux also articulates this idea when he contends that 'seule l'affiliation religieuse requiert une adhésion totale et, dans son domaine, exclusive de toute autre'. François Rigaux, "Les situations juridique individuelles dans un système de relativité générale. Cours général de droit international privé", in *Recueil des cours de l'Académie de droit international de la Haye* (Leiden: Sijthoff, 1989), 71–72.

249 Miller agrees by writing that 'we typically regard our nationality as a constituent of our identity on a par with other constituents, and the obligations that flow from it as competing with obligations arising from other sources'. When people identify with two nations, Miller does not support a policy which forces them to a choice for either country since 'national identities are not in practice treated as exclusive and overriding by their bearers, whatever certain nationalist theories may claim'. Miller, *On Nationality*, 46.

250 Peter J. Spiro, "Dual nationality and the meaning of citizenship", *Emory Law Journal* 46, no. 4 (1997): 1473–1474.

251 Hailbronner, "Nationality in public international law and European law", 36.

We may say, then, that the concept of nationality is subject to change because the idea to which it is linked—the sovereign State—is changing. Thus Franck states that: 'Multiple loyalty, in itself, is not especially remarkable … It has been the rule rather than the exception in Western civilization … What *is* remarkable is the extent to which a person's loyalty system today, for the first time in history, has become a matter of personal choice. In the early Mediterranean empire, as also in the more recent Ottoman and Habsburg empires, multiple loyalty references were imposed on persons by virtue of who they were and where they lived. They were not freely chosen'.[252] We agree with Franck that this development is clearly evidenced in the growing toleration of multiple nationality. An interesting question, particularly in the field of private international law, is the extent to which these multiple allegiances oblige a State to accept rights and obligations of its nationals that follow from the possession of another nationality (see in more detail Chapter 2).

Spiro, finally, has gone as far as to argue that multiple nationality should not merely be accepted but is even demanded by republican, communitarian and liberal conceptions[253] of citizenship. He emphasizes that imposing obstacles to naturalization 'deforms the political process by excluding greater numbers of territorial residents from participation in self-governance, retards the community identification of those who thus live among us in a second-class status, and unjustly deprives those who do not naturalize of the rights of citizenship'.[254]

This short outline of opinions with regard to multiple nationality suffices to show the controversial nature of the subject. On the one hand, it is certainly true that nationality not only entails important social, political and economic consequences, but also that it is intimately connected to individual and collective identity.[255] These emotional sentiments lead many to claim that

---

[252] Emphasis in original. Thomas M. Franck, *The Empowered Self. Law and Society in the Age of Individualism* (New York: Oxford University Press, 1999), 62. See for similar remarks concerning the subject of *citizenship* Francis Delpérée, "La citoyenneté multiple", *Annales de Droit de Louvain* 56 (1996): 261–273; Jacques Chevallier, *L'État postmoderne* (Paris: Librairie Générale de Droit et de Jurisprudence, 2003), 192 ff.

[253] See also on these conceptions Herman van Gunsteren, "Four Conceptions of Citizenship", in *The Condition of Citizenship*, ed. Bart van Steenbergen (London: Sage Publications, 1994); Blatter, *Dual Citizenship and Democracy*.

[254] Spiro, "Dual nationality and the meaning of citizenship": 1416.

[255] Boll, *Multiple Nationality and International Law*, 4. See also Miller who convingly argues that 'it would … be a mistake to suppose that, once a practice of political co-operation is in place, nationality drops out of the picture as an irrelevance—that we simply have the rights and obligations of citizens interacting with other citizens [he appears to refer to the concept of 'constitutional patriotism' as advocated by Habermas]'. Miller argues that the *prior*

nationality has to do with loyalty and allegiance. How can nationals be expected to owe loyalty to fellow nationals if some of these also hold another nationality, and therefore owe loyalty to another State? Those supporting this line of reasoning will think of multiple nationality as a very undesirable phenomenon indeed.

On the other hand, the idea of unconditional loyalty to only one collectivity clashes with State sovereignty in nationality matters. This sovereignty, which gives States great leeway in according their nationality, makes instances of multiple nationality practically inevitable. Moreover, we have seen that many countries now realize that opposing multiple nationality in a time of increased inter-State movement equals opposing a factual reality; some people just belong to different countries and/or cultures by reason of their past. In this context, it is also worth mentioning theories on postnationalism and transnationalism. These theories, as well as citizenship of the European Union, are the subject of the next section.

8. *Transnationalism,*[256] *Postnationalism and European Citizenship*[257]

Migrants may establish transnational identities[258] in liberal immigration countries if these countries do not impose on them an unconditional choice for staying or returning. Provided that the receiving country does not force

---

obligations of nationality make possible a practice of citizenship that includes elements of solidarity and distributive justice. Miller, *On Nationality*, 71–72, 162–163; David Miller, "Republicanism, National Identity, and Europe", in *Republicanism and political theory*, ed. Cécile Laborde and John Maynor (Malden, MA: Blackwell, 2008), 147–151.

256 In some of the literature also defined as 'dual nationalism', which refers to the practice of emigration countries to appeal to their nationals abroad 'as part of a national collective beyond borders for purposes of nationality unity and nationalist goals'. Faist, "Introduction: The Shifting Boundaries of the Political", 1–2.

257 See for an overview of all three concepts Jo Shaw, *The Transformation of Citizenship in the European Union. Electoral Rights and the Restructuring of Political Space* (Cambridge: Cambridge University Press, 2007), chapter 2.

258 Defined by Bauböck as 'an overlapping structure of membership in two or more polities, with significant elements of citizenship status and rights in each'. These elements would normally include local voting rights for foreign nationals, absentee voting rights for expatriates and multiple nationality. Multiple nationality, 'denizenship' (a special legal status for long-term resident foreign nationals who enjoy among other things the same social welfare rights as nationals as well as local voting rights) and 'ethnizenship' (the reverse of denizenship in that an external quasi-citizenship is granted to minorities of co-ethnic descent living abroad which includes finanancial support for mainaining, for example, a minority culture and language) are all qualified by Bauböck as modes of transnational citizenship. Both denizenship and quasi-citizenship/ethnizenship often function as stepping stones towards multiple

immigrants into full assimilation, they can maintain bonds with their original country and develop a transnational identity. Consequently, they can also make a valid claim to dual nationality: 'Migrants who are permanent residents in a receiving society but retain strong economic, social, cultural and family ties with a sending country have a plausible claim to citizenship in both polities since they are in a position where their lives will be strongly affected by political decisions in both states and where protection of their rights may depend on formal recognition as citizens of these states'.[259] The backdrop to this claim for dual nationality is the changing role of the sovereign State: 'The norms of homogenous and singular citizenship that have underpinned the Westphalian system have been gradually eroded and especially so in liberal States whose commitment to human rights, minority protection and democracy made them aware that the old conception of indivisible sovereignty clashes with their most fundamental political values'.[260] What is therefore historically new is 'the willingness of liberal democracies to recognise transnational modes of citizenship and to develop a more pluralistic public culture through policies that recognise diversity'.[261]

Also postnationalism deserves some mention here. This idea, which may be defined as 'the decline of the state as brought about by a dilution in state-based identity and the rise of non-state attachments',[262] predicts a weakened State owing to weakened national identities. In this context, the role of multiple nationality is considered an important one: although at first glance it may seem that multiple nationality in a way reinforces the idea of the nation-state because it expresses a legal bond with more than one State, the reverse could also very well be true. It is possible that multiple nationality will accelerate the phenomenon of postnationalism as it lowers the intensity of the bond between State and subject.[263] Spiro thus establishes a causality between

nationality. See Rainer Bauböck, "The Trade-off Between Transnational Citizenship and Political Autonomy", in *Dual Citizenship in Global Perspective, From Unitary to Multiple Citizenship*, ed. Thomas Faist and Peter Kivisto (New York: Palgrave Macmillan, 2007), 88. See also Thomas Hammar, "State, Nation, and Dual Citizenship", in *Immigration and the Politics of Citizenship in Europe and North America*, ed. Rogers William Brubaker (Lanham: University Press of America, 1989), 83–84; Bauböck, "Stakeholder Citizenship and Transnational Political Participation: a Normative Evaluation of External Voting": 2395–2396. For a detailed and critical overview of the strong denizenship status of legally residing foreigners in France, see Lequette, "La nationalité française dévaluée". In Lequette's view, a strong denizenship status devalues the concept of nationality.

259 Bauböck, "The Trade-off Between Transnational Citizenship and Political Autonomy", 72.

260 Ibid., 85.

261 Ibid., 75.

262 Peter J. Spiro, "Dual Citizenship: A Postnational View", ibid., 190.

263 Ibid., 189.

multiple nationality and postnationalism, but only time will tell whether he is right in predicting the following consequences: 'Insofar as citizenship comes to reflect less intensive communal bonds, the state is less likely to serve as a vehicle for robust redistributionist and rights-protective policies, which in turn will result in waning institutional power'.[264] This view of dual citizenship as a phenomenon that will undermine the state-based societal community has been called a challenge to the well-known citizenship theory developed by Marshall.[265] After all, Spiro's claim that dual citizenship undermines solidarity at the national level clashes with the Marshallian idea that citizenship has the capacity to unite individuals in a transcendent community.[266]

Others voice a different opinion and stress that the toleration of multiple nationality is accompanied by different, often contradictory, trends. While Spiro establishes a causal link between the weakened nation-state and multiple nationality, they emphasize that multiple nationality has been used by emigrant sending countries to advance nationalist goals and identities.[267] This use of multiple nationality can be interpreted as an attempt to strengthen the position of the State.

Compared to postnationalism and transnationalism—concepts that lawyers may have difficulties relating to—European citizenship is a very relevant status that has a profound impact on the perception of Member State nationality.[268] The European Union is perhaps the best example of the sovereign State making way for other (supranational) structures. This assumes concrete form in European citizenship, a status which has gained importance ever since its

---

264 Ibid., 200.

265 Peter Kivisto, "Conclusion: The Boundaries of Citizenship in a Transnational Age", ibid., ed. Peter Kivisto and Thomas Faist, 277.

266 In Marshall's definition, 'citizenship requires ... a direct sense of community membership based on loyalty to a civilisation which is a common possession'. Thomas Humphrey Marshall, *Citizenship and social class* (London: Pluto, 1992), 24.

267 Faist, "Introduction: The Shifting Boundaries of the Political", 22.

268 EU citizenship and transnationalism are nonetheless closely intertwined. Magnette, for example, interprets EU citizenship as being primarily transnational in substance. Admitting that Union citizenship carries a few rights that establish a direct link between the citizen and the Union (e.g. the right to participate in the election of the European Parliament), he feels that it is the right to freely move on the territory of the Union which represents the core of the European citizenship project. Paul Magnette, "How can one be European? Reflections on the Pillars of European Civic Identity", *European Law Journal* 13, no. 5 (2007): 12–13.

Shaw continues along the same lines of thinking, stating that 'because of the weakness of the vertical bonds, the 'static' European citizen, in contrast to the mobile transnational one, does not seem to derive many benefits from the institution of citizenship as a fundamental building block of the European Union'. Jo Shaw, "Citizenship: Contrasting Dynamics at the Interface of Integration and Constitutionalism", Working Paper University of Edinburgh 2010/14, 11.

introduction in the 1992 Maastricht Treaty.[269] The establishment of EU citizenship was indeed a unique historical moment:

> For the first time in the history of the Westphalian political order a concrete citizenship design beyond the Nation State had emerged, thereby undermining the exclusivity of national citizenship.[270]

The CJEU has declared on numerous occasions that Union citizenship is destined to become the fundamental status of Community nationals.[271] The developments in respect of Union citizenship have also instilled new dynamics in the discussion about national autonomy in nationality law[272] and it is in this light that the plea of those who advocate some EU competence in nationality law should be read. They hold the view that the more substance is given to EU citizenship, the less Member States ought to have complete autonomy in deciding who becomes a European citizen.

Article 20(1) TFEU states that 'every person holding the nationality of a Member State shall be a citizen of the Union. Citizenship of the Union shall be additional to and not replace national citizenship'.[273] From reading this definition it becomes clear that a Member State's policy towards multiple nationality is of great consequence for the access to European citizenship. If naturalization, for example, is no longer conditioned upon renunciation of the previous nationality, this is likely to increase the number of naturalizations, and consequently the number of European citizens.[274] More European citizens are also

---

269 See on the historical background of European citizenship Carlos Closa, "The concept of citizenship in the Treaty on European Union", *Common Market Law Review* 29 (1992): 1137–1169; Giovanni Kojanec, "The citizenship of the European Union", in *Feestbundel Zilverentant*, ed. F.J.A. van der Velden (Den Haag: Ministerie van Justitie-Directie Wetgeving, 1998), 133–138; Luuk van Middelaar, *De passage naar Europa. Geschiedenis van een begin* (Deventer: Historische Uitgeverij, 2009), 354 ff.

270 Dora Kostakopoulou, "European Union Citizenship: Writing the Future", *European Law Journal* 13, no. 5 (2007): 624–625.

271 For the first time in Case C-184/99 *Grzelczyk* [2001] ECR I-6193.

272 See in more detail *infra* Section 11 as well as Chapter 2.

273 Soon after the establishment of EU citizenship in the Maastricht Treaty, questions were obviously raised as to whether, and if so, to what extent, EU citizenship had limited the sovereignty of the Member States in the field of nationality. See for example Hans Ulrich Jessurun d'Oliveira and Andrew Evans, "Nationality and Citizenship", in *Human Rights and the European Community: Methods of protection*, ed. Antonio Cassese, Andrew Clapham, and Joseph Weiler (Baden-Baden: Nomos, 1991), 303.

274 See for an early discussion on the role of naturalization in acquiring Member State nationality (and thus EU citizenship) Closa, "Citizenship of the Union and nationality of Member States": 515. Closa also refers to the European Parliament's proposal to harmonize the residence periods for harmonization. The considerable differences between Member States as regards naturalization requirements were thus perceived as a problem ever since EU citizenship was established.

created when Member States allow for the unrestrained transmission of their nationality by emigrants who permanently live abroad.[275]

As European citizens enjoy the right of free movement throughout the Union,[276] every Member State is affected by the nationality law provisions of other Member States. As yet, the EU lacks competence to act in the area of nationality law, which is often justified by pointing at Member State sovereignty and the general sensitivity of the issue.[277] This does not prevent the debate on the necessity for minimum harmonization of the Member States'

---

[275] Rainer Bauböck, "Why European Citizenship? Normative Approaches to Supranational Union", *Theoretical Inquiries in Law* 8, no. 2 (2007): 473. Bauböck articulates the problem of transmitting a Member State nationality *iure sanguinis* to persons born outside the Union as follows: 'This regime creates unfair advantages for certain immigrants based on ancestry and unfair burdens for those member states that have to admit EEUSs [external EU citizens residing in third countries] created by other member states' nationality laws'.

[276] Shortly after the introduction of EU citizenship, d'Oliveira rightly noted the following: 'Whereas in the Member States the notion of citizenship historically accrued around the *political* rights of the individual, it is around the freedom of movement that the notion of Union citizenship is crystallizing' (emphasis in original). To this day he remains very critical of EU citizenship and sees the EU citizen primarily as a suppliant to whom Union citizenship is granted top down, 'just like her majesty pours out the hot chocolate to the staff at Christmas'. It seems that his main criticism is directed against the absence of a deeper political and institutional role of EU citizenship. Hans Ulrich Jessurun d'Oliveira, "Union citizenship: pie in the sky?", in *A citizens' Europe: in search of a new order*, ed. Allan Rosas and Esko Antola (London: Sage, 1995), 83; Jessurun d'Oliveira, "Europees burgerschap: dubbele nationaliteit?", 124. See also Joseph H.H. Weiler, *The Constitution of Europe. "Do the new clothes have an emperor?" and other essays on European integration* (Cambridge: Cambridge University Press, 1999), chapter 10.

We agree that EU citizenship remains a relatively weak concept in political terms; the right to vote in elections to the European Parliament and to apply to the European Ombudsman seems to mean little to the EU citizen. EU citizenship does also not entail duties, thus making it a rather pale shadow of national citizenship. However, it should be recognized that the growing body of case law on the subject of EU citizenship does, step by step, emancipate the EU citizen from being merely a market citizen (the case law on European citizenship is discussed in Chapter 2 insofar as relevant for our subject). In this connection, EU citizenship is said to slowly but steadily evolve into a fifth Treaty freedom. See Editorial, "Two-speed European citizenship? Can the Lisbon Treaty help close the gap?", *Common Market Law Review* 45 (2008): 1–11.

[277] Kochenov rightly observes that 'in failing to regulate the issue of access to EU citizenship effectively, the Member States opted for the illusion of control rather than the resolution of outstanding problems, which include, most importantly, the need to design an effective immigration policy for the Union, while ensuring that the rights of EU citizens and third-country nationals are protected'. Dimitry Kochenov, "Rounding up the Circle: The Mutation of Member States' Nationalities under Pressure from EU Citizenship", EUDO Citizenship Working Paper 2010/23, 20.

nationality laws from being in full swing.[278] In this connection, Bauböck has stressed that at present there is a low level of mobility of Union citizens. This may change, however, and when large numbers of EU citizens arrive from third countries, the need to coordinate nationality laws may outweigh to some extent the importance of self-determination.[279]

It is interesting to note that the coordination of nationality laws was exactly what happened when the Scandinavian countries started to discuss a Nordic Union citizenship after the Second World War. They agreed that a common Nordic nationality was undesirable and that Nordic Union citizenship should complement rather than replace the nationality of the participating States. Yet it was also recognized that if such a Union was created, significant differences between the States' nationality legislations could not be maintained.[280] Not only the Nordic Union example, but also the introduction of minimum standards for Third Country Nationals (TCNs) in the long-term residence directive[281] has the potential of being a forerunner for a similar development in European nationality law in general, and naturalization requirements in particular.

It thus remains to be seen whether the sovereignty argument will continue to provide sufficient justification for the near unfettered Member State autonomy in nationality matters. Proponents of a minimum degree of EU authority over domestic nationality laws acknowledge that a limitation on State sovereignty may not be to the liking of the Member States, but at the same time maintain that States will come to realize that it is in the interest of all that some basic standards be imposed.[282] These ideas on European legislation would preferably go beyond the (minimum) harmonization that has already

278 See for example Francis Delpérée, "Nationalité, droit constitutionnel et droit européen", *Annales de Droit de Louvain* 63, no. 3 (2003): 239–241; Bauböck et al., "Introduction", 15–34.

279 Bauböck, "Why European Citizenship? Normative Approaches to Supranational Union": 485.

280 Bauböck et al., "Introduction", 16. The authors give the example that in the absence of harmonization of nationality laws, the odd situation would arise that a Dane moving to Finland would enjoy equal rights there with native Finns in Nordic matters while these rights are potentially denied to foreigners born and raised in Finland.

281 Council Directive concerning the status of third-country nationals who are long-term residents, 2003/109. For a detailed analysis of this Directive, see Sergio Carrera, *In Search of the Perfect Citizen? The Intersection between Integration, Immigration and Nationality in the EU* (Leiden/Boston: Martinus Nijhoff Publishers, 2009), 171 ff.

282 De Groot refers in this respect to the initial non-compliance by Spanish courts with the ECJ ruling in *Micheletti*. Spain was apparently unhappy with the fact that it had to recognize Mr Micheletti's Italian nationality, a dual national in possession of both Italian and Argentinean nationality (see *infra* Section 11.2). In De Groot's view, it would be conceivable that Spain will plead for Community competence in the field of nationality law with the aim of

been established by the 1997 European Convention on Nationality (ECN). Should the European Union acquire legislative competence in the field of nationality, a prominent nationality law specialist has advised drawing upon the rules already drafted in the ECN.[283]

Bauböck has also argued along these lines. He identifies three approaches to give shape to European citizenship which he calls 'statist', 'unionist' and 'pluralist'.[284] The first two are readily dismissed as politically unfeasible, but the pluralist view is a more realistic option. He maintains that under the pluralist approach the sovereignty of the Member States could be constrained without reversing the present hierarchy between nationality and EU citizenship.[285] If Union citizenship as a concept is to be taken seriously, common standards should apply for access to this status and Member State autonomy should be constrained to the extent that such autonomy conflicts with commitments shared by the Member States.[286] Yet the pluralist approach does not support a reversal of the present hierarchy between national and supranational citizenship. The latter cannot under this approach be turned into the primary status, but is still meant to be complementary.

---

preventing Italian-Argentinean nationals from settling in Spain as allowed under EU law. See Gerard-René de Groot, "Negeert Spanje de Micheletti-beslissing van het Europese Hof van Justitie?", *Migrantenrecht* 13, no. 4 (1998): 123–124; Gerard-René de Groot, "Zum Verhältnis der Unionsbürgerschaft zu den Staatsangehörigen in der Europäischen Union", in *Europäisches Integrationsrecht im Querschnitt*, ed. P. Müller-Graff (Baden-Baden: Nomos, 2002), 83.

283 Gerard-René de Groot, "Towards a European Nationality Law–Vers un droit européen de nationalité. Inaugural lecture, delivered on 13 November 2003 on the occasion of the acceptance of the Pierre Harmel chair of professeur invité at the University of Liège", 2003; available from www.ejcl.org.

284 Bauböck, "Why European Citizenship? Normative Approaches to Supranational Union": 467. The statist approach corresponds to principles applied in contemporary federal democracies. The unionist approach focuses on strengthening EU citizenship by making it more important for individual bearers and more inclusionary for EU residents; it differs from a federal state model in that it seeks to emancipate Union citizenship from Member State nationality rather than integrate the latter into the former. The pluralist view does not aim at strengthening EU citizenship vis-à-vis the Member States, but instead emphasizes the autonomous value of both national and supranational citizenship.

285 Ibid., 483–484.

286 Ibid., 484. Bauböck argues that the need for common norms emerges from commitments to supranational democracy and freedom of movement: 'Even if member states create Union citizens under their own laws, they decide thereby also who will be politically represented in the legislative bodies of the Union and who will get access to all other member states of the Union. The Union formed by all states has, therefore, a legitimate interest that none of its members excludes groups with a claim to political representation or includes groups without a genuine link to any of the countries in the Union'.

The line between harmonization and Member State sovereignty may be a fine one, however. One might wonder what would be left of this sovereignty if minimum standards were to include the obligation to be more inclusive towards long-term resident immigrants (e.g. by introducing *ius soli* acquisition as well as harmonized naturalization conditions) and less inclusive towards expatriates and subsequent generations born abroad (by partly abolishing preferential regimes for co-ethnics living abroad). Indeed, such minimum standards would, by removing most of the particularities that States have introduced on account of their respective historical pasts, significantly impinge on their sovereignty in the area of nationality law.

Another debate, which is intimately linked to that on competence in nationality matters, centres around the question whether the status of Member State nationality should not be separated from that of European citizenship.[287] The latter status could, for example, be made dependent on fulfilling a given residence period in the Union. In this way, European citizenship could be acquired by TCNs who do not qualify for naturalization in individual Member States. This problem is particularly salient for the third country spouses of European citizens whose work requires them to frequently move from one EU Member State to another. Although EU law guarantees European citizens who avail themselves of free movement the right to be joined by their non-European spouses,[288] it has no say whatsoever on how these spouses can become EU citizen themselves. This is for the nationality laws of the Member States to decide.[289] Consequently, a non-European citizen who accompanies his or her European citizen spouse may have difficulties acquiring the nationality of a Member State of the EU for two reasons. First, if the couple frequently move, often the non-European spouse will not meet the conditions regarding the waiting period for naturalization in the *country of residence*; second, the trend

287 See several of the contributions in Massimo La Torre, ed., *European Citizenship: A European Challenge* (The Hague: Kluwer Law International, 1998).

288 Directive 2004/38/EC of 29 April 2004.

289 However, as De Groot points out after giving an overview of national legislation, 'in not one single Member State, a distinction is found between the situation where the non-European foreign spouse lives together with the European spouse within the European Union and the situation where they are living in a non-Member State. In the light of the free movement rights granted by the EC Treaty, such a distinction would be desirable'. In short, none of the Member States' naturalization rules take into account that the non-European spouse may have been resident for years—or even decades—in the European Union. See Gerard-René de Groot, "The access to European citizenship for third country spouses of a European citizen", in *Liber Amicorum Paul Delnoy* (Bruxelles: Larcier, 2005), 131–132.

that naturalization requirements become more stringent in several Member States—think for example of language requirements[290]—makes it difficult for the non-EU spouse to comply with these requirement if the couple does not live in the *country of origin of the EU citizen spouse.*[291]

However, ideas of separating Member State nationality from EU citizenship are (as yet) unfeasible, and perhaps even undesirable.[292] Minimum harmonization of nationality laws thus remains the most realistic option. Access to European citizenship would then still remain dependent on Member State nationality, but at least some equal access to the status of European citizen would be provided for.

In any case, we shall later see that, arguably, EU law already imposes certain constraints on Member State sovereignty in nationality matters (*infra* Section 11). Moreover, the following *obiter dictum* from *Micheletti*[293] could serve as a future basis to further curtail Member State autonomy: 'Under international law, it is for each Member State, *having due regard to Community law*, to lay down the conditions for the acquisition and loss of nationality' (emphasis added).

Although the acquisition of the nationality of a Member State remains, of course, very desirable for non-Member State nationals, it is the right of free movement as guaranteed to European citizens by Article 21 TFEU which detracts from the value of a particular nationality itself. By this we mean that it becomes crucial to hold the nationality of *a* Member State, rather than that of a *particular* Member State.[294] This also means that possessing the nationality

---

290 Costica Dumbrava, "How Illiberal are Citizenship Rules in European Union Countries?", EUDO Citizenship Working Paper 2010/50.

291 de Groot, "The access to European citizenship for third country spouses of a European citizen", 129–131.

292 Bauböck, "Why European Citizenship? Normative Approaches to Supranational Union": 485. Several arguments can be advanced against giving third country nationals direct access to EU citizenship. First, it would remove a lot of the pressure to introduce minimum standards for Member State nationality. Already possessing EU citizenship would also give third country nationals less incentive to naturalize, which would not help their integration in the Member State where they live. Finally, it would create two groups of European citizens since those not holding a Member State nationality are not represented in the Council but only in the European Parliament.

293 Case C-369/90 *Micheletti* [1992] ECR I-04239, para.10. For a pre-*Micheletti* analysis of the compatibility of the Member States' nationality laws with Community law, see Christopher Greenwood, "Nationality and the Limits of the Free Movement of Persons in Community Law", *Yearbook of European Law* 7 (1987): 193.

294 This clearly follows from a judgment which will be examined *infra* in Section 11.2.2: Case C-200/02 *Zhu and Chen* [2004] ECR I-09925.

of two or more Member States of the EU is hardly problematic if European nationality law is looked at from the perspective of access to European citizenship. A dual nationality would simply mean that the additional status of European citizen is 'founded on more than one pillar'.[295] Some also see dual nationality as a bridge between Member State nationality and EU citizenship: dual nationality contributes to the creation of solidarity, helps to transcend the national framework and, consequently, serves as a catalyst for furthering the construction of European identity.[296] Evans has gone a step further by arguing that a renunciation requirement for Member State nationals applying for naturalization in another Member State is incompatible with the European integration project.[297] In his view, 'relaxation of restrictions on possession of dual nationality seems to be demanded by the spirit, if not the letter, of Community law'.[298]

In conclusion, the previous remarks on European citizenship are evidently not intended to 'write off' the State or to trivialize in any way the importance of nationality. Though permanent residents have been given a lot of rights that in the past were only reserved to nationals, these rights can be changed at the discretion of the State and are by no means the same in every country.[299] Nationality is thus still of capital importance in being the most secure status one can have in a State. European citizenship only has an additional character, although it does give migrants from other Member States of the European Union superior rights over emigrants from third countries. It can also not be denied that the increasing reliance on European citizenship by the CJEU has given this concept more and more substance.

The *García Avello* judgment,[300] for example, which deals with European citizenship as well as dual nationality, will be discussed at length in Chapter 2.

---

295 de Groot and Vink, *Meervoudige nationaliteit in Europees perspectief*, 36.

296 Waldemar A. Skrobacki, "Dual Citizenship, European Identity and Community-Building in Europe", in *Dual Citizenship in Global Perspective, From Unitary to Multiple Citizenship*, ed. Peter Kivisto and Thomas Faist (New York: Palgrave Macmillan, 2007), 229.

297 This line of reasoning seems to have been used by Germany when it decided in 2007 to no longer provide for the loss of German nationality upon naturalization in another Member State, and to abolish the renunciation requirement for naturalizing EU citizens in Germany. See de Groot and Vink, *Meervoudige nationaliteit in Europees perspectief*, 165.

298 Andrew Evans, "Nationality Law and European Integration", *European Law Review* 16 (1991): 197.

299 Randall Hansen and Patrick Weil, "Introduction: Citizenship, Immigration and Nationality: Towards a Convergence in Europe?", in *Towards a European Nationality. Citizenship, Immigration and Nationality Law in the EU*, ed. R. Hansen and P. Weil (Hampshire: Palgrave Publishers, 2001), 2.

300 Case C-148/02 *García Avello* [2003] ECR I-11613.

Suffice it to note here that the case was decided by the ECJ on the basis of the European citizenship of the persons involved. The Court referred to the well-established case law in which it was held that 'citizenship of the Union is destined to be the fundamental status of nationals of the Member States'.[301]

9. *Does Multiple Nationality Cause Legal Problems?*

The growing trend towards acceptance of multiple nationality raises the important question whether multiple nationality causes any legal problems. Is the existence of multiple nationality really detrimental to States? After all, one might suspect that the traditional opposition is not only explainable on *emotional* grounds—the fear that multiple nationals will not feel an unconditional loyalty towards one particular State—but also for *practical* and *legal* reasons. Below we go into the problems that might ensue from multiple nationality. These have to do with loyalty, voting rights, diplomatic protection, military service and personal status.[302] We are inclined to support the view that it may be queried whether the arguments against multiple nationality, based on the aforementioned categories, provide sufficient argument for the claim that multiple nationality will inevitably pose legal problems.[303]

To begin with, the emphasis on loyalty was typical for the 19th century when State relations were unstable and when cross-border movements were still limited. Today, these arguments no longer hold the same force; it is even possible to claim that competing loyalties and affiliations constitute the characteristics of modern society. In this connection we also refer back to what was said in Section 7 about non-State loyalties and identities. These different loyalties may be perceived as legitimate, and it could be argued that one should be as tolerant to them as to the loyalty felt by a person to another State.

In the context of loyalty and State security some authors have voiced a suspicion of dual nationals and have claimed that activities such as espionage benefit from dual nationality.[304] To this it has been replied that dual nationality

301 Para. 22, in which the Court refers to Case C-413/99 *Baumbast* [2002] ECR I-07091. The reference to EU citizenship as the nationals' fundamental status has been repeated in the Court's case law on numerous occasions ever since.

302 Lagarde, *La nationalité française*, 21; Martin, "Introduction: The trend toward dual nationality", 11–18.

303 Martin, "Introduction: The trend toward dual nationality", 11–18.

304 'L' espionnage industriel, en période de paix, comme l'espionnage militaire, du temps de guerre, sont facilités par la plurinationalité en rendant insoupçonnable le donneur de renseignements, citoyen parmi d'autres'. Darras, *La double nationalité*, 396.

may, on the contrary, draw suspicion on a person and that those with treacherous intent should have an interest in avoiding dual nationality.[305]

The loyalty argument is not particularly strong when advanced in an EU context. As Hansen and Weil have argued, the European Union itself is a sign that the Member States do not take seriously a strict, exclusive definition of loyalty: 'The very project of the European integration is based on the implicit recognition of multiple loyalties—to the state of one's citizenship, to the institutions of the EU, and to citizens of other member states'.[306] As the fight against terrorism is high on the agenda, however, we may perhaps witness a renewed emphasis on loyalty in the future. For now, the terrorist acts committed in recent years seem to have impacted mainly on the civil rights of both citizens and non-citizens, and on stricter migration control measures. Thus, apart from the Netherlands,[307] 'no direct discernible impact [can as yet be witnessed] on the readiness to tolerate or even accept dual citizenship'.[308]

Multiple nationality may also give rise to problems as regards voting rights. The first argument against the right to vote for multiple nationals in their host country is that the voting behaviour of multiple nationals will be less responsible since they have an 'exit clause': there is always another country to which they can return.[309] Secondly, multiple nationals are accused of acting as puppets for other governments, representing those governments' interests in the country of residence. That there is some truth in this argument is confirmed by Jones-Correa with regard to Mexico. This country has sought to mobilize expatriates with dual nationality in the United States to further Mexican interests. The Mexican goal was to 'have a potentially significant swinging group with ties and influence with both the United States and Mexico, serving as an important linchpin in relations between the two countries'. Whether this plan has any chance of succeeding is doubtful as only a very small number of Mexican expatriates in the United States eligible for dual nationality applied for it in the past.[310] Similarly, the Turkish government expected to gain political benefits from its Turkish nationals living in Europe. Kadirbeyoglu remarks that 'the lobbying potential of migrants living in European countries has been seen as an asset by Governments in Turkey'.[311]

305 Hansen and Weil, "Introduction", 8.

306 Ibid., 7.

307 See Chapter 4, Section 8.1.

308 Faist, "Dual citizenship: Change, Prospects, and Limits", 173.

309 Martin, "Introduction: The trend toward dual nationality", 13.

310 Jones-Correa, "Under Two Flags: Dual Nationality in Latin American and its Consequences for Naturalization in the United States": 1010, 1024.

311 Kadirbeyoglu, "Changing conceptions of citizenship in Turkey", 295.

It is difficult to say whether dual nationality makes it easier for home country governments to use their dual nationals as puppets to serve their interests, or whether this accusation makes an unfounded caricature of multiple nationals. In any case, it is questionable to what extent the phenomenon of multiple nationality can be blamed for this, as also naturalized nationals who abandoned their previous nationality can be accused of voting and acting according to the preferences of their former country. After all, the absence of legal ties with the country of origin does not say anything about one's emotional attachment to it.

Another point is whether multiple nationals should be allowed to vote in the country where they are not resident.[312] It can indeed be argued that their having more nationalities gives them more political rights than mononationals.[313] Rubio-Marín takes the view that absentee voting should not be allowed. This view is not based, however, on the argument of some authors that nationals who reside abroad are not sufficiently informed or do not have a sufficient stake in the home country. Rather, Rubio-Marín thinks they can be informed and affected, but this in itself is not strong enough a reason to justify a claim to absentee voting. The right to vote should be a prerogative of residents in a country for they are affected most strongly by the exercise of public authority. She also disagrees with the argument that '"economic" citizenship and "political citizenship" should go hand in hand', meaning that the expatriates' contribution to the home country economy through remittances should be rewarded with political rights. These remittances may indeed be a great asset to the economy, but this does not justify establishing a connection between economic contribution and political rights: 'The construct of democratic citizenship … has as one of its fundamental virtues the setting of some limits on the way in which economic power … translates into political power'.[314] Other authors disagree with this view and claim that voting in two countries does not violate the principle of 'one person one vote' because votes cast by the same person in two different countries are counted only once in each election.[315]

312 See on this subject the chapter on Italy, particularly Section 6.3.

313 Martin, "Introduction: The trend toward dual nationality", 13. One should not forget, however, that multiple nationals often have no chance of voting in different countries because of a residence requirement for the exercise of this right. See Peter J. Spiro, "Political rights and dual nationality", ibid., ed. D.A Martin and Kay Hailbronner, 137.

314 Ruth Rubio Marín, "Transnational Politics and the Democratic Nation-State: Normative Challenges of Expatriate Voting and Nationality Retention of Emigrants", *New York University Law Review* 117, no. 81 (2006).

315 Bauböck, "Why European Citizenship? Normative Approaches to Supranational Union": 474. Bauböck acknowledges that this argument does not hold true for voting in a supranational union such as the EU.

Another matter concerns multiple nationals holding public office. This was heavily debated in the Netherlands in 2007 when two dual nationals (of Moroccan/Dutch and Turkish/Dutch nationality respectively) joined the government as State Secretaries. Geert Wilders's right wing 'Freedom Party' (*Partij voor de Vrijheid, PVV*) made the argument that members of both parliament and government should not be allowed to have a multiple nationality as this could cast doubt on their loyalty to the Netherlands (see also Chapter 4, Section 8.1).[316] This idea is shared by part of the population, and the incompatibility of multiple nationality and holding public office is recognized in several countries, for example Australia.[317]

Though this argument may have some merit—Turkey's position indeed seems to be that 'the more established and influential the "Euro Turks" in EU-countries get, the more they may represent Turkey and Turkish interests abroad'[318]—we are of the opinion that a general exclusion of multiple nationals from political functions would go too far. The problem can best be solved with a 'conflict-of-interest approach'.[319] Multiple nationals can be appointed to a public office, but they should refrain from exercising an office that involves the interests of the other country whose nationality they hold. On the other hand, it can also be claimed—as Spiro does—that we no longer live in a world of hostility between nation-states in which interests rarely coincide. In a globalizing world with more calls for cooperation, it is less likely for multiple

[316] For an overview and general critique of conservative nationalism (to which we count the PVV), see Miller, *On Nationality*, 124–130. Miller's main claim is that national identities are above all 'immagined' identities and subject to change over time. He thinks that 'the conservative nationalist moves from a valid premise—that a well functioning state rests upon a pre-political sense of common nationality—to a false conclusion—that this sense of common nationality can be preserved only by protecting the present sense of national identity'. Miller nonetheless acknowledges that the issue of immigration can be problematic. Despite his main claim that immigrants do not pose a threat to national identity once it is recognized that identity is always in flux, he points to two circumstances in which immigration does pose a problem, one of which is the situation where the rate of immigration is so high that there is no time for a process of mutual adjustment to occur. The PVV will argue that this is most definitely the case in the Netherlands.

[317] Kojanec, "Report on Multiple Nationality", 12. Kojanec refers to a decision by the High Court of Australia in June 1999 in which Article 44 of the Constitution was interpreted such that Australian nationals who also possessed another nationality could not be elected to the Federal Parliament.

[318] Østergaard-Nielsen, "Turkey and the 'Euro-Turks': Overseas Nationals as an Ambiguous Asset", 91. Turkey's instrumental use of Turkish emigrants in Germany has probably negatively affected their integration and has provided the opponents of dual nationality with the strong argument that this Turkish influence would only increase if dual nationality were to be allowed.

[319] Spiro, "Dual nationality and the meaning of citizenship": 1482.

nationals holding public office to be confronted with conflicting interests between the States of which they possesses the nationality.[320]

Does State practice then perhaps show that multiple nationality presents problems in the field of diplomatic protection?[321] As in so many other instances where nationality law is concerned, one starts by looking at the 1930 Hague Convention. Article 4 of the 1930 Hague Convention reads: 'A State may not afford diplomatic protection to one of its nationals against a State whose nationality such person also possesses'. Article 5 continues: 'Within a third State, a person having more than one nationality shall be treated as if he had only one. Without prejudice to the application of its law in matters of personal status and of any conventions in force, a third State shall, of the nationalities which any such person possesses, recognise exclusively in its territory either the nationality of the country in which he is habitually and principally resident, or the nationality of the country with which in the circumstances he appears to be in fact most closely connected'.[322] Article 4 represents the proponents of the 'principle of equality'[323] who take the view that 'both nationalities have equal weight and therefore none of the national States may bring a claim

[320] Spiro, "Political rights and dual nationality", 148–149.

[321] Diplomatic protection is traditionally defined as 'the right of the state to have its sovereignty respected through the *personae* of its nationals'. Under international law the State of nationality has absolute discretion to decide whether or not to exercise diplomatic protection on behalf of its national. See John Dugard, "Diplomatic Protection: Human Right or State Right?", *Australian Year Book of International Law* 24 (2005): 76, 80.

[322] In the view of Yanguas Messía, Article 4 of the Hague Convention perceives of diplomatic protection primarily as a question of public international law because it is founded on the idea of equality among States. This equality prohibits a State from exercising diplomatic protection on behalf of a national against a State of which this national also possesses the nationality. Article 5 of the Hague Convention, on the other hand, is inspired by the private international law concept of dominant nationality—a concept which was transferred to the realm of public international law in dual nationality cases. See José de Yanguas Messía, "La protection diplomatique en cas de double nationalité", in *Hommage d'une génération de juristes au Président Basdevant* (Paris: Pedone, 1960), 554.

[323] The principle of equality, also sometimes called the *rule of non-responsibility*, means that a dual national cannot make one of the countries to which he owes allegiance a defendant before an international tribunal. In other words, 'the responsibility of the respondent States may not be engaged, for otherwise the nationality of the claimant States would be given preference with no justification'. According to the *rule of dominant nationality*, 'the claim of an individual possessing the nationalities of both the claimant and the respondent States may be validly entertained at the international level if he can establish that his ties with the claimant State ... were stronger'. See Aghahosseini, *Claims of Dual Nationals and the Development of Customary International Law*, 24.

against the other'.[324] The other school—adhering to the principle of dominant nationality—is of the opinion that the nationality which an individual in fact exercises should prevail.[325] These two articles thus represent two schools of thought and international litigation on cases of dual nationality is decided by reference to either one or the other principle.[326]

Although the two articles seem to represent two fairly straighforward and separate positions, some authors regard them as being intertwined. Yanguas Messía argues that when a dual national's bond is clearly stronger with one State of nationality than with another (this is often decided on the basis of habitual residence), this State has the right to exercise diplomatic protection under the principle of dominant nationality. The other State is denied this right by virtue of the principle that a State whose nationality is not the dominant one cannot protect its dual national against another State the nationality of which this person also possesses.[327] This idea was also expressed by the United States-Italian Conciliation Commission (which was presided over by Yanguas Messía) in the influential *Mergé* Case. The Commission stated that no irreconcilable opposition exists between the principle of equality and that of effective or dominant nationality; in fact, they complement each other reciprocally.[328]

---

[324] It is generally acknowledged that a treatise written by E.B. Borchard in 1916, called 'The diplomatic Protection of Citizens Abroad', had a profound influence on the drafters of the 1930 Hague Convention. Relying on this treatise, the drafters thought that by laying down the rule of non-responsibility in Article 4 they were codifying then-existing international law. Griffin strongly disagrees with Borchard's conclusion that the rule of non-responsibility was the prevailing principle under international law at the time: 'Borchard's supposed rule is a myth—or at best an inaccurate oversimplification of the body of precedents existing when he wrote, and subsequently'. For an extensive overview of case law predating the 1930 Hague Convention, see William L. Griffin, "International Claims of Nationals of Both the Claimant and Respondent States—The Case History of a Myth", *International Lawyer* 1, no. 3 (1966–1967).

[325] van Panhuys, *The Rôle of Nationality in International Law*, 74.

[326] An overview of case law can be found in the influential *Mergé* Case of 1955 where it is explicitly stated that uniformity of precedents does not exist on the subject of dual nationality.

[327] Yanguas Messía, "La protection diplomatique en cas de double nationalité", 555. Yanguas Messia feels that a definite choice for either principle cannot be made: 'La prétention d'appliquer en tout cas le principe qui interdit à un Etat de réclamer contre un autre, par le fait d'être la personne intéressée nationale des deux Etats, sans faire entrer en jeu le principe de la nationalité effective si elle était claire, serait inadéquat et injuste. Par contre, la prétention d'appliquer en tout cas la nationalité effective tomberait plus d'une fois dans l'incertitude devant des situations douteuses'.

[328] The Commission continued as follows: 'The principle, based on the sovereign equality of States, which excludes diplomatic protection in the case of dual nationality, must yield

The traditional rule that a State cannot protect a national who is in another country of which he possesses the nationality[329]—which was the prevalent practice in the first half of the 20th century[330]—is increasingly mitigated by a State practice which focuses on the individual's dominant nationality.[331] In case the rule of the dominant nationality is applied, diplomatic protection is possible even against a State of which a dual national holds the nationality as well. Aghahosseini is of the opinion that the case law of the Iran-United States Claims Tribunal, which expresses a clear choice for the rule of dominant nationality in preference to the rule of non-responsibility,[332] will have the likely impact of reinforcing the principle of the dominant nationality as the prevailing principle for the exercise of diplomatic protection.[333] Time will tell

---

before the principle of effective nationality whenever such nationality is that of the claiming State. But is must not yield when such predominance is not proved because the first of these two principles is generally recognized and may constitute a criterion of practical application for the elimination of any possible uncertainty'. In addition, it was stated that in establishing the prevalent nationality, 'habitual residence can be one of the criteria, but not the only one. The conduct of the individual in his economic, social, political, civil and family life, as well as the closer and more effective bond with one of the two States, must also be considered'. See also Paul Weis, "Effective nationality (Nottebohm and after)", in *Liber amicorum Adolf F. Schnitzer* (Genève: Georg-Librairie de l'université, 1979), 509–510.

329 See for early examples of this practice Fromageot, *De la double nationalité des individus & des sociétés*, 82–101.

330 Zvonko R. Rode, "Dual nationals and the doctrine of dominant nationality", *American journal of international law* 59 (1959): 143; Verwilghen, "Conflits de nationalités, plurinationalité et apatridie", 454.

331 Kay Hailbronner, "Rights and duties of dual nationals: changing concepts and attitudes", in *Rights and Duties of Dual nationals - Evolutions and Prospects*, ed. David A. Martin and Kay Hailbronner (The Hague: Kluwer Law International, 2003), 23. Hailbronner refers to the cases *Canevaro* (1912) and *Mergé* (1955) in which the doctrine of the effective nationality was first established. Rode also discusses these cases and claims that the first case in international law invoking the doctrine of dominant or effective nationality was the *Drummond* case of 1834. Rode, "Dual nationals and the doctrine of dominant nationality": 140–141.

See also Ian Brownlie, "General Course on Public International Law", in *Recueil des cours de l'Académie de droit international de la Haye* (Leiden: Sijthoff, 1995), 108–109; Craig Forcese, "The Capacity to Protect: Diplomatic Protection of Dual Nationals in the 'War on Terror' ", *The European Journal of International Law* 17, no. 2 (2006): 388. Forcese also makes interesting remarks on dual nationality in the context of diplomatic protection and extradition for terrorist activities.

332 Nancy Amoury Combs, "Iran-United States Claims Tribunal. On Children and Dual Nationality: Sabet and The Islamic Republic of Iran", *Leiden Journal of International Law* 13, no. 1 (2000): 175; Aghahosseini, *Claims of Dual Nationals and the Development of Customary International Law*, 254.

333 Aghahosseini considers the choice for the dominant nationality the logical consequence of the growing acceptance of dual nationality: 'Where dual nationality is looked upon with

whether he is right, but it should also be noted that this trend had already been predicted by Rode as far back as 1959.[334]

Last but not least, an exception to the traditional rule is possible when a case involves human rights violations.[335] However, it is clearly wrong to suppose that the growth of international human rights law has made diplomatic protection lose its *raison d'être* and that it should therefore cease to exist: 'To suggest that universal human rights conventions ... provide individuals with effective remedies for the protection of their human rights is to engage in a fantasy ... Until the individual acquires comprehensive procedural rights under international law, it would be a setback for human rights to abandon diplomatic protection.'[336] Under particular circumstances diplomatic protection can even be exercised in the absence of a link of nationality.[337]

Military service may also lead to difficulties in respect of multiple nationals: a lack of loyalty on the part of dual nationals who are enrolled in the army may endanger national security. It has been shown that in the 19th century dual nationality was primarily caused by the refusal of emigrant sending States to release their emigrants from their original nationality so that male nationals (and their descendants born abroad) could be drafted for military service.[338]

Legomsky is thus probably right in stating that 'in discussions of dual nationality, conscription has been by far the single greatest practical concern

---

disdain, and the treatment of the individual by his State of nationality is considered to be no concern of international law, the application of the rule of non-responsibility ... seems quite natural. Not so where dual nationality is accepted as a very common phenomenon, and States are increasingly held responsible for the wrongs they commit against the individuals, including their own nationals. Clearly, of the two rules of non-responsibility and dominant nationality, it is the latter that is consistent with these last-mentioned conditions.' Aghahosseini, *Claims of Dual Nationals and the Development of Customary International Law*, 256.

334 Rode, "Dual nationals and the doctrine of dominant nationality": 143.

335 Hailbronner, "Rights and duties of dual nationals: changing concepts and attitudes", 22.

336 Dugard, "Diplomatic Protection: Human Right or State Right?": 76–78. See also Pieter H. Kooijmans, "Is the Right to Diplomatic Protection a Human Right?", in *Studi di diritto internazionale in onore di Gaetano Arangio-Ruiz* (Napoli: Editoriale Scientifica, 2004), 1983.

337 Hailbronner, "Nationality in public international law and European law", 73.

338 Rode, "Dual nationals and the doctrine of dominant nationality": 139–140. Rode shows that persons who naturalized abroad as well as their sons born abroad could be forced to fulfil military service in their country of origin when paying it a visit. For that reason the United States concluded a considerable number of bilateral agreements in the 19th century which 'secured the right of a naturalized citizen of the United States to return to his country of origin without being subject to punishment for failure, prior to naturalization, to respond to calls for military service.'

expressed'.[339] Some authors have argued, however, that the present stability of State relations (violence now more often occurs within States than between States) has considerably hollowed out the loyalty argument.[340] Moreover, the decline of conscription has removed one of the most important arguments against dual nationality.[341] Legomsky, who made a detailed study of dual nationality and military service, concludes from his research of State practice that dual nationals are generally permitted to serve in the military. If this policy has led to any problems, they are not apparent.[342]

Karamanoukian has given an overview of the bilateral treaties concluded by France with a number of other States which specifically addressed the problem of military service for dual nationals.[343] His survey reveals that a great number of different solutions to the problem of dual military obligations are to be found in these treaties. Sometimes it is the country of permanent residence where the dual national must fulfil his military obligations, other times

---

339 Stephen H. Legomsky, "Dual nationality and military service: strategy number two", in *Rights and Duties of Dual nationals - Evolutions and Prospects*, ed. David A. Martin and Kay Hailbronner (The Hague: Kluwer Law International, 2003), 88. See for a similar view Karamanoukian, "La double nationalité et le service militaire": 470. Karamanoukian writes that 'de toutes les consequences résultant de la double nationalité la plus fâcheuse est la possibilité de soumission des personnes se trouvant dans cette situation juridique aux obligations militaires de la part de plus d'un État'. He even goes so far as to state that 'le désir d'augmenter le nombre de soldats n'est-il pas le principal instigateur des législations sur la nationalité, donc de la pluralité de nationalités?'. Here Karamanoukian also refers to the well-known phrase by Niboyet who wrote of the French Nationality Act of 1889: 'On peut dire que désormais l'ombre du bureau de recrutement plane sur tous les texts et permet seule de les expliquer ainsi que les justifier'. In the 19th century, Fromageot already discussed a considerable body of case law dealing specifically with the problems resulting from military service and dual nationality. See Fromageot, *De la double nationalité des individus & des sociétés*, 103 ff. In the chapter on France (Section 7.1) we will pay attention to the problem of dual military service for French nationals of Algerian descent.

340 Martin, "Introduction: The trend toward dual nationality", 16–17. Legomsky agrees that international wars are now relatively infrequent and adds that because 'technological advances have made warfare less dependent on humans generally and unskilled humans in particular, conscription as a vehicle for staffing military forces is sharply down. Hence, the problem of conflicting demands for military service on dual nationals has also diminished'. See Stephen H. Legomsky, "Dual nationality and military service: strategy number two", ibid., 123.

341 Triadafilos Triadafilopoulos, "Dual Citizenship and Security Norms", in *Dual Citizenship in Global Perspective, From Unitary to Multiple Citizenship*, ed. Peter Kivisto and Thomas Faist (New York: Palgrave Macmillan, 2007), 35.

342 Legomsky, "Dual nationality and military service: strategy number two", 88.

343 Karamanoukian, "La double nationalité et le service militaire". See also Darras, *La double nationalité*, 601–630.

it is the country where he has his habitual residence and with which he is most closely connected. Still other treaties give the individual a right of election or simply provide that military service must be fulfilled 'in either country'. In short, the legal regime concerning the military service of dual nationals under these treaties is far from uniform.[344] Nevertheless, and unlike Darras,[345] Karamanoukian supports the efforts of these bilateral treaties (as well as the multilateral treaties which will be discussed presently) to find a solution to this problem.

A number of multilateral treaties have also tried to prevent multiple nationals from having to fulfil military obligations twice. The protocol to the 1930 Hague Convention as well as the second chapter of the 1963 Convention are particularly noteworthy in this respect.[346] The usefulness of this second chapter is shown by the fact that a number of States have in recent times denounced the *first* chapter of the 1963 Convention, but have decided to remain bound by the *second*. Also the ECN makes an effort to solve the problem of cumulating military obligations for multiple nationals. Article 21 ECN provides that 'persons possessing the nationality of two or more States Parties shall be required to fulfil their military obligations in relation to one of those States Parties only'. The same article in the third indent under (a) also provides that the military service shall—in the absence of a special agreement—be fulfilled in the country of the habitual residence. This solution seems to be an efficient way to prevent an accumulation of military obligations for multiple nationals. Nevertheless, some authors stress that the issue of loyalty must not be neglected. Hailbronner criticizes the provision in the ECN which allows for voluntary military service in the other country of which the multiple national

---

344 Karamanoukian, "La double nationalité et le service militaire": 473–479.

345 Darras is against bilateral treaties which try to find a solution to the cumulation of military obligations for dual nationals because they 'legalize' the phenomenon of dual nationality: 'Il existe un inconvénient majeur à rechercher la conclusion de solutions partielles en matière de plurinationalité: celui de revenir à "légaliser" le phénomène cumulatif. Les accords parcellaires finissent par entériner une situation anormale en rémediant aux abus qu'elle engendrait. En s'attaquant aux conséquences néfastes, ils deviennent le garant de la survie de la double nationalité. Ils affirment à la fois son existence et sa continuité juridique'. See Darras, *La double nationalité*, 629.

346 Article 1 of the 1930 Protocol Relating to Military Obligations in Certain Cases of Double Nationality provides as follows: 'A person possessing two or more nationalities who habitually resides in one of the countries whose nationality he possesses, and who is in fact most closely connected with that country, shall be exempt from all military obligations in the other country or countries'. Article 5 of the second chapter of the 1963 Convention reads: 'Persons possessing the nationality of two or more Contracting Parties shall be required to fulfil their military obligations in relation to one of those Parties only'.

holds the nationality. He finds it doubtful that 'a principle of free choice adequately reflects a proper balance of the interests of the individual and the society' and concludes that 'voluntary military service in a state other than the state of residence is hardly suitable to promote integration'.[347]

Finally, multiple nationality may raise legal problems when nationality is used as a connecting factor in PIL.[348] It is true that the role of habitual residence as a connecting factor has increased at the expense of nationality, but in cases concerning a person's civil status and in matters directly affecting the State, nationality is still dominant over habitual residence.[349] Use of nationality may at first sight be difficult when multiple nationals are concerned. Yet the solution commonly adopted—i.e. establishing and applying a person's most effective or dominant nationality—is considered to work well in cases involving multiple nationality.[350] The role of nationality as a connecting factor in the field of personal status and family law will be the subject of Chapter 2. At that point, we will also engage in a detailed analysis of the ruling of the European Court of Justice in *García Avello*, a case dealing with the surname of children having a dual Belgian-Spanish nationality.[351] This case, and the follow-up case *Grunkin-Paul*, had a profound impact on the place of PIL within the European Union.[352]

This section has tried to sketch some of the issues arising in relation to multiple nationality. It is undeniable that this phenomenon has quantitatively grown in importance over the years; at present there are considerably more dual nationals than in the past. This renders particularly salient the question whether the legal problems arising from this development can be overcome. Previous sections have also shown, however, that there is more to multiple nationality than just a legal perspective; multiple nationality is part of a larger

---

347 Kay Hailbronner, "Multiple Nationality and Diplomatic Protection", in *Festschrift Tugrul Ansay zum 75. Geburtstag*, ed. Sabih Arkan and Aynur Yongalik (Alphen aan den Rijn: Kluwer Law International, 2006), 119.

348 Thierry Vignal, *Droit international privé* (Paris: Dalloz, 2005), 390 ff; Dominique Bureau and Horatia Muir Watt, *Droit international privé* (Paris: Presses Universitaires de France, 2007), 405–406.

349 Verwilghen, "Conflits de nationalités, plurinationalité et apatridie", 100.

350 Castangia, *Il criterio della cittadinanza nel diritto internazionale privato*, 119. Interestingly however, Aghahosseini—member of the Iran-United States Claims Tribunal—has written in the context of *public* international law that the learned writings hardly address the difficulties in determining an individual's dominant nationality: 'Any conceptual discussion of the rule of dominant nationality has been surprisingly avoided'. Aghahosseini, *Claims of Dual Nationals and the Development of Customary International Law*, 259–260.

351 Case C-148/02 *García Avello* [2003] ECR I-11613.

352 Case C-353/06 *Grunkin-Paul* [2008] ECR I-07639.

debate on identity in the context of European integration and globalization, as our mention of transnationalism, postnationalism and European citizenship hopefully pointed out.[353] We now continue our discussion from a strictly legal perspective by examining State practice as regards multiple nationality in international law.

10. *Multiple Nationality under International Law: State Practice*

Previous sections[354] have shown that the current international law practice—which is a combination of State autonomy in nationality matters and lack of coordination of nationality laws—contributes to the existence and even growth of multiple nationality. Here we will assess the place of multiple nationality under international law by asking whether there was a specific point in time when the issue of multiple nationality began to arise in inter-state relations, and whether we can speak of a predominant attitude to multiple nationality under international law today.

It was already remarked in Section 1 that the modern concept of nationality is tied to the emergence of the nation-state, replacing feudal links with a link between an individual and a State. Yet, as Boll notes, it is impossible to indicate a specific moment in time when issues of multiple nationality emerged in international relations. He challenges, however, the prevailing opinion that multiple nationality has always been disapproved of.[355] Also the existence

---

[353] On the issue of identity in different contexts see also Elspeth Guild, *The Legal Elements of European Identity. EU citizenship and Migration Law* (The Hague: Kluwer Law International, 2004), introduction.

[354] In particular *supra* Section 4.

[355] Boll, *Multiple Nationality and International Law*, 184–186. In any case, we can say that the problem of multiple nationality came to the fore from the late 18th century onwards following the massive emigration from Europe to the Americas, and the independence of large numbers of South and North American States. These developments led to an overlap of claims to personal jurisdiction by States over individuals. Boll stresses, however, that this period in time was not characterized by a disapproval of multiple nationality as such, but by the unwillingness by many States to relinquish personal jurisdiction over emigrants.

He also disagrees with several German writers who allege that there has always been the tendency to avoid multiple nationality in Germany and that the idea was incompatible with loyalty to the German State. He points to the 1868 Bancroft Treaties and the German Delbrück law of 1913 as examples which contradict the prevailing idea that Germany has always been opposed to dual nationality. As we will discuss in more detail in the chapter on France, the French were very suspicious of the Delbrück Law which they considered was meant to allow Germans living abroad '"to acquire a nationality of pure show for the preservation of essential interests, in order to be able to be admitted to the London Stock Exchange,

of dual nationality in the relation between Spain and Latin American countries—culminating in the 20th century in a number of dual nationality treaties (see Chapter 6)—has been shown to have a long history, dating back to the period when the former colonies gained independence.[356]

For the purpose of assessing the place of multiple nationality under international law we draw heavily on the two concluding chapters of Boll's monograph *Multiple Nationality and International Law* which, in turn, were based on his thorough research of State practice towards multiple nationality. Boll's book is the most recent and comprehensive study on the subject and we have not come across literature which questions his results. On the contrary, we shall see that several of his findings have recently been confirmed by Aghahosseini. Here we present what we consider, for our purposes, to be Boll's most relevant findings.

Boll concludes that current State practice contributes to the production of multiple nationality. Although the increasing acceptance of multiple nationality lends itself to the suggestion that multiple nationality has become a virtue in itself, he thinks that such a conclusion cannot be drawn on the basis of his inquiry.[357] His findings do demonstrate, in his view, that multiple nationality is no longer an anomalous element in international relations but should rather be regarded as a 'normal' reflection of State practice.[358] Boll therefore disagrees

---

for example, or to acquire propety in Russia"—prerogatives denied to foreigners—while continuing to serve Germany, which "remained their only true homeland, by propaganda, espionage, voting and if necessary the use of arms"'. The Delbrück Law also reinforced the French idea that Germany was a racial nation, an idea that had emerged since the German annexation of Alsace-Moselle in 1870. See Weil, *How to Be French: Nationality in the Making since 1789*, 61, 187.

356 Alvarez Rodríguez, *Nacionalidad y emigración*, 117–129. The short-lived 1931 republican Constitution provided that naturalization in a Latin American country would not entail loss of Spanish nationality. However, a mechanism was already in place from the independence of former Spanish colonies which aimed at maintaining a link with Spanish emigrants. Spaniards who naturalized in a Latin American country and thereby lost Spanish nationality retained their Spanish nationality in the sense that it was automatically reacquired after a declaration of intent by the individual, renunciation of the former nationality and return to Spain (see in more detail Chapter 6).

357 According to Aghahosseini, the belief at the international level still is that 'dual nationality is not a virtue in itself, and hence should not be encouraged, but that so long as the acquisition and maintenance of nationality is left to the discretion of States, plural citizenships will exist and … will grow increasingly common. This, in turn, has led to the realization that today the appropriate policy towards the phenomenon should be, not to regard it as an evil to be avoided or eliminated, but as a fact of life the impact of which must be regulated'. Aghahosseini, *Claims of Dual Nationals and the Development of Customary International Law*, 255.

358 Boll, *Multiple Nationality and International Law*, 268.

with writers who claim that international law dictates efforts to prevent multiple nationality. He submits that there is no such rule and even if there was, his research shows that States do not respect it. This view is confirmed by other commentators.[359]

He also counters another conclusion which might be drawn from State practice as regards multiple nationality, namely the presumption that the acceptance of multiple nationality reflects an interest in sharing nationals that exceeds the municipal plane. This acceptance, he submits, has to do with specific municipal needs and interests,[360] not with wider international interests. Although agreements like those on military obligations seem to contradict such a conclusion, he maintains this is not the case. These agreements 'do not indicate that multiple nationals are treated as a category apart, but [that] military service as such is being regulated. Such agreements regulate military service, not nationality'.[361] Observations like this contain for him the essence of current State practice to accept multiple nationality. Thus, he concludes that the acceptance of multiple nationality 'does not seem inherently to reflect an acceptance of a separate status for multiple nationals, but seems instead to be premised on a practical conclusion that inter-state relations are not substantially negatively affected by multiple nationality'. Along these lines he also notes that 'acceptance of multiple nationality seems to have more to do with states' specific underlying reasons for maintaining links of nationality, as opposed to a view that multiple nationality in and of itself is a good thing'.[362]

Boll is also not willing to conclude from his inquiry that the acceptance of multiple nationality is a natural result of globalization, nor does he see the nation-state in decline.[363] His work seems to point to the contrary: from the perspective of international law at least, the nation-state is in excellent health. The reserved domain for States in respect of the attribution and loss of their nationality is even reinforced by multiple nationality. Indeed, State discretion in nationality matters on a municipal plane is strengthened by the acceptance of multiple nationality. On the other hand, the acceptance of this phenomenon reinforces the distinction between nationality on a municipal and

359 Helmut Rittstieg, "Doppelte Staatsangehörigkeit im Völkerrecht", *Neue Juristische Wochenschrift* 22 (1990): 1403; Verwilghen, "Conflits de nationalités, plurinationalité et apatridie", 168–170. Both authors agree that no rule or practice exists under international law which prohibits dual nationality.

360 The country reports in Chapters 3–6 provide ample illustration of this observation.

361 Boll, *Multiple Nationality and International Law*, 275.

362 Ibid.

363 For somewhat more theoretical observations on the alleged decline of nationality, the nation-state and national identity, see Miller, *On Nationality*, 155 ff.

international plane: 'A nationality attributed by a state is valid as such, until held against another nationality, when a test of effectivity or equality must be applied'.[364]

One might suppose that the acceptance of multiple nationality implies the existence of a rule on the international level on the recognition of nationality. However, Boll concludes that there is no clear support for either the principle of equality or that of the effective or dominant nationality.[365] The general practice starts from the assumption that in cases of protection against a *third* State the nationalities possessed by a multiple national are of equal value. The question whether protection is allowed in cases dealing with protection *by one State of nationality against another State of nationality*, is mostly answered by establishing the dominant nationality. Yet under particular circumstances both the equality and the effectivity principle are rejected. This is most clear when fundamental human rights are at stake. States are then inclined to protect their nationals even against a State of effective nationality.[366]

Another conclusion that Boll reaches as regards multiple nationality has to do with jurisdiction. He stresses that jurisdiction is first and foremost territorial. Were this different, and were nationality the ground for jurisdiction, multiple nationality would give rise to many more problems. Thus, the limited consequences of nationality under international law—international protection and the duty of admission—allow the existence of multiple nationality. Multiple nationality would probably be much more opposed if other consequences were attached to nationality. In this sense, multiple nationality can be interpreted as reinforcing the limited role of nationality on the international level. The primacy of territorial jurisdiction over jurisdiction based on nationality clearly follows from the fact that most of the obligations that individuals have towards the State are based on their territorial presence on its territory, not on nationality.[367]

Boll also makes some observations that focus on the individual. Does a right to a nationality exist for the individual and what rights ensue from nationality? Having concluded that nationality law still belongs to a State's reserved domain, he emphasizes that this means that a 'right' to a nationality

364 Boll, *Multiple Nationality and International Law*, 277–279.

365 Agahosseini concludes that the case law of the Iran-United States Claims Tribunal will have the likely impact of reinforcing the rule of dominant nationality. However, in his view there is no evidence that the rivalry between the two rules had been resolved or diminished prior to the Tribunal's involvement. Aghahosseini, *Claims of Dual Nationals and the Development of Customary International Law*, 249 ff.

366 Boll, *Multiple Nationality and International Law*, 283–285.

367 Ibid., 290 ff.

will not depend in any way on international law, but on municipal law (this view is confirmed by others, as was seen *supra* in Section 5.2). As for possible individual rights that may follow from nationality, he remarks that nationality's primary function under international law is to allocate individuals to States. International protection might be exercised as a result of nationality, but is certainly not the essential element of nationality.[368] The very weak role of the individual in matters related to nationality makes Boll disagree with those who have maintained that nationality is the link between the individual and the benefits of international law. In his opinion, 'nationality does not provide the benefits of international law, but allows the state to provide some benefit to the individual when it chooses to, or has a related obligation to other states'.[369]

Finally, one of Boll's observations in a way addresses the topic of the next chapter, i.e. multiple nationality and private international law in the EU. He writes that

> current state practice ... indicates that there is no obligation on states to "recognize" any multiple nationality of their own nationals, for the purposes of municipal law. The state may of course choose to do so. This in turn indicates that on the international plane, there is no corresponding obligation to recognise a national's foreign nationality as effective, simply because it is possessed.[370]

This statement should be kept in mind when reading the subsequent chapter on private international law and the European Union. When discussing the ECJ's ruling in *García Avello* as well as other dual nationality cases in the next chapter, we shall see that the situation is different for the specific context of the EU. For the moment suffice it to say that the ECJ dismissed Belgium's argument that it was allowed only to take into account the Belgium nationality of children who possessed both Belgian and Spanish nationality. Importantly, Boll's claim that no obligation exists for States to 'recognize' their nationals' other nationalities can thus not be maintained in an EU context.

11. *Nationality Law in Europe: The Council of Europe and the European Union*

Thus far we have seen that there are few hard and fast rules of international law in the field of nationality law. However, there are *regional* rules of customary

---

[368] Ibid., 296.
[369] Ibid., 301.
[370] Ibid., 282.

law for the Contracting Parties to treaties that were concluded under the auspices of the Council of Europe.[371] As a result of the latter's activities in the area of nationality law, some principles—such as gender equality in nationality law—can be considered to have become rules of regional customary law. Section 11.1 will focus on two nationality conventions that were instigated by the Council of Europe: The 1963 Convention on the Reduction of Cases of Multiple Nationality and Military Obligations in Cases of Multiple Nationality, and the 1997 European Convention on Nationality.[372] We shall subsequently finish this chapter by looking more closely at Member State nationality in the European Union (Section 11.2), thereby creating a bridge to the next chapter on multiple nationality in the EU.

Although the Council of Europe and the European Union are obviously different entities, we may nonetheless assume some level of interaction between the two as regards nationality. Thus Guild has said:

> Community law includes fundamental rights which form an integral part of Community law. In its search for these fundamental rights, the ECJ has had regard to other conventions which the Member States have signed and ratified … It is not impossible that the Convention on Nationality may, in due course and on further signature and ratification by Member States, take a place as an aid to the interpretation of the lawfulness of acquisition and loss of citizenship of the Union.[373]

11.1. *The 1963 Convention on the Reduction of Cases of Multiple Nationality and the 1997 European Convention on Nationality*

Here we will give a description of the activities of the Council of Europe in nationality matters, but we will limit ourselves to those activities which have a direct relation with the subject of multiple nationality. The Council of Europe's activities are not only relevant because they culminated in a number of treaties, but also for the discussion on a possible future EU competence in the field of nationality law. As was already mentioned, should the EU acquire (partial) competence in this area, it would be better to find inspiration in the long-standing activities of the Council of Europe than to start from scratch again.

---

371 de Groot and Tratnik, *Nederlands nationaliteitsrecht*, 23 ff.

372 European Treaties Series no. 43 and 166 respectively. These conventions are available from the website of the Council of Europe: www.coe.int. Also available is an up to date overview of the States who are party to the Conventions instigated by the Council of Europe.

373 Guild, *The Legal Elements of European Identity. EU citizenship and Migration Law*, 42. Indeed, in the recent *Rottmann* case the Court explicitly referred to the provisions on statelessness laid down in the ECN (see *infra* Section 11.2.3).

The Council of Europe has been active for a long time in the field of nationality, one of its accomplishments being the 1963 Convention.[374] While we have seen that some authors argued that the 1930 Hague Convention perceived multiple nationality as an unavoidable legal fact for which a solution had nonetheless to be sought,[375] the 1963 Convention had the explicit aim of preventing dual nationality for those who acquired another nationality after birth.[376] Article 1 of the 1963 Convention thus reads:

> Nationals of the Contracting Parties who are of full age and who acquire of their own free will, by means of naturalization, option or recovery, the nationality of another Party shall lose their former nationality. They shall not be authorized to retain their former nationality.

The second chapter of the 1963 Convention addressed the problem of military obligations for dual nationals by laying down the rule that a person holding the nationality of more than one Contracting Party is only required to fulfil military obligations in one of them. The 1963 Convention was quite successful and in the course of time it was ratified by 13 countries—three of which only became party to the second chapter. One by one the Contracting Parties are now renouncing the Convention, however. The most recent case is Italy where

---

374 Article 2 of the 1963 Convention was amended by a protocol of 24 November 1977 (European Treaties Series no. 095). To Article 2, which read that 'a person who possesses the nationality of two or more Contracting Parties may renounce one or more of these nationalities, with the consent of the Contracting Party whose nationality he desires to renounce', was added the phrase that 'such consent may not be withheld by the Contracting Party whose nationality a person of full age possesses ipso jure, provided that the said person has, for the past ten years, had his ordinary residence outside the territory of that Party'. Another additional protocol was also accepted (again on 24 November 1977, European Treaties Series no. 096), Article 1 of which reads that 'each Contracting Party undertakes to communicate to another Contracting Party any acquisition of its nationality by an adult or a minor who is a national of this State, which has taken place according to the conditions contained in Article 1 of the Convention'. The low number of ratifications of this latter protocol seems to be another indication that most States are not that serious about combating dual nationality. In Hammar's words: 'Without this exchange of information, enforcement of the Convention has been haphazard at best'. Hammar, "State, Nation, and Dual Citizenship", 83.

375 See *supra* Section 5.2.1.

376 Gerard-René de Groot, "Europees nationaliteitsverdrag in werking voor Nederland", *Migrantenrecht* 17, no. 1 (2002): 4. Oddly enough, in the years preceding the 1963 Convention there had been serious plans to introduce a system of multiple nationalities in Europe. In 1949 there was talk of a common European nationality and a European passport, but these ideas proved unfeasible. Instead, the alternative of a system of multiple nationality was studied. However, when in the early 1950s a Committee reported to the General Assembly of the Council of Euope on the undesirable consequences of multiple nationality, plans for multiple nationality were cancelled and an international treaty to avoid multiple nationality—the later

the 1963 Convention will no longer be in force as of 4 June 2010. Of the ten countries originally bound by the first chapter, only four of them are left.[377]

The phenomenon of multiple nationality continued to grow in the 1970s, despite the existence of the 1963 Convention. This was primarily occasioned by the introduction in Western Europe of the equality of the sexes in nationality law. Moreover, the right to free movement under the EC Treaty led to a strong migration from Southern to Northern Europe. Over time this migration, which had started in the 1950s, created a significant group of long term resident migrants who wanted to acquire the nationality of their new country for themselves and their children, without having to sever the ties with the country of origin.[378] In 1993 these developments resulted in the so-called Second Protocol to the 1963 Convention, which allowed the Contracting Parties to provide for the retention of the original nationality in a number of situations.[379]

In connection to this Second Protocol, Lagarde has pointed to an interesting paradox: although international law offers no effective right to a *single* nationality, it now in a way does recognize the right to a *dual* nationality.[380] The Second Protocol itself has always been of limited practical importance as only Italy, France and the Netherlands have ratified it.[381] The French and

1963 Convention—was drafted instead. See Federico de Castro y Bravo, "Nationalité, double et supra-nationalité", in *Recueil des cours de l'Académie de droit international de la Haye* (Leiden: Sijthoff, 1961), 610; de Groot, "The background of the changed attitude of Western European States with respect to multiple nationality", 103.

377 Seven countries ratified the 1963 Convention without reservations: Belgium (1991), Denmark (1972), France (1965), Luxembourg (1971), the Netherlands (1985), Norway (1969) and Sweden (1969). Three others made reservations: Austria (1975), Germany (1969) and Italy (1968). Ireland (1973), Spain (1987) and the UK (1971) only ratified the second chapter on military obligations. See for a systematic overview Gerard-René de Groot, "Beperking van meervoudige nationaliteit: een nieuwe afscheidssymfonie?", *Migrantenrecht* 24, no. 2 (2009): 50–52.

378 Hans Ulrich Jessurun d'Oliveira, "Het Europees Verdrag inzake Nationaliteit", in *Trends in het nationaliteitsrecht*, ed. Hans Ulrich Jessurun d'Oliveira ('s-Gravenhage: Sdu, 1998), 27; de Groot and Vink, *Meervoudige nationaliteit in Europees perspectief*, 25.

379 European Treaties Series no. 149. The Second Protocol allowed for the retention of the original nationality (1) where a national of a Contracting Party acquires the nationality of another Contracting Party on whose territory he was either born and is resident, or has been ordinarily resident for a period of time beginning before the age of 18; (2) in cases of marriage between nationals of different Contracting Parties, when one of the spouses acquires of his or her own free will the nationality of the other spouse; (3) when a national of a Contracting Party who is a minor and whose parents are nationals of different Contracting Parties acquires the nationality of one of his parents.

380 Lagarde, "Le droit à une nationalité", 148.

381 Italy and France ratified the Second Protocol on 27 January 1995 and 23 February 1995 respectively. The Protocol entered into force between these two countries on 24 March 1995.

Italian renunciation of chapter 1 of the Convention also implies renunciation of the Second Protocol however, since the latter made exceptions to the general rule laid down in Article 1 of the Convention. As a result, the Second Protocol is no longer operative as of 4 June 2010.[382] However, the Second Protocol is important in that during its drafting process the idea was conceived to come to a separate treaty containing general principles on nationality. This idea eventually materialized in the form of the European Convention on Nationality.[383]

The position in the ECN towards multiple nationality substantially differs from that in the 1963 Convention because it takes a neutral stance on the subject. The Articles 14–18 of the ECN, which are devoted to multiple nationality, were deliberately drafted in a way that neither expressly promotes nor expressly condemns multiple nationality. Neither the approach of the 1963 Convention was adopted, nor does the ECN provide for the exceptions made by the Second Protocol.[384] As almost any position on multiple nationality is

---

However, France denounced the first chapter of the 1963 Convention as well as the Second Protocol on 5 March 2008; Italy did the same on 3 June 2009. The letters with which the Permanent Representations of both countries to the Council of Europe denounced the first chapter did not contain explanations on the reasons for doing so. Information by Elise Cornu, Legal adviser of the Council of Europe, in an email message of 16 November 2010.

In the Netherlands the Protocol entered into force on 20 August 1996. In practice, the Protocol meant that a national of a State Party to the Protocol would not lose his nationality provided (1) that he fell in one of the three categories mentioned above and (2) that his country of origin had implemented the three exempted categories in its national legislation. More concretely, after the ratification by the Netherlands, French and Italian nationals who fell within one of the categories could acquire Dutch nationality without losing their nationality of origin because the nationality legislation in France and Italy does not provide for loss of their nationality upon acquisition of another nationality. The situation for Dutch nationals was somewhat different: it was only after 1 April 2003 that Dutch nationals did not lose their nationality upon acquisition of French or Italian nationality, even if they fell within one of the three categories of the Second Protocol. This can be explained by the fact that these categories were only implemented in Dutch law after 1 April 2003. For an extensive discussion of the effects of the Second Protocol, see de Groot and Vink, *Meervoudige nationaliteit in Europees perspectief*, 26.

382 Hans Ulrich Jessurun d'Oliveira, "Het zinkende schip van het Verdrag van Straatsburg 1963 en zijn Tweede Protocol", *Nederlands Juristenblad*, no. 44/45 (2009): 2877.

383 de Groot, "Europees nationaliteitsverdrag in werking voor Nederland": 5. The ECN has the potential to become a global treaty on nationality as also non-Member States of the Council of Europe who participated in the drafting process can join. This includes for example Armenia, Belarus, Canada and the United States. See Jessurun d'Oliveira, "Het Europees Verdrag inzake Nationaliteit", 9.

384 Gerard-René de Groot, "The European Convention on Nationality: a step towards a ius commune in the field of nationality law", *Maastricht Journal of European and Comparative Law* 7, no. 2 (2000): 120.

compatible with the Convention, the articles on multiple nationality cannot stand in the way of becoming party to this Convention.[385]

It must nevertheless be remarked that there has never been a strong commitment among the parties to the 1963 Convention to totally eradicate multiple nationality, despite the preamble text which tells us that it corresponds to the aims of the Council of Europe to reduce as far as possible the number of cases of multiple nationality, due to the fact that it is liable to cause difficulties. First of all, Article 1 of the Convention, which provided for the loss of original nationality upon acquisition of the nationality of another Contracting Party, was less strictly applied as time went on. Secondly, the Convention did not affect rules governing acquisition at birth, which shows that countries gave primary concern to their own interests rather than to the common interest of coordinating nationality laws. This attitude inevitably led to cases of multiple nationality. In short, the wish among States to root out multiple nationality proved less strong than the wish to regulate nationality law in the way that suited their interests best. Kojanec thus rightly remarked with regard to the 1963 Convention that 'even in the context of a regional instrument, a general exclusion of the possibility to possess multiple nationality could not be realised'.[386]

The 'realistic' position taken on multiple nationality in the ECN assumes concrete form in Article 15 which provides that 'the provisions of this Convention shall not limit the right of a State Party to determine in its internal law whether: (a) Its nationals who acquire or possess the nationality of another State retain its nationality or lose it; (b) the acquisition or retention of its nationality is subject to the renunciation or loss of another nationality'. Yet the Convention does provide, by virtue of Article 14, that 'a State Party shall allow (a) children having different nationalities acquired automatically at birth to retain these nationalities; (b) its nationals to possess another nationality where this other nationality is automatically acquired by marriage'.

Two other provisions which expressly address multiple nationality are Articles 16 and 17. The first provides that 'a State Party shall not make the renunciation or loss of another nationality a condition for the acquisition or retention of its nationality where such renunciation or loss is not possible or cannot reasonably be required'. Article 17 prescribes that 'nationals of a State Party in possession of another nationality shall have, in the territory of that State Party in which they reside, the same rights and duties as other nationals of that State Party'. In its second indent, Article 17 lays down the rule that the

---

385 de Groot and Vink, *Meervoudige nationaliteit in Europees perspectief*, 29.

386 Kojanec, "Report on Multiple Nationality", 6.

Convention's provisions on multiple nationality shall neither affect 'the rules of international law concerning diplomatic or consular protection by a State Party in favour of one of its nationals who simultaneously possesses another nationality', nor 'the application of the rules of private international law of each State Party in cases of multiple nationality'.

11.2. *Nationality and the European Union: Case C-369/90 Micheletti [1992]*[387]

If we call to mind our previous analysis of the possible constraints on State autonomy in the field of nationality law (*supra* Section 8), the question can be asked whether these (or other) constraints also exist within the specific context of the European Union.[388] In answering this question, the starting point is inevitably the Court's well-known *Micheletti* decision.

Micheletti concerned a dual Italian-Argentinean national who had been provisionally admitted to Spain for six months because he could show an Italian passport and was thus considered to be a Community national. Before expiry of the six month term, he asked for a permanent residence card because he wanted to establish himself as a dentist in Spain. The Spanish authorities refused to grant this card, however, on the basis of Spanish rules of private international law which provided that when confronted with a dual national who did not possess Spanish nationality, the nationality of the country where the person had had his habitual residence before coming to Spain should prevail. As a result, the Spanish authorities now saw Mr Micheletti as an Argentinean national, not as an Italian. The debate in *Micheletti* concerned the question whether these Spanish provisions were compatible with the EC Treaty, in particular the freedom of establishment.

In answering the preliminary question submitted to it by a Spanish court, the ECJ stated that 'it is for each Member State, *having due regard to Community law*, to lay down the conditions for acquisition and loss of nationality' (emphasis added). The Court also ruled that a Member State cannot restrict the effects of the nationality of another Member State by imposing an additional condition for recognition of that nationality with a view to the exercise of the fundamental freedoms provided for in the Treaty. Spain could therefore not make the recognition of Mr Micheletti's status of Community

[387] See Chapter 6, Section 9 for a more in-depth discussion of *Micheletti*.

[388] For a discussion of the role of EU law on the nationality laws of the Member States, see for example Frans J.A. van der Velden, "Unieburgers en staatsburgers. De invloed van het Europese gemeenschapsrecht op het nationaliteitsrecht van de lidstaten", in *De Nationaliteit in Internationaal en Europees Perspectief. Preadviezen van Prof. Mr Frans J.A. van der Velden, Prof. Mr Gerard-René de Groot en Mr Nicole Doeswijk* (Den Haag: T.M.C. Asser Press, 2004).

national subject to the condition of habitual residence in Italy. If Italy regarded him as an Italian national, even if his habitual residence had been in Argentina, so had Spain.

The Court thus precludes the Member States from restricting the exercise of the freedoms guaranteed by the Treaty by relying on the *Nottebohm* judgment, which requires a genuine link between a person and a State in order for a nationality to be an 'effective nationality'. It reasons that Member States cannot be permitted to make recognition of the status of Community national subject to a condition such as the habitual residence in the territory of the Member State of which the person holds the nationality. Any other conclusion would mean that 'the class of persons to whom the Community rules on freedom of establishment were applied might vary from one Member State to another' (para. 12).

Despite the lack of EU competence to lay down the conditions on acquisition and loss of Member State nationality[389]—and there are no signs that the EU aspires to develop such a competence[390]—several authors claim that EU law has to a limited extent whittled down Member State autonomy.[391] In addition to the Court's just-quoted statement that Member States must exercise

389 Massimo Condinanzi, Allesandra Lang, and Bruno Nascimbene, *Citizenship of the Union and Free Movement of Persons* (Leiden/Boston: Martinus Nijhoff Publishers, 2008), 9.

390 Article 20 of the Treaty on the Functioning of the European Union (TFEU), formerly the Treaty establishing the European Community (EC Treaty), more or less retained the original wording of Article 17(1) EC by providing that 'citizenship of the Union shall be additional to national citizenship and shall not replace it' (in Article 17 it could be read that EU citizenship 'shall complement and not replace national citizenship'). However, Shaw expects that this different wording will probably not make a substantial difference to the status of EU citizenship. Shaw, "Citizenship: Contrasting Dynamics at the Interface of Integration and Constitutionalism", 23.

391 See for example Hall, who writes that 'the qualitative advance in international relations which the Community represents justifies the conclusion that the Member States have entered into obligations with each other of such a nature as to limit, even more severely than in international law, their entitlement to have their dispositions of nationality unquestionably recognised for Community law purposes … The transfer of sovereignty which membership of the Community involves subjects the exercise of the Member States' power to Community supervision at least to the extent that the exercise of the power produces effects on the level of Community law'. Stephen Hall, *Nationality, Migration Rights and Citizenship of the Union* (Dordrecht/Boston/London: Martinus Nijhoff Publishers, 1995), 22–23.

On another occasion, Hall strongly hinted at the possibility of Community interference in case a conferral or withdrawal of nationality would violate any of the general principles of law protected by the ECJ: 'It is likely that the Court would refuse to apply in the field of Community law a conferral or withdrawal of nationality which is in itself repugnant to a fundamental human right'. Stephen Hall, "Loss of Union Citizenship in Breach of Fundamental Rights", *European Law Review* 21 (1996): 133.

their competence with due regard to Community law (the famous *obiter dictum*[392]), which may possibly be used to set bounds to the regulation of nationality law by the Member States, De Groot lists what he thinks are four limitations on the autonomy of EU Member States[393]:

- The nationality of a Member State cannot be lost for the sole reason of using the free movement rights that follow from one's European citizenship;
- In order to comply with Article 4(2) TEU (ex Article 10 EC), nationality cannot be accorded to large numbers of non-Member State citizens without consultation of the EU;
- EU law is violated if a Member State's provisions on the acquisition and loss of its nationality are contrary to international law. The different Member States cannot, for example, accept the loss of Member State nationality on grounds which violate international law if this loss entails that someone ceases to be a European citizen;[394]
- Lack of coordination of the nationality laws of the Member States may lead to a violation of EU law. This ground for violation of EU law will be illustrated below by way of the CJEU's *Rottmann* ruling.

In the literature on nationality and European citizenship, d'Oliveira appears to be the fiercest adversary of the idea that EU law already limits Member State discretion.[395] After having concluded that neither the Community nor other Member States have any say in how Member States regulate their nationality laws, he contends, *inter alia*, that De Groot's first point presents the world upside down:

> Whoever is a national of a Member State is a Union citizen ... Whoever is not (or no longer) a national of a Member State is not (no longer) eligible for Union citizenship.[396]

In his view, Member States are free to provide for their own provisions on loss of nationality and the ensuing loss of European citizenship will not constitute a violation of Community law. Many authors disagree—justly in our

---

[392] See already *supra* Section 8.

[393] de Groot, "Towards a European Nationality Law", 25 ff; de Groot and Vink, *Meervoudige nationaliteit in Europees perspectief*, 34.

[394] In a non-European context this loss does have to be recognized by other States in order to activate their own provisions on statelessness.

[395] Hans Ulrich Jessurun d'Oliveira, "Nationality and the European Union after Amsterdam", in *Legal issues of the Amsterdam Treaty*, ed. David O'Keeffe and Patrick Twomey (Oxford: Hart Publishing, 1999), 395–412. See also his intervention on the occasion of presentations by Van der Velden and De Groot before the Dutch International Law Association (see 'Medelingen van de Nederlandse Vereniging voor Internationaal Recht', nr. 130, 2005).

[396] Ibid., 407.

view—with the stance taken by d'Oliveira. They maintain that the exercise of Community rights should not result in sanctions—and the loss of nationality under these circumstances can rightly be called such. It is indeed hard to see how the internal market can function when the status which gives the right to free movement is lost by exercising this right.[397] Loss of nationality after prolonged residence in another Member State, even if one acquires another Member State nationality or possesses a dual nationality, would, we argue, present an enormous obstacle to the exercise of the right to free movement.[398]

Concerning De Groot's second point, d'Oliveira holds that municipal nationality laws have never been called into question by other Member States or the Community. He regards the area of nationality law as an irrelevant category in the sense of Article 10 EC.[399] De Groot has countered this argument with a reference to the Spanish dual nationality treaties which, he contends, were discussed within the Community before Spain's accession. Most recently, a similar issue arose in relation to Romania's dual nationality policy which especially benefits inhabitants of Moldova and some provinces in the Ukraine.[400] After the collapse of the communist regime, Romania 'was eager to resume ties with the Romanian Diaspora and kin-minorities abroad' and adopted a restitution policy which explicitly allowed dual nationality for certain categories of citizens.[401] This policy of restoring Romanian nationality to Moldovan and Ukrainian citizens, which created a considerable number of non-resident dual nationals, was criticized by various EU agencies in

---

397 See for example Hailbronner, "Nationality in public international law and European law", 93.

398 Curiously, d'Oliveira agrees with this line of reasoning in another context—that of the free movement of spouses in the EU. He writes that under a Community interpretation of the term 'spouse' which excludes non-married partners of EU nationals, having the effect that the latter are not allowed to be accompanied by their partners upon exercising their free movement rights, 'their willingness to avail themselves of the freedom of movement guaranteed by the Treaty will be severely reduced'. Apparently, he thinks that the loss of the nationality of origin will not severely reduce one's willingness to make use of the right to free movement as guaranteed under EU law. Hans Ulrich Jessurun d'Oliveira, "Freedom of Movement of Spouses and Registered Partners in the European Union", in *Private Law in the International Arena - Liber Amicorum Kurt Siehr* (The Hague: T.M.C. Asser Press, 2000), 528.

399 Jessurun d'Oliveira, "Nationality and the European Union after Amsterdam", 405.

400 Costanza Margiotta and Olivier Vonk, "Nationality law and European citizenship: the role of dual nationality", EUDO Citizenship Working Paper 2010/66.

401 Constantin Iordachi, "Politics of citizenship in post-communist Romania: Legal traditions, restitution of nationality and multiple memberships", in *Citizenship Policies in the New Europe* (Amsterdam: Amsterdam University Press, 2009), 188–189. See also Horváth, *Mandating identity: citizenship, kinship laws and plural nationality in the European Union*, 174–175.

2007.[402] Finally, also the British declarations on who was a British national for Community purposes were discussed with the EU authorities.[403] It thus follows from this short overview that d'Oliveira is right in stating that the European Commission has never acted under Article 10 EC in the field of nationality law; yet the above examples also demonstrate that EU bodies seem to exercise some pressure on the domestic nationality law policies of the Member States.

This section will now continue by looking more closely at the above mentioned British declarations, the legality of which was contended before the ECJ in *Kaur*. This judgment is a further demonstration of the Court's reticence to interfere in nationality matters and once again confirmed State autonomy in the area of nationality law.

11.2.1. *Case C-192/99 Kaur [2001]*

Kaur addressed the validity of British declarations which defined who was British for Community purposes. Ms Kaur, a person of Asian origin, was born in Kenya in 1948 when Kenya was a British colony (Kenya would only become independent in 1963). As a result, she acquired the status of 'citizen of the United Kingdom and Colonies' ('CUKC') under the British Nationality Act of 1948.[404] This status did not distinguish between British people who were UK-based and those who were not.[405] Many Asians who were settled in East African countries retained this status despite these countries becoming independent in the 1960s.[406] They deliberately did not acquire the nationality of the newly independent States, but retained their status of 'CUKC' because they had been assured that they would retain the right of abode (i.e. the right

---

[402] Iordachi, "Politics of citizenship in post-communist Romania: Legal traditions, restitution of nationality and multiple memberships", 203; Constantin Iordachi, "Country report: Romania", EUDO Citizenship Observatory Country Reports (2009). Iordachi remarks that 'although the European Commission has repeatedly stated that the policy of restitution of citizenship is an internal matter for Romania, several EU agencies voiced concerns that, upon Romania's accession in January 2007, the country's policy on restitution of citizenship could become an uncontrollable gate of access to the Schengen space for non-EU citizens, bypassing restrictive immigration policies'. Romania on the other hand justified its policy as 'part of the EU's program of integration with neighbouring countries', enabling the EU to exercise greater influence in the former Soviet space and to import a qualified Moldovan workforce.

[403] de Groot, "Towards a European Nationality Law", 27.

[404] Stephen Hall, "Determining the Scope ratione personae of European Citizenship: Customary International Law prevails for Now", *Legal Issues of Economic Integration*, no. 3 (2001): 355.

[405] Sawyer, "Report on the United Kingdom", 7.

[406] Ann Dummett and Andrew Nicol, *Subjects, Citizens, Aliens and Others. Nationality and Immigration Law* (London: Weidenfeld and Nicolson, 1990), 198.

to enter and remain) in the UK.[407] Yet when the UK was confronted with a strong increase in the number of Asians who moved from East Africa to the UK in the late 1960s, the Commonwealth Immigrants Act 1968 provided that from then onwards 'a British subject was free from immigration control only if he, or at least one of his parents or grandparents, was born, adopted, registered or naturalized in the United Kingdom'.[408] The UK's effort to keep these persons out had the effect that this particular group of Asians in East Africa is the largest group of British nationals not having the right of abode anywhere in the world. Although still being citizens of the UK and Colonies, they were effectively without citizenship.[409] Due to these law reforms Ms Kaur had lost her right of abode in the UK in 1968. She also did not possess 'patriality' (i.e. an ancestral connection to the UK[410]), a condition subsequently imposed in the 1971 Immigration Act; only British subjects with 'patriality' had a right of abode in the UK and were exempt from immigration control.

On the first of January 1973, at the same moment the 1971 Act came into force, the UK acceded to the EEC. A declaration was added to the Accession Treaty which stated that only those with a right of abode in the UK were to be regarded as British nationals for the purposes of Community law.

---

407 Prakash Shah, "British Nationals under Community Law: The Kaur Case", *European Journal of Migration and Law* 3 (2001): 272.

408 Dummett and Nicol, *Subjects, Citizens, Aliens and Others. Nationality and Immigration Law*, 202–203. In relation to the 1968 Act, Dummett and Nicol make the interesting observation that 'the first important inclusion, in modern nationality law, of rights derived from a female parent or grandparent, [thus] arose from a racially discriminatory measure'.

It should also be noted that in 1973 the European Commission of Human Rights concluded in a case on East Africans of Asian origin (which was not brought before the Court because the UK dealt separately with the people that had brought the claim) that the Commonwealth Immigrants Act 1968, by subjecting to immigration control citizens of the United Kingdom and Colonies in East Africa who were of Asian origin, discriminated against this group of people on grounds of their colour or race. See Jean-Yves Carlier, "Droits de l'homme et nationalité", *Annales de Droit de Louvain* 63, no. 3 (2003): 252; Sawyer, "Report on the United Kingdom", 9.

409 Shah, "British Nationals under Community Law: The Kaur Case": 272.

410 Sawyer, "Report on the United Kingdom", 8. Under the concept of patriality, only British people who were born in the UK or had a parent or grandparent who was, could enter the UK without leave. Joppke defines patriality as a mechanism that 'divided the devolving empire into a white settler and nonwhite colonial part, keeping the door open for the former but closing it on the latter'. This mechanism was strongly criticized in the UK, however, because of its racially discriminatory implications. Christian Joppke, *Selecting by Origin: Ethnic Migration in the Liberal State* (Cambridge, Massachusetts: Harvard University Press, 2005), 95.

In 1981 a new British Nationality Act was drafted which distinguished five different statuses: British citizens, British Dependent Territories citizens, British Overseas citizens, British subjects and British protected persons.[411] In practice this meant that 'citizens of the UK and colonies' who met the condition of patriality became British citizens. 'Citizens of the UK and colonies' who lived, for example, in Gibraltar and the Falkland Islands became British Dependent Territories citizens. Following the British Overseas Territories Act 2002 this group, which is now referred to as British Overseas Territories citizens, has full access to British citizenship and thus also European citizenship.[412] Ms Kaur however became a British Overseas citizen under the 1981 Act. This group did not have the right of abode in the UK.

The amended Nationality Act also made the UK decide to issue a new declaration on who was to be regarded as British nationals for the purposes of Community law. The latter declaration of 1982 replaced the one of 1972 but was of the same tenor; those who did not have the right of abode in the UK were not considered British nationals for Community law purposes. This declaration excluded British Dependent Territories citizens (except for those having a connection with Gibraltar), British Overseas citizens, British subjects without the right of abode and British protected persons. These categories therefore also do not possess European citizenship.

Let us now turn back to the specific circumstances in *Kaur*. Ms Kaur, a British Overseas citizen not having the right of abode in the UK, applied for leave to remain in the UK after several temporary periods of residence there. This application was refused, but the High Court, to which she turned for judicial review of the decision, asked the ECJ for a preliminary ruling. The questions asked concerned the effect of the British declarations and Declaration no. 2 that was annexed to the Treaty on European Union in 1992,[413] the relevance of Article 3(2) of the Fourth Protocol of the European Convention on Human Rights, and the role played by Article 18 EC in this context. We can say that the Court did not want to burn its fingers on the case and thus showed the kind of reticence in respect of nationality law that was to

[411] Shah, "British Nationals under Community Law: The Kaur Case": 271.

[412] Sawyer, "Report on the United Kingdom", 22.

[413] Declaration no. 2, which is a confirmation of customary international law, reads as follows: 'The Conference declares that, wherever in the Treaty establishing the European Community reference is made to nationals of the Member States, the question whether an individual possesses the nationality of a Member State shall be settled solely by reference to the national law of the Member State concerned. Member States may declare, for information, who are to be considered their nationals for Community purposes by way of a declaration lodged with the Presidency and may amend any such declaration when necessary'.

be expected. However, the Court's disregard of the human rights at stake in *Kaur* has been severely criticized.[414]

Ms Kaur claimed that British law infringed fundamental rights by depriving British nationals in the same situation as she was of the right to enter the territory of which they were nationals, or of rendering them effectively stateless. She referred to *Micheletti* when claiming that a State can only define the concept of national if it has due regard to Community law. This implied, in her view, the observance of fundamental rights which form an integral part of Community law. In addition, she disputed the relevance of the British declarations. The UK and others took the view that, under international law, each State alone can determine the categories of persons that it regards as its nationals. The UK stressed the importance of its declarations in the light of its colonial past.

The judgment of the Court is fairly short and disregards many of the points raised by the referring national court. After confirming State autonomy in nationality matters under international law, the Court upheld the validity of the British practice to define, in the light of its colonial past, several categories of British citizens and to confer differing rights on these categories according to their varying ties to the UK. As for the 1972 British declaration—and also the 1982 declaration, which the Court regarded as substantially designating the same categories of persons—the Court held that it had to be taken into consideration 'as an instrument relating to the Treaty for the purpose of its interpretation and, more importantly, for determining the scope of the Treaty *ratione personae*'. The adoption of the declaration, the Court continued, did not have the effect of depriving anyone of rights under Community law. Rather, these rights had never arisen in the first place. The national court was thus told to refer to the 1982 declaration in determining whether a person was a British citizens for the purposes of Community law.

Throughout this chapter we have hinted a couple of times at the possibility that the phrase from *Micheletti*, which says that the national competence to define conditions for the acquisition and loss of nationality must be exercised with due regard to Community law, could have the effect of one day limiting State autonomy in nationality law. It is clear, however, that this moment had not yet arrived in *Kaur*. Hall rightly concludes from the judgment that 'in deciding whether or not to *confer* nationality, the Member States' wide discretion under customary international law is preserved and recognition must be given to any such (non-)conferral for Community law purposes' (emphasis in

[414] Shah, "British Nationals under Community Law: The Kaur Case": 278; Helen Toner, "Annotation Case C-192/99 *Kaur* [2001]", *Common Market Law Review* 39 (2002): 890.

original).[415] Yet he continues that State discretion may not be equally wide when it comes to *withdrawing* nationality. After all, in *Kaur* the Court 'avoided holding that all nationality measures fall outside the scope of Community law and do not therefore attract the general principles of Community law of which fundamental rights are a component'.[416] Hence, the Court's conclusion that Ms Kaur had never possessed any rights under Community law leaves open the possibility that 'there may be circumstances in which a person who has already acquired the status of Member State national for Community purposes … may be protected by Community law when subject to attempts to withdraw that status'.[417]

The judgment in *Kaur* did not in any way clarify the mysterious 'due regard to Community law' phrase. Toner therefore even suggests that *Kaur* implicitly casts doubt on the scope of the limited supervision that was suggested by the phrase in *Micheletti*.[418] However, we will see below that with the *Rottmann* case the Court finally had the occasion to rule on a case involving the loss of both Member State nationality and European citizenship. The Court faced the question whether States have the same wide discretion in withdrawing nationality as they have conferring it.

Finally, before turning to the *Chen* and *Rottmann* cases, a brief word on the human rights considerations in *Kaur*. Although the Court did not devote a single word to the human rights aspect nor to the role of Article 18 EC, a number of interesting points that were raised in the literature should be mentioned here. The judgment in *Kaur* in effect ruled out 'the last possible international judicial remedy against the injustices suffered by British passport holders from East Africa consequent the Commonwealth Immigrants Act 1968'.[419] Moreover, it is observed that neither the Court nor the Advocate-General seemed to be interested in the question whether Ms Kaur had

---

415 Hall, "Determining the Scope ratione personae of European Citizenship: Customary International Law prevails for Now": 359.

416 Ibid., 360.

417 Ibid. To interpret *Kaur*, as some do, as a clear signal that the Court remains reluctant to accept any kind of review over nationality laws may be too strong a conclusion. We agree with Hall that *Kaur* concerns the conferral of nationality, and that this situation should—for the question whether any European control exists—be sharply distinguished from the withdrawal of nationality. The latter situation would arguably offer more opportunities for the Court to intervene, especially taking into account the dependence of European citizenship on Member State nationality.

418 Toner, "Annotation Case C-192/99 *Kaur* [2001]": 893.

419 Shah, "British Nationals under Community Law: The Kaur Case": 278. The consequences for Ms Kaur are quite severe, as she has no Kenyan nationality nor secure immigration and settlement rights in Kenya.

settlement elsewhere when dismissing her claim.[420] In her annotation of the case, Toner criticizes the Court's refusal to address the human rights element of the case:

> The Court has seemingly answered the first question—as to whether the Declarations are admissible and to be taken into account—without addressing the crucial qualification—as to whether, and if so what, weight should be attached to any allegation that the United Kingdom in making these declarations and excluding Mrs Kaur from British Nationality for the purposes of the Treaty infringes her fundamental rights.[421]

11.2.2. *Case C-200/02 Zhu and Chen [2004]*

The facts of the *Chen* case were very particular. Mrs Chen and her husband both worked for a Chinese undertaking and often travelled to Europe for business—the United Kingdom in particular. The couple had one child and was not allowed to have a second child under Chinese law. They came up with a very original strategy to still have a second child, however. Mrs Chen deliberately entered the UK in May 2000, when she was six months pregnant, with the aim of giving birth in Belfast. Although this city is situated in Northern Ireland, which forms part of the United Kingdom, Irish law at the time also provided for the *automatic* acquisition of Irish nationality *iure soli* to children born in Northern Ireland. Not only did Mrs Chen's child (Catherine) therefore acquire Irish nationality, the child also became a European citizen. In that capacity Catherine could make use of her right to reside in another Member State, which she did when mother and child settled in Wales, also in the UK. Although Mrs Chen and Catherine had thus never moved to another Member State, the Court held that this was not a wholly internal situation (as claimed by the Irish and UK governments) due to the fact that Catherine—an Irish national—was resident in the UK. The Court also did not agree with the UK's argument that 'Mrs Chen's move to Northern Ireland with the aim of having her child acquire the nationality of another Member State constitutes an attempt improperly to exploit the provisions of Community law'.[422] Referring to *Micheletti* and *Kaur*, the Court held that international law allows each Member State, having due regard to Community law, to lay down the

[420] Toner, "Annotation Case C-192/99 *Kaur* [2001]": 883.

[421] Ibid., 891. See in this respect also the annotation by d'Oliveira, who qualifies the British nationality law as a 'racist law'. Hans Ulrich Jessurun d'Oliveira, "Noot onder *Manjit Kaur*", *Jurisprudentie Vreemdelingenrecht* (2001): 476.

[422] Para. 34. See on the question of a possible abuse of law AG Tizzano's Opinion (para. 108 ff) and Bjørn Kunoy, "A Union of National Citizens: The Origins of the Court's Lack of *Avant-Gardisme* in the *Chen* Case", *Common Market Law Review* 43 (2006): 179–190.

conditions for the acquisition and loss of nationality. The legality of the child's acquisition of Irish nationality was therefore uncontested.[423] Finally, the ECJ decided that the mother, who was not a European citizen, had a right to reside with the child as her primary carer. Any other decision would deprive the child's right of residence of any useful effect.

For our purposes, the judgment is important in two respects. First, it once again confirmed Member State autonomy in European nationality law. More importantly, although Mrs Chen was just one of the many non-EU nationals who tried to obtain EU citizenship for their children by giving birth in Northern Ireland, her case seems to have been one of the factors that led to the abolition, by way of a referendum, of the principle of *automatic* acquisition of Irish nationality by birth in Northern Ireland—a very exceptional rule in European nationality law. This case is therefore a good example of voluntary harmonization of nationality law in Europe.

11.2.3. *Case C-135/08 Rottmann [2010]*

The most recent CJEU case in the field of nationality is *Rottmann*. The Court's ruling was eagerly awaited for the obvious reason that it was the first case brought before the Court which not only involved the loss of Member State nationality, but (consequently) also the loss of EU citizenship. Rottmann was an Austrian national by birth who acquired German nationality through naturalization in 1999, thereby losing his Austrian nationality. During the naturalization procedure, however, he had not mentioned that he was the subject of criminal proceedings in Austria. It was only after his naturalization that the German authorities were informed of Rottmann being subject to criminal proceedings, and that already in 1997 Austria had issued a warrant for his arrest. In the light of those circumstances, Rottmann's naturalization was withdrawn with retroactive effect on the ground of deception. As he had lost his Austrian nationality upon naturalization in Germany, the withdrawal of the naturalization not only rendered him stateless but also provoked the loss of European citizenship.[424]

The preliminary ruling asked for by the highest German federal administrative court consisted of two questions. First, it asked whether it was contrary to

---

423 See also Jean-Yves Carlier, "Annotation Case C-200/02 *Chen* [2004]", ibid. 42 (2005): 1127–1128.

424 It had already been questioned in the academic literature whether a criminal offence can lead to statelessness and, consequently, the loss of European citizenship for someone who has in fact never left the territory of the EU. See Gerard-René de Groot, "Notities bij de bepalingen betreffende het verlies van het Nederlanderschap", *Migrantenrecht* 18, no. 4/5 (2003): 135; Gerard-René de Groot, *Nationaliteit en rechtszekerheid* (Den Haag: Boom Juridische uitgevers, 2008), 28.

Community law that Rottmann lost his European citizenship as a result of the combined effect of the lawful withdrawal of his naturalization by the German authorities and the non-automatic recovery of his original Austrian nationality. Second, should Germany refrain altogether or temporarily from withdrawing the naturalization if or so long as that withdrawal would lead to the loss of European citizenship, or should Austria interpret and apply (or even adjust) its national law in such a way as to avoid the loss of European citizenship?

The CJEU started by making a number of predictable observations, repeating that it is for each Member State, having due regard to Community law, to lay down the conditions for the acquisition and loss of nationality.[425] Despite the fact that nationality law falls within the competence of the Member States, however, the loss of European citizenship and the rights attached to it brings the present situation within the scope of EU law.[426] Yet the reason for deciding that Rottmann's situation fell within the scope of EU law is quite radical. Rather than following AG Maduro's (conservative) argument that it was

---

[425] D'Oliveira submits that this *obiter dictum*, which by its very nature was not essential to the outcome of *Micheletti*, paved the way for *Rottmann*: '[Het obiter] was dus een schot voor de boeg, dat op gezette tijden door het Hof werd herhaald zonder dat er tot nu toe praktische gevolgen aan werden verbonden … In Rottmann is dan nu voor het eerst een praktische uitwerking ontwikkeld aan de herhaalde obiters'. In his very critical annotation he argues for a treaty revision stipulating that nationality law belongs to the 'reserved domain' of the Member States. The Court's evolution of the case law should be brought to a halt as it is in the process of reversing the relationship between nationality and EU citizenship. If the Court insists on strengthening Union citizenship, however, d'Oliveira pleads for the severance of EU citizenship from Member State nationality. Hans Ulrich Jessurun d'Oliveira, "Ontkoppeling van nationaliteit en Unieburgerschap? Opmerkingen over de *Rottmann*-zaak", *Nederlands Juristenblad*, no. 16 (2010): 1031.

[426] Para. 42. See on the question whether the case fell within the scope of EU law more extensively paras. 8–13 of AG Maduro's Opinion of 30 September 2009. The AG's reasoning is not followed by the Court. For speculations on the different situations which may fall within the scope of EU law after *Rottmann*, see Gerard-René de Groot, "Invloed van het Unierecht op het nationaliteitsrecht van de Lidstaten: Overwegingen over de Janko Rottmann-beslissing van het Europese Hof van Justitie", *Asiel- en Migrantenrecht* 1, no. 5/6 (2010): 293–300.

De Groot argues in particular that it remains unclear from *Rottmann* whether a third country national who has been naturalized in one of the Member States but who has never exercised his/her right to free movement will fall within in the scope of EU law if (s)he were to lose this 'European' nationality. If (s)he could, this would be a glaring example of judicial activism. After all, the Court would then in the particularly sensitive area of nationality law less easily conclude that a given case is a wholly internal situation. On the other hand, if this situation were not to fall within the scope of EU law then a differentiation would be made in the Member States' nationality laws between cases falling within the scope of EU law and those that do not. In De Groot's view, such a differentiation would be completely

Rottmann's exercise of his free movement right which triggered EU law,[427] the Court decided to go a step further by stating that:

> It is clear that the situation of a citizen of the Union who, like the applicant in the main proceedings, is faced with a decision withdrawing his naturalisation, adopted by the authorities of one Member State, and placing him, after he has lost the nationality of another Member State that he originally possessed, in a position capable of causing him to lose the status conferred by Article 17 EC and the rights attaching thereto falls, *by reason of its nature and its consequences*, within the ambit of European Union law (emphasis added).[428]

Several commentators feel it is this paragraph which makes *Rottmann* so important. Thus, Shaw writes that

> in *Rottmann* the connection which the Court draws between EU law and national law is the simple fact that by losing national citizenship a person will also lose EU citizenship rights. This seems to be a step beyond the approach in *Micheletti* where the Court formulated the issue thus: it is not permissible for the legislation of a Member State to restrict the effects of the grant of the nationality of another Member State by imposing an additional condition for recognition of that nationality *with a view to the exercise* of the fundamental freedoms provided in the Treaty.[429]

Kochenov builds on Shaw's statement by claiming that the classic approach of searching for a cross-border element has been trashed in *Rottmann*. In his view, the fundamental importance of the judgment resides in the fact that it has clarified the material scope of the Union citizenship provisions, i.e. the rights that are granted by the Treaty to Union citizens. The Court's statement that the situation in which Rottmann finds himself falls 'by reason of its nature and consequences' within the scope of EU law means, according to Kochenov,

---

'undeserving of belief'. As the post-*Rottmann* situation is thus not particularly clear, it is expected that the judgment will trigger a number of preliminary questions trying to ascertain its boundaries.

427 Para. 11: '... It was by making use of the freedom of movement and residence associated with Union citizenship which he enjoyed as an Austrian national that Mr Rottmann went to Germany and established his residence there in 1995, in order to initiate a naturalisation procedure. Although it was in accordance with the conditions laid down by national law that he acquired the status of German national and lost that of Austrian national, *it was therefore only after exercising a fundamental freedom conferred on him by Community law*. According to settled case-law, situations involving the exercise of the fundamental freedoms guaranteed by the Treaty, in particular those involving the freedom to move and reside within the territory of the Member States, as conferred by Article 18 EC, cannot be regarded as internal situations which have no factor linking them with Community law' (emphasis added).

428 Para. 42.

429 Emphasis in original. Shaw, "Citizenship: Contrasting Dynamics at the Interface of Integration and Constitutionalism", 18.

that '*any decision* on conferral or revocation of nationality taken by the Member States which is able to affect the EU citizenship status of an individual now falls within the scope *ratione materiae* of EU law'.[430]

Another interesting section of the judgment is where the Court tries to give some substance to the *Micheletti* statement. According to the Court,

> the proviso that due regard must be had to European Union law does not compromise the principle of international law … that the Member States have the power to lay down the conditions for the acquisition and loss of nationality, but rather enshrines the principle that, in respect of citizens of the Union, the exercise of that power, in so far as it affects the rights conferred and protected by the legal order of the Union, as is in particular the case of a decision withdrawing naturalization such as that at issue in the main proceedings, is amenable to judicial review carried out in the light of European Union law.[431]

The judicial review carried out by the Court in this case led to the conclusion that the withdrawal of Rottmann's naturalization (and consequent loss of European citizenship) *could* be compatible with European Union law: both the 1961 Convention on the Reduction of Statelessness (Article 8(2)) and the ECN (Article 7(1) and (3)) allow the deprivation of nationality when that nationality was acquired by means of fraudulent conduct.[432] Such a deprivation cannot be considered to be an arbitrary act as prohibited by the Universal Declaration of Human Rights (Article 15(2)) and the ECN (Article 4c).

Importantly, the Court adds that such withdrawal must observe the principle of proportionality. When examining a decision withdrawing naturalization, it is necessary for the national court 'to take into account the consequences that the decision entails for the person concerned and, if relevant, for the members of his family with regard to the loss of the rights enjoyed by every citizen of the Union'.[433] It will be very interesting to see how this proportionality test[434] will be interpreted by national courts in the field of nationality law. Does it, for example, imply a closer scrutiny of administrative decisions in light of the European citizenship attached to Member State nationality?[435] The

---

[430] Emphasis in original. Dimitry Kochenov, "Annotation Case C-135/08, *Rottmann* [2010]", *Common Market Law Review* 47 (2010): 1841–1842.

[431] Para. 48.

[432] This had also been argued by AG Maduro (para. 29). On these Conventions, see Hendriks and Vonk, "Mapping statelessness in the Netherlands".

[433] Para. 56.

[434] On the implications of the proportionality test (first introduced in the EU citizenship case law in *Baumbast*) see Michael Dougan, "The constitutional dimension to the case law on Union citizenship", *European Law Review* 31 (2006): 613–641.

[435] See Jo Shaw in her contribution to the EUDO citizenship forum.

Court's introduction of a proportionality test is not the only novelty in *Rottmann*, however. A 'sensational' and 'very far-reaching'[436] part of the judgment is the following:

> A Member State whose nationality has been acquired by deception cannot be considered bound, pursuant to Article 17 EC, to refrain from withdrawing naturalisation merely because the person concerned has not recovered the nationality of his Member State of origin. It is, nevertheless, for the national court to determine whether, before such a decision withdrawing naturalisation takes effect, having regard to all the relevant circumstances, observance of the principle of proportionality requires the person *concerned to be afforded a reasonable period of time to try to recover the nationality of his Member State of origin* (emphasis added).[437]

As to the second question, the Court remarked that the German withdrawal of the naturalization had not yet become definitive and that no decision had yet been taken by Austria concerning Rottmann's status. As long as no decision is taken, it is not possible for the Court to rule on the question whether this decision is contrary to EU law. Nevertheless, the Court explicitly mentions that Austria is also bound by the principles stemming from the judgment.[438]

It is hard to see how the Court could have reached a different substantive outcome in *Rottmann*; the treaties to which it referred explicitly allow statelessness which is the result of the withdrawal of a nationality acquired by means of fraudulent conduct. Nevertheless, the judgment is a very relevant addition to the Court's case law in the field of nationality law. Not only have we seen that some commentators claim that after *Rottmann* any decision on conferral or revocation of nationality taken by the Member States which is able to affect the EU citizenship status of an individual falls within the scope *ratione materiae* of EU law, but the Court's introduction of a proportionality test has also triggered a debate on the exact scope of judicial review by the CJEU on Member State nationality law. Thus, while some commentators have argued that 'the importance of the case goes far beyond its facts' and that

---

[436] de Groot, "Invloed van het Unierecht op het nationaliteitsrecht van de Lidstaten: Overwegingen over de Janko Rottmann-beslissing van het Europese Hof van Justitie": 293–300.

[437] Paras. 57–58.

[438] In para. 62 the Court states that 'it has to be borne in mind … that the principles stemming from this judgment with regard to the powers of the Member States in the sphere of nationality, and also their duty to exercise those powers having due regard to European Union law, *apply both to the Member State of naturalisation and to the Member State of the original nationality*' (emphasis added). It is therefore beyond dispute that the principles of EU law apply both to the provisions on the loss and to those on the acquisition of nationality.

'[after *Rottmann*] the legal status of EU citizenship comes across as seriously reinforced',[439] one Dutch scholar has claimed that the (procedural) proportionality test introduced in *Rottmann* does not seem to fundamentally change the balance of interests to which the Netherlands is already obliged under Dutch administrative law.[440]

The debate on the interpretation of *Rottmann* will no doubt continue for some time, and the CJEU will most likely be facing more occasions to elucidate its position on the interaction between Member State nationality and EU citizenship. The Court's reasoning in *Rottmann* has already influenced the outcome of the far-reaching *Ruiz Zambrano* migration law case,[441] which concerned Mr Ruiz Zambrano and his wife—both of Colombian nationality—and their three children, two of which were born in Belgium and only held Belgian nationality.[442] Although the parents' application for refugee status had been rejected in Belgium, they could not be sent back to Colombia under the *non-refoulement* principle in view of the civil war there. Mr Ruiz Zambrano had subsequently worked illegally for a company in Belgium for some years, and had always paid social security contributions. When he was eventually caught working illegally, he had to stop working immediately and lodged an application for unemployment benefits. When this application was rejected, the case was brought before the Belgian court which then submitted the following question to the CJEU:

> Are the citizenship provisions to be interpreted as meaning that they confer on a relative in the ascending line who is a third country national, upon whom his minor children, who are European Union citizens, are dependent, a right of residence in the Member State of which they are nationals and in which they reside, and also exempt him from having to obtain a work permit in that Member State?

The Court's reasoning in its remarkably brief judgment is simple. The children's Belgian nationality makes them European citizens and European citizenship is destined to be the fundamental status of nationals of the Member

---

439 Kochenov, "Annotation Case C-135/08, *Rottmann* [2010]": 1831, 1837.

440 Helen Oosterom-Staples, "Het internationale recht als beschermengel van de exclusieve bevoegdheden van lidstaten inzake verlies van nationaliteit?", *Nederlands Tijdschrift voor Europees Recht*, no. 6 (2010): 192.

441 Case C-34/09 *Ruiz Zambrano* [2011] ECR I-00000.

442 At the time of the children's birth in 2004 and 2005 respectively, Belgian law still provided that stateless children would acquire Belgian nationality. The Ruiz Zambrano children were stateless because Colombian law does not recognize Colombian nationality for children born outside the territory of Colombia where the parents do not take specific stepts to have them so recognized.

States. Relying then on *Rottmann*, the Court concluded that 'in those circumstances, Article 20 TFEU precludes national measures which have the effect of depriving citizens of the Union of the genuine enjoyment of the substance of the rights conferred by virtue of their status as citizens of the Union'.[443] According to the Court, both the refusal to grant a right of residence to Mr Ruiz Zambrano—which would have the effect that the children would have leave the territory of the Union to accompany their parents—and the refusal to grant him a work permit—which would similarly have the effect that the children would have leave the territory of the Union because the parents risk not having sufficient resources to provide for the family—have such an effect. *Rottmann* and *Ruiz Zambrano* represent a fundamental shift in the Court's case law, as they disconnect EU citizenship from free movement. The effect of internal measures taken by the Member States on the EU citizenship of the individuals involved is thus directly assessed by the Court in cases that used to be wholly internal situations.

Concluding Remarks

One of the main aims of this first chapter was to describe the current state of the legal concept of *nationality* in municipal and public international law, as well as the position of Member State nationality in the EU. Now that the scene is set, we may continue our analysis of *dual nationality* in PIL and EU law

[443] Para. 42. This is an aspect that distinguishes *Ruiz Zambrano* from Case C-434/09 *McCarthy*, handed down by the Court on 5 May 2011. Mrs McCarthy, a dual national holding British and Irish nationality who had always lived in England, had sought to obtain a residence right in England on the basis of her *Irish* nationality and her status as a Union citizen. This would have allowed her Jamaican husband to claim a derived right of residence under EU law, a right to which he was not entitled under UK immigration law. AG Kokott already concluded in her Opinion of 25 November 2010 that 'a Union citizen in Mrs McCarthy's position cannot rely on EU law in order to obtain for him or herself and his or her family members a right of residence in the Member State in which that Union citizen has always lived and of which he or she is a national' (para. 58). This conclusion was shared by the Court, which held that 'Article 3(1) of Directive 2004/38 is to be interpreted as meaning that that directive is not applicable to a Union citizen who has never exercised his right of free movement, who has always resided in a Member State of which he is a national and who is also a national of another Member State' (para. 43). Neither was Article 21 TFEU applicable to a Union citizen in Mrs McCarthy's position, 'provided that the situation of that citizen does not include the application of measures by a Member State that would have the effect of depriving him of the genuine substance of the rights conferred by virtue of his status as a Union citizen [*Ruiz Zambrano*] or of impeding the exercise of his right of free movement and residence within the territory of the Member States [*García Avello*]' (para. 56).

(Chapter 2) and in four different EU Member States (Chapters 3–6). Nevertheless, the subject of dual nationality proper was also regularly touched upon in this first chapter, and it was seen that it is strongly intertwined with the changing role of the nation-state due to the process of European integration as well as globalization. Hence the frequent references to dual nationality in relation to national identity, transnationalism, postnationalism, and EU citizenship. We may say that all these concepts are related and that dual nationality is therefore just one factor, albeit an important one, in the transformation process of State sovereignty.

What emerged from Chapter 1 is a trend towards a greater acceptance of dual nationality. We can safely say that at least it is no longer considered a legal anomaly which should be prevented at all costs. Rather, an increasing number of States have come to see dual nationality as a useful instrument not only for the retention of ties with an emigrant diaspora, but also for the integration of immigrants. A number of examples were mentioned of *emigration* countries (for example in Latin America[444]) which try to retain ties with their diaspora population (mainly for economic reasons) through dual nationality. On the other hand, human rights and liberal norms have increasingly imposed a (moral) obligation on *immigration* countries to be more inclusive towards immigrants. This can be done by equalizing the position of *denizens* with nationals or by adopting more inclusive nationality policies. The liberalization of naturalization policies and the toleration of dual nationality constitute important elements in making nationality laws more inclusive.[445]

These are of course rather general (and perhaps slightly one-sided) observations and it is true that dual nationality is still very much opposed in certain countries. Dual nationality remains a controversial topic and one can legitimately disagree on the emotional and psychological aspects of the concept of nationality. It is difficult to make value judgments in this respect because the feelings aroused by nationality will differ from one person to the other. The purpose of Part II of this study is therefore to give a more detailed picture of

---

[444] It was shown that Latin American countries like Mexico and Brazil now accept dual nationality in order to remain linked to their diaspora communities in the United States. We will see later on that Italy and Spain have a long tradition of allowing dual nationality, particularly for nationals who emigrated to Latin America.

[445] Faist, "Dual citizenship: Change, Prospects, and Limits", 176. Faist convincingly argues that the more 'exception groups' are created (for example refugees, children from mixed marriages and fellow EU citizens) the greater the call for legitimation of these exceptions. Not only will it become harder to justify the exceptions, the State will also be put under greater pressure by groups who claim equal treatment; this in turn will most likely lead to a further tolerance (and possibly the embrace) of dual nationality.

the domestic approach to dual nationality. In the country reports we can test whether our analysis that dual nationality is increasingly accepted and sometimes even embraced is correct for the four countries under consideration, or whether this analysis is perhaps an oversimplification. In discussing the position on dual nationality in France, Italy, the Netherlands and Spain, the country reports also pay due regard to the historical background, especially the effects of decolonization and large scale migration. Historical events often had a decisive bearing on the attitude towards dual nationality, but it will also be shown that the dominant attitude towards dual nationality in each of the countries has not been uncontested.

The country reports also provide further illustration of some of the fields (identified *supra* in Section 9) where dual nationality may possibly raise legal difficulties.[446] We discussed, for example, problems related to military obligations, diplomatic protection, voting rights, and the exercise of public office, and we have tried to show that these problems can be overcome. Despite these difficulties, the best approach is therefore, in our judgment, for States to accept dual nationality as a factual reality and to cooperate in solving the relatively minor problems that may ensue from it.

The first chapter has also clearly shown that dual nationality is an inevitable phenomenon due to the wide discretion of the State in matters of nationality. The international conventions which addressed the subject of dual nationality (the 1930 Hague Convention and the 1963 Convention in particular) failed in their half-hearted attempts to put a stop to it. States have always been more interested in adopting a nationality policy that suited their interests than in coordinating their nationality laws (and thus giving up part of their autonomy) to prevent dual nationality. Some authors have therefore argued that the increasing toleration of dual nationality on the international plane, as well as the growing awareness that dual nationality is a legal inevitability, have now made the phenomenon a 'normal' reflection of State practice.[447]

The great number of recent denunciations of the 1963 Convention marks, at least for Europe, a trend towards a growing acceptance of dual nationality. The introduction of European citizenship almost twenty years ago by the Maastricht Treaty may have had a decisive influence on this development: holding *a* Member State nationality has become more important than possessing a *particular* Member State nationality. The European citizenship attached to the possession of a Member State nationality means that the status of European citizen of someone with two or more Member State nationalities is

[446] See Chapter 1, Section 9.

[447] See *supra* Section 10.

simply 'grounded on more than one pillar'. From this perspective, the introduction of European citizenship has made dual nationality in the EU a rather non-controversial subject. On the other hand, we shall see in Chapter 2 that the approach of the ECJ in respect of dual nationality has resulted in some controversial judgments; it may even be argued that the combination of EU citizenship and the Court's approach to dual nationality has had serious consequences for the role of nationality in the Member States. Thus, despite the fact the Member States have retained their autonomy in deciding on the acquisition and loss of their nationality, Chapter 2 will show that the Court's approach to dual nationality and EU citizenship (in particular in *García Avello* and *Hadadi*) entails that Member States can no longer simply disregard other nationalities held by their nationals. This case law seriously impinges on the traditional practice that States may ignore other nationalities and give automatic preference to their own.

Let us for now assume, however, that it has become less controversial that a growing number of European citizens hold more than one Member State nationality; this is the logical result of the European integration process. What is more, the rights attached to European citizenship are the same for every European citizen regardless of the number of Member State nationalities one may possess. Yet opposition to dual nationality still exists especially when *non-European* immigrants are concerned. This view comes particularly to the fore in the context of non-European migration from countries with a strongly different culture (see also, in relation to questions of private international law, Chapter 2). It is particularly in this context that the idea of nationality as the reflection of national identity and as the expression of an undivided bond of allegiance with a State still has its adherents.

Another matter concerns the effects of some Member States' tolerant approach towards dual nationality for the access to European citizenship. This tolerant attitude is often combined with a regime of privileged access to nationality for certain categories of persons who live outside the EU. This policy creates large numbers of so-called external EU citizens resident in third countries. This important issue, which raises the question whether Member States should be completely free to adopt the nationality policy they like in a Union where European citizenship is dependent on the possession of a Member State nationality, will be addressed in much more detail in the General Conclusions at the end of Part II of this study. First, however, we need to explore the role of dual nationality in PIL and EU law.

Chapter 2

The Role of Dual Nationality in Private International Law and EU Law: The Intra-EU Context

1. *Introduction*

In this chapter we continue our discussion on the place of nationality—and more particularly dual nationality—in Private International Law (PIL) and EU law. Whereas the country reports in the subsequent chapters describe the domestic attitude towards dual nationality, and thus by definition raise the question of its (un)desirability in the relation between an individual and a State, the domain of PIL is not predominantly interested in this question. Rather, the issue in this field of the law with respect to dual nationality is to find a concrete solution to a conflict of nationalities, which can arise when nationality is used as a connecting factor. Traditionally, PIL either employs nationality or habitual residence/domicile as a connecting factor, i.e. as a criterion to decide which legal system should govern a private law relationship connected to more than one country.[1]

We will therefore start by examining the use of these connecting factors in PIL, thereby specifically focusing on the field of personal status and family law. This follows from the fact that nationality is still the dominant connecting factor in this area of law.[2] This chapter will also pay much attention to the law on surnames. Although the link with nationality may not be evident at first sight, some authors have rightly pointed to the close relationship between the laws on nationality and surnames in that they both constitute elements of one's personal status.[3]

---

1 Michael Bogdan, *Concise Introduction to EU Private International Law* (Groningen: Europa Law Publishing, 2006), 3–4.

2 Verwilghen, "Conflits de nationalités, plurinationalité et apatridie", 103.

3 Terré, "Réflexions sur la notion de nationalité": 210–212. In discussing the question whether the discipline of nationality law belongs primarily to public or private law, Terré remarks: 'Qui tend à éloigner la nationalité de la pente publiciste entend surtout marquer que le *status civitatis* doit être rapproché du *status familiae* et que la nationalité, comme le nom ou le domicile, est un des éléments de l'état de la personne'. As further evidence of the link between

In addition, the present chapter engages in a discussion on the place of PIL in the European Union, taking especially the ECJ judgment in *García Avello*[4] as a point of departure. The *Micheletti* case[5] will also be included in this discussion, for in a lot of respects it bears similarity to the former case. One of these similarities concerns the fact that both judgments intrude on domains which are still within the discretion of the Member States: nationality in *Micheletti*, personal status in *García Avello*. Another resemblance is that they both deal with national PIL rules, thereby prompting us to inquire into PIL in an EU context. The examination of these two cases, as well as a number of related judgments which do not address questions of dual nationality, will hopefully have the effect of illustrating the uneasy coexistence between PIL and EU law. This uneasiness is reflected in both cases in that the Court's interpretation of Community law flouts national PIL principles, specifically the principle of effective nationality. Other cases on dual nationality which are perhaps less known (or very recent) but still very interesting for our discussion are *Gullung*,[6] *Saldanha*,[7] *Gilly*,[8] *Mesbah*[9] and—most importantly—*Hadadi*.[10]

2. *Connecting Factors in Private International Law: Nationality Versus Domicile/Habitual Residence*

There have traditionally been two camps in the field of personal status and family law, one being in favour of domicile as a connecting factor, the other advocating nationality.[11] The preference for domicile is predominantly to be found in the Anglo-Saxon world,[12] whereas nationality is preferred in

nationality and surname he also points to the similarity between 'le principe de l'immutabilité du nom' and the concept of perpetual allegiance as used in nationality law.

4 Case C-148/02 *García Avello* [2003] ECR I-11613.

5 Case C-369/90 *Micheletti* [1992] ECR I-04239. See also Chapter 1, Section 11.2 as well as *infra* Chapter 6, Section 9.

6 Case C-292/86 *Gullung* [1988] ECR I-00111.

7 Case C-122/96 *Saldanha and MTS* [1997] ECR I-05325.

8 Case C-336/96 *Gilly* [1998] ECR I-02793.

9 Case C-179/98 *Mesbah* [1999] ECR I-07955.

10 Case C-168/08 *Hadadi* [2009] ECR I-06871.

11 Louis Isaac de Winter, "Nationality or Domicile", in *Recueil des cours de l'Académie de droit international de la Haye* (Leiden: Sijthoff, 1969). See more recently Hélène Gaudemet-Tallon, "Nationalité, status personnel et droits de l'homme", in *Festschrift für Erik Jayme, Band 1*, ed. Heinz-Peter Mansel, *et al.* (München: Sellier, 2004), 204–207.

12 David McClean and Kisch Beevers, *Morris: The Conflict of Laws* (London: Sweet & Maxwell, 2009), 29.

continental Western Europe.[13] The Netherlands, for example, traditionally adheres to nationality as a connecting factor in this area of law.[14]

We can point to several factors that have made nationality an important connecting factor in matters relating to personal status, such as personal identity or marital status. This concerns first of all the stability of nationality as compared to habitual residence (it is habitual residence rather than domicile that is the counterpart of nationality as a connecting factor). The element of stability, in turn, is closely linked to legal certainty and predictability. Use of nationality instead of habitual residence is also considered to be more appropriate as it takes into account a person's cultural identity, thereby paying due respect to fundamental human rights.[15]

A trend can be noticed however, both in the Netherlands and elsewhere, that habitual residence is assuming a more important role at the expense of nationality.[16] Strikwerda (writing in a Dutch context which does not seem

---

[13] It should be noted that the Anglo-Saxon use of domicile is in fact comparable to the continental use of nationality because it refers to 'the domicile of origin'. Foreigners living in England were regarded as having retained domile in their home country; the Anglo-saxon understanding of domicile was thus similar to the concept of nationality on the continent. See Paul Lagarde, "La nationalité et droit international privé", *Annales de Droit de Louvain* 63, no. 3 (2003): 208.

[14] Verwilghen, "Conflits de nationalités, plurinationalité et apatridie", 107; Luc Strikwerda, *Inleiding tot het Nederlandse internationaal privaatrecht* 9th ed. (Deventer: Kluwer, 2008), 72.

[15] Gaudemet-Tallon, "Nationalité, status personnel et droits de l'homme", 210. Erik Jayme writes in this connection that 'en ce qui concerne le statut personnel, l'idée de l'identité culturelle a renforcé le principe de la nationalité dans le sens que ce principe est considéré comme plus apte à tenir compte du lien culturel d'une personne avec un certain droit qu'un rattachement local. Si toutes les parties possèdent la même nationalité, l'application de leur loi nationale semble plus appropriée pour la sauvegarde de leur identité culturelle'. Erik Jayme, "Cours général de droit international privé", in *Recueil des cours de l'Académie de droit international de la Haye* (Leiden: Sijthoff, 1995), 253.

Jayme's observations go back to Mancini who, while clearly distinguishing between the nation (consisting in his own words of 'la Regione, la Razza, la Lingua, le Costumanze, la Storia, le Leggi, Le Religioni …') and the State, recognized that for the purposes of private international law nation and State had to correspond. Thus according to Jayme (quoting Mancini): 'Im internationalen Privatrecht blieb nichts anderes übrig, als die "nazionalità" stets durch die Staatsangehörigkeit zu bestimmen: "Certamente al dí d'oggi, dicendo *nazione*, dobbiamo intendere per nazione un aggregato di persone formate a *Stato*"'. Erik Jayme, *Pasquale Stanislao Mancini. Internationales Privatrecht zwischen Risorgimento und praktischer Jurisprudenz* (Ebelsbach: Verlag Rolf Gremer, 1980), 27. That said, Mancini acknowledged that the law of the country of residence could—in a subsidiary way—be applied to (in his view anomalous) cases of dual nationality. See G.C. Buzzati, "Questioni sulla cittadinanza degli italiani emigrati in America", *Rivista di diritto civile* 1 (1909): 473.

[16] Verwilghen, "Conflits de nationalités, plurinationalité et apatridie", 104.

very different from other countries) gives four reasons for this trend.[17] First, legal doctrine became more supportive of the principle of habitual residence. This influenced legal practice insofar as it led to the practice of choosing habitual residence whenever there was a problem with nationality as a connecting factor. Second, developments in respect of the position of the married woman rendered the use of nationality as a connecting factor more difficult. As women obtained an autonomous position in nationality law, the number of marriages consisting of spouses with different nationalities increased. This made nationality as a connecting factor more problematic and led to the use of habitual residence instead. Not only did a woman no longer automatically lose her original nationality upon marrying a foreigner after gender equality was secured in nationality law, she could also transmit this nationality to her children. This raised the number of children with a multiple nationality, and the phenomenon of multiple nationality is the third factor which made nationality a less suitable connecting factor. Finally, several modern Hague treaties—in contrast to the older ones—now prefer habitual residence over nationality.[18]

Despite these different factors, which all seem to favour habitual residence over nationality, the latter has not has not disappeared as a connecting factor.[19] Rather, the two connecting factors are no longer irreconcilable opposites but can be said to fulfil an equal and complementary role in the area of personal status and family law.[20]

Nationality as a connecting factor is not an autonomous notion of conflicts law, but is derivative from national law. This means that the nationality law of the country of which one claims to have the nationality—and not conflicts law itself—will decide whether one indeed possesses that nationality.[21] The situation is different for habitual residence, however. In international treaties at least, conflicts law has autonomously interpreted this term without relying on the meaning of the term in domestic law. To emphasize this autonomy,

---

[17] Strikwerda, *Inleiding tot het Nederlandse internationaal privaatrecht*, 72–73.

[18] August L.G.A. Stille, "Abweichung von der Staatsangehörigkeitsanknüpfung bei ineffektiver Staatsangehörigkeit von Monostaatern—Die aktuelle Entwicklung in den Niederlanden", in *Nation und Staat im Internationalen Privatrecht. Zum kollisionsrechtlichen Staatsangehörigkeitsprinzip in verfassungsrechtlicher und international-privatrechtlicher Sicht*, ed. Erik Jayme and Heinz-Peter Mansel (Heidelberg: C.F. Müller Juristischer Verlag, 1990), 229–230.

[19] Castangia, *Il criterio della cittadinanza nel diritto internazionale privato*, 117.

[20] Strikwerda, *Inleiding tot het Nederlandse internationaal privaatrecht*, 73.

[21] Ibid., 80; Sandrine Clavel, *Droit international privé* (Paris: Dalloz, 2009), 293.

conflicts law has developed its own terminology, which is reflected in the term 'habitual residence' instead of 'residence' or 'domicile'.[22]

Reliance on nationality as a connecting factor can give rise to certain problems. When a person is stateless, for example, nationality can obviously not be used for the purpose of connecting a person to a particular legal system. The reverse problem seems to arise in respect of multiple nationals, yet two options can provide a solution to this problem. We have seen that the first option is to let go of nationality and choose for habitual residence instead.[23] The second option, used in the Netherlands, is to search for the most effective nationality among the nationalities a person possesses.[24] Interestingly, when it comes to the *surname* of a multiple national, the principle of the effective nationality is abandoned in the Netherlands: the Dutch nationality of a Dutch multiple national will for the determination of his surname always be decisive. In Section 7 we will see how this rule is affected by the ECJ's ruling in *García Avello*.

Yet another issue concerns the question whether one's nationality should also be used as a connecting factor when there is no longer a bond between the individual and the country of which he/she holds the nationality. In the Netherlands this question was answered in the negative in a judgment by the Dutch Supreme Court.[25] The judgment introduced a 'reality test' (*realiteitstoets*) which had two important effects. In the first place, it further emphasizes the current trend towards nationality and habitual residence being of a complementary rather than a contrastive nature. Second, it shows that nationality is in some situations becoming an autonomous notion in conflicts law. In other words, one can claim to possess a nationality, and this claim can remain

---

22 Strikwerda, *Inleiding tot het Nederlandse internationaal privaatrecht*, 87.

23 Castangia, *Il criterio della cittadinanza nel diritto internazionale privato*, 118.

24 A.G.J.J. Haandrikman, "De nationaliteit in het internationaal privaatrecht", in *Nationaliteit in Volkenrecht en Internationaal Privaatrecht, Preadvies voor de Nederlandse Vereniging voor Internationaal Recht* (Deventer: Kluwer, 1981), 49. Note, however, that the nationality of the country where one also has residence has an excellent chance of being regarded the effective one. Application of either connecting factor will thus often lead to the same result.

25 Stille, "Abweichung von der Staatsangehörigkeitsanknüpfung bei ineffektiver Staatsangehörigkeit von Monostaatern", 227–228. The Dutch Supreme Court, the Hoge Raad, ruled in a divorce case of 1979 that the Portuguese nationality of two Portuguese spouses who had been living in the Netherlands for a long time was not strong enough to apply Portuguese law to the case. Though nationality was thus the initial connecting factor, the Portuguese nationality was insufficiently strong to justify its use and the Court opted for habitual residence instead.

uncontested, but the nationality can be considered too weak in practice for the purpose of using it as a connecting factor.[26]

3. *Solutions to a 'Conflict of Nationalities' in France, Italy, the Netherlands and Spain*

We saw in Chapter 1 (Section 3) that the practice adhered to by most States when confronted with dual nationals, who among other nationalities, also possess the nationality of the forum is to take into consideration only this latter nationality.[27] This section starts by looking at the criticism by part of the French doctrine to this automatic application of the nationality of the forum, and will subsequently continue with an overview of the legal practice in the three remaining countries. In this context, the question is often raised whether the increasing number of dual nationals has caused (or should cause) a change in the approach towards a conflict of nationalities in the field of PIL.

France: From an 'Autonomous' to a 'Functional' Approach in a Conflict of Nationalities?

The traditional and still prevailing French approach when two nationalities are 'en conflit' is twofold. In case of two or more foreign nationalities, the French judge looks for the most effective nationality; if one of the nationalities is the French one, however, preference is always given to this nationality.[28] Yet the automatic preference for the French nationality has not been unanimously embraced by the legal doctrine. Some authors have contrasted the traditional 'autonomous' approach with a 'functional and relative' approach, which they argue is better suited in an age in which instances of dual nationality arise more frequently than in the past.

Lagarde, who triggered this debate, defines the autonomous approach as one which tries to find a principled solution that is valid for any situation that

---

[26] Strikwerda, *Inleiding tot het Nederlandse internationaal privaatrecht*, 80.

[27] Verwilghen, "Conflits de nationalités, plurinationalité et apatridie", 429.

[28] de Geouffre de La Pradelle, "Nationalité française, extranéité, nationalités étrangères", 143, 151. De La Pradelle argues for the abolishment of the criterion of the effective nationality in a conflict between two or more foreign nationalities, for in a way it reduces one of the nationalities to a state of 'artificiality' while in practice 'un conflit de nationalités peut … exprimer exactement un conflit très réel d'effectivités … Dans ces conditions, le principe qui fait prévaloir la nationalité la plus effective, est caduc'. He therefore supports the functional approach as described in this section.

may arise. This results in a systematic (or 'mechanical'[29]) application of the nationality of the forum. The functional approach, however, seeks for a solution which is in harmony with the questions raised by the case (this may concern, for example, the enjoyment of rights or questions of jurisdiction and applicable law).[30] In other words, the functional method 'consists of putting forward not questions of nationality as such, but rather the issues that led to legal disputes over it'.[31] This may lead to a preference for another nationality than the nationality of the forum.

In suggesting this approach, Lagarde was inspired by a judgment by the French Cour de Cassation[32] in which a very open-minded solution was adopted to a case concerning French-Polish dual nationals. Faced with a French-Polish Convention the Cour de Cassation, instead of ignoring the Polish nationality as allowed under the traditional approach, referred to the spirit (*l'esprit*) of the Convention as the main criterion for the choice for either the French or the Polish nationality.[33] It recognized that the Polish court, by relying on the own (Polish) nationality, had acted as a French court would have acted had it been addressed first, and that only a 'contrôle atténué' of the foreign judgment should be exercised when deciding on the recognition of this judgment in France.[34]

---

[29] Verwilghen, "Conflits de nationalités, plurinationalité et apatridie", 446.

[30] Under the traditional approach however, 'la ou les solutions de principe retenues doivent rester indépendantes de la question de droit, extérieure au conflit de nationalités et qui en est l'enjeu'. Paul Lagarde, "Vers une approche fonctionnelle du conflit positif de nationalités", *Revue critique de droit international privé* 77, no. 1 (1988): 30–32. See for a more recent discussion of the functional approach (in connection with the ECJ judgment *Grunkin-Paul*) Paul Lagarde, "La reconnaissance mode d'emploi", in *Vers de nouveaux équilibres entre ordres juridiques: liber amicorum Hélène Gaudemet-Tallon* (Paris: Dalloz, 2008), 491.

[31] de Geouffre de La Pradelle, "Dual Nationality and the French Citizenship Tradition", 208. De La Pradelle adds: 'Under the usual method, French courts address nationality as if it were the fundamental issue in a pending case. This is appropriate when the courts are to decide if an individual is French … in other words, when French nationality itself is the issue at stake. As a method for overcoming nationality conflicts, it is entirely inappropriate'.

[32] Case *Dujaque* of 22 July 1987. See for the facts of the case Lagarde, "Vers une approche fonctionnelle du conflit positif de nationalités": 41 ff.

[33] In the search for the spirit of a Convention, 'le juge ne fait donc prévaloir systématiquement, ni la nationalité du for, ni celle qui paraît être la plus effective: il se détermine en raison de la nature des questions principales dont on l'a saisi et de celle des dispositions susceptibles de leur être appliquées'. See de Geouffre de La Pradelle, "Nationalité française, extranéité, nationalités étrangères", 150.

[34] Lagarde therefore concluded that 'la solution donnée à ce conflit n'est plus dictée par un principe general abstrait. Elle se réfère à la function que remplit la nationalité dans l'hypothèse considerée'. Lagarde, "Vers une approche fonctionnelle du conflit positif de nationalités": 41–43.

This judgment is applauded by the adherents of the functional approach for its solution to two 'situations de blocage'.[35] The first blocage concerned international treaties which were not operative (and were thus in a way paralyzed) in cases featuring dual nationality. The second problem related to the non-recognition by France of a foreign judgment concerning the personal status of French dual nationals (and vice versa in the State of which these dual nationals also possessed the nationality).[36]

In proposing the functional approach, Lagarde fundamentally questions the 'mechanical' preference for the nationality of the forum and argues that States should not be able to 'jouer sur deux tableaux à la fois'.[37] De La Pradelle articulates this idea as follows:

> A definite contradiction thus affects the way in which France has followed the general shift towards a growing tolerance of the fact of dual citizenship. It is hardly logical to adopt, through the legislature, rules of attribution that increasingly expand multiple belonging, while simultaneously refusing, through the courts, to sanction the majority of concrete manifestations of these belongings.[38]

However, subsequent case law did not continue the more liberal, open-minded approach but persisted in keeping the preference for the French nationality of those who were also in possession of another nationality. One other case is worth mentioning, though.[39] In 1990 the Tribunal de grande instance in Paris gave a judgment in a case concerning a naturalized couple of Moroccan origin (the spouses had retained their Moroccan nationality upon naturalization). Three years after their naturalization as French nationals the husband, in accordance with Moroccan law, repudiated his wife in Morocco. As the wife had agreed to this on condition that certain arrangements were made, the repudiation was not contrary to the French *ordre public*; the exequatur[40] of this decision as asked for by the husband was thus granted by the French court, which in so deciding did not take into consideration the fact that the couple also possessed French nationality. The outcome of this case, as well as the plea

---

35 Lagarde, "Le principe de proximité dans le droit international privé contemporain. Cours général de droit international privé", 83 ff.

36 Lagarde, "Vers une approche fonctionnelle du conflit positif de nationalités": 35.

37 Verwilghen, "Conflits de nationalités, plurinationalité et apatridie", 446.

38 de Geouffre de La Pradelle, "Dual Nationality and the French Citizenship Tradition", 196.

39 Yves Lequette, "Le droit international privé de la famille à l'épreuve des conventions internationales", in *Recueil des cours de l'Académie de droit international de la Haye* (Leiden: Sijthoff, 1994), 126 ff; Michel Verwilghen, "Conflits de nationalités, plurinationalité et apatridie", ibid. (1999), 447.

40 Exequatur is the permission by the judge to proceed to the execution of a foreign judgment.

for the functional approach by part of the doctrine, subsequently became the subject of severe criticism.[41]

Lequette, a strong opponent of the functional approach, points to two dangers: the functional approach violates the principle of legal certainty (by deciding on a case by case basis, 'la matière devient casuistique pure') and it disregards the role of nationality in the preservation of national identity.[42] Those who plead for a non-automatic application of the nationality of the forum are criticized for ignoring the merits of the traditional practice. In short, they are accused of ignoring the role of nationality for a country's national and social cohesion.[43] Verwilghen, who is generally sympathetic to the functional approach, thinks that the principal problem rests in its difficult applicability—the approach provides a complex answer to cases which are by definition already complex themselves. As these complex cases in fact call for a more simple approach, the functional approach mainly serves a goal in resolving 'situations de blocage'.[44]

In our view, an effectivity test is to be preferred not only over the automatic application of the nationality of the forum but also over the functional approach. Compared to the automatic preference for the *lex fori*, an effectivity

---

41 Audit rejects the functional approach, since it undermines the stability of nationality as 'une notion essentielle à la cohésion de l'ordre social'. In this context, he expresses his criticism of the 1990 judgment as follows: 'En effet, ce que l'on peut estimer inacceptable dans une décision de ce type est avant tout que des personnes ayant solicité et obtenu depuis peu une nouvelle nationalité non seulement continuent de recourir à leur statut d'origine mais demandent au surplus à l'État de leur nouvelle nationalité d'en reconnaître les effets, montrant le véritable cas qu'elles font de leur nouvelle nationalité. Bernard Audit, "Le droit international privé a fin du XXe siècle: progrès ou recul", *Revue internationale de droit comparé* 50, no. 2 (1998): 444.

42 Lequette, "Le droit international privé de la famille à l'épreuve des conventions internationales", 126ff. See also Louis d'Avout, "Jurisprudence: Hadadi", *Journal du Droit International* 137, no. 1 (2010): 178.

43 Lequette, "Le droit international privé de la famille à l'épreuve des conventions internationales", 129, 131. Lequette seriously doubts whether it is 'de bonne méthode de transformer cette donnée essentielle en un "concept caméléon" qui serait dans l'entière dépendance des règles de droit international privé' and he argues that 'les impératifs de préservation de l'identité nationale et de cohésion de la société nationale qu'a en charge le droit de la nationalité sont, en effet, sauvegardés par l'érection de la règle de la primauté de la nationalité du for au rang de principe'.

44 Michel Verwilghen, "Conflits de nationalités, plurinationalité et apatridie", ibid. (1999), 449–450. He rightly points out that the debate goes beyond a mere legal dispute: 'Ne faut-il pas voir qu'au delà de la controverse juridique ... il y a une perception différente de la vie en société contemporaine: d'une part, une approche que l'on pourrait qualifier d'internationaliste et d'ouverte; de l'autre, une conception nationaliste, car axée sur le primat de l'identité nationale à protéger, et donc l'exclusion d'"ingérences" étrangères?'.

test provides for more continuity as regards a dual national's personal status. As long as nationality is used as a connecting factor on the basis of its presumed stability, the application of the effective nationality best guarantees this stability: a dual national will generally have one quite stable effective nationality. The effectivity test also offers more stability than the functional approach. In deciding a conflict of nationalities, the latter method looks—on a case by case basis—at the function of nationality in a particular legal relationship. Consequently, the functional approach does not systematically apply either the nationality of the forum or the most effective nationality, but searches in a rather abstract way for the best solution in a given case.[45] Despite the merits of the functional approach under certain circumstances, it is in our opinion not suitable as a general approach to the conflict of nationalities.

Italy

In 1995 a reform of Italian private international law took place which also had an effect on the use of nationality as a connecting factor.[46] Article 19(2) of the current law prescribes the application of the effective nationality in a conflict between two foreign nationalities; if one of the nationalities is Italian, however, that will prevail over the non-Italian nationality.[47] This latter solution had also been in place before the modification of 1995, but the approach in a conflict between two foreign nationalities was different under the previous regime. As the previous law (of 1942) had been silent on the question of dual nationality, Italian courts developed the principle that preference was given to the nationality of the State whose criteria for the attribution of its nationality were similar to the criteria used by Italy. In practice this appears to have meant that the foreign State where *ius sanguinis* was preferred over *ius soli* (as is the case in Italy) would prevail in a conflict between different foreign nationalities.[48]

---

45 Johan Meeusen, "Bipatridie in internationaal en Europees verband", in *Met rede ontleend, de rede ontkleed. Opstellen aangeboden aan Fons Heyvaert* (Gent: Mys & Breesch, uitgevers, 2002), 232–234.

46 See Article 19 (on stateless persons, refugies and persons with a multiple nationality) of Law nr. 218 of 31 May 1995. Article 19 reads as follows: (1)'Nei casi in cui le disposizioni della presente legge richiamano la legge nazionale di una persona, se questa è apolide o rifugiata si applica la legge dello Stato del domicilio, o in mancanza, la legge dello Stato di residenza; (2) Se la persona ha più cittadinanze, si applica la legge di quello tra gli Stati di appartenenza con il quale essa ha il collegamento più stretto. Se tra le cittadinanze vi è quella italiana, questa prevale'.

47 Paolo Picone, *La riforma italiana del diritto internazionale privato* (Padova: Cedam, 1998), 270.

48 Castangia, *Il criterio della cittadinanza nel diritto internazionale privato*, 87, 121; Stefania Bariatti, "Italie", in *Nationalité et statut personnel. Leur interaction dans les traités*

At present, neither Italy nor (to our knowledge) any other State applies this rule, perhaps by reason of its nationalist connotation and 'singular arbitrariness'.[49]

The Netherlands

Dutch courts will not automatically apply the Dutch nationality in a conflict between a Dutch and a foreign nationality (an exception exists, as has already been seen, in the domain of surnames, where the Dutch nationality of a dual national is always given preference). Instead, a Dutch court will search for a dual national's effective nationality, including in a conflict between the Dutch and a foreign nationality.[50] Thus, of the four countries under discussion the Netherlands is the only country in which a stronger foreign nationality can, at the expense of the nationality of the forum, be decisive for the choice which law to apply to a given case.[51] The habitual residence and the degree of integration in the Netherlands are the most important criteria in determining the effective nationality.[52] For a short time Germany also applied the criterion of the effective nationality to Germans with a dual nationality, but this approach—introduced by the highest German courts in 1979[53]—was subsequently overturned by a reform of German private international law in 1986

internationaux et dans les législations nationales, ed. Michel Verwilghen (Bruxelles: Bruylant, 1984), 139; Fausto Pocar and Costanza Honorati, *Il nuovo diritto internazionale privato italiano* 2nd ed. (Milano: Giuffrè, 2002), 48–49. See generally on this approach of giving preference to the nationality of a State with similar criteria for the attribution of nationality Verwilghen, "Conflits de nationalités, plurinationalité et apatridie", 433–434.

49 Verwilghen, "Conflits de nationalités, plurinationalité et apatridie", 434. Or as Maury has qualified the doctrine (quoted by Verwilghen): 'On trouve l'idée, assez naïve, que la loi de l'Etat dont le tribunal dépend contient, sur la nationalité, des dispositions bonnes en elles-mêmes, supérieures *in abstracto* à toute autre'.

50 Boele-Woelki, *Die Effektivitätsprüfung der Staatsangehörigkeit im niederländischen internationalen Familienrecht*, 40.

51 This approach, which is applicable to all situations in which nationality is used as a connecting factor, is laid down in artikel 1.3 of the Conflict Law on Divorce (*Wet Conflictenrecht Echtscheiding*): 'Bezit een partij de nationaliteit van meer dan één land dan geldt als zijn nationale recht het recht van dat land waarvan hij de nationaliteit bezit, waarmede hij alle omstandigheden in aanmerking genomen de sterkste band heeft'.

52 Boele-Woelki, *Die Effektivitätsprüfung der Staatsangehörigkeit im niederländischen internationalen Familienrecht*, 42.

53 Karin Kammann, *Probleme mehrfacher Staatsangehörigkeit*, Europäische Hochschulschriften (Frankfurt am Main: Peter Lang, 1984), 52; Heinz-Peter Mansel, *Personalstatut, Staatsangehörigkeit und Effektivität*, Münchener Universitätsschriften. Reihe der Juristischen Fakultät (Band 70) (München: C.H. Beck'sche Verlagsbuchhandlung, 1988), 119.

which dictated the prevalence of the German nationality.[54] Germany currently follows the French and Italian approach.

Spain

Article 9.9 of the Spanish Civil Code (CC) decides which law should be applied to dual nationals when nationality is used as a connecting factor.[55] The Spanish legal system recognizes various forms of dual nationality[56] to which different solutions are applied when nationality is a connecting factor.

From Article 9.9 CC it follows that instances of dual nationality that are recognized under Spanish law (*situaciones de doble nacionalidad previstas en las leyes españolas*) should be distinguished from cases in which dual nationality is the result of a lack of coordination of the nationality laws of different States (*situaciones patológicas de doble nacionalidad*). Situations recognized under Spanish law are, in turn, also divided into two groups. First, the cases in which dual nationality is acquired by way of so-called dual nationality treaties; here Article 9.9 CC refers back to what these treaties provide. Second, if the treaties do not provide a solution or if the dual nationality is only unilaterally recognized by Spain, Article 9.9 CC considers as the relevant nationality for the purpose of choosing the applicable law the nationality which coincides with the last habitual residence—or in the absence of a habitual residence, the nationality that was last acquired.

54 Hans Jürgen Sonnenberger, "Anerkennung der Staatsangehörigkeit und effektive Staatsangehörigkeit natürlicher Personen im Völkerrecht und im Internationalen Privatrecht", in *Berichte der Deutschen Gesellschaft für Völkerrecht*. (Heidelberg: C.F. Müller Juristischer Verlag, 1988), 19. This law reform was generally regarded as a step backwards by the German doctrine. See Martiny, "Probleme der Doppelstaatsangehörigkeit im deutschen Internationalen Privatrecht": 1146–1147.

Article 5(1) EGBGB currently reads: 'Wird auf das Recht des Staates verwiesen, dem eine Person angehört, und gehört sie mehreren Staaten an, so ist das Recht desjenigen dieser Staaten anzuwenden, mit dem die Person am engsten verbunden ist, insbesondere durch ihren gewöhnlichen Aufenthalt oder durch den Verlauf ihres Lebens. Ist die Person auch Deutscher, so geht diese Rechtsstellung vor'.

55 Article 9.9 CC: 'A los efectos de este capítulo, respecto de las situaciones de doble nacionalidad previstas en las leyes españolas se estará a lo que determinan los tratados internacionales, y, si nada estableciesen, será preferida la nacionalidad coincidente con la última residencia habitual y, en su defecto, la última adquirida. Prevalecerá en todo caso la nacionalidad española del que ostente además otra no prevista en nuestras leyes o en los tratados internacionales. Si ostentare dos o más nacionalidades y ninguna de ellas fuera la española se estará a lo que establece el apartado siguiente'. Article 9.10 CC: 'Se considerará como ley personal de los que carecieren de nacionalidad o la tuvieren indeterminada, la ley del lugar de su residencia habitual'.

56 To be dealt with in Chapter 6.

To situations of dual nationality that are *not* recognized under Spanish law, a different approach is applied. Here the Spanish practice is to apply the *lex fori* if one of the nationalities is Spanish; if none of the nationalities are Spanish, Article 9.10 CC designates the law of the person's habitual residence as the applicable law.[57]

4. *Dual Nationals and their Surnames*

The following brief remarks on nationality as a connecting factor for the determination of one's surname[58] mainly serve as a stepping stone for a discussion of *García Avello*. Nationality is used under Dutch law as the connecting factor for the determination of a person's name. The Netherlands is party to the 1980 Treaty of Munich which entered into force in the Netherlands on 1 January 1990.[59] The Treaty refers to the conflict rules of the State of which a person possesses the nationality, yet it provides no solution to the problem of dual nationality.[60] The Dutch conflict rules in this case (*Wet Conflictenrecht Namen*) determine that Dutch law is applied to Dutch nationals; in accordance with the Treaty of Munich the conflict rules also provide that the name of a foreigner is decided in accordance with the law of the State of which he/she holds the nationality. It is important to stress that, in view of legal certainty, Dutch courts have decided that the 'reality test' (see *supra* Section 2) cannot be applied in respect of the law governing surnames. Dutch law is thus always applied to Dutch multiple nationals. Several other countries, including

57 See on the application of Article 9.9 CC Pilar Rodríguez Mateos, "La doble nacionalidad en el sistematica del derecho internacional privado", *Revista Española de Derecho Internacional* 42, no. 2 (1990): 472–477; Miguel Virgós Soriano, "Nationality and Double Nationality Principles in Spanish Private International Law System", in *Nation und Staat im Internationalen Privatrecht. Zum kollisionsrechtlichen Staatsangehörigkeitsprinzip in verfassungsrechtlicher und international-privatrechtlicher Sicht*, ed. Erik Jayme and Heinz-Peter Mansel (Heidelberg: C.F. Müller Juristischer Verlag, 1990), 251 ff; José María Espinar Vicente, *La nacionalidad y la extranjería en el sistema jurídico español* (Madrid: Civitas, 1994), 329–345; Guillermo Palao Moreno, Carlos Esplugues Mota, and Manuel De Lorenzo Segrelles, *Nacionalidad y Extranjería* 3rd ed. (Valencia: Tirant lo Blanch, 2006), 72–79; Alvarez Rodríguez, *Nacionalidad española: normativa vigente e interpretación jurisprudencial*, 141–142.

58 See generally Andrea Gattini, "Diritto al nome e scelta del nome nei casi di plurima cittadinanza", *Rivista di diritto internazionale* 79 (1996): 93–109; Mario J.A. Oyarzábal, "El nombre y la protección de la identidad. Cuestiones de Derecho Internacional Público y Privado", *Revista Prudentia Iuris* 58 (2004): 73–97.

59 Strikwerda, *Inleiding tot het Nederlandse internationaal privaatrecht*, 82.

60 Paul Lagarde, "L'oeuvre de la Commission Internationale de l'État Civil en matière de nom des personnes", in *Festschrift für Erik Jayme, Band 2*, ed. Heinz-Peter Mansel, *et al.* (München: Sellier, 2004), 1300–1301.

Belgium, adopt a similar approach.[61] This brings us to the case *García Avello*, a case with potentially far-reaching consequences. After a description of the ECJ's ruling in that case (Section 4.1) we continue with an overview of the debate aroused by this judgment (Section 4.2).

4.1. *Case C-148/02* García Avello *[2003]*

The case involved a married couple of different Member State nationalities and their two children, who possessed the nationality of both their parents. Mr García Avello, a Spanish national, and Ms Weber, a Belgian national, had married in Belgium. Their two children were later born there and held dual Belgian-Spanish nationality. In accordance with Belgian law the children had been given the name García Avello, although they were registered under the name García Weber at the Spanish consulate in Belgium. A request submitted to the Belgian authorities for a change of surname to García Weber, in order for the name to be in accordance with Spanish custom, was refused. When the couple applied for an annulment of that decision before the Conseil d'État, the latter decided to ask for a preliminary ruling by the ECJ with regard to the compatibility of the refusal with Community law.

The Court's reasoning took the following steps. It first concluded that the two children were European citizens and that European citizenship was destined to be the fundamental status of nationals of the Member States. The status of European citizen gives a right to equal treatment—subject to exceptions expressly provided for—in situations falling within the scope *ratione materiae* of the EC Treaty.

The Court went on to observe that the rules governing a person's surname are within the competence of the Member States; however, the exercise of this competence must comply with Community law. The Court emphasized that European citizenship is not intended to extend the scope *ratione materiae* to purely internal situations, but decided that a link with Community law did exist in this case: the children, nationals of one Member State, were lawfully resident in another Member State. This conclusion could not be invalidated, the Court stated, by the fact that the children also held Belgian nationality and had resided in Belgium since their birth—an argument relied on by Belgium to recognize only the children's Belgian nationality.[62] Based on this reasoning,

---

[61] Ibid., 1297.

[62] The Court refers in this respect to its decision in *Micheletti* by stating that 'it is not permissible for a Member State to restrict the effects of the grant of the nationality of another Member State by imposing an additional condition for recognition of that nationality with a view to the exercise of the fundamental freedoms provided for in the Treaty' (para. 28).

the Court held that the children could rely on Article 12 EC (now Article 18 TFEU) not to suffer discrimination on the grounds of nationality with regard to the rules governing their surname.

The next question was then whether Articles 12 and 17 EC precluded the Belgian authority from turning down the application. After stating that 'the principle of non-discrimination requires that comparable situations must not be treated differently and that different situations must not be treated in the same way'[63]—such treatment only being justified when based on 'objective considerations independent of the nationality of the persons concerned and ... proportionate to the objective being legitimately pursued', the Court addressed the question whether the García Avello children were in an identical situation to persons only holding Belgian nationality. If not, they had a right to be treated in a different manner. The Court reasoned that having different surnames under two legal systems could cause serious inconvenience at both the professional and the private level, for example concerning the legal effects of documents or diplomas. These difficulties distinguished the children from mono-Belgian nationals, yet the Court went on (in the final step in its reasoning) to consider whether the different treatment could be justified. All the arguments submitted by the Belgian State—based on social order, avoidance of confusion and the facilitation of the integration in Belgian society—were dismissed by the Court. The operative part of the judgment (*ratio decidendi*), then, was expressed as follows:

> Articles 12 and 17 must be construed as precluding ... the administrative authority of a Member State from refusing to grant an application for a change of surname made on behalf of minor children resident in that State and having dual nationality of that State and of another Member State, in the case where the purpose of that application is to enable those children to bear the surname to which they are entitled according to the law and tradition of the second Member State.[64]

---

[63] Para. 31. See for a discussion of the non-discrimination principle Giuseppa Palmeri, "Doppia cittadinanza e diritto al nome", *Europa e diritto privato* 7 (2004): 220–222.

[64] The Court's reasoning on the basis of the principle of non-discrimination has been called distorted 'because it purported to resolve a difficulty linked to the impact of cross-border mobility on individual status, whereas in fact, there was no such mobility under the facts of the case other than the dual citizenship of the children born in Belgium to a Spanish father. It did not appear unreasonable that Belgium, which was the country of citizenship and the country of domicile, sought to regulate the children's name in the same way as that of other purely Belgian children living in Belgium'. See Horatia Muir Watt, "European Federalism and the 'New Unilateralism'", *Tulane Law Review* 82 (2008): 1996–1997.

4.2. *Remarks on the (Potential) Impact of* García Avello

The considerable body of commentary on *García Avello* has interpreted this judgment from many different viewpoints—including for example cultural identity.[65] We will only focus on two elements, however. The first is the private international law dimension of the case and the impact of the decision on the national rules governing names, while the second element relates to the Court's use of the concept of European citizenship. *García Avello* fits into the category of major European citizenship cases, and further fleshes out this concept, which is gaining an increasingly high profile. Of course, we will also go into the question of the interaction between PIL and EU law. Just like *Micheletti*, this case is also crucial to assess the impact of multiple nationality in the Community framework. However, the case may not only influence the position of multiple nationals in the EU, but has the potential to bring about much more far-reaching consequences. What follows is an outline of the debate in the literature on the (possible) consequences of *García Avello*. The *Micheletti* judgment will also frequently be referred to, for it has a certain amount in common with *García Avello*.[66]

De Groot and Rutten have written on the PIL consequences of the case and conclude that the judgment in *García Avello* implies that parents of a child who possesses the nationality of more than one Member State of the EU should be given the possibility to make a choice as to the law applicable to the determination of the child's surname.[67] They also point out that the case could have consequences for other family issues as well. If a choice of law is allowed

---

[65] Horvath thinks that the judgment presents 'a boost for individual cultural identity, albeit on the basis of bureaucracy [i.e. the potential inconvenience on the professional and personal level of bearing different surnames in the EU], not respect for that identity, as such'. Psychogiopoulou argues that 'the Court's acknowledgment that strict respect for the principle of non-discrimination should not run counter to the right to one's name sent a clear message to the Member States that protection of the cultural identity of EU citizens could require specific measures on their part'. See Evangelia Psychogiopoulou, *The integration of cultural considerations in EU law and policies*, Dissertation European University Institute (Florence: EUI, 2006), 150; Enikö Horváth, *Mandating identity: citizenship, kinship laws and plural nationality in the European Union*, ibid. (Alphen aan den Rijn: Kluwer Law International, 2007), 117.

[66] For a discussion on the possible consequences of *Micheletti* on PIL see Javier Carrascosa González, "Dual nationality and Community law", *Tolleys Immigration and Nationality Law and Practice* 8 (1994): 11. In 1994 he already hinted at the possibility that the reasoning in *Micheletti* might once be applied to dual nationals in the context of civil status.

[67] Gerard-René de Groot and Susan Rutten, "Op weg naar een Europees IPR op het gebied van het personen—en familierecht", *Tijdschrift Nederlands Internationaal Privaatrecht* 22, no. 3 (2004): 275.

as to the determination of a surname on a birth certificate, then the situation should not be any different as to the consequences for the surname of the child after a parental recognition or the establishment of paternity. The judgment might also have an impact on the surname of (ex-)spouses upon the conclusion or dissolution of a marriage.[68]

The consequences of *García Avello* do not stop there, however. In De Groot's view the case not only affects the national conflict rules on names, but also the rules on recognition of decisions made in other Member States with respect to surnames. Had the children been born in Spain and had they been given a name in accordance with Spanish law, then Belgium could not have refused registration of that name, despite their holding Belgian nationality. He sees this conclusion supported by the importance which the principle of mutual recognition has gained in recent years.[69] Helms takes this argument further, arguing that the Court's reasoning cannot remain limited to multiple nationals. What would the Court have decided, for example, had the children possessed only Spanish nationality, but been born in Belgium and given a name in

[68] Gerard-René de Groot, "Towards European Conflict Rules in Matters of Personal Status", *Maastricht Journal of European and Comparative Law* 11, no. 2 (2004): 118. De Groot also mentions that an international convention which deals with the surname of (ex)-spouses, the final text of which was accepted in September 2003 after the preparatory work of the International Commission on Civil Status, is incompatible with *García Avello*. As the Convention is more restrictive than the judgment in *García Avello*—it does not give a choice of law possibility, but focuses on effective nationality and habitual residence—the Dutch government has not signed this convention. See on this convention Lagarde, "L'oeuvre de la Commission Internationale de l'État Civil en matière de nom des personnes", 1300–1305; Sergio Marchisio, "Les conventions de la commission international de l'état civil", in *Nuovi strumenti del diritto internazionale privato. Liber Fausto Pocar*, ed. Gabriella Venturini and Stefania Bariatti (Milano: Giuffrè Editore, 2009), 659–672.

In Lagarde's view, the Court overstepped the boundaries of its competence by deciding to give a choice of law to the parents. He clearly prefers a solution that is less intrusive on the national rules governing names and points in this respect to two conventions elaborated by the abovementioned International Commission on Civil Status (Lagarde's position comes as no surprise as he was the Secretary-General of this Commission (*La Commission Internationale de l'État Civil (CIEC)*) at the time these conventions were drafted). We may say that both conventions fill the gap left by the 1980 Munich Treaty in respect of multiple nationality. The first convention offers the possibility to ask for a certificate on distinct surnames, which is particularly convenient for multiple nationals. Had the convention been in force between Belgium and Spain, the result would have been that the García Avello children could prove that their name García Avello under Belgian law corresponded with their name García Weber under Spanish law. The second convention—the one also referred to by De Groot—does not provide for a choice of law, but for a system of mutual recognition. Its effect in the present case would have been that Spain was under an obligation to recognize the name given in Belgium—the country where the children are habitually resident and of which they hold the nationality.

[69] de Groot, "Towards European Conflict Rules in Matters of Personal Status": 118.

accordance with Belgium law based on their having residence there (this situation later arose in *Grunkin-Paul*, see *infra* Section 5.3)? Helms did not see a real difference between this situation and the one that actually arose in *García Avello*. He thus concluded that under those circumstances the Court could not decide any differently than it had done in *García Avello*.[70]

Finally, it is certainly not impossible that the Court's reasoning will be applied in the future when cases arise that deal with conflict and recognition rules in other matters of personal status, such as affiliation, adoption, transsexuality, marriage and divorce.[71] Ackermann echoes this view when saying that the judgment is 'based on the principle that irrespective of its private international law, a Member State has to recognize the personal status conferred upon a Union citizen by another Member State'.[72] He immediately remarks that it remains to be seen whether a combined reading of Articles 12, 17 and 18 EC Treaty will be applied to these situations as well, but the potential consequences of *García Avello* on PIL in the EU cannot be denied.

It is a matter of debate how exactly the judgment should be interpreted. Did the Court impose on Belgium an obligation to 'recognize' the Spanish surname or did it provide for a choice of applicable law?[73] The first interpretation is difficult to maintain for the following reason: if Belgium is required to recognize a name that is in accordance with the Spanish tradition, then Spain is under an obligation to recognize a name that was formed under Belgian law.[74] But why did the Court hold then that the children were allowed to a surname in accordance with Spanish tradition despite their living in Belgium and holding the nationality of that country? Does a Spanish name not violate

70 Tobias Helms, "Europarechtliche Vorgaben zur Bestimmung des Namensstatuts von Doppelstaatern: Anmerkung zu EuGH, Urteil vom 2.10.2003, C-148/02—*García Avello*", *Zeitschrift für Gemeinschaftsprivatrecht* 1 (2005): 38. Interestingly, this conclusion had already been drawn by a Dutch Court of First Instance before the case *García Avello* was brought before the ECJ. This Dutch court decided in June 2003 that two Spanish nationals who were born in the Netherlands, were there resident, and had also married there, should be given the possibility of a choice of law for their child born in the Netherlands. This judgment was later confirmed by the Court of Appeal, thereby expressly relying on the *García Avello* ruling which had been given in the meantime. See de Groot and Rutten, "Op weg naar een Europees IPR op het gebied van het personen—en familierecht": 275.

71 de Groot, "Towards European Conflict Rules in Matters of Personal Status": 119.

72 Thomas Ackermann, "Annotation Case C-148/02 *García Avello* [2003]", *Common Market Law Review* 44 (2007): 142.

73 Ibid., 152. Recognition in this context means 'a shorthand formula for the Community law obligation of a Member State not unjustifiably to deny a person a right or legal status it is lawfully entitled to under the law of another Member State'.

74 Ibid.; Paul Lagarde, "Jurisprudence: García Avello", *Revue critique de droit international privé* 93 (2004): 199–200.

Belgium's right to have its tradition respected, and should therefore Spain not recognize a name that was given under the Belgian system?

The question thus comes down to this: what made the Court decide to give preference to the Spanish name? It seems that the answer is not recognition, but a choice of applicable law for the parents; indeed, many authors conclude from the case that a choice of applicable law is allowed under the particular circumstances of *García Avello*.[75] Although the central element of the case thus concerns the issue of a choice of applicable law—and not mutual recognition—most authors also interpret the judgment as laying down an obligation of recognition (see also the remarks on mutual recognition *infra* Section 6.1).

5. García Avello *and the Related Cases* Micheletti,[76] Mesbah,[77] Konstantinidis[78] *and* Grunkin-Paul[79]

We can conclude that *García Avello*—through the use of EU citizenship—limits Member State autonomy in the field of personal status (more specifically the law on surnames), regardless of the fact that the EU does not have an express competence in this field.[80] A parallel can thus be drawn with *Micheletti*,

75 See the following general observation on the growing importance of party autonomy in European private international family law: 'Nowhere does the term "party autonomy" appear in the case-law, but a closer scrutiny shows that, under the cover of the principle of recognition known as the "country-of-origin principle", citizens have acquired the power to determine for themselves which laws will apply to their family matters'. Toni Marzal Yetano, "The Constitutionalisation of Party Autonomy in European Family Law", *Journal of Private International Law* 6, no. 1 (2010): 157.

76 Case C-369/90 *Micheletti* [1992] ECR I-04239.

77 Case C-179/98 *Mesbah* [1999] ECR I-07955.

78 Case C-168/91 *Konstantinidis* [1993] ECR I-01191.

79 Case C-353/06 *Grunkin-Paul* [2008] ECR I-07639. The case was brought a second time before the Court, after it had decided the first time that it lacked jurisdiction to answer the prelimary question. AG Jacobs did deliver an Opinion on the first occasion (30 June 2005).

It is worthy of note that neither the European judiciary nor the legal doctrine uses a consistent spelling for *García Avello* and *Grunkin-Paul*, which is ironic since both cases explicitly deal with the right to choose one's surname. Thus, although the Court and most of the literature refer to *Garcia Avello*, the Spanish doctrine and AG Sharpston in *Grunkin-Paul* use the Spanish spelling, i.e. *García Avello* (we consistently follow the Spanish doctrine, also when quoting the Court or authors using the spelling of the Court). Similarly, some of the literature refers to both *Grunkin-Paul* and *Grundkin-Paul*, sometimes even in the same article. See for example Gerard-René de Groot, "Namenrecht op drift", *Burgerzaken & Recht* 11, no. 5 (2004): 212–217.

80 Dieter Martiny, "Is Unification of Family Law Feasible or even Desirable?", in *Towards a European Civil Code*, ed. Arthur Hartkamp, *et al.* (Nijmegen: Ars Aequi Libri, 2004), 314;

also a case involving an area of law which was supposed to belong to the exclusive competence of the Member States: nationality law. As will be seen in Chapter 6, in *Micheletti* the Court did not go along with Spain's argument that Mr Micheletti's Italian nationality should be disregarded because Spanish conflict rules considered him a dominant and effective Argentinean national. The Court decided that Member States were barred from making recognition of the status of Community national subject to a condition such as the habitual residence in the territory of the Member State of which the person holds the nationality. Just as *Micheletti* restrained Spain from relying in a case coming within the scope of EU law on its particular conflict rule in respect of a multiple national who possessed the nationality of a Member State, so *García Avello* restrained Belgium from applying its conflicts rule on surnames to children who have the nationality of more than one Member State.

5.1. *Case C-179/98* Mesbah *[1999]*

One of the lesser known cases on dual nationality is *Mesbah*. In this case the Court had to give a preliminary ruling on the interpretation of Article 41(1) of the EEC-Morocco Cooperation Agreement in a dispute between Mrs Mesbah and the Belgian State. In 1995 Mrs Mesbah, a woman of Moroccan nationality who had lived with her daughter and son-in-law in Belgium since 1985, unsuccessfully applied for a disability allowance. The main reason for refusing this allowance was the fact that her daughter and son-in-law (both also of Moroccan nationality) had acquired Belgian nationality before the application for the allowance was made: the national court mistakenly assumed that this naturalization had brought about the loss of Moroccan nationality, making Mrs Mesbah the only person in the household to have retained Moroccan nationality, and that Mrs Mesbah was thus no longer to be regarded as a member of the family of a Moroccan worker (her son-in-law) for the purposes of Article 41(1) of the Agreement (it is undisputed that she would have been entitled to the allowance had her son-in-law only held Moroccan nationality).

When it became clear during the proceedings before the Court that the son-in-law had retained Moroccan nationality, the question to be answered was whether the Moroccan nationality could be relied on for the purpose of obtaining the disability allowance.[81] In other words, could Belgium ignore this worker's Moroccan nationality and treat him as having only Belgian nationality or should a line of reasoning based on *Micheletti* be followed?

Helen Oosterom-Staples, "Burgerschap van de Unie", *Nederlands tijdschrift voor Europees recht*, no. 3 (2004): 59.

[81] Para. 26.

The latter argument was put forward by the Commission, who claimed that Community law precluded Belgium from preventing family members from invoking the worker's Moroccan nationality in order to obtain a benefit under the Agreement, *on the sole ground that the worker is regarded exclusively as a Belgian national.*[82]

The Court disagreed that *Micheletti* could be applied to the case for three reasons. First, in *Mesbah* the migrant worker held, in addition to the nationality of a non-Member State, the nationality of the Member State in which he set up home and carried on his occupational activity. Second, the host State had denied the member of a worker's family the right to take advantage, not of the nationality of another Member State, but of that of a non-Member State. Finally, the claim in Mesbah did not affect freedom of movement. The ECJ pointed out that 'the purpose of the Agreement is not to enable Moroccan nationals to move freely within the community but only to consolidate the social-security position of Moroccan workers and members of their families living with them in the host Member State'.[83] The Court ruled that it is for the national court alone to determine the nationality of Mrs Mesbah son-in-law in accordance with Belgian law—in particular the Belgian nationality and private international law rules.[84]

The position of the ECJ on the subject of dual nationality thus becomes clear after a combined reading of *Micheletti* and *Mesbah*: the Italian nationality which was invoked in *Micheletti* prevented Spain from applying an effectivity test. In other words, a Community nationality will always prevail in a conflict of nationalities which falls within the scope of EU law. An effectivity test is allowed, however, in a situation like *Mesbah* where the second

82 Paras. 27–28.

83 Para. 36.

84 Para. 40. This outcome has been criticized by Groenendijk on a number of grounds: it disregards Mrs Mesbah's legal and long-term residence in Belgium; it limits her rights on the basis of her son-in-law's naturalization; and it does not take into consideration the prohibition on the grounds of nationality as laid down in the ECHR and the 1966 International Covenant on Civil and Political Rights. Carlier agrees with the Belgian decision to ignore the Moroccan nationality, for to do otherwise 'reviendrait à mettre sur un pied d'égalité la citoyenneté européenne avec l'appartenance à un Etat lié à la Communauté par un accord de coopération. Même si un tel accord entre dans le droit communautaire, l'assimilation des ressortissants de cet Etat aux citoyens européens comme critère d'effectivité en cas de pluripatridie pour supplanter la nationalité du for paraît, en l'état actuel du droit communautaire, excessif'. Kees Groenendijk, "Noot onder *Mesbah*", in *Rechtspraak Vreemdelingenrecht* (Ars Aequi Libri: Nijmegen, 1999), 367–368; Jean-Yves Carlier, "La libre circulation des personnes dans l'Union européenne", *Journal des Tribunaux. Droit Européen* (2000): 60.

nationality is that of a non-Member State, even if this nationality concerns the nationality of a country with which the EU entered a Cooperation Agreement.[85]

5.2. *Case C-168/91* Konstantinidis *[1993]*

A case that is closely related to *García Avello* is *Konstantinidis*, a pre-EU citizenship case also dealing with the surname of a Member State national. The facts were the following. Mr Konstantinidis, a Greek national, was working in Germany as a self-employed masseur and assistant hydrotherapist. When he married in 1983, his name was spelt Christos Konstadinidis in the register of marriages. In 1990 he applied for a rectification of that surname to Konstantinidis, arguing that the latter spelling indicated the most correct pronunciation of his name for German speakers. Moreover, this was the way in which his name had been transcribed in Roman characters in his Greek passport. Since the name used in the register of marriages must concur with the name in the birth certificate, the German authorities ordered a translation of the birth certificate by applying the ISO standard 18, a standard prescribed by Article 3 of the 1973 Convention on the Representation of Names and Surnames in Registers of Civil Status[86] to which both Germany and Greece were party. The transcription according to this standard would be Hréstos Kónstantinidés. Mr Konstantinidis also objected to this translation by arguing that it distorted the pronunciation of his name. The question for the ECJ to answer in a preliminary ruling was whether his rights were violated when his name was registered in Germany, against his express wishes, in a spelling that differed from the phonetic description, whereby its pronunciation was modified and distorted.

The Court stated that Article 52 (later Article 43 EC, now Article 49 TFEU) prohibited any discrimination on grounds of nationality, since it seeks to ensure that Member States treat nationals from other Member States in the same way as their own nationals. It had therefore to be determined whether the transcription rules had placed Mr Konstantinidis at a disadvantage in law or in fact compared to German nationals. The Court pointed out that although the Member States must decide on the rules on transcription of Greek names in Roman characters for the purpose of registration, these rules must not be incompatible with Article 52 of the Treaty. This would be the case 'if a Greek national is obliged to use, in the pursuit of his occupation, a spelling used in the register of civil status that modifies the pronunciation of his name and

[85] Meeusen, "Bipatridie in internationaal en Europees verband", 224.

[86] Convention no.14 of the International Commission on Civil Status.

results in a distortion that exposes him to the risk that potential clients may confuse him with other persons' (paragraph 16). The Court found this to be the case for Mr Konstantinidis and thus concluded that Article 52 had been violated.

Oosterom-Staples rightly submits that the element distinguishing the pre-EU citizenship case *Konstantinidis* from *García Avello* is Article 18 EC.[87] In *García Avello* the Court focused on the position of the children and not of the migrant father, thereby deliberately not opting for the possibility to use Article 39 to make the situation fall within the scope of Community law.[88] It was Article 18 EC, which lays down the right for European citizens to move within the territory of the Member States, that was used in *García Avello* to create a link with Community law. The Court's interpretation of European citizenship, combined with the fact that it chose this route instead of relying on the exercise of the right to freedom of movement by the children's father, reinforces the importance of European citizenship as a concept. Indeed, the route chosen by the Court matches with AG Jacobs's idea that European citizenship provided a factor 'enabling the Court to reach a decision in this case on a rather broader basis than it did in *Konstantinidis*'. The AG also argued that 'Article 17 makes clearer the applicability of the principle of non-discrimination to all situations falling within the sphere of Community law, without there being any need to establish a specific interference with a specific economic freedom'.[89]

Although the children's Spanish father had migrated to Belgium, they did not have to rely on Community legislation to live there because they also possessed the Belgian nationality of their mother. The children's situation could

[87] Oosterom-Staples, "Burgerschap van de Unie": 61. See also the interesting remark by Palmeri, who points at a paradoxical effect of European citizenship in this case. Although European citizenship is often interpreted as diminishing the importance of domestic nationality, the reliance by the Court on Articles 17 and 18 only reinforced the importance of the domestic nationality of the children. It is their status as *European citizen* that reinforces their *Spanish* nationality by allowing them the right to a name in accordance with the Spanish tradition. Palmeri, "Doppia cittadinanza e diritto al nome": 220.

[88] AG Jacobs had argued that the case fell within the sphere of Community law for two reasons. His first argument was that Mr García Avello was a *national* of a MS who had exercised his right to move and work in another MS, and a *European citizen* who had used his right to move and reside in the territory of another MS. This argument thus relied on the father having exercised his rights under Article 39 or 43 in combination with Article 18 EC. His second argument was the one that was accepted by the Court: though the children had been born in Belgium, had always resided there and had Belgian nationality, they also had the nationality of another MS; the latter fact was sufficient to make the case fall within the scope of Community law (paras. 50–52).

[89] Para. 61.

therefore have been regarded as a wholly internal situation—something also contended by Belgium—but we have seen that the Court found that there was a Community element. Such a link must still be established because Community law can not apply to internal situations, despite the long-standing call in the legal literature to abolish this rule.[90] However, by holding that there was a Community element even though the children had never exercised their free movement rights, the Court considerably narrowed down the possibility for Member States to classify situations as wholly internal when their national also possesses another Member State nationality.

5.3. *Case C-353/06* Grunkin-Paul *[2008]*

A case brought before the Court after *García Avello*, officially called *Standesamt Stadt Niebüll* but more commonly referred to as *Grunkin-Paul*, is also very relevant to the issues raised here. The Court declined jurisdiction when the case was first brought before it, but AG Jacobs nonetheless went into the substance of the case.[91] Again we begin by stating the facts.

---

[90] Hans Ulrich Jessurun d'Oliveira, "Is Reverse Discrimination Still Permissible Under the Single European Act?", in *Forty years on: The evolution of postwar private international law in Europe* (Amsterdam: Kluwer, 1990), 71–86; Niamh Nic Shuibhne, "Free movement of persons and the wholly internal rule: time to move on?", *Common Market Law Review* 39 (2002): 731–771. However, nothing points in the direction of condemining reverse discrimination. On the contrary, Article 3 of Directive 2004/38 explictly allows it by providing that the Directive shall apply to 'all Union citizens who move to or reside in a Member State other than that of which they are a national'. Van der Mei argues, however, that reverse discrimination is more a problem of national citizenship than of Union citizenship: 'The main problem of the non-mover is that he or she cannot live under one roof with a family member. The problem is not primarily that his mobile neighbour does have that right. The problem of the non-mover is not caused by the EU, but by his or her own Member State. EU law does not prohibit the legislature, policy makers and/or courts of that Member State to grant non-moving own nationals the same family reunification rights as Union law confers upon movers. The EU gives such rights to facilitate freedom of movement. Why should it also give the same rights to non-movers? In the light of the current division of powers in the field of immigration policy, solving the problem of reverse discrimination would first and foremost seem to be an issue falling within the competence of the Member States'. Anne-Pieter van der Mei, "EU-burgerschap en de reikwijdte van het verbod van discriminatie op grond van nationaliteit", *Nederlands tijdschrift voor Europees recht*, no. 8–9 (2009); Editorial, "Combating reverse discrimination: who should do the job?", *Maastricht Journal of European and Comparative Law* 16, no. 4 (2010).

[91] The ECJ declined jurisdiction because the referring Court—the Amtsgericht Niebüll—could not be regarded as exercising a judicial function. On AG Jacobs's Opinion, see Dieter Henrich, "Anerkennung statt IPR: Eine Grundsatzfrage", *IPRax* 25 (2005): 423. He points to an important part missing in the Opinion, namely the question whether a link needs to exist between the German parents and Denmark for the Danish decision to be recognized in other Member States: 'Im vorliegenden Fall war durch den Wohnsitz der Eltern und des Kindes in Dänemark

Leonhard Matthias was born in Denmark to German parents (Stefan Grunkin and Dorothee Paul). Danish rules of private international law provided that the determination of a surname was governed by the law of the person's domicile, which meant that Danish law was applied. As Danish law allows surnames to be composed of the surnames of the parents joined by a hyphen, the child was given the name Grunkin-Paul. When the parents wished to register the child in Germany, however, the name Grunkin-Paul was refused by the German authorities. German law provides that the surname of German nationals is decided by German law, concretely meaning that the name of either the father or the mother must be chosen. The Amtsgericht Niebüll subsequently submitted a question to the ECJ, asking whether the German rule was compatible with Articles 12 and 18 EC. It found the German rule hard to reconcile with the principle of freedom of movement, for it meant that a European citizen would be forced to bear different surnames in different Member States.

AG Jacobs concluded that *Grunkin-Paul* had to be distinguished from *García Avello* in the sense that Article 12 could not be used. However, he considered the position of Leonhard Matthias to be closely comparable to that of the García Avello children. The child might also encounter practical difficulties when using his right as European citizen to move and reside in the territory of the Member States. In addition to the practical difficulties, the AG also stressed that a name is a fundamental part of one's identity and private life and therefore concluded that it seems 'totally incompatible with the status and rights of a citizen of the European Union … to be required to bear different names under the laws of different Member States'.[92]

The case was brought a second time before the ECJ, and this time there were no doubts about the admissibility of the reference by a German national court for a preliminary ruling.[93] AG Sharpston concluded that Community was applicable in Leonhard Matthias's situation because the child frequently travelled between Denmark and Germany (his parents had in the meanwhile divorced and his father now lived in Germany); in travelling back and forth, he is subject to conflicting rules of both countries with regard to his surname. The AG continued by considering that a systematic practice of a Member State

---

eine Beziehung zu dem Staat gegeben, in dem der Name des Kindes eingetragen wurde. Ob die Anerkennung der Eintragung von dem Bestehen einer solchen Beziehung abhängig gemacht werden kann, ist aus dem Schlussantrag des Generalanwalts nicht eindeutig zu ersehen'.

92 Paras. 55–56.

93 Case C-353/06 *Grunkin-Paul* [2008] ECR I-07639. The Opinion was delivered by AG Sharpston on 24 April 2008.

(Germany) to refuse the surname of nationals who had been given a surname in accordance with the law of the Member State of birth and habitual residence (Denmark), was contrary to the principle of equal treatment: by virtue of this practice in situations where an individual had used the right of free movement, the right of equal treatment was not satisfied in that the criterion of habitual residence under Danish law was not given the same weight as the criterion of nationality under German law.[94] For the same reasons that had been brought forward by AG Jacobs, AG Sharpston also considered that Leonhard Matthias's right of free movement had been interfered with and that this interference could not be justified. By expressly focusing on the free movement right of the *child*, the AG countered the argument of some of the Member States that the free movement right of the parents was not interfered with. Several Member States had claimed that the parents could not 'be discouraged from moving to another Member State by the knowledge that they will be treated in the same way as if they had not exercised the right to do so'.[95]

The Court began by investigating the possible link with Community law. Referring to *García Avello*, it held that a link with Community law exists with regard to children who are nationals of one Member State and lawfully resident in another. Leonhard Matthias could thus in principle rely on Articles 12 and 18 EC. Article 12 was found not to be applicable, however, as he had not been discriminated against on grounds of nationality in Germany.[96] Yet the Court concluded that the serious inconvenience caused by the discrepancy in surnames—the Court again referred to *García Avello* on this point—was liable to hamper his freedom of movement as guaranteed under Article 18.[97] In the

---

94 See on this part of the AG's Opinion related to issues of discrimination and equal treatment Johan Meeusen, "Who is afraid of European private international law?", in *Nuovi strumenti del diritto internazionale privato. Liber Fausto Pocar*, ed. Gabriella Venturini and Stefania Bariatti (Milano: Giuffrè Editore, 2009), 696.

95 Para. 75.

96 See on this point Lagarde, who remarks that 'le critère de la nationalité n'est discriminatoire que lorsque'il conduit au refus d'un droit à raison de la nationalité, il ne l'est pas s'il fait varier le régime de ce droit en fonction de la nationalité'. Paul Lagarde, "Jurisprudence: Grunkin-Paul", *Revue critique de droit international privé* 98, no. 1 (2009): 89. See also Pieter Boeles, "Noot onder *Grunkin-Paul*", *Jurisprudentie Vreemdelingenrecht, 2008/447*; Dolores Blázquez Peinado, "Sentencia Grunkin y Paul, C-253/06", *Revista de Derecho Communitario Europeo* 33 (2009): 662; Philipp Kubicki, "Kurze Nachlese zur Rechtssache Grunkin-Paul", *Europäische Zeitschrift für Wirtschaftsrecht*, no. 11 (2009): 367.

97 This issue also played recently in Case C-208/09 *Sayn-Wittgenstein* [2010] ECR I-00000. This case of 14 October 2010 concerned an Austrian national who was adopted, as an adult, in Germany by a German national whose surname included a former title of nobility. That surname, in the femmine form—i.e. Fürstin von Sayn-Wittgenstein—was subsequently entered

Court's view, none of the arguments put forward by Germany were strong enough to justify the non-recognition of the double-barrelled surname. The operative part of the judgment therefore reads that in the circumstances of the case

> Article 18 EC precludes the authorities of a Member State, in applying national law, from refusing to recognise a child's surname, as determined and registered in a second Member State in which the child—who, like his parents, has only the nationality of the first Member State—was born and has been resident since birth.[98]

The similarities between *García Avello* and *Grunkin-Paul* are obvious and the latter is commonly regarded as a follow-up case. The effect of *Grunkin-Paul* was that Germany was under an obligation to recognize the child's double name, just as Belgium had been in *García Avello*. The case triggered a similar debate on the impact of the judgment for private international law and was also not without some controversial aspects.[99] It has for example been argued that the Court could (or even should) have reached a different outcome by forcing the Danish authorities to change Leonard Matthias's surname in accordance with the German rules on surnames.[100] This obligation could be

for the Austrian woman in the registers of civil status, but 15 years later the Austrian authorities removed the elements of the surname which indicated nobility, based on the argument that this name was incompatible with the Austrian law on the abolition of the nobility—which enjoys constitutional status. As Ilonka Fürstin von Sayn-Wittgenstein had been resident in Germany for a long time, the Court held that having her surname altered resulted in 'serious inconvenience' within the meaning of Grunkin-Paul. The Court nevertheless ruled that Austria was not precluded under Article 21 TFEU from refusing to recognize the surname which included a former title of nobilility, provided that the measures adopted by Austria were justified on public policy grounds.

98 This *ratio decidendi* thus gives answer to the question whether 'the principle of mutual recognition will remain limited to judgments and decisions in extrajudicial cases [Article 81 TFEU] or will also expand into, for example, the recognition of decisions duly taken by the public authorities of another Member State'. Gerard-René de Groot and Jan-Jaap Kuipers, "The New Provisions on Private International Law in the Treaty of Lisbon", *Maastricht Journal of European and Comparative Law* 15, no. 1 (2008): 112.

99 D'Avout is very critical of the Court's interpretation of EU citizenship in *Grunkin-Paul*. Arguing that the child's status as European citizen is dependent on his German nationality, d'Avout finds it contradictory that EU citizenship allows him to repudiate a personal status imposed by Germany law: 'L'on ne devrait donc pas pouvoir, sans contradiction, invoquer le bénéfice de la citoyenneté européene procurée par un État membre de nationalité pour répudier le statut civil impératif que cet État veut imposer à ses ressortissants personnes physiques. Si l'on veut, la nationalité est une donation avec charge; elle n'est pas seulement le tremplin qui ferait accéder à la citoyenneté pour s'effacer ensuite devant elle ….' Louis d'Avout, "Jurisprudence: Grunkin et Paul", *Journal du Droit International* 136 (2009): 214.

100 M.R. Mok, "Noot onder Grunkin-Paul", Nederlandse Jurisprudentie 2009/64.

justified by the argument that non-compliance would violate Article 18—the right to free movement. It is claimed that in *Grunkin-Paul* the Court forced Germany to accept a surname which was incompatible with German law (although this argument is questionable[101]) whilst it would not have been incompatible with Danish law to opt for the name of only one of the parents. Those following this line of reasoning argue that the Court created a situation in which 'forum shopping' is encouraged: by giving birth in Denmark, the child can receive a compound surname to which it is not entitled under the laws of other States.

The judgment in *Grunkin-Paul* stresses two aspects that already featured prominently in the discussion on *García Avello*. First, the growing significance of EU citizenship and the tension between the individual liberties guaranteed by this citizenship on the one hand and the preservation of the cultural identity of the Member States—particularly sensitive in the field of surnames—on the other.[102] Second, whether the principle of mutual recognition in combination with Article 18 can be extended to aspects of personal status that go beyond one's surname.[103] On a *material* level one might think for example of the extension of this principle to parental recognition, registered partnerships and same-sex marriages.[104] But we could also imagine a *geographical* extension; what if Leonard Matthias had been born in Norway and had been attributed a double name under Norwegian law? Would it then be necessary—in order for Community law to apply—for him to move first to Denmark (where his double name is accepted) before moving to another Member State?[105]

---

101 See para. 37 of the judgment, as well as Jürgen Rieck, "Anerkennung des Familiennamens in Mitgliedstaaten: Grunkin-Paul", *Neue Juristische Wochenschrift*, no. 3 (2009): 127–128.

102 Hans Ulrich Jessurun d'Oliveira, "Hinkende namen", *Migrantenrecht* 24, no. 2 (2009): 45. Meeusen remarks the following: 'Citizens who make use of the newly acquired freedom to move without too many restrictions over the borders, of course forget personal relationships which have all kinds of legal consequences. It would be very unsatisfactory if EC law, so to say, took away with one hand what it gave with the other. Stimulating citizens to move across the borders, and to reside in other Member States, necessarily requires that proper care is taken also of the private law effects which flow therefrom'. Meeusen, "Who is afraid of European private international law?", 692.

103 Boeles, "Noot onder *Grunkin-Paul*"; Dieter Martiny, "Anmerkung Grunkin-Paul", *Deutsche Notar-Zeitschrift*, no. 6 (2009): 456–457.

104 Lagarde, "La reconnaissance mode d'emploi", 488–450. See also Saarloos, *European private international law on legal parentage? Thoughts on a European instrument implementing the principle of mutual recognition in legal parentage*, 307 ff.

105 Lagarde, "La reconnaissance mode d'emploi", 490–491. The Norwegian example is perhaps not the most fortunate as Norway is a member of the European Economic Area (EEA). Nationals of Norway enjoy free movement rights within the territory of the EU and the EEA. Stefaan van den Bogaert, "Free movement for workers and the nationality

In this connection it should also be noted that it remains unclear from the judgment whether Germany would also be under an obligation to recognize the surname given in accordance with Danish law if the child were to no longer habitually reside in Denmark but in Germany. In that case, the argument that his freedom of movement would be violated by bearing different surnames would no longer hold true.[106]

Lagarde also takes the interesting approach of looking at *Grunkin-Paul* from a non-Community law perspective. Arguing that the fundamental justification of mutual recognition is 'le besoin de permanence du statut de la personne', the German non-recognition of the name given in Denmark would lead to a 'blocage' as described above (see Section 3). Lagarde thus again makes a plea for the functional approach because if Germany insists on applying German law to the case, there is no reason why Denmark would not insist on applying Danish law.[107]

6. *Is There A Need for Uniform European Conflict and Recognition Rules in the Field of Civil Status?*

The (potential) effects of *García Avello* (and in its wake *Grunkin-Paul*) on national conflict and recognition rules has led some authors to argue that the EU should create uniform European conflict and recognition rules in the field of civil status.[108] This could be done on the basis of Article 81 TFEU/ex Article 65 EC.[109] However, not everyone shows a preference for EU action over a reconstruction of these rules on a national level, and the *García Avello* judgment has also been severely criticized. This criticism is closely bound up with

requirements", in *Migration, Integration and Citizenship, A challenge for Europe's Future, Volume I*, ed. Hildegard Schneider (Maastricht: Forum, 2005), 63.

106 Lagarde, "Jurisprudence: Grunkin-Paul": 91.

107 Lagarde, "La reconnaissance mode d'emploi", 491.'Pour éviter le blocage de la situation, il faut que l'Allemagne accepte de reconnaître la situation créée au Danemark par des autorités qui ont appliqué leur règle de conflit comme l'auraient fait les autorités allemandes si elles avaient été saisies les premières'.

108 de Groot, "Towards European Conflict Rules in Matters of Personal Status": 119; Ackermann, "Annotation Case C-148/02 *García Avello* [2003]": 154. For a discussion of *García Avello* in the context of the 'Europeanization of PIL', see Veerle van den Eeckhout, "Tien jaar Europees internationaal privaatrecht. Een verrassende metamorfose van exotisch muurbloempje tot goed geïntegreerde deelnemer in diverse gezelschappen", *Nederlands tijdschrift voor Europees recht*, no. 11/12 (2005): 289–303.

109 de Groot and Kuipers, "The New Provisions on Private International Law in the Treaty of Lisbon": 112; Saarloos, *European private international law on legal parentage? Thoughts on a European instrument implementing the principle of mutual recognition in legal parentage*, 311.

the idea that the obligation of recognition will make private international law in the EU wither away, remaining relevant only in cases with an extracommunitarian element.[110] Indeed, a trend can be identified that erodes conflicts rules and reduces private international law in the context of the EU to jurisdiction and recognition.[111]

As said, the *García Avello* judgment has met with strong resistance—one fierce critic being Paul Lagarde. In his annotation he points out that the case is different from, for example, *Micheletti*, in the sense that there was no cross-border element involved. Whereas Mr Micheletti wanted to establish himself in a different Member State than the one of which he possessed the nationality, the same cannot be said of the García Avello children. Focusing on the specific role played by multiple nationality in these cases, we must agree with Lagarde's remark that the significant difference between both cases is that in *García Avello* dual nationality in itself creates a cross-border element—a necessary condition for the application of EU law.[112] Others have classified *García Avello* as the first case where European citizenship and a *potential* use of free movement rights suffice to make the case fall within the scope of Community law.[113]

For the sake of completion, we must also point here to two other cases in which dual nationality played a role and which, like *Micheletti*, are distinguishable from *García Avello* due to the existence of a cross-border element. The issue in *Gullung*[114] concerned the question whether a lawyer of French-German nationality who was admitted to the legal profession in Germany could rely in France on the freedom to provide services as granted under Community law.[115] *Gilly*[116] dealt with a woman of French-German nationality,

110 Hans Ulrich Jessurun d'Oliveira, "The EU and a Metamorphosis of Private International Law", in *Reform and Development of Private International Law. Essays in honour of Sir Peter North*, ed. J Fawcett (Oxford: Oxford University Press, 2002), 136.

111 Ibid., 131.

112 Lagarde, "Jurisprudence: García Avello": 197.

113 Ana Quiñones Escamez, "Derecho comunitario, derechos fundamentales y denegación del cambio de sexo y apellidos: ¿un orden público europeo harmonizador?", *Revista de Derecho Comunitario Europeo* 28 (2004): 512.

114 Case C-292/86 *Gullung* [1988] ECR I-00111.

115 In *Gullung* the Court held as follows: 'Freedom of movement for persons, freedom of establishment and freedom to provide services, which are fundamental in the Community system, would not be fully realized if a Member State were entitled to refuse to grant the benefit of the provisions of Community law to those of its nationals who are established in another Member State of which they are also a national and who take advantage of the facilities offered by Community law in order to pursue their activities in the territory of the first State by way of the provision of services' (para. 12).

116 Case C-336/96 *Gilly* [1998] ECR I-02793.

residing in France but working as a teacher in Germany. For the application of a French-German Convention on the avoidance of double taxation, it was essential to establish whether Mrs Gilly had exercised her free movement right by working in Germany while also possesing German nationality.[117]

Returning to *García Avello*, the Court's solution to the Spanish-Belgian conflict of nationalities embodies a *functional* approach to the objectives of the Treaty, but the Court thereby bypassed the two solutions commonly used in such a situation, i.e. the choice for the nationality of the forum or for the most effective nationality.[118] Lagarde apparently feels that these PIL rules were

---

[117] Here the central statement of the Court reads, with reference to *Gullung*, that 'it need merely be pointed out here that Mrs Gilly has acquired French nationality by her marriage and works in Germany whilst residing in France. She must therefore be considered in France as a worker exercising her right to freedom of movement, as guaranteed by the Treaty, in order to work in a Member State other than that in which she resides. The circumstance that she has retained the nationality of the State in which she is employed in no way affects the fact that, for the French authorities, she is a French national working in another Member State' (para. 21).

To *Gullung* and *Gilly* we may add a third one: Case C-122/96 *Saldanha and MTS* [1997] ECR I-05325. In *Saldanha* the Court had to decide on the question whether the prohibition of discrimination on grounds of nationality 'precludes a Member State [Austria] from requiring provision of security for costs [the so-called 'cautio judicatum solvi'] by a national of another Member State [United Kingdom] who is also a national of a non-member country [United States], in which he is domiciled, where that national, who is not resident and has no assets in the first Member State, has brought before one of its civil courts an action in his capacity as a shareholder against a company established in that Member State, even though such a requirement is not imposed on its own nationals who are not resident and have no assets there'. The Court first points out, with reference to *Micheletti*, that a national of a Member State who is also a national of a non-member country and who is resident in the non-member country, is not deprived of the right, as a national of that Member State, to rely on the prohibition of discrimination on grounds of nationality. It is subsequently concluded that the provision on the cautio judicatum solvi amounts to direct discrimination on grounds of nationality under the circumstances of the case because Austrian nationals are not required to provide security under that provision, even if they are not resident and have no assets in Austria. The judgment is significant in that it prevents dual nationals from being treated as second-class EU citizens: nationals of a MS can rely on the prohibition on the grounds of nationality in all situations which fall within the scope of the Treaty even if they possess a non-MS nationality and are resident in the country of that nationality. See also Kees Groenendijk, "Noot onder *Saldanha*", in *Rechtspraak Vreemdelingenrecht* (Nijmegen: Ars Aequi Libri, 1997), 328.

[118] Lagarde, "Jurisprudence: García Avello": 195. Indeed, the Court says that Article 3 of the Hague Convention, which allows a State to give preference to its own nationality when confronted with a national who also possesses another nationality, does not impose an obligation but simply provides an option. Also, the Court does not pay any consideration to another commonly applied solution under private international law, namely to look for the most effective nationality.

sidelined too readily in favour of a functional approach. This seems strange as the Court appears to use a similar reasoning (namely to look at the 'spirit' of the Treaty provisions) as was adopted by Lagarde himself when proposing the 'approche fonctionnelle' in an extra-EU context (*supra* Section 3).

The Court's broad interpretation of the EU citizenship provisions, thereby considerably extending the scope of Community law, is also criticized by Lagarde with the argument that the children's rights under Article 18 were under no serious threat.[119] In essence he questions both the validity of the wide interpretation of Articles 17 and 18 EC—which brought the case too easily within the scope of Community law—and the small regard for the national PIL rules.

By now it should have become clear that the case *García Avello* has been, and continues to be, the subject of a heated debate. Yet however one feels about the judgment, it can not be denied that the situation of private international law in the EU is in a state of flux. Meeusen identifies three characteristics of European private international law that are relevant in this respect: the focus on non-discrimination on the grounds of nationality; the impact of fundamental human rights; and the rule of mutual recognition.[120]

6.1. *The Principle of Non-Discrimination on the Grounds of Nationality, Fundamental Human Rights and the Principle of Mutual Recognition*

In the field of personal status and family law, nationality is still considered to be a valid connecting factor. However, as the prohibition of discrimination on the grounds of nationality is an important principle of Community law, application of nationality as a connecting factor can be tricky in a Community context and therefore deserves particular scrutiny.[121] Such scrutiny can be observed in *García Avello*, where the non-discrimination principle of Article 12 EC overruled the Member States' traditional conflict rules. On the whole however, the impact of the judgment on the role of nationality as a connecting factor remains limited. Nationality can still be used as a connecting factor

[119] Ibid., 197.

[120] Johan Meeusen, "Instrumentalisation of Private International Law in the European Union: Towards a European Conflicts Revolution?", *European Journal of Migration and Law* 9 (2007): 291.

[121] The use of nationality as a connecting factor was explicitly allowed by the ECJ in Case C-430/97 *Johannes v. Johannes* [1999] ECR I-03475. See also Alegría Borrás, "Prinzipien des Internationalen Familienrechts", in *Europäisches Gemeinschaftsrecht und IPR. Ein Beitrag zur Kodifikation der Allgemeinen Grundsätze des Europäischen Kollisionsrechtes*, ed. Gerte Reichelt (Wien: Manzsche Verlags—und Universitätsbuchhandlung, 2007), 63.

with respect to rules governing surnames and *García Avello* only seems to be of direct relevance to multiple nationals holding more than one Member State nationality.[122]

In connection with Article 12 EC (now Article 18 TFEU), Baratta advances the interesting claim that this is one of three provision of the Treaty on which an *implied* principle of mutual recognition of personal and family status could be construed in the future.[123] The other two provisions concern a combined reading of Article 17 and 18 EC (the EU citizenship provisions)[124] and Article 10 EC (the principle of loyal cooperation between Member States, now Article 4(3) TEU).[125] Baratta makes the caveat, however, in that the scope of the principle of mutual recognition 'concerns solely personal status accorded by the national Member State of the person involved and requires clarification for persons having a *double nationality*. A solution could be to favour the law of the State which is better suited to free movement and which better protects the person's fundamental rights' (emphasis added).[126]

Quiñonez Escamez laments the Court's interpretation of the prohibition of discrimination in *García Avello*. She concludes that if the Court had adopted the traditional solution as provided in Article 3 of the Hague Convention—which would have led to the application of Belgian law to Belgian dual nationals who were born and resident in Belgium—the outcome would have been neither discriminatory nor insensible.[127] Kohler has commented on the case in a similar vein by maintaining that the judgment flouts the general connecting

---

[122] Meeusen, "Instrumentalisation of Private International Law in the European Union: Towards a European Conflicts Revolution?": 294–295.

[123] 'It seems that legal values granted to a person by its national State cannot be denied by another Member State, in particular whenever this refusal has a negative effect on the integration of European citizens and, more generally, on their freedom to circulate and enjoy fundamental rights'. Roberto Baratta, "Problematic elements of an implicit rule providing for mutual recognition of personal and family status in the EC", *IPRax* 27 (2007): 8.

[124] Ibid., 7. 'If one reads [Articles 17 and 18] in conjunction without depriving them of any useful effect, arguably the latter right should in principle entail for that person the right to move with the personal status and family situations legally acquired in his or her Member State of origin'.

[125] Ibid., 9. 'One may query whether a Member State actually complies with the principle of loyal cooperation when it refuses a priori any recognition of the family relationships duly acquired by a European citizen according to its national legal system solely because the Member State claims the application of its own conflict of laws system'.

[126] Ibid., 11.

[127] Quiñones Escamez, "Derecho comunitario, derechos fundamentales y denegación del cambio de sexo y apellidos: ¿un orden público europeo harmonizador?": 515. See also Helms, "Europarechtliche Vorgaben zur Bestimmung des Namensstatuts von Doppelstaatern: Anmerkung zu EuGH, Urteil vom 2.10.2003, C-148/02—*García Avello*": 38.

factors used in PIL. The Court's interpretation of Article 12—namely that it amounts to discrimination to treat multiple nationals in the same way as mono-nationals if their situations differ, even when the nationality of the forum is the effective nationality or when the multiple national has his habitual residence there—comes very close to excluding the use of habitual residence as a connecting factor in cases with a Community dimension. In other words, it would only be a small step for the Court to conclude that when nationals of other Member States perceive the application of habitual residence as a connecting factor to be detrimental, such application would amount to indirect discrimination.[128]

The impact of fundamental human rights on PIL is very strongly reflected in both *García Avello* and *Grunkin-Paul*. AG Jacobs emphasized in both cases the fundamental importance of a name for a person's identity and private life.[129] These cases are thus a good illustration of the tension between national conflicts laws and the rules of the internal market, seen in the light of fundamental rights considerations.

As to mutual recognition, it is a subject of debate whether this principle should be extended to all family matters.[130] Meeusen feels that only when there is a fundamental rights dimension to it—as is for him the case in *Grunkin-Paul* but not (yet) with regard to, for example, same-sex marriages—recognition should be the rule. Fundamental rights are particularly relevant because their intervention can 'reinforce mutual recognition ... and so increase the pressure which EC law puts upon private international law'.[131] Toner, on the other hand, argues that mutual recognition of same-sex marriages would

---

[128] Christian Kohler, "Verständigungsschwierigkeiten zwischen europäischem Gemeinschaftsrecht und internationalem Privatrecht", in *Festschrift für Erik Jayme, Band 1*, ed. Heinz-Peter Mansel, *et al.* (München: Sellier, 2004), 455.

[129] Palmeri, "Doppia cittadinanza e diritto al nome": 224.

[130] For academic contributions addressing mutual recognition in a broader perspective see Jan-Jaap Kuipers, "Cartesio and Grunkin-Paul: Mutual Recognition as a Vested Rights Theory Based on Party Autonomy in Private Law", 2010; available from http://cadmus.eui.eu/dspace/bitstream/1814/13426/1/EJLS_2009_2_2_5_EN.pdf; Marzal Yetano, "The Constitutionalisation of Party Autonomy in European Family Law": 155–193; Markus Möstl, "Preconditions and limits of mutual recognition", *Common Market Law Review* 47 (2010): 405–436.

[131] Meeusen, "Instrumentalisation of Private International Law in the European Union: Towards a European Conflicts Revolution?": 298. In a similar vein, see Michael Bogdan, "Some Reflections on the Treatment of Dutch Same-Sex Marriages in European and Private International Law", in *Intercontinental Cooperation Through Private International Law*, ed. Talia Einhorn and Kurt Siehr (The Hague: T.M.C. Asser Press, 2004), 34.

constitute a form of Community law intervention which does not fundamentally threaten Member State autonomy in family law.[132]

The principle of mutual recognition is obviously an alternative to harmonization and particularly useful when harmonization is difficult or undesirable. The idea of mutual recognition figured prominently in *García Avello*. A core element of that judgment was that Belgium was under an obligation to recognize the children's Spanish nationality for the purpose of the determination of their surname; Belgium was not allowed to disregard this fact and to automatically apply its own nationality to the case.[133] Again the parallel with *Micheletti* is plain: there the Court imposed an obligation on Spain to recognize Mr Micheletti's Italian nationality, however weak that latter nationality. In this sense *García Avello* can indeed be read as a follow-up case to *Micheletti*.[134]

7. *Consequences of* García Avello *for National Rules Governing Surnames*

Thus far we have considered the (possible) impact of the *García Avello* judgment for the European context. Here we briefly focus on the concrete consequences for the national rules governing surnames. It is clear that the judgment did not condemn the use of nationality as a connecting factor for the determination of surnames. What the case does condemn is State practice on the matter of surnames which only takes into account the nationality of the forum when confronted with a multiple national who also possesses the nationality of another Member State. Consequently, the Dutch rule that Dutch nationality will always prevail in respect of Dutch multiple nationals cannot last.[135]

---

132 Helen Toner, *Partnership Rights, Free Movement, and EU Law* (Oxford: Hart Publishing, 2004), 255–256. Similarly, see Paul Lagarde, "Développements futurs du D.I.P.", *RabelsZ* 68 (2004): 235; Hans Ulrich Jessurun d'Oliveira, "How do international organisations cope with the personal *status* of their staff members? Some observations on the recognition of (same-sex) marriages in international organisations", in *Nuovi strumenti del diritto internazionale privato. Liber Fausto Pocar*, ed. Gabriella Venturini and Stefania Bariatti (Milano: Giuffrè Editore, 2009), 509. See also Gerard-René de Groot, "Private International Law Aspects Relating to Homosexual Couples", 2007; available from http://www.ejcl.org/113/article113-12.pdf.

133 We refer again to the argument sketched above that this reasoning has its flaws: if Belgium is under an obligation to recognize Spanish rules on surnames, the reverse would be true for Spain.

134 Meeusen, "Instrumentalisation of Private International Law in the European Union: Towards a European Conflicts Revolution?": 299.

135 Saarloos, *European private international law on legal parentage? Thoughts on a European instrument implementing the principle of mutual recognition in legal parentage*, 299.

The effect of the judgment for Spain is that the Spanish system of double surnames will no longer be a matter of public policy (*orden público*): a Spanish national will be able to bear a single surname if the parents are from different Member States. Formerly, Spanish nationals could under no circumstances bear a single surname, not even when Spanish nationality was acquired by naturalization.[136]

The judgment could be interpreted as having the effect of a directive.[137] The Court does not care how the Member States decide to offer a possibility to children with a multiple nationality to bear a surname to which they are entitled according to the law and tradition of one of their nationalities. This can either be done by adjusting PIL rules, by allowing a choice of law when the child is registered, or by making changes in domestic law that allow a surname in accordance with the law of the other country of which the child possesses the nationality.

8. García Avello *and Other Cases on European Citizenship*

This is not the place for a very elaborate discussion of other cases on European citizenship.[138] It may be useful, however, to place *García Avello* in the light of the general development of the case law on Articles 17 and 18 EC (now Articles 20 and 21 TFEU). In this connection, it is worth noting that many authors believe there is a movement away from the traditional idea of market

---

136 Quiñones Escamez, "Derecho comunitario, derechos fundamentales y denegación del cambio de sexo y apellidos: ¿un orden público europeo harmonizador?": 527.

137 Hans Ulrich Jessurun d'Oliveira, "Het Europese Hof activeert het Europese burgerschap", *Nederlands Juristenblad* 78 (2003): 2242–2243.

138 For general overviews of the EU citizenship case law, see Anne-Pieter van der Mei, "De juridische meerwaarde van het Burgerschap van de Europese Unie (2)", *Migrantenrecht* 18, no. 9/10 (2003); Guild, *The Legal Elements of European Identity. EU citizenship and Migration Law*, chapter 2; Noreen Burrows and Rosa Greaves, *The Advocate General and EC Law* (Oxford: Oxford University Press, 2007), chapter 10; Kostakopoulou, "European Union Citizenship: Writing the Future"; Paul Craig and Gráinne De Búrca, *EU Law. Text, Cases, and Materials* 4th ed. (Oxford: Oxford University Press, 2008), chapter 23; Francis Jacobs, "Citizenship of the European Union - A Legal Analysis", *European Law Journal* 13, no. 5 (2008); Miguel Poiares Maduro and Loïc Azoulai, eds., *The Past and Future of EU Law. The Classics of EU Law Revisited on the 50th Anniversary of the Rome Treaty* (Oxford: Hart Publishing, 2010), chapter 9.

A good overview of the role of EU citizenship in the field of social security can be found in Michael Dougan, "The Spatial Restructuring of National Welfare States within the European Union: The Contribution of Union Citizenship and the Relevance of the Treaty of Lisbon", in *Integrating Welfare Functions into EU Law: From Rome to Lisbon*, ed. U. Neergaard, R. Nielsen, and L. Roseberry (Copenhagen: DJØF Publishing, 2009); Marzo, *La dimension sociale de la citoyenneté européenne.*

citizenship—linked to the exercise of the economic free movement rights—to a citizenship that is being detached from both the exercise of an economic activity[139] and the requirement of a cross-border element.[140] This development may be in accordance with the ECJ statement that 'European citizenship is destined to be the fundamental status of nationals of the Member States',[141] but does not prevent the case law from being widely criticized. Ultimately, this disagreement boils down to a different view of the nature and future of European citizenship.[142]

The academic literature also notes that European citizenship is given further substance by interpreting this status in the light of general principles of Community law: the prohibition of discrimination on nationality, the principle of proportionality[143] and fundamental rights.[144] These principles are used as weapons by the Court to extensively interpret European citizenship, and this practice has given rise to controversial judgments—something which is true also in the field of social law.[145] Indeed, in discussing *García Avello* we

---

139 Indeed, the EU citizenship case law has granted a number of entitlements to EU citizens who are neither economically active nor economically self-sufficient (in particular non-workers, students and job-seekers). See for example Case C-456/02 *Trojani* [2004] ECR I-7573; Case C-209/03 *Bidar* [2005] ECR I-02119; Case C-184/99 *Grzelczyk* [2001] ECR I-6193; Case C-138/02 *Collins* [2004] ECR I-2703. These cases have been subject to a rich academic reflection. See for example Anastasia Iliopoulou and Helen Toner, "Annotation Case C-184/99 *Grzelczyk* [2001]", *Common Market Law Review* 39 (2002); Catherine Barnard, "Annotation Case C-209/03 *Bidar* [2005]", ibid.42 (2005); Helen Oosterom-Staples, "Annotation Case C-138/02 *Collins* [2004]", ibid.

140 Eleanor Spaventa, "Seeing the wood despite the trees? On the scope of Union citizenship and its constitutional effects", ibid.45 (2008): 44. She writes: 'There cannot be any doubt that the introduction of Union citizenship has had far-reaching effects, and that it has considerably broadened both the personal and the material scope of the Treaty. Any Union citizen falls now within the personal scope of the Treaty, regardless of an economic or cross border link. And, the rights of movement and residence conferred by Article 18(1) EC have been interpreted broadly so that Union citizens can challenge both the rules of the Member State of origin, when those affect in any way the right to move and/or reside in another Member State; and the rules of the host Member State, when they limit movement, residence or discriminate on grounds of nationality'.

141 Case C-184/99 *Grzelczyk* [2001] ECR I-6193.

142 Kohler remarks that if this development predicts the future of European citizenship, and if European citizenship is further enforced by an interpretation of Article 12 like in *García Avello*, then many areas of law that have no direct connection to the economic free movement rights become subject to Community scrutiny. See Kohler, "Verständigungsschwierigkeiten zwischen europäischem Gemeinschaftsrecht und internationalem Privatrecht", 456.

143 See on the proportionality principle in particular Dougan, "The constitutional dimension to the case law on Union citizenship": 613–641.

144 Jessurun d'Oliveira, "Het Europese Hof activeert het Europese burgerschap": 2243.

145 See generally Marzo, *La dimension sociale de la citoyenneté européenne*.

have seen that many authors remain unconvinced by the Court's reasoning and point at the dangers of the approach, for example in PIL. Meanwhile similar criticism has been voiced concerning access to social benefits.[146] Thus, the Court has generally been called upon to exercise caution in its interpretation of European citizenship, as well as to pay due regard to the system of checks and balances.[147]

The Lisbon Treaty seems to have little impact on the debate about welfare rights: 'The constitutional reform process has ... produced neither any direct and clear endorsement, nor any direct and clear rejection, of the status quo as it has evolved in the secondary legislation and through the ECJ's caselaw'.[148] However, in the context of this reform process Dougan notes that 'the Member States ... continue to stress and indeed reinforce the peculiarly sensitive nature of welfare as a field of primarily national responsibility, and to impose ever more precise limits on the powers of the Community legislature to intervene therein'. He therefore speculates that the Court will be put under increasing pressure to show greater deference to the welfare choices of the Member States.[149]

---

[146] See for a very critical approach to the Court's case law in the field of social security Christian Tomuschat, "Annotation Case C-85/96 *Martínez Sala* [1998]", *Common Market Law Review* 37 (2000): 453; Kay Hailbronner, "Union Citizenship and Access to Social Benefits", ibid. 42 (2005): 1245–1267.

[147] In this respect nationality and social security, both being bastions of national sovereignty, look much alike and the Court is advised to tread carefully in these fields. Since both the nation-state (nationality) and the welfare-state (social benefits) require a shared identity to work, we may draw an analogy between nationality law's 'genuine link' requirement and the 'real link' (i.e. 'a certain degree of integration in the host State') as expressed in Case C-209/03 *Bidar* [2005] ECR I-02119.

[148] Hence Dougan's final sentence: 'The ball, as so often, ends up back with the Court: Its vision of Union citizenship initially transformed this field of Community law; will that vision survive the tumults of the constitutional reform process unaltered?'. Dougan, "The Spatial Restructuring of National Welfare States within the European Union: The Contribution of Union Citizenship and the Relevance of the Treaty of Lisbon", 181.

Recent case law supports the view, according to Dougan, that the ECJ has lost some, though not all, of its previous confidence in developing the institution of EU citizenship. This case law is more ambivalent about the apparently well-settled 'personal circumstances test' as developed in, for example, *Grzelczyk* and *Baumbast*. Such a test was not applied recently in Case C-158/07 *Förster* [2008] ECR I-08507, para.58; Case C-123/08 *Wolzenburg* [2009] ERC I-09621, para.70. In *Rottmann*, however, the Court instructed the national court to have regard to all relevant circumstances when assessing the compatibility with EU law of the withdrawal of Rottmann's German nationality (*supra* Chapter 1, Section 11.2.3).

[149] Dougan, "The Spatial Restructuring of National Welfare States within the European Union: The Contribution of Union Citizenship and the Relevance of the Treaty of Lisbon", 183–184.

9. *Dual Nationality and the Brussels IIbis Regulation: Case C-168/08* Hadadi *[2009]*

In 2004 Van den Eeckhout, addressing the subject of dual nationality, raised the question of the exact meaning of the Court's case law in respect of dual nationality for the interpretation of a conflict of nationalities in the context of the Brussels II Regulation (which was the predecessor of Regulation 2201/2003, also referred to as Brussels IIbis Regulation).[150] This question now appears to have been answered in *Hadadi*.[151]

Hadadi concerned the divorce proceedings of a married couple, Mr Hadadi and Ms Mesko, in which the ECJ had to answer a preliminary question on the interpretation of Council Regulation No 2201/2003.[152] Both spouses were originally of Hungarian nationality, but became dual nationals after naturalization in France in 1985. On 23 February 2002, Mr Hadadi instituted divorce proceedings before a Hungarian Court. This divorce was granted on 4 May 2004, that is to say, after the Hungarian accession to the EU on 1 May 2004. Divorce proceedings that had meanwhile been started by Ms Mesko in France were initially declared inadmissible, but this decision was overturned by a

150 Veerle van den Eeckhout, "Europese bemoeienis met internationaal privaatrecht: ook ten aanzien van internationale familieverhoudingen die 'externe' aspecten vertonen?", *Nederlands tijdschrift voor Europees recht*, no. 11 (2004): 308.

151 See for an analysis Veerle van den Eeckhout, "Het beroep op het bezit van een nationaliteit in geval van dubbele nationaliteit. Enkele aantekeningen naar aanleiding van de uitspraak Hadadi (C-168/08) van het Hof van Justitie", *Nederlands tijdschrift voor Europees recht*, no. 10 (2009): 307–316.

152 Council Regulation No 2201/2003 of 27 November 2003 concerning Jurisdiction and the Recognition and Enforcement of Judgments in Matrimonial Matters and the Matters of Parental Responsibility. On 1 March 2005 this so-called 'Brussels IIbis Regulation' (sometimes also called 'Brussels IIA') repealed and replaced the 'Brussels II Regulation' (Council Regulation 1347/2000 on Jurisdiction and the Recognition and Enforcement of Judgments in Matrimonial Matters and the Matters of Parental Responsibility for Children of Both Spouses). The Regulation almost exclusively aims at the easy, unrestricted circulation of judicial decisions through mutual recognition, regardless of their content. See on these legal instruments Bogdan, *Concise Introduction to EU Private International Law*, chapter 5; Johan Meeusen, "Op weg naar een communautair internationaal familie(vermogens)recht? Enkele Europeesrechtelijke beschouwingen", in *Europees internationaal familierecht. Preadviezen van Prof. Dr Johan Meeusen en Mr G.E.Schmidt, Mededelingen van de Nederlandse Vereniging voor Internationaal Recht* (Den Haag: T.M.C. Asser Press, 2006), 54ff; Peter Stone, *EU Private International Law* (Cheltenham: Edward Elgar Publishing, 2006), chapter 16; Veerle van den Eeckhout, "Het Hof van Justitie als steun en toeverlaat in tijden van Europeanisatie van het IPR? Mogelijkheden tot aanspreken van een Europese scheidingsrechter na de uitspraak van het Hof van Justitie in de zaak *Sundelind Lopez* (C-68/07)", *Nederlands tijdschrift voor Europees recht*, no. 3 (2008).

French Appeal Court. When Mr Hadadi subsequently appealed against the Court of Appeal's decision, the French Cour de Cassation decided to ask the ECJ for a preliminary ruling on the interpretation of Article 3(1) of Regulation 2201/2003.[153]

According to the ECJ the three questions submitted by the national court essentially asked whether a Hungarian Court could have jurisdiction under Article 3(1) of the Regulation to rule in divorce proceedings between both spouses.[154] The first question submitted to the Court basically comes down to whether Article 3(1)(b) of the Regulation should be interpreted as meaning that a French court must apply French law to a case brought before it by persons who in addition to their French nationality are also both in possession of the nationality of another Member State.[155] Although the Regulation does not contain specific provisions concerning dual nationality, the ECJ held that 'where the spouses hold both the nationality of the Member State of the court seised and that of the same other Member State, that court must take into

---

[153] The discussion centers on the part of Article 3(1)(a) which grants jurisdiction to the court of the Member State 'in whose territory the spouses are habitually resident' and Article 3(1)(b), which grants jurisdiction to the court of the Member State 'of the nationality of both spouses'.

[154] We leave aside for the moment the complication that Regulation 2201/2003 was not yet in force at the time the Hungarian Court gave its judgment and that therefore a transitional provision had to be applied. In accordance with that transitional provision, the application of Regulation 2201/2003 was dependent on whether the courts of the State in which the judgment was originally given would have had jurisdiction under the Regulation. AG Kokott remarks in this connection (paras. 29 and 30) that the French court was thus faced, in applying the transitional provision, with the usual situation of adjudicating, not on its own jurisdiction, but on that of the courts of another Member State. The normal course of events would have been that each court seised examined only its own jurisdiction. If the court considered to have jurisdiction and gave judgment in the matter, that judgment must in principle be recognized in another Member State under the Regulation.

[155] We have seen in Section 3 *supra* that in France the approach prevails to only take into account a dual national's French nationality (this practice is recapitulated in d'Avout's annotation of *Hadadi*). AG Kokott did not endorse this approach in the present case (paras. 33–42), and concludes that 'Article 3(1)(b) precludes persons with dual nationality from being treated exclusively as own nationals'. The AG also refers to the so-called 'Borrás Report' to the 'Convention on Jurisdiction and the Recognition and Enforcement of Judgments in Matrimonial Matters', which was the predecessor of Regulation 2201/2003. This report (the last part of para. 33) states: 'The Convention is silent on the consequences of dual nationality, so the judicial bodies of each State will apply their national rules within the framework of general Community rules on the matter'. Though assuming the correctness of this statement, the AG distinguishes the Convention from a Regulation in that for the latter an autonomous interpretation that is based on the spirit and purpose of the provisions is to be preferred (para. 37). The question which nationality must be taken into account can thus not be determined exclusively in accordance with nationality law.

account the fact that the courts of that other Member State could, since the persons concerned hold the nationality of the latter State, properly have been seised of the case under Article 3(1)(b) of Regulation 2201/2003'.[156] Thus, Article 3(1)(b) 'precludes the court of the Member State addressed [France] from regarding spouses who each hold the nationality both of that State and of the Member State of origin as nationals only of the Member State addressed'.[157]

The Court then considered the second and third questions in which the referring court asked whether it should only take into account the most effective nationality or whether both nationalities should be taken into consideration. In the light of this chapter, in particular Section 3 which deals with the national approach in a conflict of nationalities, these are obviously fundamental questions. Ms Mesko, claiming that the French nationality of herself and her husband was certainly the effective one due to their long residence in France, argued that not applying the effective nationality would lead to a 'rush to the courts' or 'forum shopping' because Article 19 of the Regulation provides that if two courts are seised, jurisdiction lies with the court first seised.[158] Mr Hadadi maintained that an effectivity test could not be deduced from Article 3(1)(b).

The Court agreed with the latter argument by first pointing out that no hierarchy is established between the grounds of jurisdiction in Article 3(1)(a) and (b) (that is, jurisdiction on the ground of habitual residence on the one hand and nationality on the other). Second, neither the wording of Article 3(1)(b) nor its objectives nor the context of which it forms part suggest that only the effective nationality should be taken into account in applying that provision.[159] The Court held that since habitual residence is normally an essential consideration in determining the effective nationality, application of the effective nationality would create an undesirable hierarchy between

---

156 Para. 42.

157 Para. 43.

158 On the danger of forum shopping under the Brussels IIbis Regulation, see critically Meeusen, "Op weg naar een communautair internationaal familie(vermogens)recht?", 57–58; d'Avout, "Jurisprudence: Hadadi": 163; Wolfgang Hau, "Doppelte Staatsangehörigkeit im europäischen Eheverfahrensrecht (Hadadi)", *IPRax* 30, no. 1 (2010): 53.

159 The AG had referred in this context to the preamble of Regulation 2201/2003 according to which the Regulation will contribute to creating an area of freedom, security and justice, in which the free movement of persons is ensured. Thus, she concludes, the Regulation serves to enable persons who have exercised their freedom of movement to have a flexible choice of forum (paras. 55–58). This objective would be undermined by only taking into account a dual national's more effective nationality. The AG finds this view confirmed in paragraph 27 and 28 of the 'Borrás Report'.

the grounds of jurisdiction. Such a hierarchy was incompatible with the Regulation's objective of contributing to 'creating an area of freedom, security and justice, in which the free movement of persons is ensured'.[160] The Court did not refute Ms Mesko's claim that the Regulation might induce spouses to rush into seising one of the courts having jurisdiction, but disagrees that this is to be regarded as an abuse.[161]

Concluding Remarks

It has been submitted by Franck that the claim to a self-designed identity (in other words, personal self-determination) became manifest in the second half of the 20th century in a series of specific claims. These included the right 'to choose one's own nationality or nationalities, as well as trans-nation affinities, [and] to select one's preferred name and that of one's children'.[162] This quote may be considered as a concise summing up of our discussion on dual nationality thus far. Indeed, it stresses two important elements that are intricately related to the phenomenon of dual nationality: identity (both of the State and the individual) and human rights. Both elements have been subject to considerable change over the last decades; this in turn has greatly influenced the perception of dual nationality.

Thus, the human rights considerations which lay at the basis of gender equality in European nationality law from the 1970s as well as the fight against statelessness currently influence the call for the toleration of dual nationality.[163] Human rights considerations also played a role in *García Avello* and *Grunkin-Paul*; AG Jacobs particularly emphasized that a name constitutes a fundamental part of one's identity and private life. In this connection, we will also take the opportunity to repeat a statement by Aghahosseini about the effect of the increasing acceptance of dual nationality on the international

[160] Para. 47.

[161] Para. 57.

[162] Franck, *The Empowered Self. Law and Society in the Age of Individualism*, 63.

[163] Despite Faist's remark that 'if pressed to single out one key factor influencing the increase in tolerance of dual citizenship, it is perhaps the growing importance of human rights in international and national law', we have seen above that the position of nationality as a human right is not particularly strong (Chapter 1, Section 5.1). Faist himself also points to an inherent tension between citizens' rights and human rights: 'Human rights point towards open borders and a pattern of membership which is not only overlapping and nested but also gradual, with no fixed but rather porous lines, furthering the inclusion of outsiders. In contrast, citizens' rights point towards the necessity of protecting social and political orders from over-inclusion'. Faist, "Dual citizenship: Change, Prospects, and Limits", 174–176, 197.

plane.[164] He stresses that the growing importance of human rights from the Second World War onwards resulted in legal instruments under which the individual is accorded protection even against the State of which he is a national. We have seen that Aghahosseini regarded the choice for the dominant nationality as the logical consequence of the growing acceptance of dual nationality:

> Where dual nationality is looked upon with disdain, and the treatment of the individual by his State of nationality is considered to be no concern of international law, the application of the rule of non-responsibility … seems quite natural. Not so where dual nationality is accepted as a very common phenomenon, and States are increasingly held responsible for the wrongs they commit against individuals, including their own nationals. Clearly, of the two rules of non-responsibility and dominant nationality, it is the latter that is consistent with these last-mentioned conditions … It may be defensibly suggested that the Tribunal's support for the rule of dominant nationality was both a legitimate exercise of judicial function and, prompted primarily by a desire to accord the individual greater access to international justice, a theoretically laudable choice … It was also in line with the modern trend of promoting the international interests of the individual *vis-à-vis* the State … By rejecting the rule of non-responsibility, under which the nationality of the respondent State deprives the individual of international protection, and by opting for the rule of dominant nationality, under which international protection is available in cases of closer ties with the claimant State, the Tribunal clearly lent its judicial support for, and markedly contributed towards the realization of [human rights demands].[165]

The remainder of this conclusion will assess the place of dual nationality in PIL and EU law. In the conclusion to Chapter 1 we already mentioned that the ECJ handed down a number of controversial judgments in which dual nationality featured prominently. In our opinion, however, the Court rightly takes the view that the traditional PIL approach of either automatically applying the nationality of the forum or of applying an effectivity test cannot be applied in a Community context. Although the Court's reasoning (*inter alia* used in *García Avello* and *Micheletti*) has been criticized, we feel that the Court is right in adopting a functional approach to the objectives of the Treaty: it attempts to remove the barriers to the exercise of free movement by European citizens, thereby giving more substance to the concept of European citizenship. Yet we also recognize that in doing so the Court makes inroads into a number of sensitive fields, which in addition are still within the discretion of the Member States, such as nationality law and personal status.

---

[164] *Supra* Chapter 1, Section 9.

[165] Aghahosseini, *Claims of Dual Nationals and the Development of Customary International Law*, 256–258.

This chapter has shown that the issue of dual nationality also comes up in the field of PIL and EU law, often in relation to the question of identity. We feel that the role of dual nationality in these fields is slightly neglected in the literature; moreover, the issue of identity is often exclusively raised in the context of the State's rules on acquisition and loss of nationality. However, the present chapter has demonstrated that the State's identity is also affected by which legal solution is adopted in respect of a 'conflict of nationalities', i.e. when an already existing situation of dual nationality calls for a concrete solution by a court. The possible solutions to such a conflict are as fiercely debated as the preliminary question whether to accept or fight dual nationality. This follows from the fact that many authors have strong presuppositions about the role (dual) nationality in the nation-state in terms of societal cohesion and political integration. This shall be demonstrated in the subsequent country reports in the context of the State's policy towards dual nationality. However, presuppositions about the role of nationality just as well exist in the field of PIL; we need only to recall the opposing views of Lagarde/De la Pradelle and Lequette/d'Avout on how to deal with a conflict of nationalities. It was seen that Lequette's opposition to the 'functional approach' as proposed by Lagarde was based on the critique that this approach neglected the primordial function of nationality in creating national and social cohesion. The widely differing views on the best solution to such a conflict are therefore traceable to different conceptions of nationality's societal role.

The issue we will therefore focus on in this conclusion is how to deal with dual nationality in PIL when nationality is used as a connecting factor. The question was raised on a number of occasions whether it is makes sense that legislators increasingly accept dual nationality, and contribute to its existence by adopting rules which create instances of dual nationality, while courts often disregard the concrete manifestations of these belongings by automatically applying the nationality of the forum. We have just seen that it is claimed this latter approach provides legal certainty and contributes to a country's national and social cohesion. Its opponents, who instead propose the use of an effectivity test or a functional approach to a conflict of nationalities, are criticized for ignoring the merits of the long-standing practice of only taking into consideration the nationality of the forum. Their solutions are also criticized for their casuistic character.

We admit that the automatic preference for the nationality of the forum makes life easier for the courts, but do not agree that this approach contributes to the stability of a dual national's status in matters of personal status and family law. An effectivity test is indeed more casuistic, but will not violate the principle of legal certainty because a dual national normally has a quite stable effective nationality. In contrast to the traditional approach, which 'mechanically' applies the nationality of the forum, application of the effective nationality also allows taking into account the circumstances of the particular case.

From the above, it follows that the discussion on the role of nationality in the preservation of nationality identity is not only found in the domain of public law but also in the realm of private law (for our purposes primarily family law). However, the role of dual nationality is much less frequently discussed from a PIL perspective. This will also become apparent from the country reports, where the discussion on dual nationality focuses almost exclusively on its public aspects: should immigrants born in the country be automatically attributed nationality at birth (France) and should naturalisees be allowed to retain their nationality of origin (the Netherlands)? And should one allow dual nationality for former emigrants and their descendants and facilitate the acquisition of nationality for this particular group (Italy and Spain)? The role of dual nationality in PIL is rather neglected in this (heated) debate.

The focus on the public dimension of nationality is logical, though, if we bear in mind that of the four countries under consideration only the Netherlands allows for an effectivity test in a case concerning a dual national, one of whose nationalities is that of the forum. In the other three countries the nationality of the forum is automatically applied; the foreign nationalities that the dual national may possess are simply ignored. Our examination of the case law of the ECJ on dual nationality has shown that this approach (i.e. the disregard of any other Member State nationalities that the own national possesses) cannot be taken in situations of dual nationality which fall within the scope of EU law: in *Micheletti*, *García Avello* and *Hadadi*, the Court explicitly rejects both the automatic application of the nationality of the forum and the effectivity test as a solution to a conflict of Member State nationalities.

This approach was first taken by the Court in the pre-European citizenship case *Micheletti* in the context of freedom of establishment: Spain could not disregard Micheletti's Italian nationality by arguing that his Argentinean nationality was the effective one. After the introduction of European citizenship this was applied in a case which at first sight looked like a wholly internal situation: *García Avello*. Here it was decided that the status of European citizen of the García Avello children meant that Belgium (the country where they were habitually resident and of which they also held the nationality) could not simply disregard their Spanish nationality. Finally, in *Hadadi* it was held that the 'area of freedom, security and justice' in which the freedom of persons is ensured stands in the way of an effectivity test. The objective of the Brussels IIbis Regulation of offering a flexible choice of forum and of establishing an unrestricted circulation of judicial decisions through mutual recognition does not allow such a test: as habitual residence would normally be a decisive consideration in determining the effective nationality, the application of the criterion would undermine the objective of the Regulation. The only case in which a Member State was allowed to apply the own nationality in a situation of dual nationality was *Mesbah*, a case on the interpretation of the EEC-Morocco Cooperation Agreement. The fact that in *Mesbah* the second nationality concerned the nationality of a non-Member State was crucial for the Court's decision to allow Belgium to determine the case in accordance with Belgian law.

The role of dual nationality in PIL thus comes much to the fore in the ECJ case law, also because the EU has no competence to regulate on substantive issues (acquisition and loss) of Member State nationality, as was recently confirmed again in *Rottmann*.[166] This leads to an interesting conclusion: the EU influence on the Member States is not so much felt with regard to *nationality as such*—despite judgments like *Micheletti* and *Rottmann*, the EU influence on substantive issues of nationality is still weak—but especially with regard to *dual nationality*. Indeed, *García Avello* and *Hadadi* might be considered more controversial—because they actually intrude on Member State sovereignty[167]—than the former two decisions. It is thus in the domain of private international law, that is, how to deal with a conflict between two Member State nationalities, that the European influence is most strongly felt. Here the Court seriously impinges on the Member States' practice (which is moreover still in force on the international level[168]) of ignoring any dual nationality of their nationals.

With regard to the substantive nationality laws of the Member States, the EU is at present simply confronted with 27 different nationality policies of States that have a very wide discretion in the domain of nationality law. There are no signs that the EU aspires to acquire competence in this field, but the call

---

166 *Supra* Chapter 1, Section 11.2.3.

167 See the following remark by d'Avout concerning *García Avello* and *Hadadi*, and the role of dual nationality in combination with European citizenship: 'Dans l'Espace judiciaire européen, et à chaque fois qu'est en cause l'application du droit de l'Union …, le citoyen européen serait libre de se placer dans les souliers nationaux de son choix. Le hongrois, naturalisé français à sa demande, pourrait à sa guise, se faire passer en France pour un français ou un hongrois. Autrement dit—au nom du droit communautaire—il pourrait systématiquement se soustraire au traitement restrictif que son État national prétend lui imposer. *À affermir ces conjectures, la citoyenneté européenne apparaîtrait comme prenant le pas sur la citoyenneté étatique, alors même que celle-ci est constitutionnellement à la source de celle-là*' (emphasis added). d'Avout, "Jurisprudence: Hadadi": 171.

168 See Boll's analysis in Chapter 1, Section 10.

for minimum harmonization in the academic literature is becoming louder. This issue will again be raised in the country reports on Italy and Spain, for their nationality laws are so inclusive towards former emigrants and their descendants that this policy raises important questions as regards access to European citizenship. Yet Member State discretion has been severely limited by the ECJ when it comes to the recognition of the validity of other Member State nationalities (*Micheletti*), or where the recognition of decisions on personal status of dual Member State nationals are concerned (*García Avello*).

The previous observations on dual nationality bring us to a final point before proceeding to the Conclusion to Part I: how is *the general concept of nationality* affected by the abovementioned developments? Has its role been limited over the years? On the one hand, there can be no doubt that the competence to legislate in the field of nationality is still firmly in the hands of the nation-state; this was also confirmed in Chapter 1 where we discussed nationality in international law. On the other hand, a number of inroads are nonetheless made into the role of nationality. Not for nothing did Lequette call one of his contributions 'La nationalité française dévaluée'. Here we briefly mention four elements which appear to have weakened the role of nationality in recent decades.

First, the status of *denizen* has given immigrants rights that closely resemble those of nationals. One may thus seriously query whether there is still a strong incentive for immigrants to naturalize. Second, as a connecting factor nationality has been replaced by habitual residence in many fields; it has primarily maintained its role only in the domain of family law and personal status. Third, the case law of the Court of Justice does not allow the automatic application of the nationality of the forum in cases concerning dual nationals possessing more than one Member State nationality. This constitutes a serious infringement, especially taking into account the growing number of individuals in possession of several Member State nationalities. Thus, although Member States are still sovereign in deciding who their nationals are, the Court forbids them to simply ignore any other nationalities these nationals may hold. Put another way, Member States have retained full competence in deciding on the acquisition and loss of their nationality, but considerable limits have been imposed on what we may perhaps call the 'private international law component to nationality': Member States can no longer give automatic preference to their own nationality. Fourth and finally, the EU citizenship case law forms a constant threat to nationality. The more substance EU citizenship acquires, the more the different Member State nationalities are 'devalued'.

Concluding Remarks: Part I

Now that we have reached the conclusion to Part I, we should have a fairly good picture of the role of dual nationality in different fields of the law. The scene was set in Chapter 1, where we discussed the most relevant characteristics of (dual) nationality for the present study. Chapter 2 built on this by looking in more detail to dual nationality in the specific context of the EU. We discussed both the traditional private international law approach to a 'conflict of nationalities' in the four countries under discussion as well as the approach taken by the Court of Justice; in the latter's case law, Union citizenship plays a fundamental role. This study is not the place, however, for a detailed discussion of the Court's interpretation of the EU citizenship provisions. For our purposes, suffice it to say that Union citizenship is at present a non-crystallized concept with great potential.[1] The body of case law on EU citizenship is ever growing (predominantly in the field of social law) and of increasing importance.[2] In the knowledge that EU citizenship is being fleshed out by the Court, and that the Treaty connects to it the right to freely move and reside in the territory of the Union, more and more non-Member State nationals aspire to become European citizens. Yet they can only acquire this status by becoming a Member State national first. Hence, it is time to take the next step in our analysis by examining the dual nationality policies of France, Italy, the Netherlands and Spain.

The approach of these countries towards dual nationality plays an essential part in the discussion on access to Member State nationality. Accordingly, we investigate, on the one hand, whether these States allow dual nationality or whether they require naturalisees to renounce their nationality of origin upon naturalization. The renunciation requirement—commonly seen as a great obstacle to naturalization—is traditionally found in immigration countries who want to force immigrants to an unconditional choice for the new country

[1] As the EU is a constructed and flexible community, EU citizenship can never be the reflection of a pre-existing or pre-political view about community membership. Thus, most commentators see EU citizenship as a catalyst which can further the process of European integration and which can potentially help to establish a European identity. See for example Kostakopoulou, "European Union Citizenship: Writing the Future": 642. On the 'constitutional' role of EU citizenship see Shaw, "Citizenship: Contrasting Dynamics at the Interface of Integration and Constitutionalism", 8.

[2] According to Dougan, 'the introduction of Union citizenship furnished the Court with the opportunity ... to embark upon a more thorough judicial review of the relevant regulatory choices made by the Community legislature'. Dougan, "The constitutional dimension to the case law on Union citizenship": 622, 640.

of residence. Consequently, we shall see that the debate on the renunciation requirement features prominently in the Netherlands, and to a lesser extent in France. Emigration countries, on the other hand, want to maintain ties with their emigrant population. The country reports on Italy and Spain demonstrate that dual nationality is a particularly useful instrument for this purpose.

The scene is thus set for Part II: what impact does the attitude towards dual nationality have on access to Member State nationality—and consequently on EU citizenship? This attitude is especially relevant—as well as controversial—in relation to non-Member State nationals (in the conclusion to Chapter 1 we already argued that multiple nationality seems to be relatively non-controversial if it involves two or more Member State nationalities). The obvious follow-up questions are: what if Member States, by allowing dual nationality and giving preferential treatment to certain groups of non-Member State nationals residing outside EU territory, are creating EU citizens on a large scale who, importantly, do not always seem to have a particularly strong link with the Member State granting its nationality? EU citizens can freely move in the EU territory; they may move, for cultural or work-related reasons, to other Member States than the one whose nationality they acquired. In sum, each Member State is affected by the nationality policy of the others. Tensions will inevitably arise, but will this also lead to the harmonization of rules in the sensitive field of nationality law?

Part II

Country Reports on Dual Nationality: The Extra-EU Context

Introductory Remarks on the Country Reports

The reasons for including a number of country studies in this book have already been discussed in the General Introduction and in the course of Part I (in particular in the conclusions to the previous chapters). We do not want to fall in the trap of repetition, but shall instead use this occasion to make some preliminary observations on the different nationality traditions of the countries under discussion, which in the following reports are grouped into two pairs representing traditional immigration and emigration countries respectively. We also take the opportunity to stress that the short concluding remarks following the countries' analysis are merely brief recapitulations of the respective chapters. It is only in the General Conclusions that comparative remarks will be made and that the impact of the respective dual nationality policies will be assessed.

In contrast to Chapter 2, which looked at dual nationality in what we called the 'intra-EU context'—that is, a dual nationality being composed of only Member State nationalities—the country reports mainly deal with the 'extra-EU dimension'. In other words, they primarily look at the attitude towards dual nationality in relation to non-Member State nationals.

In the field of nationality law it is rather obvious to compare France with the Netherlands, both being traditional countries of immigration that have faced the question how to incorporate newcomers. It will be shown that dual nationality has not been as heavily debated in recent decades in France as it was in the Netherlands, but the Dutch controversy on multiple nationality in a way finds its French counterpart in the discussion on the role of *ius soli* in French nationality law. We will see that this discussion, which in essence centred around questions of French identity, bears some similarity with the Dutch debate on multiple nationality. The final sections of the chapter on France pay attention to this *ius soli* debate. Ernest Renan's famous 1882 essay 'Qu'est-ce qu'une nation?' proved to have lost none of its force and was frequently invoked by those who desired a *voluntary* membership of the French nation instead of the *automatic* membership *iure soli*.[1]

In fact, it will become apparent from the comparative chapters that nationality law plays a fundamental role in the domestic discussion on nationality identity. Thus, the Spanish and Italian emigration experience is still evident in their current nationality laws and is reflected in their attitude towards emigrants and their descendants, who can benefit from dual nationality and eased

[1] Weil, *How to Be French: Nationality in the Making since 1789*, 157.

access to Spanish and Italian nationality. The Italian case is in many respects similar to that of Spain. Both countries witnessed large scale emigration of their nationals in the 20th century, especially to Latin America. Spanish and Italian nationality law also manifests the will to maintain ties with former emigrants and their descendants.

The countries differ, however, in that Spain (officially) only allows multiple nationality in respect of a limited number of countries, whereas Italy wholeheartedly espoused multiple nationality in the Nationality Act of 1992, which is still in force. Another difference is perhaps the nature of both countries' bond with Latin America. In the chapter on Spain we will see that from the 1950s onwards dual nationality was explicitly accepted between Spain and Latin American countries for historical, cultural and linguistic reasons. Although concrete steps to a dual nationality regime were therefore taken under Franco's dictatorial regime, the idea of *Hispanidad* is a much longer tradition and can be traced back to the Republican Constitution of 1931.

Similar observations do not apply to the relationship between Italy and, in particular, Argentina and Brazil—the two main countries of emigration of Italian emigrants. The Italian acceptance of dual nationality can probably better be explained by the wish to maintain links with Italian emigrants abroad, and the hope that the country will benefit from this Italian diaspora. The embrace of dual nationality also fits neatly into the general picture of Italian nationality law, based as it is on the family model: the combination of dual nationality and unlimited transmission of Italian nationality *iure sanguinis* will guarantee that the 'Italian family' will not fall apart. In the words of Pastore: 'Italian nationality continues to be conceived, with regard to emigrant Italians, as an extremely tenacious bond, which nowadays is broken almost exclusively by free individual choice'.[2] The characteristic Italian emphasis on blood ties and the importance of emigrants for the Italian motherland have been articulated by Tintori with a telling metaphor: the large-scale emigration of fellow Italians was considered a painful but necessary bloodletting for the general good of the country. The lost blood was fallen back on in times of economic and political anaemia. In other words, the remittances from abroad constituted an important source of income for those who had stayed behind, and the emigrants could defend the Italian interests abroad, thereby helping to strengthen Italy's international position.[3]

---

[2] Ferruccio Pastore, "Immigration in Italy today. A community out of balance: nationality law and migration politics in the history of post-unification Italy", *Journal of Modern Italian Studies* 9, no. 1 (2004): 35.

[3] Guido Tintori, "Cittadinanza e politiche di emigrazione nell'Italia liberale e fascista. Un approfondimento storico", in *Familismo legale: come (non) diventare italiani*, ed. Giovanna Zincone (Roma-Bari: Editori Laterza, 2006), 102.

Chapter 3

France

1. *Introduction*

The choice to devote a separate chapter on dual nationality in France is perhaps not readily explainable if we start with the observation that France has generally been indifferent towards dual nationality, and that it has tolerated this phenomenon since the First World War.[1] It has been argued that the French indifference can be historically explained by the 'demographic imperative', i.e. the need for new citizens (especially after the First World War). Just like Great Britain, France was not particularly concerned whether these new French nationals retained their nationality of origin upon becoming French.[2] Others have explained the tolerant attitude towards dual nationality by a pragmatic view of (dual) nationality in France. This view considers that those who are sufficiently assimilated in France should become French and should not remain foreigners.[3] Nevertheless, the *official* toleration of dual nationality in France only came about under the Nationality Act of 1973; previous legislation, in particular the ordinance of 19 October 1945, was still characterized by hostility.[4]

Although the French position on dual nationality may thus appear abundantly clear, it would be too hasty a conclusion to suppose that the issue of dual nationality never arose throughout the previous century. In fact, it was object of discussion and controversy during the First World War, and also later in connection with dual French-Algerians. This chapter seeks to trace the French position on dual nationality and considers the different contexts in which it manifested itself.

It should also be mentioned that France has adopted a rather odd position on dual nationality in the Council of Europe, in two respects.[5] First, it is

---

1 Weil and Spire, "France", 187.

2 Weil, *How to Be French: Nationality in the Making since 1789*, 228, 237.

3 Lagarde, "La pluralité de nationalités comme moyen d'intégration des résidents étrangers: Développements en France", 2–3. See also the remarks on the French civic-republican conception of nationality in Chapter 1, Section 2.

4 Olekhnovitch, "La double nationalité": 24.

5 de Groot and Vink, *Meervoudige nationaliteit in Europees perspectief*, 145.

remarkable that France, with its long tradition of toleration of dual nationality, joined the 1963 Convention and its additional Second Protocol in the first place; second, it is strange that they were not denounced earlier.[6] France was a party to the 1963 Convention and the Second Protocol until 5 March 2009. In 1987 however, during debates on a new French Nationality Code, the *Commission de la Nationalité* unsuccessfully pleaded for the renegotiation of the first chapter of the 1963 Convention because it was thought to be outdated.[7] Lagarde also remarked in 1992 that the Strasbourg Convention violated the spirit of French nationality law ever since the 1973 reform.[8] Although this is true—the law reform of 1973 not only secured the full equality of men and women in nationality law, with obvious effects for the subject of dual nationality, but it also fully accepted dual nationality—Lagarde might have added that the French tolerance of dual nationality was developed much earlier and that the 1963 Convention was thus contrary to a long-standing tradition which tolerated dual nationality.[9] This at least is the view of Weil and Spire who, as we shall see, point out that despite its adherence to the 1963

[6] The 1963 Convention and the Second Protocol were ratified on 26 January 1965 and 23 February 1995 respectively. Their denunciation on 4 March 2008 took effect on 5 March 2009. In relation to the 1963 Convention, Costa-Lascoux rightly remarked that 'c'est entre des pays ayant des droits très proches que la plurinationalité est théoriquement impossible. En revanche, les situations de double nationalité se multiplient entre des systèmes juridiques très différents des droit européens' (she obviously refers to the Magreb countries). Jacqueline Costa-Lascoux, "L'acquisition de la nationalité française, une condition d'intégration?", in *Questions de nationalité. Histoire et enjeux d'un code*, ed. Smaïn Laacher (Paris: Éditions l'Harmattan, 1987), 104.

[7] Commission de la Nationalité, *Être français aujourd'hui et demain. Rapport remis au Premier ministre par Marceau Long, président de la commission de la Nationalité (Tome 2: Conclusions et propositions de la Commission de la Nationalité)* (Paris: Documentation française, 1988), 184; Lagarde, *La nationalité française*, 4, 31.

[8] Lagarde, "La pluralité de nationalités comme moyen d'intégration des résidents étrangers: Développements en France", 8.

[9] For all the alleged tolerance of dual nationality in France since the early 20th century, it did not mean that it was embraced as an idea. Rather, its toleration seemed inspired by pragmatic considerations related to the demographic imperative or decolonization; under different circumstances—for example in a European context—dual nationality was still particularly controversial. We would like to thank the officials working on nationality matters at the French Ministry of Justice for pointing this out. Several of these officials also see the French participation to the 1963 Convention as a counter measure to the European unification started in the 1950s, the idea being prevalent at the time that unification should not come at the expense of nationality identity. Some officials explained the late denunciation of the 1963 Convention by the wish to wait for the Council of Europe to draft a new nationality treaty. Accession to the 1997 European Convention on Nationality thus paved the way for the renunciation of the 1963 Convention. This is not a very strong argument, however, for France has not yet ratified the ECN; why France does not proceed to ratification is also a mystery to French doctrine

Convention, France has always allowed newly naturalized citizens to retain their previous nationality—except for those directly concerned by the 1963 Convention.[10] It would therefore be wrong to interpret the French adherence to the 1963 Convention as evidence of a prevailing idea in France that one should not possess more than one nationality. In practice, France long since accepted the retention of the nationality of origin upon becoming French, apart from cases where the Convention was operative.[11]

For a number of reasons it seems useful to devote somewhat more attention to 19th century nationality law in France compared to the other three countries under consideration. This particularly concerns the development of the *ius soli* principle. Not only is dual nationality a more frequent phenomenon in countries whose nationality law is at least partly based on *ius soli*,[12] we also feel that the strong position of *ius soli* in France and the general weakness of ethnic elements in the nationality discourse have had a decisive bearing on the toleration of dual nationality in France.

The first reason for concentrating in more detail on the historical background of nationality in France therefore has to do with the historical fact that France broke new ground in nationality law by abolishing *ius soli* and making *ius sanguinis* the core principle for the acquisition of French nationality. This French invention, which had a profound impact on other continental countries, has already been discussed at some length in Chapter 1 (Section 1). Secondly, at the end of the 19th century France was the only country of immigration in Europe, a fact which ultimately led to the reintroduction of *ius soli*.[13] This example was also followed by many European countries when they in turn became countries of immigration.[14] The strong position of *ius soli* makes

(see recently d'Avout in his annotation of *Hadadi*). Yet the view of the officials seems to correspond with remarks by Hall on the 1963 Convention: '[The Convention] was framed on the assumption that cases of dual or multiple nationality were a hindrance to the achievement of greater unity among the Council's members'. The 1963 Convention reflected 'a very State-centred view of European integration' which was based on the Gaullist idea of greater unity through inter-State co-operation. In Hall's view, this conception changed over time and he refers in this respect to the establishment of EU citizenship and the neutrality of the ECN on the issue of dual nationality. See Hall, "The European Convention on Nationality and the right to have rights": 599.

10 Christophe Daadouch, *Le droit de la nationalité* (Paris: Editions MB formation, 2002), 57; Weil and Spire, "France", 187.

11 Patrick Weil, *La France et ses étrangers. L'aventure d'une politique de l'immigration de 1938 à nos jours*, nouvelle édition refondue (Paris: Gallimard, 2004), 446–447.

12 Brubaker, *Citizenship and Nationhood in France and Germany*, 144.

13 Weil and Spire, "France", 187.

14 Ibid., 207.

France the archetypical example of an assimilationist and integrative country. In short, it is France's pioneering role in nationality law over the last two centuries which demands a somewhat more in-depth examination of 19th century developments in France compared to the other countries under discussion.

The comparative chapters are partly characterized by recurrent topics, for example the effect on dual nationality of gender equality in nationality law. Yet in each of the countries under consideration certain issues stand out; these are the issues we will primarily focus on. With regard to France this concerns in the first place the German Delbrück law of 1913 in relation to the question of loyalty. Another issue that draws the attention is dual nationality in relation with the decolonization process—and with Algeria in particular.[15] Lastly, we will examine the politicization of French nationality law in the 1980s.[16]

2. *Historical Overview. How* ius soli *became 'The Heart of French Nationality Law'*

According to Patrick Weil, France is different from other countries in that 'for as long as it has been defining its nationals, it has experimented with many ways of defining who is "French by birth," and has tried out virtually all possible rules for attributing or withdrawing nationality'.[17] Indeed, in the three *grandes étapes* that Weil identifies in the construction of French nationality—the 1803 Civil Code, the return of *ius soli* in 1889, and the use of nationality as an instrument in French demographic policy, especially after the First World War—it may be seen that France has regularly changed its nationality law in response to the circumstances of the time.[18]

It was seen in Chapter 1 that the roots of modern nationality law can be traced back to the French Revolution, and more particularly the 1803 Civil Code in which *ius sanguinis* was laid down as *the exclusive criterion* for the attribution of French nationality at birth. However, the deliberate break with *ius soli*—which was regarded as belonging to a feudal past—also meant that

15 The Algerian question was also the only real postcolonial immigration problem that France had to face. After all, the French empire had never been one of settlement—unlike Britain, whose postcolonial policy distinguished between privileged return settlers and non-privileged natives. See Joppke, *Selecting by Origin: Ethnic Migration in the Liberal State*, 95–96.

16 Weil and Spire, "France", 196.

17 Weil, *How to Be French: Nationality in the Making since 1789*, 3.

18 Patrick Weil, *Qu'est-ce qu'un Français? Histoire de la nationalité française depuis la Révolution* (Paris: Grasset, 2002), 16.

generations of foreigners lived in France who, although born in France, were not attributed French nationality at birth.

Ius soli would definitively return in 1889. According to Brubaker, this return is primarily to be explained by the state-centered and assimilationist understanding of French identity and less by military and demographic reasons.[19] The *ius soli* rule, as designed in 1889 and still in force today, entails the following: French nationality is attributed to a child born in France to at least one parent that was also born in France; a child born in France whose parents are neither French nor born in France will automatically acquire French nationality upon reaching the age of majority if still residing in France. In the latter case, however, French nationality can be refused.[20]

The rather late return of *ius soli* was also discussed in Chapter 1, where it was remarked that attempts were made throughout the 19th century to reintroduce *ius soli* in French nationality law. Double *ius soli* was first proposed in 1831 when an unsuccessful attempt was made to automatically attribute French nationality to male children born in France to a foreign father who himself had been born in France.[21] The resentment concerning the exemption of foreigners from military service was particularly strong in the 1820s because until 1830 the number of persons to be recruited from each region was made on the basis of a calculation of the region's total population—foreigners included. As foreigners were exempted from fulfilling military obligations, the number of conscripts drafted in regions where many foreigners clustered was in no proportion to the region's French population.[22]

The discussion on *ius soli* arose again in the aftermath of the 1848 Revolution. In 1851 a law entered into force declaring French every person born in France to foreign parents on condition that at least one of them was also born in France.[23] The fact that this law allowed for the option to renounce

---

19 Brubaker disagrees with the suggestion of many writers that military and demographic concerns were decisive for the return of *ius soli*: '*Jus soli* was not the product of a deliberate effort by the state to enlarge the population and the pool of military recruits. The problem to which the government responded by introducing and extending *jus soli* was ideological and political, not demographic or military'. The political and ideological reasons to which Brubaker refers are the 'politicized resentment … of the exemption of long-settled foreigners from military service' and the 'distinctively state-centered and assimilationist understanding of nationhood, deeply rooted in political and cultural geography and powerfully reinforced in the 1880s by the Republican program of universal primary education and universal military service'. See Brubaker, *Citizenship and Nationhood in France and Germany*, 85–86, 103.

20 Weil and Spire, "France", 187.

21 Weil, *How to Be French: Nationality in the Making since 1789*, 42.

22 Brubaker, *Citizenship and Nationhood in France and Germany*, 92.

23 Ibid., 93.

French nationality at majority—which was widely exercised to avoid military service[24]—severely limited its success, but the law itself shows the weakness of ethnic motifs in the concept of French national identity at the time. According to Brubaker, there was no principled objection to attributing French nationality to third-generation immigrants.[25]

In the absence of a principled objection against *ius soli*, it may thus come as a surprise that the more radical reform of 1889, which attributed French nationality to second-generation immigrants at majority, was very controversial owing to the general idea that the acquisition of French nationality still ought to be based on descent, and not birthplace.[26] This raises the question how the superior status of *ius sanguinis* over *ius soli* can be explained in the first place and, taking into account the general consensus on the primary status of *ius sanguinis*, how *ius soli* could come to play such a prominent role in French nationality law.

First of all, the commitment to exclusiveness of *ius sanguinis* was only superficial. *Ius sanguinis* was never affirmed on its own merits but by default: 'Its sole virtue was to be free of the defects of *jus soli*', the latter being perceived as a feudal relic which could not express any real attachments and loyalties.[27] Second, the arguments against *ius soli* concerned the absolute and unconditional form of *ius soli* to which no one gave any serious consideration.[28] Hence, in the absence of a principled argument in favour of *ius sanguinis*, and lacking any real opposition to a moderate form of *ius soli*, 'the debate of the 1880s … affords no evidence of a strong ideal commitment to an exclusively descent-based citizenship law'.[29]

Ius soli was perceived differently under the 1889 law from *ius soli* under the *Ancien Régime*, however. The 'republican' use of *ius soli* under the law of 1889 meant that 'the link with the nation no longer resulted from personal allegiance to the king but from upbringing within French society'.[30] A person's link with France was thus guaranteed by one's past residence on the territory. It was residence combined with socialisation (i.e. the acquisition of social

24 Weil, *How to Be French: Nationality in the Making since 1789*, 43.

25 Brubaker, *Citizenship and Nationhood in France and Germany*, 93. Brubaker writes that the transformation of long-term immigrants into Frenchmen was accepted by all and was part of a 'nonpartisan cultural idiom, not a partisan ideology'. Hence, 'the French nation-state was clearly understood by the elite as something that could, in principle accommodate new accessions through immigration'.

26 Ibid., 96.

27 Ibid.

28 Ibid., 97.

29 Ibid.

30 Weil, *How to Be French: Nationality in the Making since 1789*, 52–53.

codes) in French society which had by this time become the foundation of French nationality.[31]

Nevertheless, a moderate ethnicization[32] of French nationality can be witnessed from the 1860s onwards and particularly after the French defeat in the Franco-Prussian war of 1870.[33] This ethnicization was triggered by a revaluation of the French universalist and rationalist tradition. France was left in such a weak and vulnerable position after the war that the universalist claim—perfectly reconcilable with French patriotism when France had been the dominant power in Europe—now stood in the way of the development of a form of patriotism that mirrored the changed geopolitical situation.[34] Rather than universalist ambitions, France was in need of 'a particularist patriotism, a *reserrement*, a contraction and concentration of values and commitments'.[35] The institutions of school and army became particularly important in arousing these patriotic feelings.[36]

Still, the ethnic line of thinking remained too weak to seriously question the more deeply rooted assimilationist features of French nationhood. Brubaker therefore lists the 'rhetoric of inclusion' and the 'weakness of ethnicity' as essential elements in the continuity of French nationality law.[37] As a result, the legislation of 1889 has survived ever since (even during the Second World War under Vichy) and the *ius soli* for second-generation immigrants has remained untouched.[38] We may thus agree with the statement that 'French nationality law as it currently exists was essentially established by 1889'.[39]

The third phase in the construction of French nationality, as identified by Weil, was the use of nationality law in demographic policy. France faced a demographic deficit from the end of the 19th century until the end of the 1930s, a problem which became particularly pressing after the First World War.[40] Due to the large number of war casualties[41] there was a serious need for new (male) citizens. This so-called 'demographic imperative' first of all meant

31 Ibid.

32 The ethnic conception of nationality was addressed in Chapter 1, Section 2.

33 Brubaker, *Citizenship and Nationhood in France and Germany*, 100.

34 Ibid.

35 Ibid.

36 Dominique Colas, *Citoyenneté et nationalité* (Paris: Gallimard, 2004), 114.

37 Brubaker, *Citizenship and Nationhood in France and Germany*, 110–112.

38 Weil, *How to Be French: Nationality in the Making since 1789*, 169–170.

39 Weil and Spire, "France", 187.

40 Weil, *La France et ses étrangers*, 23.

41 Wesseling, *Frankrijk in oorlog, 1870–1962*, 183. Of the countries participating in the First World War, France suffered the most casualties: 1,3 million French were killed and 4,2 million were wounded.

that measures were taken to increase the birth rate and to lower the infant mortality rate.[42] These were measures aimed at the middle and long term, however; in the short term France began to encourage immigration.[43]

Yet in spite of population growth, not nearly enough people were becoming French nationals for the liking of the French State. In 1927 this led to the most liberal legislation the French Republic has ever known.[44] The express goal of the law—the creation of a 100,000 new French nationals each year through naturalization—was to be achieved by a reduction of the waiting period for naturalization from ten to three years.[45] The law indeed had the immediate effect of doubling the number of naturalizations in 1928.[46] The policy of massive naturalization adopted under the law of 1927 was indifferent to the fact whether new French persons kept their original nationality or not. Weil therefore traces the traditional French indifference towards dual nationality back to the law of 1927. A debate on dual nationality did arise around the time of the First World War, however, in relation to the German Delbrück law of 1913.[47] This law is the subject of Section 3.

The demographic imperative also had an important effect on the status of married women. As France had lost twice as many Frenchwomen as it had gained between 1914 and 1924,[48] it was decided under the law of 1927 that a Frenchwoman marrying a foreigner kept her French nationality (and the possibility to transmit this nationality to her children) unless she explicitly opted for that of her husband.[49] We will come back to this issue in Section 5 which is dedicated to the equality of the sexes in French nationality law.

From the mid-1930s the idea of selecting foreigners on the basis of national and ethnic criteria became publicly discussed, obviously due to the rise of fascism.[50] The main spokesperson for this line of thinking was Georges Mauco, a leading expert on immigration, who in his doctoral thesis of 1932 classified the assimilability of foreigners on the basis of ethnicity.[51] As we shall see in

---

42 Weil, *How to Be French: Nationality in the Making since 1789*, 63.

43 Weil and Spire, "France", 190.

44 Ibid.

45 Weil, *How to Be French: Nationality in the Making since 1789*, 55, 68.

46 Ibid., 225. In the period 1928–1933, 125,000 adults and 155,000 children were naturalized.

47 Ibid., 235–237.

48 Ibid., 64. France had become a country of immigration and 'the overrepresentation of men among immigrants had meant that many more French women were transformed into foreigners by marriage than foreign women into Frenchwomen'.

49 Raymond Boulbès, *Droit français de la nationalité* (Paris: Sirey, 1957), 269; Weil, *How to Be French: Nationality in the Making since 1789*, 64, 202.

50 Weil, *How to Be French: Nationality in the Making since 1789*, 72.

51 Ibid., 76. Although Mauco recognized that 'ce n'est pas le sang qui est le lien de la grande solidarité nationale, c'est l'esprit', in his doctoral thesis of 1932 he defended an immigration

Section 4, Mauco remained an influential figure in the years to come but his ideas were not put into practice: until 1939 the French naturalization policy did not take into consideration criteria of national, ethnic, racial and religious origin.[52] It was only under the Vichy regime that those advocating a racist and restrictionist policy would gain the upper hand at the expense of those who supported a policy of openness in nationality and immigration matters.[53]

A new nationality law was drafted in 1945 which again made amendments to the position of the married women in nationality matters. The nationality Act of 1945 provided that a foreign woman who married a Frenchman was automatically granted French nationality and did not—unlike the law of 1927—allow her to express her own choice. Under the law of 1945 French women retained their nationality upon marriage with a foreigner; children born to a French mother were also French even if they had been born abroad.[54] The new nationality law also extended the waiting period for naturalization from three to five years, although this period was considerably reduced for a number of categories.[55]

Nationality matters in the 1960s were dominated by the decolonization process, in particular Algerian independence. In 1973—the end of a liberal period in French nationality law—French nationality law was modified to ensure the definitive equality of the sexes both in terms of marriage and transmission of nationality.[56]

3. *Nationality Law during the Great War (1914–1918): The Fear of the German Delbrück Law*

The Great War (1914–1918) triggered a strong French paranoia towards naturalized persons of enemy origin (Germans, Austrians and Ottomans).[57] The principal cause of the French fear was the Delbrück Law of 22 July 1913.

policy based on ethnicity. This argument, in turn, was based on his survey on the degree of assimilability of different nationalities in which Arabs had the lowest score and Belgians the highest. See Georges Mauco, *Les étrangers en France. Leur rôle dans l'activité économique* (Paris: Armand Colin, 1932), 556.

52 Weil, *How to Be French: Nationality in the Making since 1789*, 82.

53 Ibid., 88, 108. The essence of the 'Vichy law', a law on nationality passed on 23 July 1940, was to allow—without the need to indicate a particular cause—the withdrawal of French nationality that had been acquired under the liberal law of 1927.

54 Ibid., 141.

55 Ibid.

56 Ibid., 151.

57 Ibid., 61.

This law incorporated dual nationality in German law by granting the option to request authorization to retain German nationality upon naturalization abroad on condition, however, of prior authorization by the German government (Article 25(2) of the Delbrück law).[58] Male candidates only acquired such authorization if they agreed to carry out their German military service.[59] The link with Germany was in principle maintained indefinitely because German nationality was also transmitted to children of German emigrants without any specific act required on their part.[60]

Alfred Weil has attributed the German position towards dual nationality on the international level to the existence of a kind of 'dual nationality' on the domestic level. He argued that inhabitants of the German States were in sense dual nationals because the nationality of the German empire was dependent on possession of the nationality of one of the German States. As more nationalities simultaneously existed within the German Empire itself, it was

---

58 An English translation of Article 25 can be found in Thiesing, "Dual allegiance in the German law of nationality and American citizenship": 488. Article 25(1) reads as follows: 'A German who has neither his domicile nor permanent residence in Germany loses his nationality upon the acquisition of a foreign nationality where the latter is acquired on his voluntary application'. Article 25(2) continues: '[German] nationality is not lost by one who before acquiring foreign nationality has applied for and obtained the written consent of the competent authorities of his home State to retain such nationality. Before this consent is given, the German Consul is to be heard'.

Thiesing's description of the parliamentary debate is also useful for a better understanding of the motives that lay behind the Delbrück Law—named after the German Minister of the Interior at the time. According to Thiesing, widespread consent existed on the undesirability of dual nationality, also where German nationals were concerned. However, it was also recognized that in exceptional circumstances it would nonetheless serve the German interest if dual nationality were allowed. These circumstances would arise, for example, when a German was automatically granted another nationality in a country that applied *ius soli*, or if a German acquired a foreign nationality to protect his economic interests. As several countries allegedly did not allow foreigners to acquire real property, retention of German nationality should be possible upon naturalization in these countries. In the specific case of naturalization in the United States, Thiesing alleges that a general consensus exists among German as well as American jurists that 'a German subject loses his German nationality *ipso jure* upon the acquisition of American citizenship for the simple reason that the conferring of the American national character is conditioned upon the unequivocal renunciation … of any prior allegiance by taking the oath of allegiance in a formal court proceeding'. The author also points to Article 36 of the Delbrück Law, which provides that existing treaties (such as the Bancroft Treaties) are not affected by the law. See Alfred Weil, "La double nationalité en droit allemand avant et après la loi du 22 juillet 1913", *Revue critique de droit international privé* 11–12 (1915–1916): 147; Thiesing, "Dual allegiance in the German law of nationality and American citizenship": 488–495.

59 Weil, *How to Be French: Nationality in the Making since 1789*, 186.

60 Weil, "La double nationalité en droit allemand avant et après la loi du 22 juillet 1913": 149.

only logical that Germany would also allow dual nationality in relation to other States.[61]

Darras mentions the Delbrück law as an example of 'la double nationalité offensive': in their effort to 'dominate', States may encourage their emigrants to acquire another nationality while retaining their original nationality. They may do so for cultural and political reasons, but the predominant motivation seems to be of an economic nature: the emigrants' economic integration in the receiving country, which is furthered by acquiring its nationality, will economically benefit the home country. He then contrasts this form of dual nationality with 'la double nationalité defensive', which refers to States (Arab States in particular) that adhere to the idea of perpetual allegiance[62]—called by Darras 'le totalitarisme étatique'. In the latter case, dual nationality is the result of a State's refusal to let go of its nationals even if they acquire another nationality; although the possibility to surrender the nationality of origin is sometimes allowed for, such requests are very seldom granted.[63]

Given the general consensus at the time that cases of dual nationality were undesirable, it comes as no great surprise that the Delbrück law was strongly criticized in the literature.[64] Yet the criticism specifically targeted the fact that

---

[61] Ibid., 142–143. After German unification, the nationality of the German empire was simply added to one's status as national of a particular German State. In the words of Alfred Weil, who also points to the interconnectedness of the two concepts: '[La nationalité d'Empire] s'est simplement superposée aux anciennes nationalités, sans les absorber … Donc pas de nationalité allemande sans la nationalité d'un des États qui composent l'Empire; pas de nationalité particulière sans nationalité d'Empire; l'une et l'autre sont étroitement liées et ne peuvent exister qu'ensemble'.

[62] See in this connection the statement by King Hassan II of Morocco, who recalled in 1997 that every Moroccan, whether living in Morocco or abroad, is tied to Morocco through the principle of allegiance: 'Nous (Roi du Maroc) ne sommes pas uniquement dépositaires de la responsabilité vis-à-vis de nos sujets à l'intérieur du Maroc mais […] nous sommes également lies par la *Beïa* (allégeance) aux Marocains résidant à l'étranger'. Quoted in Zoubir Chattou and Mustapha Belbah, *La double nationalité en question. Enjeux et motivations de la double appartenance* (Paris: Karthala, 2002), 19–20. See also Gianluca P. Parolin, *Citizenship in the Arab World. Kin, Religion and Nation-State* (Amsterdam: Amsterdam University Press, 2009), 93.

[63] In the words of Darras, the defensive form of dual nationality ('le totalitarisme étatique') is 'orientée vers la défense de la politique nationale' and imposes 'la permanence de son allégeance aux ressortissants expatriés' whereas the offensive form is 'attentive aux moyens de réaliser la domination … et assure une implantation active dans le pays étranger'. See Darras, *La double nationalité*, 13–35, 392.

[64] See for example Richard W. Flournoy, "Observations on the new German law of nationality", *American journal of international law* 8 (1914): 477–486; David Jayne Hill, "Dual citizenship in the German imperial and state citizenship law", ibid.12 (1918): 357. In respect of the Delbrück law, Jayne Hill remarks that 'although it is contrary to the generally accepted idea of a single allegiance, dual citizenship is here recognized as a perfectly normal status'.

the law was unique in its unilateral and explicit support for dual nationality among German emigrants who naturalized abroad. It was considered a selfish, nationalist act of the German government, which seemed 'to carry the principle of dual nationality further than it [had] ever been carried before'.[65] Although the Delbrück law seemed first and foremost an instrument designed to protect German emigrants who for economic reasons had to adopt the nationality of their host country but did not want to sever their ties with Germany,[66] Makarov acknowledges that other States suspected from the start that not only economic grounds but also political motives[67] lay behind the adoption of this law.[68] Castro y Bravo also stresses the law's nationalist character, and thinks that its most remarkable aspect consists in the fact that the country whose nationality is acquired is misled because the renunciation of German nationality is ineffective under German law.[69]

In spite of all the criticism expressed in respect of the Delbrück law, it should be emphasized that under this law German nationality was for the first time lost upon acquisition of another one, admittedly with the possibility of keeping German nationality if the German authorities granted permission. Under the previous legislation German nationality was in principle lost after ten years of residence abroad, but this hardly ever happened as loss could easily be circumvented in three ways. First, by requesting a 'certificat d'indigénat' before leaving Germany (possession of this document normally meant that the ten year period would never start to run). Loss of German nationality could also be prevented by registering at a German consulate abroad or by bringing a short visit to Germany. As a result, before the entry into force of the Delbrück law a German would normally end up with a dual nationality upon naturalization abroad.[70] Alfred Weil therefore stressed that the Delbrück law did not introduce a new principle in German law. True, under French law at

---

65 Richard W. Flournoy, "Observations on the new German law of nationality", ibid.8 (1914): 478.

66 Alvarez Rodríguez, *Nacionalidad y emigración*, 36.

67 It should be recalled that this was around the time of the Dreyfus affaire which divided France in the 1890s and early 1900s. Alfred Dreyfus, a French captain, had been wrongly accused and convicted for spying for Germany. It was only after Émile Zola wrote his '*J'accuse*' that the case was re-opened and that Dreyfus was exonerated and reinstated in the army. In brief, the subject of espionage was very topical at the time.

68 Alexander Makarov, *Deutsches Staatsangehörigkeitsrecht. Kommentar* (Frankfurt a.M: Alfred Metzner Verlag, 1966), 135. The author also quotes (in German) the parliamentary debate as described above by Thiesing.

69 de Castro y Bravo, "Nationalité, double et supra-nationalité", 602.

70 'L'Allemand, en acquérant une nationalité étrangère, ne faisait que la cumuler avec l'ancienne'Weil, "La double nationalité en droit allemand avant et après la loi du 22 juillet 1913": 144–146.

the time, French nationality was lost upon naturalization abroad, but this was not necessarily the case under German law. With the Delbrück law however, which introduced automatic loss of German nationality upon naturalization abroad and only allowed dual nationality under exceptional circumstances, German law was thus actually more in line with French law than it had been under the previous German legislation.[71]

The Delbrück Law reinforced the French perception that Germany was a racial nation, an idea that had taken root since the annexation of Alsace-Moselle by Germany in 1870.[72] The French were strongly concerned that the French economy and finance system had been infiltrated under the influence of the 'Delbrück strategy'.[73] As a response, two laws were passed in 1915 and 1917 which allowed for stripping French nationality from naturalized persons of enemy origin.[74] In 1918 a special service was called into being, the service for the control of naturalized persons, which investigated naturalization cases, but the service quickly disappeared after the armistice of November 1918.[75] A proposal to amend the law of 1889 in a way that would rule out the possibility of dual nationality did not materialize.[76]

4. *French Nationality Law after the Second World War*

Demographic concerns also played a role after the Second World War and France was again eager to receive new immigrants.[77] Two ordinances were adopted on 19 October and 2 November 1945; together they provided the rules on access to French nationality and the conditions for entry and residence for immigrants.[78] The ordinance of 19 October established a new Nationality Act whilst the latter—for the first time—established a comprehensive text on State action in the field of immigration.[79] The ordinance of

[71] Ibid., 148.

[72] Weil, *How to Be French: Nationality in the Making since 1789*, 187.

[73] Ibid., 62.

[74] Makarov, *Deutsches Staatsangehörigkeitsrecht. Kommentar*, 135. Makarov remarks that these laws were clearly a deliberate response to the Delbrück law. He quotes Duvergier's *Collection complète des lois, décrets, ordonnances et règlements* of 1915, where it is stated that 'cette hypothèse de déchéance a été envisagée principalement en considération de la loi allemande du 22 juillet 1913, dite loi Delbruck, laquelle dispose qu'un Allemand peut avoir l'autorisation de se faire naturaliser à l'étranger tout en conservant la nationalité d'origine'.

[75] Weil, *How to Be French: Nationality in the Making since 1789*, 62.

[76] Ibid., 61.

[77] Weil, *La France et ses étrangers*, 80.

[78] Ibid., 79.

[79] Ibid.; Weil and Spire, "France", 191.

November 1945 was characterized by an open, liberal approach on the issue of immigration and integration of immigrants and their children—regardless of their country of origin.[80] When it came to naturalization, however, mostly other European nationals (Italians, Poles and Spaniards) were naturalized in the period 1945–1963. The naturalization policy in these years was grounded on selection based on ethnic criteria: certain nationalities (mostly European) were considered easier to assimilate.[81]

Selection on the basis of ethnicity can be traced back to the racist and antisemitic ideas of Georges Mauco (secretary general of the High Committee of the Population), who earlier in 1945 had proposed a plan to select immigrants on the basis of origin. A quota system was to be introduced which gave preference first to 'Nordics', then 'Mediterraneans', and finally Slavs. Immigration by other nationalities was to be 'strictly limited to individual cases presenting exceptional interest'.[82] Although this plan had been approved by Mauco's own *Haut Comité de la population* and the French government, the Council of State had prevented this plan from materializing.[83] Selection of immigrants on the basis of their origin was thus never officially implemented and the administration did not (at least not formally) distinguish according to national origin of immigrants. The practical implementation of the selection procedure, however, did benefit immigrants from certain countries.[84] As a result, in 1974 immigration in France was 'kaleidoscopic' with large immigrant groups from the Mediterranean (758,000 Portuguese, 497,000 Spaniards and 462,000 Italians) and from the Maghreb (710,000 Algerians, 260,000 Moroccans and 139,000 Tunisians).[85] We can thus safely conclude that we should distinguish between a post-war *naturalization* policy which selected on ethnic criteria and an *immigration* policy that did not.

The large numbers of 'Maghrebians' show the profound impact of the decolonization process on post-war immigration. Most colonies had gained independence by 1960, which resulted in the modification of the conditions for entry into France for immigrants from former colonies. In 1961 a new law no longer required good health and legal residence as conditions for entry. The same law also increased the possibilities for naturalization without residence

80 Weil and Spire, "France", 191.

81 Ibid., 192.

82 Weil, *La France et ses étrangers*, 72.

83 Weil, *How to Be French: Nationality in the Making since 1789*, 152.

84 As the National Immigration Office, which had to recruit foreign laborers, had its seat in Milan, it was more likely that Italians rather than, for example, Turks were recruited. See Weil, *La France et ses étrangers*, 81.

85 Weil, *How to Be French: Nationality in the Making since 1789*, 152.

requirements.[86] Consequently, 'the former colonial population became an increasingly important part of the newly naturalised French population'.[87] Since 1992 'Maghrebians' have constituted more than 40 percent of new French nationals. The number of European naturalisees has dropped from 95 percent in the aftermath of the Second World War to 20 percent in 1993.[88]

5. *Equality of the Sexes in French Nationality Law*

We have seen that the 1803 Civil Code had a major impact on nationality law, since it provided for the first time that nationality was transmissible through parentage, in other words through *ius sanguinis*. Yet the transmission of nationality was a male prerogative and the status of women was actually lowered under the 1803 Civil Code. Under the Civil Code a woman lost her French nationality upon marrying a foreigner, even if she continued to live in France, while under the *Ancien Régime* she had been able to keep her nationality.[89] The weakened position of women under the Civil Code can perhaps be attributed to Napoleon Bonaparte's notorious misogyny.[90]

We have also already touched upon the fact that the position of women in French nationality law improved after the First World War.[91] However, it was only in 1973 that women gained a completely independent position in French nationality law and became equal to men, both with regard to marriage and to the transmission of nationality to their children.[92] The strengthened position of women under the law of 1927 primarily served a demographic purpose and

86 Weil and Spire, "France", 194.

87 Ibid.

88 Ibid., 197–198.

89 Weil, *How to Be French: Nationality in the Making since 1789*, 194.

90 Napoleon was actively involved in the drafting process of the Civil Code, attending fifty-seven out of 109 meetings. According to Mclynn, the Code Civil gave the death blow to feminist aspirations that had arisen in the aftermath of the Revolution. In his view, 'the most reactionary aspect of the Code … was its treatment of women' at the root of which lay Napoleon's misogyny and hostility to female emancipation. Napoleon is heard to have declared that 'women these days require restraint. They go where they like, do what they like. It is not French to give women the upper hand. They have too much of it already'. Another illustration of his hostility to female emancipation is his reply to the question which woman in history he admired most: Whoever has borne the most children. See Frank McLynn, *Napoleon: a biography* (London: Pimlico, 1998), 163, 256–257.

91 See *supra* Section 2. We also touched on gender equality in nationality law in Chapter 1, Section 6.

92 Belorgey, "Le droit de la nationalité: évolution historique et enjeux", 66; Weil, *How to Be French: Nationality in the Making since 1789*, 195, 206.

was not inspired by the idea of equality of the sexes.[93] Be this as it may, the law greatly contributed to gender equality in French nationality law and did so in respect of both French and foreign women. An initial proposal had still provided that foreign women who married a Frenchman would automatically acquire French nationality, while this was no longer the case for French women who married a foreigner (the latter could nonetheless decide to take their husband's nationality). This proposal was criticized for serving merely the French demographic exigency instead of endorsing the ideal of gender equality.[94] Under pressure from this argument, the proposal was modified and the law of 1927 as it was finally adopted guaranteed foreign women the same right as had been granted to French women.[95]

The law of 1945, however, subsequently meant a step backwards in respect of the position of the woman in nationality law. In the period 1945–1973 familialism triumphed over feminism and the 'demographic logic was applied at full strength'.[96] The effect was that, in order to let the population grow, foreign women marrying French men automatically became French. As statistics showed that after the law reform of 1927 some 70 percent of foreign women had still (voluntarily) adopted the French nationality of their husbands, the legislator thought that by reversing the law of 1927 on this point it was merely 'bringing the law into agreement with objective facts'.[97] Under the law of 1945 French women retained their nationality, however, upon marriage with a foreigner.[98] This was again ostensibly based on statistics, according to which hardly 5% of French women chose the nationality of their foreign husband.[99]

6. *Questions of Nationality Law Relating to the Decolonization Process*

After the Second World War the French colonies gained independence one after the other. Space considerations unfortunately do not permit a comprehensive discussion of the decolonization effects on French nationality law, however. Section 7 will therefore only focus on the Algerian question, while

---

93 Lagarde, *La nationalité française*, 176.

94 On the feminist struggle for the improvement of the position of women in French nationality law, see generally Elisa Camiscioli, "Intermarriage, Independent Nationality, and the Individual Rights of French Women. The law of 10 August 1927", *French Politics, Culture and Society* 17, no. 3–4 (1999): 52–71.

95 Weil, *How to Be French: Nationality in the Making since 1789*, 202–203.

96 Ibid., 205–206.

97 Lagarde, *La nationalité française*, 179.

98 Boulbès, *Droit français de la nationalité*, 273.

99 Lagarde, *La nationalité française*, 179.

the present section consists of general and introductory remarks concerning the effects on French nationality on the decolonization of territories other than Algeria.

Questions of nationality obviously had to be addressed when the French colonies gained independence. The starting point in answering such questions is to consult the bilateral treaties concluded between France and its former colonies which transferred sovereignty to the newly independent State. In cases where these treaties are silent on questions of nationality, one may have recourse to Article 17-8 of the French Civil Code which provides as follows:

> Nationals of the ceding State domiciled in the annexed territories on the day of the transfer of sovereignty acquire French nationality, unless they actually establish their domiciles outside those territories. Under the same reservation, French nationals domiciled in the ceded territories on the day of the transfer of sovereignty lose that nationality.[100]

From this we can conclude that domicile—and not place of birth—is decisive where questions of nationality in relation to former colonies are concerned.[101]

It should first of all be remarked that questions of nationality were not raised in relation to States where French authority had merely been superposed. The States where France had not tried to replace national sovereignty by its own—and which were thus officially sovereign countries, even though the French dominion was nonetheless as pervasive there as in countries that had been officially colonized—concerned Morocco, Tunisia, Cambodia, Cameroun and Togo. Consequently, the problem of the re-allocation of the inhabitants of these territories after decolonization did not arise: the original inhabitants had always kept the nationality of their respective States and had never acquired French nationality.[102]

Questions of nationality did arise in connection with other territories. In order to solve these questions, bilateral treaties were concluded with Tunisia[103]

---

[100] Ibid., 201. 'Les nationaux de l'État cédant, domiciliés dans les territoires annexés au jour du transfert de la souveraineté acquièrent la nationalité française, à moins qu'ils n'établissent effectivement leur domicile hors de ces territoires. Sous la même réserve, les nationaux français, domiciliés dans les territoires cédés au jour du transfert de la souveraineté perdent cette nationalité'. For the English translation of the nationality provisions in the French Civil Code see http://eudo-citizenship.eu/ (select France under the country profiles).

[101] Ibid.

[102] Paul Lagarde, "De quelques conséquences de la décolonisation sur le droit français de la nationalité", in *Mélanges Savatier* (Paris: Dalloz, 1965), 512.

[103] It was explained above that French authority had merely been superimposed in Tunisia. The only purpose of the bilateral treaty was to accord Tunisia the right to lay down its own rules in nationality law. See Lagarde, *La nationalité française*, 212.

and Vietnam on 3 June and 16 August 1955 respectively, but not with the former colonies in Africa (*Afrique noire et Madagascar*) nor with Algeria.[104] As to the former colonies in Africa, it was simply a lack of time which prevented the conclusion of treaties on nationality law. Lagarde explains that in order to join the United Nations, the former colonies wanted to have their independence proclaimed as soon as possible. Independence would have been delayed by difficult negotiations concerning the allocation of people.[105] Although questions of nationality were certainly the subject of bilateral negotiations, the conditions at the time were thus such that the former African colonies were not eager to start concrete negotiations on a bilateral nationality treaty.[106]

As attempts to solve nationality matters through bilateral treaties proved unsuccessful, the normal recourse would be to the abovementioned provision from the French Civil Code. However, the application of Article 13 CC—the predecessor of Article 17-8 CC—would have had the politically unacceptable effect that those who were French by origin and wanted to remain in the former colony would lose their French nationality without being guaranteed the nationality of the newly independent State.[107] According to Foyer, it was also expected that the majority of French nationals domiciled in the former colony would one day return to France. What is more, the former colonies had little intention of granting their nationality to these French nationals, and France obviously had no say whatsoever in who was granted the nationality of the new States. Applying Article 13 CC would thus have had the effect of rendering stateless tens of thousands of persons.[108] France therefore unilaterally decided to rule out the application of Article 13 CC with regard to two categories. The first category concerned persons domiciled in overseas territories (law 60-752 of 28 July 1960); the second affected those domiciled in Algeria (ordinance 62-825 of 21 July 1962).

---

104 Ibid., 211–213, 281.

105 Lagarde, "De quelques conséquences de la décolonisation sur le droit français de la nationalité", 513. Lagarde also points to another reason why the former colonies were not eager to conclude a treaty on nationality: 'Une convention aurait normalement conduit à une ventilation entre ceux qui restaient Français et ceux qui prenaient la nationalité du nouvel État, et par la même aurait brisé les liens qui, sans convention, continuaient d'unir à la France les populations des anciens territoires d'outre-mer'.

106 Jean Foyer, "Problèmes de droit international privé dans les relations entre la France et les nouveaux États africains d'expression française", in *Travaux du comité français de droit international privé, 1958–1962*, 144.

107 Lagarde, *La nationalité française*, 213.

108 Foyer, "Problèmes de droit international privé dans les relations entre la France et les nouveaux États africains d'expression française", 145.

The law of 28 July 1960 and the ordinance of 21 July 1962 distinguished between those who were in possession of a full French nationality and those who—though never having ceased being French subjects—only had their French nationality recognized (or 'conserved'[109]) on condition of establishing domicile in France.[110] This distinction between 'Français de plein droit' on the one hand and 'Français sous condition de reconnaissance' on the other (hereafter we translate 'reconnaissance' as recognition[111]) was made on the basis of ethnic origin, in other words, by distinguishing between 'les originaires du territoire de la République française[112] et les non-originaires'.[113]

The ordinance of 21 July 1962 concerning Algeria will be examined in the next section. Here we will content ourselves with discussing the law of 28 July 1960. Suffice it to note for now that due to the heterogeneity of the Algerian population the ordinance of 21 July 1962 adopted a different criterion than ethnic origin for the allocation of people to France. Not only was the European share in the Algerian population much bigger, it also consisted of such diverse groups as French nationals, Europeans, Jews, autochthones Muslims governed by French law and autochtone Muslims governed by local law. As a result, the ordinance of 21 July 1962 could not use the criterion of ethnic origin and opted for the criterion of 'statut personnel' instead.[114]

---

[109] Lagarde, *La nationalité française*, 221.

[110] Ibid., 213. For remarks on the fact that the establishment of separate categories of French nationals seems to infringe on the unitary character of French nationality, see Lagarde, "De quelques conséquences de la décolonisation sur le droit français de la nationalité", 529.

[111] Spire and Weil translate the 'déclaration de reconnaissance' as a 'declaration of acceptance'. See Weil and Spire, "France", 194.

[112] Foyer, "Problèmes de droit international privé dans les relations entre la France et les nouveaux États africains d'expression française", 146. Foyer defines the 'originaire' as 'toute personne dont l'un des ascendants était né sur le territoire de la République Française tel qu'il est actuellement constitué [in 1962 that is]'. The 'orginaire' can also be described in the negative, which is done by Lagarde when he defines the 'non-originaire' as 'ceux qui ne sont ni originaires du territoire de la République française, ni conjoints veufs ou veuves de ces derniers, ni descendants des uns ou des autres'. Lagarde thus defines the 'originaire' in a broader sense than Foyer.

[113] Lagarde, *La nationalité française*, 214–216. See also Foyer who writes that a person of non-French origin had a '"nationalité française de jouissance" et non pas "d'exercise", car il ne peut pas … exercer les droits attachés à la qualité de français'. Foyer, "Problèmes de droit international privé dans les relations entre la France et les nouveaux États africains d'expression française", 148.

[114] Lagarde, "De quelques conséquences de la décolonisation sur le droit français de la nationalité", 521–522.

6.1. *The Law of 28 July 1960 and the 'Recognition' Procedure*

Under the law of 28 July 1960 the 'originaires' were allowed to retain their French nationality even if the nationality of the country of residence was acquired. The law thus deliberately created dual nationals.[115] As for the 'non-originaires', these could acquire full French nationality through recognition of French nationality, but this was conditional upon two requirements: the applicant was required to establish domicile in France as proof of his 'francisation' and make a statement before a French judge for the purpose of having his French nationality recognized.[116]

The law of 1960 was of a very inclusive nature in the sense that the recognition could be exercised by all those 'de statut civil de droit local'[117] and their descendants. Although there was no generation limit under the law of 1960, the ordinance of 1962 did limit the recognition to those 'de statut civil de droit local' and their children—in other words, only to the first generation.[118]

Neither the law of 28 July 1960 nor the ordinance of 21 July 1962 provided for a time limit for exercising the right to recognition, which is strange because their explicit purpose was to allow those who felt connected to France when independence was proclaimed to retain their French nationality. The question was rightly raised at the time why one should still be able to exercise a recognition several decades after independence,[119] and the recognition of French nationality was therefore eventually subjected to a time limit. In respect of Algeria, the time limit for applying for recognition of French nationality expired on 23 March 1967;[120] for Afrique noir and Madagascar the deadline expired on 31 July 1973.[121]

Although the law of 9 January 1973 abolished the recognition procedure, it simultaneously introduced the possibility of 'réintégration par déclaration'.[122]

---

115 Foyer, "Problèmes de droit international privé dans les relations entre la France et les nouveaux États africains d'expression française", 147.

116 Ibid.

117 This means that they were governed by local law, not by French law. See also *infra* Section 7.1.

118 Lagarde, "De quelques conséquences de la décolonisation sur le droit français de la nationalité", 535.

119 Ibid.

120 By virtue of a law of 20 December 1966.

121 By virtue of a law of 9 January 1973. See Lagarde, *La nationalité française*, 213, 221.

122 According to Costa-Lascoux, 'la déclaration de nationalité, acte authentique souscrit devant le juge du Tribunal d'instance ou le consul, est un droit pour le déclarant. Une fois remplies les conditions fixées par la loi, il suffit d'exprimer la volonté de réclamer la nationalité française pour l'obtenir'. She also points out that two categories can make use of the 'déclaration

Curiously, this has been translated by Weil and Spire as 'reintegration by decree'.[123] As opposed to the recognition procedure, the 'réintégration par déclaration' (which would later to be abolished by the law of 22 July 1993[124]), had no retroactive effect and was dependent upon the prior authorization of the Minister charged with naturalizations—authorization which could, however, only be refused for 'indignité' or 'défaut d'assimilation'.[125]

What then was the exact legal nature of this recognition? First of all, it was beyond all doubt that the recognition had retroactive effect; the applicant was thus considered never to have ceased being French. One remained French on the same title as before, however, meaning for example that the 'reconnaissance' did not transform a French nationality acquired through naturalization into a French nationality by origin.[126]

At first sight the term '*reconnaissance*' seems to refer to a discretionary power of the French State to recognize a person's French nationality, which seems to be confirmed by the fact that the State also enjoyed the right of opposition.[127] However, one can also claim that '*reconnaissance*' is essentially a right, although it was admittedly subject to the State's limited power of

de réintégration dans la nationalité française': 1) La personne qui, française d'origine, a perdu sa nationalité par mariage ou par acquisition d'une nationalité étrangère; 2) les originaires des territoires d'outre-mer qui ont accédé à l'indépendance. Pour ceux-ci, il s'agit évidemment d'une réintégration après avoir perdu la nationalité française en raison de la résidence à la date de l'indépendance sur des territoires anciennement sous souveraineté française'. Costa-Lascoux, "L'acquisition de la nationalité française, une condition d'intégration?", 99–100.

123 Weil and Spire, "France", 194. Lagarde distinguishes the acquistion of French nationality 'par déclaration' from acquisition 'par décret'. The former is 'un droit pour l'intéressé mais que celui-ci doit exercer pour le rendre efficace', while the latter form of acquistion 'suppose une demande de l'intéressé à laquelle le pouvoir politique apporte une réponse discrétionnaire'. Paul Lagarde, "La nationalité française rétrécie (commentaire critique de la loi du 22 juillet 1993 réformant le droit de la nationalité)", *Revue critique de droit international privé* 82, no. 4 (1993): 538. See also Guiho who refers to the 'réintégration par déclaration' as a right for the individual whilst the 'réintégration par décret' is more similar to naturalization, allowing a wider 'pouvoir d'appréciation' for the government. Pierre Guiho, *La nationalité*, Guides essentiels (Paris: L'hermès, 1996), 58.

124 According to Lagarde, the 'réintégration par déclaration' could no longer be justified in 1993—thirty years after independence. Its abrogation was thus opportune. Lagarde, "La nationalité française rétrécie": 556.

125 Lagarde, *La nationalité française*, 226.

126 Ibid., 222–224.

127 The power to oppose recognition was abolished in 1961 in respect of the law of 28 July 1960, but would remain in place for the ordinance of 21 July 1962. See Lagarde, "De quelques conséquences de la décolonisation sur le droit français de la nationalité", 534–535.

opposition.[128] It can further be argued that the declarative character of the procedure (fulfilling the conditions seemed to create a *fait accompli*) as well as the fact that the application for recognition was made on a person's own initiative meant that recognition was essentially a procedure by which a person recognized his or her French nationality.[129]

7. *The Algerian Question and the Controversy Surrounding* ius soli

In the vast French colonial empire Algeria occupied a special place as it was legally and administratively part of French territory. It was divided into three *départments*, each headed by a prefect who received orders from Paris. Algeria was also the only settlement to which many French as well as other Europeans moved with the intention of permanently settling.[130] In 1830 France had intervened in Algeria, allegedly to revenge an incident of 1827 when the bey, the Algerian ruler, slapped the French consul's nose with a fly-flap for non-payment of Algerian grain supplies.[131] The other—more plausible—explanation is that the unpopular Bourbon regime attempted to save the monarchy by a military expedition which would evoke the successes of the Napoleonic wars. Moreover, merchants from Marseille were complaining bitterly about the damage inflicted by Algerian pirates to their commerce.[132]

---

128 Ibid. According to Bilbao, '[la reconnaissance] constitue un droit, sous réserve du pouvoir d'opposition du Gouvernement'.

129 In Foyer's words, 'il se la reconnaît à lui-même en quelque sorte'. Foyer, "Problèmes de droit international privé dans les relations entre la France et les nouveaux États africains d'expression française", 147. Lagarde describes the legal nature of the '*reconnaissance*' as follows: 'La nationalité française des personnes astreintes à déclaration leur est conservée *sous la condition suspensive de la reconnaissance*' (emphasis in original). See Lagarde, "De quelques conséquences de la décolonisation sur le droit français de la nationalité", 538; Lagarde, *La nationalité française*, 222.

130 Wesseling distinguishes three forms of colonial administration: protectorates, colonies and colonial territories that are part of the motherland. Morocco and Tunisia, for example, were French protectorates, which meant that there were (officially) independent States. In *protectorates* the local ruler remained in power as far as internal affairs were concerned; foreign affairs were a matter for the colonial power, however. In the French *colonies*, the colonial power was in charge of both internal and foreign affairs. The only French colony which was considered part of France was Algeria. In practice, however, the subdivision into different forms of colonial administration was stripped of its meaning, as the colonial powers also intervened in the internal affairs of their protectorates when this suited their interests. The French thus exercised the same influence in Morocco and Tunisia as they did in Algeria. See H.L. Wesseling, *Europa's koloniale eeuw* (Amsterdam: Uitgeverij Bert Bakker, 2003), 61–62.

131 Ibid., 117–118.

132 Ibid., 118. Algerian piracy in the Mediterranean was a long-standing problem. Readers who are familiar with Cervantes's *Don Quijote* will remember the story of the prisoner of war in

Under French annexation the native Muslims and Jews in Algeria were considered French subjects (and were thus presumed to be French), yet they did not have full French nationality, nor was there a procedure by which they could obtain it.[133] Whilst from the 1850s onwards France began facilitating the naturalization of foreigners in Algeria, the naturalization of Muslims and Jews was very problematic. Naturalization of these groups 'could not take place without overturning their civil laws, which are at the same time religious laws'.[134] A majority of Algerian Jews, however, came to seriously demand naturalization and in 1870 they were naturalized *en masse*. A similar naturalization policy could not be adopted in respect of Muslims, who from the French point of view simply could not become French. Otherwise, the original French minority would suddenly find itself amidst two million new French nationals and how, then, to justify the domination of this minority over the new French nationals? Consequently, Algerian Muslims were left with only one possibility to become French: individual naturalization.[135]

The return of *ius soli* in the law of 1889 also covered the territory of Algeria. Children of the *European* population who were born in Algeria to a parent born in Algeria were now French at birth. This was important for two reasons. First, France had given up all hope that the French population in Algeria could be increased by colonization. Second, few Europeans naturalized into French nationality despite the easy conditions for naturalization.[136] The result was that the foreign European population in Algeria had exceeded the French population by 1881.[137]

chapters 39–41 ('Donde el cautivo cuenta su vida y sucesos'). This episode was probably inspired by Cervantes's own five-year experience as a prisoner in Algeria after having been captured by Algerian pirates while making the journey from Naples (where he lived in exile) to Barcelona in 1575. See Jean Canavaggio, *Don Quichotte du livre au mythe. Quatre siècles d'errance* (Paris: Fayard, 2005), 11; Donald McCrory, *Cervantes. De schepper van Don Quichot* (Amsterdam: Atheneum-Polak&Van Gennep, 2005), 67.

133 Weil, *How to Be French: Nationality in the Making since 1789*, 208. Bruschi writes: 'Celui appelé "indigène" ne pouvait accéder à la pleine qualité de Français qu'après avoir renoncé à son statut personnel. C'est sur cette base que furent distingués le Français-citoyen et le Français-sujet … Les Français-sujets n'étaient definés que négativement, il s'agissait de ceux qui n'étaient pas citoyens français mais qui, en habitant dans un territoire français, avaient la nationalité française. Ils n'avaient qu'une nationalité diminuée qui ne les faisait jouir ni des droits politiques, ni des droits civils français'. Bruschi, "Droit de la nationalité et égalité des droits de 1789 à la fin du XIXe siècle", 42–43.

134 Quoted in Weil, *How to Be French: Nationality in the Making since 1789*, 208–209.

135 Ibid., 210–212.

136 Patrick Weil, "Le statut des musulmans en Algérie coloniale. Une nationalité française dénaturée", EUI Working Paper 2003/03, 5.

137 Weil, *How to Be French: Nationality in the Making since 1789*, 213–214.

Article 2 of the law of 1889 stated explicitly, however, that the law did not apply to the Algerian Muslims.[138] Not only was naturalization more difficult for them as compared to European foreigners, their children born in Algeria still had to go through naturalization proceedings whereas double *ius soli* applied to children of European foreigners born in Algeria.[139]

Only very small numbers of Algerian Muslims made a request for naturalization. This is commonly explained by the fact that the acquisition of French nationality obliged them to respect the French Civil Code, meaning that they could no longer practicise traditional customs incompatible with that code. As this would come down to renouncing Islam itself, naturalization was hardly an option.[140] Algerian Muslims were not, unlike the inhabitants of some French communes in Senegal, naturalized 'in the status', which allowed someone to become fully French while at the same time retaining a personal status which was in conformity with religious prescriptions. Nor were they given an individual right to French nationality if only they renounced their personal status and declared themselves governed by French law, a right that had been accorded to natives in French settlements in India. The fact that renunciation of the personal status of Muslim was not sufficient for acquiring French nationality—unlike other colonial subjects, the Algerian Muslims' only option was thus the difficult and uncooperative naturalization procedure—reveals in Weil's view that the status of Muslim had a strong ethno-political character rather than merely a civil or religious one.[141]

A law of February 1919 did try to improve the legal position of the Algerian Muslims.[142] Although this law perceived of naturalization as a right instead of a favour, it kept in place the conditions for naturalization.[143] These conditions had been rather stringent and the effect of the law of 1919 in terms of

[138] Weil, "Le statut des musulmans en Algérie coloniale. Une nationalité française dénaturée", 5.

[139] Weil, *How to Be French: Nationality in the Making since 1789*, 214, 219.

[140] Ahmed Lourdjane, "Les musulmans originaires d'Algérie peuvent-ils bénéficier de la double nationalité: française et algérienne?", *Revue juridique et politique, Indépendance et coopération* 21 (1967): 297.

[141] Weil, *How to Be French: Nationality in the Making since 1789*, 215–219. The local administrators were so uncooperative, and even downright discouraging, that only 2,400 Algerian Muslims naturalized in the period 1865–1915.

[142] Paul Sumien, "Algérie", in *Répertoire de droit international*, ed. A. De la Pradelle and J.P. Niboyet (Paris: Librairie du Recueil Sirey, 1929), 365.

[143] Ibid., 365–366. The naturalization procedure as instituted by a senatus-consult of 1865 and decrees of 1866 and 1876 remained in force. See on this procedure Sumien, who, moreover, also stresses that one of the law's objectives was to turn naturalization from a favour into a right 'dont l'exercise n'est pas soumis à l'appréciation de l'autorité administrative, et sur lequel l'autorité judiciaire n'a un droit de contrôle que pour constater si les conditions prévues par la loi sont réunies'.

acquisition of French nationality by Muslims was thus understandably weak. The restrictive nature of access to full French nationality meant that other aspects of the law of 1919 came to be emphasized, such as voting rights on a municipal level without possessing French nationality.[144]

European migration to Algeria, which had been considerable during the course of the 19th century and only decreased after the First World War, was concentrated in the northern port towns.[145] In 1890 half a million Europeans lived in Algeria and by 1954 this had risen to one million. The majority was French, but many Spaniards, Italians, Maltese and Germans had also decided to settle in Algeria. In absolute figures the European population grew, but as the Muslim population grew faster (it constituted eight million people in 1954), the European share in the total population decreased.[146] Although the Algerian Muslims were French subjects, an overwhelming majority did not possess a full French nationality.[147] At the time of Algerian independence (1962) only some ten thousand Muslims were fully French. The vast majority of Algerian Muslims could only remain French after Algerian independence by availing themselves of the recognition procedure.[148]

After the Second World War, Algerian Muslims started moving to metropolitan France in great numbers. Between 1949 and 1955 there were 180,000 Algerian Muslims compared to 160,000 workers from all other foreign nationalities combined.[149] Algerians could move to metropolitan France because they had been attributed French citizenship under the French Constitution of the Fourth Republic of 27 October 1946, yet they were denied full rights of citizenship.[150]

---

144 Weil, *How to Be French: Nationality in the Making since 1789*, 221–222.

145 Wesseling, *Frankrijk in oorlog, 1870–1962*, 289.

146 Ibid., 290.

147 Their status as French subject for example meant that they could not be expulsed and that they were allowed to practice as a lawyer. It also had the effect that an Algerian Muslim could not be qualified as a foreigner in legal proceedings; consequently, he could not be asked to provide a cautio judicatum solvi (a security for the costs of legal proceedings). See Sumien, "Algérie", 365. As to the question of French diplomatic protection on behalf of Algerian Muslims, Weil remarks that 'théoriquement, lorsqu'il se trouve à l'étranger, [the Algerian Muslim] est sous la protection d'un consul français; mais c'est une protection toute théorique dans la mesure où il n'a pas le droit de quitter son village sans autorisation!'. Weil, "Le statut des musulmans en Algérie coloniale. Une nationalité française dénaturée", 10.

148 Weil, *How to Be French: Nationality in the Making since 1789*, 225.

149 Ibid., 153.

150 Lagarde, "De quelques conséquences de la décolonisation sur le droit français de la nationalité", 513; Weil, *La France et ses étrangers*, 84; Joppke, *Selecting by Origin: Ethnic Migration in the Liberal State*, 110; Alexis Spire, "D'une colonie à l'autre. La continuation des structures coloniales dans le traitement de la migration algérienne en France après 1945", in *L'esclavage,*

After a bloody struggle, the Évian agreements of 18 March 1962 established Algerian independence and made Algeria a sovereign, independent State.[151] These agreements extended the free movement between France and Algeria to nationals of both countries. As France still thought at the time that many French would remain in Algeria, it saw free movement primarily as an emergency escape route for Europeans but also for Algerians who had supported France.[152] It soon became clear, however, that this free movement benefited Algerians seeking work in France to the detriment of other nationalities. Consequently, France attempted to slow Algerian immigration by signing treaties with Yugoslavia, Turkey, Portugal, Morocco and Tunisia which favoured immigration from these countries.[153]

The Évian agreements did not fully address questions of nationality. They only covered the *pied noirs* (French Algerians) by providing that they could acquire Algerian nationality after a three year transitory period. Nothing was decided concerning the Algerian Muslims, Algeria being opposed to dual nationality (for reasons of state building) as well as to a system of option rights (for fear that Algerians would exercise this right *en masse* and provoke a massive exodus to France).[154]

Boushaba provides clear evidence of the diametrically opposed position on the question of dual nationality between France and Algeria. Before the Évian agreements were signed, two proposals had been advanced in which dual nationality featured prominently. France initially proposed dual nationality for the Europeans who would remain in Algeria after the country's independence. Interestingly, Boushaba remarks that this proposal entailed that the French nationality would only be 'en sommeil'[155]—that is, non effective ('il ne

la colonisation, et après ... France, États-Unis, Grande-Bretagne, ed. Patrick Weil and Stéphane Dufoix (Paris: Presses Universitaires de France, 2005), 388. In the words of Marzo: 'L'article de la Constitution de 1946 disposait que « tous les nationaux français et les ressortissants de l'Union française ont la qualité de citoyen de l'Union française qui leur assure la jouissance des droits et des libertés garantis par le préambule de la Constitution ». En vertu de l'article 60 de la même Constitution, la citoyenneté de l'Union française s'appliquait aux ressortissants de la France métropolitaine, des départements et des territoires d'Outre-mer, des États associés (protectorats) et des territoires associés (territoires sous tutelle)'. This citizenship included all kinds of social and labour rights, but 'la qualité de citoyen de l'Union française n'emportait pas sur le territoire métropolitain, la reconnaissance du droit de suffrage'. Marzo, *La dimension sociale de la citoyenneté européenne*, 53–54.

151 Wesseling, *Frankrijk in oorlog, 1870–1962*, 289–316.

152 Weil, *La France et ses étrangers*, 85.

153 Ibid., 89–90.

154 Lagarde, "De quelques conséquences de la décolonisation sur le droit français de la nationalité", 515; Lagarde, *La nationalité française*, 213.

155 Compare with the idea of the 'dormant' nationality under the Spanish-Latin American dual nationality treaties in Chapter 6, Section 3.

jouera pas' in the words of Boushaba)—while living in Algeria; it would only be activated when the dual national established residence in France.[156] France thought it was important that these Europeans also acquired Algerian nationality, for otherwise they would become a minority in Algeria, possessing only limited rights.[157] For several reasons Algeria nonetheless rejected the idea of dual nationality. As legal reasons it advanced that the system of 'automatic' dual nationality as proposed by France would violate the 1930 Hague Convention. Article 1 of that Convention, which allows each State to determine under its own law who are its nationals, would be violated if Algeria were forced to grant its nationality to 'undesirable' individuals. In other words, Algeria wanted to have the freedom to deny Algerian nationality to certain people. Second, it pointed to the international consensus on the undesirability of dual nationality.[158] In addition, Algeria opposed granting the special status of dual nationality to whichever minority, even if the foreign nationality was in fact only 'en sommeil'. Dual nationality was thought incompatible with 'l'unité du peuple algérien'.[159]

The Algerian position concerning dual nationality also meant that a second French proposal, which was more moderate in that it secured dual nationality only to very specific categories, was doomed to fail.[160] As France and Algeria could not agree on questions of nationality, both countries would eventually legislate unilaterally on these matters.

7.1. *Unilateral Action by France: The Ordinance of 21 July 1962 and the Predominance of Personal Status over Origin*

For the purpose of allocating persons to France, the ordinance of 21 July 1962 had recourse to the criterion of personal status.[161] People living in Algeria had traditionally been either 'de statut civil de droit commun', which meant that they were governed by French law in matters of private law,[162] or 'de statut civil de droit local'. Almost the whole of the native Muslim population was

[156] Zouhir Boushaba, *Nationalité et double nationalité dans les rapports Franco-Algeriens*, Thèse pour le doctorat en droit (Marseille: L'Université d'Aix-Marseille, 1991), 179.

[157] Ibid.

[158] Ibid., 180.

[159] Ibid., 185.

[160] Ibid., 182–183.

[161] Paul Lagarde, "Le droit français de la nationalité", in *Nationality laws in the European Union - Le droit de la nationalité dans l'Union Européene*, ed. Bruno Nascimbene (Milano: Giuffrè Editore, 1996), 329.

[162] Lagarde, "De quelques conséquences de la décolonisation sur le droit français de la nationalité", 522.

governed by local law, despite their status as French subjects.[163] An Algerian Muslim could nevertheless renounce application of local law in two ways: a partial renunciation by which he declared himself governed by French law in a specific situation, or a total renunciation by naturalizing into a full French national.[164]

The French and European populations, as well as the native population which had adopted a French lifestyle and was therefore regarded with hostility by the new Algerian government,[165] were governed by French law. As persons could easily be distinguished on the basis of the applicable law, it was only logical to allocate to France those who had always been governed by French law. In the words of Lagarde: 'The intention was therefore not to discriminate on racial or religious grounds, but to find a realistic criterion'.[166] In this connection is has also been remarked that by a sort of reversal of conditions and consequences, nationality is now no longer a connecting factor to determine personal status, but the other way round.[167]

Article 1 of the ordinance of 21 July 1962, which would later become Article 32-1 of the Civil Code, provided that:

> French persons of civil status of general law who were domiciled in Algeria on the date of the official announcement of the results of the poll for self-determination keep French nationality whatever their situation with respect to Algerian nationality may be.[168]

Several authors point out that the application of this ordinance created many cases of dual nationality.[169]

---

163 Lourdjane, "Les musulmans originaires d'Algérie peuvent-ils bénéficier de la double nationalité: française et algérienne?": 298.

164 As Sumien points out, except for these two situations, 'il n'y a pas d'autres moyens pour le musulman de se soustraire à son statut personnel'. Sumien, "Algérie", 376.

165 Lourdjane points out that as far as their legal status was concerned, their position hardly differed from the 'European' Algerians. After Algerian independence, they also acquired Algerian nationality under Algerian law and thus became dual nationals, provided of course that they did not renounce Algerian nationality. See Lourdjane, "Les musulmans originaires d'Algérie peuvent-ils bénéficier de la double nationalité: française et algérienne?": 295–298.

166 'L'intention n'était donc pas d'établir une discrimination sur une base racial ou religieuse mais de trouver un critère réaliste'. Lagarde, *La nationalité française*, 218.

167 'Par une sorte de renversement des conditions et des conséquences, la nationalité n'est plus ici le facteur de rattachement du statut personnel, c'est le dernier qui devient un critère d'accès à la nationalité'. Carlier, "Droits de l'homme et nationalité": 248–249.

168 'Les Français de statut civil de droit commun domiciliés en Algérie à la date de l'annonce officielle des résultats du scrutin d'autodétermination conservent la nationalité française, quelle que soit leur situation au regard de la nationalité algérienne'.

169 Lagarde, "De quelques conséquences de la décolonisation sur le droit français de la nationalité", 523; Lourdjane, "Les musulmans originaires d'Algérie peuvent-ils bénéficier de la

The distinction between 'Français de plein droit' and 'Français sous condition de reconnaissance' was also made with regard to persons who lived in Algeria. Whereas those 'de statut civil de droit commun' were recognized as 'Français de plein droit',[170] those 'de statut civil de droit local' were subject to recognition of their French nationality.[171] Article 2 of the ordinance of 21 July 1962 laid down the conditions for recognition of one's French nationality—French nationality often being referred to in the literature as the 'quality of being French' (*qualité de Français*). Recognition was essentially dependent on two elements: one had to have possessed the quality of being French before Algerian independence, and to have established domicile in France.[172] As this category had also been attributed Algerian nationality, persons falling within this category were dual nationals provided that Algerian nationality was not explicitly renounced.[173]

Algerian Muslims who lived in France and were of age could thus automatically become French by signing a 'déclaration de reconnaissance'. They therefore had 'superior' rights over other foreigners.[174] Few made use of this possibility, however, as it was seen as a betrayal of Algeria; they would also lose the 'statut personnel' by which they had been governed in Algeria (the overwhelming majority was not governed by French law in matters of private

double nationalité: française et algérienne?": 295; Olekhnovitch, "La double nationalité": 17. Wesseling remarks, however, that the internal fight in Algeria between French Algerians (*pied noirs*) and Algerian Muslims had become very violent around the time of the Évian agreements. In the aftermath of these agreements there were hardly any French Algerians left in Algeria. Whether there were thus many French dual nationals living in Algeria after Algerian independence can thus be questioned. See Wesseling, *Frankrijk in oorlog, 1870–1962*, 311–312.

170 The effects of decolonization constitute the major part of the heavy workload at the (relatively small) nationality department of the French Ministry of Justice. The department is flooded with requests for French nationality by Algerian Muslims alleging to descend from a person who was of 'statut civil de droit commun'. After all, Algerian Muslims who were governed by French law at the time of independence were 'Français de plein droit'. The officials at the ministry have the difficult task of checking whether the ancestor was indeed governed by French law at the time of independence. Also the birth certificates of those who allegedly descend from this ancestor have to be checked. One file can potentially involve dozens of people. We thank Muriel Pouzet El Masry of the Ministry for this information.

171 Lagarde, *La nationalité française*, 220.

172 Ibid., 221. Domicile is to be understood as 'une résidence stable et permanente coïncidant avec le centre des attaches familiales et des occupations professionnelles'.

173 Lourdjane, "Les musulmans originaires d'Algérie peuvent-ils bénéficier de la double nationalité: française et algérienne?": 295, 300.

174 Weil, *How to Be French: Nationality in the Making since 1789*, 154.

law).[175] It was seen in Section 6.1 *supra* that recognition was abolished for Algerian Muslims in 1967, but that this procedure was subsequently replaced by one which allowed Algerian Muslims to become French through 'réintégration par déclaration' which required five years' residency.[176]

The effects of Algerian independence remained a salient issue in the following years. The economic crisis in the late 1970s led to plans for a forced return policy of North Africans (Algerians in particular) who were long term residents in France.[177] The plan was never executed owing to large scale opposition—both in open and discreet ways by numerous organisations and institutions—but its goal had been the forced return of 500,000 foreigners in five years.[178]

In the early 1980s, Algerians again were at the centre of debate when it became clear that children born in France to Algerian parents who had themselves been born in Algeria before 1962 (we recall that Algeria was officially part of France and composed of three *départements*, which made the situation different for Algerians compared to, for example, Moroccans) were automatically French under the double *ius soli* rule.[179] It is this controversial context—French nationality was attributed automatically, without the possibility of renunciation, to children of Algerian parents who had sometimes fought for Algerian independence—which is of particular interest for our discussion of dual nationality.

In 1982 the first group of male Algerian children who had also become French under the double *ius soli* rule were called up for military service in both countries. The year 1982 would prove to be a turning point in the nationality conflict between France and Algeria. Until then, the problem of dual nationality had been nothing more than a possible problem of identity for French-Algerian children and their parents, or a diplomatic problem between France and Algeria.[180] However, in the absence of a bilateral agreement on

---

[175] In the period between 1 January 1963 and 30 October 1966, only 50,700 people signed a 'déclaration de reconnaissance'. See Lourdjane, "Les musulmans originaires d'Algérie peuvent-ils bénéficier de la double nationalité: française et algérienne?": 299–300.

[176] Weil and Spire, "France", 194.

[177] See for a detailed discussion Weil, *La France et ses étrangers*, 150 ff.

[178] Weil, *How to Be French: Nationality in the Making since 1789*, 154.

[179] Weil and Spire, "France", 195. The following quote illustrates the point well: 'By a sort of historical irony, from 1962 the double ius soli that applied in metropolitan France allowed all children born in France to a parent born in Algeria to be French from birth, without distinction of origin. As for the status of their children, all the former inhabitants of Algeria—French nationals, Jewish or Muslim subjects—were equal, retroactively'. See Weil, *How to Be French: Nationality in the Making since 1789*, 225.

[180] Weil, *How to Be French: Nationality in the Making since 1789*, 155.

military service, the double *ius soli* rule which had caused this situation came under attack from different sides. The Algerians insisted on an amendment of this rule (laid down in Article 23 of the Nationality Code) in such a way that Algerian children born in France would no longer fall under the provision. This was unacceptable for France as it meant denying that Algeria had been part of French territory until 1962. Such a move could be interpreted by part of French public opinion as a *de facto* recognition of the illegitimacy of the former French presence in Algeria.[181] Yet France was apparently willing to conclude a bilateral treaty with Algeria which would have given Algerians falling within the scope of Article 23 a free choice as to which nationality they wanted to possess.[182] The French Right (which included Le Pen's emerging National Front) also attacked double *ius soli*—as well as single *ius soli*—because French nationality was not to be 'imposed' but should be 'chosen'.[183]

Before we continue with the controversy around *ius soli*, we shall conclude this section by noting that the Franco-Algerian animosity over dual military obligations did blow over. An agreement on military service was finally signed on 11 October 1983, allowing French-Algerian nationals to comply with their obligations in either France or Algeria.[184] The choice of where to fulfil military obligations was thus left to the individual. This choice would have no consequences in terms of employment, residence rights or possession of the nationality of the country where the dual national did not decide to meet his military obligations.[185] Eventually, Algeria gave in, and adopted a different attitude towards their nationals in France: it recognized the definitive settlement of Franco-Algerians in France and began to see dual nationality as a useful lobbying instrument in the way that was discussed in Chapter 1 (Section 7).[186] France, on the other hand, was content with the bilateral solution for it meant that the French tradition of double *ius soli* remained untouched.[187]

---

[181] Weil, *La France et ses étrangers*, 234.

[182] Ibid., 233.

[183] Weil, *How to Be French: Nationality in the Making since 1789*, 155–157.

[184] Weil, *La France et ses étrangers*, 235.

[185] Darras, *La double nationalité*, 626.

[186] The adherence to the idea of perpetual allegiance and the acceptance of dual nationality by former French colonies (in particular Islamic countries) also served another purpose: 'Pour ces États, c'est aussi une façon de proclamer leur indépendence face aux anciennes puissances coloniales. La double nationalité devient le moyen de faire reconnaître "malgré tout" sa souveraineté quand bien même le retour des "émigrés" créerait plus de difficultés au pays d'origine qu'un gain réel'. Costa-Lascoux, "L'acquisition de la nationalité française, une condition d'intégration?", 106.

[187] Weil, *How to Be French: Nationality in the Making since 1789*, 156.

8. *The 1980s and 90s: Attacks on the French* ius soli *Tradition*

We have just seen that a significant part of the French political right challenged the long-standing French tradition of *ius soli*. The writings of Ernest Renan, who claimed that a nation is based on a choice on the part of its members,[188] were frequently invoked. According to this view, by the mid-1980s the military and demographic arguments for *ius soli* had disappeared. When the political right won the legislative elections of 1986, it therefore proposed to make acquisition of French nationality by children of non-French parents subject to a voluntary act; this would also allow the State some leeway in 'selecting' its new nationals.[189] This idea was also advocated by part of the academic literature of the time. Darras thought that the automatic acquisition of French nationality must be prevented at all cost; foreigners should only become French by manifesting their wish to become French. He opposed the automatic acquisition of French nationality to the point of advocating the abolishment of all *ius soli* elements from French law.[190]

Weil has shown in a detailed fashion how different developments took the edge off the proposal to end the automatic attribution of French nationality.[191] Abolishment of double *ius soli* had been opposed from the beginning by influential bodies in the administration (the Bureau of Nationality) and the Council of State. As a result, the proposal was moderated and double *ius soli* was maintained.[192] Another element of the proposal, which proposed that children of foreign parents would no longer acquire French nationality at the age of majority but would have to manifest their desire to become French between the ages of sixteen and twenty-three instead, was also strongly criticized by the left and by anti-discrimination organizations. However, it was a concurrence of circumstances with led to the withdrawal of this part of the proposal as well. The reform of the Nationality Code happened to coincide with university reform. As the latter aroused much protest, Prime Minister Chirac thought it

---

188 Renan argued the following in his famous lecture at the Sorbonne on 11 March 1882: 'Dans l'ordre d'idées que je vous soumets, une nation n'a pas plus qu'un roi le droit de dire à une provence: "Tu m'appartiens, je te prends." Une province, pour nous, ce sont ces habitants; si quelqu'un en cette affaire a droit d'être consulté, c'est l'habitant. Une nation n'a jamais un véritable intérêt à s'annexer ou à retenir un pays malgré lui. Le voeu des nations est, en définitive, le seul critérium légitime, celui auquel il faut toujours en revenir'. See Ernest Renan, *Qu'est-ce qu'une nation? (et autres textes choisis et présentés par Joël Roman)* (Paris: Presses Pocket, 1992), 55.

189 Weil, *How to Be French: Nationality in the Making since 1789*, 157–158.

190 Darras, *La double nationalité*, 954–955.

191 Weil, *How to Be French: Nationality in the Making since 1789*, 156–167.

192 Ibid., 158–159.

wise to abandon the nationality reform altogether and to instead have a special commission investigate the possibility for a reform of French nationality law.[193]

This commission, which was presided over by Marceau Long and which held televised public hearings that were of great importance for the public debate, gave a report in 1988 which was well received by both the political right and left.[194] Overall, the commission steered a middle course. On the one hand, it proposed, for example, that acquisition of French nationality at majority should be chosen (between the ages of sixteen and twenty-one) and not imposed; on the other hand, it advised that the conditions for acquisition be relaxed compared to the legislation in force. The commission's report has been qualified as 'a call for a vigorous and open French community';[195] its overall objective was to 'allow people to exercise free choice, not to prevent them from becoming French'.[196]

The commission's proposal was transformed into a law (law of 22 July 1993) whose main feature was that the acquisition of nationality at the age of majority was made dependent on a manifestation of desire to become French.[197] Although the modification was in fact modest—acquisition of French nationality was not made more difficult but only became dependent on an expressed desire to become French—Weil points out that the law broke with 'a deeply rooted egalitarian practice of recognition' that had been in force since 1889.[198]

---

193 Lagarde, "La nationalité française rétrécie": 537; Weil, *How to Be French: Nationality in the Making since 1789*, 160.

194 Weil, *How to Be French: Nationality in the Making since 1789*, 160–161.

195 M. Moreau, "Nationalité: française. Propos en marge du rapport de la Commission de la Nationalité", in *La condition juridique de l'étranger, hier et aujourd'hui. Actes du Colloque organisé à Nimègue les 9–11 mai 1988 par les Facultés de Droit de Poitiers et de Nimègue* (Nijmegen: Faculteit der Rechtsgeleerdheid, 1988), 31.

196 Weil, *How to Be French: Nationality in the Making since 1789*, 161. The commission itself thought that the approach adopted would also 'évite le développement des cas de double nationalité subie et non désirée'. See Commission de la Nationalité, *Être français aujourd'hui et demain. Rapport remis au Premier ministre par Marceau Long, président de la commission de la Nationalité (Tome 2: Conclusions et propositions de la Commission de la Nationalité)*, 187.

197 See critically on this law Lagarde, "La nationalité française rétrécie": 536, 548. His criticism is directed most of all to the fact that the manifestation of the desire to become French as stipulated in the law of 1993 is not accompanied by an obligation for the administration to individually inform potential French nationals to take this step. The law is considerably more restrictive on this point than the commission's proposal. For positive comments on this law, and the 'manifestation de volonté' in particular, see Lequette, "La nationalité française dévaluée", 381 ff.

198 Weil, *How to Be French: Nationality in the Making since 1789*, 163. See also Lagarde, who maintains that whatever the merits of the new 'conception élective' of French nationality,

The modification had an important effect, however, for the question of dual nationality. As the acquisition of French nationality was now dependent on a manifestation of will, this could result in the loss of the nationality of origin when the country of origin provided for such loss upon voluntary acquisition of another nationality.[199]

In 1998, when the left again came to power, the law of 1993 was submitted to an evaluation.[200] This resulted in revisions which were designed to bring about a better synthesis between the principle of equality as instituted under the law of 1889 and the principle of autonomy of will as introduced in 1993.[201] The law of 16 March 1998 reaffirmed the principle of equality for children of foreign parents by providing that they would automatically become French again at the age of eighteen if they had lived there during adolescence.[202] Also the principle of autonomy of will was reinforced because children could now, through their manifestation of the will to be French, anticipate at an earlier moment (from the age of thirteen to eighteen) the State's recognition of their French nationality. A second way in which autonomy of will was strengthened was the right to decline the acquisition of French nationality six months before and one year after the eighteenth birthday.[203] In 1998 a long debate thus ended in favour of *ius soli* or, in the words of Weil, 'the logic adopted in 1889

this conception had never been part of French law. The rules on French nationality law 'n'ont jamais été déduites d'une conception théorique et aprioristique de la nation française'. Lagarde, "La nationalité française rétrécie": 538.

Also in his appearance before the nationality commission, Lagarde strongly rejected the claim that historically the principle of *ius sanguinis* had been dominant and that foreigners who wanted to become French had been compelled to submit a 'déclaration positive': 'La tradition de l'ancienne France, et, sur ce point, la tradition concordante des Constitutions révolutionnaires, c'était que ceux qui étaient français, les régnicoles, comme on disait autrefois, c'étaient, avant tout, les personnes nées en France et qui résidaient en France. Il est vrai que le Code Napoléon en 1804 a renversé cet état du droit et a accordé une sorte d'exclusivité au droit du sang … Mais toute l'évolution postérieure au Code Napoléon et qui commence dès le milieu du XIXe siècle a tendu à faire remonter le droit du sol à côté du droit du sang pour aboutir à un certain équilibre'. See Commission de la Nationalité, "Audition de Paul Lagarde", in *Être français aujourd'hui et demain. Rapport remis au Premier ministre par Marceau Long, président de la commission de la Nationalité (Tome1: Les auditions publiques)* (Paris: Documentation française, 1988), 115.

199 Paul Lagarde, "La loi du 16 mars 1998 sur la nationalité: une réforme incertaine", *Revue critique de droit international privé* 87, no. 3 (1998): 384, footnote 312.

200 Ibid., 380–381.

201 Weil, *How to Be French: Nationality in the Making since 1789*, 165–167.

202 Ministère de la Justice, *La nationalité française. Recueil des textes législatifs et réglementaires, des conventions internationales et autres documents* (Paris: Ministère de la Justice, 2002), 9.

203 Weil, *How to Be French: Nationality in the Making since 1789*, 167.

presupposing the progressive integration of the children and grandchildren of immigrants seems no longer to be in question today'.[204]

9. *Concluding Remarks*

This chapter has shown that the role of nationality in French society is a hotly debated issue in the academic literature (see in particular the different views of Lagarde and Darras, although it should be stressed that the latter stands quite alone in his views). As for dual nationality, this status became *de iure* accepted with the 1973 Nationality Act. *De facto* it had been accepted for most part of the 20th century, except for countries that were, like France, bound by the 1963 Convention. Cases of dual nationality were also deliberately created in the wake of the French decolonization process.

Residence and socialization are the foundation of the French nationality policy; whether one retains another nationality upon becoming French is of little concern to the French State. Unlike Italy, whose acceptance of dual nationality is mainly to be explained by its relation with former emigrants (see Chapter 5), France seems to perceive of dual nationality as an instrument in the integration policy. The fact that a renunciation requirement upon naturalization is absent in French nationality law (unlike in the Netherlands, see the next chapter), also means that France, as far as dual nationality is concerned, does not pose additional hindrances to the acquisition of French nationality by immigrants and their children. This chapter also gave us the chance to illustrate a number of issues that were identified in Chapter 1 as being related to the question of dual nationality. This concerned the question of loyalty (the French position in relation to the German Delbrück law of 1913) and the problem of military service for dual nationals (the issue of Franco-Algerian dual nationals).

---

[204] Ibid.

Chapter 4

The Netherlands

1. *Introduction*

At various points in this study we can observe a trend towards greater politicization of nationality law. Yet nowhere in the four countries under consideration can this trend be witnessed more clearly than in the Netherlands. The 'turmoil around a naturalisation decree'—that of former Dutch MP Ayaan Hirsi Ali—even led to the fall of a Dutch government on 30 June 2006.[1] This chapter will attempt to demonstrate in the Dutch case how, in the words of Groenendijk, the question of dual nationality has become a typical example of the 'political power to define'. By this he means the power of politicians to qualify certain migration issues as a problem, thereby creating a very concrete (yet hitherto non-existent) problem for those affected.[2] Moreover, it is also shown that the political discussion on dual nationality from the 1980s to the present is undeniably characterized by selectivity and political symbolism.[3] In the course of this chapter we will see that the current obligation to renounce the nationality of origin upon naturalization produces many inconsistencies. The renunciation requirement, and its underlying objective of forcing immigrants to make an exclusive choice for the Netherlands, is almost unanimously

[1] Hans Ulrich Jessurun d'Oliveira, "Turmoil around a naturalisation decree or how the Dutch cabinet stumbled over a pebble", in *Vers de nouveaux équilibres entre ordres juridiques: liber amicorum Hélène Gaudemet-Tallon* (Paris: Dalloz, 2008), 319–333. When it was discovered that Hirsi Ali had provided false personal data upon naturalization, the Minister for Immigration and Integration concluded that she had never acquired Dutch nationality. Eventually, however, Hirsi Ali kept her Dutch nationality because it was shown that she was allowed under Somali law to bear the name that she had used upon naturalization; Hirsi Ali herself did not know that she was in fact allowed to bear the 'false' name which was entered in her naturalization decree.

[2] Kees Groenendijk, "Achterstand, dubbele nationaliteit en betrouwbare informatie: drie persoonlijke herinneringen voor Frans Zilverentant", in *Feestbundel Zilverentant*, ed. F.J.A. van der Velden (Den Haag: Ministerie van Justitie-Directie Wetgeving, 1998), 86.

[3] Hans Ulrich Jessurun d'Oliveira, "Alweer plannen om de afstandseis bij naturalisatie uit te breiden", *Nederlands Juristenblad*, no. 43 (2004): 2236; Anita Böcker, Kees Groenendijk, and Betty de Hart, "De toegang tot het Nederlanderschap, effecten van 20 jaar beleidswijzigingen", ibid., no. 3 (2005): 157.

rejected by the legal doctrine[4] but politicians seem little impressed by the legal arguments or stern facts and statistics that are brought forward.

At present, dual nationality is almost exclusively discussed in an immigration context. De Hart therefore explains the Dutch policy towards dual nationality from the 1990s onwards as follows: 'Overall, dual citizenship was treated as a cultural issue, and as relevant only to ethnic minorities, which is arguably the reason why the possibility of holding dual nationality as a rule was finally rejected'.[5] Indeed, Dutch nationals have to give up their nationality upon foreign naturalization, just as foreigners have to surrender their nationality of origin upon naturalization in the Netherlands. By placing dual nationality in a context of integration, however, a different view of dual nationality could nonetheless be adopted for foreign immigrants on the one hand and Dutch emigrants on the other. In other words, as the retention of Dutch nationality upon naturalization abroad did not pose an integration problem in the Netherlands, dual nationality among Dutch emigrants was not frowned upon. Dutch nationals who permanently live abroad can therefore retain their Dutch nationality, even if they hold a dual nationality.

Although applicants for naturalization in the Netherlands in principle have to renounce their nationality of origin, the list of exceptions to the renunciation requirement has continued to grow over time. In fact, during the period from 1998–2006 a large majority of 65 percent fell under one of the exceptions and was, consequently, allowed to retain the nationality of origin upon naturalization in the Netherlands.[6] It is therefore subject to doubt whether the renunciation requirement is a successful instrument in the fight against dual nationality.

The 1963 Convention plays an important role in this chapter. The Netherlands is still party to the 1963 Convention, but has also ratified the Second Protocol. The exceptions from this Protocol have been implemented in Dutch law as a general rule, meaning that they do not exclusively apply in relation to countries that are also party to the Second Protocol. Section 8.1 focuses more closely on these exceptions.

As Dutch law in practice departs so frequently from the renunciation requirement, it can be queried whether the government itself still believes—as it has often argued—that the prevention of dual nationality is a principle of international law. Although ten countries were bound by the first chapter of

---

[4] See for example Hans Ulrich Jessurun d'Oliveira, "Dubbelzinnigheden over dubbele nationaliteit", in *Woorden als daden. Commentaar en opinies* (Deventer: Kluwer, 2004), 132; Pieter Boeles, "Het nut van nationaliteit", *Nederlands Juristenblad*, no. 42 (2007): 2671.

[5] de Hart, "The End of Multiculturalism: The End of Dual Citizenship?", 81.

[6] de Groot and Vink, *Meervoudige nationaliteit in Europees perspectief*, 120–126.

the 1963 Convention in its heyday, consistent plans to totally eradicate dual nationality have never been elaborated within the Council of Europe. Not only did Article 1 of the first chapter already have a quite narrow scope, some countries even made reservations to it, and again others—like the Netherlands—decided to join the Second Protocol, implying that they no longer supported the harsh line adopted under Article 1. As a consequence, it appears that the Dutch participation to the 1963 Convention is of a pragmatic rather an ideological nature. The 1963 Convention serves as a pretext which makes possible the claim that an international consensus exists on the need to prevent dual nationality.[7] The spirit of Article 1 of the 1963 is subsequently infringed upon at the domestic level depending on the particular (societal and political) circumstances of the time. Inroads into the prohibition of dual nationality are so frequently made that it becomes difficult to make a convincing argument that the Netherlands still adheres to the ideological objective of Article 1. It remains to be seen how long the tactics of claiming international consensus on the undesirability of dual nationality based on the existence of the 1963 Convention can last, as the Convention's 'Farewell Symphony' is already being played.[8] A mere four countries are currently bound by the 1963 Convention, with Denmark and Norway being the only ones to apply the Convention without exceptions.[9] Hence, it becomes increasingly difficult to refer the 1963 Convention as proof of an international consensus on the undesirability of dual nationality.

The following sections will give a historical overview of the Dutch position on dual nationality, starting with the attitude towards this phenomenon under the 1892 Act and its successor, the 1985 Act. We then continue with an examination of the important modifications to Dutch nationality law that were brought about in 2003, and conclude with an enumeration of partly materialized proposals and controversies that arose on the subject of dual nationality after 2003.

Although dual nationality has been primarily debated in relation to the Dutch integration policy, we will also discuss the situation for Dutch emigrants and the consequences of the independence of the former Dutch colonies Indonesia (the Dutch East Indies) and Surinam. The latter subject may not feature as prominently in the nationality literature as do issues that have a direct bearing on the integration and minority policy. It should be interesting

---

[7] This was also the opinion of Frans Zilverentant, an acknowledged nationality law expert formerly working at the Dutch Ministry of Justice (personal conversation, Voorschoten, the Netherlands, 22 July 2009).

[8] de Groot, "Beperking van meervoudige nationaliteit: een nieuwe afscheidssymfonie?": 52.

[9] Austria made a reservation in respect of Article 1 of the 1963 Convention.

nonetheless to see whether the Dutch relation with the former colonies concerning nationality law differs from the other countries discussed in this study.

2. *The Dutch Nationality Act of 1892* (Wet op het Nederlanderschap en het ingezetenschap 1892)

It was mentioned in Chapter 1 (Section 3) that for most of the 19th century the Netherlands had two sets of rules concerning nationality.[10] The nationality provisions of the 1838 Dutch Civil Code were used in matters concerning civil law (and other fields such as private international law, migration law, extradition law and penal law); a special nationality law of 1850 (*Wet op het Nederlanderschap*) defined Netherlands nationality for the exercise of civic rights (active and passive suffrage and the appointment to government functions).[11] This division was abolished on 1 July 1893 when the 1892 Nationality

---

[10] For the sake of completion, it should be mentioned that the first proper Dutch nationality law was the *Wetboek Napoleon ingerigt voor het Koningrijk Holland*, which entered into force on 1 May 1809 and which was heavily inspired by the French Civil. The *Wetboek Napoleon* was short-lived and was replaced by the French Code Civil on 1 March 1811 when the Netherlands came under French rule. The French Code Civil would remain in force until the promulgation of the Dutch 1838 Civil Code. See de Groot and Tratnik, *Nederlands nationaliteitsrecht*, 38.

[11] In the mid-19th century, Dutch nationality (*Nederlanderschap*) as an independent legal status had crystallized to the point that the 1848 Constitution dictated that a special law should lay down the rules concerning it (the future 1850 law). The idea that Dutch nationality should be the expression of legal belonging to the Dutch nation-state had gained much force throughout the 19th century, yet an independent legal notion of Dutch nationality had not yet developed under the previous 1815 Constitution. Strictly speaking, this Constitution did not contain rules on Dutch nationality. It distinguished between different categories of Dutch nationals, of which only those born Dutch (*inboorlingen*) could exercise high public office. The question whether a person was Dutch could thus only be answered in an indirect way, namely by verifying whether this person had a right to exercise high public office under the Constitution. The 1848 Constitution abolished this distinction.

To sum up, we can say that acquisition of Dutch nationality through naturalization was only of interest in the 19th and beginning of the 20th century for those (men) who aspired to hold a public office or wanted to exercise their suffrage, in other words those who were financially well off and highly educated. Until the First World War, when the economic crisis led to protectionist measures in the labour market, Dutch nationality was of no importance for the right to reside and work in the Netherlands. Until then, the idea had prevailed that foreigners could reside in the Netherlands on condition that they were no burden to others and possessed sufficient financial means. This changed, however, with the outbreak of the First World War. The economic and political uncertainties inherent to the war led to a growing interest in Dutch nationality among the foreign population, no longer exclusively by well off

Act entered into force (*Wet op het Nederlanderschap en het ingezetenschap 1892*).

The issue of dual nationality was decisive for a number of modifications to Dutch nationality law that were brought about by the 1892 Act. Under the 1838 Civil Code the *ius soli* principle was in place and Dutch nationality was, accordingly, acquired by children whose foreign parents (in the majority of cases of German origin) were permanent residents in the Netherlands. As these children also acquired the nationality of their foreign parents, they were dual nationals. The government, however, increasingly saw the existence of dual nationality as a situation to be avoided and calls for the abolishment of *ius soli* became stronger, ultimately leading to the decision not to incorporate the *ius soli* principle in the 1892 Act. Children born to foreign parents were thus forced to naturalize in order to become Dutch, although spouses and children were automatically naturalized upon naturalization of their husband and father respectively.[12] Yet the choice for *ius sanguinis* in the 1892 Act was not exclusively inspired by the negative feelings towards the allegedly feudal *ius soli* principle and the phenomenon of dual nationality. It was also clearly an ideological choice and the intrinsic value of *ius sanguinis* itself made it 'the right principle' to foster loyal and nationalist feelings. The embrace of *ius sanguinis* at the time shows a changing perception of the Dutch nation, because children born to foreign parents were no longer automatically assumed to feel loyal towards the Dutch State.[13]

Heijs remarks that the Dutch interest in issues relating to dual nationality was first aroused in the 1850s. The most important debate in nationality matters at the time concerned the question whether or not to allow the retention

---

and highly educated foreigners, but also by those working in low skilled professions. See O. Moorman van Kappen, "Les concepts précurseurs de "nationalité" dans le droit néerlandais jusqu'au milieu du 19ième siècle", in *La condition juridique de l'étranger, hier et aujourd'hui. Actes du Colloque organisé à Nimègue les 9–11 mai 1988 par les Facultés de Droit de Poitiers et de Nimègue* (Nijmegen: Faculteit der Rechtsgeleerdheid, 1988), 203; Eric Heijs, *Van vreemdeling tot Nederlander. De verlening van het Nederlanderschap aan vreemdelingen 1813–1992*, Dissertatie Katholieke Universiteit Nijmegen (Amsterdam: Het Spinhuis, 1995), 15–60 and 84–85; de Groot, *Handboek Nieuw Nationaliteitsrecht*, 36–39.

12 Heijs, *Van vreemdeling tot Nederlander*, 67–68 and 100–101. The 1892 Act did contain a double *ius soli* provision, but Dutch nationality was only granted to the third generation foreigners (the second generation born in the Netherlands) if they were otherwise stateless. The practical effect of this provision was therefore negligible. The absence of *ius soli* in the nationality legislation obviously had an impact on the naturalization policy. Whilst in the years 1850–1890 only three percent of naturalisees had been born in the Netherlands, this had become 25 percent in the years 1890–1940.

13 Ibid., 67.

of the original nationality upon naturalization in the Netherlands. Whilst there were States which did not allow the retention of their nationality upon foreign naturalization, there were also those who did, for example Great Britain. Consequently, the naturalization in the Netherlands of a number of British nationals, who thereby acquired dual nationality, gave rise to parliamentary debate. Initially, the government argued that only Dutch law was relevant in naturalization cases and that foreign law was immaterial to the decision to grant naturalization to foreigners who applied for Dutch nationality. Although the parliament agreed with this reasoning, the government changed its mind in 1860 and from then on the renunciation requirement was strictly applied and subsequently incorporated in the 1892 Act.[14] These events will prove to be a recurrent theme in Dutch thinking about dual nationality: should Dutch law and Dutch interests be the exclusive criterion in the naturalization policy, or do foreign nationality laws also play a role? In other words, should the acceptance of dual nationality be a part of the naturalization policy when it is in the Dutch interest to incorporate the foreign population, or should naturalization be refused when the foreign applicant is unwilling or unable to relinquish the nationality of origin?

While the renunciation requirement upon naturalization in the Netherlands was strictly enforced, the 1892 Act allowed the retention of Dutch nationality for Dutch nationals permanently living abroad as well as their descendants, despite the rule that Dutch nationality was lost after ten years' residency abroad. A declaration stating the wish to remain Dutch lodged before the expiry of this ten year term was sufficient to retain Dutch nationality.[15]

After fierce criticism, the loss provision of the 1892 Act was modified in 1910. Dutch nationals born in the Netherlands or in Dutch colonies no longer lost Dutch nationality after ten years' residency abroad. The rule remained in place, however, for Dutch nationals not born in the Netherlands or in the colonies because it could still serve the purpose of testing the strength of the bond with the Netherlands. The modification of the provision on the loss of Dutch nationality owing to permanent residence abroad thus facilitated the retention of Dutch nationality. This policy can partly be explained by the hope that Dutch interests abroad could be better promoted by a stronger and larger Dutch presence there.[16]

Only in 1953 was *ius soli* reintroduced in Dutch nationality law: second generation foreigners born in the Netherlands were automatically granted

---

[14] Ibid., 50–53, 74.

[15] Ibid., 75–77.

[16] Ibid., 77–79.

Dutch nationality (double *ius soli*). Those who had criticized the absence of *ius soli* in the 1892 Act were proved correct in predicting that the Netherlands would face large colonies of permanent foreign residents in the future if children born in the Netherlands to foreign parents no longer acquired Dutch nationality by birth on Dutch soil. The problem was particularly serious in the Dutch-Belgian border region, but the intended plan to conclude a Dutch-Belgian agreement on facilitated naturalization of each other's nationals who lived across the border was eventually rejected. Rather than employing the method of naturalization however, which was considered an instrument for individual cases, it was decided that the second generation born in the Netherlands should automatically acquire Dutch nationality again.[17] It is important to stress that this rule had retroactive effect to 1 July 1893 (the moment the 1892 Act entered into force).[18]

The perception of dual nationality had also changed over the years. The hostile attitude that had triggered the abolishment of *ius soli* back in 1892 had turned into indifference, even in the knowledge that instances of dual nationality would inevitably increase with the reintroduction of *ius soli* elements. As a justification for the toleration of dual nationality, the government pointed to the 1930 Hague Convention, which was claimed to allow dual nationality by providing that each State is competent to decide who its nationals are. (This argument once more proves the ambiguous position of this convention on the issue of dual nationality: the convention simply lends itself to different interpretations.) Yet the toleration of dual nationality for third generation foreigners did not mean a departure from the general policy that dual nationality should be prevented. The opposition to dual nationality was simply to give way to the prevalent objective of the double *ius soli* rule to include the permanent foreign population and to relieve the pressure on the naturalization office.[19]

---

[17] More precisely, the double *ius soli* rule of 1953 provided that Dutch nationality was acquired by a child born in the Netherlands to a father resident there who had himself been born to a mother residing in the Netherlands at the time of the birth of her son. Children born out of wedlock acquired Dutch nationality if born to a mother who was resident in the Netherlands at the time of the child's birth and who herself had been born to a mother resident in the Netherlands at the time of her daughter's birth. As the decisive factor under this rule is *parental residence* and not *place of birth*, it is perhaps better to describe this rule as acquisition *iure domicilii*. See Gerard-René de Groot and Carlos Bollen, "Netherlands nationality law", in *Nationality laws in the European Union - Le droit de la nationalité dans l'Union Européene*, ed. Bruno Nascimbene (Milano: Giuffrè Editore, 1996), 552.

[18] Heijs, *Van vreemdeling tot Nederlander*, 134–135.

[19] Ibid., 135–136.

3. *Decolonization: The Independence of Indonesia and Surinam*

In the comparative chapters of this book considerable attention is paid to the current relation of the four States with their former colonies and with expatriates abroad. It is therefore worth examining the Dutch reaction to decolonization, and how this was expressed in its nationality legislation. Yet we remark at the outset that we will not encounter a spectacular system of dual nationality as exists in Spain, nor a situation in which instances of dual nationality were created on a large scale after decolonization, as in France. The treaties on the allocation of nationals between the Netherlands and its former colonies (Indonesia and Surinam) emphatically do not allow for a system of dual nationality. In what follows, we provide a historical overview of both former colonies and touch upon the nationality arrangements made after decolonization.

3.1. *The Nationality Status of the Native Population of the Dutch East Indies during Colonization and the Nationality Arrangements after Decolonization*

The Netherlands ruled the Dutch East Indies from 1596 until 1942, apart from the period 1795–1816 during which these territories were occupied by France and later by England. There was, however, a substantial difference in the way the Dutch East Indies were ruled when the Dutch returned to power in 1816 as compared to the situation before.[20]

The VOC and the WIC, two Dutch companies which in the early 17th century had been given trading monopolies by the Dutch States General in the East and West respectively, were commercial enterprises that also exercised some political functions, including concluding treaties with Indonesian rulers.[21] These commercial undertakings perished in the late 18th century and the Dutch colonies were occupied by foreign powers in the years following the French Revolution.[22] A change of perception took root in the aftermath of the Napoleonic wars and the Congress of Vienna when European governments became interested in ruling their colonies themselves rather than depending on commercial undertakings for this purpose.[23]

---

20 Wesseling, *Europa's koloniale eeuw*, 27.

21 Ibid., 20–22. From the State's viewpoint, this was an attractive system because the companies were themselves responsible for administration costs. Other European States would follow the Dutch example by setting up their own companies in the first half of the 17th century.

22 Ibid., 103.

23 Ibid., 136–141.

Since the Dutch East Indies were of great importance to the Netherlands, the Indonesian declaration of independence of 17 August 1945 was not accepted. Yet despite two military interventions, euphemistically called 'police interventions' (*politionele acties*), and under pressure from the United States and the United Nations, the Netherlands finally recognized the independent Republic of Indonesia—New Guinea excluded—on 27 December 1949. The question of New Guinea, which had been under permanent and effective Dutch rule since 1898,[24] was settled by a treaty concluded on 15 August 1962; on 1 May 1963 Indonesia could add New Guinea to its territory.[25]

What kind of arrangements were made over time concerning the nationality status of the native population in the Dutch East Indies? Under the 1838 Civil Code, Dutch nationality was acquired by persons born in the Netherlands or the colonies to parents who had their permanent residence there. The implications of this rule for the native population in the Dutch East Indies had been discussed in parliament during the debate prior to the promulgation of the Civil Code. It turned out that the native population was covered by the provision from the Civil Code and consequently possessed Dutch nationality for the purposes of private law, penal law, extradition law (they could not be extradited to third countries) and diplomatic protection (the Netherlands could exercise diplomatic protection on their behalf).[26] Slaves, however, were not covered by the 1838 Civil Code's provision on nationality. This was justified by the government with the argument that slaves, by nature, did not have the ability to establish residency and could therefore not possibly fall under the provision.[27] Heijs points out that the parliament—avowedly content with the government's statement—initially let the matter drop, but that the subject was raised again during the debate on the 1848 Constitution. On that occasion, it was decided that the native population in the Dutch East Indies was to be excluded from the nationality law of 1850, which defined Dutch nationality for the exercise of civic rights.[28]

---

24 Ibid., 325.

25 Renata Henriette de Haas-Engel, *Het Indonesisch Nationaliteitsrecht*, Dissertatie Universiteit Maastricht (Deventer: Kluwer, 1993), 3–7. For an illustration of the effects of this independence in the field of nationality law, see the fictional case 'Een Nieuw-Guinese Chinees' in Gerard-René de Groot, *Achtentwintig Nederlanders? Bewerkte adviezen en casus over de toepassing van de Nederlandse nationaliteitswetgeving* ('s-Gravenhage: Elsevier Overheid, 2007), 179–190.

26 de Haas-Engel, *Het Indonesisch Nationaliteitsrecht*, 150.

27 Heijs, *Van vreemdeling tot Nederlander*, 34–35. The government writes that they are not persons but objects (*non sunt personae sed res*).

28 Ibid., 35. A very small number of MPs argued that extending political membership to the native population—a harmless proposal because the natives would not be able to fulfil the

When the two regulations on Dutch nationality—the 1838 Civil Code and the 1850 Nationality Act—were replaced by the 1892 Nationality Act, the question was again asked whether the native population of the Dutch East Indies possessed Dutch nationality. It was decided that they should be excluded, but this exclusion was highly problematic from the perspective of international law; Dutch subjects were turned into aliens or rendered stateless, implying that diplomatic protection could no longer be exercised on behalf of these former subjects.[29] Only in 1910 was a bond of international law again created with the native population by giving them them the status of 'Dutch subject non-Dutch national'. De Haas-Engel mentions that international law made no distinction between Dutch nationals under the 1892 Act and 'Dutch subject non-Dutch national' under the Act from 1910—the Act that introduced this status.[30]

In the Dutch East Indies themselves a central government was in place. The Dutch-Indonesian society was a segregated one and race was the criterion on which the social, economic and political structure was based.[31] This 'race-criterion'—based on the assumption that different societal groups had different legal needs—was implemented in the 1854 Dutch East Indies' Constitution (the so-called *Regeringsreglement*), thereby establishing two legal categories: 'Europeans and assimilated' (mostly Christians), and 'natives and assimilated' (consisting of the native population, Arabs, Chinese, Mohammedans and pagans).[32] Both categories had their own private and public law, which created a dualism that would (be it in mitigated form) last until the recognition of Indonesian independence by the Netherlands in 1949.[33]

Indonesian independence obviously changed the nationality arrangements as described above. The main principle of the allocation treaty, supported by

---

numerous additional requirements—would at least have a positive symbolical effect: in theory, the native population would have political rights; in practice, this policy would pose no danger to the Netherlands as the native population could not meet the financial and residence requirements. Yet the government found it self-evident that the native population was excluded from having political rights under the 1850 Act.

29 Ibid., 70.

30 Hence, the exclusive aim of the 1910 Act was to re-establish a link under international law with the native population. In 1892 they had been made aliens and the 1910 Act now made them subjects again—be it second-class ones. The 1910 Act should thus emphatically not be interpreted as rehabilitation to 'full' Dutch nationality. See de Haas-Engel, *Het Indonesisch Nationaliteitsrecht*, 100–101.

31 Ibid., 74; Heijs, *Van vreemdeling tot Nederlander*, 70.

32 van Oers, de Hart, and Groenendijk, "Netherlands", 393.

33 Heijs, *Van vreemdeling tot Nederlander*, 70.

both the Dutch and Indonesian delegation, was straightforward: those belonging to the Dutch nation would remain Dutch; those with a stronger bond with Indonesia would acquire Indonesian nationality. As this division had already taken shape under the 1910 Act with the introduction of the status 'Dutch subject non-Dutch national', allocation was not a difficult task.[34] The native population (70 million people) acquired Indonesian nationality without any possibility of remaining Dutch subjects. The 250,000 Dutch nationals residing in Indonesia remained Dutch, but the majority had an option right to Indonesian nationality. For several reasons, the Dutch government expected and hoped that many of them would use this right. In the first place, the socio-economic conditions in the Netherlands were such that emigration was encouraged. Large-scale migration from Indonesia to the Netherlands was therefore to be prevented at all costs. In addition, the group in possession of the option right—i.e. those born in Indonesia or resident there for more than six months—was discouraged from coming to the Netherlands for fear that they could not be integrated.[35] In the end, only 13,600 people opted for Indonesian nationality (31,000 if we take into account the women and children that were automatically included in the option right exercised by their husband and father respectively).[36]

We can conclude, then, that a system of dual nationality between the Netherlands and Indonesia was never seriously considered. From the Dutch point of view, immigration from Indonesia should be prevented. Dutch nationals with strong bonds with Indonesia were also encouraged to remain in Indonesia and to opt for Indonesian nationality.[37] Moral considerations towards the native population in respect of nationality law did not play any role in the aftermath of decolonization. After all, the Dutch East Indies had always been a segregated society in which the 'natives and assimilated' were never treated on the same footing as the 'Europeans and assimilated'. Indonesia, on the other hand, adopting the perspective of a newly independent State, was preoccupied chiefly with nation building. Neither dual nationality nor a system of option rights would be conducive to this objective.

---

[34] de Haas-Engel, *Het Indonesisch Nationaliteitsrecht*, 126; Heijs, *Van vreemdeling tot Nederlander*, 121–122.

[35] Heijs, *Van vreemdeling tot Nederlander*, 123.

[36] Ibid., 126.

[37] Ibid., 130. In the absence of an option right to Dutch nationality for the native population in Indonesia, the government promised to adopt a generous naturalization policy. In practice, however, such a policy was never implemented, since it was qualified as incompatible with the restrictive immigration policy at the time.

3.2. *The Nationality Status of the Native Population of Surinam during Colonization and the Nationality Arrangements after Decolonization*

Surinam became a Dutch colony on the basis of the 1667 Peace Treaty of Breda which stipulated that the island Manhattan, hitherto a Dutch settlement bearing the name 'New Netherlands' (*Nieuw Nederland*), would be ceded to the British.[38] The Netherlands received Surinam in return, a territory which would become independent on 25 November 1975.

In contrast to the native inhabitants in the Dutch East Indies, who did not have Dutch nationality under the 1892 Act, the inhabitants of Surinam and the Dutch Antilles were in possession of Dutch nationality and had also been so under the 1838 Civil Code and the 1850 Nationality Act.[39] Immigration had always been an important factor for the prospering of Surinam. In the beginning of the 20th century, for example, many workers from the Dutch East Indies (Java in particular) had been recruited in Surinam. This specific group of natives from the Dutch East Indies had, unlike the rest of the native population of the Dutch East Indies, the possibility to acquire Dutch nationality after Indonesian independence.[40]

In 1954 the Netherlands, Surinam and the Dutch Antilles entered a new interrelationship as the Kingdom of the Netherlands. Its legal basis was the Charter for the Kingdom of the Netherlands (*Statuut voor het Koninkrijk der Nederlanden*) which entered into force on 29 December 1954.[41] For our purposes, it is sufficient to note that the Charter provided that matters of nationality concerned the whole of the Kingdom of the Netherlands; none of the

---

[38] Wesseling, *Europa's koloniale eeuw*, 22; A.Th. van Deursen, *De last van veel geluk. De geschiedenis van Nederland, 1555–1702* (Amsterdam: Uitgeverij Bert Bakker, 2004), 250–251.

[39] van Oers, de Hart, and Groenendijk, "Netherlands", 393. Different treatment of the native populations of Surinam and the Netherlands Antilles was possible because they were much smaller in number than the Indonesian population.

[40] Heijs, *Van vreemdeling tot Nederlander*, 121, 144. More specifically, the children of the many labourers from the Dutch East Indies born after the entry force of the 1892 Act did no longer automatically acquire Dutch nationality by birth on Dutch territory. In 1927 they were given the status 'Dutch subject non-Dutch national', however. This status was replaced in 1951 by full Dutch nationality on condition that they had not yet chosen for Indonesian nationality after Indonesian independence.

[41] de Groot and Bollen, "Netherlands nationality law", 545. In 1986 Aruba separated itself from the other Islands comprising the Dutch Antilles and obtained the status of a separate country within the Kingdom. As of 10 October 2010 the Dutch Antilles no longer exist. Sint-Maarten and Curaçao became autonomous countries within the Kingdom of the Netherlands (a so-called 'status aparte'), while Bonaire, Sint-Eustasius and Saba became 'special municipalities' of the Netherlands.

three countries could thus independently decide on rules concerning acquisition and loss of nationality. Consequently, the double *ius soli* which was in place in the Netherlands also applied in Surinam and the Dutch Antilles. Moreover, the need for a bigger Surinam population led to a facilitated naturalization policy there. The combined effect of this nationality settlement was that the overwhelming majority of the population of Surinam was in possession of Dutch nationality by the late 1960s.[42]

Until the mid-1960s the Netherlands was not particularly worried about the majority of the Surinam population possessing Dutch nationality. At that moment in time some 11,000 Dutch nationals of Surinam descent lived in the Netherlands, but this number started to increase rapidly, rising to 30,000 in 1970.[43] The Dutch government was alarmed by the growing immigration from Surinam, yet an admission policy for Dutch nationals of Surinam descent was—due the colonial past and the moral obligations ensuing from it—politically and morally indefensible.[44] As a consequence of this uncontrollable immigration, the Netherlands was more than happy to cooperate when Surinam announced at the beginning of 1974 that it was striving to declare independence within two years.[45]

This wish for independence as expressed by the Surinam government had a dramatic effect, however. Many Dutch nationals of Surinam descent preferred a transfer to the Netherlands over the political uncertainty surrounding Surinam independence. The Netherlands once more tried to install an admission regime, which again proved politically and morally unfeasible. As a result, on 25 November 1975 the number of Dutch nationals of Surinam descent had doubled to 100,000 compared to early 1974, when Surinam had for the first time openly announced that it strived for independence.[46]

---

[42] Heijs, *Van vreemdeling tot Nederlander*, 145.

[43] Ibid.

[44] Interestingly, some members of the Dutch government thought that a unilateral policy on the admission of nationals from Surinam would be a violation of rules of international law. In this context, they referred to the issue of the British nationals of Asian descent in East Africa and their admission to the UK (see for this situation our discussion in Chapter 1 of the ECJ judgment *Kaur*). Ahmad Ali concludes, however, that there were no rules of international law in the early 1970s which would have prevented the Netherlands from introducing such an admission policy. See Hamied A. Ahmad Ali, *De Toescheidingsovereenkomst inzake nationaliteiten tussen Nederland en Suriname*, Dissertatie Universiteit Utrecht (s'-Gravenhage: Sdu, 1998), 288–289.

[45] Heijs, *Van vreemdeling tot Nederlander*, 146; Ahmad Ali, *De Toescheidingsovereenkomst inzake nationaliteiten tussen Nederland en Suriname*, 288.

[46] Heijs, *Van vreemdeling tot Nederlander*, 146.

Surinam gained independence on 25 November 1975. Again an allocation treaty was drafted, the main principle of which was again straightforward: those with a strong link to the Dutch nation would remain Dutch; those whose lives were primarily connected with the Surinam nation and territory were to acquire the nationality of that country. In practice, this meant that all Dutch nationals born in Surinam and there resident on 25 November 1975 acquired Surinam nationality. Dutch nationals born in Surinam to parents who had not been born in Surinam (but for example in the Netherlands or the Dutch Antilles) were given the possibility to opt for Dutch nationality within one year after Surinam independence. This was justified by the fact that this group might feel more closely connected to the Netherlands than to Surinam. All those who did not fall under this exception definitively lost their prior Dutch nationality.[47] Moreover, as had been the case under the Dutch-Indonesian allocation treaty, neither Surinam nor the Netherlands believed in a system of dual nationality.[48]

This course of affairs was strongly criticized by the opposition in the Surinam parliament and in the legal literature.[49] Aside from the group mentioned above, the allocation treaty did not contain a general right to opt for Dutch nationality, nor did it contain a system of dual nationality. It was called a discriminatory treaty by the Surinam opposition because those who could afford to travel to the Netherlands before 25 November 1975 were allowed to keep Dutch nationality.[50] The opposition was possibly also afraid of a 'brain

47 Ibid., 147–149. This had implications also for those who descended from the native population of the Dutch East Indies and who were subsequently brought to Surinam as labour immigrants at the beginning of the 20th century. They did not have the possibility to remain Dutch, although their cultural background made it not all that evident that they should be allocated to Surinam.

48 Under Article 2(1) of the allocation treaty, acquisition of Surinam nationality resulted in the loss of Dutch nationality. Under Article 2(2) the reverse applied for the acquisition of Dutch nationality. Both nationalities were thus mutually exclusive and dual nationality was not allowed under the treaty. While the Netherlands was not eager to welcome new immigrants, Surinam had its own reasons for opposing a system of dual nationality. As Ahmad Ali rightly points out, the function of nationality as an instrument to define the personal substratum of States is of particular importance in the case of State succession. This argument against dual nationality is further strengthened in the Surinam case by the fact that the population was composed of many ethnic groups. The exclusive possession of Surinam nationality would therefore be conducive to the unifying and nation building process in the newly independent State. See Ahmad Ali, *De Toescheidingsovereenkomst inzake nationaliteiten tussen Nederland en Suriname*, 58.

49 D'Oliveira has criticized the treaty's position on dual nationality for not taking into account the will of the individuals concerned. Jessurun d'Oliveira, "Het Europees Verdrag inzake Nationaliteit", 37–38.

50 Heijs, *Van vreemdeling tot Nederlander*, 148.

drain' if the Surinam elite were to leave for the Netherlands before Surinam independence. In any case, despite efforts to encourage a return to Surinam,[51] very few of the Dutch nationals of Surinam descent who had retained Dutch nationality returned there in the end.[52] The ties with Surinam remained strong, however, ultimately leading to talk about dual citizenship—although not dual nationality.[53]

4. *The Equality of the Sexes in Dutch Nationality Law*

In keeping with the nationality laws of most other States, the Netherlands for a long time adhered to a 'unitary system', i.e. a system under which children only acquired the nationality of their father. The first significant attack on this principle came about on 1 March 1964 when the 1892 Act was amended in such a way that a foreign woman marrying a Dutch man no longer automatically acquired Dutch nationality. She did have a right of election, however, and was not subject to a renunciation obligation upon exercising that right.[54] In reverse, a Dutch woman could now keep her Dutch nationality upon marriage with a foreigner, even if she also acquired her husband's nationality. Just as with the introduction of *ius soli* in 1953, the government was indifferent to the unavoidable rise of dual nationals resulting from this modification.[55]

---

[51] An important feature of the allocation treaty between the Netherlands and Surinam was the issue of remigration. In order to facilitate remigration, Article 5 of the treaty allowed Dutch nationals of Surinam descent to opt for Surinam nationality within ten years after Surinam independence. This would result in the loss of Dutch nationality, however. They could also at any time return to Surinam and would automatically acquire Surinam nationality after two years' residency there. See Ahmad Ali, *De Toescheidingsovereenkomst inzake nationaliteiten tussen Nederland en Suriname*, 289, 298.

[52] Heijs, *Van vreemdeling tot Nederlander*, 150.

[53] Hamied A. Ahmad Ali, "Surinaamse emigranten. Duaal burgerschap, onvoorwaardelijke toelating en gelijke behandeling", in *Collected Essays in honour of Kees Groenendijk* (Nijmegen: Wolf Legal Publishers, 2008), 154. Although there are no signs that this plan will materialize in the near future, a 'Dual Citizenship Act Surinam Emigrants' (*Wet Duaal Burgerschap Surinaamse Emigranten*) was drafted by Kees Groenendijk in 2004, the essence of which resides in the right for Surinam emigrants to establish themselves at all times in Surinam and to be treated (with exceptions) as Surinam nationals.

[54] Foreign men marrying a Dutch woman did not have such an option right, however. They were subject to the regular naturalization procedure. See de Hart, *Onbezonnen vrouwen. Gemengde relaties in het nationaliteitsrecht en het vreemdelingenrecht*, 81.

[55] A law of 14 November 1963 introduced this modification, thereby anticipating the ratification on 6 November 1966 of the 1957 UN Convention on the Status of Married Women. A previous law of 21 December 1936 (which entered into force on 1 July 1937) had achieved

Although this step to bring about a transition from a 'système unitaire' to a 'système dualiste' was of great consequence, it was not until 1 January 1985—when the 1892 Act was replaced by a new nationality Act—that true gender equality was finally secured. It is only as of 1985 that Dutch women can transmit their nationality to their children.[56] The discussion in Western Europe in the 1970s on the equality of men and women in nationality law—France and Germany, for example, fully abolished the unitary system in 1973 and 1975 respectively—had also been picked up in the Netherlands. Below we will set out the main points in the Dutch discussion on gender equality in nationality law in the years preceding the 1985 Act, restricting ourselves to the relevant aspects of this discussion for the matter of dual nationality. A discussion held within the Dutch Association of Comparative Law in 1977 on the occasion of a comparative study presented by De Groot is particularly instructive in this regard, as it presents an elaborate examination of the possibilities to prevent multiple nationality. (It should be emphasized that De Groot would later change his position on dual nationality; he now embraces the concept.)[57]

De Groot presented the choice in favour or against dual nationality as one of principle. Although his whole study was imbued with the idea that men and women should be treated equally in nationality matters, he did not advocate a

a more modest result by providing that a Dutch woman would not lose her nationality if she did not acquire her foreign husband's nationality upon marriage. See Gerard-René de Groot, *Gelijkheid van man en vrouw in het nationaliteitsrecht. Preadvies uitgebracht voor de Nederlandse Vereniging voor Rechtsvergelijking* (Deventer: Kluwer, 1977), 50–52.

56 This equalization of the position of women in Dutch nationality law came about at the expense of foreign women. Until 1985 foreign women who married a Dutchman could, unlike foreign men marrying a Dutch woman, opt for Dutch nationality. This right was not granted to foreign men for fear of 'sham marriages'. What happened in 1985 was a 'negative equalization' in the sense that the option right was revoked altogether; the foreign spouse (men as well as women) could now only apply for Dutch nationality after having lived together for three years or after three years of marriage. See de Hart, *Onbezonnen vrouwen. Gemengde relaties in het nationaliteitsrecht en het vreemdelingenrecht*, 82–83. D'Oliveira has shown that equality of the sexes in nationality law was still very controversial in 1976. The minister then in office argued against equalizing the position of men and women because 'this would have the unintended effect of making Dutch women excessively attractive for large groups of aliens on the move'. In other words, it was feared that 'sham marriages' would be concluded for the sole purpose of obtaining Dutch nationality. Hans Ulrich Jessurun d'Oliveira, "The Artifact of 'Sham Marriages'", *Yearbook of Private International Law* 1 (1999): 55–56.

57 See for example de Groot, "Een pleidooi voor meervoudige nationaliteit": 100–105. Yet De Groot's paper was written at a time when—witness the many ratifications of the 1963 Convention in the late 1960s and early 1970s—wide consensus still existed on the undesirability of dual nationality.

general toleration of the cumulation of nationalities. Since he perceived the matter to be one of principle (seeming to say that dual nationality was either good or bad), a choice in favour of dual nationality would imply not only its toleration but also its promotion.[58] In other words, not only should one tolerate this status for spouses and children in mixed marriages, but also in every other case thinkable. And not only should it be tolerated. After all, if dual nationality were seen as a good thing, nothing would stand in the way of actively promoting it. As he did not wish to take responsibility for the fundamental alteration of nationality law if this position towards dual nationality were to be implemented, he supported the line taken by the 1963 Convention (which had already been signed by the Netherlands but was not yet ratified).

In his endeavour to reconcile full gender equality in nationality law with a prohibition on dual nationality, De Groot proposed several solutions.[59] One of these entailed the obligation for a dual national from birth to choose between his or her nationalities at a certain age. He acknowledged, however, that this proposal was problematic as it would require extensive international coordination. Thus doubting the feasibility of this proposal, he suggested instead a system which would provide for the automatic loss of nationality upon proof that the dual national had severed the ties with a country of which he/she possessed the nationality. This would be the case, for example, after a long residence abroad. De Groot clearly preferred another solution, however, which combined the elements of *ius sanguinis* and *ius soli*: a child born to parents of different nationalities should in principle not acquire a nationality *iure sanguinis* but *iure soli*. More specifically, the child should acquire the nationality of the country of birth which corresponded to the nationality of one of the parents. In this proposal *ius sanguinis* played a subsidiary role and was only to be used to avoid a child's statelessness if it was born in a country of which neither parent possessed the nationality—a situation which could easily arise when one of the parents worked abroad in the service of the State of his or her nationality. The proposal's weak spot was that dual nationality would still come about when the different States, the nationalities of which the parents possessed, would attribute both their nationality to a child born in a third country.

De Groot's reasoned rejection of multiple nationality was not shared by the majority of discussants at the time, who countered his ideas with arguments

58 de Groot, *Gelijkheid van man en vrouw in het nationaliteitsrecht*, 72–73.

59 Ibid., 84–88.

which would later also be espoused by De Groot himself.[60] D'Oliveira (whose ever-continuing amicable polemic with De Groot in nationality matters seems to find its origin here) did not support a principled choice against plural nationality, primarily because he objected to the loss of nationality independent of the will of the individual. In addition, he did not understand the intolerance towards the phenomenon. In his view, several principles of nationality law were simply irreconcilable with each other: an unconditional support for the principle of gender equality in nationality law implied a (partial) sacrifice of other principles, such as the prevention of dual nationality.[61] The elimination of cases of dual nationality was not a goal to which this equality should be subordinated. This view was supported by Zilverentant, a nationality law specialist working at the Ministry of Justice, who also argued that the opposition to dual nationality should give way to full equality of men and women in nationality law.[62]

It has already been seen in Chapter 1 that the 1963 Convention provided that 'nationals of the Contracting Parties who are of full age and who acquire of their own free will, by means of naturalization, option or recovery, the nationality of another Party shall lose their former nationality'. Although the Convention thus only has a bearing on those who acquire a nationality after birth, the toleration of dual nationality for children from mixed marriages violates the spirit of the Convention, to say the least. This conspicuous contradiction gave rise to doubt in the literature over the desirability of ratifying the 1963 Convention.[63] Nevertheless, resistance to ratification was of no use:

---

60 See Gerard-René de Groot, "Eenenveertig jaren nationaliteitsrecht", *Burgerzaken & Recht* 5, no. 6 (1998): 146–152; de Groot, "Vingt et un ans après: De gelijke behandeling van man en vrouw in het nationaliteitsrecht", 71–77.

61 Nederlandse Vereniging Voor Rechtsvergelijking, *Debat over het preadvies 'Gelijkheid van man en vrouw in het nationaliteitsrecht' van Mr. G.R. de Groot in het kader van de Nederlandse Vereniging Voor Rechtsvergelijking* (Deventer: Kluwer, 1978), 38–39. See also Hans Ulrich Jessurun d'Oliveira, "Nederlanders, wie zijn dat?", *Nederlands Juristenblad*, no. 24 (1977): 590. On that occasion, he had already supported dual nationality, not only for the substantial benefits that accrue from dual nationality for the dual national, but also for the osmosis of sovereign States it would supposedly create. From the fact that dual nationals belong to the personal substratum of more than one State, it followed in d'Oliveira's view that the phenomenon of dual nationality may fade the personal boundaries between States.

62 F.Th. Zilverentant, "Polemiek over de gelijkheid van man en vrouw in het nationaliteitsrecht", *Burgerzaken* (1982): 1–2; de Groot, "Eenenveertig jaren nationaliteitsrecht": 148.

63 D'Oliveira in particular was very vocal about the undesirability of ratifying the 1963 Convention. In his view, only the second chapter on military obligations was worth ratifying; the first chapter took too harsh a position on dual nationality. Moreover, he criticized the ambiguous position on dual nationality if one would ratify a convention which aimed at reducing dual nationality while simultaneously advocating the equality of the sexes in

despite all the well-founded criticism, the 1963 Convention entered into force on 10 June 1985. Endorsement of the 1963 Convention seemed not only to clash with the equality of the sexes in nationality law, however. It also appeared incompatible with another feature of the new Nationality Act: the 'minorities' policy' intended to improve the legal status of non-Dutch minorities. We will come to speak of this in the next section, which is dedicated to the 1985 Act.

5. *The Dutch Nationality Act of 1985*

On 1 January 1985, the Nationality Act of 1892 was succeeded by a new nationality law.[64] For our purposes the 1985 Act (hereafter sometimes abbreviated as DNA) is important mainly for three reasons: the introduction of equality of men and women in nationality law, the idea that the legal position of minorities should be improved, and the incorporation of the principal objective of the 1963 Convention, i.e. the reduction of cases of dual nationality. Reconciling these different objectives in the new nationality law may seem difficult at first sight, and it will be shown below that this was indeed the case.

Having discussed the debate on gender equality in Dutch nationality in the previous section, we will give it fairly brief treatment here. In accordance with the European trend at the time, the 1985 Act introduced a dualist system: children would now also acquire the nationality of the mother at birth.[65]

---

nationality law. D'Oliveira refers in this respect also to Ko Swan Sik, who had recently argued before the Dutch Association on International Law that the objections against dual nationality were of an emotional-political rather than a legal nature; he also refers to a commission report advising on matters of international law, which had advised against ratification of the 1963 Convention. We may thus conclude that the ratification of 1963 Convention was widely opposed amongst academics. See Ko Swan Sik, "Nationaliteit en het volkenrecht", 3–42; Hans Ulrich Jessurun d'Oliveira, "De herziening van ons nationaliteitsrecht", *Nederlands Juristenblad*, no. 9 (1982): 347.

[64] In the late 1970s the Netherlands planned to ratify three Conventions: the 1961 UN Convention on the Reduction of Statelessness, the 1963 Convention and the 1973 Bern Convention on the Reduction of Statelessness. As ratification of these conventions required the 1892 Act to be changed on many points, a new Act became a necessity. See Jessurun d'Oliveira, "De herziening van ons nationaliteitsrecht": 246. See for the English translation of the Nationality Act by the author of the present study http://eudo-citizenship.eu (select the Netherlands under the country profiles).

[65] The equality of the sexes also had important effects in the field of alien law: children born to a foreign father and a Dutch mother were longer aliens; in addition, the non-Dutch parent acquired a stronger residence right in the Netherlands through the Dutch nationality of his children. See Kees Groenendijk, "Le rôle changeant de la nationalité pour la condition juridique de l'étranger", in *La condition juridique de l'étranger, hier et aujourd'hui. Actes du*

A transitory provision provided that the children of Dutch mothers who were still minors when the 1985 Act entered into force and did not possess Dutch nationality, could opt for Dutch nationality between 1 January 1985 and 1 January 1988. Children who had already reached the age of majority did not have such an option right.[66] This has most recently changed, however, and an option right has been granted to foreigners born before 1 January 1985 to a mother who was Dutch at the time of birth while the father was not (see also *infra* Section 8.1).[67] It is estimated that up to 90,000 latent Dutch nationals could avail themselves of this option right. It should nevertheless be stressed that since Dutch women used to lose their nationality upon marriage with a foreigner until 1 January 1964, the requirement that the mother held Dutch nationality at the time of birth may, in certain cases, give rise to difficulties in this regard.[68]

In addition, the 1985 Act introduced a right to opt for Dutch nationality for children born in the Netherlands to foreign parents. They could exercise this right between the age of 18 and 25, provided that they had been residing on Dutch territory since birth.[69] It is hard to understand how the fact that this option right was not conditioned on the renunciation of the nationality of origin was still thought compatible with the spirit of 1963 Convention, which provided that 'nationals of the Contracting Parties who are of full age and who acquire of their own free will, by means of … option … the nationality of another Party shall lose their former nationality'.[70]

The option right for second generation foreigners was part of a new way of thinking about the Dutch integration policy. Until the early 1980s no coherent policy to promote immigrant integration had been developed.[71] A country of

---

Colloque organisé à Nimègue les 9–11 mai 1988 par les Facultés de Droit de Poitiers et de Nimègue (Nijmegen: Faculteit der Rechtsgeleerdheid, 1988), 111.

66 Although the Nationality Act set the age of majority at 18 years, it is important to stress that the Civil Code provided until 1989 that one attained the age of majority at 21. It is therefore not surprising that the transitory provision of Article 27(2) granted an option right to the children of Dutch mothers below the age of 21 years. See de Groot and Bollen, "Netherlands nationality law", 568.

67 Dutch Official Journal (*Staatsblad*) 2010, 242.

68 See in more detail EUDO citizenship news of 12 July 2010 (http://eudo-citizenship.eu).

69 Ruud van den Bedem, "Towards a System of Plural Nationality in the Netherlands", in *From Aliens to Citizens. Redefining the Status of Immigrants in Europe*, ed. Rainer Bauböck (Aldershot: Avebury, 1994), 96.

70 See also Hans Ulrich Jessurun d'Oliveira, "Burgers en buitenlui", *Nederlands Juristenblad*, no. 41 (1983): 1304.

71 Han Entzinger, "The Rise and Fall of Multiculturalism: The Case of the Netherlands", in *Toward Assimilation and Citizenship: Immigrants in Liberal Nation-States*, ed. Christian Joppke and Eva Morawska (Basingstoke: Palgrave Macmillan, 2003), 61.

emigration in the years immediately following the Second World War, the Netherlands had not been particularly concerned at the time with developing an immigration policy. Immigration became a reality from the 1950s, when the Netherlands was confronted with immigrants from its (former) colonies, Indonesia and Surinam, and guest-workers from the Mediterranean.[72] The guest-workers were initially thought to work in the Netherlands on a temporary basis only—hence the adoption of an active return policy—but most of the welfare state provisions were also made available to them and they were encouraged to preserve their cultural identity. All in all, a two-pronged policy was in place. On the one hand, a return policy was implemented in respect of temporary migrants; on the other hand, a policy of hospitality and inclusiveness was adopted concerning access to welfare state provisions.[73]

In 1979 an influential report was published by the Scientific Council for Government Policy (*Wetenschappelijke Raad voor het Regeringsbeleid*) which concluded that most immigrants would stay in the Netherlands on a permanent basis.[74] The report advised an inclusive policy towards these immigrants and the government acted accordingly by initiating a minority policy. This policy aimed at the equal participation of minorities in society and would create a multi-ethnic society in which migrants were primarily perceived in terms of their group membership, and not so much as individuals.[75] In hindsight, these years were the heydays of the multicultural policy, though it is doubtful whether the policy was ever based on a principled multiculturalism. De Hart suggests that the multicultural policies 'were based on a pragmatism that would later be labelled as multiculturalism in public and scientific discourse'.[76]

In order to strengthen the minorities' legal position, naturalization was simplified and actively promoted under the 1985 Act. It also became more of a

72 de Hart, "The End of Multiculturalism: The End of Dual Citizenship?", 79.

73 Entzinger, "The Rise and Fall of Multiculturalism: The Case of the Netherlands", 61; de Hart, "The End of Multiculturalism: The End of Dual Citizenship?", 79.

74 1979 report on ethnic minorities by the Scientific Council for Government Policy.

75 Entzinger, "The Rise and Fall of Multiculturalism: The Case of the Netherlands", 62. The aim of the minority policy was 'integration with retention of identity'. In other words, the Netherlands was to become a multi-ethnic society in which minorities would live in harmony with the majority and where they had equal opportunities.

76 de Hart, "The End of Multiculturalism: The End of Dual Citizenship?", 80. Entzinger makes similar observations about developments in the early 1990s: 'The Netherlands appeared to have a 'silent majority', weary of multiculturalism, but unwilling to speak up until then, probably fearing to be accused of racism'. See Entzinger, "The Rise and Fall of Multiculturalism: The Case of the Netherlands", 71.

right than a favour.[77] Questions on what it meant to become Dutch were not addressed, however; the political climate at the time was fearful of nationalist feelings.[78] The renunciation requirement remained a condition for naturalization, although an exception was made for those from whom this could not reasonably be asked.[79] However, not only did the renunciation requirement—a strong disincentive for naturalization—seem incompatible with an inclusive policy, but by exempting certain categories from the renunciation obligation the Netherlands reinforced the already ambiguous position on the question of dual nationality.[80] This further illustrates the extent to which the whole subject is characterized by incoherence and arbitrariness in the Netherlands. Whether a person is allowed to possess another nationality alongside the Dutch one should not depend, in our view, on particular individual circumstances, or on a foreign law which does not allow for the renunciation of nationality. For the sake of equality, there should be no space for a policy which makes the possession of a dual nationality dependent on such arbitrary factors. Rather, it should depend on equal and predictable criteria which are easily applicable in

---

77 Under the 1985 Act, naturalization was granted by Royal Decree rather than by a formal Act. A naturalization request also had to be dealt with within one year after receiving the request. In addition, the naturalization procedure became increasingly decentralized. Since 1996 municipalities prepare the naturalization files and issue an advice. The Immigration and Naturalization Service in turn marginally tests the advice and finally decides on the file. See Böcker, Groenendijk, and de Hart, "De toegang tot het Nederlanderschap, effecten van 20 jaar beleidswijzigingen": 85–86.

78 See critically A.V.M. Struycken, "Acquisition et perte de la nationalité néerlandaise", in *La condition juridique de l'étranger, hier et aujourd'hui. Actes du Colloque organisé à Nimègue les 9–11 mai 1988 par les Facultés de Droit de Poitiers et de Nimègue* (Nijmegen: Faculteit der Rechtsgeleerdheid, 1988), 6. 'Le gouvenement a hésité à assumer son rôle qui consiste à dire à quelles réalités dans le monde contemporain correspond l'idée de patrie, et a risqué de méconnaître les besoins spirituels que pourraient éprouver les Néerlandais sur ce point'.

79 van Oers, de Hart, and Groenendijk, "Netherlands", 405–406. The exemption from the renunciation requirement for three categories had already been laid down in a 1977 circular and had been applied since. These categories included (1) persons whose country of origin did not allow renunciation, (2) refugees who could not be expected to contact the authorities of their country of origin, and (3) persons who would suffer disproportional financial damage as a result of the renunciation of their original nationality.

80 This was also the opinion of the Social Democrats, Progressive Liberals and small left-wing parties, who argued that the renunciation requirement was not in tune with an inclusive minority policy. Moreover, they thought dual nationality would be a useful instrument in the re-emigration of temporary migrants. More generally, the parties called into question the renunciation requirement from an equality perspective. After all, in practice Dutch law permitted dual nationality in numerous cases. See de Hart, "The End of Multiculturalism: The End of Dual Citizenship?", 87.

practice. Presently, however, the devil is in the detail.[81] It is evident that the acceptance of dual nationality would take away much of the incoherence and arbitrariness that currently surrounds the subject.

6. *The Fall of Multiculturalism and the Continuing Debate on the Renunciation Requirement*

In 1989 another report on immigration was published which broke with the multicultural tradition. Entzinger has remarked about this second influential report by the Scientific Council for Government Policy that 'the emphasis on culture … was only very limited, relegating it to a private affair'.[82] The report thus criticized the government for its emphasis on multiculturalism and stressed the need for immigrant participation.[83] It also recommended not to impose too difficult conditions for naturalization and to allow dual nationality.[84] Indeed, research had shown that the renunciation requirement was the

[81] This can be illustrated by the fictional 'Constaninescu case', in which a married couple with two minor children had their Dutch naturalization decree withdrawn for non-compliance with the obligation to renounce their nationality of origin. Renunciation was very problematic because the country of origin required each individual to pay €2,500, thus €10,000 in total. Due to legal technicalities, Dutch nationality could still be saved for one of the parents as well as for the two minor children if this parent would pay the €2,500 required for renunciation: minor children are normally included in the naturalization decree of a parent under Article 11(1) DNA; moreover, the minor children themselves are not required to renounce their nationality of origin under Article 15 DNA as this article only refers to persons who have attained the age of majority. The parent who did not renounce the nationality of origin would lose Dutch nationality, but could in time apply again for Dutch nationality as the spouse of a Dutch national. Renunciation of the nationality of origin is not required because spouses of Dutch nationals who acquire Dutch nationality are exempted from this requirement under Article 9(3)d DNA. See de Groot, *Achtentwintig Nederlanders? Bewerkte adviezen en casus over de toepassing van de Nederlandse nationaliteitswetgeving*, 51–56.

[82] 1989 report on the immigrant policy by the Scientific Council for Government Policy. See Entzinger, "The Rise and Fall of Multiculturalism: The Case of the Netherlands", 70.

[83] Ibid. We also have to take into account that the minority policy based on the multicultural model had become more difficult due to the minorities becoming more numerous and more heterogeneous in the 1980s. See for a critique of multiculturalism (in the context of a defence of the concept of nationality) Miller, *On Nationality*, 133 ff. Miller accuses multiculturalism of both overlooking the need and desire on the part of ethnic minorities to fully belong to the national community and of making unrealistic demands on the majority; in the absence of a shared identity (which in his view can only be provided by nationality), the kind of trust that is required for solidarity across groups will also be absent.

[84] de Hart, "The End of Multiculturalism: The End of Dual Citizenship?", 88.

greatest obstacle to naturalization.[85] The government followed these recommendations by deciding to remove all unnecessary obstacles to naturalization, including the renunciation requirement. As of 1 January 1992, it was no longer required to give up the nationality of origin, yet this situation would be short-lived. On 1 October 1997 the renunciation requirement was reintroduced, though on that occasion the list of exceptions to the renunciation requirement was greatly expanded.[86] What exactly happened as regards this volatile dual nationality policy was the following.

Although the government (a coalition consisting of Christian Democrats and Social Democrats under Prime Minister Lubbers) did not at first subscribe to the report's recommendation of allowing dual nationality, it later changed its mind by adopting a policy which it described as 'a shift from the prevention to the limitation of dual nationality'.[87] The Christian Democrats later confessed, however, that they had always remained hostile towards dual nationality, and that the change of policy had been a compromise with the Social Democrats. The latter would give up their plan to grant non-Dutch immigrants voting rights in parliamentary elections[88] if the Christian Democrats promised to support dual nationality (local franchise had already been introduced in 1985).[89] The Social Democrats in particular were strong proponents of the toleration of dual nationality. They argued that international mobility created multiple and transnational identities among migrants, with

85 Ruud van den Bedem, "Plural nationality seen from the perspective of concerned minorities", in *Plural nationality: Changing attitudes* (Conference at the European University Institute, Florence: 1992), 6. For a survey in Dutch see Ruud van den Bedem, *Motieven voor naturalisatie; Waarom vreemdelingen uit diverse minderheidsgroepen wel of niet kiezen voor naturalisatie* (Arnhem: Gouda Quint, 1993).

86 Frans J.A. van der Velden, "De circulaire inzake de afstandsverklaring", in *Trends in het nationaliteitsrecht*, ed. Hans Ulrich Jessurun d'Oliveira ('s-Gravenhage: Sdu, 1998), 114; de Groot and Vink, *Meervoudige nationaliteit in Europees perspectief*, 118.

87 de Hart, "The End of Multiculturalism: The End of Dual Citizenship?", 87.

88 This proposal can be seen in the light of the prevalent idea in the 1980s not to force Dutch nationality on immigrants. Rather, the policy in these years was to create a denizenship status for immigrants by eliminating all forms of different treatment between nationals and non-nationals. Hence, long-term foreign residents could enter the public service (with the exception of the police and the army) and were treated in the same way as Dutch nationals with regard to the social security system. See Entzinger, "The Rise and Fall of Multiculturalism: The Case of the Netherlands", 65.

89 de Hart, "The End of Multiculturalism: The End of Dual Citizenship?", 89. See for a similar debate in Sweden Mikael Spang, "Pragmatism All the Way Down? The Politics of Dual Citizenship in Sweden", ibid., 106, 120. Sweden is one of the very rare examples of a country where the *de facto* toleration of dual nationality ultimately led to its principled acceptance.

multiple nationality being the expression of this development.[90] The Christian Democrats, on the other hand, never ideologically supported dual nationality. The strong popular demand for immigrant integration forced them to make a choice between two evils, however. They were forced to either accept dual nationality by abolishing the renunciation requirement, or to accept political participation for non-Dutch immigrants. In the end, they decided that the abolishment of the renunciation requirement was the lesser evil.

It is perhaps strange that a political compromise lay at the root of a policy shift on such a sensitive subject like immigration and minorities. However, the Dutch political landscape—traditionally built around the need to reach consensus and compromise—may account for this. In the words of De Hart: 'The need to build coalitions among parties with very different ideologies has led to a political culture of pragmatic consensus-building, even in the case of moral issues'.[91]

The political compromise on dual nationality meant that the renunciation requirement was abolished on 1 January 1992.[92] This decision was initially laid down in a ministerial memorandum, but the government prepared legislation to formalize this policy by modifying the 1985 Act.[93] It was during these years and in this particular context that the government began to seriously doubt the desirability of the restraints imposed by the 1963 Convention on the Dutch policy.[94] To our knowledge, this was the only period in which the government appeared at all uncomfortable with the 1963 Convention. After all, the toleration of dual nationality for immigrants in general—inspired by the assumption that this was an important step in their integration process—seemed to make obsolete the principle that dual nationality should be prevented concerning nationals of States that were, like the Netherlands, bound by the 1963 Convention. Though this awkward position in respect of the 1963 Convention has, as far as this writer is aware, never materialized in concrete proposals for

---

[90] Jan-Jaap Kuipers, *Het Debat omtrent Meervoudige Nationaliteit in de Tweede Kamer 1983–2007* (Maastricht University: Faculty of Law, 2007), 12.

[91] de Hart, "The End of Multiculturalism: The End of Dual Citizenship?", 84.

[92] Maarten Vink, "The Limited Europeanization of Domestic Citizenship Policy: Evidence from the Netherlands", *Journal of Common Market Studies* 39, no. 5 (2001): 886.

[93] van der Velden, "De circulaire inzake de afstandsverklaring", 111–112.

[94] Hans Ulrich Jessurun d'Oliveira, "Het 'meerdere', een regeringsnotitie over meervoudige nationaliteit", *Nederlands Juristenblad*, no. 43 (1991): 1735–1736. He goes so far as to state that the government did not want to stay bound by the 1963 Convention for ideological reasons, and that it was seriously investigating ways to withdraw from the Convention without harming the friendly relations with other States. D'Oliveira strongly supported this move, arguing that the other States bound by the Convention would be relieved and follow the Dutch withdrawal from this 'half-hearted' Convention.

its denunciation, the Dutch support for the Second Protocol at least shows a distancing from the line taken in the 1963 Convention.

Paradoxically, the rise in naturalizations in the years following 1992—and therefore indirectly the success of an inclusive integration policy as advocated by the Scientific Council for Government Policy on numerous occasions—led to a reconsideration among the Christian Democrats and the Conservative Liberals of their position on dual nationality. The waiver of the renunciation requirement was shown to have a significant effect, in particular on Turkish immigrants.[95] The naturalization quota among Turks rose to 20 percent in 1992 and dropped to 5 percent again when the renunciation requirement was reintroduced in 1997.[96]

As said, the Christian Democrats and Conservative Liberals were not particularly enthusiastic about the rise of naturalizations. To their mind, Dutch nationality was being granted too easily and should not be an instrument to stimulate integration. Acquisition of Dutch nationality ought rather be the final step in a successfully completed integration process.[97] At the time of writing, the parties at the right side of the political spectrum still adhere to this line of thinking, while the left wing parties continue to support the idea that dual nationality facilitates immigrant integration.

The growing opposition to dual nationality for the reasons sketched above coincided with a growing opposition to the multicultural model in the 1990s. The idea took root that the State had been too soft on immigrants under the minority policy of the 1980s.[98] Yet not only did the multicultural model become discredited in the 1990s, a report on naturalization among immigrants also called into question the use of naturalization as an indicator for the degree of integration among immigrants. According to the report, the motives for naturalization were of a pragmatic nature; naturalization numbers would therefore not constitute a real indicator of the degree of integration of immigrants.[99] The already growing resistance against dual nationality, further reinforced by the conclusion of the report on the motives for naturalization, made dual nationality a politically sensitive and risky subject, ultimately leading

[95] The effects of the new policy were negligible for citizens from Morocco and Suriname. Morocco does not allow renunciation of its nationality while Suriname citizens automatically lose their nationality upon naturalization abroad. See de Hart, "The End of Multiculturalism: The End of Dual Citizenship?", 90.

[96] van Oers, de Hart, and Groenendijk, "Netherlands", 418.

[97] de Hart, "The End of Multiculturalism: The End of Dual Citizenship?", 91.

[98] Ibid., 80.

[99] 1996 report on minorities by the Social Cultural Planning Bureau (*Sociaal en Cultureel Planbureau*). See ibid., 93.

(in 1997) to the withdrawal of the Bill which would have officially deleted the renunciation requirement from the 1985 Act.[100] This was not the end of the dual nationality debate in the Netherlands, however.

7. *Dutch Emigrants and Dual Nationality under the 1985 Act*

In the foregoing section we mentioned that the Dutch discussion on dual nationality took place in the context of integration.[101] As a result, different policies could be adopted for foreign immigrants and Dutch emigrants since the latter did not pose an integration problem. However, this different policy for Dutch emigrants was only adopted after a long and polemical discussion. During the debates on the 1985 Act, the idea had initially been conceived to treat immigrants and emigrants on an equal footing. In other words, the intolerance towards dual nationality should apply as much to immigrants who wanted to become Dutch as to Dutch emigrants who lived and naturalized abroad.[102] Consequently, in spite of vehement and sustained protests, the 1985 Act introduced the rule that Dutch nationality was automatically lost after ten years' residency abroad, on condition that the Dutch national affected also possessed another nationality. Under this rule, there was no possibility to avoid this loss by making a declaration of continuation—a possibility which existed under the 1892 Act. Furthermore, the general rule was maintained that voluntary acquisition of a foreign nationality entailed the loss of Dutch nationality. This meant that from 1992, immigrants who lived in the Netherlands could possess a dual nationality while Dutch emigrants would lose their nationality upon foreign naturalization.[103]

The principal spokesman of the opposition to the automatic loss of Dutch nationality was Mackaay, a Dutch law professor working in Canada. Supported by many other Dutch nationals living and working abroad, he contested the government's position that permanent foreign residence renders the bond

---

[100] Böcker, Groenendijk, and de Hart, "De toegang tot het Nederlanderschap, effecten van 20 jaar beleidswijzigingen": 161–163. In the years following 1997, it became clear that the renunciation requirement had important effects. Fewer Turks applied for naturalization and those who did would only do so on condition that Turkish nationality could be retained. This is clearly shown by the fact that Turkish nationality was retained in 100 percent of the Turkish naturalization cases. We may therefore properly assume that the renunciation requirement is indeed a particularly strong disincentive to naturalization.

[101] See *supra* Section 1.

[102] de Hart, "The End of Multiculturalism: The End of Dual Citizenship?", 87.

[103] Ibid., 90.

with the Netherlands weak or non-existent.[104] With his systematic rebuttal of the government's arguments against dual nationality, he convincingly argued that the retention of Dutch nationality for Dutch nationals abroad who also possessed another nationality did not pose insurmountable problems.[105] He also pointed to a paradox in the policy; the government, by taking away Dutch nationality for the group under consideration, was obviously not willing to take back Dutch nationals who lived abroad on a permanent basis. Yet the expatriates' feelings of attachment to the Netherlands were still strong to the extent that they would not naturalize abroad if this entailed the loss of their Dutch nationality. The Dutch policy thus actually discouraged them from taking up a foreign nationality, thereby hindering their integration abroad. The upshot of this policy might thus well be, so Mackaay argued, that large groups of Dutch mono-nationals lived abroad who never applied for the nationality of their country of residence for fear of losing Dutch nationality. This was a very strange situation for a group of persons of which the government thinks that they have permanently left the Netherlands and will never return. Mackaay was right in wondering how this was compatible with the government's premise 'gone is gone'.[106]

Although the protests by Mackaay and others were unsuccessful at the time, the subject was again put on the agenda ten years later. In 1995 the first Dutch nationals who had permanent residence abroad would lose their Dutch nationality under the rule introduced in the 1985 Act. Again they pleaded in great numbers for the toleration of dual nationality. The matter had already been raised in 1992, when the government prepared the Bill to formally abolish the renunciation requirement for naturalisees. The Council of State warned the government that this legislation would entail unequal treatment of Dutch nationals as they would still be subject to automatic loss of Dutch nationality upon naturalization abroad. As a result, the Bill that would allow dual nationality by abolishing the renunciation requirement for immigrants was adapted to also allow dual nationality for Dutch emigrants.[107] However, as this Bill had not entered into effect (and would never do so), Dutch nationals had no choice but to submit a renewed plea for dual nationality to parliament in 1995.

---

104 Ejan Mackaay, "Bipatridie: een kijkje uit den vreemde", *Nederlands Juristenblad*, no. 36 (1982): 993.

105 Ejan Mackaay, "Verlies van het Nederlanderschap voor emigranten", *Nederlands Juristenblad*, no. 41 (1983): 1319–1320.

106 Mackaay, "Bipatridie: een kijkje uit den vreemde": 993.

107 Anita Böcker, Kees Groenendijk, and Betty de Hart, "De toegang tot het Nederlanderschap, effecten van 20 jaar beleidswijzigingen", ibid., no. 3 (2005): 159; de Hart, "The End of Multiculturalism: The End of Dual Citizenship?", 90.

Curiously, their pleas were now greeted with positive reactions from opposing political horizons. The Conservative Liberals supported dual nationality for Dutch emigrants with the argument that it should be up to the receiving country to allow dual nationality or not. Some have rightly pointed to a contradiction in this position. The Conservative Liberals had always argued that nationality should express an indivisible and exclusive bond between an individual and a State. Such a conception of nationality is incompatible with the idea that Dutch nationality can be preserved upon foreign naturalization. After all, voluntary naturalization abroad is a strong indication that someone feels more closely linked to another country than with the Netherlands.[108] The Christian Democrats came to the same conclusion but used a different line of reasoning. To their mind, since Dutch emigrants did not pose an integration issue, dual nationality for this group was not a problem.[109] Also the left-wing parties took the side of the Dutch emigrants because it would make their case for dual nationality for immigrants stronger.[110]

The equality argument—dual nationality cannot be opposed as regards Dutch emigrants but tolerated in respect of immigrants—was unsuccessful, however. When the Bill was withdrawn in 1997, the provision on the automatic loss of Dutch nationality was finally amended and concessions were made to Dutch emigrants who lived abroad; the Bill reintroduced the renunciation requirement, however.[111] A parliamentary majority saw dual nationality for Dutch emigrants and immigrants as distinct matters. 'The wish of Dutch emigrants to retain Dutch citizenship was never questioned, regardless of the motives involved, whether these were instrumental … or emotional'.[112]

108 Kuipers, *Het Debat omtrent Meervoudige Nationaliteit in de Tweede Kamer 1983–2007*, 21.

109 The fact that a relatively large part of Dutch expatriates appear to vote for the Conservative Liberals or the Christian Democrats may also have had something to do with these two parties changing their minds on the issue of dual nationality.

110 van Oers, de Hart, and Groenendijk, "Netherlands", 407.

111 The original Bill which allowed dual nationality for both immigrants and emigrants was passed in the Second Chamber but rejected in the Senate (where Christian Democrats and Liberal Conservatives had a majority). Böcker, Groenendijk, and de Hart, "De toegang tot het Nederlanderschap, effecten van 20 jaar beleidswijzigingen": 159. A salient detail is that Ernst Hirsch Ballin, who had prepared the Bill as Minister of Justice, abstained from voting on his own Bill while being a senator in 1997. See Kees Groenendijk and Eric Heijs, "Nationality Law in the Netherlands", in *Towards a European Nationality. Citizenship, Immigration and Nationality Law in the EU*, ed. Randall Hansen and Patrick Weil (Hampshire: Palgrave Publishers, 2001), 160.

112 de Hart, "The End of Multiculturalism: The End of Dual Citizenship?", 92. Under the current Nationality Act (Article 15) Dutch emigrants still lose their nationality upon foreign naturalization (see *infra* Section 8.1). Dual nationals no longer automatically lose Dutch nationality after having permanently resided abroad for more than ten years,

8. *Modifications to Dutch Nationality Law by the 2003 Act*

The previous section has shown that the Bill of 1993, which tolerated dual nationality by abolishing the renunciation requirement, was withdrawn in 1997. Yet it would be a mistake to think that things were simply put back to the pre-1992 situation as far as dual nationality was concerned. The debate on dual nationality would soon be reopened, but in the meantime Dutch nationality would, in 2003, undergo substantial modifications.[113]

In the discussion on important amendments to the 1985 Nationality Act (which would be brought about by the 2003 Act),[114] Dutch nationality was predominantly perceived in ethnic and cultural terms. As a result, the general attitude towards naturalization became more restrictive. As for the requirements for naturalization, knowledge of Dutch language and society became strongly emphasized.[115] This is not to say that the debate took on very strong nationalist tones. Rather, it seemed a legitimate reaction against a policy which demanded very little of immigrants.

From 1 October 1997 the renunciation requirement was enforced again, be it with all kinds of new exceptions.[116] Important in this respect is that the 2003 Act implemented the premises of the Second Protocol of 1996 in a general way into Dutch nationality law. We return to this in more detail below (Section 8.1), but for the present, we note that this meant that these important

---

however. Dutch nationality can also be transmitted to foreign-born generations and dual nationality is allowed in this case.

113 Gerard-René de Groot and Carlos Bollen, "Nationality Law of the Kingdom of the Netherlands in International Perspective", *Netherlands Yearbook of International Law* 35 (2004): 207.

114 The 2003 Act, which made substantial modifications to the 1985 Act, was adopted by the Upper House in December 2000 and entered into force on 1 April 2003.

115 de Hart, "The End of Multiculturalism: The End of Dual Citizenship?", 93–94.

116 Groenendijk and Heijs submit that the effect of the reintroduction 'appears to have been limited as dispensation has been granted to 13 categories of applicants, notably nationals of states that do not allow their nationals to renounce their nationality, nationals of states that are party to the Second Protocol of the 1963 Strasbourg Convention, persons born in the Netherlands, persons married to a Dutch national, recognized refugees, persons who would suffer substantial financial damage as a result of renouncing their nationality, persons who can only renounce their nationality after engaging in military service or buying their way out of military service, and persons who can prove that they have special and valid reasons for not renouncing their foreign nationality. In practice the overwhelming majority of applicants are in one of these categories'. They also remark that 'these rules may generally penalize female immigrants, who often have less property, fewer pension rights and no obligation to engage in military service'. Groenendijk and Heijs, "Nationality Law in the Netherlands", 148.

exceptions apply to any person who acquired Dutch nationality, and not just to nationals of other parties to the Second Protocol. Although one still has to renounce the nationality of origin, then, upon naturalization in the Netherlands, around 65 percent of the naturalisees fall within one the exception categories. All in all, the number of Dutch nationals with a dual nationality has increased from around 600,000 in 1998 to more than a million in 2007.[117]

Finally, the 2003 Act made a very important amendment to the rule on *ex lege* loss of Dutch nationality after having permanently resided for ten years outside the Netherlands, the Dutch Antilles or Aruba. From this rule it followed that in the period 1985–2003 Dutch dual nationals permanently residing abroad could not retain Dutch nationality, even if the bond with the Netherlands had remained strong. Since 2003, however, loss of Dutch nationality no longer exists when the Dutch dual national 'is in possession of a Netherlands passport not older than ten years or a certificate of possession of [Dutch] nationality which is not older than ten years'.[118] This means that the Dutch dual national needs only to renew the proof of his/her Dutch nationality before the expiry of the ten year term. Importantly, this rule on the loss of nationality does not apply to Dutch dual nationals who are permanently residing in another EU Member State. The government explicitly legitimized this exemption with the argument that the loss of Dutch nationality could hinder free movement if the person concerned did not possess the nationality of another Member State.[119]

8.1. *Developments after 2003: More Proposals, Amendments and Controversies*

The position concerning dual nationality under the current Nationality Act can hardly be called the result of a crystallized debate. The topic still regularly crops up and continues to excite considerable debate. This is evinced by the following enumeration of proposals (some of which recently materialized) and controversies surrounding dual nationality, many of which were also the subject of public debate in the media:

- Proposal to withdraw Dutch nationality from Moroccan-Dutch nationals who have committed criminal offences (2002);
- Reintroduction of the renunciation requirement for migrants marrying a Dutch national and for second generation immigrants; proposal to

117 de Groot and Vink, *Meervoudige nationaliteit in Europees perspectief*, 9.

118 Gerard-René de Groot and Maarten Vink, "Loss of Citizenship. Trends and Regulations in Europe", EUDO Citizenship Observatory Country Reports (2010), 31.

119 Ibid.

withdraw Dutch nationality from dual nationals who have 'inflicted serious damage to the essential interests of the Kingdom of the Netherlands' (2004–2005);

- Controversy surrounding the appointment of two State Secretaries of Moroccan-Dutch and Turkish-Dutch nationality (2007);
- Proposal to introduce the renunciation requirement for a specific category of persons who make use of their option right to Dutch nationality. Foreigners who were not born in the Netherlands, who have reached the age of majority, and who have resided in the Netherlands, the Dutch Antilles or Aruba since the age of four, should in principle give up their nationality of origin when opting for Dutch nationality (2008/2010). The government which proposed these modifications (Balkenende IV) fell on 20 February 2010,[120] but the proposal was accepted by the Dutch Lower and Upper House on 26 January and 15 June 2010 respectively, and has entered into force on 1 October 2010.[121]

The common thread that unites these proposals and controversies is evident: they concern immigrants, not emigrants. In the Dutch view, the wish among Dutch emigrants to retain Dutch nationality is perceived as legitimate. Although one loses Dutch nationality when acquiring another one, Dutch nationality can under certain circumstances be retained even in the case of permanent residence abroad.[122] Various scholars have pointed to the lack of symmetry which is brought about by increasingly asking immigrants to give up their original nationality while allowing the retention of Dutch nationality under comparable circumstances abroad.[123] In the literature one thus repeatedly finds the observation that Dutch nationality law applies a double standard, although it is also recognized that political considerations allow for some asymmetry.[124] However, a differentiation between immigrants and

---

120 On 14 October 2010 Mark Rutte succeeded Jan Peter Balkenende as Prime Minister of the Netherlands. His minority government consists of Christian Democrats and Liberal Conservatives and is dependent on the support by Geert Wilders's Freedom Party. For the goverment's plans in the field of nationality law, see EUDO citizenship news of 19 October 2010 (http://eudo-citizenship.eu).

121 See for the amendments the *Dutch Official Journal* (*Staatsblad*) 2010, 242. See also EUDO citizenship news of 12 July 2010.

122 Article 15 DNA.

123 Jessurun d'Oliveira, "Alweer plannen om de afstandseis bij naturalisatie uit te breiden": 2236; de Hart, "The End of Multiculturalism: The End of Dual Citizenship?", 92.

124 Hans Ulrich Jessurun d'Oliveira, "Veel lawaai om een klutsei", *Nederlands Juristenblad*, no. 3 (2006): 141.

emigrants should only be justifiable for compelling reasons. In the words of d'Oliveira, 'asymmetry is suspect'.[125]

Proposal to Withdraw Dutch Nationality from Moroccan-Dutch Nationals who Have Committed Criminal Offences

It was Hilbrand Nawijn—Minister of Immigration and Integration and member of the LPF (*Lijst Pim Fortuyn*), the political party of the assassinated politician Pim Fortuyn—who came forward with this proposal in 2002 in order to expel criminal juveniles to Morocco. Although the measure never materialized and met from the outset with strong criticism, including from Prime Minister Jan-Peter Balkenende, De Hart perceived the suggestion as marking an important change in thinking about dual nationality, for it entails the idea that immigrants, 'although naturalized or perhaps even born with dual citizenship, can be expelled to the country of origin because they did not behave according to Dutch cultural norms and values. It treats Dutch nationals differently based on their lineage'.[126] Below we will see, however, that a subsequent Bill adopted these ideas by providing for the withdrawal of Dutch nationality from dual nationals who had 'inflicted serious damage to the essential interests of the Kingdom of the Netherlands'.

Reintroduction of the Renunciation Requirement for Migrants Marrying a Dutch National and for Second Generation Immigrants

The proposal to ban dual nationality for third generation immigrants who have acquired Dutch nationality under the double *ius soli* rule was introduced in October 2003.[127] This proposal, in respect of which we can argue that it was not in tune with rules of international law,[128] was enthusiastically embraced by Rita Verdonk—the new Minister of Immigration and Integration. Yet she did not stop here but went on to propose even more far-reaching measures in her crusade against dual nationality.[129] This finally resulted in a proposal to reintroduce the renunciation requirement for migrants who had married a Dutch national and for second generation immigrants.

---

[125] Jessurun d'Oliveira, "Alweer plannen om de afstandseis bij naturalisatie uit te breiden": 2233.

[126] de Hart, "The End of Multiculturalism: The End of Dual Citizenship?", 95.

[127] Kamerstukken 2003/2004, 29 200 VI, nr. 81. The parliamentary debate can be consulted on www.tweedekamer.nl. See also Betty de Hart, "Meervoudige nationaliteit, integratie en terrorisme", *Migrantenrecht* 19, no. 8 (2004): 295.

[128] The proposal seemed to be unaware of the fact that the Netherlands cannot decide on the attribution of the nationality of other States. The reader will know that the attribution of nationality falls within the exclusive competence of the State and that intrusion by other States is not allowed.

[129] de Hart, "The End of Multiculturalism: The End of Dual Citizenship?", 95.

In 2004 Minister Verdonk presented her proposals to fight dual nationality.[130] It aimed at reintroducing the renunciation requirement for migrants marrying a Dutch national and for second generation migrants who are either born in the Netherlands or have been resident in the Netherlands for at least five years before reaching the age of majority.[131] Indeed, these categories correspond with the exceptions inspired by the Second Protocol, yet the Protocol itself remained in force under the proposal. This may perhaps need some explanation.

The exceptions from the Second Protocol are implemented in Article 9(3)a DNA. This provision remained untouched by the proposal. However, the exceptions from the Second Protocol have also served as inspiration for a number of exceptions to the general renunciation requirement under Dutch law (Article 9(3)b–d DNA). These exceptions—which were thus merely inspired by the Second Protocol and do not constitute the implementation of the Protocol into Dutch law[132]—were the object of Verdonk's proposal.[133] Yet the preamble to the Second Protocol makes clear that it is inspired by the need to complete the integration of immigrants through the acquisition of the nationality of their State of residence, the desirability of unity of nationality in the same family, and the fact that the conservation of the original nationality is an important factor in achieving these objectives. The government's proposal thus seemed incompatible with the tenor of the preamble. If the government was serious about allowing naturalisees to only have a link of nationality with the Netherlands, the most logical step would have been to not only abolish the exceptions that were inspired on the Second Protocol, but to denounce the Protocol itself as well.[134]

Some authors have raised the question whether the proposal was compatible with Article 6(4) ECN, which provides that Contracting States shall

---

130 Kamerstukken 2004/2005, 30 166 (R 1795), nr. 2, 'Wijziging van de Rijkswet op het Nederlanderschap tot beperking van meervoudige nationaliteit en tot invoering van het verlies van het Nederlanderschap wegens het toebrengen van ernstige schade aan de essentiële belangen van het Koninkrijk of van een of meer van zijn landen'. Bill 30 166 was withdrawn on 12 December 2007 (See Kamerstukken 2007–2008, 30 166 (R 1795), nr. 26).

131 de Groot and Vink, *Meervoudige nationaliteit in Europees perspectief*, 9.

132 D'Oliveira speaks of these exceptions as 'the product of the generalization of the premises of the Second Protocol' ('zij zijn het product van de veralgemening van de uitgangspunten van het Tweede Protocol'). See Jessurun d'Oliveira, "Veel lawaai om een klutsei": 140.

133 Article 9(3)b-d DNA accords exemption from the renunciation requirement for the following categories: (1) the applicant was born in the Netherlands, the Dutch Antilles or Aruba; or (2) the applicant has, as a minor, lived for at least five years in the Netherlands, the Dutch Antilles or Aruba; or (3) the applicant is married to a Dutch national.

134 Jessurun d'Oliveira, "Veel lawaai om een klutsei": 139.

facilitate the acquisition of their nationality *inter alia* to the two categories that were targeted by the proposal. Is a State allowed to revoke a previous facilitation of the acquisition of its nationality without violating Article 6(4) ECN?[135] Others have pointed to a glaring inconsistency in the proposal. We have seen that Article 9(3)b–d DNA provided for a number of exemptions from the requirement to renounce the nationality of origin upon acquiring Dutch nationality. In Article 15(2) DNA we find the same exemptions, but this time in reverse, namely exemptions from the loss of Dutch nationality upon acquisition of a foreign nationality. In other words, although Article 15(1) DNA states the general rule that Dutch nationality is lost when one acquires a foreign nationality, Article 15(2) provides for a number of exceptions which are the mirror image of Article 9(3)b–d.[136] The 'astonishing' inconsistency lies in the fact that foreigners will in some cases have to renounce their nationality of origin upon acquisition of Dutch nationality, but can recover their original nationality without having to give up their Dutch nationality because they are covered by Article 15(2).[137]

As the government did not advance arguments for focusing on these two specific categories, it is hard to understand what lay behind this decision. The best guess is that the proposal was primarily based on the pragmatic idea that only targeting these specific categories would substantially decrease the number of dual nationals. It is open to doubt whether this is a strong argument. In fact, the Minister's note itself already indicated that of all the exceptions to the renunciation requirement upon naturalization, the two categories only constituted 14 percent (12 percent for marriage and 2 percent for the second generation) while in 32 percent of the cases naturalisees were exempted from this requirement because they could rely on the fact that their country of origin did not allow renunciation.[138]

Leaving aside for the moment the arbitrary nature of the proposal—acquisition of Dutch nationality by option was not covered[139]—the plan could also very well have proved counterproductive. D'Oliveira points to comparative research which consistently shows that people only apply for naturalization if

[135] de Hart, "Meervoudige nationaliteit, integratie en terrorisme": 297; Jessurun d'Oliveira, "Alweer plannen om de afstandseis bij naturalisatie uit te breiden": 2235.

[136] Under Article 15(2) DNA, Dutch nationality is not lost by a Dutch national who acquires another nationality in the following cases: (1) he or she was born in the country of the other nationality; (2) or had lived there for at least five years as a minor; or (3) is married to a person who possesses that other nationality.

[137] de Groot and Schneider, "Die zunehmende Akzeptanz von Fällen mehrfacher Staatsangehörigkeit in West-Europa", 79–80.

[138] de Hart, "Meervoudige nationaliteit, integratie en terrorisme": 294–295.

[139] Jessurun d'Oliveira, "Veel lawaai om een klutsei": 143.

they can retain their original nationality.[140] Hence, a more stringent enforcement of the renunciation requirement will have the opposite effect to the one intended. Instead of creating mono-Dutch nationals who have renounced their nationality of origin, the proposal creates large groups of mononationals without Dutch nationality.[141]

Another proposal in Verdonk's Bill envisaged the withdrawal of Dutch nationality from dual nationals who had 'inflicted serious damage to the essential interests of the Kingdom of the Netherlands'. It has been subject to discussion whether such withdrawal is in accordance with rules of international law. The argument runs as follows. For a nationality to be effective under international law, a 'genuine link' must exist with the State of which one possesses the nationality. In the case of dual nationals who possess Dutch nationality, the loss of Dutch nationality is highly undesirable from the perspective of international law when only a nationality remains which does not represent such a 'genuine link'. This situation may arise in relation to second-generation immigrants.[142] Consequently, it can be argued that such a person is rendered *apatride de fait* (one is left with a non-effective nationality), which is prohibited under *ius cogens* (i.e. peremptory norms of international law).[143]

Others have convincingly countered this argument. First, they refer to private international law where a 'recessive' nationality (the opposite of a 'dominant' nationality) can often still be used as a connecting factor. This 'recessive' nationality is certainly not without meaning and the person in possession

140 The government ignores these academic conclusions by arguing in an explanatory note that 'the renunciation requirement has no bearing on an applicant's willingness to naturalize'. See ibid., 140.

141 Jessurun d'Oliveira, "Alweer plannen om de afstandseis bij naturalisatie uit te breiden": 2235.

142 Gerard-René de Groot, "Het ontnemen van het Nederlanderschap wegens terroristische activiteiten", in *Crossing borders, Essays in European and Private International Law, Nationality Law and Islamic Law in honour of Frans van der Velden*, ed. Paulien van der Grinten and Ton Heukels (Deventer: Kluwer, 2005), 218. The argument is also made by Boele-Woelki who writes: 'Personen die die Staatsangehörigkeit eines Landes besitzen, in dem sie noch nie gewesen sind und dessen Sprache sie nicht einmal beherrschen, sind überzeugende Beispiele für das Bestehen einer nur formellen inhaltslosen Staatsangehörigkeit. Diese Fälle sind nicht selten, betrachtet man die von den Gastarbeitern im Gastland geborenen und aufgewachsene Generation'. Boele-Woelki, *Die Effektivitätsprüfung der Staatsangehörigkeit im niederländischen internationalen Familienrecht*, 50.

In this context (i.e. second-generation migrants who may possibly lose the nationality of the country of birth) we may also refer to the situation in Germany, where the current law of 2000 imposes a obligation on dual nationals who acquired German *iure soli* to choose for either German or the foreign nationality between the age of 18 and 23.

143 de Groot, "Het ontnemen van het Nederlanderschap wegens terroristische activiteiten", 218.

of this nationality is certainly not stateless from the point of view of private international law.[144] More generally, it is argued that a dual national's loss of an effective nationality does not imply that the other nationality is non-effective. The Moroccan nationality of a second generation Moroccan-Dutch national who lives in the Netherlands, for example, may not be the dominant one from a Dutch perspective, but is definitely not seen as non-effective from a Moroccan perspective. This nationality will thus normally constitute a 'genuine link' with Morocco under international law. Were this different, Morocco would be under no obligation to allow its nationals entry and residence on its territory, not even when they had lost their other nationalities and were only in possession of Moroccan nationality.[145]

Although it can therefore be concluded that the proposal to withdraw Dutch nationality from dual nationals who have committed terrorist acts does not violate international law, it is very unlikely that they can be expulsed to the country of which they still possess the nationality. Human rights considerations will often stand in the way of deportation because the deportee may suffer inhuman treatment, especially in countries which are under authoritarian rule and who are themselves fighting (religious) terrorism.[146]

Controversy Surrounding the Appointment of Two State Secretaries with Dual Nationality

When a new government (the fourth government under Prime Minster Balkenende) took office in February 2007, a new controversy arose over dual nationality as two State Secretaries were in possession of a dual nationality.[147] This time, however, the backdrop of the discussion was not integration but loyalty. It was argued by nationalist political parties—more in particular those at the extreme political right and left as well as the Conservative

---

144 Hans Ulrich Jessurun d'Oliveira, "Ontneming van Nederlanderschap als zet in de terrorismebestrijding", *Migrantenrecht*, no. 10 (2006): 358.

145 Ibid., 358–359.

146 Kees Groenendijk, "Minister Verdonk: Grote woorden, minder daden en riskante ideeën", *Nederlands Juristenblad*, no. 24 (2006): 1309. Other arguments against the proposal that we can think of concern the fact that dual nationals are discriminated because only this group can lose Dutch nationality (loss of nationality is not allowed under Dutch law if this results in statelessness). In addition, nationals of Arab countries, who can normally not surrender their nationality, cannot escape extradition by giving up their nationality, while many citizens from other countries can. See also Audrey Macklin, "The Securitisation of Dual Citzenship", in *Dual Citizenship in Global Perspective, From Unitary to Multiple Citizenship*, ed. Peter Kivisto and Thomas Faist (New York: Palgrave Macmillan, 2007), 61.

147 It concerned Ms Albayrak and Mr Aboutaleb, both members of the Social Democratic Party, who in addition to their Dutch nationality possessed Turkish and Moroccan nationality respectively.

Liberals—that members of parliament and government should not be allowed to hold a dual nationality, or else they could be accused of double loyalties and interests.[148] Geert Wilders's right wing 'Freedom Party' took the most radical stance in this debate, proposing to ban dual nationality not only from national politics, but also from provincial and local representative bodies, the judiciary, diplomatic corps, policy force, and the military service.[149]

D'Oliveira points to an awkward matter in this discussion on dual nationality of high public figures, namely the undeniable fact that the Dutch queen Beatrix, like her mother (Juliana) and grandmother (Wilhelmina) before her, possesses British nationality. This fact 'is based upon a British statute of 1705, attributing British nationality to [Sophia] Electress of Hanover and to "all Persons lineally descending from her, born or thereafter born." The statute was abrogated in 1948, with the effect that all persons lineally descending from Sophia before 1948 had acquired British nationality—including, among some four hundred persons, the German emperor Wilhelm II.'[150] This statute of 1705 was in fact a special law attributing British nationality to the protestant Sophia in order to exclude the Roman Catholic branches of the House of Stuart from succession to the British throne.[151] Despite the controversy

---

148 Kuipers, *Het Debat omtrent Meervoudige Nationaliteit in de Tweede Kamer 1983–2007*, 24.

149 Geert Wilders and Sietse Fritsma, 'Een ambassadeur kan niet voor twee landen optreden', *Trouw* (Dutch daily newspaper) of 24 March 2007. See also Martin Bosma, *De schijn-élite van de valse munters* (Amsterdam: Uitgeverij Bert Bakker, 2010), 137, 221. It is worthy of note that the subject of (dual) nationality is not addressed in a similarly critical book on the *German* multicultural society. See Thilo Sarrazin, *Deutschland schafft sich ab. Wie wir unser Land aufs Spiel setzen* (München: Deutsche Verlags-Anstalt, 2010).

150 Jessurun d'Oliveira, "Book review of Alfred Boll's 'Multiple Nationality and International Law'": 922.

151 This statute was more or less rediscovered in the mid 1950s when Prince Ernst August of Hanover, who lineally descended from Sophia, wished to see his British nationality confirmed. The case was finally brought before the House of Lords which confirmed the Court of Appeal's ruling that Prince Ernst August was indeed a British citizen. For the Dutch Royal family this meant, in the words of C. d'Olivier Farran, that 'H.M. Queen Juliana, her mother Princess Wilhelmina, and the four young Dutch princesses are all now in the eyes of English law British. H.R.H. Prince Bernhard seems to be one of the few protestants royalties not descended from Sophia, but so intricately complicated are royal genealogies through intermarriage, that it is quite possible that he may be. On the other hand the Belgian royal family, though descended from Sophia, are not within the Act, being Roman Catholics'. See C. d'Olivier Farran, "The Dutch royal family is British!", *Nederlands tijdschrift voor internationaal recht* 4 (1956): 54; Jessurun d'Oliveira, "Nationaliteit en koninklijk huis", 148–151.

Also the children of the four princesses (this includes the future Dutch King Willem-Alexander) seem to possess British nationality, but their children in turn do not. See for the very technical details Hans Ulrich Jessurun d'Oliveira, "Beatrix is ook Brits",

surrounding the dual nationality of high public figures, 'no political party, though faced with a glaring inconsistency in its treatment of the queen versus lesser mortals, has as yet invited the queen to renounce her British nationality'.[152]

New Amendments Restricting Dual Nationality in the Netherlands

A very recent amendment[153] has introduced the renunciation requirement for a specific category of persons who make use of the option right to Dutch nationality. Foreigners who were not born in the Netherlands, who have come of age, and who have resided in the Netherlands, the Dutch Antilles or Aruba since the age of four, should in principle give up their nationality of origin when opting for Dutch nationality.[154] The government claims that their prolonged and permanent residence in the Netherlands renders ineffective their bond with the country of origin, and submits that 'the renunciation requirement is inspired by the argument that a national's rights and duties are thereby better brought into conformity with his factual situation'.[155] The requirement does not apply to any of the other categories of persons having an option right to Dutch nationality; the general exemptions from the renunciation requirement as laid down in the law also apply, however, for this newly created category of persons who have to surrender their nationality of origin.

In explaining the purpose of the amendment, the government emphasized that it does not reflect some kind of 'vendetta' against dual nationals (in contrast to previous proposals concerning dual nationality, we might add). Instead, the amendment is meant to clarify the nationality position of those

---

HP/De Tijd, 16 December 2005. The article is also available from http://www.maxpam.nl/category/buitenhof/.

152 Jessurun d'Oliveira, "Book review of Alfred Boll's 'Multiple Nationality and International Law'": 922. Queen Beatrix was not amused when d'Oliveira hinted at her dual nationality in a coincidental personal meeting during a literary award ceremony. She referred to it as 'a mere hype', but when d'Oliveira confessed to be the source of this hype she turned away, saying that this was a subject for another occasion. This proved to him that the queen is perfectly aware of her dual nationality. The anecdote can be found in Jessurun d'Oliveira, "Beatrix is ook Brits".

153 *Staatsblad* 2010, 242.

154 In consequence, a renunciation requirement is introduced for those falling under Article 6(2)e DNA. This concerns a relatively small group. Between 2004 and 2008, 3125 persons who acquired Dutch nationality fell in this category. See Kamerstukken II, 2008/2009, 31813 (R1873), nr. 6, at 9. This group constitutes around 9 percent of the total number of acquisitions of Dutch nationality through option. See for statistics de Groot and Vink, *Meervoudige nationaliteit in Europees perspectief*, 119.

155 'De afstandsverplichting wordt ingegeven door het argument dat rechten en plichten van de burger die het betreft beter in overeenstemming worden gebracht met zijn feitelijke situatie'.

who allegedly 'no longer have an effective bond with the country of which they also hold the nationality'.[156] A mere emotional bond is emphatically not regarded by the government as an effective bond in a legal sense.[157] The government's position is criticized by left wing parties (*Groen Links* and *SP*) for its disregard of individual choice. In other words, who is the government to decide whether one still has an effective bond with the country of origin?

In response to the Council of State's view that it was unclear why the renunciation requirement could not be imposed as well on other categories having an option right to Dutch nationality, the government clarified its position. As for minors who opt for Dutch nationality, the government explained that a renunciation requirement for this category would be incompatible with its own interpretation of Article 8 of the Convention on the Rights of the Child: 'As the government feels that Article 8 of the Convention gives rise to far-reaching efforts to protect the identity of the child, renunciation is not required upon the exercise of the option right by a minor child'.[158] In this connection it should be observed that it is strange, to say the least, that foreign minor children who are included in the naturalization decree of a parent can retain this parent's foreign nationality while the parent him/herself has to renounce this nationality upon naturalization in the Netherlands.

The renunciation requirement will also not be imposed on foreigners who have reached the age of majority and were born in the Netherlands, the Dutch Antilles or Aruba. Although the government was of the opinion that also this category lacks an effective bond with the country of origin, it nonetheless felt that 'the assessment between the respect for new and existing rights leads to another outcome'.[159]

Other important modifications of the new law which are relevant for our purposes concern the introduction of a renunciation requirement for *naturalization* applicants who have lived uninterruptedly in the Netherlands, the Dutch Antilles and Aruba for five years before coming of age, as well as the withdrawal of Dutch nationality from dual nationals who have been irrevocably convicted of a crime that has seriously harmed the interests of the Kingdom (the legal instruments as referred to in the new Article 14(2) lay down the crimes for which one can be deprived of Dutch nationality). The amended

[156] Debate in the Dutch Upper House on 15 June 2010 (Eerste Kamer 32, 1380).

[157] Eerste Kamer, 2009–2010, 31 813 (R1873), at 4.

[158] 'Het kabinet ziet in artikel 8 IVRK aanleiding om de identiteit van het kind vergaand te beschermen en vereist daarom geen afstand bij optie door een minderjarig kind'. See Kamerstukken II, 2008/2009, 31813 (R1873), nr. 4, at 3.

[159] 'De afweging tussen respect voor bestaande en nieuw te verwerven rechten leidt echter tot een andere uitkomst'. See Kamerstukken II, 2008/2009, 31813 (R1873), nr. 4, at 3.

Nationality Act also provides for full gender equality in Dutch nationality by granting an option right to so-called 'latent' Dutch nationals, i.e. foreigners born before 1 January 1985 to a mother who was Dutch at the time of birth while the father was not (see in more detail *supra* Section 5).[160] The government explicitly allows dual nationality for the category of latent Dutch nationals.[161]

The current Dutch government, headed by Prime Minister Rutte and installed on 14 October 2010, issued a proposal in March 2011 which aims at reducing dual nationality by first of all submitting all categories which have an option right to Dutch nationality to the renunciation requirement, except stateless persons and latent Dutch nationals.[162] The government also proposes to withdraw the exceptions to the renunciation requirement under Article 9(3) DNA, apart from exceptions to which the Netherlands is bound by international treaties. In addition, the Second Protocol to the 1963 Convention is to be denounced as the Netherlands is the only Contracting State left. Finally, foreign minor children who are included in the naturalization decree of a parent are also subjected to the renunciation requirement.

9. *Concluding Remarks*

From this chapter we can draw the conclusion that dual nationality has never been fully accepted in the Netherlands, aside from a half-hearted tolerance on the basis of a compromise in the years 1992–1997. On the other hand, the opposition to dual nationality has not prevented the phenomenon from growing. Statistics show that the number of dual nationals has substantially increased and that a large majority of those who acquire Dutch nationality through naturalization are able to keep their nationality of origin. The countless proposals and attempts to put a halt to the increasing number of dual

160 Betty de Hart, Hermie de Voer, and Stans Goudsmit, "Latente Nederlanders: discriminatie van kinderen van Nederlandse moeders in het nationaliteitsrecht", *Nederlands Juristenblad*, no. 17 (2006); Gerard-René de Groot, "Een optierecht voor latente Nederlanders", *Asiel- en Migrantenrecht* 1, no. 8 (2010); Betty de Hart, "Dubbele nationaliteit: verschil moet er zijn", ibid., no. 9.

161 Tweede Kamer 43, 4179.

162 See for the government's recent plan of 28 March 2011 to amend the DNA http://www.internetconsultatie.nl/nationaliteitsrecht/document/300. See critically on these plans, Ernst Hirsch Ballin, "Burgerrechten. Rede uitgesproken bij de aanvaarding van het ambt van hoogleraar in de rechten van de mens aan de Universiteit van Amsterdam op 9 september 2011"; available from http://www.oratiereeks.nl/upload/pdf/PDF-2406weboratie_Hirsch_Balin2.pdf.

nationals have been unsuccessful. It is therefore to be hoped, also for the sake of legal certainty and coherence, that the Netherlands rethink its position and adopt a more balanced and well-thought out view of dual nationality which is less swayed by the issues of the day.

We are not suggesting that dual nationality cannot be objected to on good grounds, yet one problem will always remain when the renunciation requirement is part of the nationality policy: such a policy can never lay claim to equality as long as the country of origin has a decisive say on the question whether its nationality can be renounced. In the knowledge that some applicants cannot renounce their nationality upon foreign naturalization, and that children born from mixed marriages are allowed to hold two nationalities, it is in our opinion unjustified to ask for renunciation in respect of those who can. As the Netherlands has no say whatsoever on the nationality law of another country, intermediate solutions which—as we have seen—try to combat dual nationality for particular categories, will never lead to a satisfying outcome. Such attempts will always remain inconclusive and their (presumed) merits do in our view not outweigh their defects.

The debate on dual nationality will probably continue for some time as it is linked to what is perhaps the most topical discussion at the moment in the Netherlands: immigration and integration. We will have to wait and see how this discussion develops, but many prominent politicians and scholars have felt compelled to join in the debate. In doing so, they have sometimes also expressed their ideas on dual nationality. Former Prime Minister Lubbers, for example, still supports dual nationality and finds it wrong to ask someone to choose between two different nationalities. He argues that in the Netherlands there should be room to feel both Dutch and Moroccan.[163] Scheffer, a leading scholar on immigration who triggered the debate on immigration and integration in 2000 with his newspaper article 'The Multicultural Drama',[164] shows himself tolerant in respect of the phenomenon by not endorsing the idea that loyalty towards the Netherlands is incompatible with having a dual nationality. In Scheffer's view, there are many dual nationals who—by supporting the public cause or serving in the army for example—show a great identification with the Netherlands. To deny this commitment will lead to nothing but grudges and resentment, according to him.[165]

The scholars De Groot and Vink conclude in their study 'Multiple nationality in a European perspective'—written at the request of the Advisory

---

[163] Ruud Lubbers, *De vrees voorbij* (Amsterdam: De Bezige Bij, 2007), 57.

[164] Paul Scheffer, 'Het multiculturele drama', *NRC Handelsblad* (Dutch daily newspaper), 29 January 2000.

[165] Paul Scheffer, *Het land van aankomst* (Amsterdam: De Bezige Bij, 2007), 429.

Committee on Aliens Affairs (*Adviescommissie voor Vreemdelingenzaken*, ACVZ)—that 'the fact that a person has a genuine and effective bond with more than one country is something which is becoming increasingly accepted in our time of migration, not only in European nationality law but also in the overwhelming majority of the eighteen countries studied in this report. For a growing number of Dutch nationals this fact is also shown to constitute part of their life'.[166] In its advisory report to the Minister of Justice,[167] the ACVZ adopts a strikingly favourable view of dual nationality. We end this chapter with one of its recommendations, which is worth quoting in its entirety:

> The ACVZ urges that the Netherlands adopt the position favoured by the vast majority of European countries, which no longer consider it relevant whether a person's naturalization creates a situation of multiple nationality. In this light, the ACVZ does not consider that there is any point in seeking to restrict multiple nationality in the regulations governing nationality or in insisting on the relinquishment of the original nationality. Indeed, the ACVZ believes that the full acceptance of multiple nationality could actually have a positive impact on the extent to which new Dutch nationals identify with the Netherlands and on their integration into Dutch society.[168]

166 'Dat een persoon daadwerkelijke en effectieve banden met meer dan één land kan hebben, is een gegeven dat in deze tijd van migratie in toenemende mate wordt geaccepteerd, niet alleen in het Europese nationaliteitsrecht, maar inmiddels ook door de overgrote meerderheid van de door ons bestudeerde achttien staten. Voor een groeiend aantal Nederlanders blijkt dit feit ook een deel van hun leven te zijn'. See de Groot and Vink, *Meervoudige nationaliteit in Europees perspectief*, 130.

167 In this advisory report, called 'Dutch nationality in a world without frontiers', the ACVZ relies on the report by De Groot and Vink as well as a report which studied the sociological aspects to multiple nationality: Jaco Dagevos, *Dubbele nationaliteit en integratie* (Den Haag: Sociaal Cultureel Planbureau, 2008). According to this report, no differences exist between mono-Dutch nationals and dual nationals with respect to, for example, unemployment, professional level and the mastery of the Dutch language. Dual nationals do identity themselves less with the Netherlands and spent less time with the autochthonous Dutch population compared to those who only hold Dutch nationality. Most significantly, the report shows that dual nationals are considerably more integrated in Dutch society than those who only possess the nationality of their country of origin. The latter are more frequently unemployed, speak the Dutch language less well, feel less at home in the Netherlands and indicate more often that they intend to return to their country of origin.

168 Adviescommissie voor vreemdelingenzaken, *Nederlanderschap in een onbegrensde wereld. Advies over het Nederlandse beleid inzake meervoudige nationaliteit* (Den Haag: ACVZ, 2008), 55.

Chapter 5

Italy

1. *Introduction*

This chapter studies the attitude towards dual nationality in Italy, an attitude which is closely related to the country's emigration history. Before engaging substantively with this issue, however, we will give an overview of the most salient features of Italian nationality law from the beginning of the 20th century to the present (Sections 2–5). In addition to examining the Italian position on dual nationality, we will thus also touch upon many general aspects of Italian nationality law. Particularly important in this respect is the sharply differing way in which Italian nationality is accessible to Italian co-ethnics on the one hand, and immigrants of non-Italian descent on the other. The family model on which Italian law is based assumes concrete form in the very lenient provisions for co-ethnics, while the provisions concerning immigrants of non-Italian descent are particularly severe.

Another feature of this family model that until recently stood out was the very easy access to Italian nationality through marriage. While in other countries marriages of conveniences were regarded as a serious problem, marriage with an Italian national entailed a right to Italian nationality after six months of marriage if the couple lived in Italy and three years if they lived abroad. Since July 2009, however, the former period has been raised to two years and thus the persistence of the couple's bond is being tested prior to the grant of Italian nationality.[1]

Italy has had two Nationality Acts in the 20th century. The 1912 Act and the 1992 Act (laws 555/1912 and 91/92), the latter being the nationality legislation in force at the time of writing. The key to understanding Italian nationality law is realizing that it embodies a family orientated model—i.e. a model in which nationality and citizenship are reserved for members who belong to

---

[1] Giovanna Zincone and Marzia Basili, "Report on Italy", EUDO Citizenship Observatory Country Reports (2009), 2. The law (called the 'Security Act') is available from http://www.parlamento.it/parlam/leggi/09094l.htm.

a national community by descent.[2] The Italian motives for pursuing this family model, which was already present under the 1912 Act, yet assumed even greater importance under the current law, will be treated in detail in this chapter.[3]

In the first place, the principle of *ius sanguinis* (and until recently *ius conubii*, i.e. acquisition by marriage) is the central way to acquire Italian nationality under the current 1992 Act. Second, the law expresses a strong co-ethnic preference for foreigners of Italian descent. Finally, the acceptance of dual nationality is consistent with the family model since it keeps intact family ties. Other forms of obtaining Italian nationality, for example by *ius soli* or naturalization, play a very marginal role because the conditions are very hard to meet. This is especially true for immigrants who are third country nationals: they have to fulfil a ten year residence requirement if they want to naturalize. The residence requirement is four years for nationals of EU Member States and only three years for persons who can prove to be of Italian descent. However, since European citizens who live in another Member State than their own tend to make relatively few applications for naturalization, the use of the term 'immigrant' in this chapter can generally be understood as referring to those permanent residents in Italy who want to acquire Italian nationality but are neither of Italian descent nor European citizens. Since this category does not enjoy a form of privileged access to Italian nationality, as on the contrary 'ethnic' Italians and European citizens do, the literature sometimes also refers to this category as 'non-privileged immigrants'.

Both Spain and Italy have been criticized in the academic literature for looking too much to the past when shaping their respective nationality laws.[4]

---

[2] Marta Arena, Bruno Nascimbene, and Giovanna Zincone, "Italy", in *Acquisition and Loss of Nationality, Policies and Trends in 15 European Countries*, ed. Rainer Bauböck, *et al.* (Amsterdam: Amsterdam University Press, 2006), 329. The preferential treatment of EU Member State nationals and the ratification of the Second Protocol to the 1963 Convention can also be seen as the expression of a family model, namely the larger 'European family'. See Giovanna Zincone, "Due pesi e due misure: pronipoti d'Italia e nuovi immigrati", in *Familismo legale: come (non) diventare italiani*, ed. Giovanna Zincone (Roma-Bari: Editori Laterza, 2006), 20.

[3] On the role of Italian regions in recruiting co-ethnic immigrants from Latin America, see Guido Tintori, *Fardelli d'Italia? Conseguenze nazionali e transnazionali delle politiche di cittadinanza italiane* (Roma: Carocci, 2009), 50 ff.

[4] Andrea De Bonis and Marco Ferrero, "Dalla cittadinanza etno-nazionale alla cittadinanza di residenza", *Diritto, Immigrazione e Cittadinanza* 5, no. 2 (2004); Bruno Nascimbene, "Proposte di riforma delle norme sulla cittadinanza", *Rivista di diritto internazionale privato e processuale* 40, no. 2 (2004); Giovanna Zincone, "Premessa (preface)", in *Familismo legale. Come (non) diventare italiani*, ed. Giovanna Zincone (Roma-Bari: Editori Laterza, 2006). For a more

Even when it had become plain that the two countries were in fact no longer countries of emigration but of immigration, their nationality laws continued to be marked by a co-ethnic preference. The conditions for acquisition by *ius soli* or naturalization are particularly hard to meet in Italy, a country which figures amongst the EU Member States with the most restrictive nationality law policy in respect of immigrants. Whereas many other countries have liberalized their nationality law and have become more inclusive towards immigrants, such a trend cannot be discerned in Italy. On the contrary, law 91/92 imposed more stringent conditions on acquisition *iure soli* compared to its predecessor of 1912.

Many commentators take issue with the family model as expressed in the law. On the one hand, access to nationality has been facilitated in respect of persons who do not take part in Italian society and who often have no link with Italy other than having an Italian forebear. In addition, the law was until recently also very lenient on another facet of the family model: acquisition by marriage. On the other hand, the severe conditions of the 1992 Act discourage immigrants who work and reside in Italy from attempting to obtain Italian nationality. Although these immigrants are *de facto* part of Italian society, the route to nationality is fraught with obstacles, conveying the clear message that they are not regarded as potential nationals and citizens.

The legal discrepancy between 'ethnic' Italians and non-privileged immigrants is perceived as a risk to the coherence of Italian society. The distinction between these two groups is also clearly reflected in the issue of voting rights. Italians abroad can vote in Italian elections and have special representatives in the Italian *national* parliament.[5] Yet even proposals to grant non-Italian immigrants voting rights in *local* elections have not become law (EU citizens, however, have this right under Article 22 TFEU). The right to vote for Italians abroad may even have the effect of reinforcing the privileged position of co-ethnics. Since they have special representatives to defend their interests, it is not inconceivable that the co-ethnic preference of Italian law will be furthered in the future.[6] The recent past has shown that the senators representing Italians abroad were decisive in establishing a majority for the coalition after the 2006 elections. As long as these senators—who will obviously support a

---

cautious approach to the acquisition of Italian nationality by immigrants, see Vincenzo Lippolis, "La doppia cittadinanza nel disegno di legge Amato: perché non ripensarci?", *Quaderni Costituzionali* 26 (2006): 803–805.

[5] Italians who are resident abroad have both active and passive suffrage in national elections. They are represented by six senators and 12 MPs. See in more detail *infra* Section 6.3.

[6] Zincone, "Il perché del presente e gli auspici per il futuro che potrebbe essere migliore", 147.

further 'ethnicization' of nationality law—play a crucial political role, it is unlikely that the co-ethnic attitude of Italian legislation will change.[7]

The following sections on the role of dual nationality in Italy are structured as follows. To start with, we will consider the creation of the Italian nation-state and the 'Great Migration'. A brief description of these historical events has been weaved in because their effects are clearly reflected in Italian nationality law. We will then deal with the link between the large scale emigration and the deliberations on a new nationality law policy leading to the 1912 Act. A close look at this period of large scale emigration is warranted in order to understand the choice for adopting a nationality law which focuses on Italian co-ethnics. With this historical background in mind, we then turn our attention to more recent developments such as the introduction of gender equality in Italian nationality law, the 1992 Act and law 459/2001, which gave the right to vote to Italians resident abroad. The family model remains central to the conception of Italian nationality and the strong focus on co-ethnics has led some authors to depict the current law as an 'ethnic law'.[8] The inclusion of immigrants through nationality law, however, is a challenge that Italy has only recently started to confront. We will see that proposals addressing immigrants who want to obtain Italian nationality, for example by giving a wider role to the *ius soli* principle, remained unpassed.

2. *The 19th Century: The Formation of the Italian Nation-State and the 'Great Migration'*

Italy only became a unitary nation-state in 1861, the Kingdom of Piedmont being the driving force behind the unification. Until then, Italy had been a nation in search of a State. Due to this fact, the concept of the Italian State was rooted in the idea of the nation.[9]

---

[7] Arena, Nascimbene, and Zincone, "Italy", 360.

[8] Gerardo Gallo and Guido Tintori, "Come si diventa cittadini italiani. Un approfondimento statistico", in *Familismo legale: come (non) diventare italiani*, ed. Giovanna Zincone (Roma-Bari: Editori Laterza, 2006), 111.

[9] Arena, Nascimbene, and Zincone, "Italy", 336. The idea that Italy was already a nation before 1861 seems to be contradicted somewhat by Koenig-Archibugi, who quotes the well-known aphorism at the time of the unification that 'Italy has been made, now we must make the Italians'. According to him, a strong nationalist feeling was lacking in pre-unitary Italy, and the country was characterized by political fragmentation and social diversity. Nationalism only emerged later in the 19th century and remained limited to the elites; it never became a mass phenomenon. See Mathias Koenig-Archibugi, "National and European Citizenship: The Italian Case in Historical Perspective", *Citizenship Studies* 7, no. 1 (2003): 88.

Despite Italy's unification, certain territories that were culturally considered to belong to Italy—such as Veneto, Trento and Dalmatia—were yet to be incorporated into the newly formed country. Taking into account the existence of 'Italians' outside the new Italian State, one would thus expect the 1865 Civil Code (CC) to contain specific provisions for co-ethnics. However, the Civil Code did not specifically focus on co-ethnics, perhaps for diplomatic reasons: granting Italian nationality to minorities in neighbouring countries would not be a wise thing to do, as it could be interpreted as an indirect claim to those territories.[10] The 1865 Civil Code did try to retain Italian nationality for Italian emigrants and their descendants. Dual nationality was prohibited by virtue of Article 11(2) CC, however. Children of Italian emigrants who had acquired another nationality *iure soli* should thus have lost Italian nationality, but informally they were allowed to retain this nationality since priority was given to the *ius sanguinis* principle as laid down in Article 4 CC. Furthermore, Article 6 CC read that a child born abroad to a parent who had lost his Italian nationality before the child's birth was a foreigner. Such a child could still obtain Italian nationality, though, on condition of establishing domicile in Italy. Interestingly, the 1865 Civil Code thus imposed residence as a requirement. Residence therefore formed the link between national belonging and societal belonging. It will be seen that this would change in the years to come.[11]

2.1. *The 'Great Migration' (1880–1930)*

Italy (together with Ireland) has historically been Europe's emigration country par excellence, much more so than Spain. During the time of the 'Great Migration' from Europe to non-European countries, Italian emigrants outnumbered emigrants from Spain by approximately 9 million to 4 million.[12] The three main non-European destinations for Italian emigrants were Argentina, Brazil and the United States. An almost equal number of Italian emigrants remained in Europe, however. In the period 1876–1915 slightly more than 6 million Italian emigrated to other European countries, the main destinations being France, Germany and Switzerland. In the same period, around 7,3 million Italians emigrated to countries outside Europe. From 1876–1895 Argentina and Brazil were the most popular destination among

[10] Zincone, "Due pesi e due misure: pronipoti d'Italia e nuovi immigrati", 36. See on Italian nationality in the years preceding unification G.C. Buzzati, "Note sulla cittadinanza", *Rivista di diritto civile* 8 (1916): 485–506.

[11] Zincone, "Due pesi e due misure: pronipoti d'Italia e nuovi immigrati", 36.

[12] Christopher Duggan, *A Concise History of Italy* (Cambridge: Cambridge University Press, 2007), 20.

Italian emigrants and together received more than a million Italians. The period 1895–1915, however, shows a sharp increase in the number of Italian emigrants going to the United States: from 450,000 between 1876–1895 to almost 3,7 million between 1895–1915.[13]

For the purpose of this chapter it is more interesting to focus our attention on overseas emigration—in particular to Latin America—rather than Italian emigration within Europe. The reason is of course the strong co-ethnic preference of Italian nationality law: former Italian emigrants and their descendants, whose overseas emigration often turned out to be *permanent*, can nonetheless easily acquire Italian nationality. This is even more important for those who emigrated to Argentina and Brazil than to the United States, as the former two are known for their recurrent economic crises. The possibility of escaping to Europe with an Italian passport is thus an attractive option which many have made use of. It is estimated that between three and four million Italians are living abroad. Yet not only those possessing Italian nationality are interested in the Italian motherland. Pugliese notes a growing interest among the third and fourth generation descendants of Italian emigrants in their family history and Italian culture. This trend involves tens of millions of people.[14]

Our focus on Latin America as an emigration destination does not mean that we treat European emigration as being of little importance; quantitatively, emigration within Europe was even more important than overseas emigration. European migration nonetheless had a more temporary character. Between 1876–1975, 13,5 million Italian emigrants remained in Europe, whereas 11,5 million emigrated to North and South America. These statistics do not take into account the number of Italians returning to Italy in the end, however. With regard to the emigration to the United States it is estimated that about 50 percent returned to Italy at some point.[15] This percentage seems to be the same for non-European emigration by Italians on the whole.[16]

Overseas migration became less expensive and much faster after the introduction of the steam ship in 1860. The passage from Europe to the United States took 44 days by sailing vessel, while it took a steam ship only 14 days.

---

[13] Rudolph J. Vecoli, "Negli Stati Uniti", in *Storia dell'emigrazione Italiana*, ed. Piero Bevilaqua, Andreina De Clementi, and Emilio Franzina (Roma: Donzelli, 2002), 56; Patrizia Audenino and Maddalena Tirabassi, *Migrazioni Italiane. Storia e storie dall'Ancien régime a oggi* (Milano: Bruno Mondadori, 2008), 23.

[14] Enrico Pugliese, *L'Italia tra migrazioni internazionali e migrazioni interne* (Bologna: Il Mulino, 2002), 15.

[15] Audenino and Tirabassi, *Migrazioni Italiane. Storia e storie dall'Ancien régime a oggi*, 49, 67.

[16] Tintori, "Cittadinanza e politiche di emigrazione nell'Italia liberale e fascista", 58.

Important for the choice of destination were the countries' immigration policies and economic opportunities. In Argentina, for example, the Latin American country with most Italian immigrants, immigration increased enormously in the 1880s because of the unification of the country, expansion of the territory which allowed the cultivation of many more hectares of land, the construction of a railroad system and the invention of a cooling system which allowed the transportation of frozen meat.[17] Also the (informal) mechanisms and dynamics of the emigration process were important for the emigrants' choice where to go. The presence in the United States or Latin America of family and friends who had already made the journey to the 'New World' facilitated the decision to emigrate. Those who had stayed behind in Italy were often stimulated to make the overseas passage themselves; letters sent to Italy often contained prepaid tickets for those who also wished to make the journey.[18]

In Brazil's São Paulo region most Italian emigrants ended up working at coffee plantations under slave like conditions, including child labour (slavery was only abolished in Brazil in 1888).[19] Italians from Northern Italy normally emigrated as a family and looked for work in the agricultural sector. As much of the work on the fields was done in groups of families, there was no strong disproportion between the number of men and women in the countryside. On the other hand, it was characteristic of Southern Italy that mostly unmarried men without families emigrated; they searched for work in the cities rather than the countryside.[20]

Immigration law in the United States became much more restrictive in the interwar period. Moreover, Northern European immigrants were preferred at the expense of South and Eastern Europeans. The number of Italian immigrants in the United States dropped from 5,7 million between 1911–1920 to slightly less than 530,000 in the period 1931–1941. The restrictive immigration policy in the United States forced many Italians to choose Latin America instead. Argentina became the country of destination for 700,000 Italians in the years 1916–1945, but in the same period a million Italians nonetheless emigrated to the United States.[21]

In Argentina, it became increasingly more difficult from the 1920s onwards to distinguish the Italian-Argentineans from the rest of Argentinean

[17] Audenino and Tirabassi, *Migrazioni Italiane. Storia e storie dall'Ancien régime a oggi*, 21, 62.

[18] Ibid., 69.

[19] Gianfausto Rosoli, "La crise des relations entre l'Italie et le Brésil: la grande naturalisation (1889–1896)", *Revue Européenne des Migrations Internationales* 2, no. 2 (1986): 73.

[20] Audenino and Tirabassi, *Migrazioni Italiane. Storia e storie dall'Ancien régime a oggi*, 62.

[21] Ibid., 80–81, 88.

population due to a process of 'argentinizzazione'; in the preceding years, however, the Italian influence in Argentina had been so profound—both in terms of its share in the population and in the strong presence of Italian enterprises—that the country was called by some 'Italia transoceanica'.[22] This nickname is fully understandable, taking into account that 3,5 million Italians arrived in Argentina between 1830–1950, while the total population of Argentina around the 1850s consisted only of one million people. At the start of the 20th century, around 12 percent of Argentina's population was of Italian descent (by comparison: in the United States, Italians never constituted more than 2,5 percent of the population).[23] The number of Italian arrivals in Argentina was not always higher than the number of departures, though. The numerous Argentinean crises caused many to leave. An economic crisis in 1890 for example resulted in some 58,000 Italians leaving the country, with only 16,000 entering.[24]

Finally, it is important to stress the role of emigration during the 'Great Migration' in the development of Italian unification. This unification only came about in 1861 and Lonni argues that the resulting tensions and conflicts were attenuated by the large-scale emigration. The small communities of Italians all around the world were the object of common concern as well as pride. Although the loss of people was at first sight an impoverishment, in fact it fostered a stronger cohesion of those who remained, thereby contributing to the idea that the unification of Italy was now firmly rooted.[25]

3. *The Influence of Emigration on Italian Nationality and Migration Law*

In this section we will try to sketch an outline of the political deliberations after the 'Great Migration', which culminated in the Italian emigration law

22 Ibid., 85.

23 Fernando Devoto, "In Argentina", in *Storia dell'emigrazione Italiana*, ed. Piero Bevilaqua, Andreina De Clementi, and Emilio Franzina (Roma: Donizelli, 2002), 25.

24 Ibid., 36.

25 Ada Lonni, "Histoire des migrations et identité nationale en Italie", *Revue Européenne des Migrations Internationales* 9, no. 1 (1993): 32. Weil points out that a similar development occurred in Germany: 'The Prussians, Bavarians, and Rhenans who lived abroad, far from the internal divisions that opposed them in Germany, were perceived—and perceived themselves—as Germans from a single country; in their compatriots' eyes, they represented the unity of a new country which, like Italy, made a unifying symbol of its émigrés'. Weil, *How to Be French: Nationality in the Making since 1789*, 186.

of 1901 and the Nationality Act of 1912. In writing this part we have drawn heavily upon the work of Tintori, who has studied the political considerations on which these laws were based. To be sure, the ethnic and nationalist elements in Italian nationality law have a long history. Yet he also shows that it is mistaken to assume that emigration with the retention of Italian nationality has always been unanimously advocated in Italy. From a historical perspective, the ethnic and nationalist characteristics have often been the subject of political and academic criticism.

Tintori starts at the end of the 19th century, the time when Italy began to experience massive emigration due to the extreme poverty of its population. He points to three different strands of thought in Italy with respect to emigration.[26] First, emigration was opposed by some parts of the ruling classes under the influence of large landowners who had an interest in keeping emigration numbers low: by maintaining a surplus of workers, wages could be kept down. The industrialist lobby, however, which was closely connected to the transport sector, supported emigration as it would benefit transport companies. The political compromise reached between these two powerful interest groups led to the ambiguous position of allowing emigration, while at the same time offering little legal protection to emigrants. The practical aspects of emigration were largely left to the market, without any government interference or assistance.

A second strand of thought perceived of emigration as an instrument for nationalist expansion. As opposed to other European countries which colonized through military force,[27] Italy had the idea of using emigration to its commercial advantage by creating 'free colonies' (*colonie libere*). The aim was to encourage emigration to certain countries in order to create such a prevalent Italian influence that one could almost speak of colonization.

The third position on emigration was what can be called a nationalist *familismo*: an indissoluble bond existed with Italians abroad to whom Italy had a moral debt since it had not been able to offer them a future in the homeland. Ideas of nationalist *familismo* and nationalist expansionism remained strong over time, whereas the opposition to emigration quickly lost much of its force. Especially the nationalist *familismo*, which spoke to Italian sentiment, was to become an important influence on the future of Italian nationality law.

The consequences of this large scale migration on nationality law became clear fairly quickly. The reason was that the position of Italian emigrants

---

[26] Tintori, "Cittadinanza e politiche di emigrazione nell'Italia liberale e fascista", 52–55.

[27] The Italian colonies have never been of great importance.

in nationality matters became confused by the simultaneous application of the Italian *ius sanguinis* principle (Article 4 of the 1865 Civil Code) and the *ius soli* principle in place in most countries of emigration. Probably the most well-known example of this clash between the *ius sanguinis* and the *ius soli* principle was the Brazilian 'Great Naturalization' in the 19th century. In order to increase the population, the 1891 Brazilian Constitution stated that any child born in Brazil acquired Brazilian nationality *iure soli*. In addition, Brazilian nationality was 'forced upon' foreigners who lived in Brazil and who had not declared their intention to keep their original nationality within six months after the Constitution came into force.[28] As Italy's opposition to this Brazilian practice turned out to be largely ineffective, it decided to adopt another strategy. Instead of opposing the loss of Italian nationality upon naturalization in Brazil, Italy decided to facilitate the recovery of Italian nationality. This strategy, which had been used before by Germany, saved Italy from the useless attempt of preventing the naturalization of its nationals in Brazil.

If dual nationality was officially not possible under Italian law,[29] it occurred frequently enough in practice. Italy made efforts to preserve Italian nationality for emigrants by allowing the transmission of Italian nationality *iure sanguinis*. Yet it also took offence to the voluntary acquisition of another nationality and perceived this decision as a definitive choice against Italy. Applications for reacquisition of Italian nationality after voluntary acquisition of another one were therefore hardly ever successful. As a result, the majority which did not want to lose Italian nationality kept the Italian authorities uninformed about the acquisition of another nationality, thereby creating confusion as to their nationality position.[30]

---

[28] See generally Rosoli, "La crise des relations entre l'Italie et le Brésil: la grande naturalisation (1889–1896)": 69–90. The large scale naturalization was opposed by Italy and a number of other European countries (Portugal, France and the Austro-Hungarian empire), but to no avail. Rosoli shows that although Brazilian nationality could be refused, this was strongly discouraged. Moreover, the poor Italian immigrant population did not really seem to care or were ignorant of their naturalization; Italian elites in Brazil, on the other hand, whose interests had become linked to the Brazilian State, generally did not oppose the 'Great Naturalization'. As a matter of fact, this large scale automatic naturalization was not without historical precedent. French nationality was automatically conferred upon hundreds or even thousands of foreigners resident in France in the years 1790–1795. See Weil, *How to Be French: Nationality in the Making since 1789*, 16.

[29] Article 11(2) and (3) of the 1865 Civil Code provided for the loss of Italian nationality upon acquiring another nationality or rendering military service for another country.

[30] Tintori, "Cittadinanza e politiche di emigrazione nell'Italia liberale e fascista", 60–61.

During drafting a new emigration law—which would become the law of 1901[31]—the Italian nationality legislation was also subject of discussion. Some MPs held the minority view that Italy should release its nationals from their Italian nationality and encourage the acquisition of the nationality of their new country. This could in the end lead to a bond between Italy and Argentina similar to that between Great-Britain and the United States. The majority, however, was of the opinion that loss of Italian nationality would also mean the loss of feelings for Italy. This was unacceptable due to Italy's dependence on remittances. In the short term, the retention of Italian nationality was thus of the utmost importance. Yet on the long term, Italy wished to establish economic and commercial bonds with the countries of emigration. For that purpose, it would be highly desirable if Italian emigrants possessed the nationality of those countries, but at the same time still fostered feelings for Italy.[32] These nationalist and expansionist ideas were shared by an overwhelming majority in parliament and led to the objective of creating 'free colonies'—countries where the Italian influence was so pervasive that it resembled colonization—for the benefit of the Italian motherland.[33]

Against this backdrop, the 1901 law contained special provisions on Italian nationality and military service.[34] First of all, Article 33 provided that Italians abroad were excused from military service in Italy during peace time. Article 35 abrogated Article 11(3) of the 1865 CC, which provided for the loss of Italian nationality of Italians who had worked for a foreign government (this included, for example, participating in the construction of railroads which were state property) or had served in a foreign military. The abrogation of this provision meant that Italian nationality was saved for a considerable category of persons.[35] However, as Article 11(2) was not abrogated, acquisition of another nationality still resulted in loss of Italian nationality. Buzzatti found this particularly worrying because Latin American countries attributed their nationality very easily to new immigrants.[36] In recognition of the fact that a person could legitimately be claimed by both the country of origin and the country of residence, Buzzati argued unsuccessfully for the official acceptance of dual nationality, and thus the abrogation of Article 11(2), at the first session

[31] Law n. 23, 31 January 1901.

[32] Tintori, "Cittadinanza e politiche di emigrazione nell'Italia liberale e fascista", 62–65.

[33] Ibid., 66–67.

[34] Ibid., 67–71.

[35] Buzzati, "Questioni sulla cittadinanza degli italiani emigrati in America": 451–452.

[36] Ibid., 452.

of the Congress of Italians living abroad, held in 1908 (*prima Sezione del Congresso degli italiani all'estero*[37]).[38]

In Buzzatti's view, the retention of Italian nationality would not be void of meaning. Not only could the Italian State provide financial credit and offer help to Italians abroad in fields such as education and public health, Italian nationality should—and this is the more radical aspect of Buzzati's view—prevail over domicile in matters of personal status and family law.[39] Finally, Article 36 of the law of 1901 facilitated the acquisition of Italian nationality by children born abroad who had not opted for Italian nationality within one year after coming of age (Article 6 CC). These children could now obtain Italian nationality on condition of establishing residence in Italy.

Even though the law was supported by a large majority in the Lower House, highly critical voices were heard in the Senate.[40] Some pointed out that the new provisions contradicted international obligations to prevent dual nationality, and proponents of the law were accused of performing a masquerade regarding the underlying aim for the legislative modifications. The idea of founding 'free colonies', which would lead to economic and political ties with the countries of emigration, was an illusion according to these critics. They argued that those who emigrated were part of a poor and hardly educated part of society; in other words, they would not be able to further Italian interests abroad—be they economical or political. The critics of the law contended that nationalist expansionism was the real motive behind the modifications and they predicted that the abrogation of a provision such as the above mentioned

---

37 A second session was held in 1911. The goal of the congress was 'de maintenir la confraternité et la bonne intelligence parmi les Italiens dispersés dans le monde et de reserrer les liens de solidarité avec la mère patrie'. See E.S. Zeballos, "De la nationalité et de la naturalisation dans la République Argentine", *Journal de droit international* 45 (1918): 29–30. Others point out that the task of the congress was a 'studio delle riforme da consigliarsi alle leggi che regolano attualmente l'istituto della cittadinanza e del servizio militare nei riguardi del movimento migratorio'. Quoted in N. Samama, *Secondo congresso degli italiani all'estero. Tema primo. Il problema della cittadinanza specialmente nei rapporti degli italiani all'estero* (Firenze: Tipografia Enrico Ariani, 1911), 5.

38 Buzzati, "Questioni sulla cittadinanza degli italiani emigrati in America": 456, 462–463. He admitted that the acceptance of dual nationality would raise a number of new legal questions, but argued that also the permanent migration to Latin American was a new phenomenon, calling for new approaches. He tried to put dual nationality—and the opposition to this phenomenon—in a historical perspective by pointing at the fact that the right to migrate and the right to change nationality were also not so long ago regarded as 'legal heresies'.

39 Ibid., 471. Buzzati uses, among others, the classic argument that nationality is a stable criterion whereas domicile is not.

40 Tintori, "Cittadinanza e politiche di emigrazione nell'Italia liberale e fascista", 71–74.

Article 11(3) CC would not lead to Italian emigrants exercising a high public office abroad. Instead, the law would serve the expansionist objective of those advocating a dispersion of as many Italians around the world as possible.

Soon after the enactment of the 1901 emigration law, plans were made for a new Nationality Act.[41] First of all, there was general dissatisfaction concerning the 1901 law—the provision on military service, for example, was now deemed too wide and was thought to encourage expatriation. More importantly, it was thought that a new law should bring to even greater prominence the two central principles of Italian nationality law discussed at the beginning of this section: the nationalist/sentimentalist *familismo* and the expansionist nationalism.[42] In other words, the attainment of these objectives could be realized more successfully with a new nationality law than with the old emigration law. This new nationality law should first of all express a moral debt towards Italian emigrants; it was therefore imperative to facilitate the recovery of Italian nationality. Furthermore, under the influence of the expansionist strand of thinking the objective of founding 'free colonies' was brought more to the fore. The ideas of the principal spokesman of this line of thinking, Nicola Apuzzo, were quite pretentious and opportunistic: emigration was the manifestation of 'the need for expansion', and the economic interests of Italians abroad could serve as a pretext for political intervention abroad.[43]

4. *Law 555/1912: A Response to the 'Great Migration'*

The 1912 Act was mainly an answer to the 'Great Migration', the principal objective being to retain Italian nationality for Italian emigrants. This not only meant the unlimited transmission of Italian nationality *iure sanguinis*, but also dual nationality for those possessing another nationality *iure soli*.[44] Nevertheless, when discussing the Bill in parliament the Minister of Justice

[41] The need for a special law on nationality was also one of the main conclusion at the 1908 Congress of Italians living abroad. See Samama, *Secondo congresso degli italiani all'estero. Tema primo. Il problema della cittadinanza specialmente nei rapporti degli italiani all'estero*, 6.

[42] Tintori, "Cittadinanza e politiche di emigrazione nell'Italia liberale e fascista", 76.

[43] Ibid., 80.

[44] The Bill explicitly recognized the unlimited transmission of Italian nationality *iure sanguinis* as a general principle but did not, however, provide anything on dual nationality. The absence of a provision on dual nationality was criticized by Samama, who stressed that dual nationality—due to the rapid increase of people possessing this status—was the very subject that should have been addressed by the law. For the Bill as well as Samama's commentary, see Samama, *Secondo congresso degli italiani all'estero. Tema primo. Il problema della cittadinanza specialmente nei rapporti degli italiani all'estero*, 126–142.

did his utmost to deny that this law would lead to dual nationality, merely stating that the *ius sanguinis* provision would possibly only lead to 'conflicts of nationality'—not to dual nationality.[45] This was obviously not a very strong argument.

The ambiguity concerning the position on dual nationality—theoretically the 1912 law would not lead to dual nationality, but in practice it did—was enhanced by the wording of Article 7 of the 1912 Act, reading that Italians born abroad who also possessed the nationality of the country of birth *could* give up their Italian nationality when coming of age. There was thus no obligation to do so. Also Article 8 would in practice lead to dual nationality as it was interpreted in a way that Italian nationality was not lost if 'the foreign nationality was acquired without the express wish of the individual'. Many articles were thus worded in a way which left ample room for interpretation, which in turn allowed Italian policy makers plenty of opportunities to retain Italian nationality for emigrants and their descendants.[46]

As was to be expected, the recovery of Italian nationality was rather easy under the 1912 Act.[47] Article 9(2) provided for the reacquisition subject to two conditions: renunciation of the other nationality and one year residence in Italy. However, by virtue of Article 9(3) reacquisition was even *automatic* after two years of residence in Italy if the ground for loss of Italian nationality had been the acquisition of a foreign nationality. The same article even made reacquisition possible after two years of residence in a third State (i.e. neither Italy nor the country of nationality).[48] The recovery of Italian nationality obviously resulted in a dual nationality if the individual was not required under the law of the other country to give up that nationality upon reacquiring the Italian one.

A minority of critics of the 1912 Act lamented the fact that the needs of Italian emigrants had not sufficiently been taken into account. We have seen that the aim of the 1912 Act was to retain Italian nationality for emigrants. However, especially the second generation emigrants had pleaded for a facilitation of the loss of Italian nationality because they felt they were

45 Tintori, "Cittadinanza e politiche di emigrazione nell'Italia liberale e fascista", 88.

46 Ibid., 90. Weil mentions on this subject that the Italian law of 1912 went much further than the German Delbrück law which would be adopted a year later. The Italian law only allowed the loss of Italian nationality through a voluntary act whilst the Delbrück law in principle provided for the loss of German nationality for those who naturalized abroad, admittedly with the possibility to keep German nationality if prior authorization had been obtained. See Weil, *How to Be French: Nationality in the Making since 1789*, 186.

47 Tintori, "Cittadinanza e politiche di emigrazione nell'Italia liberale e fascista", 96–97.

48 Stefania Bariatti, *La disciplina giuridica della cittadinanza italiana* (Milano: Giuffrè Editore, 1989), 37.

'condemned' to Italian nationality. The 'life sentence' of Italian nationality was attacked most fiercely by Cabrini, who claimed that there ought to be only two scenarios: either the attraction of the Italian motherland was so great that Italians would return spontaneously, or the attraction of the new country prevailed—in which case the retention of Italian nationality would merely be 'a rope around the emigrant's neck'.[49]

Cabrini's view that Italian nationality was often considered a burden by Italian emigrants turned out to be true during the fascist years. The fascist regime made an appeal to the nationalist sentiments of Italian emigrants, but these emigrants only supported Italian projects if it served their own social and economic cause in the country of immigration. If not, they did not feel compelled to further the Italian cause. It was thus clear that emigrants, when put to the test, saw their future in their new country of residence.[50]

Finally, since dual nationality was *de facto* tolerated by Italy, many Italians residing abroad possessed two nationalities. This fact called for the regulation of military service, particularly with countries where many Italians resided. From 1938 Italy therefore concluded a number of treaties on military service concerning dual nationals.[51] The 1938 Italian-Argentinean Treaty provided that persons born in Argentina to Italian parents—and vice versa persons born in Italy to Argentinean parents—were exempt from fulfilling their military service in Italy during peace time on condition of proof that their military obligations under Argentinean law had been met. Under the French-Italian Treaty of 1953 a different system was adopted, which allowed the individual the choice to comply with his military obligations in the French or Italian army. Compulsory military service in Italy was abolished by law 331/2000.[52]

If we try to summarize the attitude towards multiple nationality until 1992—the current law 91/92 explicitly allows dual nationality—we can say

---

49 Tintori, "Cittadinanza e politiche di emigrazione nell'Italia liberale e fascista", 96–97. See also the following statement by Quadri: 'Certo è, comunque, che il legislatore del 1912 si è troppo ispirato ad una tendenza missionaria e protettrice che non si confà ad un legislatore particolare; come pure ha ecceduto nel consentire la conservazione e il recupero della cittadinanza italiana, sì da farne assai spesso una specie di cittadinanza "di riserva", che non corrisponde in alcun modo alla vita reale dei soggetti'. Quadri, "Cittadinanza", 323.

50 Tintori, "Cittadinanza e politiche di emigrazione nell'Italia liberale e fascista", 99.

51 Treaties were concluded for example with Argentina (1938), France (1953) and Brazil (1958). See generally Mario Giuliano, "Accordi internazionali bilaterali relativi al servizio militare", *Rivista di diritto internazionale privato e processuale* 1 (1965): 329–331; Roberta Clerici, "L'Italia e i nuovi accordi sul servizio militare", ibid. 13 (1977): 679–685.

52 Adriana Sabato, *La cittadinanza italiana. Disciplina e profili operativi* (Santarcangelo di Romagna: Maggioli Editore, 2006), 207.

that it was not permitted under the 1865 Civil Code, although it was tolerated in practice. The issue of multiple nationality became increasingly relevant when Italy was confronted from the 1890s onwards with massive emigration, in particular to countries in Latin America. Most of these countries applied the *ius soli* principle and sometimes even imposed automatic naturalization upon immigrants.

Neither was a definite solution on multiple nationality adopted under the 1912 Act. Even though Italian nationality should have been lost under particular circumstances, the 1912 law bears witness to the wish to maintain strong ties with Italian emigrants. It thus gave preference to the *ius sanguinis* principle at the expense of the prohibition of dual nationality. In short, the matter of dual nationality was never clearly decided and for many emigrants their Italian nationality became a spare nationality.[53]

5. *The 1970s and 80s: Gender Equality in Italian Nationality Law*

Gender equality in nationality law is an important cause of dual nationality.[54] Italian nationality law provided in Article 10(3) of the 1912 Act that Italian women would lose their nationality upon marriage with a foreigner if the husband possessed a nationality which was transmitted to her by virtue of the marriage. This implied that Italian nationality was not lost if the husband was stateless.[55] Women could also not transmit their nationality to their children due to the principle of *ius sanguinis a patre* (Article 1(1) 1912 Act).

From the 1970s the question was increasingly raised—in particular by the women's movement—whether these rules did not conflict with the principle of gender equality. In 1975 the rule under which an Italian woman would lose Italian nationality upon marrying a foreigner was declared unconstitutional by the Italian Constitutional Court.[56] The woman's legally inferior position in nationality law violated the principle of non-discrimination on the ground of sex as laid down in Article 3 of the 1947 Constitution.[57] The Court pointed to

53 Arena, Nascimbene, and Zincone, "Italy", 338.

54 We touched upon the role of gender equality in Chapter 1, Section 6.

55 Article10(3): 'La donna cittadina che si marita ad uno straniero perde la cittadinanza italiana, sempreché il marito possieda una cittadinanza che per il fatto del matrimonio a lei si comunichi'.

56 Ruling by the Constitutional Court, 16 April 1975, n. 87. For the text of the ruling see Bariatti, *La disciplina giuridica della cittadinanza italiana*, 251–253.

57 The Italian Constitution came into force on 1 January 1948. Article 3 reads: 'All citizens have the same social dignity and are equal before the law regardless of their sex, race, language, religion, political opinions, social and personal conditions'.

the unacceptability of the loss of Italian nationality irrespective of the will of the woman concerned, and in addition concluded that this practice violated Article 29 of the Constitution (the moral and legal equality of spouses). Moreover, it was ruled that the problems resulting from the loss of nationality (e.g. the ineligibility for jobs for which Italian nationality is required and the loss of legal protection which is reserved for Italian nationals) might discourage women from contracting a marriage or from dissolving an existing one.

In 1983 another judgment by the Constitutional Court declared unconstitutional the fact that Italian women could not transmit their nationality to their children (violation of Articles 3 and 29 of the Constitution). This ruling had the effect that a child now acquires Italian nationality if either the father or the mother possesses Italian nationality.[58] Although the equality of spouses would give rise to a growing incidence of dual nationality—which Italy tried to prevent, as the Court remarked, by having ratified the 1963 Strasbourg Convention on 4 October 1966—this did not justify tolerating the inequality of men and women concerning the transmission of nationality to their children. In sum, the implications of gender equality overrode the inclination to avoid multiple nationality. This judgment had retroactive effect to 1 January 1948, when the Constitution entered into force.

Following these two important rulings by the Constitutional Court, both Italian family law and nationality law were modified. The rule that Italian women no longer lost their nationality upon marrying a foreigner was codified in the Civil Code in the same year.[59] The 1912 Act was modified by law 123/1983, which stated in Article 5 that minor children acquired Italian nationality if either their father or mother was Italian. However, if this resulted in a dual nationality, one nationality should be chosen upon coming of age.[60] This rule was, in turn, amended by law 180/86 which postponed the obligation to opt for one nationality until the new Nationality Act would come into

[58] Ruling by the Constitutional Court, 9 February 1983, n. 30. For the text of the ruling see Bariatti, *La disciplina giuridica della cittadinanza italiana*, 286–289.

[59] Law 19 March 1975, n. 151, reform of family law. Article 143-*ter* …: 'Cittadinanza della moglie. La moglie conserva la cittadinanza italiana, salvo sua espressa rinunzia, anche se per effetto del matrimonio o del mutamento di cittadinanza da parte del marito assume una cittadinanza straniera'.

[60] Article 5 of Legge 21 aprile 1983 n. 123: 'È cittadino italiano il figlio minorenne, anche adottivo, di padre cittadino o madre cittadina. Nel caso di doppia cittadinanza, il figlio dovrà optare per una sola cittadinanza entro un anno dal raggiungimento della maggiore età'. By virtue of Article 1 of this law, the foreign or stateless spouse of an Italian national could also acquire Italian nationality after spending six months on Italian territory or after three years of marriage.

force.[61] This was to become the 1992 Act, which allows multiple nationality by virtue of Article 11.[62] Thus, the obligation for dual nationals to choose one of their nationalities upon reaching the age of majority did not become part of the 1992 Act.

6. *The Favourable Attitude towards Italian Co-Ethnics: Laws 91/1992, 379/2000, 124/2006 and 459/2001*

With the 1992 Act, Italian law for the first time explicitly allows multiple nationality. Though it had already been *de facto* accepted for a long time, the acceptance *de iure* of dual nationality is still qualified by Kojanec as a salient aspect of the present law, in particular because it illustrates the global move from a half-hearted toleration of the phenomenon to—at least in the Italian case—a wholehearted embrace.[63] Law 91/92 has also brought to greater prominence the principle of *ius sanguinis* as well as the co-ethnic predilection for foreigners of Italian origin. These elements were also incorporated in subsequent nationality law reforms—laws 379/2000 and 124/2006—which, as we shall see in this section, aim at the reacquisition of Italian nationality by particular categories of foreigners. Nascimbene notes on law 124/2006 that its objective was inspired by political and social reasons; it is supposed to be an answer to the tormented national history of the territories Istria, Fiume and Dalmatia from the end of the Second World War to the collapse of the Federal Republic of Yugoslavia, and the subsequent need to rearrange territories as well as persons.[64] Alongside these two laws of 2000 and 2006 addressing Italian co-ethnics, another law—law 459/2001—introduced voting rights for Italians living abroad.

This section is structured as follows. First, we will present the general features of law 91/92 (Section 6.1). Then, the modes of acquisition of Italian

---

[61] Article 1 of Legge 15 maggio 1986, n. 180, amending Article 5 of Legge 21 aprile 1983 n. 123: 'Il termine per l'esercizio dell'opzione di cui all'art. 5, secondo comma, della l. 21 aprile 1983 n. 123, è prorogato fino alla data di entrata in vigore della nuova legge organica sulla cittadinanza'.

[62] Article 11: 'A citizen who already has, or has acquired or re-acquired a foreign citizenship shall retain Italian citizenship, but may renounce the latter where he or she resides or establishes residence abroad'.

[63] Giovanni Kojanec, *Nuove norme sulla cittadinanza italiana: Riflessi interni ed internazionali* (Milano: Franco Angeli, 1995), 16.

[64] Bruno Nascimbene, "Proposte a favore dell'acquisto o riacquisto della cittadinanza italiana da parte di connazionali residenti in Slovenia e Croazia", *Rivista di diritto internazionale privato e processuale* 41, no. 2 (2005): 372.

nationality upon request will be examined (6.1.1). This merits some discussion because it clearly shows the different treatment of Italian co-ethnics on the one hand and foreigners of non-Italian descent on the other. Finally, we will explore the two more recent laws which favour foreigners of ethnic descent (6.2), as well as the law which grants voting rights to Italians abroad (6.3).

6.1. *Law 91/1992: Towards a Further 'Ethnicization' of Italian Nationality Law*

Just like the 1912 Act, the present nationality law allows an unrestricted transmission of Italian nationality to Italians born abroad. This rule, combined with the acceptance of dual nationality will—just like the regime under the 1912 Act—create many 'latent Italians' residing abroad. Compared to the 1912 Act the modes of acquisition of Italian nationality by immigrants who are neither of Italian descent nor from EU countries became more rigid under the present law; in contrast, the reacquisition of Italian nationality for emigrants and their descendants has been facilitated. The law is said to be the embodiment of the '"myth of productive return", namely the groundless hypothesis that emigrants would come back with human and financial capital capable of enriching the economy of the country'.[65]

Joppke has made interesting remarks about the parliamentary debate over the 1992 Act, which according to him was characterized by a rhetoric of transnationalism, globalization and anti-statism. His impression was, furthermore, that the 'ethical obligation' towards Italian emigrants who suffered hardship in the general interest of Italy was clearly secondary to the sentimental and cultural value expressed by the tie of nationality. In sum, the 1992 Act was a measure 'to strengthen the sense of Italian nationness, separate from and beyond the state, in a world of increased mobility and movement across borders'.[66] Joppke's perception seems to be supported by Zincone, who has described the 1992 Act as a schizophrenic 'delayed-action provision', concealing a 'discreet nationalism'.[67]

The adoption of the 1992 Act was a delayed measure because Italy, by reinforcing the *ius sanguinis* elements in the 1992 Act, behaved as if it were a country of emigration, whilst in reality it had been a country of immigration since 1973. As this fact was also increasingly recognized by Italian politics, a pro-immigrant law was passed in 1990, showing that the political

65 Arena, Nascimbene, and Zincone, "Italy", 346.

66 Joppke, "Citizenship between De- and Re-ethnicization (1)": 451.

67 Arena, Nascimbene, and Zincone, "Italy", 345–347.

climate was not hostile to immigrants. The 1992 Act, however, reinforced the generous attitude towards foreigners of Italian descent, but is less generous towards immigrants than its predecessor of 1912. Indeed, this is a schizophrenic choice: the law testifies to a clear co-ethnic preference in the absence of clear motives for favouring foreigners of Italian descent; moreover, public opinion did not consider co-ethnic preference to be a valid criterion for acquisition of Italian nationality.[68] In the absence of clear grounds for favouring co-ethnics, the 1992 Act should thus at best be regarded as a form of 'discreet nationalism'—an idea which is moreover shared across party ideologies: 'After fascism, nationalist sentiments could not be expressed in the open and therefore became discreet and concealed themselves under the myth of emigration and gratitude to emigrants'.[69]

We shall see that two conceptions of Italian nationality exist: one that is inclusive towards Italian co-ethnics and one which favours more inclusive measures for immigrants of non-Italian descent. Up till now, there have been concrete plans to achieve both objectives, but only the first line of thinking has been successful. In this respect, it is useful to take a close look at the different modes of acquiring Italian nationality upon request. This will show how the difference between co-ethnics and immigrants of non-Italian descent works out in practice.

6.1.1. *The Modes of Acquisition of Italian Nationality Upon Request: Embracing Emigrants and Bashing Immigrants?*

Gallo and Tintori list five modes of 'non-automatic' acquisition of Italian nationality under the 1992 Act, i.e. acquisition which is dependent on the will of the applicant.[70] These modes are acquisition by:

1. Marriage (Article 5);
2. Birth and prolonged residence in Italy (Article 4(2));
3. Ordinary naturalization (Article 9(1));
4. Reacquisition (Article 13);
5. Descent from former Italians (ministerial circular K.28.1 of 8 April 1991);
6. Extraordinary naturalization (Article 9(2)).

Although the modes under 3, 4 and 6 above allow for administrative discretion, the others do not. The different modes will be discussed in turn, except for the extraordinary naturalization (naturalization awarded to a person who

---

[68] Zincone, "Il perché del presente e gli auspici per il futuro che potrebbe essere migliore", 144.
[69] Arena, Nascimbene, and Zincone, "Italy", 345.
[70] Gallo and Tintori, "Come si diventa cittadini italiani. Un approfondimento statistico", 112.

has rendered eminent services to Italy or represents an exceptional interest to the State); the latter form of acquisition is not of great interest for our discussion.

Mode 1: Acquisition by Marriage

Acquisition of nationality by marriage was until recently very easy under the 1992 Act.[71] Italian nationality was acquired after six months' residency in Italy or after three years if the married couple lived abroad. For those of non-Italian descent, marriage is by far the most common way to obtain Italian nationality. If we compare the numbers of acquisition by marriage to those of ordinary naturalization, the former outnumbers the latter by a ratio of 9:1.[72]

Modes 2 and 3: Birth and Prolonged Residence in Italy and Ordinary Naturalization

Articles 4(2) and 9(1) clearly evidence how Italian law favours ethnic Italians. By virtue of the first Article, persons whose (grand)parent was Italian by birth can—on condition of having legally resided in Italy for two years before coming of age—freely opt for Italian nationality. The same article also shows how difficult it is for a child of non-privileged immigrant parents to have an option right to Italian nationality after he/she reaches the age of majority: the law requires *birth in Italy* as well as a *legal and uninterrupted* residence until the person comes of age.[73]

---

71 Since July 2009, however, the six month period is raised to two years and the persistence of the couple's bond is tested upon the grant of Italian nationality. See *supra* Section 1. Article 5(1) now reads: 'The foreign or stateless spouse of an Italian citizen may acquire Italian citizenship if, after the marriage, he or she has been legally resident for at least two years in the territory of the Republic, or after three years from the marriage if he or she has been residing abroad, where, upon the adoption of the decree referred to in Article 7 paragraph 1, the marriage has not been dissolved or annulled or has not ceased to have civil effects and there is no legal separation'. The Italian translation of the 1992 Act is available from http://eudo-citizenship.eu (select Italy under the country profiles).

72 Gallo and Tintori, "Come si diventa cittadini italiani. Un approfondimento statistico", 119.

73 Article 4(1): 'An alien or stateless person, whose father or mother, or direct ancestors in the second degree were citizens by birth, shall become a citizen: c) if, having reached the age of majority, he or she has had legal residence for at least two years in the territory of the Republic, and declares within one year his or her intention to acquire Italian citizenship'.

Article 4(2): 'Aliens born in Italy, who have been legally resident on a continuous basis therein until they have reached the age of majority, shall become citizens where they declare their intention to acquire Italian citizenship within one year of such date'.

A similar regime is in place as regards ordinary naturalization: three years of legal residence in Italy is required of persons whose Italian (grand)parent is either Italian by birth or was born in Italy. In respect of nationals of EU Member States the residence term is four years. Foreign immigrants who are neither of Italian descent nor EU citizen need to fulfil ten years of legal residence before being eligible to Italian nationality.[74]

Mode 4: Reacquisition

As for Italians who at some point lost their nationality, Article 17 of the 1992 Act[75] introduced a programme for the reacquisition of Italian nationality. The programme—the deadline of which was postponed from 1994 to 1997—led to 163,756 people reacquiring Italian nationality while living abroad.[76] Although Article 17 is no longer in force, the possibility to recover Italian nationality is still possible under two other laws, law 379/2000 and 124/2006 (see *infra*).

Mode 5: Descent from Former Italian Nationals (riconoscimento dello status civitatis italiano) under Ministerial Circular K.28.1 of 8 April 1991

In recent years the number of people who recovered Italian nationality or acquired it through descent from an Italian ancestor has increased considerably. Pastore may have been right in a publication of 2001 that at the time the total number of former nationals and their descendants who recovered Italian nationality was likely to be small, as the implementation of the 1992 law 'fortuitously corresponded to a period of strong economic growth and political

[74] Article 9(1): 'Italian citizenship may be granted …:
a) to aliens whose father or mother or one of whose direct ancestors to the second degree were citizens by birth, or aliens who were born in the territory of the Republic and, in both cases, have been legally resident therein for at least three years, subject to the provisions of Article 4, paragraph 1, subparagraph (c); ...
d) to citizens of a Member State of the European Community who have been legally resident in the territory of the Republic for at least four years;
f) to aliens who have been legally resident in the territory of the Republic for at least ten years'.

[75] Article 17(1): 'Any person who has lost Italian citizenship under the provisions of Articles 8 and 12 of the Act 12 June 1912 n. 555, or for not having made the choice provided for by Article 5 of the Act 21 April 1983 n. 123, may re-acquire it by making a declaration to that effect within two years of the entry into force of the present Act'. We recall that Italian nationality was only lost under the 1912 Act in case of renunciation of Italian nationality or after voluntary acquisition of another nationality.

[76] Zincone, "Due pesi e due misure: pronipoti d'Italia e nuovi immigrati", 8.

stability in the main Latin American receiving countries'. Current statistics, however, show that this has changed.[77]

The principal cause has been the success of the method of acquiring Italian nationality under the ministerial circular, which laid down the procedure for the recognition of Italian nationality with regard to descendants of Italian emigrants. This circular is still in force and was not amended by law 91/1992.[78] Its essence resides in the fact that those who are descended from an Italian emigrant and to whom was attributed another nationality *iure soli*, but who never renounced Italian nationality, transmit Italian nationality to their descendants.[79] It was only from 1948 that this rule also applies to women, who from that moment on could also transmit Italian nationality.[80] As Italian nationality was passed on without restrictions, even a person who can prove descent from an Italian who emigrated before the unification of Italy (1861) is entitled to Italian nationality, provided that the Italian ancestor was alive at the time of Italy's unification.[81]

In the period 1998–2007 an incredible number of 786,000 people acquired Italian nationality because they could prove their descent from an Italian ancestor.[82] They only needed to 'revive' Italian nationality, which could even

---

[77] Ferruccio Pastore, "Migration Law and International Migration: The Italian Case", in *Towards a European Nationality. Citizenship, Immigration and Nationality Law in the EU*, ed. Randall Hansen and Patrick Weil (Hampshire: Palgrave Publishers, 2001), 103. Tintori shows, however, that the socio-economic difficulties in Argentina (2001) and Uruguay (2002) led to a strong increase of applications for the recognition of Italian nationality. Tintori, *Fardelli d'Italia? Conseguenze nazionali e transnazionali delle politiche di cittadinanza italiane*, 67.

[78] Bariatti, *La disciplina giuridica della cittadinanza italiana*, 187.

[79] Alessio remarks that the overwhelming majority of Italians born abroad (this concerns tens of millions of persons) were never registered at Italian consulates in the country of birth. They were thus unknown to the Italian Register of Population. Marcello Alessio, "La doppia cittadinanza come problema 'quantitativo' ", 2000; available from http://www.umanesimolatino.it/fondazionecassamarca/05_emigrazione/convegni/con_treviso.html.

[80] Gallo and Tintori, "Come si diventa cittadini italiani. Un approfondimento statistico", 127. The circular itself states that the combined effect of Articles 1 and 7 of law 555/1912 provides for 'the concrete possibility that Italian descendants of the second, third and fourth generation and even further possess Italian nationality'.

[81] Guido Menghetti, "Problematiche relative agli immigrati dall'Argentina", 2002; available from www.interno.it. Menghetti states: 'Giova evidenziare che è fondato giuridicamente il riconoscimento della cittadinanza anche ai discendenti di un soggetto emigrato da uno degli Stati preunitari prima della proclamazione del Regno d'Italia alla condizione che fosse vivente alla data del 17/3/1861 (proclamazione del Regno)'.

[82] The statistics show that the economic and political situation in Latin American countries is of the utmost relevance for the number of people deciding to have their Italian nationality recognized: 60 percent of those who 'revived' their Italian nationality were from Argentina and Brazil, countries which experienced economic and political difficulties at the time.

be done at a consulate abroad.[83] Although Gallo and Tintori list this particular regime under the denominator 'acquisition of nationality', they recognize that one cannot properly speak of acquisition. Rather, the Italian nationality is 'revived' or, in other words, one's Italian *status civitatis* is recognized.[84]

Gallo and Tintori, who refer to the assessment by the Italian Ministry of Foreign Affairs that there were 60 million people of Italian descent living around the world in 1994, estimate that at least 30 million of them can prove their Italian descent, and thus have an Italian nationality which only needs to be 'revived'.[85] However, it is doubtful that those who acquire Italian nationality in this way will take up residence in Italy. The European citizenship that is derived from Italian nationality allows them to establish themselves in countries to which they are culturally and linguistically more related, such as Spain and Portugal (this was already illustrated by the *Micheletti* case in Chapter 1, Section 11.2). They also move to London in great numbers.[86] Moreover, Italian nationality allows them to travel to the United States without an entry visa.[87] The great irony of the Italian policy, then, is that other States may be much more affected by this policy than Italy itself.[88]

The large number of applications abroad has led to 'an administrative paralysis' at many Italian consulates in Argentina and Brazil; applicants need to wait at least two years for the completion of their procedure. As a result, an increasing number of people decide to take another route that is open to them: they take up residence in Italy and address the municipality where they reside with their request.[89] This development has had a negative impact on Italian

---

See Tintori, *Fardelli d'Italia? Conseguenze nazionali e transnazionali delle politiche di cittadinanza italiane*, 10.

83 Gallo and Tintori, "Come si diventa cittadini italiani. Un approfondimento statistico", 128.

84 Ibid., 115.

85 Ibid., 133.

86 Tintori, *Fardelli d'Italia? Conseguenze nazionali e transnazionali delle politiche di cittadinanza italiane*, 60.

87 Ibid., 12–13. Although many Latin Americans legally enter the US with their Italian passport, a very large number decide to remain there as illegal residents. As a result, the US has become suspicious of Italians from Latin America, which can obviously have negative effects for 'true' Italians born in Latin America to temporary Italian migrants. This example shows how the Italian nationality policy for co-ethnics in Latin America can have seriously negative effects on 'true' Italians (temporarily) living abroad.

88 Ibid., 84. Of those who have their Italian nationality recognized only 5–10 percent move to Italy. The majority remains in the country of origin (55–60 percent) and merely uses the Italian passport as a 'life insurance'. However, 30–40 percent use their Italian passport to move to another country than Italy.

89 Gallo and Tintori, "Come si diventa cittadini italiani. Un approfondimento statistico", 131–132.

municipalities as well as immigrants of Italian descent themselves. The many applications had the same paralyzing effect on the administration of Italian municipalities as it had on Italian consulates abroad. The application procedure can also have dramatic effects on immigrants who—sometimes lured to Italy upon payment of considerable sums of money by intermediaries who are silent about the cumbersome procedure—enter Italy as foreigners and cannot work during the time in which their request for Italian nationality is assessed. What is more, they will often have resided illegally in Italy before being recognized as Italians because their tourist visa will most probably have expired while waiting for the decision by the Italian authorities.[90]

6.2. *Laws 379/2000*[91] *and 124/2006*[92]

The reacquisition regime under Article 17 of law 91/1992 was copied in law 379/2000, the latter seemingly being aimed at Italian majorities that lived in parts of the former 19th century Austro-Hungarian Empire. Persons born and formerly resident in territories which belonged to the Austro-Hungarian Empire before 16 July 1920 are granted the right to acquire Italian nationality under law 379/2000. The law also applies to their descendants. Initially, the application deadline was set at five years after the entry into force of the law (20 December 2000), but this was extended by decree no. 273/2005 with another five years until 20 December 2010.[93] The territories to which the law refers comprise territories that are now part of Italy or territories which belonged to Italy but became part of Yugoslavia after the Second World War. The persons eligible under this law can live anywhere in the world (it thus also applies to Italian overseas emigrants), apart from Austria.[94]

Law 124/2006 is similar to law 379/2000 in that it allows for the (re)acquisition of Italian nationality to former Italian nationals who were resident in territories that formerly belonged to Italy but that became part of Yugoslavia after the Second World War. The territories involved—Istria, Fiume and

[90] Tintori, *Fardelli d'Italia? Conseguenze nazionali e transnazionali delle politiche di cittadinanza italiane*, 57.

[91] Available from http://www.parlamento.it/parlam/leggi/00379l.htm. A short English commentary is available from http://www.trentininelmondo.it/cittadinanza/chi_ne_ha_diritto_en.asp, the site of 'Trentini Nel Mondo' (Natives of Trento in the world).

[92] Available from http://www.parlamento.it/parlam/leggi/06124l.htm.

[93] http://www.trentininelmondo.it/cittadinanza/documenti/Liv_3_d_l_273_2005.pdf.

[94] Zincone, "Due pesi e due misure: pronipoti d'Italia e nuovi immigrati", 8. This can be explained, according to Zincone, by the presumption that if the person is resident in Austria, he or she is of Austrian origin.

Dalmazia—are now part of Croatia. There are also differences with law 379/2000, however. First, law 124/2006 contains no deadline for application. Second, in order to be eligible one needs to have been Italian and resident in these territories at the time when they were ceded to the former Yugoslav Republic by the 1947 Paris Peace Treaty and the 1975 Osimo Treaty. Another difference is that descendants of former Italian nationals—although eligible to Italian nationality under this law—must comply with language and cultural requirements. This law thus displays, according to Nascimbene, a move from an objective to a subjective understanding of 'Italianness'. In other words, whilst an objective, ethnic conception prevailed in the past to be eligible for Italian nationality, law 124/2006 stresses a subjective, sentimental aspect by requiring cultural and linguistic knowledge.[95]

6.3. *Law 459/2001: Voting Rights for Italians Resident Abroad*[96]

By now it should be sufficiently clear that the unlimited transmission of nationality to generations of Italians living abroad is a typical feature of Italian law. The bond between Italy and its emigrants thus persists indefinitely. Until recently, however, 'the unlimited persistence of the bond of national identity across the generations had rather limited consequences, at least until eventual return to Italy'.[97] This has changed with the entry into force of law 459/2001 on 6 January 2002, which turned a mere hereditary nationality into a real political tie with Italy. The parliament accepted the Bill with a lot of rhetoric, emphasizing the wide consent among both the majority and the opposition that this Bill would be of great historical significance in fulfilling the citizenship rights of Italians living abroad.[98]

Italians resident abroad—who are represented by six senators and 12 MPs—are divided into four different foreign constituencies (Article 6 of law 459/2001):

95 Nascimbene, "Proposte a favore dell'acquisto o riacquisto della cittadinanza italiana da parte di connazionali residenti in Slovenia e Croazia": 375.

96 Available from http://www.parlamento.it/leggi/01459l.htm. For practical and constitutional objections to this law, see Enrico Grosso, "Riflessioni a prima lettura sulla nuova legge in materia di voto dei cittadini all'estero"; available from www.forumcostituzionale.it/site/index3.php?option=content&task..; Enrico Grosso, "Il voto all'estero: tra difficoltà applicative e dubbi di costituzionalità", *Quaderni Costituzionali* 22, no. 2 (2002).

97 Pastore, "Immigration in Italy today. A community out of balance: nationality law and migration politics in the history of post-unification Italy": 35.

98 Grosso, *Riflessioni a prima lettura sulla nuova legge in materia di voto dei cittadini all'estero.*

1) Europe (including Russia and Turkey);
2) South America;
3) North and Central America;
4) Africa, Asia, Oceania and Antarctica.

Quantitatively, the number of senators and MPs seems rather negligible.[99] Each constituency is represented by one senator and one MP, while the other senators and MPs are distributed among the constituencies on the basis of the number of Italians resident there. Grosso argues that this is a ludicrous division.[100] Why should the interests of the Italian community in Africa be better represented by a senator from Australia (which he claims will always be the case since the Italian population in Australia is so much larger than that in Africa, Asia or Antarctica) than by an ordinary Italian senator? Grosso predicts that the system will benefit particular territories with many Italians; they will monopolize the representation of Italians abroad at the expense of territories with a less densely Italian population. Consequently, he fears that the law will not serve the cause of representing the interests of Italians around the world, but only that of clearly defined territories.[101]

7. *Attempts to Reform Italian Nationality Law to the Benefit of Non-Privileged Immigrants*

It was said in the previous section that the co-ethic strand of thinking has prevailed over the last decades and that little was achieved that benefited

[99] Article 56 of the Constitution: 'The Chamber of Deputies is elected by direct and universal suffrage. The number of Deputies is six hundred and thirty, twelve of which are elected in the Overseas Constituency. All voters who have attained the age of twenty-five on the day of elections are eligible to be Deputies. The division of seats among the electoral districts, with the exception of the number of seats assigned to the Overseas Constituency, is obtained by dividing the number of inhabitants of the Republic, as shown by the latest general census of the population, by six hundred eighteen and distributing the seats in proportion to the population in every electoral district, on the basis of whole shares and the highest remainders'.

Article 57 of the Constitution: 'The Senate of the Republic is elected on a regional basis, with the exception of the seats assigned to the Overseas Constituency. The number of Senators to be elected is three hundred and fifteen, six of which are elected in the Overseas Constituency. No Region may have fewer than seven Senators; Molise shall two, Valle d'Aosta one. The division of seats among the Regions, with the exception of the number of seats assigned to the Overseas Constituency, in accordance with the provisions of the preceding Article, is made in proportion to the population of the Regions as revealed in the most recent general census, on the basis of whole shares and the highest remainders'.

[100] Grosso, *Riflessioni a prima lettura sulla nuova legge in materia di voto dei cittadini all'estero.*

[101] Grosso, "Il voto all'estero: tra difficoltà applicative e dubbi di costituzionalità": 348.

immigrants of non-Italian descent. On the contrary, the conditions imposed on this group have simply become more stringent. However, there have been proposals (in particular by the centre-left parties) to reduce the discrimination in respect of immigrants who do not fall within one of the privileged categories of Italian nationality law. A 1999 proposal by Livia Turco, Minister of Social Affairs, was particularly favourable to minors by providing, *inter alia*, that a child born in Italy to immigrant parents who were legally resident could acquire Italian nationality from the age of five; the proposal also contained the introduction of double *ius soli*. Furthermore, the rigorous naturalization requirements—legal and uninterrupted residence until reaching the age of eighteen—were to be abolished.[102]

A number of factors doomed these proposals to fail.[103] First, the two most powerful lobby groups in the migration field—catholic organizations and employers' associations—were not primarily interested in granting nationality to immigrants. The main focus of most catholic organizations was on legalizing immigrants and providing them with the most basic rights. The acquisition of nationality was considered a 'luxury' and not a basic need, and thus took second place.[104] The employers' associations, on the other hand, were confronted with Italy's aging population as well as a need for manpower and thus advocated an increase of legal migration.

This position contrasted with public opinion, which wanted to put a stop to immigration but which was at the same time prepared to improve the position of (undocumented) immigrants already present in Italy by granting them nationality and citizenship rights. It is against this backdrop that the government had recourse to what Zincone has called 'false substitutes': immigration is demanded by the market and can therefore not be stopped, yet at the same time public opinion turned sharply against further immigration. To please public opinion, it was therefore decided to limit the rights of immigrants.

Again in 2006 a centre-left government adopted a draft Bill which focused on immigrants and which contained a number of favourable provisions[105]: a reduction of the required period of residence from ten to five years before

---

102 Zincone, "Il perché del presente e gli auspici per il futuro che potrebbe essere migliore", 147.

103 Arena, Nascimbene, and Zincone, "Italy", 349–351.

104 For the immigration problematic in Italy, see Giovanna Zincone, "Illegality, Enlightenment and Ambiguity: A Hot Italian Recipe", *South European Society and Politics* 3, no. 3 (1998): 45–82.

105 This Bill was drafted by the Minister of Interior, Giuliano Amato, and is therefore also called the Amato reform. The text of the proposal, which was accepted by the government in August 2006, is available from http://www.governo.it/Governo/Provvedimenti/dettaglio.asp?d=28863.

a naturalization application could be lodged; moreover, children born in Italy to foreign parents could obtain Italian nationality if at least one of the parents had been legally resident in Italy for five years without interruption. On the other hand, the proposal also included elements that had already been introduced elsewhere in Europe, such as more stress on language requirements and measures against marriages of convenience.[106]

What is interesting about the Italian case is that, unlike many other countries, the nationality and migration policies do not fundamentally differ depending on whether the political right or left is in power.[107] One can say, on the one hand, that the Italian left and right rhetorically follow the traditional distinction as articulated by Joppke:

> The political left, true to its universalist vocation, generally supports de-ethnicized citizenship rules, which lower the threshold of citizenship acquisition for immigrants. By contrast, the political right, more on the side of "being" then of "becoming", generally supports re-ethnicized citizenship rules, strengthening the ties with members abroad even across foreign-born generations.[108]

Yet the Italian case also proves, on the other hand, the general left-right consensus in traditional emigration countries on a favourable policy towards co-ethnics abroad. Law 379/2000, for example, came into being under a centre-left government.[109]

---

[106] Measures against marriages of conveniences were indeed taken in the Security Act of 15 July 2009. See *supra* Section 1.

[107] Weil argues that this can be explained as follows: 'When the dominant feeling, under the effect of uncertain borders, territorial disputes, or a tradition or continuing practice of emigration, is that an important part of the constitutive population lives beyond the country's borders, the adoption of measures for the legal inclusion of children or even grandchildren of immigrants is politically very difficult'. Weil, *How to Be French: Nationality in the Making since 1789*, 192.

[108] Joppke, "Citizenship between De- and Re-ethnicization (1)": 432. Significantly in this connection, Gianfranco Fini—a prominent member of the former right wing *Alleanza Nazionale*, which merged with Berlusconi's *Forza Italia* into *Popolo della Libertà* (PdL) or People of Liberty Party in March 2009, and which generally favours an 'ethnicization' of nationality law—is seemingly beginning to have doubts about the co-ethnic elements in Italian nationality. During his travels to Latin America as Minister of Foreign Affairs, his own experience with people of Italian descent opened his eyes. These people often did not speak a word of Italian and admitted to apply for Italian nationality mainly to be able to move to the United States or other European countries than Italy. Fini must thus be aware of the fact that the effects of Italian law may have a deeper impact on other countries than on Italy itself. See Gallo and Tintori, "Come si diventa cittadini italiani. Un approfondimento statistico", 135.

[109] Christian Joppke, "Comparative Citizenship: A Restrictive Turn in Europe?", *Law & Ethics of Human Rights* 2, no. 1 (2008): 37.

It is thus characteristic of Italy that the policy in the field of nationality and migration is one of continuity, regardless of the political constellation. Although it is true that only the political left has stood up for immigrants with concrete legislative proposals in 2000 and 2006, the above has shown that in the end it gave in to societal pressure. At the same time, the political right, traditionally more anti-immigrant, is also susceptible to the influence of lobby groups because it is partly composed of Catholics and free market entrepreneurs. Immigration flows therefore do not necessarily diminish under right wing governments and favourable co-ethnic laws are not only passed when a centre-right government is in power (law 124/2006), but under centre-left governments as well (law 379/2000).

8. *Concluding Remarks*

The discussion above has shown that the legislator's attention in matters of nationality has been narrowly focused on the acquisition of Italian nationality by co-ethnics. Attempts to reform the law for the benefit of non-privileged immigrants have failed to yield concrete results. At the time of writing, the fourth Berlusconi government (elected in April 2008) does not seem interested in reforming nationality law, and certainly not for the benefit of long-term residents and their children.[110]

The literature generally speaks out against the one-sided developments in Italian nationality law since 1992. The consequences of the marked contrast between, on the one hand, the facilitated acquisition of Italian nationality by people who have no link with Italy other than being the descendant of an Italian emigrant, and the lack of appropriate rules to include long term residents on the other, are evident: children born in Italy to foreign parents and integrated in Italian society are worse off when it comes to the acquisition of Italian nationality than descendants of Italian emigrants who have no clear

[110] Zincone and Basili, "Report on Italy", 2. It should be admitted, however, that nationality reform was put on the agenda again in May 2009 by Gianfranco Fini of Berlusconi's PdL, resulting in a bipartisan Bill with the Democratic Party (the Sarubbi-Granata Bill) which *inter alia* tried to reduce the residence requirement for naturalization, to strengthen *ius soli*, and to facilitate the acquisition of nationality by minors born and/or educated in Italy. This Bill was drastically amended, however, by the Constitutional Committee of the Chamber of Deputies following proposals by Bertolini, an MP of the PdL; curiously, the amended text is even more restrictive than the present nationality law, since the language and integration measures are kept while the innovative features (*ius soli*, shorter residence requirements) are abandoned. See EUDO Citizenship news of 23 October 2009 and 5 January 2010 (http://eudo-citizenship.eu/).

link with Italy. What is more, the latter group often applies for Italian nationality for instrumental reasons[111]—such as the contingent European citizenship. In the General Conclusions we explain the particularly worrying aspect of this policy from a European perspective. The co-ethnic preference is, however, likely to be sustained in the near future, taking into account legislative developments such as laws 379/2000 and 124/2006. Furthermore, the special representatives for Italians abroad may reinforce the further 'ethnicization' of a law which is already predisposed to favouring those who are considered to belong to the 'Italian family'.

[111] This is also recognized by Italian consulates. See Tintori, *Fardelli d'Italia? Conseguenze nazionali e transnazionali delle politiche di cittadinanza italiane*, 82.

Chapter 6

Spain

1. *Introduction*

This chapter is dedicated to the quite particular attitude towards dual nationality in Spain. Although Spain may be characterized as a country which is at least in principle opposed to dual nationality,[1] it has been more than willing to accept dual nationality with countries to which it feels closely connected, in particular the countries in Latin America. To that end, dual nationality treaties were concluded between Spain and Latin American countries in the 1950s and 1960s, creating the possibility of acquiring a dual nationality. Yet under this system, the two nationalities could never be active at the same time: the nationality of the country where the dual national was permanently resident was active, while the other was a so-called 'dormant' or 'hibernating' nationality.

In addition to the dual nationality treaties—dubbed the 'conventional route' or *vía convencional*—subsequent modifications to Spanish nationality legislation allowed another route for obtaining dual nationality. This way of acquiring dual nationality—known as the 'legal route' or *vía legal*—is different from the conventional route in that it allows both nationalities to be active at the same time. The legal intricacies of both the conventional and the legal route will be discussed at considerable length in this chapter.

For the greater part of the 20th century, Spain was an emigrant sending country—in particular to Latin America. Like many other European countries, however, Spain has become a net recipient of immigrants.[2]

---

[1] Acquisition of Spanish nationality is in theory only possible after renunciation of the original nationality. It was already mentioned, however, that the renunciation requirement has not been enforced since 1971 (see Chapter 1, Section 6). As a result, upon naturalization in Spain one can keep the other passport with the possibility of renewal. Spain does also not inform the country of origin of the naturalization of one of its nationals in Spain. If the country of origin provides for the automatic loss of nationality for nationals who naturalize abroad, the Spanish practice thus has the effect that this provision is not activated.

[2] For a detailed discussion of migration issues in Spain see Carrera, *In Search of the Perfect Citizen? The Intersection between Integration, Immigration and Nationality in the EU*, chapter 5.

Nevertheless, this transition from an emigration country to an immigration country—the turning point being the mid-1980s—is not reflected in Spanish nationality law today. The provisions on nationality law were modified on several occasions since the 1980s, but this was predominantly done to firm up the bonds with countries with which Spain is historically and culturally connected.

Another prominent feature of Spanish nationality law concerns the provisions dealing with the facilitated (re)acquisition of Spanish nationality for Spanish emigrants and their descendants. This attitude is often referred to as a 're-ethnicization' of nationality law in the sense that the descendants of expatriates are given preferential treatment with respect to the acquisition of nationality.[3] These modifications were made in order to fulfil the clearly worded constitutional mandate which requires that 'the State shall protect the social and economic rights of Spanish workers abroad, and enact a policy to facilitate their return' (Article 42 Spanish Constitution, hereafter abbreviated as CE).

Spanish law has adopted a very inclusive attitude to Latin Americans and some other groups, as well as to Spanish emigrants and their descendants. This attitude contrasts with the exclusive approach towards immigrants who do not belong to these categories, for whom a residence period of ten years, as well as a (theoretical) renunciation of the original nationality upon naturalization, is required. As a result, Spain is invariably listed in country reports among the European countries with a restrictive nationality law.

The dual nationality treaties are a prominent feature of Spanish nationality law, but Italy also concluded such a treaty with a Latin American country, namely Argentina. As it is commonly acknowledged that this treaty of 1973 was inspired by the Spanish-Argentinean treaty, it makes sense to discuss the Italian-Argentinean treaty in this chapter (see Section 8). On that occasion, we shall also pay attention to treaties concluded between Portugal and some of its former colonies. These treaties do not address the issue of dual nationality, however, but accord far-reaching citizenship rights to the nationals of the contracting parties.

Finally, we also address in more detail the important *Micheletti* decision of the European Court of Justice, which deals with nationality law in general and the issue of dual nationality in particular (Section 9). The *Micheletti* judgment is discussed here, and not in Chapter 2 where we discussed ECJ case law on dual nationality, because of the facts: Mr Micheletti was an Italian-Argentinean national who wished to establish himself in Spain as a dentist. As the case

[3] Joppke, "Comparative Citizenship: A Restrictive Turn in Europe?": 2.

illustrates the attitude towards dual nationality in Spain and Italy, it forms an intrinsic part of this chapter.

2. *The Spanish Phenomenon of Dual Nationality*

According to Fernández Rozas, dual nationality can be approached in two ways.[4] In the first place, it can be seen as an anomaly that results from the lack of coordination between two States who simultaneously consider a person to be their subject. A typical example of this situation is the possession of dual nationality owing to the application of both the principle of *ius sanguinis* and *ius soli*. Children of parents whose country applies the *ius sanguinis* principle will acquire a dual nationality when they are born in a country which grants nationality by birth on its territory. Other examples can of course be given, but these situations have in common that dual nationality is created unintentionally; it is the lack of coordination between two or more legal systems that is creating dual nationality.

It has also been seen throughout this study that dual nationality has become more frequent in Western Europe ever since the unitary system was replaced by a dualistic system, thus allowing women to retain their original nationality upon marrying a foreigner. Spanish nationality law was modified in 1982 in order to comply with the constitutional prohibition of discrimination on the grounds of sex (Article 14 CE). Moreover, Article 17.1 of the Civil Code (hereafter CC) abolished discrimination against women in respect of nationality by allowing Spanish women to transmit their nationality to their children.[5] Although gender equality in nationality law is an important cause for dual nationality, we will not elaborate on that topic in this chapter because it has been a common feature in Western Europe since the 1980s.[6] Instead, we will focus on aspects that are truly characteristic of the Spanish approach to dual nationality.

Although multiple nationality is frequently seen as an anomaly, it can also be a goal to be pursued. Seen in this light, States can expressly recognize and support this phenomenon. Particular bonds can exist between States, justifying the possession of dual nationality of each other's nationals; dual

---

[4] José Carlos Fernández Rozas, *Derecho español de la nacionalidad* (Madrid: Editorial Tecnos, 1987), 235–238. See also Mariano Aguilar Benítez de Lugo, "Doble nacionalidad", *Boletín de la Facultad de Derecho* 10–11 (1996): 220–221.

[5] Ruth Rubio Marín, "Spain", in *Acquisition and Loss of Nationality, Policies and Trends in 15 European Countries*, ed. Rainer Bauböck, *et al.* (Amsterdam: Amsterdam University Press, 2006), 488.

[6] See Chapter 1, Section 6.

nationality can also be a means to protect nationals living abroad. These considerations led Spain to conclude treaties on dual nationality with a number of Latin American countries from the 1950s onwards. Article 1 of these treaties provides that Spaniards can acquire the nationality of the Latin American country concerned without losing Spanish nationality. Conversely, Latin Americans can obtain Spanish nationality without losing their original nationality.

The first dual nationality treaty, concluded between Spain and Chile, entered into force on 28 October 1958. Other treaties were subsequently concluded with the following Latin American countries (the date indicates when the treaty was ratified by Spain)[7]: Peru (15 December 1959), Paraguay (15 December 1959), Guatemala (25 January 1962), Nicaragua (25 January 1962), Bolivia (25 January 1962), Ecuador (22 December 1964), Costa Rica (21 January 1965), Honduras (23 February 1967), the Dominican Republic (16 December 1968) and Argentina (2 February 1970). A final treaty, concluded between Spain and Colombia, was ratified on 7 May 1980.

Dual nationality has for a long time played a leading role in Spanish law.[8] The idea of dual nationality could already be found in Article 24 of the Spanish Republican Constitution of 1931, which distinguished two types of dual nationality.[9] In the first place, nationals from Portugal and Latin American countries could, on condition of reciprocity, acquire Spanish nationality when residing in Spain without losing their original nationality. Second, the provision allowed Spaniards to naturalize in these countries without having to renounce their Spanish nationality, but only if this was not prohibited under the laws of those countries. Under this regime, called the *doble nacionalidad automática*, there was no reciprocity requirement.[10] The Republican

7 Juan Aznar Sanchez, *La doble nacionalidad (doctrina, convenios, legislación, jurisprudencia)* (Madrid: Marcial Pons, 1977), 28–29. The text of the dual nationality treaties is available from http://www.lanacionalidadespanola.com/Convenios-de-Doble-nacionalidad-firmados-por-Espana/32.

8 Aurelia Alvarez Rodríguez, "Binacionalidad en el ordenamiento español y su repercusión en la Union Europea", in *Estudios de derecho europeo privado*, ed. Juan María Díaz Fraile and Registrales Centro de Estudios (Madrid: J. San José, 1994), 109.

9 Article 24 of the 1931 Constitution reads: 'A base de una reciprocidad internacional efectiva y mediante los requisitos y trámites que fijará una ley, se concederá ciudadanía a los naturales de Portugal y países hispánicos de América, comprendido el Brasil, cuando así lo soliciten y residan en territorio español, sin que pierdan ni modifiquen su ciudadanía de origen. En estos mismos países, si sus leyes no lo prohíben, aun cuando no reconozcan el derecho de reciprocidad, podrán naturalizarse los espanoles sin perder su nacionalidad de origen'.

10 José Pérez de Vargas Muñoz, "Cuestiones de doble nacionalidad", *Revista de Derecho Privado* 12 (2002): 889–910.

Constitution was not granted long life and Article 24 was never implemented,[11] yet the ideas from the Republican Constitution on dual nationality were adopted by the Franco government,[12] thereby laying the foundation for the dual nationality treaties.[13]

3. *The Background of the Treaties on Dual Nationality*

In 1954 a modification of the Spanish Civil Code made it possible to conclude dual nationality treaties.[14] Article 22 stated that, if expressly agreed on by a treaty, the acquisition of the nationality of a Latin American country or the Philippines would not produce the loss of Spanish nationality. The reverse was true when a national of a Latin American country or the Philippines acquired Spanish nationality.[15]

Three reasons underlie the decision to draft treaties on dual nationality in the 1950s and 60s. In the first place, the still very strong historical and cultural ties between Spain and Latin America.[16] Especially during the first years of the Franco dictatorship, the cultural policy was very much determined by the shared Spanish-Latin American history.[17] In 1947 the *Instituto de Cultura*

---

[11] Virgós Soriano, "Nationality and Double Nationality Principles in Spanish Private International Law System", 239.

[12] The idea appealed to Franco because it would in a sense re-establish the former Spanish empire. In fact, the period 1833–1931, during which Spain lost many of its colonial territories, was in Franco's view to be erased from Spanish history. See Juan Pablo Fusi, *Franco. Autoritarismo y poder personal* (Madrid: Grupo Santillana de Ediciones, 2001), 41.

[13] Fernández Rozas, *Derecho español de la nacionalidad*, 240.

[14] The preambule to this law of 1954 contains the following paragraph: 'Y como tributo a la honda realidad social derivada de la peculiar condición de la persona por pertenecer a la comunidad de los pueblos iberoamericanos y filipino, y en fortalecimiento de sus vinculos, se sienta excepcionalmente el principio de la doble nacionalidad, en base al cual preceptúase que la adquisición de la nacionalidad de países integrantes de dicha comunidad no producirá pérdida de la nacionalidad española, *cuando así se haya convenido expresamente*' (emphasis added). See for the preamble's text María Teresa Echezarreta Ferrer, ed., *Legislacíon sobre nacionalidad*, 4th ed. (Madrid: Tecnos, 2003), 102–103.

[15] Article 22 of the 1954 Civil Code: 'No obstante lo dispuesto en el párrafo primero, la adquisición de la nacionalidad de un país iberoamericano o de Filipinas no producirá la perdida de la nacionalidad española cuando así se haya convenido expresamente con el Estado cuyo nacionalidad se adquiere. Correlativamente y siempre que mediase convenio que de modo expreso así lo establezca, la adquisición de la nacionalidad española no implicará la pérdida de la de origen, cuando esta última fuera de la de un país iberoamericana o de Filipinas'.

[16] Elisa Pérez Vera, "El sistema español de doble nacionalidad", in *Emigración y Constitución*, ed. José Ignacio Cases Méndez (Madrid: Instituto Español de Emigración, 1983), 73–74.

[17] Joppke rightly points to a distinction between Spain and other former colonial powers. Francoist Spain, a pariah in a democratic postwar Western Europe, was looking for

Hispánica was established with the objective of preserving the spiritual bond between the people composing the cultural Ibero-American community.[18] From this perspective, the dual nationality treaties were an expression of the idea of *Hispanidad.*[19]

A second reason was the emigration of many Spaniards to Latin America. Spain was a very poor country after the Second World War and emigration was seen as a way to escape poverty. There had always been Spanish migration to Latin America, the total number of Spanish emigrants to Latin America being estimated at almost 3,3 million in the period 1880–1930.[20] The 19th century in general was a period of massive emigration: 50 million Europeans emigrated between 1815 and 1930.[21]

It is subject to debate whether this emigration was caused primarily due to internal circumstances in Spain, or whether the external attraction of Latin America was decisive (the so-called push-pull model); it is questionable though whether it is worth drawing a sharp distinction between push and pull factors, as the internal and external motives seem to be intertwined.[22] Sánchez Alonso nevertheless concludes that Spanish emigrants did not randomly pick a Latin American country as their place of destination. The fact that the overwhelming majority went to Argentina, Cuba, Brazil and Uruguay (the countries are put in order of popularity) shows that the emigrants' choice was influenced by what they knew of the particular situation in each of these

an alternative sphere of influence. This led to 'the rebuilding of postcolonial ties that had been ruptured more than half a century ago', which is 'rather different from the standard postcolonial *problématique* of regulating the transition from empire to nation-state'. Joppke, *Selecting by Origin: Ethnic Migration in the Liberal State*, 112–113.

18 Valentina Fernández Vargas, "Últimas oleadas y cierre del proceso", in *Historia General de la Emigración Española a Iberoamérica* (Madrid: Historia 16, 1992), 616.

19 In his classic study of the Spanish-Argentinean treaty, Boggiano defines the 'hispánico' in a somewhat bombastic manner and emphasizes the shared values rather than a common descent: 'El ser hispánico … aspira a su *despliegue en lo universal*, por *el habla castellana*, la *fe católica* y un singular *temple ético en el vivir y sostener las proprias convicciones* … Los *hispánicos* son los empeñados en una empresa futura y común inspirada en la cultura hispánica con vocación universal y perenne. No son los vinculados tan solo por lazos de sangre a los españoles y americanos. Hay hispánicos descendientes de italianos, alemanes, eslavos o sajones' (emphasis in original). Antonio Boggiano, *La doble nacionalidad en derecho internacional privado* (Buenos Aires: Ediciones Depalma, 1973), 35–37.

20 Consuelo Naranjo, "El aluvión, 1880–1930", in *Historia General de la Emigración Española a Ibéroamerica* (Madrid: Historia 16, 1992), 178–186.

21 Blanca Sánchez Alonso, *Los Determinantes de la Emigración Española, 1880–1930*, Dissertation History Department (Florence: European University Institute, 1993), 1.

22 Ibid., 227.

countries.[23] In short, the decision to emigrate as well as the intensity of the emigration was determined by internal factors; the conditions in the receiving countries were responsible for the choice of destination and the strong fluctuations in migration waves.[24]

The emigration to Latin America—and the problems posed by this development—inspired the Argentinean Juan Carlos Garay to propose a distinction between nationality and citizenship.[25] In his view, nationality was a natural fact expressing a person's sociological belonging (culture, traditions etc.) to a particular country. A nationality existed independently of person's will and could not be changed; Garay was also expressly opposed to dual nationality. His proposal did not allow a change of *nationality*, but he suggested instead that one could acquire a different *citizenship*, namely by meeting requirements related to residence and work in another country.[26] Citizenship would entail political rights such as suffrage. The separation of the concepts of nationality and citizenship was devised to meet the problems of European migration to Argentina: immigrants could maintain their nationality of origin but still participate politically and economically as citizens in Argentinean life.[27] The Italian-Argentinean treaty, although allowing dual nationality, to a certain extent follows this reasoning. It stipulates that the nationality where the dual national is not domiciled is a 'dormant' nationality, meaning that the dual national cannot exercise public and private law rights in that country. He thus has two citizenships of a different value (*cittadinanze disuguali*). The distinction between an active and a dormant nationality was abolished by an additional protocol to the treaty that was signed in 2005 (see *infra* Section 8).[28]

---

[23] Ibid.

[24] Ibid., 237.

[25] Mario J.A. Oyarzábal, "Il Protocollo aggiuntivo che modifica l'Accordo italo-argentino sulla cittadinanza", *Rivista di diritto internazionale* 90, no. 3 (2007): 755.

[26] de Castro y Bravo, "Nationalité, double et supra-nationalité", 613–614.

[27] See also Buzzati, who argued that although Italian emigrants had become strongly linked to their new country of residence from an economic perspective, this had not weakened in any way their 'italianità'. Buzzati, "Questioni sulla cittadinanza degli italiani emigrati in America": 457–458.

[28] Article 3 of the additional protocol: 'Le persone che si sono avvalse o si avarranno dell'Accordo potranno esercitare i diritti politici attribuiti dai rispettivi ordinamenti ai propri residenti all'estero. Le persone che, in base ai rispettivi ordinamenti siano considerate come argentini ed italiani, non potranno ricoprire allo stesso tempo incarichi pubblici e/o elettivi nel territorio di entrambe le Parti. Nel caso che i rispettivi ordinamenti siano incompatibili, si applicherà la normativa del luogo di residenza'. On the Italian-Argentinean treaty and the additional protocol, see Oyarzábal, "Il Protocollo aggiuntivo che modifica l'Accordo italo-argentino sulla cittadinanza": 749–758.

Garay's theory has been criticized for proposing the impossible: no country could grant foreigners full political rights since this would allow them, for example, to have a say in the specific moral values of a people, or to exercise the highest public functions.[29] Instead of citizenship, De Yanguas therefore proposed to grant foreigners what he calls 'citadinage' (*vecindad* in Spanish). 'Citadinage' would include local voting rights and equality in matters of civil law.[30] De Yanguas argued that his proposal, under which important rights are decoupled from nationality, also solved the problem of 'forced naturalization', which refers to the emigrant's almost 'compulsory' acquisition of a foreign nationality for economic reasons.[31]

The Spanish emigration after the Second World War would reach its peak in the 1950s and 1960s. This is illustrated by migration statistics provided by Fernández Vargas.[32] The number of Spanish republican refugees that fled to Latin America in the period 1939–1946 is estimated at around 30,000. Some additional 25,000 Spaniards emigrated to Latin American for economic reasons, of which almost 15,000 returned to Spain in the end.[33] The Latin American countries were generally cautious and reticent with respect to the admittance of Spanish immigrants; the ideological ideas of the political refugees were unwanted and the labour market was to be protected against new workers who would compete with the national population.[34]

The years 1947 and 1948 show a considerable increase in the number of Spanish emigrants, but the massive wave of Spanish emigration starts in 1949 and ends in 1958.[35] The yearly total of Spanish emigrants constantly fluctuates between 40,000 and 60,000 in this period. Spanish emigration thus increased enormously compared to the years 1939–1946. Moreover, the number of Spaniards returning to Spain was much lower: 23 out of every 100 compared to 55 of every 100 in the period 1939–1946. The family reunification with Spanish emigrants who remained in Latin American obviously reinforced the total number of emigrants. The most popular countries remained Argentina, Brazil and Uruguay, as well as newcomer Venezuela.

---

29 José de Yanguas Messía, "La double nationalité en Amerique", *Revue de droit international et de législation comparée* 57 (1925): 365.

30 Ibid., 366.

31 Ibid., 367.

32 Fernández Vargas, "Últimas oleadas y cierre del proceso", 579–614.

33 As clandestine emigration is not included in these statistics, the number of emigrants will be considerably higher in reality.

34 Fernández Vargas, "Últimas oleadas y cierre del proceso", 582.

35 Ibid., 584.

The period from 1959 onwards was characterized by emigration to other European countries. Between 1960 and 1965, little more than a 100,000 Spaniards migrated to the four Latin American countries mentioned above, but 400,000 migrated within Europe. The years from 1966 and 1975 show a spectacular decline of emigration to Latin America. This can partly be explained by the 1971 Spanish Emigration Law which focused on Europe rather than Latin America.[36] Only 55,000 Spaniards emigrated to Latin America out of a total emigrant population of 812,000. In the period 1976–1989 the number of Spaniards emigrating to Latin America had shrunk to only 20,000, in particular owing to the economic and political crises in most Latin American countries.

The decision to emigrate was facilitated by the existence of the dual nationality treaties: Spanish nationality was not lost upon acquisition of the nationality of a country with which a treaty on dual nationality had been concluded. This system was also advantageous for the emigrant's integration in his new country because he was not restrained from applying for the nationality of the country of emigration.[37]

The third and final reason for drafting dual nationality treaties was that Spain found itself in an internationally isolated position during Franco's dictatorship. To strengthen its position, and to establish economic growth, Spain sought to forge a tighter link with Latin America. In order to achieve this goal, Spain pursued an emigration policy, first to Latin America, and later to Western Europe.[38]

3.1. *The Content of the Treaties on Dual Nationality*

Let us now turn to the content of the dual nationality treaties. In spite of minor differences, they have two elements in common.[39] First of all, not all nationals of the contracting States have the possibility to acquire a dual nationality. The treaties read, sometimes with different wordings, that only those who are nationals by origin of one of the contracting parties are eligible for a dual

---

[36] Ibid., 589.

[37] Rafael Arroyo Montero, "Modificación de los convenios sobre doble nacionalidad como instrumentos de integración (los Protocolos adicionales concluidos entre España y Costa Rica de 23 de octubre de 1997 y entre España y Nicaragua de 12 de noviembre de 1997)", in *Actas de las XVIII Jornadas de la Asociación Española de Profesores de Derecho Internacional y Relaciones Internacionales*, 193.

[38] Rafael Calduch Cervera, "La Emigración a Iberoamérica y la Política Exterior Española (1898–1975)"; available from http://www.incipe.org/Espa%F1oles%20de%20ambas%20orillas.pdf.

[39] Pérez de Vargas Muñoz, "Cuestiones de doble nacionalidad": 889–910.

nationality.[40] Article 1 of the treaty concluded between Spain and Chile thus speaks of 'Spaniards born in Spain and Chileans born in Chile'. Article 1 of the Spanish-Argentinean treaty adopts a different wording and talks about 'Spaniards and Argentineans 'by origin' (*de origen*).[41] Second, all treaties provide those who lost their nationality of origin upon acquisition of another one with the possibility to rely on the treaty in order to still obtain a dual nationality.

It should be emphasized that the treaties do not facilitate the acquisition of another nationality (the Spanish-Guatemalan treaty was an exception, see *infra* Section 7). Article 1 of the treaties states that in order to acquire the nationality of either country, the conditions of the nationality legislation of the country concerned must be satisfied. The treaties themselves thus merely provide for the possibility to acquire a dual nationality and refer to national legislation for the exact requirements that have to be met in order to acquire another nationality.[42] Spanish nationality legislation does facilitate the acquisition of Spanish nationality for Latin Americans by virtue of Article 22 CC. This category can acquire Spanish nationality after two years of residence in Spain, instead of the normal period of ten years.

Article 3 of the treaties is an important provision which makes clear that a dual national can never be subject to two different legislations at the same time.[43] It provides that the legislation to be applied to the exercise of public and private law rights (in particular diplomatic protection, the conferral of passports and all political, social and labour rights) is that of the country where the dual national has his domicile. The other nationality is 'dormant' (often referred to in Spanish literature as *una nacionalidad*

---

[40] Aznar Sanchez, *La doble nacionalidad*, 32–33. See critically on the distinction between nationals by birth and nationals by naturalization Boggiano, *La doble nacionalidad en derecho internacional privado*, 51–52.

[41] Virgós Soriano points out that nationals of origin refers to persons who are nationals 'by birth'. Naturalized persons are thus excluded from the treaties. This is confirmed by Aguilar. See Virgós Soriano, "Nationality and Double Nationality Principles in Spanish Private International Law System", 241; Aguilar Benítez de Lugo, "Doble nacionalidad": 226–227.

[42] Arroyo Montero, "Modificación de los convenios sobre doble nacionalidad como instrumentos de integración", 194.

[43] Article 3 of the Spanish-Argentinean treaty: 'Para las personas a que se refieren los artículos anteriores, el ejercicio de los derechos públicos y privados y, en especial, la protección diplomática y el otorgamiento de pasaportes y todos los derechos políticos, civiles, sociales y laborales, se regirán por las leyes del país que otorga la nueva nacionalidad. Por la misma legislación se regulará el cumplimiento de las obligaciones militares, entendiéndose como cumplidas las satisfechas en el país de origen'.

durmiente/hibernada or *en estado de latencia*).[44] This latter nationality is activated when the person takes up residence in the country of the dormant nationality. Activation of one nationality automatically means that the other is turned into a hibernating one. Article 4 provides a solution to the situation in which a dual national moves to a third country.[45] In that case, the domicile for the purposes of the treaty is presumed to be the last place of domicile in one of the countries party to the treaty.

Finally, a brief word should be devoted to Spanish private international law. Article 9.9 CC decides which law should be applied to dual nationals when nationality is used as a connecting factor.[46] In case the dual nationality is acquired by way of the dual nationality treaties, Article 9.9 CC refers back to what the treaties provide. In the absence of international treaties or when they do not provide a solution, Article 9.9 CC considers as the effective nationality the one that coincides with the last habitual residence (we return to this article when discussing *Micheletti* in Section 9).

4. *The Spanish Constitution of 1978*

The 1978 Constitution is of the utmost importance for our examination of dual nationality in Spain. The reason is that Article 11.3 CE created, in addition to the *vía convencional* (referring to the acquisition of dual nationality under the dual nationality treaties), the *vía legal*.[47] Article 11.3 CE reads as follows (our translation):

---

[44] No discussion exists with respect to the *effects* of the hibernating nationality: it is not activated until domicile is established in the country of that nationality. Until then, the hibernating nationality does not entail any civil or political rights. Discussion exists, however, as to the exact *status* of the hibernating nationality. Espinar Vicente argues that the hibernating nationality has in fact disappeared because it does not produce any civil or political effects ('una nacionalidad hibernada que no surte effectos civiles ni políticos, más que hibernada hay que considerla desaparecida'). Others, like de Castro y Bravo, do not share this opinion, but merely see the hibernating nationality as the one that is not preponderant. See de Castro y Bravo, "Nationalité, double et supra-nationalité", 628; Espinar Vicente, *La nacionalidad y la extranjería en el sistema jurídico español*, 333–334.

[45] Article 4 of, for example, the Spanish-Argentinean treaty reads: 'En el caso de que una persona que goce de la doble nacionalidad traslade su residencia al territorio de un tercer Estado, se entenderá por domicilio, a los efectos de determinar la dependencia política y la legislación aplicable, el último que hubiera tenido en el territorio de una de las partes contratantes'.

[46] See also Chapter 2, Section 3.

[47] Elena Cano Bazaga, "La doble nacionalidad con los países iberoamericanos y la constitución de 1978"; available from http://www.us.es/cidc/mesas/estadoHumanos.htm; Aznar Sanchez, *La doble nacionalidad*, 45; Pérez Vera, "El sistema español de doble nacionalidad", 80–81.

> The State can conclude dual nationality treaties with Latin American countries or with countries that have had or will have a particular bond with Spain. In these countries, even if a reciprocal right is not granted to their own nationals, Spaniards will be able to naturalize without losing their original nationality.[48]

The first sentence refers to the dual nationality treaties that could be concluded. The second sentence has reference to the so-called 'automatic dual nationality'. This means that a Spaniard can acquire the nationality of a country with which Spain has a special bond without losing his Spanish nationality. In that case, the existence of a dual nationality treaty is not required, although the existence of such a treaty obviously indicates that a special bond with Spain exists.

Until the enactment of article 11.3 of the Constitution, Spanish legislation only accepted one type of dual nationality, namely the *doble nacionalidad convencional*. Article 11.3 CE was the first provision to allow dual nationality that was not regulated by a convention.[49] We have seen that the idea of an 'automatic dual nationality' was already part of Article 24 of the 1931 Constitution. However, Vargas Muñoz states that the 1978 Constitution creates more possibilities for Spaniards to acquire a dual nationality compared to the 1931 Constitution.[50] One of the conditions in Article 24 of the 1931 Constitution for obtaining a dual nationality—the fact that the legislation of the country of which the Spaniard acquired the nationality should not prohibit dual nationality—is waived by the 1978 Constitution. Under the present Constitution, a Spaniard maintains Spanish nationality irrespective of other States' approval. Spanish law thus considers that, independently of the laws of other countries, Spaniards can naturalize in the countries referred to in Article 11.3 CE without losing Spanish nationality.[51] Consequently, the special dual nationality

---

48 'El estado podrá concertar tratados de doble nacionalidad con los países iberoamericanos o con aquellos que hayan tenido o tengan una particular vinculación con España. En estos mismos países, aun cuando no reconozcan a sus ciudadanos un derecho recíproco, podrán naturalizarse los españoles sin perder su nacionalidad de origen'.

49 Aguilar Benítez de Lugo, "Doble nacionalidad": 233–234. Aguilar's statement that the 'doble nacionalidad convencional' and the 'doble nacionalidad automática' belong to one and the same category, i.e. 'doble nacionalidad como sistema', is representative for the Spanish legal doctrine. All the remaining instances of dual nationality are qualified by the doctrine as 'doble nacionalidad anómala/patológica'. See also Palao Moreno, Esplugues Mota, and De Lorenzo Segrelles, *Nacionalidad y Extranjería*, 72.

50 Pérez de Vargas Muñoz, "Cuestiones de doble nacionalidad": 889–910.

51 One jurisdiction, in this case the Spanish one, can thus consider a particular individual to be a dual national, whereas the other State does not because it does not recognize the Spanish nationality. This situation is not unusual due to the wide discretion of States in regulating their nationality legislation. See Fernández Rozas, *Derecho español de la nacionalidad*, 243.

treaties with these countries—which made an exception to the general prohibition of dual nationality—were no longer necessary. This does not mean that the dual nationality treaties were abrogated by the constitutional provision. The treaties are still in force, and Article 11.3 CE even expressly refers to them.[52]

Unlike other countries, Spain does not have a separate Nationality Act but deals with the matter in the Civil Code.[53] After 1978 the articles dealing with nationality law (Articles 17–26 CC) have been amended on a number of occasions.[54] We shall discuss these amendments in Sections 10–13, but it should be mentioned here that shortly after the enactment of the 1978 Constitution the Civil Code was modified by law 51/1982 in order to bring the law into agreement with Article 11.3 CE. Article 23.4 of law 51/1982 provided that the acquisition of the nationality of a Latin American country, Andorra, the Philippines, Equatorial Guinea and Portugal did not produce loss of Spanish nationality.[55] Article 23 CC of law 18/1990 later granted the reverse right to nationals of these countries who acquired Spanish nationality: they were exempted from the general renunciation requirement.

Although Spain does not require renunciation of previous nationality upon acquisition of Spanish nationality with respect to the abovementioned group of countries, it will depend on the nationality law of these countries whether this nationality is in fact lost or not. With regard to the countries mentioned in Article 24.1 of the Spanish Civil Code Andorra, Guatemala, Honduras and Panama have a rule in force providing for the automatic loss of the original nationality upon acquisition of a foreign nationality.[56] In Bolivia, Brazil, Chile, Colombia, Cuba, El Salvador, the Philippines, Paraguay, Peru, Portugal and Venezuela, however, naturalization in another country does not automatically entail the loss of nationality. These countries do allow voluntary renunciation in such a case, something that is not possible under the laws of Argentina, Costa Rica, the Dominican Republic, Ecuador, Mexico, Nicaragua and Uruguay. These latter countries do not have a rule ordering the automatic loss of nationality upon naturalization, nor

52 Aguilar Benítez de Lugo, "Doble nacionalidad": 230.

53 Javier Carrascosa González, *Curso de Nacionalidad y Extranjería*, ed. Javier Carrascosa González, Antonia Durán Ayago, and Beatriz L. Carrillo Carrillo (Madrid: Colex, 2008), 43.

54 Amendments were made by laws 51/1982, 18/1990, 29/1995, 36/2002 and 52/2007.

55 'La adquisición de la nacionalidad de países iberoamericanos…, no es bastante para producir, conforme a este apartado, la pérdida de la nacionalidad española de origen'.

56 See the annex providing an overview of the consequences for the nationality of origin upon naturalization in the Netherlands in de Groot and Vink, *Meervoudige nationaliteit in Europees perspectief*, 166 ff.

do they allow the voluntary renunciation of their nationality by their nationals.[57]

5. *Differences Between the Conventional and the Legal Routes to Dual Nationality* (vía convencional/vía legal)

As from the enactment of the 1978 Constitution, there were two ways of acquiring dual nationality—the *vía convencional* and the *vía legal*. However, it makes a big difference which system is relied upon in order to obtain a dual nationality. Under the *vía convencional*, one of the nationalities is 'dormant', as the treaties do not allow both nationalities to be active at the same time. Under the *vía legal*, however, both nationalities are fully active.[58]

Those who had relied on the dual nationality treaties could only activate their latent nationality if they met the conditions laid down in the dual nationality treaty concerned. As mentioned before, domicile determined which of the nationalities was active. The domicile could be changed by taking up habitual residence in the country of the other contracting party.[59] A Chilean, for example, who also possessed a latent Spanish nationality would thus need to move his habitual place of residence to Spain in order to activate his Spanish nationality.[60] Only then he would be able to exercise his civil and political rights and obtain a Spanish passport. While living outside Spain, he was in theory a Spaniard, but was not entitled to a Spanish passport.[61] Those who had a latent Spanish nationality were as a consequence regarded as foreigners at the Spanish border when they wanted to enter Spain.[62] If they wanted to come to Spain as a tourist or establish themselves in Spain, they were subject to

57 We have divided the countries into groups based on the general rule in place. Exceptions to this rule are possible, however.

58 'Los [españoles] que utilizaron el sistema de la *doble nacionalidad automática* mantendrán en plenitud su nacionalidad española, que coexistirá con la del Estado de acogida'. Pérez de Vargas Muñoz, "Cuestiones de doble nacionalidad": 889–910.

59 Article 4 of the Chilean-Spanish treaty articulates the requirement as follows: 'Este domicilio puede cambiarse sólo en el caso de traslado de la residencia habitual al otro país contratante'.

60 Aznar explains that 'domicilio' is the place where a person establishes habitual residence with the intention of staying there permanently ('el domicilio es el lugar donde la persona establece su residencia habitual con ánimo de permanencia'). Aznar Sanchez, *La doble nacionalidad*, 34.

61 Aurelia Alvarez Rodríguez, "Principios inspiradores y objetivos de la nueva reforma del derecho español de la nacionalidad: Las principales novedades de la ley 36/2002 de 8 de octubre", *Revista de derecho migratorio y extranjería* 1 (2002): 24.

62 Cano Bazaga, *La doble nacionalidad con los países iberoamericanos y la constitución de 1978.*

Spanish migration law.[63] It also seems that under the dual nationality treaties Spaniards who possess a dual nationality and are resident in Latin America need a visa to enter Spain. Espinar Vicente points to the fact that only the treaty between Spain and Guatemala, by virtue of Article 8, exempts those who rely on the treaty from a visa obligation.[64] No such article is to be found in the other treaties.

Another category of Spaniards should also be mentioned, namely those who renounced Spanish nationality upon acquisition of another nationality. These former Spaniards do not possess Spanish nationality, not even a dormant one. Paradoxically, however, these former Spaniards can more easily reactivate Spanish nationality compared to those who had kept a latent Spanish nationality. This is because they are not bound by the requirements laid down in the dual nationality treaties, and are only required to meet the conditions in Article 26 CC.[65] This article does not require the return to Spain for the reacquisition of Spanish nationality.[66]

The legal regime sketched above led to a particularly strange situation: it was harder for a Spaniard to activate a latent Spanish nationality than it was for a former Spaniard who had voluntarily renounced Spanish nationality to reacquire it.[67] It is thus clear that the modifications to the Spanish dual nationality regime brought about after 1978 put Spaniards who had relied on the conventional route in a less favourable position than Spaniards who had relied on the legal route, or Spaniards who had even renounced Spanish nationality. In the first place, the group that had used the conventional route could only

---

63 Alvarez Rodríguez, "Principios inspiradores y objetivos de la nueva reforma del derecho español de la nacionalidad: Las principales novedades de la ley 36/2002": 61.

64 Espinar Vicente, *La nacionalidad y la extranjería en el sistema jurídico español*, 337. Article 8 of the treaty reads: 'Las personas que gocen de los beneficios de este Convenio no necesitarán de visado para entrar en el territorio de cualquiera de los Estados contratantes, bastando que tengan pasaporte válido expedido por las autoridades del país de su último domicilio'.

65 The following requirements need to be complied with in order to reacquire Spanish nationality under Art 26 CC: 'b) declarar ante el encargado del Registro Civil su voluntad de recuperar la nacionalidad española c) inscribir la recuperación en el Registro Civil'.

66 Under Article 26 of law 18/1990, the reacquisition of Spanish nationality was still conditional upon the return to Spain. Yet this condition was dispensed with when Spanish emigrants or their children 'pretended to reside in Spain' while actually living abroad. As the law required no proof whatsoever of actual residence in Spain, Spanish nationality could be reacquired while living abroad. The residence requirement was subsequently abolished by law 29/1995. See Arroyo Montero, "Modificación de los convenios sobre doble nacionalidad como instrumentos de integración", 197. See also Aurelia Alvarez Rodríguez, *Guía de la nacionalidad española* 2nd ed. (Madrid: Ministerio de Trabajo y Asuntos Sociales, 1996), 137.

67 Arroyo Montero, "Modificación de los convenios sobre doble nacionalidad como instrumentos de integración", 197.

activate Spanish nationality by taking up residence again in Spain. No such requirement was imposed on those who had acquired dual nationality via the legal route. What is more, the position of those who had acquired a dual nationality under one of the treaties was even less advantageous in relation to those who had renounced Spanish nationality. For these former Spaniards, it was easy to reacquire Spanish nationality because they were not bound by the provisions in the dual nationality treaties. Most importantly, they were not required to move back to Spain in order to reacquire Spanish nationality. To resolve this imbalance it was decided to draft additional protocols to the dual nationality treaties.[68]

6. *The Additional Protocols to the Dual Nationality Treaties*

Drafting the additional protocols to the dual nationality treaties was done solely on the Spanish initiative.[69] As explained above, Spaniards who had taken the conventional route were after the enactment of the 1978 Constitution and the subsequent modification of Spanish nationality law in a less favourable position compared to those who had relied on the legal route.

A distinction must be made between two types of protocol. First, there are the protocols between Spain and Nicaragua (18 March 1999), Costa Rica (1 December 1998) and Bolivia (1 February 2002).[70] Article 2 of the protocol with Nicaragua, for example, states that Nicaraguans and Spaniards who relied on the treaty in the past can renounce its application. The result is that a Nicaraguan can activate a latent Spanish nationality without establishing domicile in Spain.[71] The protocol put these Spaniards in the same position as Spaniards who obtained Nicaraguan nationality after the entry into force of the 1978 Constitution.[72]

Second, protocols were established with Honduras (1 December 2000), Guatemala (7 February 2001), Paraguay (1 March 2001), Peru (1 December 2001), the Dominican Republic (1 February 2002), Colombia (1 July 2002)

[68] Cano Bazaga, *La doble nacionalidad con los países iberoamericanos y la constitución de 1978.*

[69] Arroyo Montero, "Modificación de los convenios sobre doble nacionalidad como instrumentos de integración", 198.

[70] The dates mentioned in this section correspond with the entry into force of the protocols.

[71] Although it may appear from reading the protocols that Spanish nationality is lost upon renunciation of the treaty, the contrary is true: Spanish nationality is in fact activated. After all, Article 11.3 CE provides that acquisition of the nationality of a Latin American country does not produce the loss of Spanish nationality.

[72] Cano Bazaga, *La doble nacionalidad con los países iberoamericanos y la constitución de 1978.*

and Argentina (1 October 2002). These protocols read that passports and other documents that serve as means of identification can be obtained and renewed in both countries or in both countries at the same time. These protocols therefore do not speak of a renunciation of the treaty, but make it possible to obtain a Spanish passport without having to move to Spain.[73]

These two different sets of protocols thus have the effect of turning a latent Spanish nationality into an active one. Consequently, those who had used the conventional route have been placed on an equal footing with those who had used the legal route. In addition, those who formerly only held a latent Spanish nationality are now also European citizens, even when not residing in Spain. We shall see below in the section on *Micheletti* that the ECJ did not object to the concurrent possession of two nationalities. The protocols are thus perfectly compatible with EU law.

7. *Particularities Concerning the Spanish-Guatemalan Treaty*

The dual nationality treaty between Spain and Guatemala was also modified, although for partly different reasons than those mentioned for the other protocols. The Spanish-Guatemalan treaty had been the only treaty which actually facilitated the acquisition of dual nationality, instead of merely providing for the possibility of having one.[74] It was sufficient for a Spaniard who wanted to acquire Guatemalan nationality to establish domicile[75] in Guatemala and to express the wish to acquire that nationality.[76] The treaty did not impose the establishment of *residence* as a condition for the acquisition of the other

---

[73] Mario J.A. Oyarzábal, "El Protocolo Adicional al Convenio de nacionalidad entre España y Argentina. Un análisis desde la perspectiva argentina", *Revista Española de Derecho Internacional* 56, no. 2 (2004).

[74] Pérez Vera, "El sistema español de doble nacionalidad", 79; Espinar Vicente, *La nacionalidad y la extranjería en el sistema jurídico español*, 336–337.

[75] The term domicile is not used in the same way here as in the other treaties. As mentioned before, domicile and habitual residence were normally equated. However, in the Spanish-Guatemalan treaty the domicile and habitual residence are disconnected. It is thus possible under the treaty to acquire Spanish and Guatemalan nationality respectively by only establishing domicile, and not habitual residence, in the other country.

[76] Article 1 of the Spanish-Guatemalan treaty: 'Los españoles y los guatemaltecos por nacimiento podrán adquirir la nacionalidad guatemalteca o española, respectivamente, por el solo hecho de establecer domicilio en Guatemala o en España, según el caso, declarar ante la autoridad competente su voluntad de adquirir dicha nacionalidad y hacer la inscripción en los registros que determinen las Leyes o disposiciones gubernativas del país de que se trate'.

nationality. Vargas Muñoz has therefore stated that this treaty in fact gave an option right to the other nationality.[77]

Two protocols that entered into force on 18 March 1996 and 7 February 2001 respectively put an end to this privileged situation. The reason for drafting these protocols was the fact that many Guatemalans had only acquired Spanish nationality for reasons of convenience while looking for a job in Spain, something that was seen as undesirable from the Spanish perspective.[78]

Article 3 of the first protocol reads that domicile should be interpreted as the place where one resides habitually. Spanish or Guatemalan nationality is thus only acquired after a 'residencia legal, permanente y continuada', which represented a 180 degree turn compared to the original treaty. Also the second protocol made another substantial change. Article 1 of the second protocol renders the acquisition of another nationality dependent on the national legislation.[79] Consequently, Guatemalans will only be able to acquire Spanish nationality if they have resided permanently in Spain for two years. This is the residence requirement for Latin American under Spanish law. The second protocol thus abolished the 'option right' that was part of the original treaty.

8. *Interlude: The Italian-Argentinean Treaty on Dual Nationality and the Bilateral Treaties Concluded between Portugal and Some of its Former Colonies*

Italy and Argentina signed a treaty on dual nationality on 29 October 1971, which entered into force on 12 September 1974.[80] This treaty provided for the possibility of acquiring a dual nationality, in spite of Article 8 of law 555/1912 (the Italian law on nationality then in force) which (at least officially) provided for the loss of Italian nationality after the voluntary acquisition of another one. Dual nationality was allowed under Italian nationality legislation in 1992, however, and both countries subsequently discussed the possibility of a revision of the treaty in December 2002. On 16 August 2005 these

---

77 Pérez de Vargas Muñoz, "Cuestiones de doble nacionalidad": 899–910.

78 Ibid.

79 Article 1 of the second protocol: 'Los guatemaltecos y los españoles de origen podrán adquirir la nacionalidad guatemalteca y española, respectivamente, sin perder su nacionalidad de origen, por el solo hecho de establecer domicilio en España o en Guatemala, según sea el caso, de conformidad con la legislación interna de cada una de las Partes'.

80 Antonio Filippo Panzera, *Limiti internazionali in materia di cittadinanza*, Pubblicazioni della facoltà giuridica dell'università di Bari (Napoli: Editore Jovene, 1984), 221.

deliberations resulted in an additional protocol to the treaty.[81] Nevertheless, it seems that the desired outcome of the proposed amendment to the treaty had already been achieved informally before the additional protocol was officially discussed (see *infra* Section 8.2).

The provisions of the Italian-Argentinean treaty on dual nationality are substantially the same as those in the Spanish-Argentinean treaty.[82] Thus, the Italian-Argentinean treaty also applies the distinction between an active and a dormant nationality. The dormant nationality can only be activated by taking up residence in the country of that nationality. Moreover, like its Spanish-Argentinean counterpart, the treaty does not apply to Italians and Argentineans who are dual nationals by birth.[83] It was seen in the chapter on Italy, however, that although Article 8 of the 1912 Act did not allow a person to maintain Italian nationality after voluntarily acquiring another one, Article 1 provided for the transmission of Italian nationality *iure sanguinis*. This led to dual nationality by birth for many children of Italian emigrants, since they also acquired a Latin American nationality *iure soli*.

Another similarity between the treaties on dual nationality is that they do not deal with the mode of acquisition of the nationality of the parties to the treaties. However, an important difference between Spain and Italy is that the Spanish Civil Code specifically grants facilitated access to Spanish nationality for Latin Americans. This is not the case under Italian legislation: the residence term to be fulfilled for naturalization is the same for Argentineans as for anyone else. The fact that Argentineans may in many cases still have eased access to Italian nationality is not because of their Argentinean nationality, but because they are able to prove descent from an Italian forebear.

8.1. *Italian Academic Reactions to the Dual Nationality Treaty*

Unlike in Spain, where the legal doctrine is particularly positive and understanding about the treaties on dual nationality,[84] the conclusion of the

---

[81] Oyarzábal, "Il Protocollo aggiuntivo che modifica l'Accordo italo-argentino sulla cittadinanza": 749.

[82] Tulio Treves, "Costituzione e accordo italo-argentino sulla cittadinanza", *Rivista di diritto internazionale privato e processuale* 11 (1975): 296–297; Mario J.A. Oyarzábal, "La revisione dell'accordo italo-argentino di doppia cittadinanza", ibid.41 (2005): 102.

[83] However, in the context of the Spanish-Argentinean treaty (on which the Italian-Argentinean treaty is based) Virgós Soriano takes the deviant position that the dual nationality treaties can also apply to dual nationals by birth. Virgós Soriano, "Nationality and Double Nationality Principles in Spanish Private International Law System", 241.

[84] See for example Adolfo Miaja de la Muela, "Los convenios de doble nacionalidad entre España y algunas republicas americanas", *Revista de derecho internacional* 18 (1966): 381–410.

Italian-Argentinean treaty attracted much criticism in the Italian literature. It is submitted that this has to do with the different relationship between Spain and Italy (on the one hand) and the Latin American countries (on the other). For Spain, the introduction of dual nationality is very much a reflection of the historical and cultural ties, and a way of showing that the country wants to maintain its close ties with Latin America. Italy does not have similarly strong ties. The dual nationality treaty is merely an attempt to keep alive the bond with Italian emigrants to Argentina.

As just said, Italian jurists were critical of the Italian-Argentinean dual nationality treaty. It is worth discussing some of their objections, particularly because this criticism is absent among Spanish commentators. First, there were complaints about the scope of the treaty.[85] It is maintained that a treaty specifically dealing with the nationality of both countries should also address the question of dual nationality acquired at birth—a situation which arises much more frequently compared to dual nationality acquired after naturalization. However, this is not the case as Article 1 of the treaty refers to Italians and Argentineans by birth who can acquire Argentinean and Italian nationality respectively. Morelli sees the exclusion of this group of dual nationals as a missed opportunity to resolve the problems resulting from dual nationality acquired at the time of birth.

Second, the idea of a 'dormant nationality' has been objected to because its significance is not clear. It is claimed that introducing a latent nationality will only complicate matters, and that facilitating the recovery of the Italian nationality in case of loss would have been a better solution. The confusion on how to interpret the status of the 'dormant nationality' can also be illustrated by the fact that some authors see this nationality as in suspense,[86] whereas others[87] regard this nationality as lost (yet with the possibility of very easy recovery by taking up residence in the country of which the nationality was lost).

A third point that has attracted criticism is the alleged unconstitutionality of the treaty. It is argued that the Italian Constitution does not allow the suspension of rights that are guaranteed by constitutional provisions. As the Constitution only knows one category of nationals, so the argument goes, any rule infringing on the unitary character of Italian nationality (i.e. every national has all the rights and duties resulting from the possession of Italian nationality), as the treaty does by creating a category of 'suspended citizens'

85 M. Morelli, "L'accordo di cittadinanza italo-argentino: un'occassione mancata", *Rivista di diritto internazionale* 60 (1977): 153.

86 Ibid.

87 Treves, "Costituzione e accordo italo-argentino sulla cittadinanza": 298.

(*cittadini sospesi*), violates the Constitution. Moreover, the treaty is discriminatory to naturalisees because only nationals by birth can rely on it.

Treves has replied to this latter point of criticism by relying on his above-mentioned assumption that Italian nationality is lost upon acquisition of Argentinean nationality, although it can easily be obtained again by taking up residence in Italy. He argues, quite artificially in our view, in the following way: Every Italian acquiring another nationality loses his Italian nationality (remember that he thinks of the 'dormant nationality' as a lost nationality). Only the Italian national by birth can rely on the treaty to easily recover Italian nationality. However, there is no discrimination if you only allow an Italian by birth to rely on the treaty and not, for example, a naturalized Italian who acquired Argentinean nationality, because there is a different treatment of *foreigners*, not of Italians. As Italian nationality is lost, there can never be discrimination because the persons involved are no longer Italians.

It is distinctive for the Italian literature on the Italian-Argentinean treaty that the content of the 'dormant nationality' is so heavily debated. To our knowledge, this discussion does not feature prominently in the Spanish literature—if it is not altogether absent. Again, it is submitted that this shows that the Spanish doctrine is particularly satisfied with the legal recognition of the bonds with Latin America as reflected in the dual nationality treaties.

8.2. *Italy's Current Approach to Dual Nationality and the Additional Protocol to the Italian-Argentinean Dual Nationality Treaty*

The Italian-Argentinean treaty on dual nationality became irrelevant after the Italian reform of nationality law as brought about by law 91/92.[88] Article 11 of this law allowed dual nationality for Italians by stating that Italian nationality will not be lost by the sole fact of acquiring another nationality. It needs to be said that the treaty had been of little relevance to Argentina.[89] Except for the period of military dictatorship between 26 May 1978 and 19 April 1984, a period in which Argentinean law provided for the loss of Argentinean nationality upon acquisition of another nationality unless otherwise provided by an international treaty, Argentinean law never allowed for the renunciation of

[88] Kojanec, *Nuove norme sulla cittadinanza italiana*, 36. It must also be emphasized that very few Italians relied on the treaty in the past. In the first twenty years after the entry into force of the treaty only twenty Italians relied on it. See Giovanni Papperini, *Immigrazione e cittadinanza: Permessi di soggiorno per lavoro e studio, Adozione di minori stranieri, Apolidi e rifugiati, Pratiche per l'ottenimento della cittadinanza italiana, Documenti, Visti, Formalita doganali* (Milano: Pirola, 1987), 214.

[89] Oyarzábal, "La revisione dell'accordo italo-argentino di doppia cittadinanza": 103; Oyarzábal, "Il Protocollo aggiuntivo che modifica l'Accordo italo-argentino sulla cittadinanza": 750.

Argentinean nationality. Moreover, it was decided after the fall of the dictatorship that loss of Argentinean nationality occasioned by the abovementioned law was invalid and without any legal effect. In summary, the dual nationality treaties with Spain and Italy did not have any effect on Argentineans as Argentinean nationality cannot be renounced. For those who had lost Argentinean nationality during the dictatorship, a rule was later adopted stating that this loss was invalid.

Let us come back to the reason why Italy wanted a treaty revision. Oyarzábal rightly observes that the revision was the result of Italy having accepted dual nationality in the 1992 Act.[90] In other words, the new norms concerning dual nationality adopted under the 1992 Act rendered obsolete the treaty of 1971.[91] As Italy did not want to renounce the treaty, however, a modification was necessary to undo the discrimination between Italian nationals falling under the scope of the new norms, on the one hand, and Italians governed by the treaty, on the other. The solution proposed was the same as the one adopted in the protocol between Spain and, amongst others, Nicaragua: those who had relied on the treaty could revoke its application with the effect that their position was equated with those who had obtained a foreign nationality after the entry into force of law 91/92. Although this solution would not be adopted, Italians could revoke the application of the treaty owing to an agreement between the Italian embassy in Argentina and the Argentinean Ministry of Foreign Affairs in 1994.[92] The result of that agreement was that Italians governed by the treaty are in possession of all the rights granted under Italian law.[93]

The additional protocol that would eventually be concluded on 16 August 2005 does not adopt the abovementioned solution of renunciation of the treaty. Rather, the protocol seems inspired by the Spanish-Argentinean protocol. For those who had relied on the treaty in the past, Article 2 provides for the possibility of acquisition and renewal of passports and other travel documents in both countries, also simultaneously.[94]

---

90 Oyarzábal, "La revisione dell'accordo italo-argentino di doppia cittadinanza": 103.

91 Oyarzábal, "Il Protocollo aggiuntivo che modifica l'Accordo italo-argentino sulla cittadinanza": 750.

92 Kojanec, *Nuove norme sulla cittadinanza italiana*, 36.

93 Ibid. Kojanec, quoting part of the agreement, writes: 'I cittadini italiani che hanno effettuato una dichiarazione nel senso di voler avvalersi dell'Accordo ..., possono agli effetti dell'ordinamento italiano, revocare tale dichiarazione e, da quel momento, essere considerati, nell'ambito di tale ordinamento, in possesso di tutti i diritti da questo previsti, conformemente ai principî della Costituzione Italiana'.

94 Article 2 of the additional protocol: 'Le persone che si sono avvalse dell'Accordo possono farsi rilasciare o rinnoverare i propri passaporti e altri documenti di viaggio in entrambi i

8.3. *Bilateral Treaties Concluded between Portugal and Some of its Former Colonies*

Portuguese doctrine recognizes that one can approach dual nationality in distinct ways. First, the uncoordinated interplay between different municipal nationality laws can lead to the attribution of different nationalities to a person. Such a multiple claim on an individual was, as we have seen, historically seen as an anomaly to be avoided. Second, multiple nationality can be pursued as a goal between different peoples, and thus reflects a development whereby individuals are allowed to identify with more than one State. Under the second approach, multiple nationality is no longer the inconvenient effect of State autonomy, but the object of legislation and—in the form of bilateral treaties—international cooperation.[95]

If this is the doctrinal opinion in Portugal, one would expect to also encounter dual nationality treaties between Portugal and its former colonies.[96] This is not the case, however. Although bilateral treaties exist between Portugal, on the one hand, and Brazil and some African countries, on the other, it is important to stress that these treaties are not about multiple nationality, but merely accord rights to nationals of the other contracting State that are normally

paesi, anche contemporaneamente'. From the fact that only express mention is made in the protocol of the right to simultaneously renew one's passport in both countries, Oyarzábal concludes that other rights mentioned in the original treaty (e.g. social and labour rights) are still subject to the original norms as laid down in the treaty. These rights can therefore not be exercised simultaneously in both countries. See Oyarzábal, "Il Protocollo aggiuntivo che modifica l'Accordo italo-argentino sulla cittadinanza": 753–754.

95 Moura Ramos, "La double nationalité d'après le droit portugais": 183.

96 These treaties are discussed in Rui Manuel Moura Ramos, *Do direito português da nacionalidade* (Coimbra: Coimbra Editora, 1984), 222, footnote 379; Rui Manuel Moura Ramos, "La double nationalité et les liens spéciaux avec d'autres pays (Colonies précédentes, unions d'états, etc…) Les développements et les perspectives au Portugal", in *Plural Nationality: Changing attitudes* (Conference at the European University Institute, Florence: 1992), 15; Rui Manuel Moura Ramos, "Le droit portugais de la nationalité", in *Nationality laws in the European Union - Le droit de la nationalité dans l'Union Européene*, ed. Bruno Nascimbene (Milano: Giuffrè Editore, 1996), 605.

For a description of Portuguese nationality law in English, see Rui Manuel Moura Ramos, "Migratory movements and nationality law in Portugal", in *Towards a European nationality: citizenship, immigration and nationality law in the EU*, ed. Randall Hansen and Patrick Weil (Hampshire: Palgrave Publishers, 2001); Joppke, *Selecting by Origin: Ethnic Migration in the Liberal State*, 129–144; Maria Ioannis Baganha and Constança Urbano de Sousa, "Portugal", in *Acquisition and Loss of Nationality, Policies and Trends in 15 European Countries*, ed. Rainer Bauböck, *et al.* (Amsterdam: Amsterdam University Press, 2006); Olivier Vonk, *Portuguese nationality law*, Master's thesis (Maastricht: Faculty of Law, 2007); Nuno Piçarra and Ana Rita Gil, "Report on Portugal", EUDO Citizenship Observatory Country Reports (2009).

reserved for the own nationals. Although application of these treaties will thus emphatically not have the effect of creating dual nationality, it has been argued that the wide scope of the rights granted under the Portuguese-Brazilian treaty in particular, leads to similar results as when a dual nationality treaty had been concluded.[97]

Portugal and Brazil signed the Convention on Equal Rights and Obligations on 7 September 1971 (ratified by Portugal on 22 April 1972). The essence of this Convention is that Portuguese in Brazil and Brazilians in Portugal have the same rights and duties as the host State's nationals, apart from the rights that the Constitutions of both countries reserve for those who hold the nationality by birth. The 1971 Convention was the origin of the creation of a form of 'Lusophone citizenship', which was subsequently laid down in Article 15(3) of the 1976 Portuguese Constitution.[98] That article gave nationals of Lusophone countries, on condition of reciprocity, rights that were not accessible to other foreigners (with the exception of higher positions in the government, and service in the armed forces and the diplomatic corps). Article 15(3) was drafted in this way in order to make this 'Lusophone citizenship' also possible for the nationals of the former African colonies. However, the 'Lusophone citizenship' only exists in relation to Brazil, as only that country meets the reciprocity condition. It is thus interesting to see that Portugal responded to the decolonization from a perspective of citizenship and not of nationality.[99]

The Luso-Brazilian citizenship status created by the 1971 Treaty has been strengthened by another treaty that calls for friendship, cooperation and consultation (ratified by Portugal on 14 December 2000).[100] Moreover, Article 15(3) of the Constitution was reworded and extended the range of political rights available to citizens.[101] As only Brazil has thus far met the condition of reciprocity, Brazilians permanently living in Portugal enjoy the same political

---

[97] Moura Ramos, "La double nationalité d'après le droit portugais": 207. Moura Ramos writes: 'Il faut sitôt reconnaître que l'étendue des droits par rapport auxquels l'égalité est admise est bien majeure que celle qu'on reconnaît d'habitude dans les traits de ce genre ... On dirait ainsi que les résultats du traité sont bien proches de ceux auxquels on serait amené si l'on reconnaîssait la double nationalité'.

[98] Ioannis Baganha and Urbano de Sousa, "Portugal", 460.

[99] Ibid.

[100] Piçarra and Gil, "Report on Portugal", 28.

[101] Article 15(3) of the Portuguese Constitution reads: 'With the exceptions of appointment to the offices of President of the Republic, President of the Assembly of the Republic, Prime Minister and President of any of the supreme courts, and of service in the armed forces and the diplomatic corps, in accordance with the law and subject to reciprocity, such rights as are not otherwise granted to foreigners shall apply to citizens of Portuguese-speaking states who reside permanently in Portugal'.

rights as Portuguese nationals, without having to acquire Portuguese nationality. Although Brazilians are excluded from a few positions (e.g. president of the Republic), it is possible for them to be elected as Member of Parliament without having Portuguese nationality.

The bilateral treaties concluded with a number of African countries do not have as far-reaching consequences as the Luso-Brazilian treaty.[102] Although the starting point was the equal treatment of the nationals of the contracting States, this remained limited to rights of an economic and social nature. Equal status with regard to political rights has, to date, not been feasible.[103] Moreover, Portugal has a different relationship with each African country, which is expressed in the treaties accordingly.

With Cape Verde and Guinea-Bissau, Portugal concluded the same treaty on the equal treatment of each other's nationals and their possessions.[104] It is the most far-reaching treaty with an African country, although it is of such a nature that it could just as well have been concluded with a country with which Portugal did not share a common history and language.[105] A treaty on cooperation and friendship exists with São Tomé e Principe and provides for equal treatment concerning access to employment.[106] The least interesting treaties are those with Mozambique and Angola, which only provide for cooperation.[107]

9. *Case C-369/90* Micheletti *[1992]*

Although the essence of the *Micheletti* judgment was already discussed in Chapter 1 (Section 11.2), it is very interesting for our discussion on Spanish and Italian nationality law to dwell a little more on this case. Mr Micheletti was born in Argentina to Italian parents. Consequently, he possessed two nationalities: Argentinean nationality *iure soli* and Italian nationality by virtue of the *ius sanguinis* principle.[108] He had obtained a dental qualification in Argentina, which was recognized by Spain on the basis of an agreement with

---

102 Moura Ramos, "Migratory movements and nationality law in Portugal", 225.

103 Moura Ramos, "La double nationalité et les liens spéciaux avec d'autres pays", 21.

104 'Acordo especial regulador do estatuto de pessoas e regime dos seus bens', ratified on 5 July 1976 and 7 January 1977 respectively.

105 Moura Ramos, "La double nationalité d'après le droit portugais": 210.

106 'Acordo geral de amizade e cooperação', ratified by Portugal on 24 January 1976.

107 'Acordo geral de cooperação', ratified by Portugal on 12 December 1975 and 9 February 1979 respectively.

108 The statement in an earlier publication that Mr Micheletti had acquired dual nationality by relying on the Italian-Argentinean dual nationality treaty is clearly wrong. See Olivier Vonk,

Argentina, and had been provisionally admitted to Spain for six months because he could show an Italian passport and was thus considered to be a Community national.[109] Before expiry of the six month term, he requested a permanent residence card as he wanted to establish himself as a dentist in Spain. At that point in time, the Spanish authorities refused to grant this card on the basis of Articles 9.9 and 9.10 of the Spanish Civil Code. Those articles provided that when confronted with a dual national who did not possess Spanish nationality, the nationality of the country where the person had had his habitual residence before coming to Spain should prevail. As a result, the Spanish authorities saw Mr Micheletti as an Argentinean national, not as an Italian.

The debate in *Micheletti* concerned the question whether these Spanish provisions were incompatible with the Treaty, in particular the freedom of establishment.[110] The Spanish court asking the preliminary question recognized that Italy could autonomously decide who its nationals were, while Spain could at the same time autonomously lay down rules on how to deal with dual nationality. However, the same court also acknowledged that the Italian and Spanish rules could clash with each other, leading to a violation of Community law, if Spain would not recognize the effectiveness of Mr Micheletti's Italian nationality.[111]

In its answer to the preliminary question, the ECJ stated that it is for each Member State, having due regard to Community law, to lay down the conditions for acquisition and loss of its nationality. The Court also ruled that a Member State cannot restrict the effects of the nationality of another Member State by imposing an additional condition for recognition of that nationality with a view to the exercise of the fundamental freedoms provided for in the Treaty. Spain could not therefore make the recognition of Mr Micheletti's status of Community national subject to the condition of habitual residence in Italy. If Italy regarded him as an Italian national, even if his habitual residence had been in Argentina, so must Spain.

"Latijns-Amerikaanse Spanjaarden en het Europees burgerschap", *Migrantenrecht*, no. 5 (2006).

109 In the pre-Lisbon literature, the term 'Community national' was generally used as a shorthand for the national of a Member State or an EU citizen. The reader may, consequently, want to read EU citizen where reference is made of Community national in this section.

110 Hans Ulrich Jessurun d'Oliveira, "Annotation Case C-369/90 *Micheletti* [1992]", *Common Market Law Review* 30 (1993): 624.

111 José Luis Iglesias Buhigues, "Doble nacionalidad y Derecho comunitario: A propósito del asunto C-369/90, Micheletti, [1992]", in *Hacia un nuevo orden internacional y europeo. Estudios en homenaje al profesor don Manuel Díez de Velasco* (Madrid: Editorial Tecnos 1993), 956.

The Court thus precluded the Member States from restricting the exercise of the freedoms guaranteed by the Treaty by relying on the *Nottebohm* judgment, which requires a genuine link between a person and a State in order for a nationality to be an 'effective nationality'.[112] Community law therefore imposes clear limits on the power of Member States to regulate situations involving dual nationals; the Member State nationality of a dual national who also possesses a non-Member State nationality will always prevail.[113] The Court reasoned that Member States cannot be permitted to make recognition of the status of Community national subject to a condition such as the habitual residence in the territory of the Member State of which the person holds the nationality. Any other conclusion would mean that 'the class of persons to whom the Community rules on freedom of establishment were applied might vary from one Member State to another'.[114] The Court continued by reasoning that Directive 73/148, on which Mr Micheletti relied, only allowed a Member State to ask for the presentation of an identity card or passport for admission on its territory. If the individual can present such a document showing that he is a Community national, this quality cannot be contested by the Member State whose territory he wants to enter.

From the *Micheletti* case we can therefore conclude that in a number of cases Member States are prevented from applying their private international law rules.[115] First, these rules cannot be applied in a situation like *Micheletti* where a person has both a Member State and a non-Member State nationality. Second, a State cannot have recourse to these rules when dealing with a situation in which a person has two Member State nationalities if application of these rules would lead to the conclusion that EU law would not apply. It is when a person shows two non-Member State nationalities that private international law can apply, for only that situation truly addresses a 'conflict of nationalities' which does not affect EU law.

Let us elaborate some more on the point of the effectiveness of the nationality. AG Tesauro's Opinion expressed a strong rejection of the application of the criterion of effective nationality in the present case, arguing that the origin of effective nationality could be traced back to a 'romantic period' of

---

112 Ibid., 966; Jessurun d'Oliveira, "Annotation Case C-369/90 *Micheletti* [1992]": 625; Kojanec, "Report on Multiple Nationality", 11.

113 Iglesias Buhigues, "Doble nacionalidad y Derecho comunitario: *Micheletti*", 966.

114 Para. 12.

115 Nuria Bouza I Vidal, "El ámbito personal de aplicación del derecho de establecimiento en los supuestos de doble nacionalidad: comentario a la Sentencia del TJCE de 7 de julio de 1992 en el caso Micheletti c. Delegación del Gobierno de Cantabria (As. C-369/90)", *Revista de Instituciones Europeas* 20 (1993): 573; Carrascosa González, "Dual nationality and Community law": 7–8.

international relations (what exactly is meant by this remains unclear), in particular diplomatic protection.[116] The AG pointed to Article 52 EC (now Article 49 TFEU) and concluded that the article does not impose a choice between two nationalities. Community law therefore does not make one nationality prevail over the other on the basis of residence. The approach taken by the AG, and subsequently by the Court, has been criticized by Ruzié.[117] Arguing from a public international law perspective, he maintains that Mr Micheletti could not 'legitimately' claim Italian nationality, given that this nationality was not the effective one. Contrary to the AG's perception of effective nationality as belonging to a 'romantic' past, he is of the opinion that the principle does not lack 'realism'; if applied by each Member State, it would assuage the fear of the ECJ that there would be variable rules within the Community with regard to the recognition of the nationality of a Member State.[118]

Yet Ruzié's criticism that the Court is rather extensively interpreting the notion of Community national in *Micheletti* appears to be unfounded. We can first of all point to Article 8 of the Maastricht Treaty—although, admittedly, this only came into force after *Micheletti*[119]—which states that 'every person holding the nationality of a Member State shall be a citizen of the Union'. Moreover, Mr Micheletti had acted in conformity with Directive 73/148, which merely required presentation of a passport for admission to Spanish territory. The Court of Justice was thus not, in our opinion, extending the scope of the notion of Community national by not applying the effective nationality criterion. On the contrary, the outcome in *Micheletti* seems the most suitable solution for guaranteeing the freedoms guaranteed by the Treaty to dual nationals who have the nationality of a Member State and of a non-Member State. It is clear why Ruzié disagreed with the Court's approach as it failed, in his view, to protect the interests of 'real' Community nationals in a time of unemployment in the Community.[120] Applying the criterion of the effective nationality to decide who is a Community citizen would obviously serve to protect these interests.

What, then, is the particular relevance of the *Micheletti* decision for this chapter? Leaving aside the fact that the decision is probably the most

---

116 Para. 5 of the AG's Opinion.

117 David Ruzié, "Nationalité, effectivité et droit communautaire", *Revue générale de droit international public* 97 (1993): 109–113.

118 Ibid., 113.

119 On the other hand, the Court was obviously aware of the wording of the EU citizenship provisions in the Maastricht Treaty at the time of handing down the judgment on 7 July 1992 (the Treaty had been signed on 7 February and entered into force on 1 November 1993).

120 Ruzié, "Nationalité, effectivité et droit communautaire": 116.

important ruling by the ECJ on the issue of dual nationality, the case is interesting because of the role played by the dual nationality treaties.

It must be said that Spain complicated the case enormously by wrongly alleging in the first place that Mr Micheletti possessed dual nationality based on the Italian-Argentinean treaty.[121] We have seen that this was not the case because Micheletti was a dual national by birth. Spain subsequently relied on the Italian-Argentinean treaty to see whether he should be regarded as an Italian national who could enjoy the freedom of establishment in Spain. It concluded, in accordance with its own Spanish-Argentinean treaty, that his Italian nationality was 'dormant' because his habitual residence had been in Argentina. The reliance placed on the Italian-Argentinean treaty is remarkable because it had been clear from the beginning that this treaty was not applicable: Italy had always maintained that Mr Micheletti was an Italian national by birth.

The *Micheletti* decision also raised the question whether Community law could restrict Spain's competence to regulate the issue of dual nationality by means of the dual nationality treaties. In other words, could Community law, in addition to the prohibition for one Member State to impose limits on the effects of a nationality granted by another Member State, also limit the regulation of its *own nationality* if a person possessed both this nationality and the nationality of a non-Member State?[122] What would happen, for example, in the hypothetical situation[123] that a Spanish-Argentinean national, whose Spanish nationality was latent under the dual nationality treaty and who was living in Argentina, wanted to establish himself in France?[124] This looks to be a legitimate question because the doctrine of the 'effective nationality' does not seem to apply in Community law. Moreover, the concept of a latent nationality does not seem to fit the Community law picture; application of Community law only requires the possession of a Member State nationality, without any further requirements and conditions.[125]

121 Iglesias Buhigues, "Doble nacionalidad y Derecho comunitario: *Micheletti*", 956.

122 Ibid., 965–966; Carrascosa González, "Dual nationality and Community law": 9.

123 The dual national will have the practical problem of not possessing a Spanish passport; as a result, he is not able to identify himself as a Community national. We recall that granting a passport is done under the dual nationality treaties by the country where the dual national has his domicile, in this case Argentina. To establish himself in France, the dual national will thus first have to 'activate' his Spanish nationality by taking up residence in Spain. Once he can identify himself as a Community national, he can freely establish himself anywhere in the Community.

124 Iglesias Buhigues, "Doble nacionalidad y Derecho comunitario: *Micheletti*", 965–966.

125 Ibid., 966–967.

Carrascosa has therefore argued that a State, although free to establish the conditions for acquisition and loss of its own nationality, cannot impose any restrictions on the effectiveness of that nationality for Community purposes. Consequently, if a Latin American obtained a dual nationality by acquiring Spanish nationality, the Spanish nationality cannot be put in a dormant state that would deny the dual national the exercise of the fundamental freedoms guaranteed by Community law.[126] Relying on *Micheletti*, Carrascosa argues that a Member State cannot impose additional conditions on a dual national who possesses that Member State's nationality before recognizing that nationality for the purpose of exercising the freedoms under the Treaty.

Although it has been regretted by some that the ECJ did not deal in *Micheletti* with the compatibility of the dual nationality treaties with Community law,[127] there is no longer any need to wait for a case dealing with this question. Spain has, in part due to the *Micheletti* decision, concluded the protocols that amended the dual nationality treaties (see *supra* Section 6). These protocols were drafted primarily to equalize the position of dual Spanish-Latin American nationals who had acquired this dual nationality by relying on the conventional route with those who had obtained this dual nationality by following the legal route. Another reason seems to be, however, that the *Micheletti* decision proved that the ECJ had no problem with the concurrent possession of two active nationalities. There was thus no longer the need, if indeed there ever had been in the first place, for Spain to adhere to the rule of one active and one dormant nationality. Spain may have thought that if Community law only required Mr Micheletti to show an Italian passport to identify himself as an Italian, Community law would not oppose the grant of Spanish passports to all those with a dormant Spanish nationality. This is, as we have seen, exactly the approach taken in some protocols, whereas others simply allow the renunciation of the treaties, resulting in the revival of Spanish nationality—a Spanish passport included.

---

[126] It should be remarked that exactly the opposite argument was made by Pérez Vera on the occasion of Spain's accession to the EC. She argued that the dual nationality treaties were fully compatible with Community law because a dual national's Spanish nationality would always be 'dormant' if the person did not have domicile in Spain. She thus reassured the Community that a dual national would never have two active nationalities at the same time. Consequently, the dual national did not have any rights under Community law as long as he did not live in Spain. See Elisa Pérez Vera, "El sistema español de doble nacionalidad ante la futura adhesión de España a las Comunidades Europeas", *Revista de instituciones europeas* 8 (1981): 685–703. Carroscosa doubts whether this interpretation is still valid after the *Micheletti* decision, for it denies dual nationals rights under EU law.

[127] Alvarez Rodríguez, "Binacionalidad en el ordenamiento español y su repercusión en la Union Europea", 97.

10. *Developments in Spanish Nationality Law after the Enactment of the 1978 Constitution: Modification of Spanish Nationality Law by Law 51/1982*

Now that the Italian and Portuguese bilateral treaties have been discussed, as well as the ECJ's judgment in *Micheletti*, it is time to come back to the provisions in the Spanish Civil Code on dual nationality. These provisions were modified several times after the enactment of the 1978 Constitution.[128] In the next four sections we will systematically discuss the different modifications, starting with law 51/1982. This law recognized four different forms of dual nationality:

1. Dual nationality in consequence of emigration (Section 10.1.1);
2. Dual nationality acquired during minority and retained after reaching the age of majority (*la emancipación*) (10.1.2);
3. Dual nationality owing to the acquisition of the nationality of a country with which Spain is historically and/or geographically connected (10.1.3);
4. Dual nationality acquired under the dual nationality treaties (10.1.4).

Only the last mode of acquiring dual nationality demands cooperation with another State. The others do not require this cooperation and thus reflect situations in which Spanish law recognizes the existence of dual nationality independently of the legal regime of another State.[129] Before addressing these four different ways in which Spanish law recognizes dual nationality, we want to point to Article 22.1 of law 51/1982. This article requires only two years' residency in Spain for the naturalization of nationals by origin from Latin American countries, Andorra, the Philippines, Equatorial Guinea, Portugal or Sephardic Jews.[130]

---

128 Both the DGRN and the majority of Spanish doctrine are of the opinion that the constitutional provision did not require a modification of the Civil Code in order to have legal effect. Article 11.3 CE thus had immediate effect and provisions in the Civil Code that were incompatible with Article 11.3 CE were revoked. See Aguilar Benítez de Lugo, "Doble nacionalidad": 236.

129 Fernández Rozas, *Derecho español de la nacionalidad*, 246.

130 The inclusion of Sephardic Jews may come as a surprise. Although they were not mentioned in the original Bill, the 'Grupo Socialistas de Cataluña' managed to include them through an amendment. This was done based on the cultural link (e.g. through the Spanish language) that certain members of this ethnic group still have with Spain. Moors (*moriscos*) were excluded, however, because—despite being expulsed from Spain as well in the 15th century—they would no longer have such a link with Spain. See Pérez de Vargas Muñoz, "Cuestiones de doble nacionalidad": 889–910.

This provision can also be regarded as a delayed compliance with the mandate of Article 23 of the Republican Constitution of 1931. This article provided that a law would lay down

10.1.1 There are two ways in which dual nationality can be obtained as a result of emigration. First, if one acquires another nationality without losing the Spanish one. Article 23.1 CC states that Spanish nationality is not lost when another nationality is acquired for reasons relating to emigration.[131] The second way to acquire a dual nationality is by reacquisition of Spanish nationality. This possibility can be used by emigrants who had lost Spanish nationality upon acquisition of another nationality before the entry into force on 19 August 1982 of law 51/1982. A transitory provision determines that Spanish nationality can be reacquired without having to renounce the nationality acquired in the country of emigration. Taken together, these two provisions make sure that Spanish emigrants are treated equally regardless of whether they emigrated before or after the entry into force of law 51/1982.[132]

However, law 52/1982 did not clearly state who exactly was covered by the abovementioned rules. As a consequence, the *Centro Directivo* (General Directorate of Registries and Notaries)[133] was required to interpret the notion of 'emigración' in order to determine the scope of application of the rules. From its interpretation it is clear that the Directorate includes family members who follow the emigrant.[134] Importantly, however, it can also be concluded

the procedure for eased access to Spanish nationality for persons of Spanish origin who were living abroad ('una ley establecerá el procedimiento que facilite la adquisición de la nacionalidad a las personas de origin español que residan en el extranjero'). We know about the unfortunate history of the Republican Constitution and that its provisions were never implemented. However, a special regime had already been in place for Sephardic Jews until 31 December 1930 (under a Royal Decree of 20 December 1924) through which Sephardic Jews could acquire Spanish nationality at a Spanish consulate abroad—mainly through the link of the Spanish language. See Pedro García Valdés, "El problema sefardí a través de la Constitución de la República española", *Revista general de legislación y jurisprudencia* 162 (1933): 756–764.

131 Article 23.1 CC: 'No … perderán [la nacionalidad española] cuando justifiquen ante los Registros Consular o Central que la adquisición de la nacionalidad extranjera se produjo, por razón de emigración'. The underlying reason for this provision is to protect emigrants living in countries with which Spain did not conclude a dual nationality treaty. See Rubio Marín, "Spain", 448.

132 Fernández Rozas, *Derecho español de la nacionalidad*, 246.

133 The *Centro Directivo* or General Directorate of Registries and Notaries (D.G.R.N.) plays an important role in Spanish nationality law. As there are few articles in the Civil Code dedicated to nationality law, which are moreover often vaguely worded, the Directorate has produced guidelines which are essential to interpreting the legislation. See Rubio Marín, "Spain", 480.

134 Fernández Rozas, *Derecho español de la nacionalidad*, 249. The Directorate comes with the following interpretation of the term emigration: 'Este concepto de emigración ha de entenderse en su sentido propio, es decir, ha de referirse al español, que especialmente por motivos laborales o profesionales, traslada su residencia habitual al extranjero, así como a los familiares que le sigan'.

from the Directorate's decisions that children of an emigrant who are born abroad are not covered by this interpretation of 'emigration'. The reason advanced by the Directorate is that these children do not 'follow' the emigrant to the country of emigration, and consequently are not sufficiently integrated into Spanish society.[135] Thus, despite the willingness to protect Spanish emigrants abroad, on a more practical level the need was felt to restrain the acquisition of dual nationalities.[136] Although children of Spanish emigrants born abroad were excluded from the scope of Article 23.1 CC, they were potentially covered by Article 23.2 CC, which provided that children who since their childhood had been in possession of both the Spanish and another nationality only lost their Spanish nationality by explicit renunciation. Alvarez Rodríguez shows in an inventory of decisions by the Directorate, however, that only in two out of twenty-five cases where the child was born abroad could Spanish nationality be retained. The main problem seems to be the fact that Article 23.2 CC only applies to children who acquired the nationality of the country of birth before coming of age, whilst in practice this nationality is mostly acquired after the age of majority.[137]

10.1.2 This category deals with Spaniards who possessed also another nationality during minority. Under law 51/1982 they do not lose their Spanish nationality when coming of age, unless they explicitly renounce this nationality.[138]Although this form of dual nationality had always been permitted, it was now for the first time explicitly laid down in Spanish nationality law.[139]

10.1.3 As was mentioned above, Article 11.3 of the 1978 Constitution reads that Spaniards can acquire the nationality of a Latin American country and countries which have, or will have, a special bond with Spain, without losing Spanish nationality.[140] This constitutional provision was further elaborated by

---

[135] Ibid., 251–252.

[136] Aurelia Alvarez Rodríguez, "Doble nacionalidad. Jurisprudencia española de DIPr", *Revista de derecho internacional* 40 (1988): 154–155. 'Nuestro Ordenamiento ha sido muy sensible a estas situaciones involuntarias de residencia en el extranjero por parte de estas personas [i.e. Spanish emigrants] permitiéndoles mantener la nacionalidad española aunque hayan obtenido la nacionalidad de acogida. Sin embargo, la gran sensibilidad del legislador hacia los emigrantes de origen español residentes fuera de España se corresponde con el sentido eminentemente práctico de los órganos que han tenido que frenar el entusiasmo por la doble nacionalidad'.

[137] Ibid., 157.

[138] Article 23 CC in the wording of law 51/1982: 'Cuando se trate de españoles que ostenten desde su menor edad, además, una nacionalidad extranjera, sólo perderán la nacionalidad española, si, un vez emancipados, renunciaren expresamente a ella en cualquier momento'.

[139] Fernández Rozas, *Derecho español de la nacionalidad*, 256.

[140] *Supra* Section 4.

Article 23.4 CC of law 51/1982. By virtue of this article, Spaniards who acquired the nationality of a Latin American country, Andorra, the Philippines, Equatorial Guinea, Portugal, or countries with which Spain will conclude dual nationality treaties, only lose Spanish nationality if this nationality is expressly renounced.[141] This article was a new provision in Spanish nationality law. Under previous legislation, Spanish nationality was still lost upon acquisition of the nationality of one of the abovementioned countries.[142]

This particular way of acquiring dual nationality was only possible after the entry into force of Article 23.4 CC. No transitory provision existed such as the one we have seen with dual nationality as a consequence of emigration (*supra* Section 10.1.1). In case the nationality of one of the countries just mentioned had been acquired before Article 23.4 CC had entered into force, Spanish nationality was lost. These former Spaniards could plead, however, that they had applied for the other nationality for reasons relating to emigration. If successful in their plea, they still acquired dual nationality, not under Article 23.4 CC but under the transitory provision that was mentioned above in relation to dual nationality acquired as a result of emigration.[143]

10.1.4 Article 23.4 CC *inter alia* stated that Spaniards who acquired the nationality of a Latin American country only lost Spanish nationality if they expressly renounced it. If Spanish nationality was not renounced, both nationalities were active simultaneously.[144] This evidently conflicts with the 12 dual nationality treaties. After all, the essence of these treaties resided in the fact that different nationalities could never be active at the same time; one of the nationalities was always 'dormant'.

The *Centro Directivo* had to provide a solution to this contradiction, and it proposed to use a provision from the dual nationality treaties. The treaties contain a provision which calls for periodic consultation on matters relating to the treaty.[145] This possibility was not used, however, until the additional

---

[141] The final part of Article 23 CC reads: 'La adquisición de la nacionalidad de países iberoamericanos, Andorra, Filipinas, Guinea Ecuatorial y Portugal o de aquellos con los que se concierte un tratado de doble nacionalidad, sólo producirá pérdida de la nacionalidad española de origen cuando el interesado así lo declare expresamente en el Registro Civil una vez emancipado'.

[142] Fernández Rozas, *Derecho español de la nacionalidad*, 258.

[143] Ibid., 259.

[144] It might not be apparent that both nationalities are active simultaneously when reading Article 23.4 CC. See for further clarification ibid., 259–265.

[145] Article 8 of the Spanish-Nicaraguan treaty: 'Ambos gobiernos se consultarán periódicamente con el fin de estudiar y adoptar las medidas conducentes para la mejor y uniforme interpretación y aplicación de este convenio, así como las eventuales modificaciones y adiciones de común acuerdo se estimen convenientes'. See also Aurelia Alvarez Rodríguez,

protocols were drafted.[146] Another solution thus had to be found. The only possibility for Spaniards who had relied on the dual nationality treaties in the past was to prove that the other nationality was acquired as a result of emigration. In this way, the transitory provision could be used. If this proof could not be produced, the only way to activate the latent nationality was to return to Spain.[147]

11. *Modification of Spanish Nationality Law by Law 18/1990*

Not too long after law 51/1982 Spanish nationality legislation was again modified, this time by law 18/1990. First of all, Article 24.1 CC should be mentioned.[148] This article is almost identical with Article 23.4 CC of law 51/1982. The article's tenor is the same: acquisition of the nationality of a Latin American country, Andorra, the Philippines, Equatorial Guinea or Portugal will not produce the loss of Spanish nationality.

Secondly, law 18/1990 also provides a solution for those who had acquired the nationality of a Latin American country, Andorra, the Philippines, Equatorial Guinea, and Portugal before the entry into force of law 51/1982. Article 26.1.b of law 18/1990 reads that a Spanish nationality that had been lost could only be reacquired after renunciation of the other nationality.[149] However, *naturales* of the countries mentioned in Article 24 are exempted from the renunciation requirement. The *Centro Directivo* subsequently decided that Spaniards who had acquired the nationality of one of these countries were covered by this exemption.

Article 26.1.b offers relief to two groups of Spaniards. The first group consists of those who before the entry into force of law 51/1982 on 19 August 1982 had acquired the nationality of one of the countries mentioned in

---

"Modificación del convenio de doble nacionalidad entre España y Nicaragua", *Revista de Emigración e Inmigración*, no. 540 (1999). In her contribution she mentions that Article 8 of the dual nationality treaties was the basis for the additional protocols.

146 Fernández Rozas, *Derecho español de la nacionalidad*, 265.

147 Ibid.

148 Article 24.1 CC: 'La adquisición de la nacionalidad de países iberoamericanos, Andorra, Filipinas, Guinea Ecuatiorial o Portugal, no es bastante para producir, conforme a este apartado, la pérdida de la nacionalidad española de origen'.

149 Article 26.1.b) CC: 'Quien haya perdido la nacionalidad española podrá recuperarla cumpliendo los siguientes requisitos : Declarar ante el encargado del Registro Civil su voluntad de recuperar la nacionalidad española y su renuncia, salvo que se trate de naturales de los países mencionados en el artículo 24, a la nacionalidad anterior'.

Article 24.1 CC.[150] The second group is comprised of Spaniards who acquired such nationality after 19 August 1982, but had renounced their Spanish nationality on that occasion. Both groups of former Spaniards are given the opportunity under this article to reacquire Spanish nationality. Spaniards who had obtained another nationality before the entry into force of Article 23.4 CC, but after enactment of Article 11.3 CE, were thus no longer discriminated against.

In the third place, a new provision was introduced by law 18/1990. This provision, Article 23.b CC, exempts nationals of the countries mentioned in Article 24.1 CC from the renunciation requirement upon acquisition of Spanish nationality. Consequently, the dual nationality treaties need no longer be used by this group as the Spanish Civil Code now allows the retention of the original nationality.[151]

One may wonder what the effect of all these developments in Spanish nationality law has been on the dual nationality treaties. Alvarez Rodríguez comes to the conclusion that the treaties were hardly effective anymore when law 51/1982 came into force; with the entry into force of law 18/1990 however, they lost all effect.[152] Her explanation is the following: Spaniards who obtained the nationality of a country in Latin America after 1982 did not lose Spanish nationality, and what is more, both nationalities were active simultaneously. This clearly violated the essence of the dual nationality treaties. After 1990 Latin Americans could, regardless of whether their country had concluded a dual nationality treaty with Spain, acquire Spanish nationality without being asked to renounce their nationality of origin. This possibility was offered by Article 23.b CC. Thus, the dual nationality treaties did not provide any advantage to either Spaniards or Latin Americans compared to the provisions in the Spanish Civil Code.

Alvarez Rodríguez also makes clear the importance of the additional protocols. Before the protocols were drafted, she had put forward a proposal which provided a solution for Spaniards who lived in Latin America and who had relied on the dual nationality treaties in the past, but who now wanted to possess two fully active nationalities. She proposed that these Spaniards renounce the treaty, thereby losing Spanish nationality. Next, they could rely on Article 26 CC, which neither demands the return to Spain nor the renunciation of

150 The relevant date is now no longer 19 August 1982, but 29 December 1978 (the moment the Constitution entered into force). After all, Article 11.3 CE already provided that Spaniards did not lose Spanish nationality upon acquiring a Latin American nationality.

151 Palao Moreno, Esplugues Mota, and De Lorenzo Segrelles, *Nacionalidad y Extranjería*, 74.

152 Alvarez Rodríguez, *Guía de la nacionalidad española*, 134–135.

their other nationality for the reacquisition of Spanish nationality.[153] When the additional protocols were discussed in Section 6, it was seen that some protocols adopted Alvarez Rodríguez's suggestion to allow the renunciation of the treaty.[154]

11.1. *The Future of the Dual Nationality Treaties*

All the aforementioned developments in Spanish nationality law have made the dual nationality treaties lose much of their relevance. After the enactment of the 1978 Constitution and the subsequent modifications of the nationality law provisions in the Civil Code, it made more sense to use the legal instead of the conventional route. After all, the legal route allowed for the possession of two active nationalities.

Despite the diminished relevance of the Spanish-Latin American treaties, some feel that dual nationality treaties may still be useful to Spain. Vargas Muñoz, for example, has pointed to the fact that Article 11.3 of the Constitution still refers to the possibility of concluding such treaties with (European) countries with which Spain has a special bond. He considers it useful to conclude dual nationality treaties with countries to which many Spaniards have emigrated, so that they can acquire the nationality of the country of emigration—which makes their life in the country of residence easier—without having to lose Spanish nationality; such treaties also stimulate European integration.[155] This suggestion to conclude European dual nationality treaties now seems somewhat outdated, however, as more and more European States explicitly allow dual nationality, particularly for fellow European citizens.

12. *Modification of Spanish Nationality Law by Law 36/2002*

Law 36/2002, which entered into force on 9 January 2003, has also significantly modified Spanish nationality law. The primary aim of this modification was to redress some disadvantages for Spanish emigrants and their descendants.[156] In the following, we shall discuss some of these modifications.[157]

---

153 Ibid., 136–137.

154 See *supra* Section 11.

155 Pérez de Vargas Muñoz, "Cuestiones de doble nacionalidad": 889–910.

156 Alvarez Rodríguez, "Principios inspiradores y objetivos de la nueva reforma del derecho español de la nacionalidad: Las principales novedades de la ley 36/2002": 47.

157 An English translation of the current nationality provisions in the Spanish Civil Code is available from http://eudo-citizenship.eu (select Spain under the country profiles).

Article 20.1.b CC is a very favourable provision for children of Spanish emigrants.[158] They can opt for Spanish nationality if either the father or the mother was Spanish by origin[159] and was born in Spain.[160] No age-limit is imposed concerning this right to opt for Spanish nationality. What is more, the option right can be exercised outside Spain. The practical effects of this article have been nicely illustrated by De Groot, who mentions that Fidel Castro—whose father was born in the Spanish province Galicia in the 19th century—could opt for Spanish nationality without having to leave Cuba.[161]

Article 22.2.f CC is beneficial to children and grandchildren of emigrants who originally possessed Spanish nationality.[162] Children and grandchildren who were born outside Spain can acquire Spanish nationality after one year residence in Spain, provided that either a parent or grandparent was Spanish by origin (if the father or mother who was Spanish by origin was also born in Spain Article 20.1.b CC applies).[163] It is important to note, however, that applicants are (at least in theory) required to renounce the previous nationality

---

158 Article 20.1 CC: 'Tienen derecho a optar por la nacionalidad española a) las personas que estén o hayan estado sujetas a la patria potestad de un español b) aquellas cuyo padre o madre hubiera sido originariamente español y nacido en España'. See Palao Moreno, Esplugues Mota, and De Lorenzo Segrelles, *Nacionalidad y Extranjería*, 49.

159 Lara Aguado has called the distinction between Spaniards by origin and naturalized Spaniards an intolerable and unconstitutional discrimination. Law 36/2002 was meant to comply with the constitutional mandate expressed in Article 42 CE, i.e. facilitating the acquisition of Spanish nationality by descendants of Spanish emigrants. However, by distinguishing between naturalized Spaniards and Spaniards by origin, the law treats differently two categories that were in the same position. This, in her opinion, amounts to discrimination. See Angeles Lara Aguado, "Nacionalidad e Integración Social: a propósito de la Ley 36/2002 de 8 de octubre", *La Ley* 24, no. 5694 (2003): 1449–1450. Whether this is a strong argument is doubtful, as the Constitution itself also makes this distinction when stating that only Spaniards by origin cannot be deprived of their nationality (Article 11.2 CE).

160 Alvarez Rodríguez, "Principios inspiradores y objetivos de la nueva reforma del derecho español de la nacionalidad: Las principales novedades de la ley 36/2002": 62–63. This article was not new as law 29/1995 already contained a temporary provision of the same tenor. The present article is not a temporary provision, however. The Spanish daily newspaper *El País* reports that five years after entry into force of the provision some 30,000 Cubans had relied on it to acquire Spanish nationality. 'Los nietos de los exiliados hacen fila', *El País*, 30 December 2008.

161 de Groot, "Towards a European Nationality Law", 23.

162 This article introduced the transmission of Spanish nationality by a grandparent. Until then, the article only referred to parents, thus excluding the third generation. See Rubio Marín, "Spain", 497.

163 Article 22.1: 'Para la concesión de la nacionalidad por residencia se requiere que ésta haya durado diez años'. Article 22.2: 'Bastará el tiempo de un año para: f) El nacido fuera de España de padre o madre, abuelo o abuela, que originariamente hubieran sido españoles'.

under Article 22.2.f as well as Article 20.1.b CC unless that nationality concerns the nationality of a Latin American country, Andorra, the Philippines, Guinea or Portugal (Article 23.b CC).[164]

Another provision that was modified is Article 24.1 CC. This provision allows Spaniards who acquire another nationality (regardless of being an emigrant or not) and who habitually reside abroad to maintain Spanish nationality. To that purpose, they are required to declare within three years after acquisition of the other nationality that they wish to maintain Spanish nationality.[165]

Finally, Article 26 CC was changed. Previously, Article 26.1.b contained a renunciation requirement upon reacquisition of Spanish nationality, although persons possessing the nationality of one of the countries mentioned in Article 24 CC were exempted from this requirement. Article 26 CC of law 36/200 no longer imposes a renunciation requirement.[166] One should be aware, however, that a general renunciation requirement upon acquisition of Spanish nationality is still part of Spanish law. Article 26 CC is only applicable to those who reacquire Spanish nationality after having lost it at some point.

Article 26 CC also facilitates the reacquisition of Spanish nationality for Spanish emigrants and their children. Unlike other Spaniards who lost their nationality, this category does not need to be legally resident in Spain in order to reacquire Spanish nationality.[167]

12.1. *The Objective of Law 36/2002: To Repair the Injustice Suffered by Spanish Emigrants*

The modifications by law 36/2002 had a clear aim: to remedy the injustice suffered by Spanish emigrants and their descendants who were forced to emigrate at a time when the economical and political situation was difficult in Spain.[168] Spanish nationality was hardly ever transmitted to a child of Spanish emigrants who was born abroad.[169] Law 36/2002, drafted on the initiative of

---

164 Alvarez Rodríguez, "Principios inspiradores y objetivos de la nueva reforma del derecho español de la nacionalidad: Las principales novedades de la ley 36/2002": 85.

165 Ibid., 73.

166 Ibid., 73–74.

167 Article 26.1 CC: 'Quien haya perdido la nacionalidad española podrá recuperarla cumpliendo los siguientes requisitos: a) Ser residente legal en España. Este requisito no será de aplicación a los emigrantes ni a los hijos de emigrantes….'

168 Lara Aguado, "Nacionalidad e Integración Social: a propósito de la Ley 36/2002 de 8 de octubre": 1450.

169 Alvarez Rodríguez, "Principios inspiradores y objetivos de la nueva reforma del derecho español de la nacionalidad: Las principales novedades de la ley 36/2002": 61.

the Popular Party (*Partido Popular*), was meant to comply with the mandate of Article 42 of the Constitution which states that 'the State shall protect the social and economic rights of Spanish workers abroad, and enact a policy to facilitate their return.'[170]

Although the legal doctrine generally praises the attempt to remedy the injustice suffered by Spanish emigrants, some criticize the law for not taking into account that Spain has in fact become a country of immigration. Law 36/2002 exclusively focuses on the reacquisition of Spanish nationality for Spanish emigrants and their descendants.[171] Proposals by the Socialist Party (*Grupo Parlamentario Socialista*) and United Left (*Izquierda Unida*) did recognize, however, that Spain had to face the fact that many immigrants were permanently resident on its territory and needed to become part of Spanish society. Their proposals aimed at fulfilling the constitutional mandate in respect of Spanish emigrants, but also made an attempt to make Spanish nationality more inclusive for immigrants.[172]

The group of persons that can benefit from the modifications by law 36/2002 is potentially large, but Spanish doctrine agrees on the need to facilitate reacquisition of Spanish nationality for this group.[173] To non-Spanish eyes, however, some of the provisions that are welcomed by Spanish doctrine seem rather over-inclusive. Upon reading the Fidel Castro example, many would find it hard to see why Castro should be eligible for Spanish nationality (and thus European citizenship) only on the basis of his father being born in 19th century Spain. The absence of both an age limit and a residence requirement in Spain may seem overgenerous, taking into account that Spanish nationality law not only affects Spain but all the other Member States of the EU as well.

---

170 Articles 11 and 42 of the Constitution are the only constitutional provisions expressly referring to nationality. They are the expression of two important features of Spanish nationality law. Firstly, the existence of an Ibero-American community, which permits a system of dual nationality (Article 11.3 CE); secondly, the constitutional obligation to protect Spanish emigrants. See Rubio Marín, "Spain", 487–488.

171 Alvarez Rodríguez, "Principios inspiradores y objetivos de la nueva reforma del derecho español de la nacionalidad: Las principales novedades de la ley 36/2002": 85; Lara Aguado, "Nacionalidad e Integración Social: a propósito de la Ley 36/2002 de 8 de octubre": 1455.

172 Alvarez Rodríguez, "Principios inspiradores y objetivos de la nueva reforma del derecho español de la nacionalidad: Las principales novedades de la ley 36/2002": 57. The proposal of the Socialist Party included among other measures an extension of the *ius soli* principle: children born in Spain to foreign parents acquire Spanish nationality if at least one parent is legally resident in Spain. It also suggested reducing the required residence term for naturalization from ten to five years. The proposal of the United Left is very similar to that of the Socialist Party.

173 See for example Lara Aguado, "Nacionalidad e Integración Social: a propósito de la Ley 36/2002 de 8 de octubre": 1445.

Law 36/2002 once more proves that nationality law still falls within the exclusive competence of the Member States. This is also taken for granted by the commentators, who do not—or only very marginally—consider the impact of these modifications to the EU at large. The settlement of the moral debt owed to Spanish emigrants is deemed to be of greater importance than the potential effect of creating large numbers of European citizens. The favourable provisions for Spanish expatriates are generally welcomed and sometimes even criticized for not sufficiently facilitating the acquisition of Spanish nationality.[174]

On the other hand, Spain faces the reality of being a country of immigration. Since the mid-1980s Spain has transformed from an emigration country into a net recipient of immigrants, yet none of the nationality laws since passed have responded to this change. The (re)acquisition of Spanish emigrants and their descendants has continually been prioritized.[175] The preferential treatment given to expatriates—expressed in the acceptance of dual nationality with regard to this group and the very short (or absent) residence period required—contrasts with the lack of initiatives to include immigrants who are neither of Spanish descent nor belong to a privileged category enjoying facilitated access to Spanish nationality.[176]

13. *Law 52/2007 and Option Rights to Spanish Nationality*

The most recent change to Spanish nationality law has been brought about by law 52/2007 (The Historical Memory Act or *Ley de Memoria Histórica*), which introduces two important modifications.[177] In the first place, it grants an option right to Spanish nationality to children whose father or mother was Spanish by origin without requiring, however, that the Spanish father or mother was also born in Spain.[178] This had still been required under law

[174] Ibid., 1456.

[175] Rubio Marín, "Spain", 489–490.

[176] Spain applies a double *ius soli* (Article 17 CC) but not a simple *ius soli*. Children born in Spain to first generation immigrants can acquire a derived Spanish nationality, however, after one year of legal residence (Article 22.2 CC). Yet they do not acquire a Spanish nationality by origin, which has important consequences as Spaniards by origin and their descendants often find themselves in a privileged position.

[177] See the 'disposición adicional séptima: adquisición de la nacionalidad española', which is available from http://www.mpr.es/Documentos/textoleymemoria.htm#exposicion.

[178] Carrascosa González, *Curso de Nacionalidad y Extranjería*, 93. Carrascosa points to the motivation to law 52/2007, which only requires the parent to be Spanish by origin. The option right is thus created in view of Spanish emigration and not necessarily for

36/2002. Law 52/2007 seems to meet the doctrinal complaints in respect of law 36/2002 which had criticized the requirement that the parent had to be born in Spain.[179] Second, an option right is granted to the grandchildren of Spaniards by origin that lost or had to renounce Spanish nationality as a result of exile (this includes exile for both political and economic reasons) during the Civil War or the Franco dictatorship.[180] It is important to note that the option right in law 52/2007 is only a temporary provision which does therefore not modify Articles 17–26 of the Civil Code. Applicants can only make use of the provision as from 27 December 2008 until 27 December 2010.[181]

Many have already made use of the possibilities offered by the Historical Memory Act. It is estimated that half a million persons are eligible for Spanish nationality under the provisions of law 52/2007. The newspaper *El País* reports that children and grandchildren of Spaniards who went in exile for political or economic reasons[182] between 18 July 1936 (the beginning of the Civil War) and 31 December 1955 (the official end of the postwar period) will have the possibility of opting for Spanish nationality.[183]

In Cuba alone, around 150,000 persons qualify for Spanish nationality under the Historical Memory Act (referred to in Cuba as 'law for grandchildren'). 20 percent of them qualify as grandchildren of a Spanish exiles; the overwhelming majority, however, benefits from the fact that the requirement that their Spanish parent was born in Spain has been waived.[184] Many of those who obtain a Spanish passport do not consider moving to Spain, however. An important reason for applying for a Spanish passport is the possibility

---

descendants of Spaniards who left Spain because of the Civil War or Franco's dictatorship. (See Carrascosa's quote of the 'exposición the motivos', reading that 'la presente ley amplía la posibilidad de adquisición de la nacionalidad española a los descendientes hasta el primer grado de quienes hubiesen sido originariamente españoles. Con ello se satisfece una legítima pretensión de la emigración española, que incluye singularmente a los descendientes de quienes perdieron la nacionalidad española por el exilio a consecuencia de la Guerra Civil o la Dictadura'.)

179 Lara Aguado, "Nacionalidad e Integración Social: a propósito de la Ley 36/2002 de 8 de octubre": 1456.

180 Carrascosa González, *Curso de Nacionalidad y Extranjería*, 94.

181 Ibid.

182 The inclusion of economic emigrants in a law so clearly political as the *Ley de Memoria Histórica* has aroused a debate in Spain. Political refugees, although of the opinion that those who emigrated for economic reasons are also entitled to Spanish nationality, criticize the fact that this law seems to equalize political exile with economic exile. See 'El gobierno ofrece la nacionalidad a medio millón de exiliados de Franco', *El País*, 1 November 2008.

183 'El gobierno ofrece la nacionalidad a medio millón de exiliados de Franco', *El País*, 1 November 2008.

184 'Los nietos de los exiliados hacen fila', *El País*, 30 December 2008.

of entering the United States (in particular Miami) without a visa. Also the mere 'mental' possibility of being able to emigrate to Spain is important.[185] Another country with many Spanish exiles is Argentina, where around 300,000 people are eligible for Spanish nationality under law 52/2007.[186]

The creation of new Spaniards who do not live in Spain also raises questions on voting rights. Although there seems to be a general consensus that these Spaniards living outside Spain have the right to vote in Spanish elections, no agreement exists on the question whether voting can only take place at consulates or also by mail. The number of new Spaniards is potentially large and thus forms a considerable electorate. Political parties therefore compete for their favour and accuse each other of adopting opportunistic policies towards the issue of absentee voting.[187]

14. *Concluding Remarks*

This chapter has examined the development of dual nationality in Spain from 1931 to the present. We have seen that one of the distinct features of the Spanish dual nationality policy, the *conventional route* in which one of the two nationalities was dormant, lost much of its relevance when the *legal route* subsequently allowed both nationalities to be active at the same time. The discrepancy between these two ways of acquiring a dual nationality led to additional protocols that modified the dual nationality treaties. These protocols sought to equalize the position of those who had relied on the conventional route with those who had used the legal route. Subsequent modifications to Spanish nationality law were aimed at repairing the injustice suffered by Spaniards who had emigrated in the past for political or economic reasons, thereby losing their Spanish nationality.

Pérez Vera had argued at the time of Spain's accession to the EC that the Spanish dual nationality system should be accepted by other Member States because the Spanish nationality of a dual national would always be dormant if the person did not have domicile in Spain. The ECJ's decision in *Micheletti* made such considerations irrelevant, however. Since the judgment confirmed Member State autonomy in regulating nationality matters, there was no need for Spain to uphold a system which only allowed for one active nationality.

[185] 'Los nietos de los exiliados hacen fila', *El País*, 30 December 2008.

[186] 'Consulados a la espera de refuerzos', *El País*, 30 December 2008.

[187] 'Blanco dice que el sufragio en urna niega el derecho al vota a al mayoría de la emigración', *El País*, 20 December 2008.

This autonomy also meant that the effects of the nationality of a Member State cannot be restricted by other Member States. In other words, the possession of the nationality of a Member State is a fact that has to be recognized by the others. The recognition of this nationality cannot be subject to any additional conditions.

Although the question whether the autonomy of Member States in deciding who their nationals are should in some way be restrained will not be discussed here[188] it is remarkable that Spanish legal doctrine gives hardly any consideration to the consequences of all the modifications discussed in this chapter to the EU at large. The autonomy in nationality law as confirmed in *Micheletti* has been fully used by Spain to modify Spanish law in a way which created the possibility of acquiring Spanish nationality for many descendants of Spanish emigrants. Yet taking into consideration the politically sensitive issue of Spanish emigration, encroaching on Member State autonomy in matters of nationality will be difficult.[189]

Several commentators have nonetheless expressed the hope that the different modifications to Spanish law to the benefit of Spanish emigrants will be followed-up by measures that will benefit immigrants.[190] They argue that Spanish law should no longer exclusively look to the past, but ought to focus on the future. It was seen in the chapter on Italy that a similar sort of criticism was expressed concerning the Italian attitude towards emigrants and immigrants.

188 See Chapter 1, Section 8, as well as the General Conclusions.

189 Vonk, "Latijns-Amerikaanse Spanjaarden en het Europees burgerschap": 195.

190 Ruth Rubio Marín and Irene Sobrino, "Report on Spain", EUDO Citizenship Observatory Country Reports (2009), 27–28.

General Conclusions

Let us briefly recall the reasons for undertaking this study called 'Dual Nationality in the European Union'. Our main objective was to explore the subject of dual nationality, particularly against the background of the status of European citizenship. This status is, as we have seen, still dependent on holding the nationality of a Member State of the EU. Union citizenship not only entails the right to freely move and reside on the territory of the Member States, but the Court of Justice has also handed down a great number of judgments that have considerably strengthened the rights of EU citizens.

It was argued that the increasing number of dual nationals has led to the growing importance of dual nationality on two different levels. These we have called the intra- and extra-EU context. The former refers to a situation of dual Member State nationality; in the latter context, dual nationality is composed of a Member State and a non-Member State nationality. It was claimed that on both these levels it is precisely the combination of *dual nationality* with *European citizenship* which has a significant impact on the EU. It is also in this respect that the present study differs from others: the intra-context (and to a lesser extent the extra-context) are rather neglected in the dual nationality literature, which focuses either on dual nationality in international law, its role on the municipal level or its relation with other phenomena that are allegedly weakening the nation-state, such as transnationalism and postnationalism.

As for the intra dimension, it is sometimes claimed that holding different Member State nationalities is no longer controversial because of the supranational European citizenship attached to the nationality of each Member State. Under this view, it has become essential to hold *a* Member State nationality; the question which one is only of secondary importance. After all, dual Member State nationality does not entail more rights as far as EU citizenship is concerned; it just provides a more solid base, since the status of EU citizen is 'grounded on more than one pillar'. Although we agree with this reasoning, it must be stressed that the Court's case law concerning situations of dual Member State nationality has been strongly criticized because it impinged on the traditional private international law (PIL) approach in the Member States. Holding more Member State nationalities may therefore be uncontroversial (and perhaps even desirable) from the perspective of European integration, but the Court's approach to 'conflicts of nationalities' nonetheless effectively means an inroad into the traditional PIL practice of the Member States; hence also the very critical commentaries by PIL specialists on *García Avello* and *Hadadi*.

As was seen in Chapter 2, where we analysed the Court's case law, this inroad consists in the fact that the Court does not permit Member States to simply ignore other Member State nationalities their nationals may possess. In short, despite the Court's lack of competence to directly interfere with the conditions on acquisition and loss of Member State nationality, it does impinge on another important aspect, namely how to deal with a 'conflict of nationalities'. We have therefore speculated that cases like *García Avello* and *Hadadi*—which only indirectly addressed nationality issues—have perhaps had a greater direct impact on questions of nationality than the recent *Rottmann* case which expressly focused on such questions. Indeed, the Court's case law seems to weaken the position of the Member States' nationalities, not because the Court interferes with the conditions on acquisition and loss, but because Member States have less control over their own nationality when their nationals are dual Member State nationals. The PIL consequences hereof should definitely not be neglected. Despite our approval of this case law (see Chapter 2), the Court's approach will obviously become all the more relevant as the number of dual Member State nationals increases.

The remainder of this conclusion now continues with the extra-EU context, that is, dual nationality consisting of a Member State and a non-Member State nationality. The country reports particularly addressed this issue. In the General Introduction it was stated that the country reports primarily served two purposes. First, the detailed inquiry into the attitude towards dual nationality in two immigration and two emigration countries would allow us to test (at least for the countries under consideration) the general observation in the literature that dual nationality is becoming increasingly accepted and sometimes even embraced. Second, the comparative chapters offered an illustration of the problems that have arisen over the years in relation to dual nationality. Topics concerned loyalty to the State, military service, voting rights, and the exercise of public office. With the country reports in mind, it is now time to present our findings and to draw some general conclusions, especially in relation to one of the main themes of this study: the role of dual nationality in acquiring European citizenship through a Member State's nationality.

As said, the academic literature identifies the trend that a growing number of emigration countries use dual nationality as an instrument to maintain bonds with an expatriate population. Immigration countries, on the other hand, feel increasingly compelled—under the pressure of human rights considerations—to adopt more inclusive nationality laws; the toleration of dual nationality is generally part of a more inclusive policy towards immigrants. The literature acknowledges, though, that this picture is a generalization and that contradictory trends can also be witnessed. The country reports, by giving a detailed historical overview of the discussion on dual nationality from the beginning of the 20th century in four countries, were designed to illustrate this discussion in two traditional immigration countries (France and the Netherlands) and two traditional emigration countries (Italy and Spain).

We feel that it would go too far, however, to regard the distinction between immigration and emigration countries as described above as a sort of hypothesis to which we test the four countries under discussion. This distinction was merely used as a point of departure, and the fact that our findings do or do not correspond with it says nothing about its validity as a general distinction. In other words, it has not been our objective to draw general conclusions from the country reports as regards State practice of immigration and emigration States on the subject of dual nationality; States have too wide a discretion in nationality law, and the subject has become so politicized in recent times (and thus susceptible to change), that trying to make too broad generalizations on State practice on the basis of the comparative chapters will in our view not be very fruitful. We will therefore keep our ambitions modest by trying to draw some comparative conclusions from the country reports in this study.

France and the Netherlands have for a long time had to address the quesion of how to incorporate newcomers in their societies through nationality law (Spain and Italy, although currently also countries of immigration, have only recently started to confront this question). In France the discussion centred around the very inclusive *ius soli* principle, reintroduced in 1889 after its abolishment by the 1803 Civil Code. The assimilationist understanding of French identity lay at the basis of this reintroduction: residence combined with socialization in French society ought to be the foundation of French nationality law. This idea came under attack in the 1980s and 90s by the political right, which argued that membership of the French nation should depend on a voluntary act and not on the automatic acquisition of French nationality at birth or upon attaining the age of majority. Yet the *ius soli* tradition proved strong enough to resist these ideas and remains the heart of French nationality law to this day.

In this debate on the French nation and French identity, dual nationality was conspicuous by its absence, which may be explained by the long-standing toleration of dual nationality. After all, in the days of the demographic imperative, France was in desperate need of a greater population; whether these 'reinforcements' retained their nationality of origin was of little concern to France. The indifference towards dual nationality can therefore be traced back to the law of 1927, or perhaps even to the 1803 Civil Code, as the latter did not make acquisition of French nationality dependent upon loss of the nationality of origin. In this connection, it is perhaps strange that France was a party to the 1963 Convention for so long. This, in turn, may be explained by the need to preserve a French identity in a unified Europe. The initial success of the 1963

Convention may therefore be interpreted as a countermeasure to the European integration process started in the 1950s. It was apparently more controversial at the time to hold the nationality of another EU Member State than that of a non-EU State.

In the course of the 20th century, the issue of dual nationality was at least on two occasions the subject of debate. First in relation to the German Delbrück law of 1913, which allowed Germans to retain their nationality upon foreign naturalization. Although this law seems to have served mainly as a means to retain bonds with the German emigrant population, France feared that Germans who naturalized into French nationality would deliberately infiltrate the French system during the First World War. It is unclear to what extent these were legitimate concerns, but it proves the controversial nature of dual nationality in times of war.

Closely linked to the aspect of loyalty is that of conscription. The second occasion when dual nationality was a hot issue concerned French-Algerian children who after Algerian independence had been attributed French nationality by reason of the double *ius soli* rule under French law. In the early 1980s, the first dual nationals were called up for military service in both countries, which turned the issue of dual nationality into more than a possible diplomatic conflict or a problem of identity for the dual nationals involved. On the contrary, it became a very concrete problem for which a solution had to be found. A bilateral treaty on military obligations was finally concluded, however, showing that the problem of cumulative military obligations for dual nationals can be overcome.

Concerning the subject of dual nationality after decolonization, we may observe different positions in France and the Netherlands. Whereas the former created dual nationality on a large scale after decolonization, the Netherlands and its former colonies (Indonesia and Surinam) all had their reasons to reject dual nationality, as well as a system of option rights. In hindsight, the French position may seem remarkable in that dual nationality was thus a common phenomenon in the 1960s in relation to the former colonies while France at the same time became party to the 1963 Convention, which had been drafted to fight dual nationality in Europe.

From the French chapter we may conclude that the issue of dual nationality probably raises most concerns (and for obvious reasons) in relation to conscription and loyalty in times of war. However, as we pointed out in Chapter 1, there are several factors which render this subject less salient compared to the past. First, at present there is a far greater stability of State relations, with violence occurring more frequently within States than between States. Second, the fact that the military is now less dependent on humans and more on technology makes that the problem of conflicting demands for military service on dual nationals has diminished. General State practice seems to be that dual nationals are allowed to serve in the military. This policy has not led to any apparent problems.

In the Netherlands dual nationality featured prominently in the nationality debate since the 1850s and a renunciation requirement was strictly applied from then onwards. Yet the Dutch discussion was characterized by a recurrent question: should Dutch law and Dutch interests be the exclusive criterion in the naturalization policy, or do foreign nationality laws also play a role? Or to put it differently: should the acceptance of dual nationality be part of the naturalization policy when it is in the Dutch interest to incorporate the foreign population, or should naturalization be refused when the foreign applicant is unwilling or unable to relinquish the nationality of origin? It has been demonstrated that this question is the subject of an uninterrupted debate on dual nationality since the 1970s.

We can discern a contradictory trend in the Netherlands. On the one hand, it has become more tolerant on dual nationality by the adherence to the Second Protocol to the 1963 Convention and the introduction of a great many exceptions to the official renunciation requirement. On the other hand, the numerous controversies that have arisen since 2003 show that dual nationality is certainly not generally supported.

In this writer's submission, the Dutch policy on dual nationality is characterized by incoherence, inequality and lack of transparency. It is therefore desirable that the rules on dual nationality should be adapted in a way which makes them easier to apply. We also lament the fact that the subject has become so politicized in recent years and that nationality law in general has become the subject of frequent change. It is very doubtful, though, whether nationality law will become less politicized in the present political climate. On the contrary, it is hard to keep up with all the proposed amendments. One can thus expect that nationality law will remain the object of frequent modification in the near future, due to the hotly debated topic of immigration and integration.

The issue of loyalty to the Dutch State also arose in the Netherlands on at least two occasions. A law was passed in June 2010 which allows the withdrawal of Dutch nationality from dual nationals who had inflicted serious damage to the interests of the Netherlands, in particular by committing terrorist acts. Although we concluded that this is allowed under international law (whether it is desirable from the perspective of equal treatment of nationals is a different matter), this proposal may be difficult to execute because of human rights considerations: expulsion to countries which are often under authoritarian rule and which are confronted with terrorism themselves may lead to inhuman treatment. Another occasion concerned the appointment in 2007 of two dual nationals as State Secretaries in the Dutch government. Only a small parliamentary minority took the view, however, that members of parliament and government who possess a dual nationality implicitly cast doubt on their loyalty to the Netherlands. In this context, it is also remarkable that Queen Beatrix holds British nationality and that to date no political party has called on her to give it up.

In Italy dual nationality was definitively embraced by the 1992 Act, both for immigrants and emigrants. The toleration of dual nationality for Italian emigrants has a long history and is a reflection of the family model on which Italian nationality law is based. The very inclusive policy towards co-ethnics starkly contrasts with the exclusive policy towards immigrants. This is also reflected in the fact that Italians abroad can vote in Italian elections and have special representatives in the *national* parliament, whereas immigrants do not even have voting rights in *local* elections.

A remarkable difference exists between Italy and the Netherlands. In the former, the conditions for becoming Italian are harder to meet for immigrants compared to the Netherlands. Italy is only tolerant in one respect: naturalisees are allowed to retain their nationality of origin. In the Netherlands, however, the retention of the original nationality has been the very point of contention over the last decades. This example shows that a rather inclusive policy towards immigrants does not necessarily have to go hand in hand with the toleration of dual nationality.[1]

The Italian family model is supported by both the political right and left, yet this consensus is quite common in traditional emigration countries. However, Italy has been a country of immigration for quite some time now. The discrepancy between the treatment of 'ethnic' Italians, on the one hand, and non-privileged immigrants, on the other, can be criticized for the risk that it poses to the coherence of Italian society: certain persons who do not take part in Italian society have relatively easy access to Italian nationality through the 'ethnic' Nationality Act of 1992, whilst others who do take part have to meet very severe conditions to become Italian. One may rightly ask the question whether Italian law does not look to the past too much, and whether the present rules do not exclude a large group that significantly contributes to the Italian economy and society.

[1] Compare also Germany, which has one of the most liberal *ius soli* regimes in Europe, yet still adheres to the principle of avoiding dual nationality. Gerdes, Faist, and Rieple, "'We are All "Republican" Now': The Politics of Dual Citizenship in Germany", 46–47.

These observations equally apply to the situation in Spain, although there are also differences. Spain has a long tradition of explicitly accepting dual nationality in relation to Latin American countries on the basis of the idea of *Hispanidad*. This idea can be traced back to the 1931 Constitution—although it was not implemented at that time—and laid the groundwork for the dual nationality treaties concluded from the 1950s onwards. It was shown in Chapter 6 that Spain moved from a dual nationality system in which one nationality was in a 'dormant' state to a system in which both nationalities could be active at the same time. The Spanish doctrine had explicitly argued on the occasion of Spain's accession to the EC that the former system was compatible with Community law because of the very fact that Latin American Spaniards who lived in Latin America would not have an active Spanish nationality. In other words, unless these dual nationals lived in Spain, they were not Community nationals. This consideration became irrelevant after *Micheletti* as the judgment confirmed Member State autonomy in nationality law and thus allowed Spain to modify the conventional regime. We have seen that this resulted in the 1990s in a number of protocols amending the dual nationality treaties.

Another difference with Italy concerns the fact that Spain's inclusive policy towards Latin Americans does not particularly seem to burden other Member States. In the knowledge that most of the Latin American countries are Spanish speaking, Spain will be the primary destination if they decide to move to Europe. As far as Italy is concerned, however, it is probably not too bold a suggestion that its inclusive attitude towards emigrants and their descendants does not affect Italy as strongly as it affects other Member States.

It is particularly the Italian and Spanish approach to certain categories of persons residing outside the EU which brings us to one of the main themes of this study: *Member State autonomy in the field of nationality law in a Union where those holding European citizenship—an additional status to Member State nationality—can avail themselves of free movement and rely on the substantial body of EU citizenship case law.* The most striking illustration of this problem is probably still the *Micheletti* judgment, which showed that the Italian policy concerning co-ethnics may be a bigger burden on other EU Member States than on Italy itself. The Latin Americans eligible for Italian nationality use this nationality to settle in countries that are culturally and linguistically more related to their home country in the Americas. Those who descend from an Italian forebear and apply for Italian nationality explicitly recognize themselves that this decision is inspired primarily by the European citizenship connected to Italian nationality, and by the possibility to travel to the US without an entry visa.

It thus follows that the *Micheletti* case is still very relevant to our discussion on the relation between Member State nationality and European citizenship. In fact, Italy at present experiences its own '*Micheletti* situation' in that it is confronted with large-scale migration by nationals from a non-EU Member State (Moldova) who benefit from a very inclusive dual nationality policy by a Member State (Romania).[2] In other words, Italy presently faces a similar problem with which it burdened Spain some twenty years ago in the *Micheletti* case.

The instrumental acquisition of Italian and Romanian nationality in order to acquire the status of European citizen is clearly problematic in a European Union where free movement is one of the core objectives. The importance of free movement is also constantly stressed by the CJEU, which in different contexts has explicitly rejected an effectivity test in a conflict of Member State nationalities (see the conclusion to Chapter 2). In other words, once a third country national (TCN) acquires the nationality of a Member State, other Member States cannot argue that this Member State nationality is not the effective one. In situations falling within the scope of EU law, the Member State nationality will simply prevail over non-Member State nationalities.

It was stressed on numerous occasions that the EU has no competence in the field of nationality law. The CJEU has also not ruled against the toleration of dual nationality by the Member States. On the contrary, the Italian practice towards dual nationality was explicitly allowed in *Micheletti* and the Court ruled on that occasion that Member States could not restrict the principle of free movement by imposing additional criteria for the recognition of another Member State's nationality. This may seem obvious given the wide consensus on the principle of international law that each State is autonomous in deciding who its nationals are, but it evidently gives rise to tensions in an EU context: a great many rights are dependent on the possession of a Member State nationality, yet each Member State has a near-total freedom in deciding who holds this nationality.

Micheletti shows the problems that arise if every Member State adopts its own inclusive dual nationality policy to groups outside the EU. These groups may often not go to the Member State of which they hold the nationality, but move to others where there is work or to which they feel culturally and linguistically more connected. In other words, the descendants of Italian emigrants who, as we saw, established themselves in Argentina and Brazil in the early 20th century may use their Italian nationality to move to Spain or Portugal, but not Italy; Moldovans do not go to Romania, but move on to Italy.

---

[2] See Chapter 1, Section 11.2. On the situation of Romanians in Italy, see Cara Uccellini, "Romanian migration to Italy. Insiders and outsiders", in *Globalisation, Migration, and the Future of Europe. Insiders and Outsiders*, ed. Leila Simona Talani (London: Routledge, 2012).

A similar development of granting privileged access to nationality can be discerned in Bulgaria, where a special regime is in place for ethnic Bulgarians from neighbouring countries (Macedonia and Moldova in particular). This policy has led to a sharp increase of naturalization applications, also because the renunciation requirement was waived in 2001. The travel opportunities offered by the Bulgarian passport are again explicitly mentioned as the main motivation for applying for Bulgarian nationality.[3]

We feel that this is a highly problematic situation, especially taking into account that an effective bond with the Member State granting the nationality is often lacking. It may be questioned whether the legal tradition in traditional sending States of maintaining ties with the emigrant population, based on political or economic grounds, and sometimes on feelings of guilt, should be possible in a Union where Member States are so inter-dependent on each other through the European citizenship attached to each of their nationalities. The same objection is also true of Member States (in Eastern Europe) who for historical reasons easily grant their nationality to co-ethnics in neighbouring States.

As nationality law belongs to the reserved domain of each individual Member State, there is no mechanism which allows the EU to control the number of European citizens. A considerable number of Member States currently combine a preferential acquisition regime with the acceptance of dual nationality. This allows many individuals to become European citizen through the acquisition of a Member State nationality and retain their nationality of origin. It is often even possible to acquire the nationality of a Member State while living outside the EU. This creates large groups of external EU citizens residing in third countries whose EU citizenship is not based on a nationality reflecting a real link with an EU Member State.

We mentioned two striking examples that clearly illustrate this problem. The first concerned Fidel Castro, who could opt for Spanish nationality without having to leave Cuba merely because his father was born in 19th century Spain. As for Italy, even a person who can prove descent from an Italian who emigrated before the unification of Italy in 1861 is automatically entitled to Italian nationality, provided that the Italian ancestor was alive at the time of Italy's unification. The very generous provisions for certain groups are particularly questionable if we realize that many Member States have nationality laws that are restrictive towards non-privileged immigrants who live and contribute to the society in which they live. From the perspective of the EU, it is should be highly undesirable that a great number of individuals become

[3] Daniel Smilov and Elena Jileva, "Report on Bulgaria", EUDO Citizenship Observatory Country Reports (2009).

European citizens for instrumental reasons while others who may have been resident in the EU for a long time experience difficulties in acquiring this status because they live in a Member State with a restrictive nationality policy. In this connection, we have also pointed at the difficulties for non-EU spouses of EU citizens who frequently move within the Union to acquire their own independent EU citizenship status. This again stands in sharp contrast to the extremely easy access by some groups that have no real link with the EU whatsoever.

The foregoing explains the reason for the call for minimum harmonization of nationality law in the EU.[4] Two examples of such harmonization have been referred to in this study. First, the long-term residents directive achieved minimum harmonization as regards the status of TCNs in the EU. Second, the Nordic Union, created after the Second World War, recognized the need for harmonization of individual nationality laws if a common Nordic Union citizenship were created.

It is often asserted that the Member States will never give up their autonomy in nationality law as this would effectively be the beginning of a federal Europe. Nationality being one of the core elements of State independence, their sovereignty and existence are put in jeopardy when giving up part of this autonomy. In short, the sensitivity of nationality would militate against the idea of harmonization in this field. A strong argument can be mounted for a contrary point of view, however, according to which the Member States will become increasingly aware that it is in the interest of all to set minimum standards in the field of nationality law, for example concerning the conditions for naturalization.[5] In effect, we have tried to argue that setting minimum standards will not divest Member States of their general competence in this field. Minimum harmonization would also not mean the end of the concept of

[4] See the 'main recommendations' directed towards Member State governments and the European Union in Bauböck et al., "Introduction", 30 ff.

[5] If the EU aspires to exercise more influence in matters of nationality, it is urged to cooperate with the Council of Europe in setting up minimum standards in nationality law. In other words, rather than starting from scratch again, the EU should encourage Member States to sign and ratify the 1997 European Convention on Nationality. We share De Groot's view that the Council of Europe—due to its long-standing activities in nationality law—could be made responsible for the general harmonization attempts, thereby leaving the EU to concentrate on points that the Council of Europe cannot decide on. This involves, for example, EU rules which stipulate that residence in other Member States should be taken into account when assessing naturalization applications. This hypothesis, that is, the cooperation of the EU and the Council of Europe, shows that the form of harmonization as has been going on for some years now under the auspices of the Council of Europe will not lead to the abolition of the Member States' nationality laws. See de Groot, "Towards a European Nationality Law", 42–46.

nationality and the incorporation of the Member States in a federal Europe. On the contrary, nationality would remain the essential link between an individual and a State on the international plane, and European citizenship would remain dependent on Member State nationality.[6] Minimum harmonization would therefore not do away with Member State competence, but would be a collective effort to counter the serious negative effects on the EU at large of the different nationality laws presently in force in the EU. In our view, these negative effects are twofold. First, there are TCNs who cannot demonstrate a real link with the EU but who can nonetheless (unjustly) acquire EU citizenship through the nationality of a Member State. Second, there are TCNs who can demonstrate such a link but who, for different reasons, have difficulties acquiring the nationality of a Member State;[7] consequently, also EU citizenship is out of reach. Although minimum harmonization would—despite its modest ambition—admittedly constitute a significant inroad into the autonomy of the Member States, it might solve some of the conspicuous problems raised by dual nationality in a Union which at present allows every individual Member State an unrestrained discretion in creating external EU citizens residing in third countries.[8]

It is true that the European Commission has no competence to act in nationality matters; nor does it appear to have sought to acquire such competence.[9] Yet it remains to be seen to what extent an ever expanding Union with

[6] It was argued in Chapter 1 that disconnecting the link between Member State nationality and EU citizenship would not only remove the pressure on Member States to impose minimum standards; it would also give TCNs less incentive to naturalize, thereby hindering their integration in the country of residence.

[7] These difficulties consist in naturalization requirements that are particularly hard to meet (for example long residence periods for naturalization; a renunciation requirement; language and society tests that are part of the naturalization procedure). We also referred to the fact that non-EU spouses of EU citizens who frequently move in the territory of the Union will find themselves in a problematic situation. They may not be able to acquire the nationality of the *country of residence* because they move again to another Member State before fulfilling the waiting period for naturalization; it may also be difficult to acquire the nationality of the *EU citizen spouse* because naturalization conditions (for example language requirements) have become much stricter in recent years. More generally, it may be questioned to what extent language tests will still make sense after the establishment of EU citizenship. After all, language tests were introduced on the assumption that immigrants would stay after naturalization; EU citizenship, on the other hand, allows newly naturalized immigrants to move to other Member States, also if they do not speak their language. See Chapter 1, Section 8 for further details.

[8] de Groot, "Towards a European Nationality Law", 35.

[9] See most recently COM (2010) 603: 'On progress towards effective EU citizenship 2007–2010'.

increasing geographic mobility of EU citizens can do without some limitations on Member State autonomy. This question has become all the more pressing for two reasons: the Union is exerting a growing influence in the field of immigration law[10] and European citizenship is occupying an increasingly important place in the case law of the CJEU. To date, the Commission and the Court have been very reticent to interfere in the field of nationality law, although we have seen that behind the scenes the EU seems to exert some pressure on the nationality policy of some Member States.

On another occasion, we have argued that the different dual nationality policies will very likely create growing tensions between different Member States, possibly leading to a case brought before the CJEU.[11] As a result of the great number of Moldovans living in Italy, the Italian Minister for European Affairs has hinted at the fact that the Romanian (dual) nationality policy in respect of Moldovans may impact both the demographic equilibrium and migration fluxes in Europe. He called on the European Commission to closely watch this situation. It can thus be speculated that in the absence of concrete EU action, the lack of coordination of nationality laws may at some point lead to the Member States' disregard of *Micheletti*.[12] In other words, they may possibly refuse to recognize nationalities that have been duly granted under the laws of other Member States.

It does not seem too far-fetched to argue that a case may be brought before the Court in which a Member State (e.g. Italy) argues that another Member State's dual nationality policy (e.g. Romania) is in breach of the principle of loyal cooperation under Article 4(2) TEU (note that Spain could use the same argument against Italy).[13] Romania will then rebut that its autonomy in the

---

10 See for example Bernd Martenczuk and Servaas van Tiel, eds., *Justice, Liberty, Security: New Challenges for EU External Relations* (Brussels: VUB Press, 2008); Steve Peers, "Legislative Update: EU Immigration and Asylum Competence and Decision-Making in the Treaty of Lisbon", *European Journal of Migration and Law* 10 (2008): 219–247.

11 Costanza Margiotta and Olivier Vonk, "Nationality law and European citizenship: the role of dual nationality", in *Globalisation, Migration, and the Future of Europe. Insiders and Outsiders*, ed. Leila Simona Talani (London: Routledge, 2012). Also available in a shorter and slightly less elaborate version in Italian: Costanza Margiotta and Olivier Vonk, "Doppia cittadinanza e cittadinanza duale: normative degli Stati membri e cittadinanza europea", *Diritto, Immigrazione e Cittadinanza*, no. 4 (2010).

12 It is recalled that Spanish courts initially disregarded the ECJ's ruling in *Micheletti* (Chapter 1, Section 8).

13 In a different context, namely that of statelessness in the *Rottmann* case, Kochenov has argued that 'the principle of Union loyalty might be the right instrument to explore in pushing the Member States towards limited coordination [of their nationality laws]. At least, statelessness should definitively be made an impossible outcome of playing with different EU nationalities. EU loyalty could be construed in such a way that the Member States are bound

domain of nationality law follows from the principle that the EU respects the national identities of the Member States as laid down in Article 4(3) TEU.[14] Such a case would give the Court the possibility to decide in a situation where two national identities are at stake (note that Italy would invoke Article 4(2) precisely because it feels that its own national identity is being affected by the Romanian dual nationality policy concerning Moldovans). In the absence of legislative harmonization of the nationality laws of the Member States, it can be speculated that the criteria developed by the Court to decide the above-sketched case may be the start of a concrete harmonization process, initiated by the Court. In any case, this short hypothetical (but not wholly unimaginable) example shows how untenable the situation of exclusive Member State competence in the field of nationality has become.

In conclusion, it has been shown that the near unfettered Member State discretion in the field of nationality law can have significant negative effects, especially for other Member States than the one granting its nationality. What we can safely assume is that this will increasingly provoke conflicts between different EU Member States. The future will tell whether these effects, collectively felt by all the Member States, are experienced as a burden that is strong enough an incentive to give up part of the autonomy in nationality law and to establish some minimum standards. Much will depend on the number of external EU citizens arriving from third countries: the more external EU citizens enter the territory of the Union on the basis of a nationality expressing no real link with a Member State, the more this will probably be perceived as a serious problem affecting the EU at large. It is not unlikely that when this happens, the call for the harmonization of the Member States' nationality laws will gather momentum.

---

to coordinate their nationality regulation at least to such a minimal extent that the outcome of statelessness and the loss of EU citizenship be made impossible in the EU'. Kochenov, "Annotation Case C-135/08, *Rottmann* [2010]": 1846.

14 Article 4(2) TEU (ex Article 6(3) EC) reads: 'The Union shall respect the equality of Member States before the Treaties as well as their national identities …'. Article 4(3) TEU (ex Article 10 EC) continues: 'Pursuant to the principle of sincere cooperation, the Union and the Member States shall, in full mutual respect, assist each other in carrying out tasks which flow from the Treaties. The Member States shall take any appropriate measure, general or particular, to ensure fulfilment of the obligations arising out of the Treaties or resulting from the acts of the institutions of the Union. The Member States shall facilitate the achievement of the Union's tasks and refrain from any measure which could jeopardise the attainment of the Union's objectives'.

Bibliography

Case Law of the Court of Justice of the European Union

Case C-292/86 *Gullung* [1988] ECR I-00111.
Case C-369/90 *Micheletti* [1992] ECR I-04239.
Case C-168/91 *Konstantinidis* [1993] ECR I-01191.
Case C-122/96 *Saldanha and MTS* [1997] ECR I-05325.
Case C-336/96 *Gilly* [1998] ECR I-02793.
Case C-179/98 *Mesbah* [1999] ECR I-07955.
Case C-430/97 *Johannes v. Johannes* [1999] ECR I-03475.
Case C-184/99 *Grzelczyk* [2001] ECR I-6193.
Case C-192/99 *Kaur* [2001] ECR I-01237.
Case C-224/98 *D'Hoop* [2002] ECR I-6191.
Case C-413/99 *Baumbast* [2002] ECR I-07091.
Case C-148/02 *García Avello* [2003] ECR I-11613.
Case C-138/02 *Collins* [2004] ECR I-2703.
Case C-200/02 *Zhu and Chen* [2004] ECR I-09925.
Case C-456/02 *Trojani* [2004] ECR I-7573.
Case C-209/03 *Bidar* [2005] ECR I-02119.
Case C-353/06 *Grunkin-Paul* [2008] ECR I-07639.
Case C-158/07 *Förster* [2008] ECR I-08507.
Case C-123/08 *Wolzenburg* [2009] ERC I-09621.
Case C-168/08 *Hadadi* [2009] ECR I-06871.
Case C-135/08 *Rottmann* [2010] ECR I-01449.
Case C-208/09 *Sayn-Wittgenstein* [2010] ECR I-00000.
Case C-34/09 *Ruiz Zambrano* [2011] ECR I-00000.
Case C-434/09 *McCarthy* [2011] ECR I-00000.

Literature

Ackermann, Thomas, "Annotation Case C-148/02 *García Avello* [2003]", *Common Market Law Review* 44 (2007): 141–154.

Adviescommissie voor vreemdelingenzaken, *Nederlanderschap in een onbegrensde wereld. Advies over het Nederlandse beleid inzake meervoudige nationaliteit* (Den Haag: ACVZ, 2008).

Aghahosseini, Mohsen, *Claims of Dual Nationals and the Development of Customary International Law. Issues Before the Iran-United States Claims Tribunal* (Leiden/Boston: Martinus Nijhoff Publishers, 2007).

Aguilar Benítez de Lugo, Mariano, "Doble nacionalidad", *Boletín de la Facultad de Derecho* 10–11 (1996): 219–262.

Ahmad Ali, Hamied A., *De Toescheidingsovereenkomst inzake nationaliteiten tussen Nederland en Suriname*, Dissertatie Universiteit Utrecht (s'-Gravenhage: Sdu, 1998).

——, "Surinaamse emigranten. Duaal burgerschap, onvoorwaardelijke toelating en gelijke behandeling", in *Collected Essays in honour of Kees Groenendijk* (Nijmegen: Wolf Legal Publishers, 2008), pp. 153–159.

Alessio, Marcello, "La doppia cittadinanza come problema 'quantitativo' ", 2000. Available from http://www.umanesimolatino.it/fondazionecassamarca/05_emigrazione/convegni/con_treviso.html.

Alvarez Rodríguez, Aurelia, "Doble nacionalidad. Jurisprudencia española de DIPr", *Revista de derecho internacional* 40 (1988): 152–161.

—, *Nacionalidad y emigración* (Madrid: La Ley, 1990).

—, "Binacionalidad en el ordenamiento español y su repercusión en la Union Europea", in *Estudios de derecho europeo privado*, eds. Juan María Díaz Fraile and Registrales Centro de Estudios (Madrid: J. San José, 1994), pp. 27–120.

—, *Guía de la nacionalidad española*. 2nd ed (Madrid: Ministerio de Trabajo y Asuntos Sociales, 1996).

—, "Modificación del convenio de doble nacionalidad entre España y Nicaragua", *Revista de Emigración e Inmigración*, no. 540 (1999).

—, "Principios inspiradores y objetivos de la nueva reforma del derecho español de la nacionalidad: Las principales novedades de la ley 36/2002 de 8 de octubre", *Revista de derecho migratorio y extranjería* 1 (2002): pp. 47–86.

—, *Nacionalidad española: normativa vigente e interpretación jurisprudencial* (Cizur Menor, Navarra: Thomson/Aranzadi, 2008).

Amoury Combs, Nancy, "Iran-United States Claims Tribunal. On Children and Dual Nationality: Sabet and The Islamic Republic of Iran", *Leiden Journal of International Law* 13, no. 1 (2000): 173–191.

Ancel, Marc, "Les conflits de nationalités. Contribution à la recherche d'une solution rationnelle des cas de multi-nationalité", *Journal de droit international* 64 (1937): 19–40.

Arena, Marta, Bruno Nascimbene, and Giovanna Zincone, "Italy", in *Acquisition and Loss of Nationality, Policies and Trends in 15 European Countries*, eds. Rainer Bauböck, Eva Ersbøll, Kees Groenendijk and Harald Waldrauch (Amsterdam: Amsterdam University Press, 2006), pp. 329–366.

Arendt, Hannah, *The Origins of Totalitarianism* (New York: Schocken Books, 2004).

Arroyo Montero, Rafael "Modificación de los convenios sobre doble nacionalidad como instrumentos de integración (los Protocolos adicionales concluidos entre España y Costa Rica de 23 de octubre de 1997 y entre España y Nicaragua de 12 de noviembre de 1997)", in *Actas de las XVIII Jornadas de la Asociación Española de Profesores de Derecho Internacional y Relaciones Internacionales*, pp. 193–199.

Audenino, Patrizia, and Maddalena Tirabassi, *Migrazioni Italiane. Storia e storie dall'Ancien régime a oggi* (Milano: Bruno Mondadori, 2008).

Audit, Bernard, "Le droit international privé a fin du XXe siècle: progrès ou recul", *Revue internationale de droit comparé* 50, no. 2 (1998): 421–448.

Aznar Sanchez, Juan, *La doble nacionalidad (doctrina, convenios, legislación, jurisprudencia)* (Madrid: Marcial Pons, 1977).

Baratta, Roberto, "Problematic elements of an implicit rule providing for mutual recognition of personal and family status in the EC", *IPRax* 27 (2007): 4–11.

Bariatti, Stefania, "Italie", in *Nationalité et statut personnel. Leur interaction dans les traités internationaux et dans les législations nationales*, ed. Michel Verwilghen (Bruxelles: Bruylant, 1984), pp. 123–142.

—, *La disciplina giuridica della cittadinanza italiana* (Milano: Giuffrè Editore, 1989).

Barnard, Catherine, "Annotation Case C-209/03 *Bidar* [2005]", *Common Market Law Review* 42 (2005): 1465–1489.

Barry, Brian, *Culture and Equality. An Egalitarian Critique of Multiculturalism* (Cambridge: Polity Press, 2001).

Baty, Th., "La double nationalité est-elle possible?", *Revue de droit international et de législation comparée* 7 (1926): 622–632.

Bauböck, Rainer, "Stakeholder Citizenship and Transnational Political Participation: a Normative Evaluation of External Voting", *Fordham Law Review* 75, no. 5 (2007): 2393–2447.

—, "The Trade-off Between Transnational Citizenship and Political Autonomy", in *Dual Citizenship in Global Perspective, From Unitary to Multiple Citizenship*, eds. Thomas Faist and Peter Kivisto (New York: Palgrave Macmillan, 2007), pp. 69–92.

—, "Why European Citizenship? Normative Approaches to Supranational Union", *Theoretical Inquiries in Law* 8, no. 2 (2007): 452–488.

Bauböck, Rainer, Eva Ersbøll, Kees Groenendijk, and Harald Waldrauch, "Introduction", in *Acquisition and Loss of Nationality, Policies and Trends in 15 European Countries*, eds. Rainer Bauböck, Eva Ersbøll, Kees Groenendijk and Harald Waldrauch (Amsterdam: Amsterdam University Press, 2006).

——, eds., *Acquisition and Loss of Nationality, Policies and Trends in 15 European Countries* (Amsterdam: Amsterdam University Press, 2006).

Bauböck, Rainer, Bernhard Perchinig, and Wiebke Sievers, eds., *Citizenship policies in the New Europe* (Amsterdam: Amsterdam University Press, 2009).

Belorgey, Jean-Michel, "Le droit de la nationalité: évolution historique et enjeux", in *Questions de nationalité. Histoire et enjeux d'un code*, ed. Smaïn Laacher (Paris: Éditions l'Harmattan, 1987), pp. 61–79.

Benedek, Wolfgang, "Nationality decrees in Tunis and Morocco (Advisory Opinion)", in *Encyclopedia of Public International Law*, ed. R Bernhardt (Amsterdam: Elsevier, 1997), pp. 510–511.

Blatter, Joachim K., "Dual Citizenship and Democracy", 2009. Available from http://www.unilu.ch/files/Dual-Citizenship-and-Democracy-wp01.pdf.

Blázquez Peinado, Dolores, "Sentencia Grunkin y Paul, C-253/06", *Revista de Derecho Communitario Europeo* 33 (2009): 649–664.

Böcker, Anita, Kees Groenendijk, and Betty de Hart, "De toegang tot het Nederlanderschap, effecten van 20 jaar beleidswijzigingen", *Nederlands Juristenblad*, no. 3 (2005): 157–164.

Boele-Woelki, Katharina, *Die Effektivitätsprüfung der Staatsangehörigkeit im niederländischen internationalen Familienrecht*, Dissertation Freie Universität Berlin (Deventer: Kluwer, 1981).

Boeles, Pieter, "Noot onder *Grunkin-Paul*", *Jurisprudentie Vreemdelingenrecht, 2008/447.*

——, "Het nut van nationaliteit", *Nederlands Juristenblad*, no. 42 (2007): 2666–2671.

Bogdan, Michael, "Some Reflections on the Treatment of Dutch Same-Sex Marriages in European and Private International Law", in *Intercontinental Cooperation Through Private International Law*, eds. Talia Einhorn and Kurt Siehr (The Hague: T.M.C. Asser Press, 2004), pp. 24–35.

——, *Concise Introduction to EU Private International Law* (Groningen: Europa Law Publishing, 2006).

Boggiano, Antonio, *La doble nacionalidad en derecho internacional privado* (Buenos Aires: Ediciones Depalma, 1973).

Boll, Alfred Michael, *Multiple Nationality and International Law* (Leiden/Boston: Martinus Nijhoff Publishers, 2007).

Borrás, Alegría, "Prinzipien des Internationalen Familienrechts", in *Europäisches Gemeinschaftsrecht und IPR. Ein Beitrag zur Kodifikation der Allgemeinen Grundsätze des Europäischen Kollisionsrechtes*, ed. Gerte Reichelt (Wien: Manzsche Verlags- und Universitätsbuchhandlung, 2007), pp. 55–67.

Bosma, Martin, *De schijn-élite van de valse munters* (Amsterdam: Uitgeverij Bert Bakker, 2010).

Bosniak, Linda, "Multiple nationality and the postnational transformation of citizenship", in *Rights and Duties of Dual nationals - Evolutions and Prospects*, eds. David A. Martin and Kay Hailbronner (The Hague: Kluwer Law International, 2003), pp. 27–48.

Boulbès, Raymond, *Droit français de la nationalité* (Paris: Sirey, 1957).

Boushaba, Zouhir, *Nationalité et double nationalité dans les rapports Franco-Algeriens*, Thèse pour le doctorat en droit (Marseille: L'Université d'Aix-Marseille, 1991).

Bouza I Vidal, Nuria, "El ámbito personal de aplicación del derecho de establecimiento en los supuestos de doble nacionalidad: comentario a la Sentencia del TJCE de 7 de julio de 1992 en el caso Micheletti c. Delegación del Gobierno de Cantabria (As. C-369/90)", *Revista de Instituciones Europeas* 20 (1993): 563–581.

Brøndsted Sejersen, Tanja, "'I Vow to Thee My Countries' - The Expansion of Dual Citizenship in the 21st Century", *International Migration Review* 42, no. 3 (2008): 523–549.

Brownlie, Ian, "General Course on Public International Law", in *Recueil des cours de l'Académie de droit international de la Haye* (Leiden: Sijthoff, 1995), pp. 13–227.

——, *Principles of Public International Law*. 6th ed (Oxford: Oxford University Press, 2003).

Brubaker, Rogers, *Citizenship and Nationhood in France and Germany* (Cambridge, Massachusetts: Harvard University Press, 1992).

Bruschi, Christian, "Droit de la nationalité et égalité des droits de 1789 à la fin du XIXe siècle", in *Questions de nationalité. Histoire et enjeux d'un code*, ed. Smaïn Laacher (Paris: Éditions l'Harmattan, 1987), pp. 21–59.
Bureau, Dominique, and Horatia Muir Watt, *Droit international privé* (Paris: Presses Universitaires de France, 2007).
Burrows, Noreen, and Rosa Greaves, *The Advocate General and EC Law* (Oxford: Oxford University Press, 2007).
Buzzati, G.C., "Questioni sulla cittadinanza degli italiani emigrati in America", *Rivista di diritto civile* 1 (1909): 445–474.
—, "Note sulla cittadinanza", *Rivista di diritto civile* 8 (1916): 485–506.
Cabaleiro, Ezequiel, "La doble nacionalidad", *Revista general de legislación y jurisprudencia*, no. 212 (1962): 7–75.
Calduch Cervera, Rafael, "La Emigración a Iberoamérica y la Política Exterior Española (1898–1975)". Available from http://www.incipe.org/Espa%F1oles%20de%20ambas%20orillas.pdf.
Camiscioli, Elisa, "Intermarriage, Independent Nationality, and the Individual Rights of French Women. The law of 10 August 1927", *French Politics, Culture and Society* 17, no. 3–4 (1999): 52–71.
Canavaggio, Jean, *Don Quichotte du livre au mythe. Quatre siècles d'errance* (Paris: Fayard, 2005).
Cano Bazaga, Elena, "La doble nacionalidad con los países iberoamericanos y la constitución de 1978". Available from http://www.us.es/cidc/mesas/estadoHumanos.htm.
Carlier, Jean-Yves, *Autonomie de la Volonté et Statut Personnel* (Bruxelles: Bruylant, 1992).
—, "La libre circulation des personnes dans l'Union européenne", *Journal des Tribunaux. Droit Européen* (2000): 54–60.
—, "Droits de l'homme et nationalité", *Annales de Droit de Louvain* 63, no. 3 (2003): 243–257.
—, "Annotation Case C-200/02 *Chen* [2004]", *Common Market Law Review* 42 (2005): 1121–1131.
Carrascosa González, Javier, "Dual nationality and Community law", *Tolleys Immigration and Nationality Law and Practice* 8 (1994): 7–12.
—, *Curso de Nacionalidad y Extranjería*. Javier Carrascosa González, Antonia Durán Ayago and Beatriz L. Carrillo Carrillo (Madrid: Colex, 2008).
Carrera, Sergio, *In Search of the Perfect Citizen? The Intersection between Integration, Immigration and Nationality in the EU* (Leiden/Boston: Martinus Nijhoff Publishers, 2009).
Castangia, Isabella, *Il criterio della cittadinanza nel diritto internazionale privato* (Napoli: Casa Editrice Dott. Eugenio Jovane, 1983).
Chan, Johannes M.M., "The right to a nationality as a human right. The current trend towards recognition", *Human Rights Law Journal* 12, no. 1–2 (1991): 1–14.
Chattou, Zoubir, and Mustapha Belbah, *La double nationalité en question. Enjeux et motivations de la double appartenance* (Paris: Karthala, 2002).
Chevallier, Jacques, *L'État postmoderne* (Paris: Librairie Générale de Droit et de Jurisprudence, 2003).
Churchill, Winston S., *The Second World War, vol. 2* (London: Cassell & Co., 1949).
Çinar, Dilek, and Harald Waldrauch, "Austria", in *Acquisition and Loss of Nationality, Policies and Trends in 15 European Countries*, eds. Rainer Bauböck, Eva Ersbøll, Kees Groenendijk and Harald Waldrauch (Amsterdam: Amsterdam University Press, 2006), pp. 19–61.
Clavel, Sandrine, *Droit international privé* (Paris: Dalloz, 2009).
Clerici, Roberta, "L'Italia e i nuovi accordi sul servizio militare", *Rivista di diritto internazionale privato e processuale* 13 (1977): 679–685.
Closa, Carlos, "The concept of citizenship in the Treaty on European Union", *Common Market Law Review* 29 (1992): 1137–1169.
—, "Citizenship of the Union and nationality of Member States", *Common Market Law Review* 32 (1995): 487–518.
Cogordan, George, *La nationalité au point de vue des rapports internationaux* (Paris: L. Larose et Forcel, 1890).

Colas, Dominique, *Citoyenneté et nationalité* (Paris: Gallimard, 2004).

Commission de la Nationalité, "Audition de Paul Lagarde", in *Être français aujourd'hui et demain. Rapport remis au Premier ministre par Marceau Long, président de la commission de la Nationalité (Tome1: Les auditions publiques)* (Paris: Documentation française, 1988), pp. 113–129.

——, *Être français aujourd'hui et demain. Rapport remis au Premier ministre par Marceau Long, président de la commission de la Nationalité (Tome 2: Conclusions et propositions de la Commission de la Nationalité)* (Paris: Documentation française, 1988).

Condinanzi, Massimo, Allesandra Lang, and Bruno Nascimbene, *Citizenship of the Union and Free Movement of Persons* (Leiden/Boston: Martinus Nijhoff Publishers, 2008).

Costa-Lascoux, Jacqueline, "L'acquisition de la nationalité française, une condition d'intégration?", in *Questions de nationalité. Histoire et enjeux d'un code*, ed. Smaïn Laacher (Paris: Éditions l'Harmattan, 1987), pp. 81–118.

Courbe, Patrick, *Le nouveau droit de la nationalité*. 2nd ed (Paris: Dalloz, 1998).

Craig, Paul, and Gráinne De Búrca, *EU Law. Text, Cases, and Materials*. 4th ed (Oxford: Oxford University Press, 2008).

d'Argent, Pierre, "Nationalité et droit international public", *Annales de Droit de Louvain* 63, no. 3 (2003): 221–231.

d'Avout, Louis, "Jurisprudence: Grunkin et Paul", *Journal du Droit International* 136 (2009): 207–216.

——, "Jurisprudence: Hadadi", *Journal du Droit International* 137, no. 1 (2010): 163–183.

d'Olivier Farran, C., "The Dutch royal family is British!", *Nederlands tijdschrift voor internationaal recht* 4 (1956): 52–56.

Daadouch, Christophe, *Le droit de la nationalité* (Paris: Editions MB formation, 2002).

Dagevos, Jaco, *Dubbele nationaliteit en integratie* (Den Haag: Sociaal Cultureel Planbureau, 2008).

Darras, Loïc, *La double nationalité*, Thèse pour le doctorat en droit (Paris: Université Paris II, 1986).

De Bonis, Andrea, and Marco Ferrero, "Dalla cittadinanza etno-nazionale alla cittadinanza di residenza", *Diritto, Immigrazione e Cittadinanza* 5, no. 2 (2004): 49–63.

de Castro y Bravo, Federico, "Nationalité, double et supra-nationalité", in *Recueil des cours de l'Académie de droit international de la Haye* (Leiden: Sijthoff, 1961), pp. 521–634.

de Geouffre de La Pradelle, Géraud, "Nationalité française, extranéité, nationalités étrangères", in *Mélanges dédiés à Dominique Holleaux* (Paris: Librairie de la Cour de Cassation, 1990), pp. 135–155.

——, "Dual Nationality and the French Citizenship Tradition", in *Dual Nationality, Social Rights and Federal Citizenship in the US and Europe*, eds. Randall Hansen and Patrick Weil (New York: Berghahn Books, 2002), pp. 191–212.

de Groot, Gerard-René, *Gelijkheid van man en vrouw in het nationaliteitsrecht. Preadvies uitgebracht voor de Nederlandse Vereniging voor Rechtsvergelijking* (Deventer: Kluwer, 1977).

——, *Staatsangehörigkeitsrecht im Wandel* (Köln: Heymanns, 1989).

——, "Eenenveertig jaren nationaliteitsrecht", *Burgerzaken & Recht* 5, no. 6 (1998): 146–152.

——, "Negeert Spanje de Micheletti-beslissing van het Europese Hof van Justitie?", *Migrantenrecht* 13, no. 4 (1998): pp. 123–124.

——, "Vingt et un ans après: De gelijke behandeling van man en vrouw in het nationaliteitsrecht", in *De meerwaarde van de rechtsvergelijking. Opstellen aangeboden aan prof. H.U. Jessurun d'Oliveira bij gelegenheid van zijn afscheid als bestuurslid van de Nederlandse Vereniging voor Rechtsvergelijking*, ed. E.H. Hondius (Deventer: Kluwer, 1999), pp. 71–77.

——, "The European Convention on Nationality: a step towards a ius commune in the field of nationality law", *Maastricht Journal of European and Comparative Law* 7, no. 2 (2000): 117–157.

——, "Europees nationaliteitsverdrag in werking voor Nederland", *Migrantenrecht* 17, no. 1 (2002): 4–13.

——, "Zum Verhältnis der Unionsbürgerschaft zu den Staatsangehörigen in der Europäischen Union", in *Europäisches Integrationsrecht im Querschnitt*, ed. P. Müller-Graff (Baden-Baden: Nomos, 2002), pp. 67–86.

——, "The background of the changed attitude of Western European States with respect to multiple nationality", in *New concepts of citizenship: residential/regional citizenship and dual nationality*, eds. Atsushi Kondo and Charles Westin (Stockholm: CEIFO, 2003), pp. 99–119.
——, *Handboek Nieuw Nationaliteitsrecht* (Deventer: Kluwer, 2003).
——, "Notities bij de bepalingen betreffende het verlies van het Nederlanderschap", *Migrantenrecht* 18, no. 4/5 (2003): 133–147.
——, "Towards a European Nationality Law – Vers un droit européen de nationalité. Inaugural lecture, delivered on 13 November 2003 on the occasion of the acceptance of the Pierre Harmel chair of professeur invité at the University of Liège", 2003. Available from www.ejcl.org.
——, "Namenrecht op drift", *Burgerzaken & Recht* 11, no. 5 (2004): 212–217.
——, "Towards European Conflict Rules in Matters of Personal Status", *Maastricht Journal of European and Comparative Law* 11, no. 2 (2004): 115–119.
——, "The access to European citizenship for third country spouses of a European citizen", in *Liber Amicorum Paul Delnoy* (Bruxelles: Larcier, 2005), pp. 93–133.
——, "Geschiedenis van het Nederlandse nationaliteitsrecht in de negentiende eeuw", in *Wordt voor Recht gehalden, Opstellen ter gelegenheid van vijfentwintig jaar Werkgroep Limburgse Rechtsgeschiedenis*, eds. A.M.J.A. Berkvens and Th.J. van Rensch (Maastricht: Werkgroep Limburgse Rechtsgeschiedenis, 2005), pp. 375–420.
——, "Het ontnemen van het Nederlanderschap wegens terroristische activiteiten", in *Crossing borders, Essays in European and Private International Law, Nationality Law and Islamic Law in honour of Frans van der Velden*, eds. Paulien van der Grinten and Ton Heukels (Deventer: Kluwer, 2005), pp. 215–230.
——, "Towards a European Nationality Law", in *Migration, Integration and Citizenship, A Challenge for Europe's Future*, ed. Hildegard Schneider (Maastricht: Forum, 2005), pp. 13–53.
——, "Een pleidooi voor meervoudige nationaliteit", *Migrantenrecht* 21, no. 3 (2006): 100–105.
——, *Achtentwintig Nederlanders? Bewerkte adviezen en casus over de toepassing van de Nederlandse nationaliteitswetgeving* ('s-Gravenhage: Elsevier Overheid, 2007).
——, "Private International Law Aspects Relating to Homosexual Couples", 2007. Available from http://www.ejcl.org/113/article113-12.pdf.
——, *Nationaliteit en rechtszekerheid* (Den Haag: Boom Juridische uitgevers, 2008).
——, "Beperking van meervoudige nationaliteit: een nieuwe afscheidssymfonie?", *Migrantenrecht* 24, no. 2 (2009): 50–52.
——, "Een optierecht voor latente Nederlanders", *Asiel- en Migrantenrecht* 1, no. 8 (2010): 411–416.
——, "Invloed van het Unierecht op het nationaliteitsrecht van de Lidstaten: Overwegingen over de Janko Rottmann-beslissing van het Europese Hof van Justitie", *Asiel- en Migrantenrecht* 1, no. 5/6 (2010): 293–300.
de Groot, Gerard-René, and Carlos Bollen, "Netherlands nationality law", in *Nationality laws in the European Union - Le droit de la nationalité dans l'Union Européene*, ed. Bruno Nascimbene (Milano: Giuffrè Editore, 1996), pp. 545–597.
——, "Nationality Law of the Kingdom of the Netherlands in International Perspective", *Netherlands Yearbook of International Law* 35 (2004): 205–250.
de Groot, Gerard-René, and Nicole Doeswijk, "Nationaliteitsrecht en het Internationale Recht", in *De Nationaliteit in Internationaal en Europees Perspectief. Preadviezen van Prof. Mr Frans J.A. van der Velden, Prof. Mr Gerard-René de Groot en Mr Nicole Doeswijk* (Den Haag: T.M.C. Asser Press, 2004), pp. 45–99.
de Groot, Gerard-René, and Jan-Jaap Kuipers, "The New Provisions on Private International Law in the Treaty of Lisbon", *Maastricht Journal of European and Comparative Law* 15, no. 1 (2008): 109–114.
de Groot, Gerard-René, and Susan Rutten, "Op weg naar een Europees IPR op het gebied van het personen- en familierecht", *Tijdschrift Nederlands Internationaal Privaatrecht* 22, no. 3 (2004): 273–282.
de Groot, Gerard-René, and Hildegard Schneider, "Die zunehmende Akzeptanz von Fällen mehrfacher Staatsangehörigkeit in West-Europa", in *Japanischer Brückenbauer zum deutschen Rechtskreis* (Berlin: Duncker & Humblot, 2006), pp. 65–80.

de Groot, Gerard-René, and Matjaz Tratnik, *Nederlands nationaliteitsrecht*. 4th ed, Studiepockets privaatrecht (Deventer: Kluwer, 2010).

de Groot, Gerard-René, and Maarten Vink, *Meervoudige nationaliteit in Europees perspectief: een landenvergelijkend overzicht*, Voorstudie voor de Adviescommissie voor Vreem delingenzaken (Den Haag: ACVZ, 2008).

——, "Loss of Citizenship. Trends and Regulations in Europe", EUDO Citizenship Observatory Country Reports (2010), pp. 1–53.

de Haas-Engel, Renata Henriette, *Het Indonesisch Nationaliteitsrecht*, Dissertatie Universiteit Maastricht (Deventer: Kluwer, 1993).

de Hart, Betty, *Onbezonnen vrouwen. Gemengde relaties in het nationaliteitsrecht en het vreemdelingenrecht*, Dissertatie Katholieke Universiteit Nijmegen (Amsterdam: Aksant, 2003).

——, "Meervoudige nationaliteit, integratie en terrorisme", *Migrantenrecht* 19, no. 8 (2004): 293–299.

——, "The End of Multiculturalism: The End of Dual Citizenship? Political and Public Debates on Dual Citizenship in the Netherlands (1980–2004)", in *Dual Citizenship in Europe: From Nationhood to Societal Integration*, ed. Thomas Faist (Aldershot: Ashgate, 2007), pp. 77–102.

——, "Dubbele nationaliteit: verschil moet er zijn", *Asiel- en Migrantenrecht* 1, no. 9 (2010): 456–463.

de Hart, Betty, Hermie de Voer, and Stans Goudsmit, "Latente Nederlanders: discriminatie van kinderen van Nederlandse moeders in het nationaliteitsrecht", *Nederlands Juristenblad*, no. 17 (2006): 932–939.

de Winter, Louis Isaac, "Nationality or Domicile", in *Recueil des cours de l'Académie de droit international de la Haye* (Leiden: Sijthoff, 1969), pp. 347–504.

Del Vecchio, Anna Maria, "Alcuni rilievi in tema di nazionalità e di cittadinanza nel contesto internazionale", *Rivista internazionale dei diritti dell'uomo* 10, no. 1 (1997): 7–24.

——, "La considerazione del principio di effettività nel vincolo di nazionalità e di cittadinanza doppia o plurima (e problematiche relative)", *Rivista internazionale dei diritti dell'uomo* 13, no. 1 (2000): 11–31.

Delpérée, Francis, "La citoyenneté multiple", *Annales de Droit de Louvain* 56 (1996): 261–273.

——, "Nationalité, droit constitutionnel et droit européen", *Annales de Droit de Louvain* 63, no. 3 (2003): 233–241.

Dethloff, Nina, "Doppelstaatsangehörigkeit und Internationales Privatrecht", *Juristenzeitung*, no. 2 (1995): 64–73.

Devoretz, Don J., "The Economics of Citizenship: A Common Intellectual Ground for Social Scientists?", *Journal of Ethnic and Migration Studies* 34, no. 4 (2008): 679–693.

Devoto, Fernando, "In Argentina", in *Storia dell'emigrazione Italiana*, eds. Piero Bevilaqua, Andreina De Clementi and Emilio Franzina (Roma: Donizelli, 2002), pp. 25–46.

Donner, Ruth, *The Regulation of Nationality in International Law*. 2nd ed (New York: Transnational Publishers Inc., 1994).

Dougan, Michael, "The constitutional dimension to the case law on Union citizenship", *European Law Review* 31 (2006): 613–641.

——, "The Treaty of Lisbon 2007: winning minds, not hearts", *Common Market Law Review* 45 (2008): 617–703.

——, "The Spatial Restructuring of National Welfare States within the European Union: The Contribution of Union Citizenship and the Relevance of the Treaty of Lisbon", in *Integrating Welfare Functions into EU Law: From Rome to Lisbon*, eds. U. Neergaard, R. Nielsen and L. Roseberry (Copenhagen: DJØF Publishing, 2009), pp. 147–187.

Dugard, John, "Diplomatic Protection: Human Right or State Right?", *Australian Year Book of International Law* 24 (2005): 75–91.

Duggan, Christopher, *A Concise History of Italy* (Cambridge: Cambridge University Press, 2007).

Dumbrava, Costica, "How Illiberal are Citizenship Rules in European Union Countries?", EUDO Citizenship Working Paper 2010/50, pp. 1–37.

Dummett, Ann, and Andrew Nicol, *Subjects, Citizens, Aliens and Others. Nationality and Immigration Law* (London: Weidenfeld and Nicolson, 1990).

Echezarreta Ferrer, María Teresa, ed., *Legislacíon sobre nacionalidad.* 4th ed (Madrid: Tecnos, 2003).

Editorial, "Two-speed European citizenship? Can the Lisbon Treaty help close the gap?", *Common Market Law Review* 45 (2008): 1–11.

——, "Combating reverse discrimination: who should do the job?", *Maastricht Journal of European and Comparative Law* 16, no. 4 (2010).

Entzinger, Han, "The Rise and Fall of Multiculturalism: The Case of the Netherlands", in *Toward Assimilation and Citizenship: Immigrants in Liberal Nation-States,* eds. Christian Joppke and Eva Morawska (Basingstoke: Palgrave Macmillan, 2003), pp. 59–86.

Espinar Vicente, José María, *La nacionalidad y la extranjería en el sistema jurídico español* (Madrid: Civitas, 1994).

Evans, Andrew, "Nationality Law and European Integration", *European Law Review* 16 (1991): 190–215.

Faist, Thomas, "Social Citizenship in the European Union: Nested Membership", *Journal of Common Market Studies* 39, no. 1 (2001): 37–58.

——, "Dual citizenship: Change, Prospects, and Limits", in *Dual Citizenship in Europe: From Nationhood to Societal Integration,* ed. Thomas Faist (Aldershot: Ashgate, 2007), pp. 171–200.

——, "The Fixed and Porous Boundaries of Dual Citizenship", in *Dual Citizenship in Europe: From Nationhood to Societal Integration,* ed. Thomas Faist (Aldershot: Ashgate, 2007), pp. 1–43.

——, "Introduction: The Shifting Boundaries of the Political", in *Dual Citizenship in Global Perspective, From Unitary to Multiple Citizenship,* eds. Thomas Faist and Peter Kivisto (New York: Palgrave Macmillan, 2007), pp. 1–23.

——, ed., *Dual Citizenship in Europe: From Nationhood to Societal Integration* (Aldershot: Ashgate, 2007).

Faist, Thomas, Jürgen Gerdes, and Beate Rieple, "Dual Citizenship as a Path-Dependent Process", *International Migration Review* 38, no. 3 (2004): 913–944.

Faist, Thomas, and Peter Kivisto, eds., *Dual Citizenship in Global Perspective, From Unitary to Multiple Citizenship* (New York: Palgrave Macmillan, 2007).

Fernández Rozas, José Carlos, *Derecho español de la nacionalidad* (Madrid: Editorial Tecnos, 1987).

Fernández Vargas, Valentina, "Últimas oleadas y cierre del proceso", in *Historia General de la Emigración Española a Iberoamérica* (Madrid: Historia 16, 1992).

Flournoy, Richard W., "Observations on the new German law of nationality", *American Journal of International Law* 8 (1914): 477–486.

Forcese, Craig, "The Capacity to Protect: Diplomatic Protection of Dual Nationals in the 'War on Terror'", *The European Journal of International Law* 17, no. 2 (2006): 369–394.

Foyer, Jean, "Problèmes de droit international privé dans les relations entre la France et les nouveaux États africains d'expression française", in *Travaux du comité français de droit international privé, 1958–1962.*

Franck, Thomas M., *The Empowered Self. Law and Society in the Age of Individualism* (New York: Oxford University Press, 1999).

——, "Multiple citizenship: autres temps, autres moeurs", in *Mélanges en l'honneur de Nicolas Valticos* (Paris: Éditions A. Pedone, 1999), pp. 149–158.

Fromageot, Henri, *De la double nationalité des individus & des sociétés* (Paris: A. Rousseau, 1892).

Fusi, Juan Pablo, *Franco. Autoritarismo y poder personal* (Madrid: Grupo Santillana de Ediciones, 2001).

Galicki, Z.W., "Does the right to a nationality belong to the catalogue of human rights?", in *Feestbundel Zilverentant,* ed. F.J.A. van der Velden (Den Haag: Ministerie van Justitie-Directie Wetgeving, 1998), pp. 69–73.

Gallo, Gerardo, and Guido Tintori, "Come si diventa cittadini italiani. Un approfondimento statistico", in *Familismo legale: come (non) diventare italiani,* ed. Giovanna Zincone (Roma-Bari: Editori Laterza, 2006), pp. 107–138.

García Valdés, Pedro, "El problema sefardí a través de la Constitución de la República española", *Revista general de legislación y jurisprudencia* 162 (1933): 756–764.

Gattini, Andrea, "Diritto al nome e scelta del nome nei casi di plurima cittadinanza", *Rivista di diritto internazionale* 79 (1996): 93–109.

Gaudemet-Tallon, Hélène, "Nationalité, status personnel et droits de l'homme", in *Festschrift für Erik Jayme, Band 1*, eds. Heinz-Peter Mansel, Thomas Pfeiffer, Herbert Kronke, Christian Kohler and Rainer Hausmann (München: Sellier, 2004), pp. 205–221.

Gerdes, Jürgen, Thomas Faist, and Beate Rieple, " 'We are All "Republican" Now': The Politics of Dual Citizenship in Germany", in *Dual Citizenship in Europe: From Nationhood to Societal Integration*, ed. Thomas Faist (Aldershot: Ashgate, 2007), pp. 45–76.

Giuliano, Mario, "Accordi internazionali bilaterali relativi al servizio militare", *Rivista di diritto internazionale privato e processuale* 1 (1965): 329–331.

Green, Simon, "Between Ideology and Pragmatism: The Politics of Dual Nationality in Germany", *International Migration Review* 39, no. 4 (2005): 921–952.

Greenwood, Christopher, "Nationality and the Limits of the Free Movement of Persons in Community Law", *Yearbook of European Law* 7 (1987): 185–210.

Griffin, William L., "International Claims of Nationals of Both the Claimant and Respondent States - The Case History of a Myth", *International Lawyer* 1, no. 3 (1966–1967): 400–423.

Groenendijk, Kees, "Le rôle changeant de la nationalité pour la condition juridique de l'étranger", in *La condition juridique de l'étranger, hier et aujourd'hui. Actes du Colloque organisé à Nimègue les 9–11 mai 1988 par les Facultés de Droit de Poitiers et de Nimègue* (Nijmegen: Faculteit der Rechtsgeleerdheid, 1988), pp. 101–115.

——, "Noot onder *Saldanha*", in *Rechtspraak Vreemdelingenrecht* (Nijmegen: Ars Aequi Libri, 1997), pp. 328–329.

——, "Achterstand, dubbele nationaliteit en betrouwbare informatie: drie persoonlijke herinneringen voor Frans Zilverentant", in *Feestbundel Zilverentant*, ed. F.J.A. van der Velden (Den Haag: Ministerie van Justitie-Directie Wetgeving, 1998).

——, "Noot onder *Mesbah*", in *Rechtspraak Vreemdelingenrecht* (Ars Aequi Libri: Nijmegen, 1999), pp. 367–370.

——, "Minister Verdonk: Grote woorden, minder daden en riskante ideeën", *Nederlands Juristenblad*, no. 24 (2006): 1308–1311.

Groenendijk, Kees, and Eric Heijs, "Nationality Law in the Netherlands", in *Towards a European Nationality. Citizenship, Immigration and Nationality Law in the EU*, eds. Randall Hansen and Patrick Weil (Hampshire: Palgrave Publishers, 2001), pp. 143–172.

Grosso, Enrico, "Riflessioni a prima lettura sulla nuova legge in materia di voto dei cittadini all'estero". Available from www.forumcostituzionale.it/site/index3.php?option=content&task...

——, "Il voto all'estero: tra difficoltà applicative e dubbi di costituzionalità", *Quaderni Costituzionali* 22, no. 2 (2002): 346–348.

Guerrero, José Gustave, *La Codification du Droit International. La Première Conférence (La Haye, 13 mars - 12 Avril 1930)* (Paris: A. Pedone, 1930).

Guiguet, Benoît, *Citoyenneté et nationalité: limites de la rupture d'un lien*, Thèse pour le doctorat en droit (Florence: European University Institute, 1997).

——, "Citizenship and nationality: tracing the French roots of the distinction", in *European Citizenship: A European Challenge*, ed. Massimo La Torre (The Hague: Kluwer Law International, 1998), pp. 95–111.

Guiho, Pierre, *La nationalité*, Guides essentiels (Paris: L'hermès, 1996).

Guild, Elspeth, *The Legal Elements of European Identity. EU citizenship and Migration Law* (The Hague: Kluwer Law International, 2004).

Haandrikman, A.G.J.J., "De nationaliteit in het internationaal privaatrecht", in *Nationaliteit in Volkenrecht en Internationaal Privaatrecht, Preadvies voor de Nederlandse Vereniging voor Internationaal Recht* (Deventer: Kluwer, 1981), pp. 43–65.

Hailbronner, Kay, "Rights and duties of dual nationals: changing concepts and attitudes", in *Rights and Duties of Dual nationals - Evolutions and Prospects*, eds. David A. Martin and Kay Hailbronner (The Hague: Kluwer Law International, 2003), pp. 19–26.

——, "Union Citizenship and Access to Social Benefits", *Common Market Law Review* 42 (2005): 1245–1267.

——, "Germany", in *Acquisition and Loss of Nationality, Policies and Trends in 15 European Countries*, eds. Rainer Bauböck, Eva Ersbøll, Kees Groenendijk and Harald Waldrauch (Amsterdam: Amsterdam University Press, 2006), pp. 213–251.

——, “Multiple Nationality and Diplomatic Protection”, in *Festschrift Tugrul Ansay zum 75. Geburtstag*, eds. Sabih Arkan and Aynur Yongalik (Alphen aan den Rijn: Kluwer Law International, 2006), pp. 117–124.

——, “Nationality in public international law and European law”, in *Acquisition and Loss of Nationality, Policies and Trends in 15 European Countries*, eds. Rainer Bauböck, Eva Ersbøll, Kees Groenendijk and Harald Waldrauch (Amsterdam: Amsterdam University Press, 2006), pp. 35–104.

Hall, Stephen, *Nationality, Migration Rights and Citizenship of the Union* (Dordrecht/Boston/London: Martinus Nijhoff Publishers, 1995).

——, “Loss of Union Citizenship in Breach of Fundamental Rights”, *European Law Review* 21 (1996): 129–143.

——, “The European Convention on Nationality and the right to have rights”, *European Law Review* 24 (1999): 586–602.

——, “Determining the Scope ratione personae of European Citizenship: Customary International Law prevails for Now”, *Legal Issues of Economic Integration*, no. 3 (2001): 355–360.

Hammar, Thomas, “State, Nation, and Dual Citizenship”, in *Immigration and the Politics of Citizenship in Europe and North America*, ed. Rogers William Brubaker (Lanham: University Press of America, 1989), pp. 81–95.

Hansen, Randall, and Patrick Weil, “Introduction: Citizenship, Immigration and Nationality: Towards a Convergence in Europe?”, in *Towards a European Nationality. Citizenship, Immigration and Nationality Law in the EU*, eds. R. Hansen and P. Weil (Hampshire: Palgrave Publishers, 2001), pp. 1–23.

——, “Introduction”, in *Dual nationality, Social Rights and Federal Citizenship in the US and Europe*, eds. Randall Hansen and Patrick Weil (New York: Berghahn Books, 2002), pp. 1–15.

Hau, Wolfgang, “Doppelte Staatsangehörigkeit im europäischen Eheverfahrensrecht (Hadadi)”, *IPRax* 30, no. 1 (2010): 50–53.

Hecker, Hellmuth, *Staatsangehörigkeit im Code Napoléon als europäisches Recht: die Rezeption des Französischen Code Civil von 1804 in Deutschland und Italien in Beziehung zum Staatsangehörigkeitsrecht* (Hamburg und Frankfurt am Main: A. Metzner, 1980).

Heijs, Eric, *Van vreemdeling tot Nederlander. De verlening van het Nederlanderschap aan vreemdelingen 1813–1992*, Dissertatie Katholieke Universiteit Nijmegen (Amsterdam: Het Spinhuis, 1995).

Helms, Tobias, “Europarechtliche Vorgaben zur Bestimmung des Namensstatuts von Doppelstaatern: Anmerkung zu EuGH, Urteil vom 2.10.2003, C-148/02 - *García Avello*”, *Zeitschrift für Gemeinschaftsprivatrecht* 1 (2005): 36–39.

Hendriks, Karel, and Olivier Vonk, “Mapping statelessness in the Netherlands”, UNHCR report (2011). Available in Dutch and English from www.unhcr.nl.

Henrich, Dieter, “Anerkennung statt IPR: Eine Grundsatzfrage”, *IPRax* 25 (2005): 422–424.

Hirsch Ballin, Ernst, “Burgerrechten. Rede uitgesproken bij de aanvaarding van het ambt van hoogleraar in de rechten van de mens aan de Universiteit van Amsterdam op 9 september 2011”. Available from http://www.oratiereeks.nl/upload/pdf/PDF-2406weboratie_Hirsch_Balin2.pdf.

Hool, Frédéric-Henri, *Les effets de la double nationalité en droit suisse* (Neuchâtel: Editions du Griffon, 1949).

Horváth, Enikö *Mandating identity: citizenship, kinship laws and plural nationality in the European Union*, Dissertation European University Institute (Alphen aan den Rijn: Kluwer Law International, 2007).

Howard, Marc Morjé, “Variation in Dual Citizenship Policies in the Countries of the EU”, *International Migration Review* 39, no. 3 (2005): 697–720.

——, “Comparative Citizenship: An Agenda for Cross-National Research”, *Perspectives on Politics* 4, no. 3 (2006): 443–455.

Huntington, Samuel P., *Who are we? The challenges to America's national identity* (New York: Simon & Schuster, 2004).

Iglesias Buhigues, José Luis, “Doble nacionalidad y Derecho comunitario: A propósito del asunto C-369/90, Micheletti, [1992]”, in *Hacia un nuevo orden internacional y europeo.*

Estudios en homenaje al profesor don Manuel Díez de Velasco (Madrid: Editorial Tecnos 1993), pp. 953–967.

Iliopoulou, Anastasia, and Helen Toner, "Annotation Case C-184/99 *Grzelczyk* [2001]", *Common Market Law Review* 39 (2002): 609–620.

Ioannis Baganha, Maria, and Constança Urbano de Sousa, "Portugal", in *Acquisition and Loss of Nationality, Policies and Trends in 15 European Countries*, eds. Rainer Bauböck, Eva Ersbøll, Kees Groenendijk and Harald Waldrauch (Amsterdam: Amsterdam University Press, 2006), pp. 435–476.

Iordachi, Constantin, "Country report: Romania", EUDO Citizenship Observatory Country Reports (2009), pp. 1–22.

——, "Politics of citizenship in post-communist Romania: Legal traditions, restitution of nationality and multiple memberships", in *Citizenship Policies in the New Europe* (Amsterdam: Amsterdam University Press, 2009), pp. 177–209.

Itzigsohn, José, "Migration and Transnational Citizenship in Latin America: The Cases of Mexico and the Dominican Republic", in *Dual Citizenship in Global Perspective, From Unitary to Multiple Citizenship*, eds. Peter Kivisto and Thomas Faist (New York: Palgrave Macmillan, 2007), pp. 113–134.

Jacobs, Francis, "Citizenship of the European Union - A Legal Analysis", *European Law Journal* 13, no. 5 (2008): 591–610.

Jayme, Erik, *Pasquale Stanislao Mancini. Internationales Privatrecht zwischen Risorgimento und praktischer Jurisprudenz* (Ebelsbach: Verlag Rolf Gremer, 1980).

——, "Cours général de droit international privé", in *Recueil des cours de l'Académie de droit international de la Haye* (Leiden: Sijthoff, 1995), pp. 13–267.

Jayne Hill, David, "Dual citizenship in the German imperial and state citizenship law", *American journal of international law* 12 (1918): 356–363.

Jessurun d'Oliveira, Hans Ulrich, "Nederlanders, wie zijn dat?", *Nederlands Juristenblad*, no. 24 (1977): 589–598.

——, "De herziening van ons nationaliteitsrecht", *Nederlands Juristenblad*, no. 9 (1982): 245–256.

——, "Burgers en buitenlui", *Nederlands Juristenblad*, no. 41 (1983): 1301–1310.

——, "Tendenzen in Europees nationaliteitsrecht", *Nederlands Juristenblad*, no. 11–12 (1989): 357–361.

——, "Is Reverse Discrimination Still Permissible Under the Single European Act?", in *Forty years on: The evolution of postwar private international law in Europe* (Amsterdam: Kluwer, 1990), pp. 71–86.

——, "Het 'meerdere', een regeringsnotitie over meervoudige nationaliteit", *Nederlands Juristenblad*, no. 43 (1991): 1734–1741.

——, "Annotation Case C-369/90 *Micheletti* [1992]", *Common Market Law Review* 30 (1993): pp. 623–637.

——, "Union citizenship: pie in the sky?", in *A citizens' Europe: in search of a new order*, eds. Allan Rosas and Esko Antola (London: Sage, 1995), pp. 58–84.

——, "Het Europees Verdrag inzake Nationaliteit", in *Trends in het nationaliteitsrecht*, ed. Hans Ulrich Jessurun d'Oliveira ('s-Gravenhage: Sdu, 1998), pp. 7–47.

——, "The Artifact of 'Sham Marriages'", *Yearbook of Private International Law* 1 (1999): 49–83.

——, "Nationality and the European Union after Amsterdam", in *Legal issues of the Amsterdam Treaty*, eds. David O'Keeffe and Patrick Twomey (Oxford: Hart Publishing, 1999), pp. 395–412.

——, "Freedom of Movement of Spouses and Registered Partners in the European Union", in *Private Law in the International Arena - Liber Amicorum Kurt Siehr* (The Hague: T.M.C. Asser Press, 2000), pp. 527–543.

——, "Noot onder *Manjit Kaur*", *Jurisprudentie Vreemdelingenrecht* (2001): 474–477.

——, "The EU and a Metamorphosis of Private International Law", in *Reform and Development of Private International Law. Essays in honour of Sir Peter North*, ed. J Fawcett (Oxford: Oxford University Press, 2002), pp. 111–136.

——, "Het Europese Hof activeert het Europese burgerschap", *Nederlands Juristenblad* 78 (2003): 2242.

——, "Alweer plannen om de afstandseis bij naturalisatie uit te breiden", *Nederlands Juristenblad*, no. 43 (2004): 2232–2238.
——, "Dubbelzinnigheden over dubbele nationaliteit", in *Woorden als daden. Commentaar en opinies* (Deventer: Kluwer, 2004), pp. 132–133.
——, "Europees burgerschap: dubbele nationaliteit?", in *Asser Colloquium Europees Recht, 33e zitting, 2003* (The Hague: T.M.C. Asser Press, 2004), pp. 91–125.
——, "Nationaliteit en koninklijk huis", in *Woorden als daden. Commentaar en opinies* (Deventer: Kluwer, 2004), pp. 148–153.
——, "Beatrix is ook Brits," *HP/De Tijd*, 16 December 2005.
——, "Ontneming van Nederlanderschap als zet in de terrorismebestrijding", *Migrantenrecht*, no. 10 (2006): 352–361.
——, "Veel lawaai om een klutsei", *Nederlands Juristenblad*, no. 3 (2006): 138–143.
——, "Book review of Alfred Boll's 'Multiple Nationality and International Law' ", *The American Journal of International Law* 101 (2007): 922–928.
——, "Turmoil around a naturalisation decree or how the Dutch cabinet stumbled over a pebble", in *Vers de nouveaux équilibres entre ordres juridiques: liber amicorum Hélène Gaudemet-Tallon* (Paris: Dalloz, 2008), pp. 319–333.
——, "Het zinkende schip van het Verdrag van Straatsburg 1963 en zijn Tweede Protocol", *Nederlands Juristenblad*, no. 44/45 (2009): 2876–2879.
——, "Hinkende namen", *Migrantenrecht* 24, no. 2 (2009): 41–46.
——, "How do international organisations cope with the personal *status* of their staff members? Some observations on the recognition of (same-sex) marriages in international organisations", in *Nuovi strumenti del diritto internazionale privato. Liber Fausto Pocar*, eds. Gabriella Venturini and Stefania Bariatti (Milano: Giuffrè Editore, 2009), pp. 505–531.
——, "Ontkoppeling van nationaliteit en Unieburgerschap? Opmerkingen over de *Rottmann*-zaak", *Nederlands Juristenblad*, no. 16 (2010): 1028–1033.
Jessurun d'Oliveira, Hans Ulrich, and Andrew Evans, "Nationality and Citizenship", in *Human Rights and the European Community: Methods of protection*, eds. Antonio Cassese, Andrew Clapham and Joseph Weiler (Baden-Baden: Nomos, 1991), pp. 299–350.
Jones-Correa, Michael, "Under Two Flags: Dual Nationality in Latin American and its Consequences for Naturalization in the United States", *International Migration Review* 35, no. 4 (2001): 997–1029.
——, "Seeking shelter: Immigrants and the Divergence of Social Rights and Citizenship in the United States", in *Dual Nationality, Social Rights and Federal Citizenship in the US and Europe*, eds. Randall Hansen and Patrick Weil (New York: Berghahn books, 2002), pp. 233–263.
Joppke, Christian, *Immigration and the Nation-State. The United States, Germany, and Great Britain* (Oxford: Oxford University Press, 1999).
——, "Citizenship between De- and Re-ethnicization (1)", *European Journal of Sociology* 44, no. 3 (2003): 429–458.
——, *Selecting by Origin: Ethnic Migration in the Liberal State* (Cambridge, Massachusetts: Harvard University Press, 2005).
——, "Comparative Citizenship: A Restrictive Turn in Europe?", *Law & Ethics of Human Rights* 2, no. 1 (2008): 1–41.
Kadirbeyoglu, Zeynep, "Changing conceptions of citizenship in Turkey", in *Citizenship policies in the new Europe* eds. Rainer Bauböck, Bernhard Perchinig and Wiebke Sievers (Amsterdam: Amsterdam University Press, 2007), pp. 293–311.
——, "National Transnationalism: Dual Citizenship in Turkey", in *Dual Citizenship in Europe: From Nationhood to Societal Integration*, ed. Thomas Faist (Aldershot: Ashgate, 2007), pp. 127–146.
Kammann, Karin, *Probleme mehrfacher Staatsangehörigkeit*, Europäische Hochschulschriften (Frankfurt am Main: Peter Lang, 1984).
Karamanoukian, Aram, "La double nationalité et le service militaire", *Revue générale de droit international public* 78 (1974): 459–484.
Kivisto, Peter, "Conclusion: The Boundaries of Citizenship in a Transnational Age", in *Dual Citizenship in Global Perspective, From Unitary to Multiple Citizenship*, eds. Peter Kivisto and Thomas Faist (New York: Palgrave Macmillan, 2007), pp. 272–287.

Ko Swan Sik, *De meervoudige nationaliteit* (Leiden: Sijthoff, 1957).
——, "Nationaliteit en het volkenrecht", in *Nationaliteit in Volkenrecht en Internationaal Privaatrecht, Preadvies voor de Nederlandse Vereniging voor Internationaal Recht* (Deventer: Kluwer, 1981), pp. 3–42.
——, "Book review of Alfred Boll's 'Multiple Nationality and International Law' ", *Netherlands International Law Review* 55 (2008): 407–414.
Kochenov, Dimitry, "Rounding up the Circle: The Mutation of Member States' Nationalities under Pressure from EU Citizenship", EUDO Citizenship Working Paper 2010/23.
——, "Annotation Case C-135/08, *Rottmann* [2010]", *Common Market Law Review* 47 (2010): 1831–1846.
Koenig-Archibugi, Mathias, "National and European Citizenship: The Italian Case in Historical Perspective", *Citizenship Studies* 7, no. 1 (2003): 85–109.
Kohler, Christian, "Verständigungsschwierigkeiten zwischen europäischem Gemeinschaftsrecht und internationalem Privatrecht", in *Festschrift für Erik Jayme, Band 1*, eds. Heinz-Peter Mansel, Thomas Pfeiffer, Herbert Kronke, Christian Kohler and Rainer Hausmann (München: Sellier, 2004), pp. 445–459.
Kojanec, Giovanni, *Nuove norme sulla cittadinanza italiana: Riflessi interni ed internazionali* (Milano: Franco Angeli, 1995).
——, "The citizenship of the European Union", in *Feestbundel Zilverentant*, ed. F.J.A. van der Velden (Den Haag: Ministerie van Justitie-Directie Wetgeving, 1998), pp. 133–138.
——, "Report on Multiple Nationality", (2000).
Kooijmans, Pieter H., "Is the Right to Diplomatic Protection a Human Right?", in *Studi di diritto internazionale in onore di Gaetano Arangio-Ruiz* (Napoli: Editoriale Scientifica, 2004), pp. 1975–1984.
Kortmann, C.A.J.M., "La nationalité et les fonctions politiques et publiques aux Pays-Bas", in *La condition juridique de l'étranger, hier et aujourd'hui. Actes du Colloque organisé à Nimègue les 9–11 mai 1988 par les Facultés de Droit de Poitiers et de Nimègue* (Nijmegen: Faculteit der Rechtsgeleerdheid, 1988), pp. 59–65.
Koslowski, Rey, *Migrants and Citizens. Demographic Change in the European State System* (Ithaca, NY: Cornell University Press, 2000).
——, "Challenges of international cooperation in a world of increasing dual nationality", in *Rights and Duties of Dual nationals - Evolutions and Prospects*, eds. D.A Martin and Kay Hailbronner (The Hague: Kluwer Law International, 2003), pp. 157–182.
Kostakopoulou, Dora, "European Union Citizenship: Writing the Future", *European Law Journal* 13, no. 5 (2007): 623–646.
Kovács, Mária M., "The Politics of Dual Citzenship in Hungary", in *Dual Citizenship in Global Perspective, From Unitary to Multiple Citizenship*, eds. Peter Kivisto and Thomas Faist (New York: Palgrave Macmillan, 2007), pp. 92–112.
Kubicki, Philipp, "Kurze Nachlese zur Rechtssache Grunkin-Paul", *Europäische Zeitschrift für Wirtschaftsrecht*, no. 11 (2009): 366–369.
Kuipers, Jan-Jaap, *Het Debat omtrent Meervoudige Nationaliteit in de Tweede Kamer 1983–2007* (Maastricht University: Faculty of Law, 2007).
——, "Cartesio and Grunkin-Paul: Mutual Recognition as a Vested Rights Theory Based on Party Autonomy in Private Law", 2010. Available from http://cadmus.eui.eu/dspace/bitstream/1814/13426/1/EJLS_2009_2_2_5_EN.pdf.
Kunoy, Bjørn, "A Union of National Citizens: The Origins of the Court's Lack of *Avant-Gardisme* in the *Chen* Case", *Common Market Law Review* 43 (2006): 179–190.
La Torre, Massimo, ed., *European Citizenship: A European Challenge* (The Hague: Kluwer Law International, 1998).
Lagarde, Paul, "De quelques conséquences de la décolonisation sur le droit français de la nationalité", in *Mélanges Savatier* (Paris: Dalloz, 1965), pp. 511–544.
——, "Le principe de proximité dans le droit international privé contemporain. Cours général de droit international privé", in *Recueil des cours de l'Académie de droit international de la Haye* (Leiden: Sijthoff, 1986).
——, "Vers une approche fonctionnelle du conflit positif de nationalités", *Revue critique de droit international privé* 77, no. 1 (1988): 29–54.

——, "L'accession des immigrés à la nationalité du pays d'accueil de le problème de la double nationalité", in *Immigrés et réfugiés dans les démocraties occidentales, défis et solutions*, ed. D. Turpin (Paris: Economica, 1989), pp. 199–213.
——, "La pluralité de nationalités comme moyen d'intégration des résidents étrangers: Développements en France", in *Plural Nationality: Changing attitudes* (Conference at the European University Institute, Florence, 1992).
——, "La nationalité française rétrécie (commentaire critique de la loi du 22 juillet 1993 réformant le droit de la nationalité)", *Revue critique de droit international privé* 82, no. 4 (1993): 535–563.
——, "Le droit à une nationalité", in *Droit et libertés fondamentaux*, eds. Rémy Cabrillac, Marie-Anne Frison-Roche and Thierry Revet (Paris: Dalloz, 1996), pp. 143–156.
——, "Le droit français de la nationalité", in *Nationality laws in the European Union - Le droit de la nationalité dans l'Union Européene*, ed. Bruno Nascimbene (Milano: Giuffrè Editore, 1996), pp. 309–336.
——, *La nationalité française*. 3rd ed (Paris: Dalloz, 1997).
——, "La loi du 16 mars 1998 sur la nationalité: une réforme incertaine", *Revue critique de droit international privé* 87, no. 3 (1998): 379–401.
——, "La nationalité et droit international privé", *Annales de Droit de Louvain* 63, no. 3 (2003): 205–219.
——, "Développements futurs du D.I.P.", *RabelsZ* 68 (2004): 225–243.
——, "Jurisprudence: García Avello", *Revue critique de droit international privé* 93 (2004): 192–202.
——, "L'oeuvre de la Commission Internationale de l'État Civil en matière de nom des personnes", in *Festschrift für Erik Jayme, Band 2*, eds. Heinz-Peter Mansel, Thomas Pfeiffer, Herbert Kronke, Christian Kohler and Rainer Hausmann (München: Sellier, 2004), pp. 1291–1305.
——, "La reconnaissance mode d'emploi", in *Vers de nouveaux équilibres entre ordres juridiques: liber amicorum Hélène Gaudemet-Tallon* (Paris: Dalloz, 2008), pp. 481–501.
——, "Jurisprudence: Grunkin-Paul", *Revue critique de droit international privé* 98, no. 1 (2009): 86–93.
Lara Aguado, Angeles, "Nacionalidad e Integración Social: a propósito de la Ley 36/2002 de 8 de octubre", *La Ley* 24, no. 5694 (2003): 1444–1460.
Le Gouvernement du Grand-Duché de Luxembourg, *The Luxembourg Nationality Law of 23 October 2008* (Luxembourg: Imprimerie Centrale, 2009).
Lefebvre, Edwige Liliane, "Republicanism and Universalism: Factors of Inclusion or Exclusion in the French Concept of Citizenship", *Citizenship Studies* 7, no. 1 (2003): 15–36.
Legomsky, Stephen H., "Dual nationality and military service: strategy number two", in *Rights and Duties of Dual nationals - Evolutions and Prospects*, eds. David A. Martin and Kay Hailbronner (The Hague: Kluwer Law International, 2003), pp. 79–134.
Lequette, Yves, "Le droit international privé de la famille à l'épreuve des conventions internationales", in *Recueil des cours de l'Académie de droit international de la Haye* (Leiden: Sijthoff, 1994).
——, "La nationalité française dévaluée", in *L'avenir du droit. Mélanges en hommage à François Terré* (Paris: Dalloz, 1999), pp. 349–392.
Levitt, Peggy, "Variations in Transnational Belonging: Lessons from Brazil and the Dominican Republic", in *Dual Nationality, Social Rights and Federal Citizenship in the US and Europe*, eds. Randall Hansen and Patrick Weil (New York: Berghahn books, 2002), pp. 264–289.
Liebich, André, "Introduction: the vicissitudes of citizenship in the new EU states", in *Citizenship Policies in the New Europe*, eds. Rainer Bauböck, Bernhard Perchinig and Wiebke Sievers (Amsterdam: Amsterdam University Press, 2007), pp. 17–40.
——, "How Different is the "New Europe"? Perspectives on States and Minorities", *CEU Political Science Journal* 3, no. 3 (2008): 269–292.
Lippolis, Vincenzo, "La doppia cittadinanza nel disegno di legge Amato: perché non ripensarci?", *Quaderni Costituzionali* 26 (2006): 803–805.
Lodder, G.G., *Vreemdelingenrecht in vogelvlucht*. 3rd ed (Den Haag: Sdu uitgevers, 2008).

Lonni, Ada, "Histoire des migrations et identité nationale en Italie", *Revue Européenne des Migrations Internationales* 9, no. 1 (1993): 29–46.

Lourdjane, Ahmed, "Les musulmans originaires d'Algérie peuvent-ils bénéficier de la double nationalité: française et algérienne?", *Revue juridique et politique, Indépendance et coopération* 21 (1967): 295–300.

Lubbers, Ruud, *De vrees voorbij* (Amsterdam: De Bezige Bij, 2007).

Mackaay, Ejan, "Bipatridie: een kijkje uit den vreemde", *Nederlands Juristenblad*, no. 36 (1982): 993.

——, "Verlies van het Nederlanderschap voor emigranten", *Nederlands Juristenblad*, no. 41 (1983): 1319–1322.

Macklin, Audrey, "The Securitisation of Dual Citzenship", in *Dual Citizenship in Global Perspective, From Unitary to Multiple Citizenship*, eds. Peter Kivisto and Thomas Faist (New York: Palgrave Macmillan, 2007), pp. 42–66.

Magnette, Paul, *Citizenship: the history of an idea* (Colchester: ECPR Press, 2005).

——, "How can one be European? Reflections on the Pillars of European Civic Identity", *European Law Journal* 13, no. 5 (2007): 664–679.

Makarov, Alexander, "Règles générales du droit de la nationalité", in *Recueil des cours de l'Académie de droit international de la Haye* (Leiden: Sijthoff, 1949), pp. 269–376.

——, "Le droit d'option en cas de double nationalité dans les conventions internationales", in *Liber amicorum J.P.A. François* (Leiden: Sijthoff, 1959), pp. 194–202.

——, *Allgemeine Lehren des Staatsangehörigkeitsrechts*. 2nd ed (Stuttgart: Kohlhammer, 1962).

——, *Deutsches Staatsangehörigkeitsrecht. Kommentar* (Frankfurt a.M: Alfred Metzner Verlag, 1966).

Mansel, Heinz-Peter, *Personalstatut, Staatsangehörigkeit und Effektivität*, Münchener Universitätsschriften. Reihe der Juristischen Fakultät (Band 70) (München: C.H. Beck'sche Verlagsbuchhandlung, 1988).

Marchisio, Sergio, "Les conventions de la commission international de l'état civil", in *Nuovi strumenti del diritto internazionale privato. Liber Fausto Pocar*, eds. Gabriella Venturini and Stefania Bariatti (Milano: Giuffrè Editore, 2009), pp. 659–672.

Margiotta, Costanza, and Olivier Vonk, "Nationality law and European citizenship: the role of dual nationality", EUDO Citizenship Working Paper 2010/66.

——, "Doppia cittadinanza e cittadinanza duale: normative degli Stati membri e cittadinanza europea", *Diritto, Immigrazione e Cittadinanza*, no. 4 (2010): 13–34.

——, "Nationality law and European citizenship: the role of dual nationality", in *Globalisation, Migration, and the Future of Europe. Insiders and Outsiders*, ed. Leila Simona Talani (London: Routledge, 2012), pp. 208–223.

Marshall, Thomas Humphrey, *Citizenship and social class* (London: Pluto, 1992).

Martenczuk, Bernd, and Servaas van Tiel, eds., *Justice, Liberty, Security: New Challenges for EU External Relations* (Brussels: VUB Press, 2008).

Martin, David A., "Introduction: The trend toward dual nationality", in *Rights and Duties of Dual nationals - Evolutions and Prospects*, eds. David A. Martin and Kay Hailbronner (The Hague: Kluwer Law International, 2003), pp. 3–18.

Martin, David A., and Kay Hailbronner, eds., *Rights and duties of dual nationals: changing concepts and attitudes* (The Hague: Kluwer Law International, 2003).

Martiny, Dieter, "Probleme der Doppelstaatsangehörigkeit im deutschen Internationalen Privatrecht", *Juristenzeitung*, no. 23 (1993): 1145–1150.

——, "Is Unification of Family Law Feasible or even Desirable?", in *Towards a European Civil Code*, eds. Arthur Hartkamp, Martijn Hesselink, Ewoud Hondius, Carla Joustra, Edgar du Perron and Muriel Veldman (Nijmegen: Ars Aequi Libri, 2004), pp. 307–333.

——, "Anmerkung Grunkin-Paul", *Deutsche Notar-Zeitschrift*, no. 6 (2009): 450–458.

Marzal Yetano, Toni, "The Constitutionalisation of Party Autonomy in European Family Law", *Journal of Private International Law* 6, no. 1 (2010): 155–193.

Marzo, Claire, *La dimension sociale de la citoyenneté européenne*, Thèse pour le doctorat en droit (Florence: European University Institute, 2009).

Mauco, Georges, *Les étrangers en France. Leur rôle dans l'activité économique* (Paris: Armand Colin, 1932).

McClean, David, and Kisch Beevers, *Morris: The Conflict of Laws* (London: Sweet & Maxwell, 2009).

McCrory, Donald, *Cervantes. De schepper van Don Quichot* (Amsterdam: Atheneum-Polak&Van Gennep, 2005).

McLynn, Frank, *Napoleon: a biography* (London: Pimlico, 1998).

Meeusen, Johan, "Bipatridie in internationaal en Europees verband", in *Met rede ontleend, de rede ontkleed. Opstellen aangeboden aan Fons Heyvaert* (Gent: Mys & Breesch, uitgevers, 2002), pp. 219–234.

—, "Op weg naar een communautair internationaal familie(vermogens)recht? Enkele Europeesrechtelijke beschouwingen", in *Europees internationaal familierecht. Preadviezen van Prof. Dr Johan Meeusen en Mr G.E.Schmidt* (Den Haag: T.M.C. Asser Press, 2006), pp. 5–70.

—, "Instrumentalisation of Private International Law in the European Union: Towards a European Conflicts Revolution?", *European Journal of Migration and Law* 9 (2007): 287–305.

—, "Who is afraid of European private international law?", in *Nuovi strumenti del diritto internazionale privato. Liber Fausto Pocar*, eds. Gabriella Venturini and Stefania Bariatti (Milano: Giuffrè Editore, 2009), pp. 685–700.

—, "The Grunkin and Paul Judgment of the ECJ, or How to Strike a Delicate Balance between Conflict of Laws, Union Citizenship and Freedom of Movement in the EC", *Zeitschrift für Europäisches Privatrecht* 18, no. 1 (2010): 186–201.

Menghetti, Guido, "Problematiche relative agli immigrati dall'Argentina", 2002. Available from www.interno.it.

Miaja de la Muela, Adolfo, "Los convenios de doble nacionalidad entre España y algunas republicas americanas", *Revista de derecho internacional* 18 (1966): 381–410.

Mill, John Stuart, "Nationality", in *Utilitarianism, Liberty, Representative Government*, ed. H.B. Acton (London: Dent, 1972), pp. 359–366.

Miller, David, "The Ethical Significance of Nationality", *Ethics* 98, no. 4 (1988): 647–662.

—, *On Nationality* (Oxford: Clarendon Press, 1995).

—, "In Defence of Nationality", in *Citizenship and National Identity* (Cambridge: Polity Press, 2000).

—, "Republicanism, National Identity, and Europe", in *Republicanism and political theory*, eds. Cécile Laborde and John Maynor (Malden, MA: Blackwell, 2008), pp. 133–158.

Ministère de la Justice, *La nationalité française. Recueil des textes législatifs et réglementaires, des conventions internationales et autres documents* (Paris: Ministère de la Justice, 2002).

Mok, M.R., "Noot onder Grunkin-Paul", Nederlandse Jurisprudentie 2009/64.

Mole, Nuala, "Multiple nationality and the European convention on human rights", Report for the 2nd European conference on nationality, Challenges to national and international law on nationality at the beginning of the new millenium (2001), pp. 129–147.

Moorman van Kappen, O., "Les concepts précurseurs de "nationalité" dans le droit néerlandais jusq'au milieu du 19ième siècle", in *La condition juridique de l'étranger, hier et aujourd'hui. Actes du Colloque organisé à Nimègue les 9–11 mai 1988 par les Facultés de Droit de Poitiers et de Nimègue* (Nijmegen: Faculteit der Rechtsgeleerdheid, 1988), pp. 197–207.

Moreau, M., "Nationalité: française. Propos en marge du rapport de la Commission de la Nationalité", in *La condition juridique de l'étranger, hier et aujourd'hui. Actes du Colloque organisé à Nimègue les 9–11 mai 1988 par les Facultés de Droit de Poitiers et de Nimègue* (Nijmegen: Faculteit der Rechtsgeleerdheid, 1988), pp. 21–35.

Morelli, M., "L'accordo di cittadinanza italo-argentino: un'occassione mancata", *Rivista di diritto internazionale* 60 (1977): 152–160.

Möstl, Markus, "Preconditions and limits of mutual recognition", *Common Market Law Review* 47 (2010): 405–436.

Moura Ramos, Rui Manuel, "La double nationalité d'après le droit portugais", *Boletim da facultade de direito da Universidade de Coimbra* 59 (1983): 181–211.

—, *Do direito português da nacionalidade* (Coimbra: Coimbra Editora, 1984).

—, "La double nationalité et les liens spéciaux avec d'autres pays (Colonies précédentes, unions d'états, etc…) Les développements et les perspectives au Portugal", in *Plural Nationality: Changing attitudes* (Conference at the European University Institute, Florence, 1992).

——, "Le droit portugais de la nationalité", in *Nationality laws in the European Union - Le droit de la nationalité dans l'Union Européene*, ed. Bruno Nascimbene (Milano: Giuffrè Editore, 1996), pp. 599–637.

——, "Migratory movements and nationality law in Portugal", in *Towards a European nationality: citizenship, immigration and nationality law in the EU*, eds. Randall Hansen and Patrick Weil (Hampshire: Palgrave Publishers, 2001), pp. 214–229.

Muir Watt, Horatia, "European Federalism and the 'New Unilateralism'", *Tulane Law Review* 82 (2008): 1983–1998.

Naranjo, Consuelo, "El aluvión, 1880–1930", in *Historia General de la Emigración Española a Ibéroamerica* (Madrid: Historia 16, 1992).

Nascimbene, Bruno, "Proposte di riforma delle norme sulla cittadinanza", *Rivista di diritto internazionale privato e processuale* 40, no. 2 (2004): 555–564.

——, "Proposte a favore dell'acquisto o riacquisto della cittadinanza italiana da parte di connazionali residenti in Slovenia e Croazia", *Rivista di diritto internazionale privato e processuale* 41, no. 2 (2005): 371–376.

——, ed., *Nationality laws in the European Union - Le droit de la nationalité dans l'Union Européene* (Milano: Giuffrè Editore, 1996).

Nederlandse Vereniging Voor Rechtsvergelijking, *Debat over het preadvies 'Gelijkheid van man en vrouw in het nationaliteitsrecht' van Mr G.R. de Groot in het kader van de Nederlandse Vereniging Voor Rechtsvergelijking* (Deventer: Kluwer, 1978).

Niboyet, Marie-Laure, and Géraud De Geouffre de La Pradelle, *Droit international privé*. 2nd ed (Paris: LGDJ, 2009).

Nic Shuibhne, Niamh, "Free movement of persons and the wholly internal rule: time to move on?", *Common Market Law Review* 39 (2002): 731–771.

O'Leary, Síofra, *The evolving concept of Community citizenship: from the free movement of persons to Union citizenship* (The Hague: Kluwer Law International, 1996).

Oeter, Stefan, "Effect of nationality and dual nationality on judicial cooperation, including treaty regimes such as extradition", in *Rights and Duties of Dual Nationals*, eds. David A. Martin and Kay Hailbronner (The Hague: Kluwer Law International, 2003), pp. 55–77.

Olekhnovitch, Georges, "La double nationalité", *Droit et économie* (1991): 15–25.

Oosterom-Staples, Helen, "Burgerschap van de Unie", *Nederlands tijdschrift voor Europees recht*, no. 3 (2004): 57–61.

——, "Annotation Case C-138/02 *Collins* [2004]", *Common Market Law Review* 42 (2005): 205–223.

——, "Het internationale recht als beschermengel van de exclusieve bevoegdheden van lidstaten inzake verlies van nationaliteit?", *Nederlands Tijdschrift voor Europees Recht*, no. 6 (2010): 188–194.

Orentlicher, Diane F., "Citizenship and National Identity", in *International Law and Ethnic Conflict*, ed. David Wippman (Ithaca: Cornell University Press, 1998), pp. 296–325.

Østergaard-Nielsen, Eva, "International Migration and Sending Countries", in *International Migration and Sending Countries: Perceptions, Policies and Transnational Relations*, ed. Eva Østergaard-Nielsen (New York: Palgrave Macmillan, 2003), pp. 3–30.

——, "Turkey and the 'Euro-Turks': Overseas Nationals as an Ambiguous Asset", in *International Migration and Sending Countries: Perceptions, Policies and Transnational Relations*, ed. Eva Østergaard-Nielsen (New York: Palgrave Macmillan, 2003), pp. 77–98.

Oyarzábal, Mario J.A., "El nombre y la protección de la identidad. Cuestiones de Derecho Internacional Público y Privado", *Revista Prudentia Iuris* 58 (2004): 73–97.

——, "El Protocolo Adicional al Convenio de nacionalidad entre España y Argentina. Un análisis desde la perspectiva argentina", *Revista Española de Derecho Internacional* 56, no. 2 (2004): 579 ff.

——, "La revisione dell'accordo italo-argentino di doppia cittadinanza", *Rivista di diritto internazionale privato e processuale* 41 (2005): 101–106.

——, "Il Protocollo aggiuntivo che modifica l'Accordo italo-argentino sulla cittadinanza", *Rivista di diritto internazionale* 90, no. 3 (2007): 749–758.

Palao Moreno, Guillermo, Carlos Esplugues Mota, and Manuel De Lorenzo Segrelles, *Nacionalidad y Extranjería*. 3rd ed (Valencia: Tirant lo Blanch, 2006).

Palmeri, Giuseppa, "Doppia cittadinanza e diritto al nome", *Europa e diritto privato* 7 (2004): 217–230.

Panzera, Antonio Filippo, *Limiti internazionali in materia di cittadinanza*, Pubblicazioni della facoltà giuridica dell'università di Bari (Napoli: Editore Jovene, 1984).

Papperini, Giovanni, *Immigrazione e cittadinanza: Permessi di soggiorno per lavoro e studio, Adozione di minori stranieri, Apolidi e rifugiati, Pratiche per l'ottenimento della cittadinanza italiana, Documenti, Visti, Formalita doganali* (Milano: Pirola, 1987).

Parolin, Gianluca P., *Citizenship in the Arab World. Kin, Religion and Nation-State* (Amsterdam: Amsterdam University Press, 2009).

Parry, Clive, "Some considerations upon the protection of individuals in international law", in *Recueil des cours de l'Académie de droit international de la Haye* (Leiden: Sijthoff, 1956), pp. 653–726.

Pastore, Ferruccio, "Migration Law and International Migration: The Italian Case", in *Towards a European Nationality. Citizenship, Immigration and Nationality Law in the EU*, eds. Randall Hansen and Patrick Weil (Hampshire: Palgrave Publishers, 2001), pp. 95–117.

——, "Immigration in Italy today. A community out of balance: nationality law and migration politics in the history of post-unification Italy", *Journal of Modern Italian Studies* 9, no. 1 (2004): 27–48.

Peers, Steve, "Legislative Update: EU Immigration and Asylum Competence and Decision-Making in the Treaty of Lisbon", *European Journal of Migration and Law* 10 (2008): 219–247.

Pérez de Vargas Muñoz, José, "Cuestiones de doble nacionalidad", *Revista de Derecho Privado* 12 (2002): 889–910.

Pérez Vera, Elisa, "El sistema español de doble nacionalidad ante la futura adhesión de España a las Comunidades Europeas", *Revista de instituciones europeas* 8 (1981): 685–703.

——, "El sistema español de doble nacionalidad", in *Emigración y Constitución*, ed. José Ignacio Cases Méndez (Madrid: Instituto Español de Emigración, 1983), pp. 71–90.

——, "Citoyenneté de l'Union européene, nationalité et conditions des étrangers", in *Recueil des cours de l'Académie de droit international de la Haye* (Leiden: Sijthoff, 1996), pp. 243–425.

Piçarra, Nuno, and Ana Rita Gil, "Report on Portugal", EUDO Citizenship Observatory Country Reports (2009), pp. 1–45.

Picone, Paolo, *La riforma italiana del diritto internazionale privato* (Padova: Cedam, 1998).

Pocar, Fausto, and Costanza Honorati, *Il nuovo diritto internazionale privato italiano*. 2nd ed (Milano: Giuffrè, 2002).

Poiares Maduro, Miguel, and Loïc Azoulai, eds., *The Past and Future of EU Law. The Classics of EU Law Revisited on the 50th Anniversary of the Rome Treaty* (Oxford: Hart Publishing, 2010).

Preuss, Ulrich K., "Citizenship and the German Nation", *Citizenship Studies* 7, no. 1 (2003): 37–55.

Price, Roger, *A concise history of France*. 2nd ed (Cambridge: Cambridge University Press, 2005).

Psychogiopoulou, Evangelia, *The integration of cultural considerations in EU law and policies*, Dissertation European University Institute (Florence: EUI, 2006).

Pugliese, Enrico, *L'Italia tra migrazioni internazionali e migrazioni interne* (Bologna: Il Mulino, 2002).

Quadri, Rolando, "Cittadinanza", in *Novissimo Digesto Italiano*, eds. Antonio Azara and Ernesto Eula (Torino: Unione Tipografico, 1957), pp. 306–335.

Quiñones Escamez, Ana, "Derecho comunitario, derechos fundamentales y denegación del cambio de sexo y apellidos: ¿un orden público europeo harmonizador?", *Revista de Derecho Comunitario Europeo* 28 (2004): 507–529.

Randelzhofer, Albrecht, "Nationality", in *Encyclopedia of Public International Law*, ed. R. Bernhardt (Amsterdam: Elsevier, 1997), pp. 501–510.

Renan, Ernest, *Qu'est-ce qu'une nation? (et autres textes choisis et présentés par Joël Roman)* (Paris: Presses Pocket, 1992).

Rezek, José Francisco, "Le droit international de la nationalité", in *Recueil des cours de l'Académie de droit international de la Haye* (Leiden: Sijthoff, 1986), pp. 337–400.

Rieck, Jürgen, "Anerkennung des Familiennamens in Mitgliedstaaten: Grunkin-Paul", *Neue Juristische Wochenschrift*, no. 3 (2009): 125–129.

Rigaux, François, "Les situations juridique individuelles dans un système de relativité générale. Cours général de droit international privé", in *Recueil des cours de l'Académie de droit international de la Haye* (Leiden: Sijthoff, 1989), pp. 9–407.

Rittstieg, Helmut, "Doppelte Staatsangehörigkeit im Völkerrecht", *Neue Juristische Wochenschrift* 22 (1990): 1401–1405.

——, "Dual Citizenship: Legal and Political Aspects in the German Context", in *From Aliens to Citizens. Redefining the Status of Immigrants in Europe*, ed. Rainer Bauböck (Aldershot: Avebury, 1994), pp. 111–120.

Rode, Zvonko R., "Dual nationals and the doctrine of dominant nationality", *American journal of international law* 59 (1959): 139–144.

Rodríguez Mateos, Pilar, "La doble nacionalidad en el sistematica del derecho internacional privado", *Revista Española de Derecho Internacional* 42, no. 2 (1990): 463–493.

Rosoli, Gianfausto, "La crise des relations entre l'Italie et le Brésil: la grande naturalisation (1889–1896)", *Revue Européenne des Migrations Internationales* 2, no. 2 (1986): 69–90.

Rubio Marín, Ruth, "Spain", in *Acquisition and Loss of Nationality, Policies and Trends in 15 European Countries*, eds. Rainer Bauböck, Eva Ersbøll, Kees Groenendijk and Harald Waldrauch (Amsterdam: Amsterdam University Press, 2006), pp. 477–515.

——, "Transnational Politics and the Democratic Nation-State: Normative Challenges of Expatriate Voting and Nationality Retention of Emigrants", *New York University Law Review* 117, no. 81 (2006).

Rubio Marín, Ruth, and Irene Sobrino, "Report on Spain", EUDO Citizenship Observatory Country Reports (2009), pp. 1–30.

Ruzié, David, "Nationalité, effectivité et droit communautaire", *Revue générale de droit international public* 97 (1993): 107–120.

Saarloos, Kees Jan, *European private international law on legal parentage? Thoughts on a European instrument implementing the principle of mutual recognition in legal parentage*, Dissertatie Universiteit Maastricht (Maastricht: Océ Business Services, 2010).

Sabato, Adriana, *La cittadinanza italiana. Disciplina e profili operativi* (Santarcangelo di Romagna: Maggioli Editore, 2006).

Sahlins, Peter, *Unnaturally French. Foreign Citizens in the Old Regime and After* (Ithaca: Cornell University Press, 2004).

Samama, N., *Secondo congresso degli italiani all'estero. Tema primo. Il problema della cittadinanza specialmente nei rapporti degli italiani all'estero* (Firenze: Tipografia Enrico Ariani, 1911).

Sánchez Alonso, Blanca, *Los Determinantes de la Emigración Española, 1880–1930*, Dissertation History Department (Florence: European University Institute, 1993).

Sarrazin, Thilo, *Deutschland schafft sich ab. Wie wir unser Land aufs Spiel setzen* (München: Deutsche Verlags-Anstalt, 2010).

Sawyer, Caroline, "Report on the United Kingdom", EUDO Citizenship Observatory Country Reports (2009), pp. 1–44.

Sawyer, Caroline, and Brad K. Blitz, eds., *Statelessness in the European Union* (Cambridge: Cambridge University Press, 2011).

Scheffer, Paul, *Het land van aankomst* (Amsterdam: De Bezige Bij, 2007).

Shah, Prakash, "British Nationals under Community Law: The Kaur Case", *European Journal of Migration and Law* 3 (2001): 271–278.

Shaw, Jo, "Citizenship: Contrasting Dynamics at the Interface of Integration and Constitutionalism", Working Paper University of Edinburgh 2010/14, pp. 1–31.

——, *The Transformation of Citizenship in the European Union. Electoral Rights and the Restructuring of Political Space* (Cambridge: Cambridge University Press, 2007).

Skrobacki, Waldemar A., "Dual Citizenship, European Identity and Community-Building in Europe", in *Dual Citizenship in Global Perspective, From Unitary to Multiple Citizenship*, eds. Peter Kivisto and Thomas Faist (New York: Palgrave Macmillan, 2007), pp. 227–246.

Smilov, Daniel, and Elena Jileva, "Report on Bulgaria", EUDO Citizenship Observatory Country Reports (2009), pp. 1–26.

Sonnenberger, Hans Jürgen, "Anerkennung der Staatsangehörigkeit und effektive Staatsangehörigkeit natürlicher Personen im Völkerrecht und im Internationalen Privatrecht", in *Berichte der Deutschen Gesellschaft für Völkerrecht*. (Heidelberg: C.F. Müller Juristischer Verlag, 1988), pp. 9–36.

Spang, Mikael, "Pragmatism All the Way Down? The Politics of Dual Citizenship in Sweden", in *Dual Citizenship in Europe: From Nationhood to Societal Integration*, ed. Thomas Faist (Aldershot: Ashgate, 2007), pp. 103–125.

Spaventa, Eleanor, "Seeing the wood despite the trees? On the scope of Union citizenship and its constitutional effects", *Common Market Law Review* 45 (2008): 13–45.

Spire, Alexis, "D'une colonie à l'autre. La continuation des structures coloniales dans le traitement de la migration algérienne en France après 1945", in *L'esclavage, la colonisation, et après … France, États-Unis, Grande-Bretagne*, eds. Patrick Weil and Stéphane Dufoix (Paris: Presses Universitaires de France, 2005), pp. 387–409.

Spiro, Peter J., "Dual nationality and the meaning of citizenship", *Emory Law Journal* 46, no. 4 (1997): 1411–1485.

——, "Political rights and dual nationality", in *Rights and Duties of Dual nationals - Evolutions and Prospects*, eds. D.A Martin and Kay Hailbronner (The Hague: Kluwer Law International, 2003), pp. 135–152.

——, "Dual Citizenship: A Postnational View", in *Dual Citizenship in Global Perspective, From Unitary to Multiple Citizenship*, eds. Thomas Faist and Peter Kivisto (New York: Palgrave Macmillan, 2007), pp. 189–203.

Stille, August L.G.A., "Abweichung von der Staatsangehörigkeitsanknüpfung bei ineffektiver Staatsangehörigkeit von Monostaatern - Die aktuelle Entwicklung in den Niederlanden", in *Nation und Staat im Internationalen Privatrecht. Zum kollisionsrechtlichen Staatsange hörigkeitsprinzip in verfassungsrechtlicher und international-privatrechtlicher Sicht*, eds. Erik Jayme and Heinz-Peter Mansel (Heidelberg: C.F. Müller Juristischer Verlag, 1990), pp. 223–235.

Stone, Peter, *EU Private International Law* (Cheltenham: Edward Elgar Publishing, 2006).

Strikwerda, Luc, *Inleiding tot het Nederlandse internationaal privaatrecht*. 9th ed (Deventer: Kluwer, 2008).

Struycken, A.V.M., "Acquisition et perte de la nationalité néerlandaise", in *La condition juridique de l'étranger, hier et aujourd'hui. Actes du Colloque organisé à Nimègue les 9–11 mai 1988 par les Facultés de Droit de Poitiers et de Nimègue* (Nijmegen: Faculteit der Rechtsgeleerdheid, 1988), pp. 3–19.

Sumien, Paul, "Algérie", in *Répertoire de droit international*, eds. A. De la Pradelle and J.P. Niboyet (Paris: Librairie du Recueil Sirey, 1929), pp. 360–389.

Terré, François, "Réflexions sur la notion de nationalité", *Revue critique de droit international privé* 64 (1975): 197–214.

Thiesing, Theo. H., "Dual allegiance in the German law of nationality and American citizenship", *Yale Law Journal* 27, no. 4 (1918): 479–508.

Tintori, Guido, "Cittadinanza e politiche di emigrazione nell'Italia liberale e fascista. Un approfondimento storico", in *Familismo legale: come (non) diventare italiani*, ed. Giovanna Zincone (Roma-Bari: Editori Laterza, 2006), pp. 52–106.

——, *Fardelli d'Italia? Conseguenze nazionali e transnazionali delle politiche di cittadinanza italiane* (Roma: Carocci, 2009).

Tomuschat, Christian, "Annotation Case C-85/96 *Martínez Sala* [1998]", *Common Market Law Review* 37 (2000): 449–457.

Toner, Helen, "Annotation Case C-192/99 *Kaur* [2001]", *Common Market Law Review* 39 (2002): 881–893.

——, *Partnership Rights, Free Movement, and EU Law* (Oxford: Hart Publishing, 2004).

Tratnik, Matjaz, *Het Nationaliteitsrecht in de Oosteuropese Landen*, Dissertatie Universiteit Maastricht (Deventer: Kluwer, 1989).

Treves, Tulio, "Costituzione e accordo italo-argentino sulla cittadinanza", *Rivista di diritto internazionale privato e processuale* 11 (1975): 294–300.

Triadafilopoulos, Triadafilos, "Dual Citizenship and Security Norms", in *Dual Citizenship in Global Perspective, From Unitary to Multiple Citizenship*, eds. Peter Kivisto and Thomas Faist (New York: Palgrave Macmillan, 2007), pp. 27–41.

Uccellini, Cara, "Romanian migration to Italy. Insiders and outsiders", in *Globalisation, Migration, and the Future of Europe. Insiders and Outsiders*, ed. Leila Simona Talani (London: Routledge, 2012), pp. 101–123.

van den Bedem, Ruud, "Plural nationality seen from the perspective of concerned minorities", in *Plural nationality: Changing attitudes* (Conference at the European University Institute, Florence, 1992).

——, *Motieven voor naturalisatie; Waarom vreemdelingen uit diverse minderheidsgroepen wel of niet kiezen voor naturalisatie* (Arnhem: Gouda Quint, 1993).

——, "Towards a System of Plural Nationality in the Netherlands", in *From Aliens to Citizens. Redefining the Status of Immigrants in Europe*, ed. Rainer Bauböck (Aldershot: Avebury, 1994), pp. 95–109.

van den Bogaert, Stefaan, "Free movement for workers and the nationality requirements", in *Migration, Integration and Citizenship, A challenge for Europe's Future, Volume I*, ed. Hildegard Schneider (Maastricht: Forum, 2005), pp. 55–72.

van den Eeckhout, Veerle, "Europese bemoeienis met internationaal privaatrecht: ook ten aanzien van internationale familieverhoudingen die 'externe' aspecten vertonen?", *Nederlands tijdschrift voor Europees recht*, no. 11 (2004): 302–310.

——, "Tien jaar Europees internationaal privaatrecht. Een verrassende metamorfose van exotisch muurbloempje tot goed geïntegreerde deelnemer in diverse gezelschappen", *Nederlands tijdschrift voor Europees recht*, no. 11/12 (2005): 289–303.

——, "Het Hof van Justitie als steun en toeverlaat in tijden van Europeanisatie van het IPR? Mogelijkheden tot aanspreken van een Europese scheidingsrechter na de uitspraak van het Hof van Justitie in de zaak *Sundelind Lopez* (C-68/07)", *Nederlands tijdschrift voor Europees recht*, no. 3 (2008): 84–90.

——, "Het beroep op het bezit van een nationaliteit in geval van dubbele nationaliteit. Enkele aantekeningen naar aanleiding van de uitspraak Hadadi (C-168/08) van het Hof van Justitie", *Nederlands tijdschrift voor Europees recht*, no. 10 (2009): 307–316.

van der Mei, Anne-Pieter, "De juridische meerwaarde van het Burgerschap van de Europese Unie (2)", *Migrantenrecht* 18, no. 9/10 (2003): 318–324.

——, "EU-burgerschap en de reikwijdte van het verbod van discriminatie op grond van nationaliteit", *Nederlands tijdschrift voor Europees recht*, no. 8-9 (2009): 275–287.

van der Velden, Frans J.A., "De circulaire inzake de afstandsverklaring", in *Trends in het nationaliteitsrecht*, ed. Hans Ulrich Jessurun d'Oliveira ('s-Gravenhage: Sdu, 1998).

——, "Unieburgers en staatsburgers. De invloed van het Europese gemeenschapsrecht op het nationaliteitsrecht van de lidstaten", in *De Nationaliteit in Internationaal en Europees Perspectief. Preadviezen van Prof. Mr Frans J.A. van der Velden, Prof. Mr Gerard-René de Groot en Mr Nicole Doeswijk* (Den Haag: T.M.C. Asser Press, 2004), pp. 1–43.

van Deursen, A.Th., *De last van veel geluk. De geschiedenis van Nederland, 1555–1702* (Amsterdam: Uitgeverij Bert Bakker, 2004).

van Gunsteren, Herman, "Four Conceptions of Citizenship", in *The Condition of Citizenship*, ed. Bart van Steenbergen (London: Sage Publications, 1994), pp. 36–48.

van Middelaar, Luuk, *De passage naar Europa. Geschiedenis van een begin* (Deventer: Historische Uitgeverij, 2009).

van Oers, Ricky, Betty de Hart, and Kees Groenendijk, "Netherlands", in *Acquisition and Loss of Nationality, Policies and Trends in 15 European Countries*, eds. Rainer Bauböck, Eva Ersbøll, Kees Groenendijk and Harald Waldrauch (Amsterdam: Amsterdam University Press, 2006), pp. 391–434.

van Panhuys, Haro F., *The Rôle of Nationality in International Law* (Leiden: A.W. Sühoff, 1959).

van Waas, Laura, *Nationality Matters. Statelessness under international law* (Antwerp: Intersentia, 2008).

Vecoli, Rudolph J., "Negli Stati Uniti", in *Storia dell'emigrazione Italiana*, eds. Piero Bevilaqua, Andreina De Clementi and Emilio Franzina (Roma: Donzelli, 2002), pp. 55–84.

Verwilghen, Michel, "Conflits de nationalités, plurinationalité et apatridie", in *Recueil des cours de l'Académie de droit international de la Haye* (Leiden: Sijthoff, 1999).

——, ed., *Nationalité et statut personnel. Leur interaction dans les traités internationaux et dans les législations nationales* (Bruxelles: Bruylant, 1984).

Vignal, Thierry, *Droit international privé* (Paris: Dalloz, 2005).

Vink, Maarten, "The Limited Europeanization of Domestic Citizenship Policy: Evidence from the Netherlands", *Journal of Common Market Studies* 39, no. 5 (2001): 875–896.

——, *Limits of European Citizenship. European Integration and Domestic Immigration Policies* (Hampshire: Palgrave Macmillan, 2005).

Virgós Soriano, Miguel, "Nationality and Double Nationality Principles in Spanish Private International Law System", in *Nation und Staat im Internationalen Privatrecht. Zum kollisionsrechtlichen Staatsangehörigkeitsprinzip in verfassungsrechtlicher und international-privatrechtlicher Sicht*, eds. Erik Jayme and Heinz-Peter Mansel (Heidelberg: C.F. Müller Juristischer Verlag, 1990), pp. 237–258.

Vonk, Olivier, "Latijns-Amerikaanse Spanjaarden en het Europees burgerschap", *Migrantenrecht*, no. 5 (2006): 187–195.

——, *Portuguese nationality law*, Master's thesis (Maastricht: Faculty of Law, 2007).

——, "De rol van dubbele nationaliteit voor toegang tot het Unieburgerschap en voor rechts- en forumkeuzebevoegdheid in het Europese internationaal privaatrecht", *Nederlands Juristenblad*, no. 27 (2011): 1760–1766.

Weil, Alfred, "La double nationalité en droit allemand avant et après la loi du 22 juillet 1913", *Revue critique de droit international privé* 11–12 (1915–1916): 142–158.

——, "La nationalité dans les rapports de l'Allemagne avec les Etats-Unis et les traités Bancroft", *Journal de droit international* 44 (1917): 424–435; 899–910.

Weil, Patrick, "Le statut des musulmans en Algérie coloniale. Une nationalité française dénaturée", EUI Working Paper 2003/03, pp. 1–17.

——, *Qu'est-ce qu'un Français? Histoire de la nationalité française depuis la Révolution* (Paris: Grasset, 2002).

——, *La France et ses étrangers. L'aventure d'une politique de l'immigration de 1938 à nos jours*, nouvelle édition refondue (Paris: Gallimard, 2004).

——, *How to Be French: Nationality in the Making since 1789*. trans. Catherine Porter (Durham: Duke University Press, 2008).

Weil, Patrick, and Randall Hansen, eds., *Towards a European Nationality. Citizenship, Immigration and Nationality Law in the EU* (Hampshire: Palgrave Publishers, 2001).

——, eds., *Dual Nationality, Social Rights and Federal Citizenship in the US and Europe* (New York: Berghahn Books, 2002).

Weil, Patrick, and Alexis Spire, "France", in *Acquisition and Loss of Nationality, Policies and Trends in 15 European Countries*, eds. Rainer Bauböck, Eva Ersbøll, Kees Groenendijk and Harald Waldrauch (Amsterdam: Amsterdam University Press, 2006), pp. 187–211.

Weiler, Joseph H.H., *The Constitution of Europe. "Do the new clothes have an emperor?" and other essays on European integration* (Cambridge: Cambridge University Press, 1999).

Weis, Paul, "Effective nationality (Nottebohm and after)", in *Liber amicorum Adolf F. Schnitzer* (Genève: Georg-Librairie de l'université, 1979), pp. 501–512.

——, *Nationality and statelessness in international law*. 2nd revised ed (Alphen aan den Rijn: Sijthoff & Noordhoff, 1979).

Wesseling, H.L., *Europa's koloniale eeuw* (Amsterdam: Uitgeverij Bert Bakker, 2003).

——, *Frankrijk in oorlog, 1870–1962* (Amsterdam: Uitgeverij Bert Bakker, 2007).

Wihtol de Wenden, Catherine, *Citoyenneté, nationalité et immigration* (Paris: Arcantère Éditions, 1989).

Yanguas Messía, José de, "La double nationalité en Amerique", *Revue de droit international et de législation comparée* 57 (1925): 364–368.

——, "La protection diplomatique en cas de double nationalité", in *Hommage d'une génération de juristes au Président Basdevant* (Paris: Pedone, 1960), pp. 547–558.

Zamoyski, Adam, *Rites of Peace. The Fall of Napoleon & the Congress of Vienna* (London: Harper Perennial, 2007).

Zeballos, E.S., "De la nationalité et de la naturalisation dans la République Argentine", *Journal de droit international* 45 (1918): 19–38; 526–539.

Ziemele, Ineta, *State Continuity and Nationality: The Baltic States and Russia. Past, Present and Future as Defined by International Law* (Leiden/Boston: Martinus Nijhoff Publishers, 2005).
Zilbershats, Yaffa, *The Human Right to Citizenship* (Ardsley, New York: Transnational Publishers, Inc, 2002).
Zilverentant, F.Th., "Polemiek over de gelijkheid van man en vrouw in het nationaliteitsrecht", *Burgerzaken* (1982): 1–2.
Zincone, Giovanna, "Illegality, Enlightenment and Ambiguity: A Hot Italian Recipe", *South European Society and Politics* 3, no. 3 (1998): 45–82.
——, "Due pesi e due misure: pronipoti d'Italia e nuovi immigrati", in *Familismo legale: come (non) diventare italiani*, ed. Giovanna Zincone (Roma-Bari: Editori Laterza, 2006), pp. 3–51.
——, "Il perché del presente e gli auspici per il futuro che potrebbe essere migliore", in *Familismo legale: come (non) diventare italiani*, ed. Giovanna Zincone (Roma-Bari: Editori Laterza, 2006), pp. 139–164.
——, "Premessa (preface)", in *Familismo legale. Come (non) diventare italiani*, ed. Giovanna Zincone (Roma-Bari: Editori Laterza, 2006).
Zincone, Giovanna, and Marzia Basili, "Report on Italy", EUDO Citizenship Observatory Country Reports (2009), pp. 1–23.

Index

www.ingramcontent.com/pod-product-compliance
Lightning Source LLC
LaVergne TN
LVHW020651300926
849161LV00004B/888